TENEMENT

the Bone Orchard
MYTHOS

IMAGE COMICS, INC.

Robert Kirkman – Chief Operating Officer
Erik Larsen – Chief Financial Officer
Todd McFarlane – President
Marc Silvestri – Chief Executive Officer
Jim Valentino – Vice President

Eric Stephenson – Publisher / Chief Creative Officer
Nicole Lapalme – Vice President of Finance
Leanna Caunter – Accounting Analyst
Sue Korpela – Accounting & HR Manager
Lorelei Bunjes – Vice President of Digital Strategy
Emilio Bautista – Digital Sales Coordinator
Dirk Wood – Vice President of International Sales & Licensing
Ryan Brewer – International Sales & Licensing Manager
Alex Cox – Director of Direct Market Sales
Jon Schlaffman – Specialty Sales Coordinator
Margot Wood – Vice President of Book Market Sales
Chloe Ramos – Book Market & Library Sales Manager
Kat Salazar – Vice President of PR & Marketing
Deanna Phelps – Marketing Design Manager
Drew Fitzgerald – Marketing Content Associate
Heather Doornink – Vice President of Production
Ian Baldessari – Print Manager
Drew Gill – Art Director
Melissa Gifford – Content Manager
Erika Schnatz – Senior Production Artist
Wesley Griffith – Production Artist
Rich Fowlks – Production Artist
IMAGECOMICS.COM

Publication design by Steve Wands

KAW

JEFF LEMIRE
ANDREA SORRENTINO

DAVE STEWART
colorist

STEVE WANDS
letterer & designer

GREG LOCKARD
editor

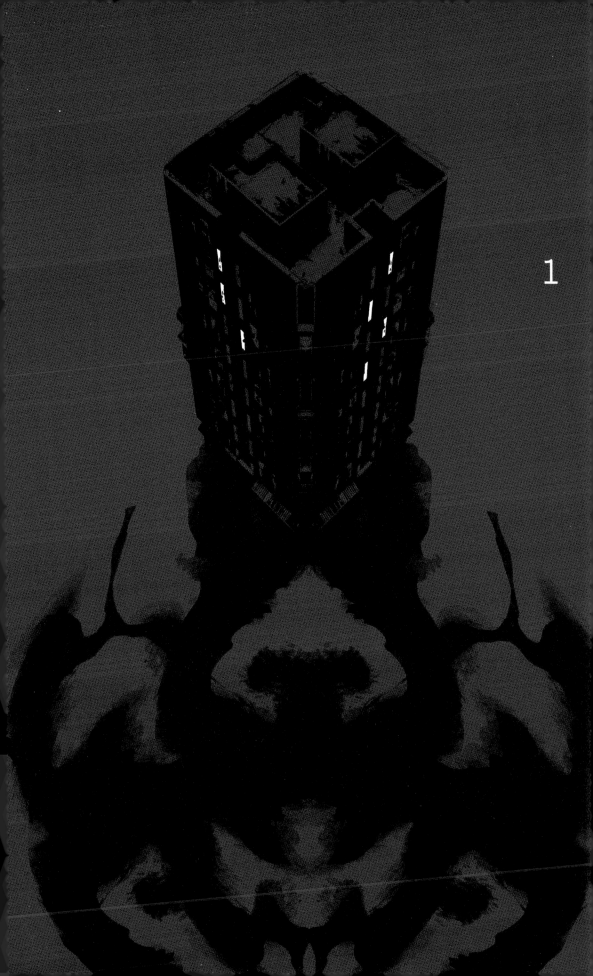

1

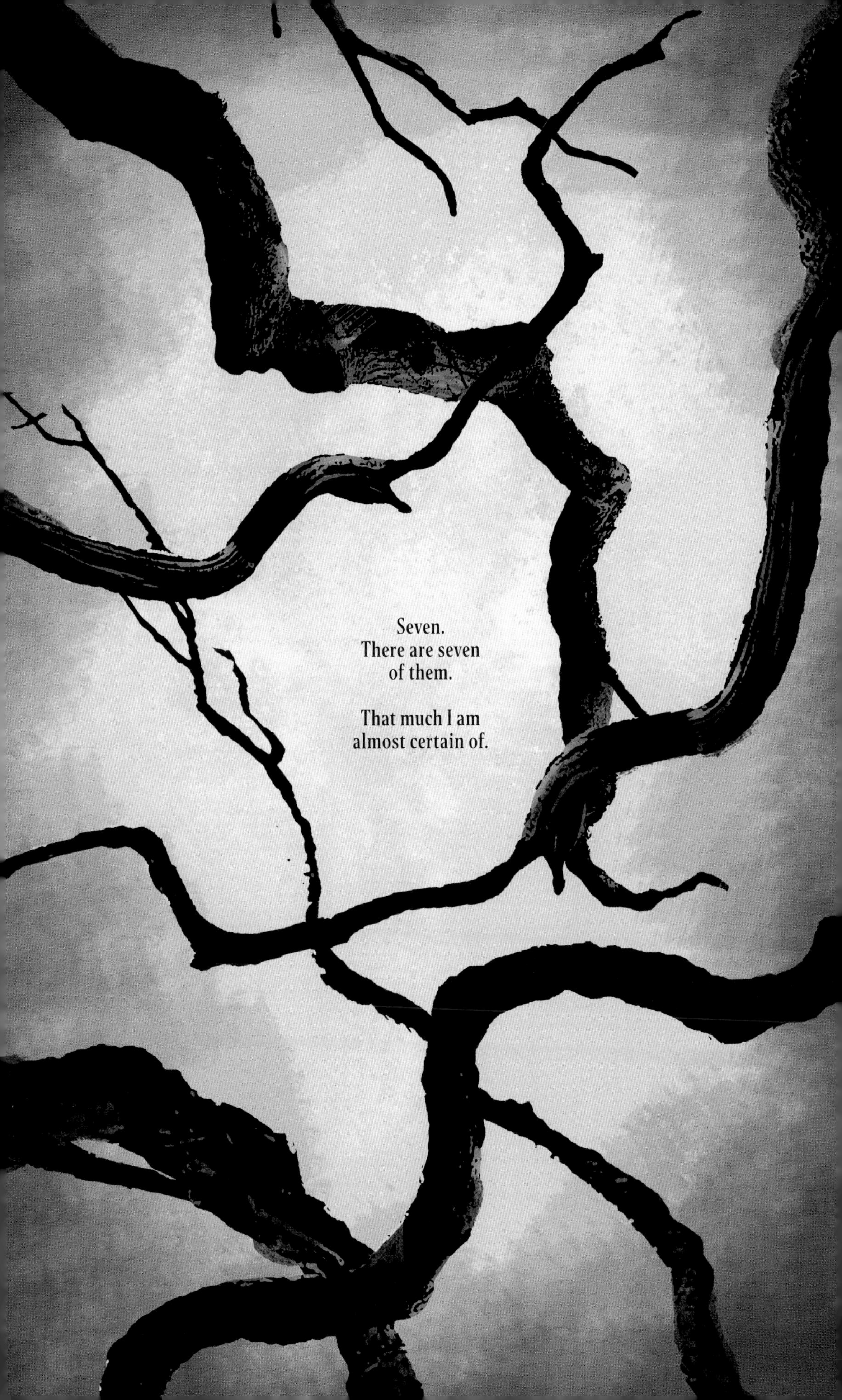
Seven.
There are seven
of them.

That much I am
almost certain of.

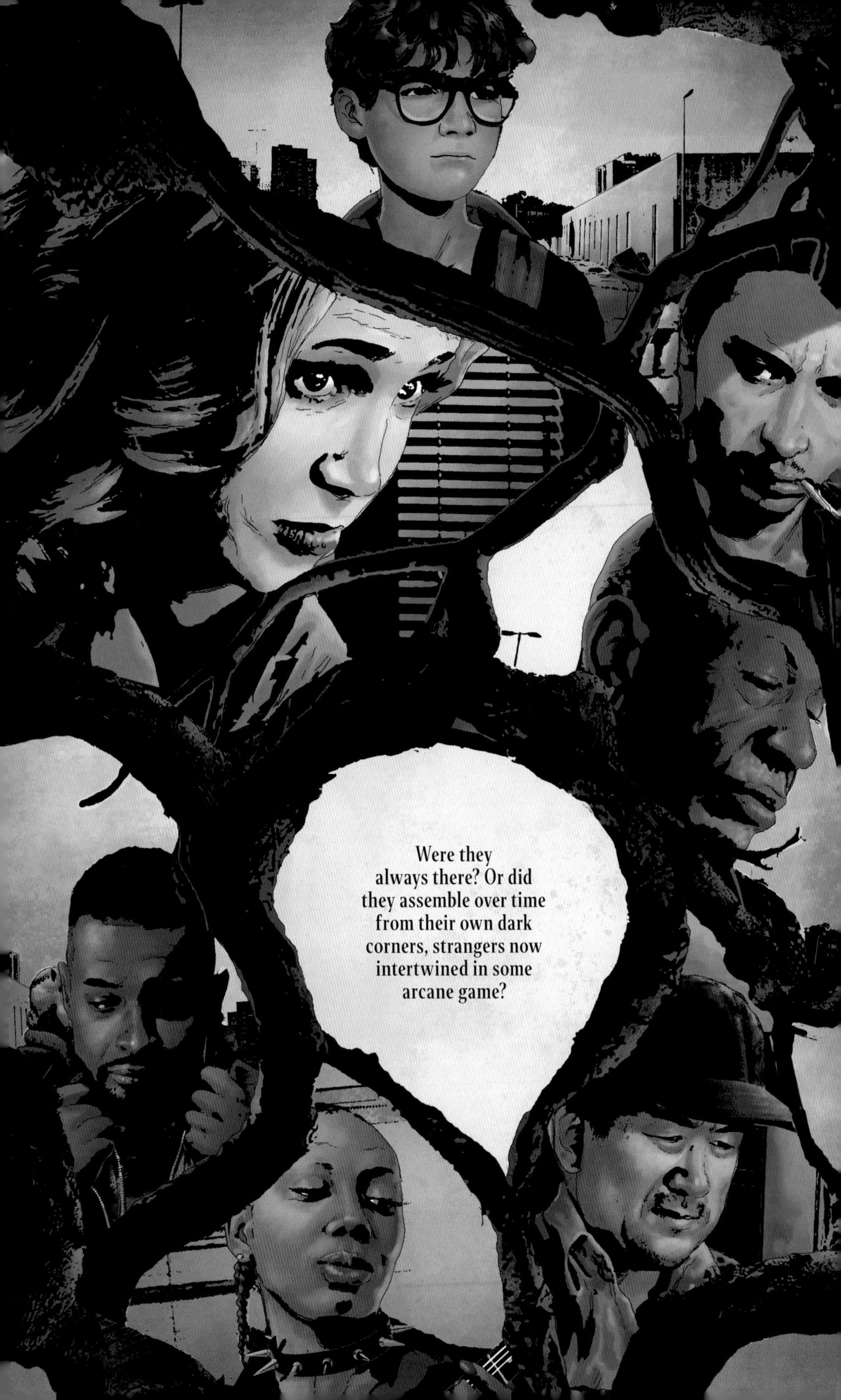
Were they always there? Or did they assemble over time from their own dark corners, strangers now intertwined in some arcane game?

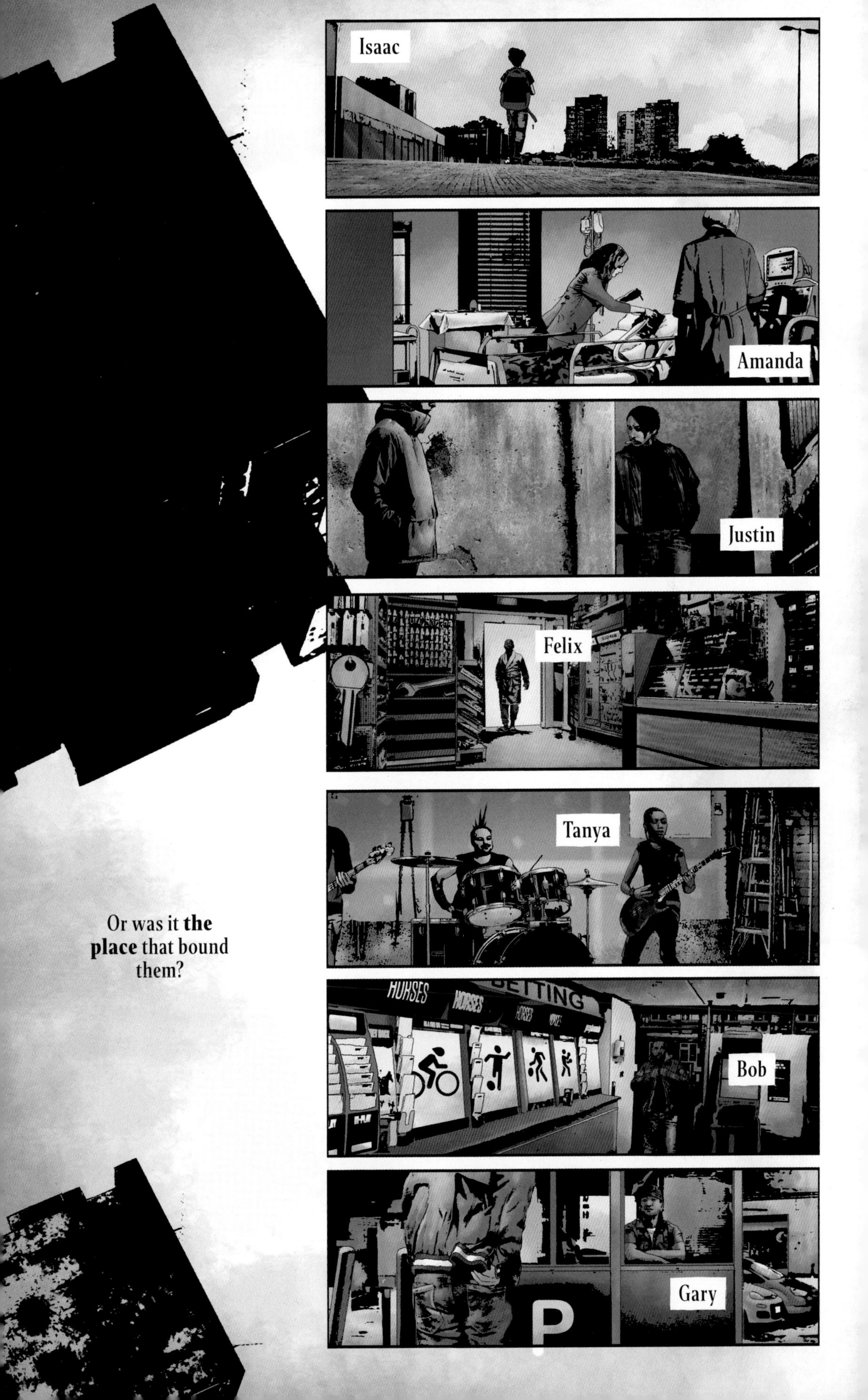
Isaac
Amanda
Justin
Felix
Tanya
Or was it **the place** that bound them?
Bob
Gary

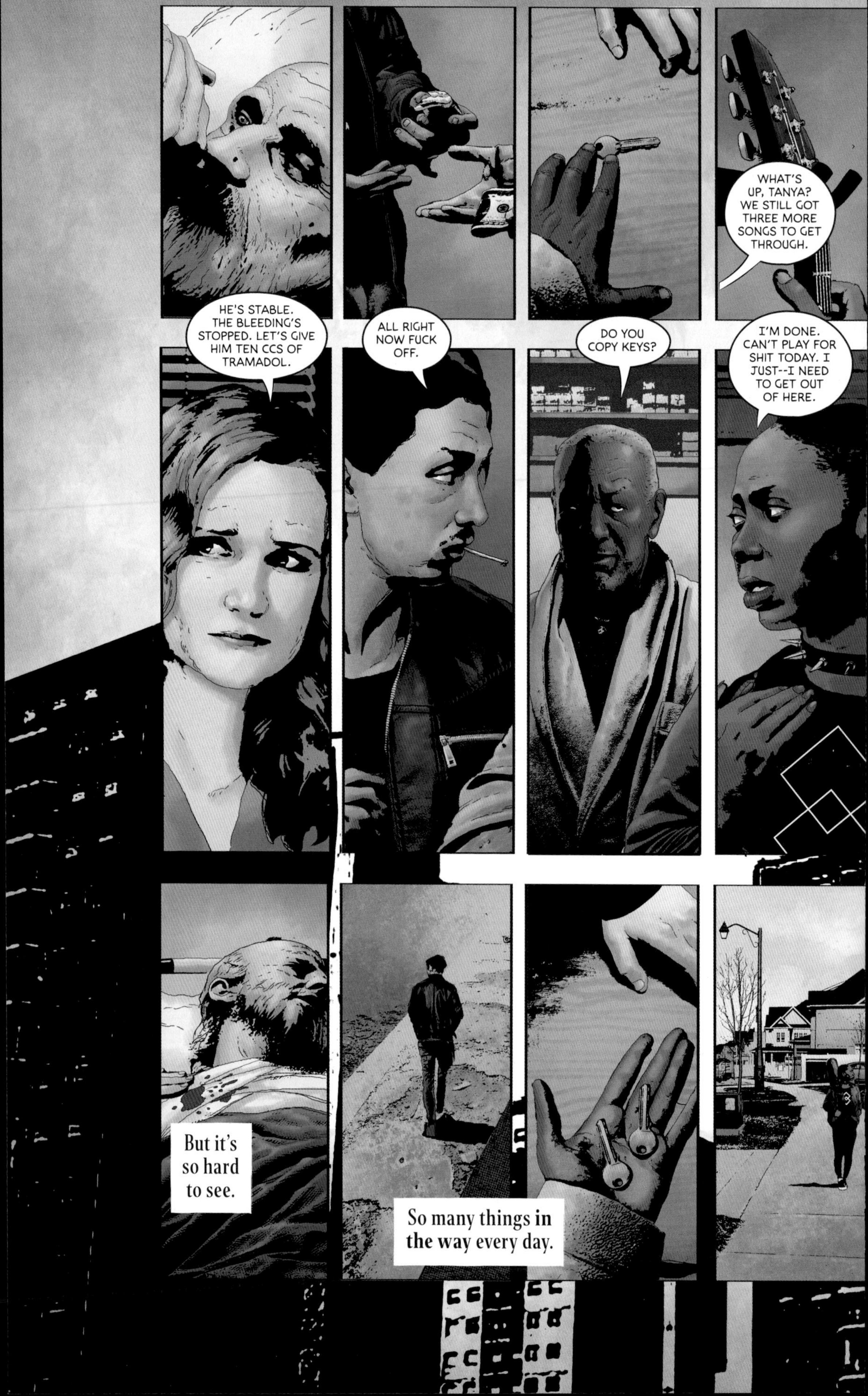
WHAT'S UP, TANYA? WE STILL GOT THREE MORE SONGS TO GET THROUGH.
HE'S STABLE. THE BLEEDING'S STOPPED. LET'S GIVE HIM TEN CCS OF TRAMADOL.
ALL RIGHT NOW FUCK OFF.
DO YOU COPY KEYS?
I'M DONE. CAN'T PLAY FOR SHIT TODAY. I JUST--I NEED TO GET OUT OF HERE.
But it's so hard to see.
So many things in the way every day.

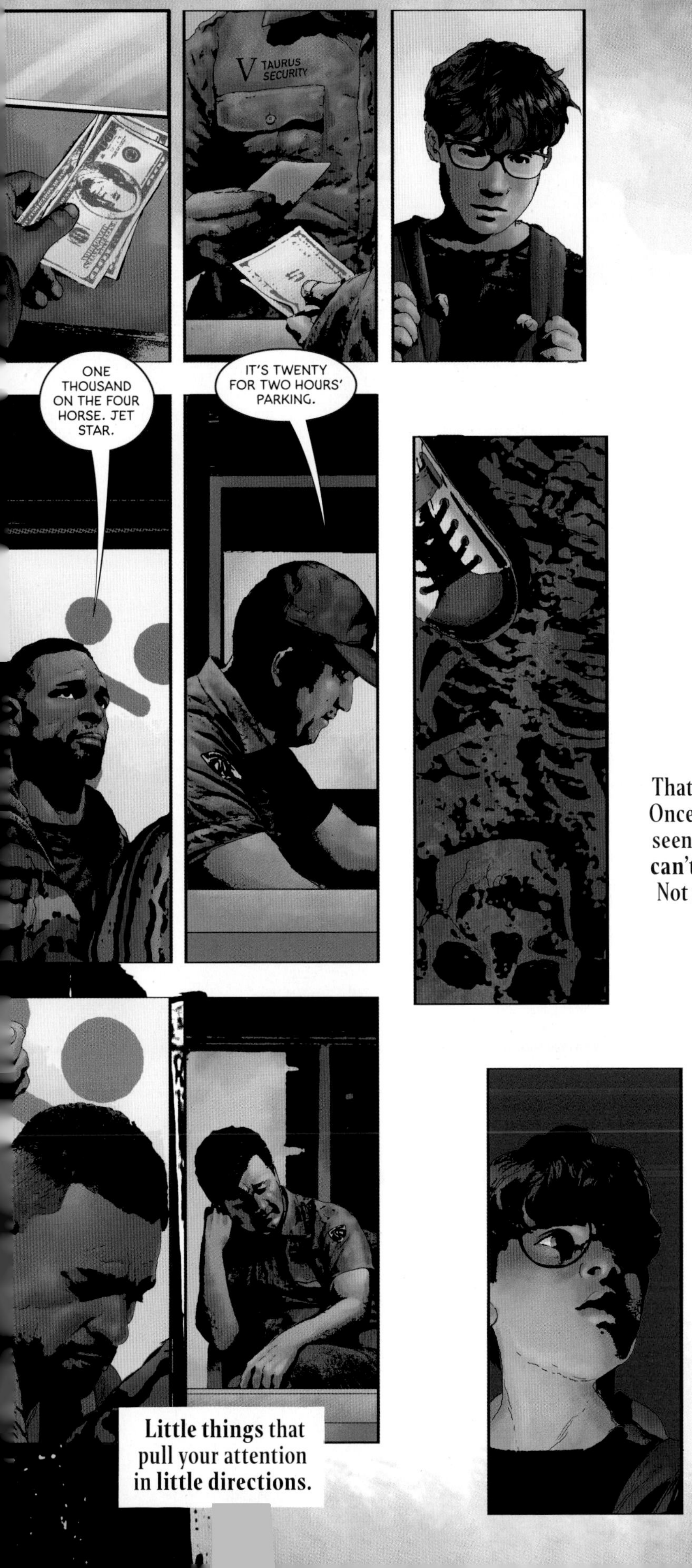
V TAURUS SECURITY
ONE THOUSAND ON THE FOUR HORSE. JET STAR.
IT'S TWENTY FOR TWO HOURS' PARKING.
That place. Once you've seen it, you can't leave. Not really.
Little things that pull your attention in little directions.
But if you can look past all that...if you can really see...there is just nothingness beyond...and that's where the true terror lies.

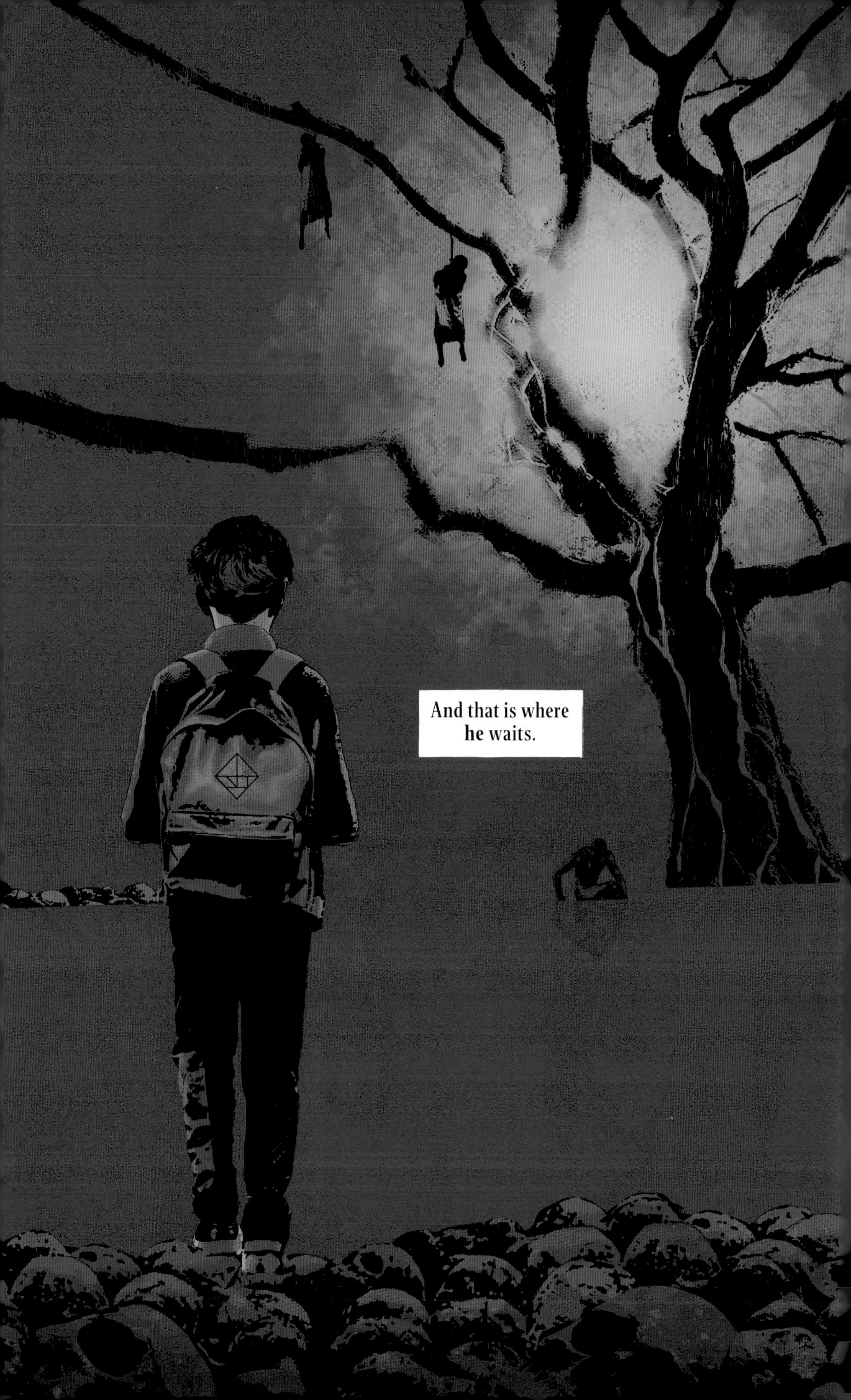
And that is where he waits.

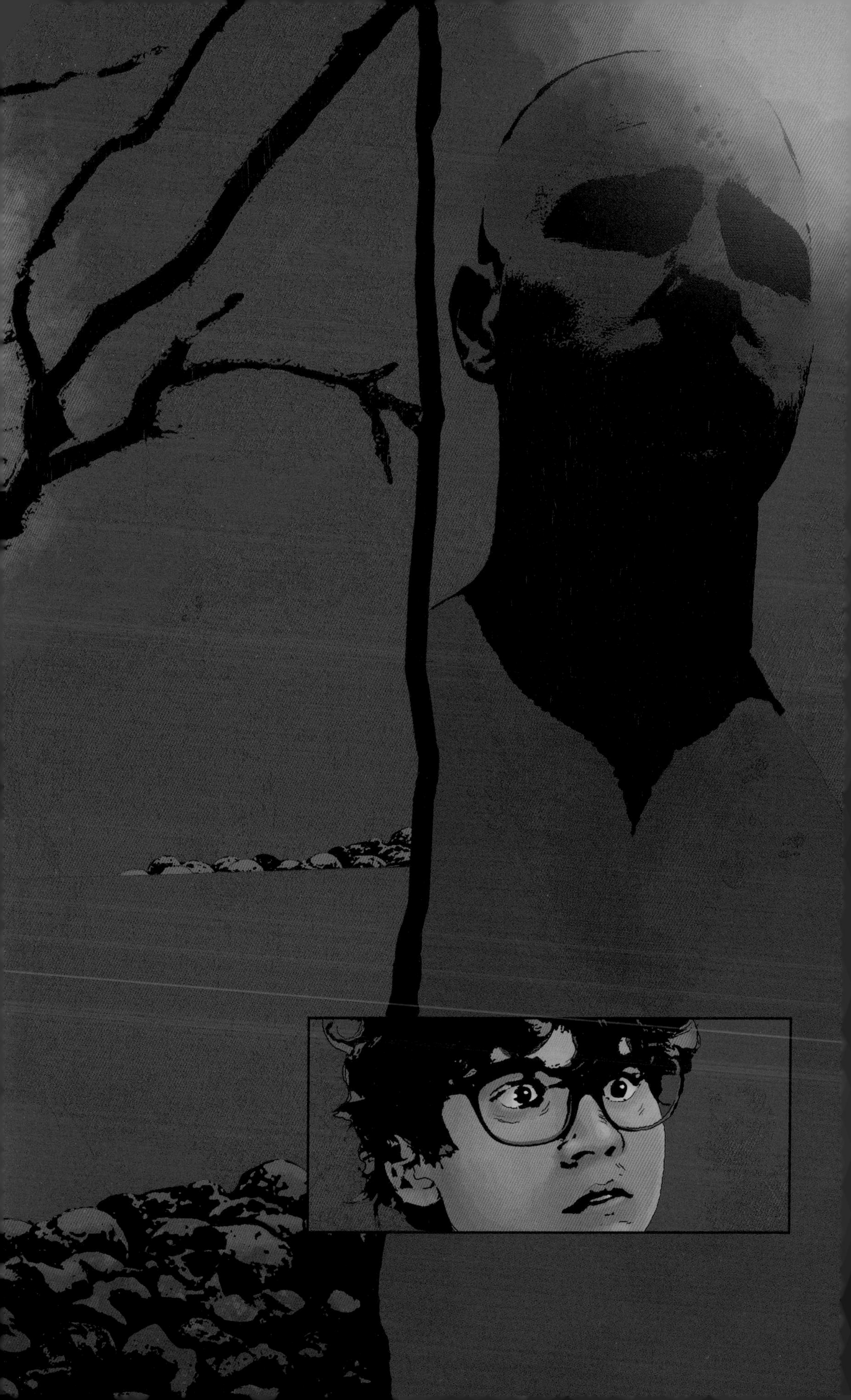

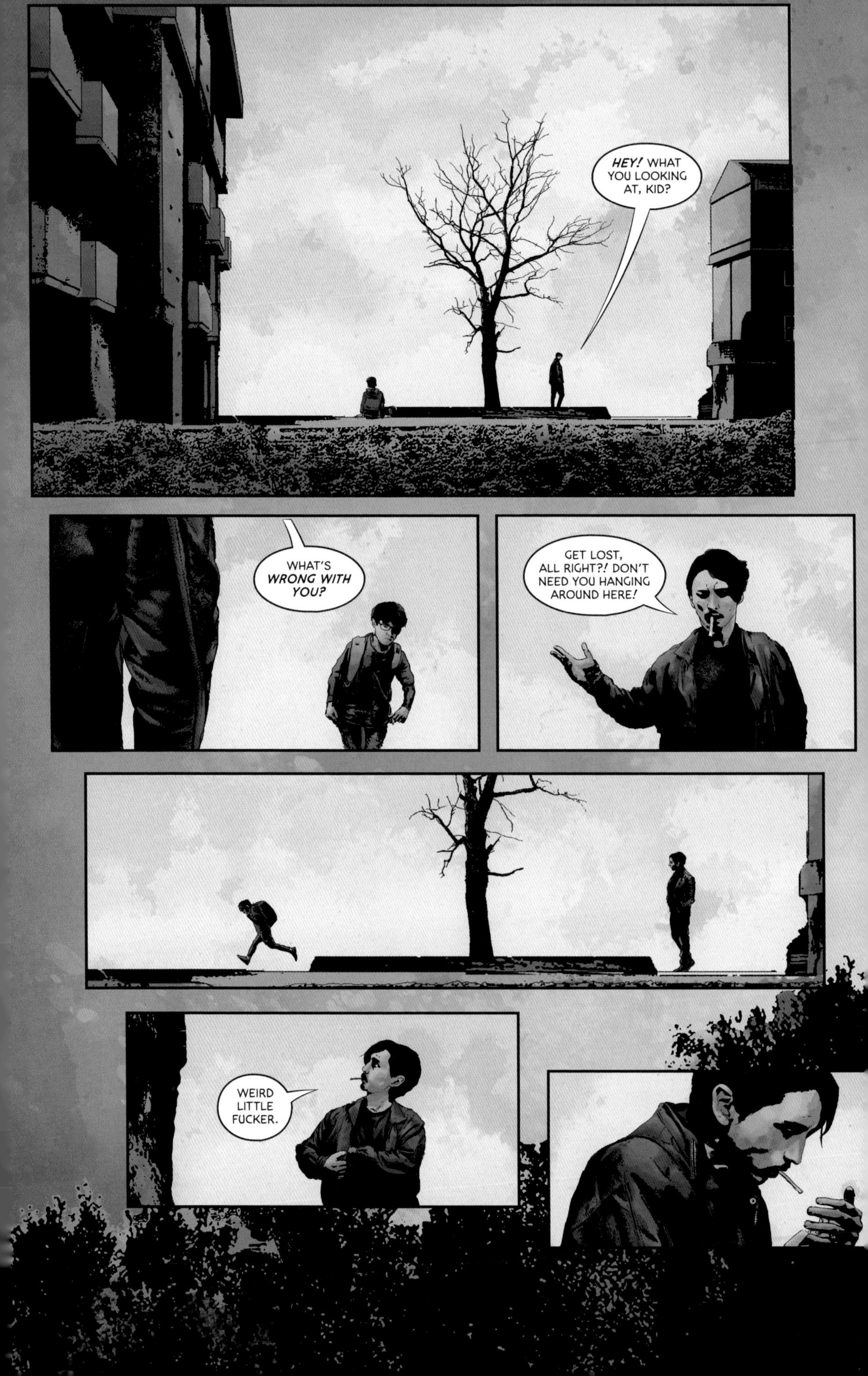
HEY! WHAT YOU LOOKING AT, KID?
WHAT'S WRONG WITH YOU?
GET LOST, ALL RIGHT?! DON'T NEED YOU HANGING AROUND HERE!
WEIRD LITTLE FUCKER.

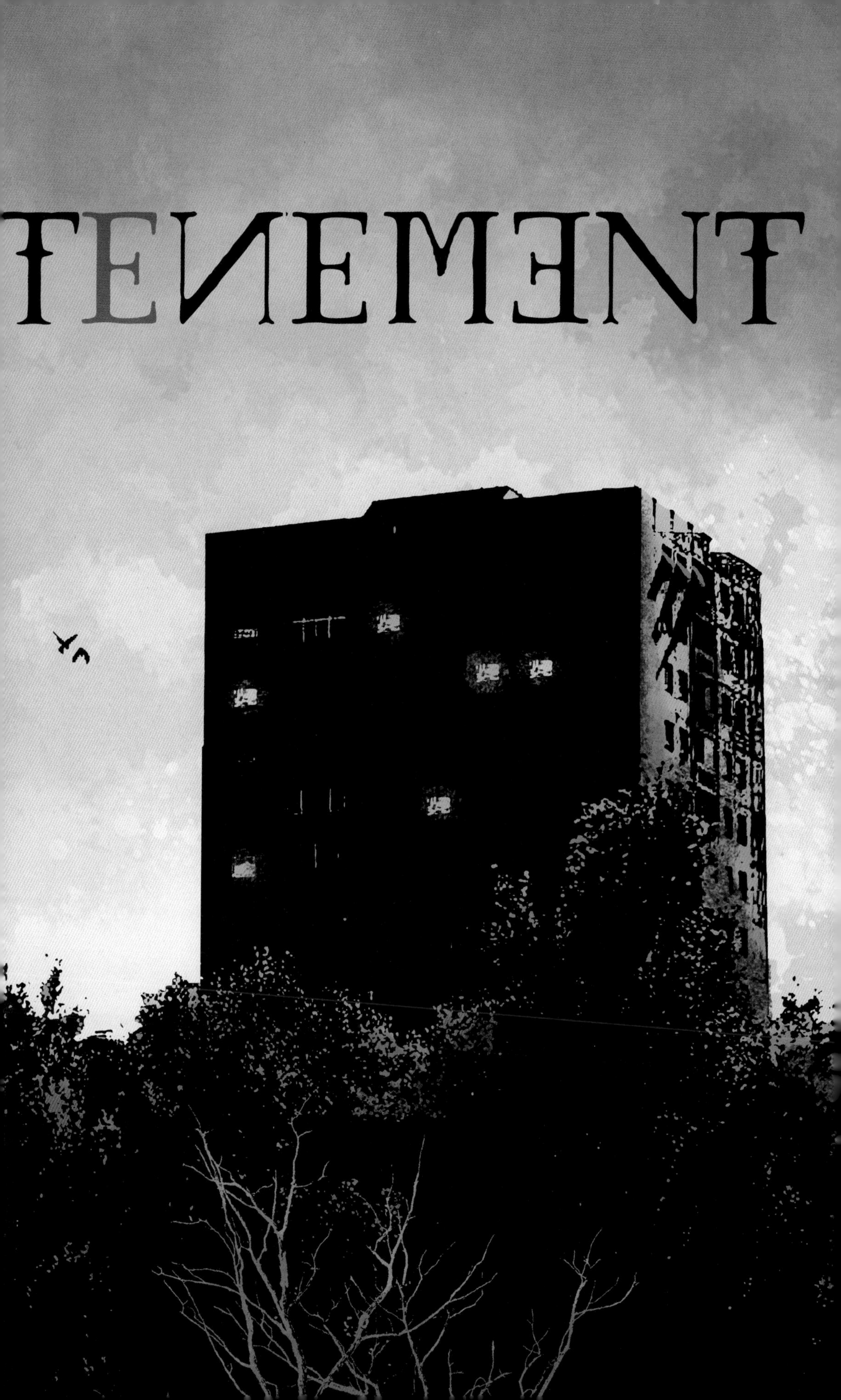
TENEMENT

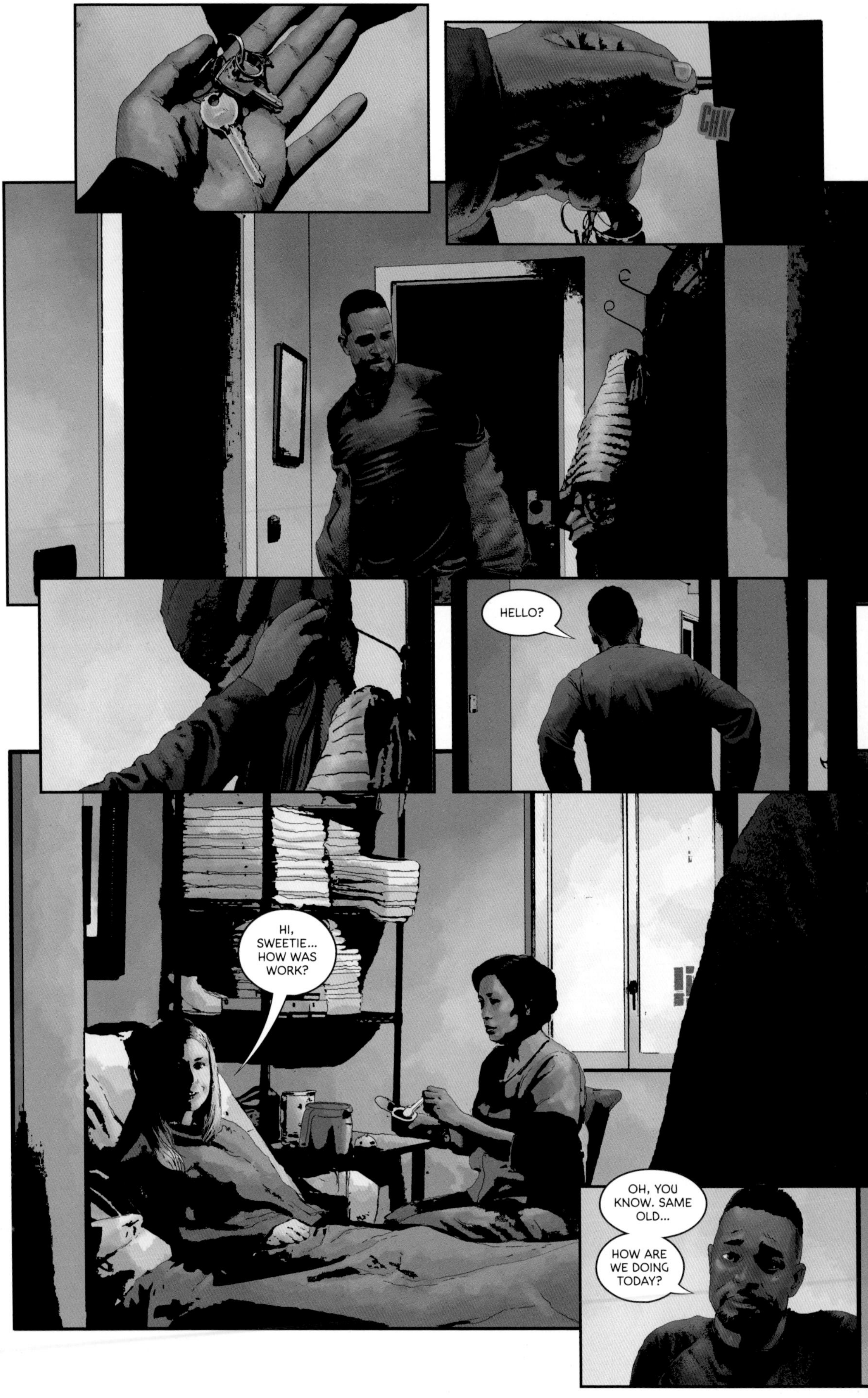
CHK
HELLO?
HI, SWEETIE... HOW WAS WORK?
OH, YOU KNOW. SAME OLD...
HOW ARE WE DOING TODAY?

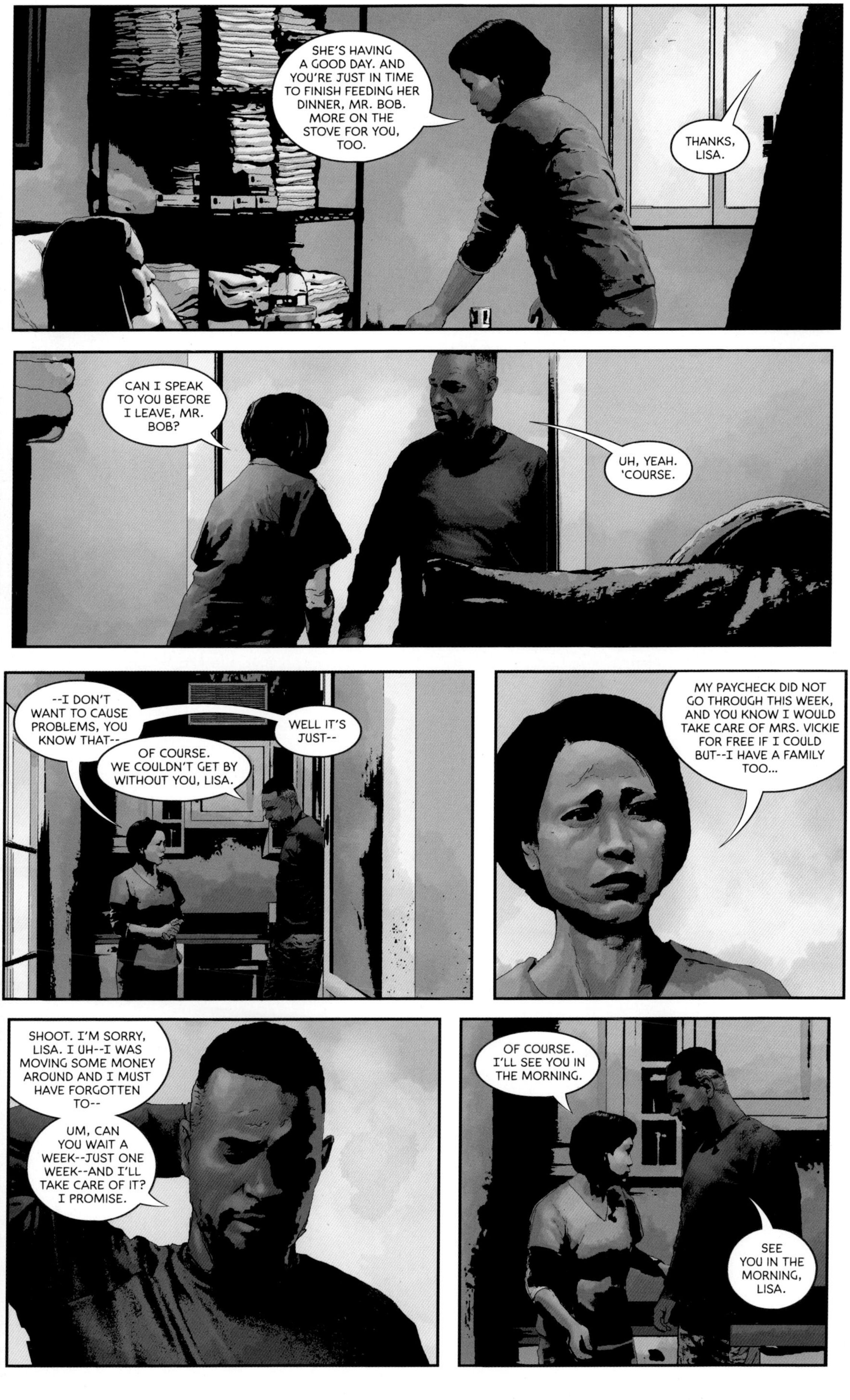
SHE'S HAVING A GOOD DAY. AND YOU'RE JUST IN TIME TO FINISH FEEDING HER DINNER, MR. BOB. MORE ON THE STOVE FOR YOU, TOO.
THANKS, LISA.
CAN I SPEAK TO YOU BEFORE I LEAVE, MR. BOB?
UH, YEAH. 'COURSE.
WELL IT'S JUST--
--I DON'T WANT TO CAUSE PROBLEMS, YOU KNOW THAT--
OF COURSE. WE COULDN'T GET BY WITHOUT YOU, LISA.
MY PAYCHECK DID NOT GO THROUGH THIS WEEK, AND YOU KNOW I WOULD TAKE CARE OF MRS. VICKIE FOR FREE IF I COULD BUT--I HAVE A FAMILY TOO...
SHOOT. I'M SORRY, LISA. I UH--I WAS MOVING SOME MONEY AROUND AND I MUST HAVE FORGOTTEN TO--
UM, CAN YOU WAIT A WEEK--JUST ONE WEEK--AND I'LL TAKE CARE OF IT? I PROMISE.
OF COURSE. I'LL SEE YOU IN THE MORNING.
SEE YOU IN THE MORNING, LISA.

FINAL NOTICE

...T PAST DUE

OXYGEN CANISTER
$ 1056.92

SHIT.

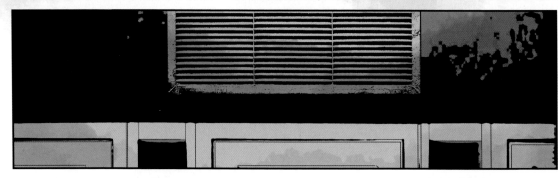

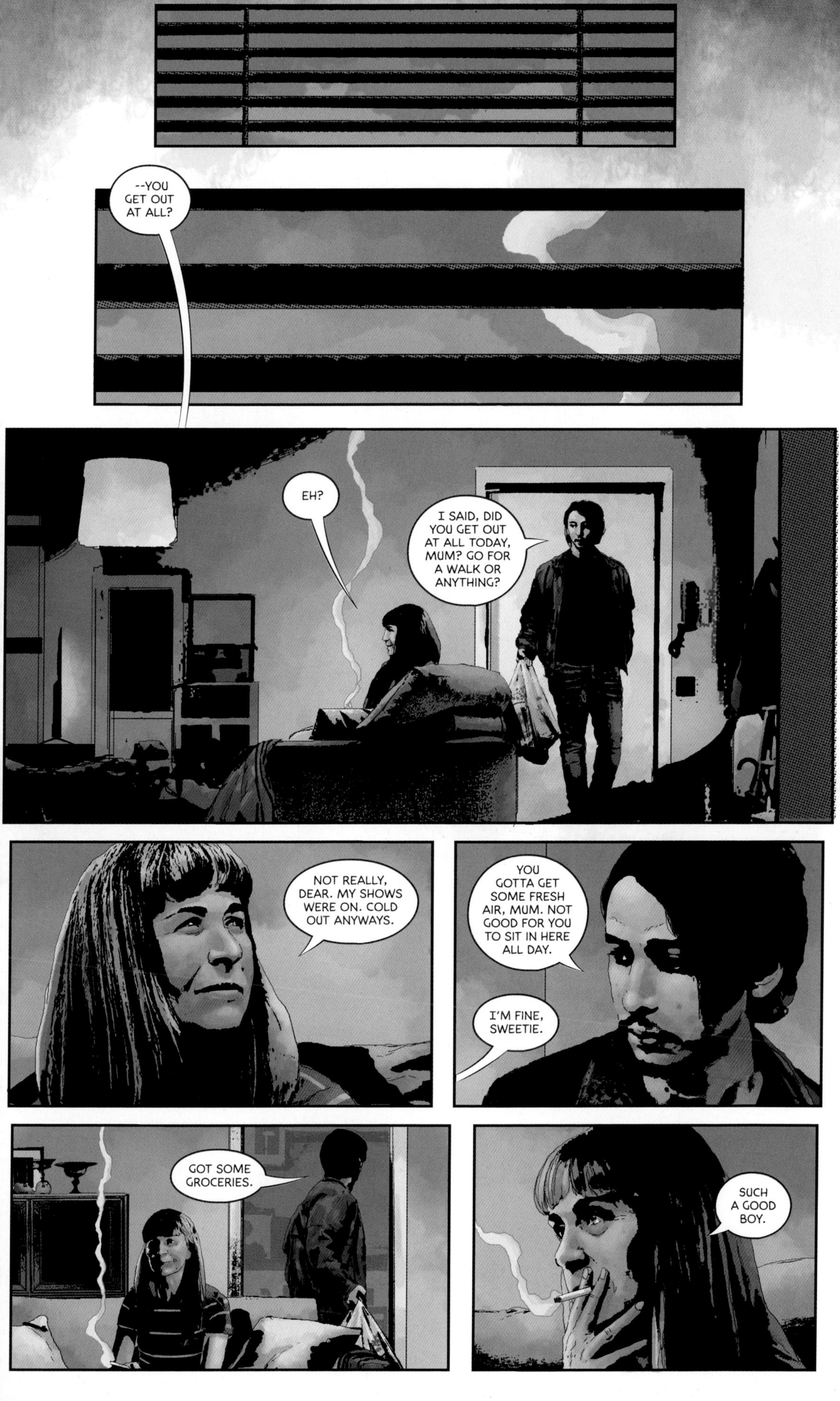
--YOU GET OUT AT ALL?
EH?
I SAID, DID YOU GET OUT AT ALL TODAY, MUM? GO FOR A WALK OR ANYTHING?
NOT REALLY, DEAR. MY SHOWS WERE ON. COLD OUT ANYWAYS.
YOU GOTTA GET SOME FRESH AIR, MUM. NOT GOOD FOR YOU TO SIT IN HERE ALL DAY.
I'M FINE, SWEETIE.
GOT SOME GROCERIES.
SUCH A GOOD BOY.

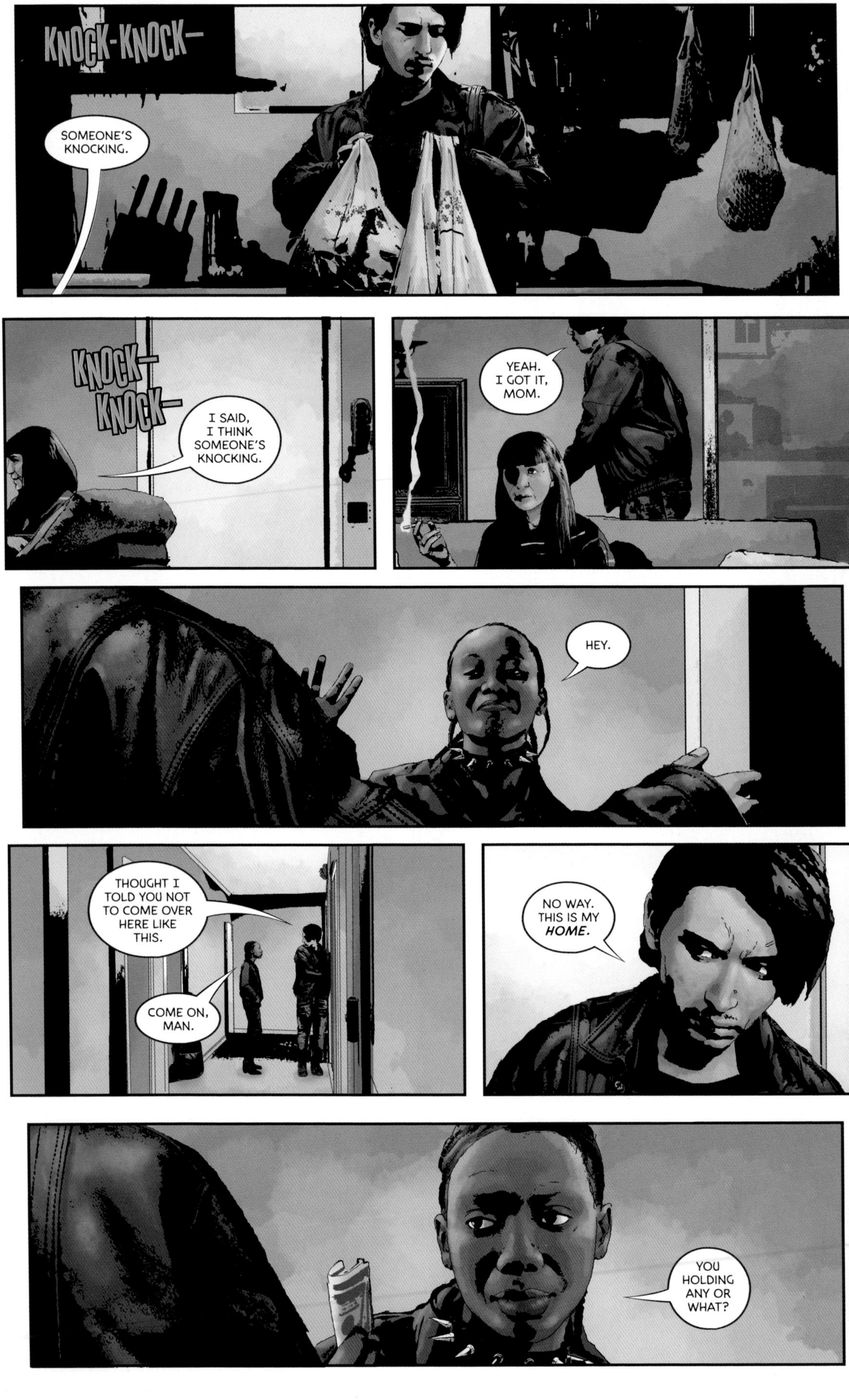
KNOCK-KNOCK-
SOMEONE'S KNOCKING.
KNOCK-KNOCK-
I SAID, I THINK SOMEONE'S KNOCKING.
YEAH. I GOT IT, MOM.
HEY.
THOUGHT I TOLD YOU NOT TO COME OVER HERE LIKE THIS.
COME ON, MAN.
NO WAY. THIS IS MY *HOME.*
YOU HOLDING ANY OR WHAT?

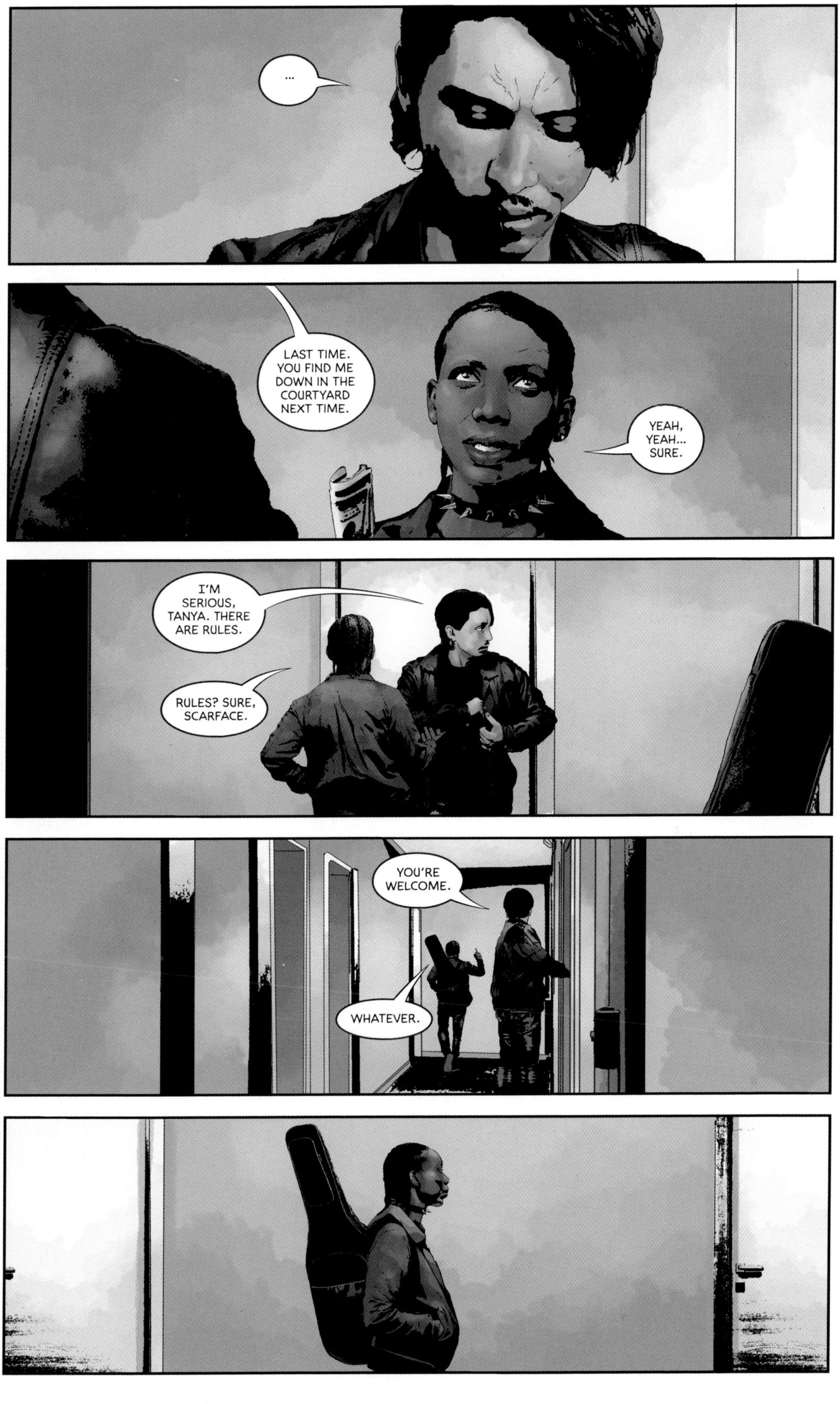
...
LAST TIME. YOU FIND ME DOWN IN THE COURTYARD NEXT TIME.
YEAH, YEAH... SURE.
I'M SERIOUS, TANYA. THERE ARE RULES.
RULES? SURE, SCARFACE.
YOU'RE WELCOME.
WHATEVER.

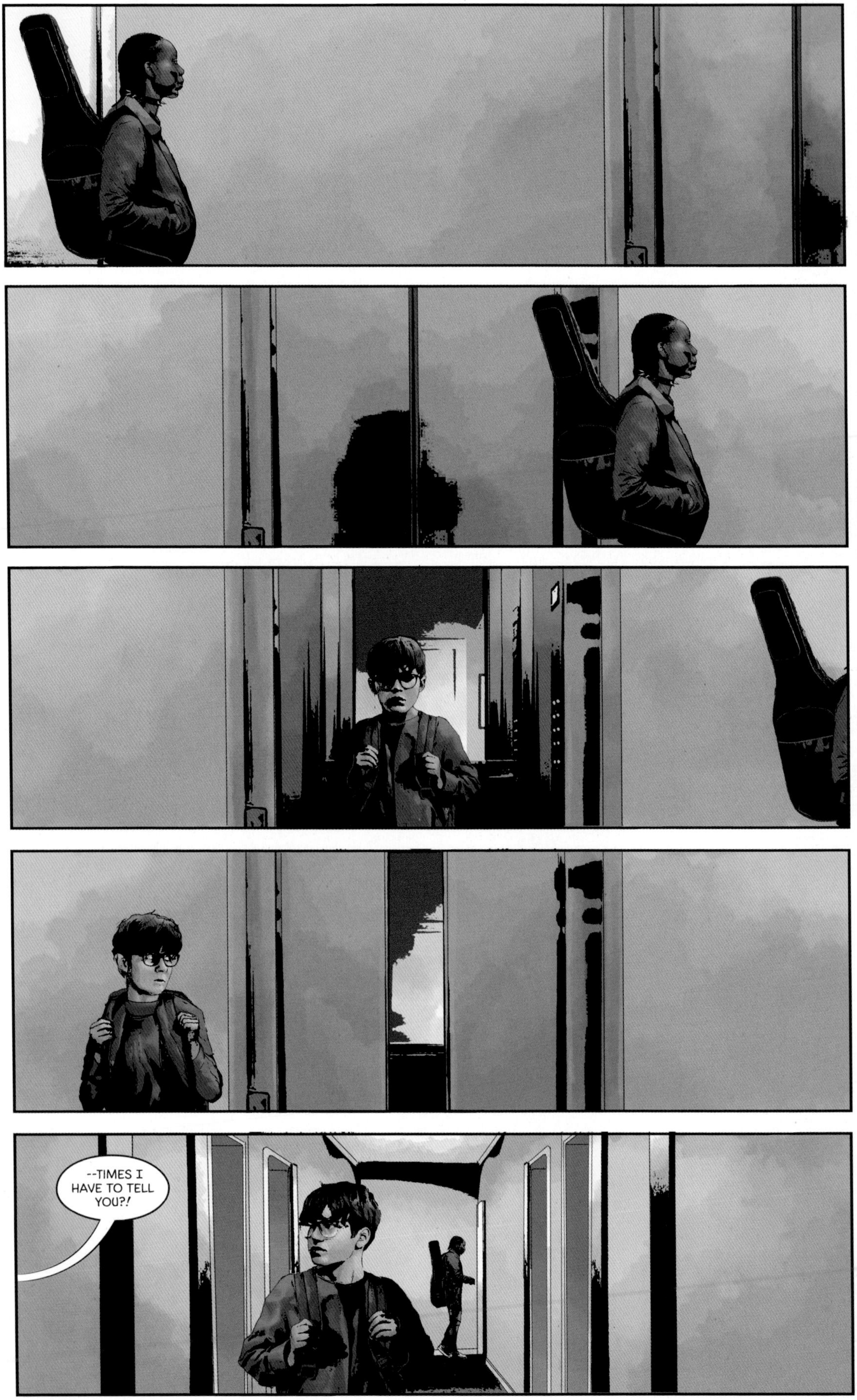
--TIMES I HAVE TO TELL YOU?!

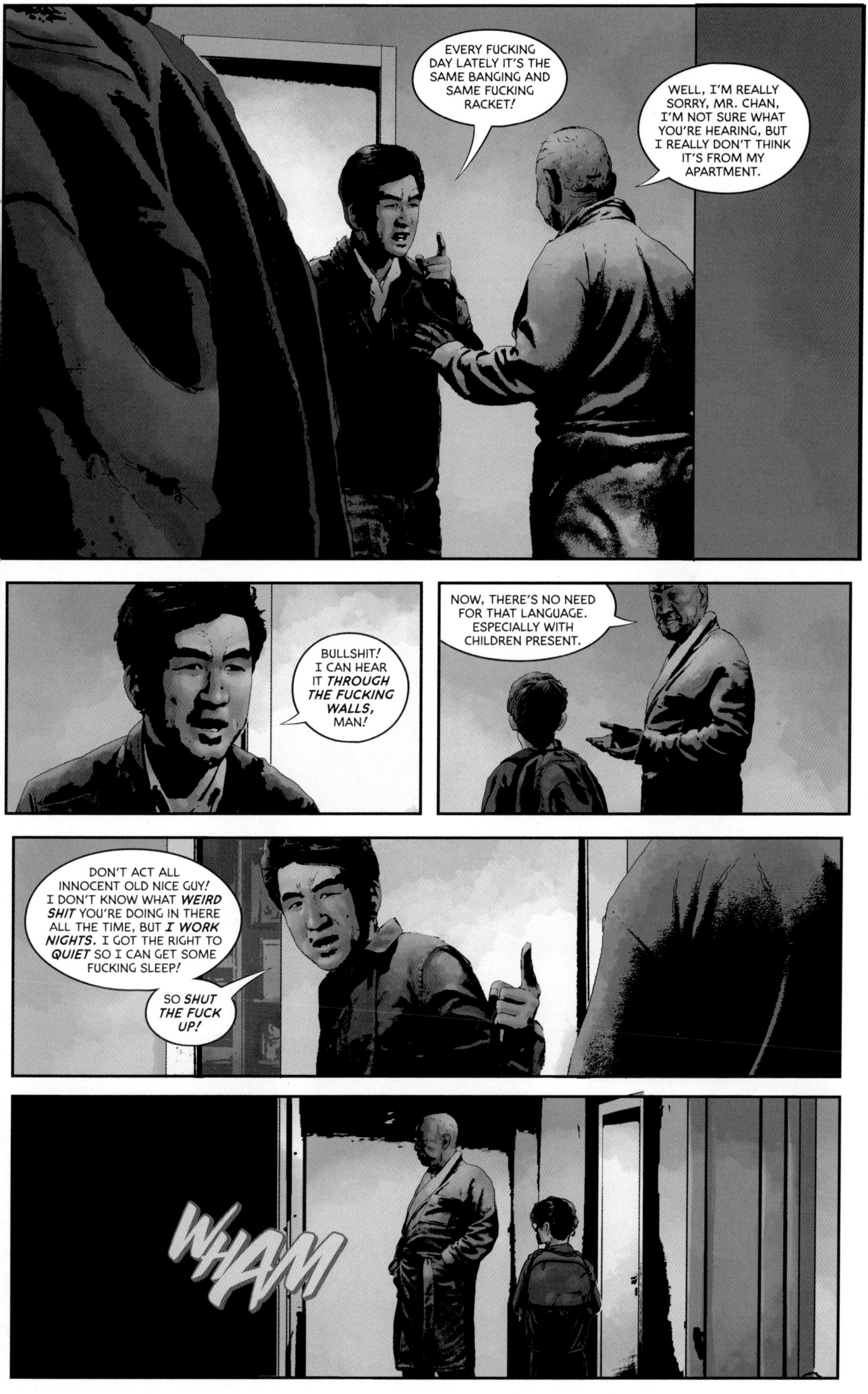
EVERY FUCKING DAY LATELY IT'S THE SAME BANGING AND SAME FUCKING RACKET!
WELL, I'M REALLY SORRY, MR. CHAN, I'M NOT SURE WHAT YOU'RE HEARING, BUT I REALLY DON'T THINK IT'S FROM MY APARTMENT.
BULLSHIT! I CAN HEAR IT THROUGH THE FUCKING WALLS, MAN!
NOW, THERE'S NO NEED FOR THAT LANGUAGE. ESPECIALLY WITH CHILDREN PRESENT.
DON'T ACT ALL INNOCENT OLD NICE GUY! I DON'T KNOW WHAT WEIRD SHIT YOU'RE DOING IN THERE ALL THE TIME, BUT I WORK NIGHTS. I GOT THE RIGHT TO QUIET SO I CAN GET SOME FUCKING SLEEP!
SO SHUT THE FUCK UP!
WHAM

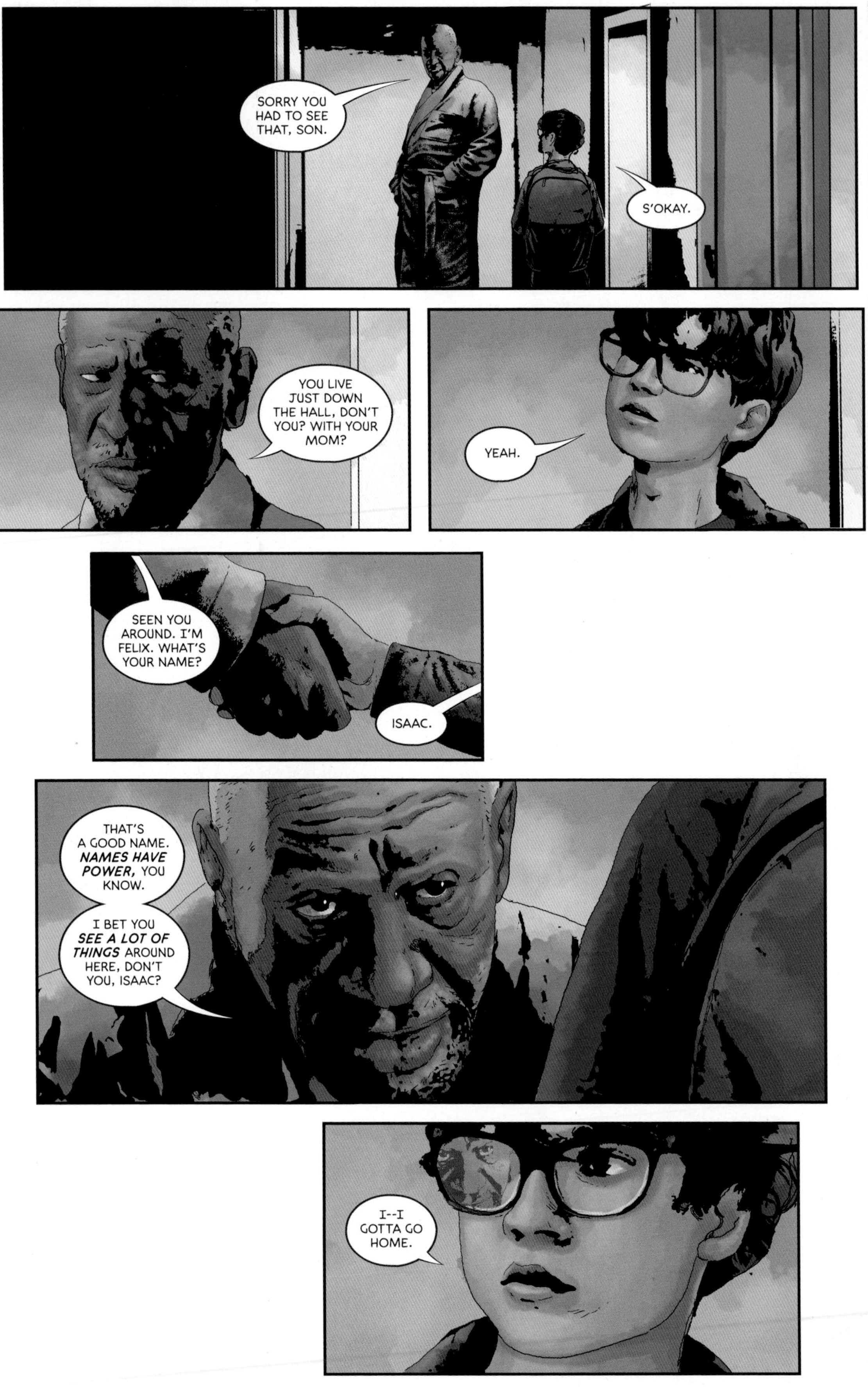
SORRY YOU HAD TO SEE THAT, SON.
S'OKAY.
YOU LIVE JUST DOWN THE HALL, DON'T YOU? WITH YOUR MOM?
YEAH.
SEEN YOU AROUND. I'M FELIX. WHAT'S YOUR NAME?
ISAAC.
THAT'S A GOOD NAME. ***NAMES HAVE POWER,*** YOU KNOW.
I BET YOU ***SEE A LOT OF THINGS*** AROUND HERE, DON'T YOU, ISAAC?
I--I GOTTA GO HOME.

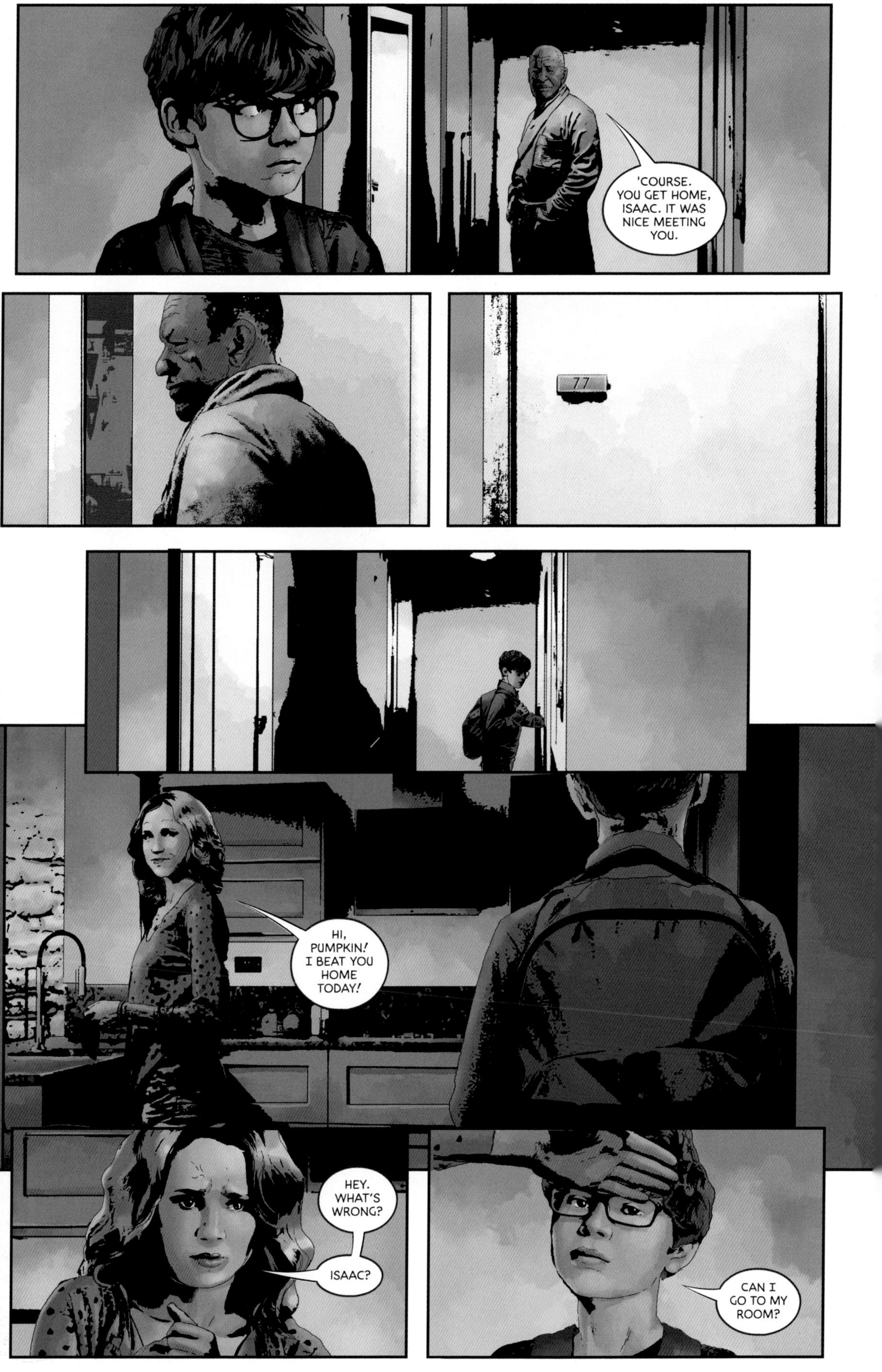
'COURSE. YOU GET HOME, ISAAC. IT WAS NICE MEETING YOU.
77
HI, PUMPKIN! I BEAT YOU HOME TODAY!
HEY. WHAT'S WRONG?
ISAAC?
CAN I GO TO MY ROOM?

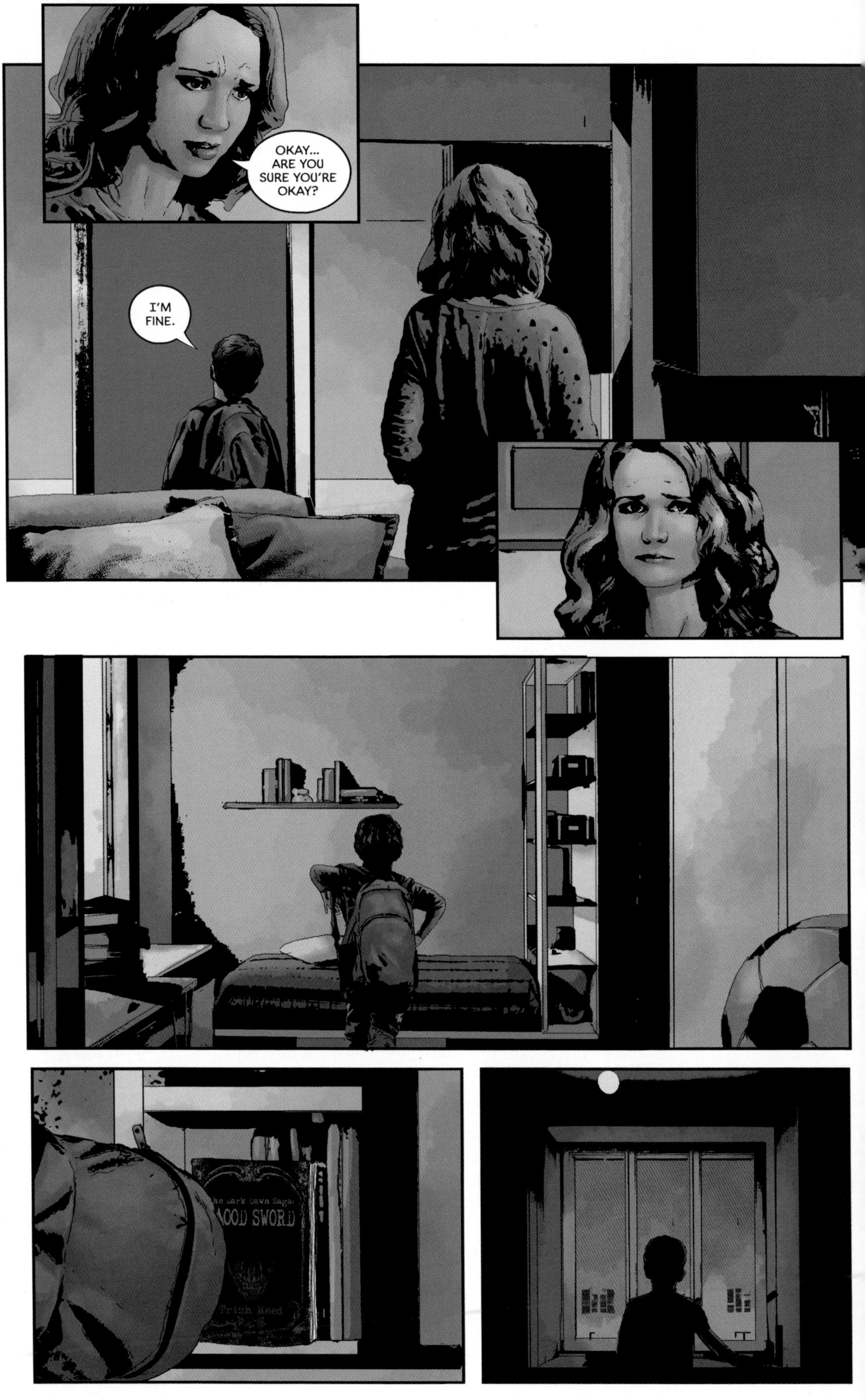
OKAY... ARE YOU SURE YOU'RE OKAY?
I'M FINE.

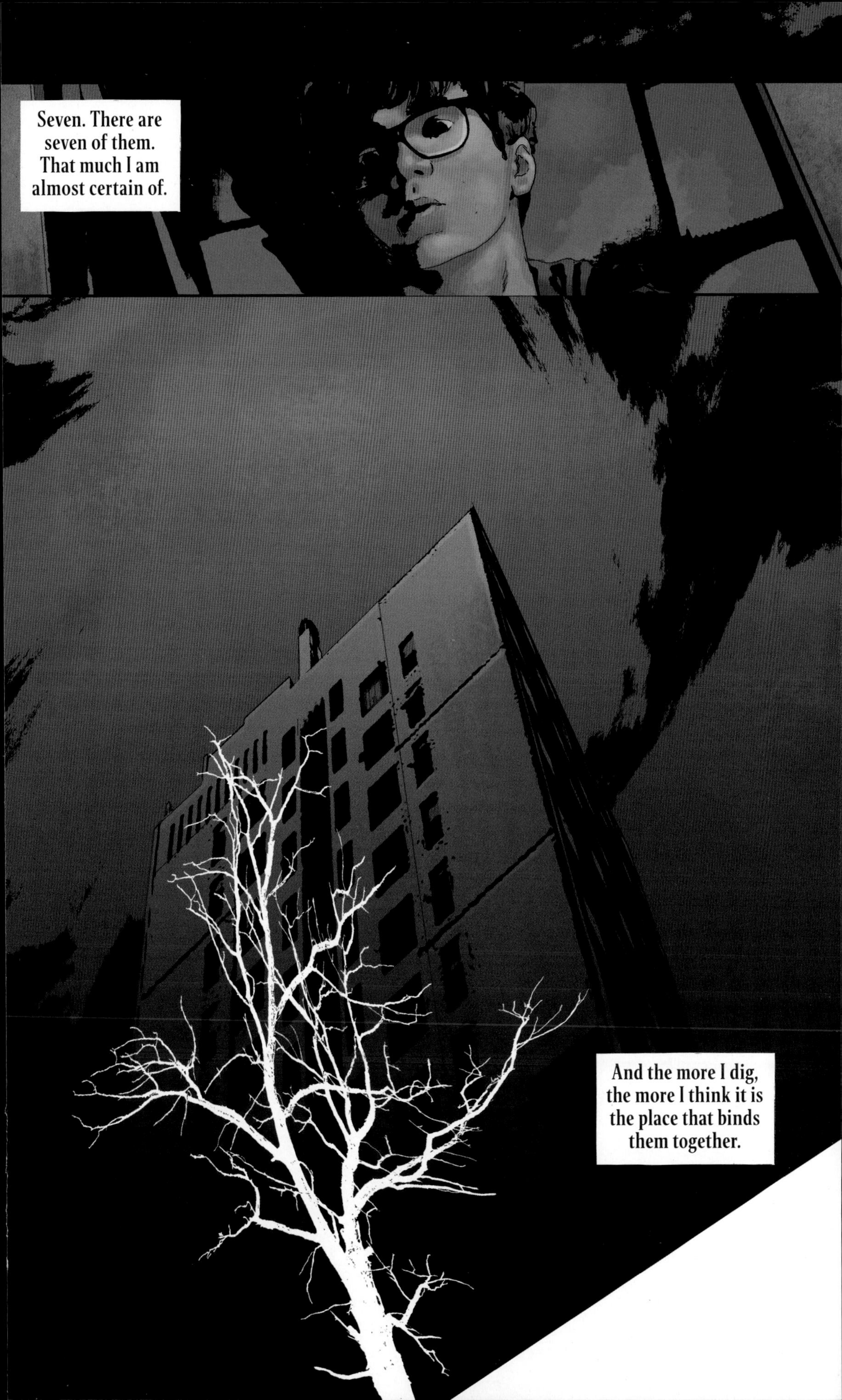
Seven. There are seven of them. That much I am almost certain of.
And the more I dig, the more I think it is the place that binds them together.

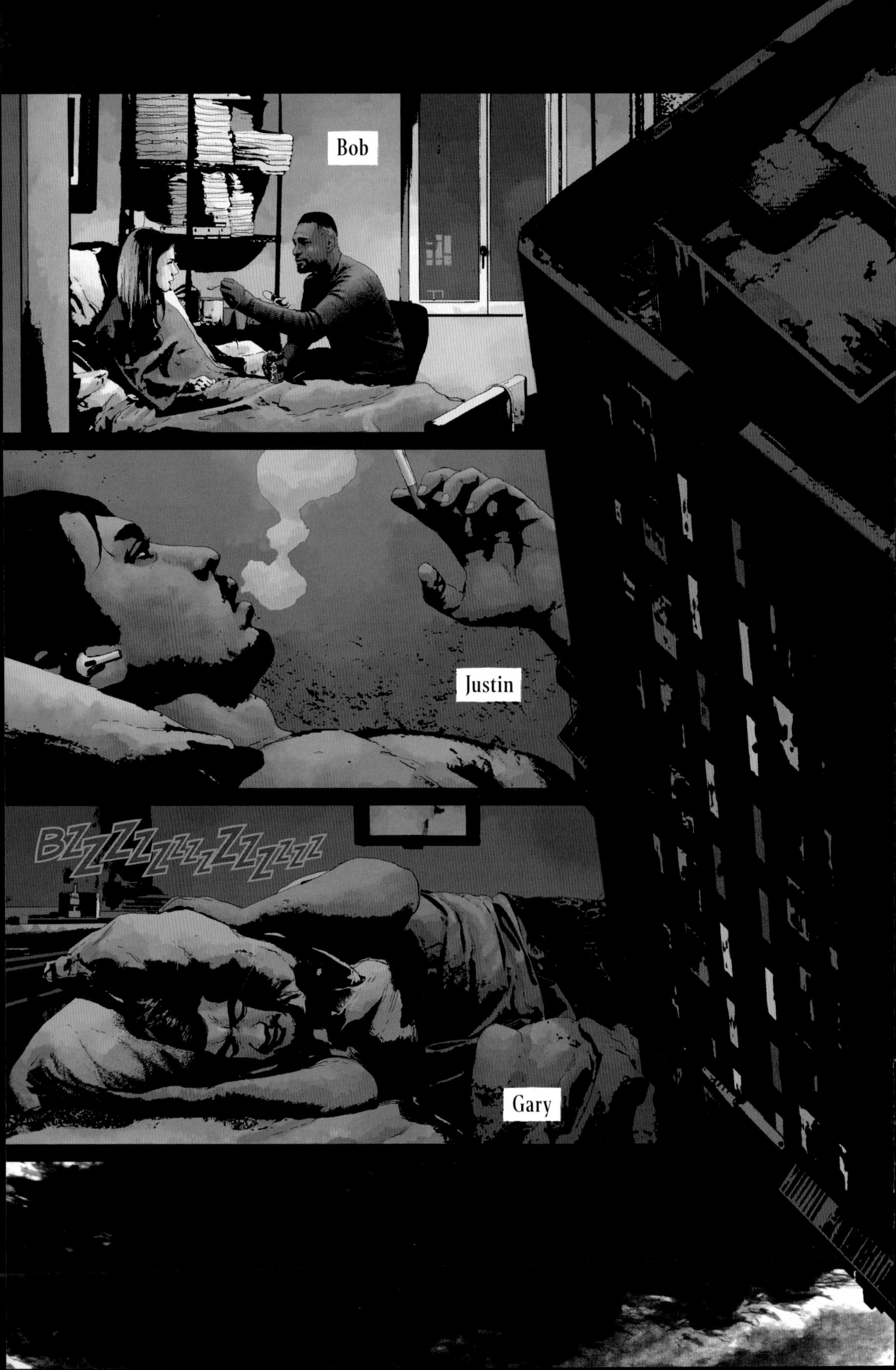

Bob
Justin
BZZZZzzzzZZZzzzz
Gary

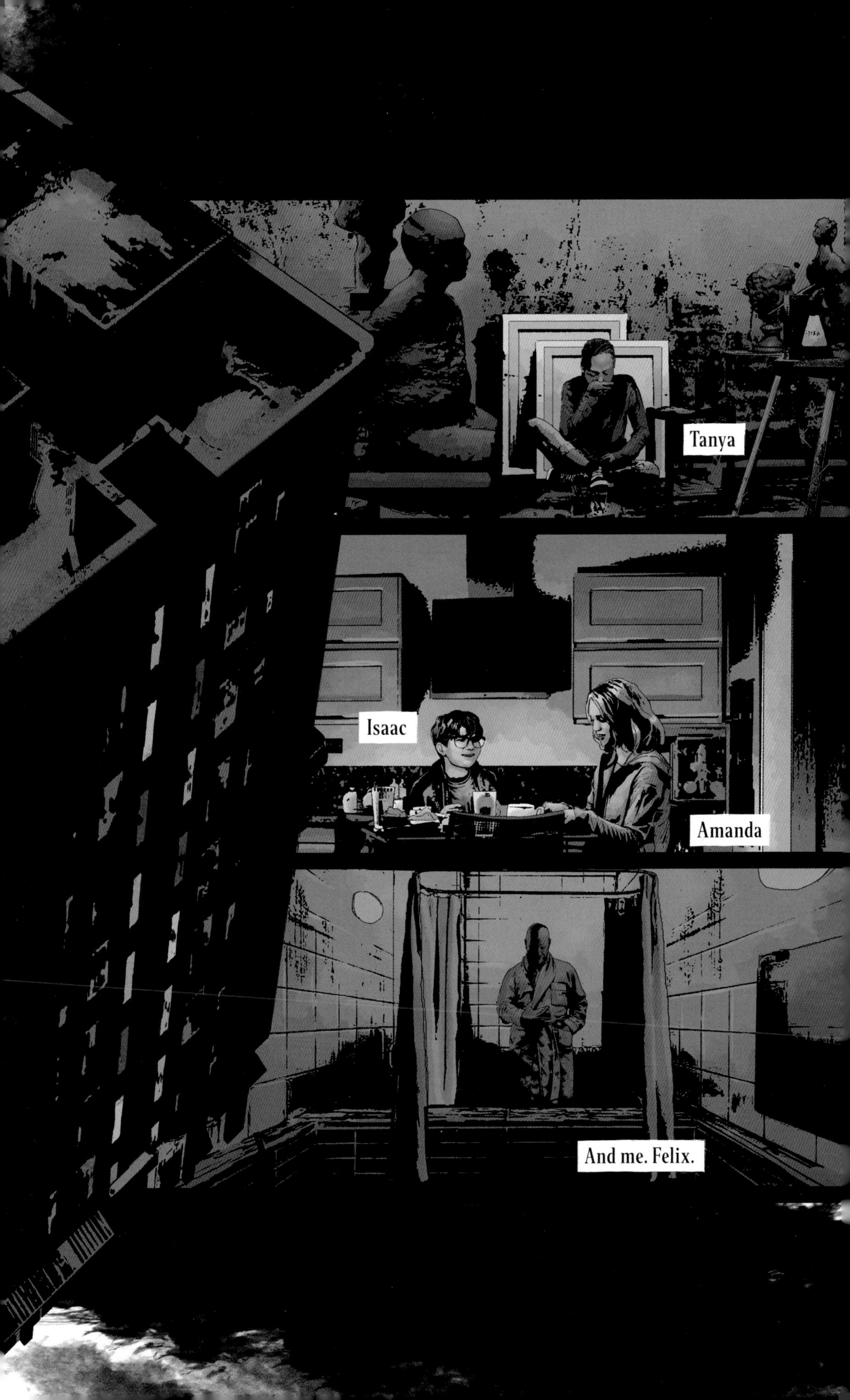
Tanya
Isaac
Amanda
And me. Felix.

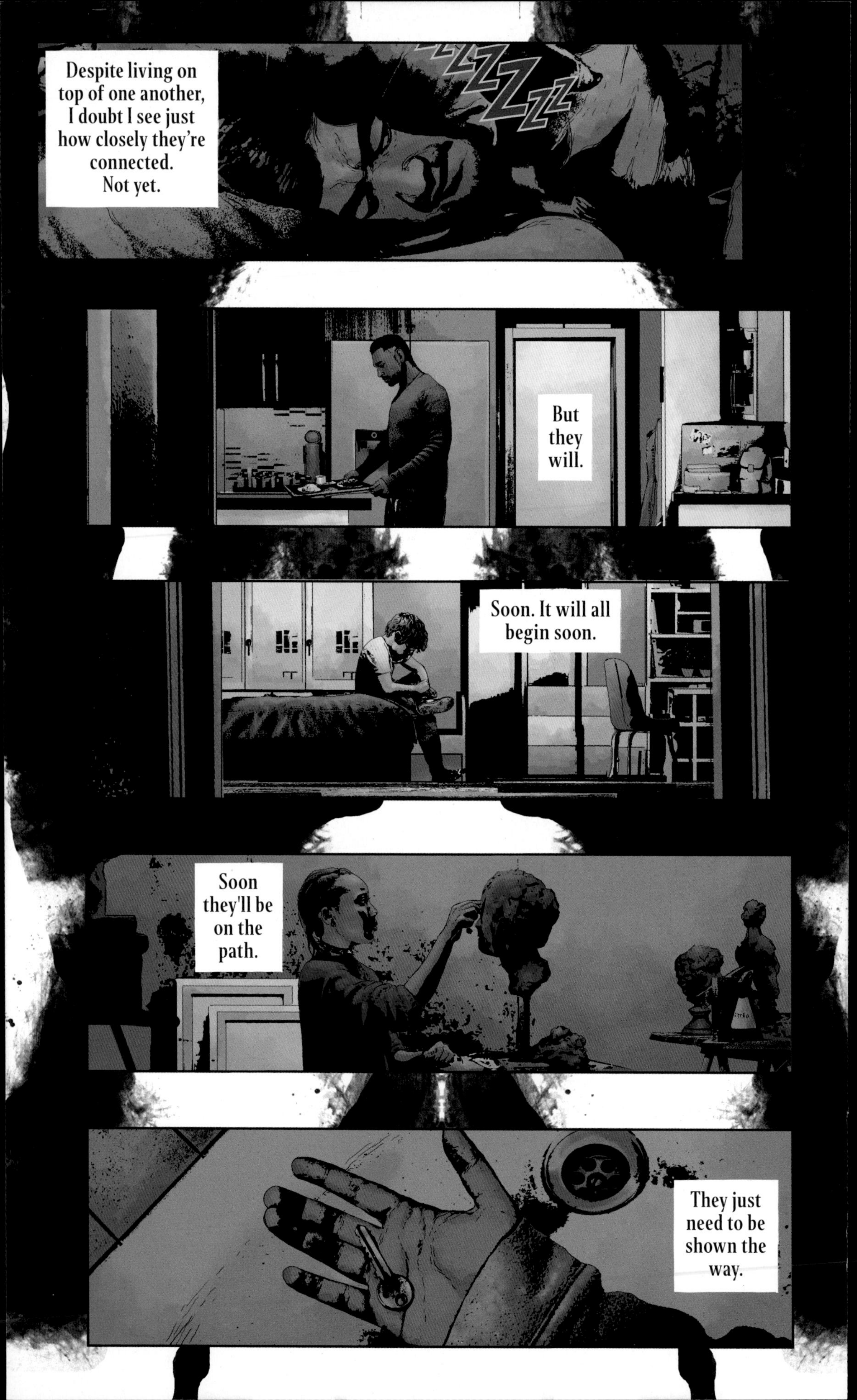
Despite living on top of one another, I doubt I see just how closely they're connected. Not yet.
ZZZZZ
But they will.
Soon. It will all begin soon.
Soon they'll be on the path.
They just need to be shown the way.

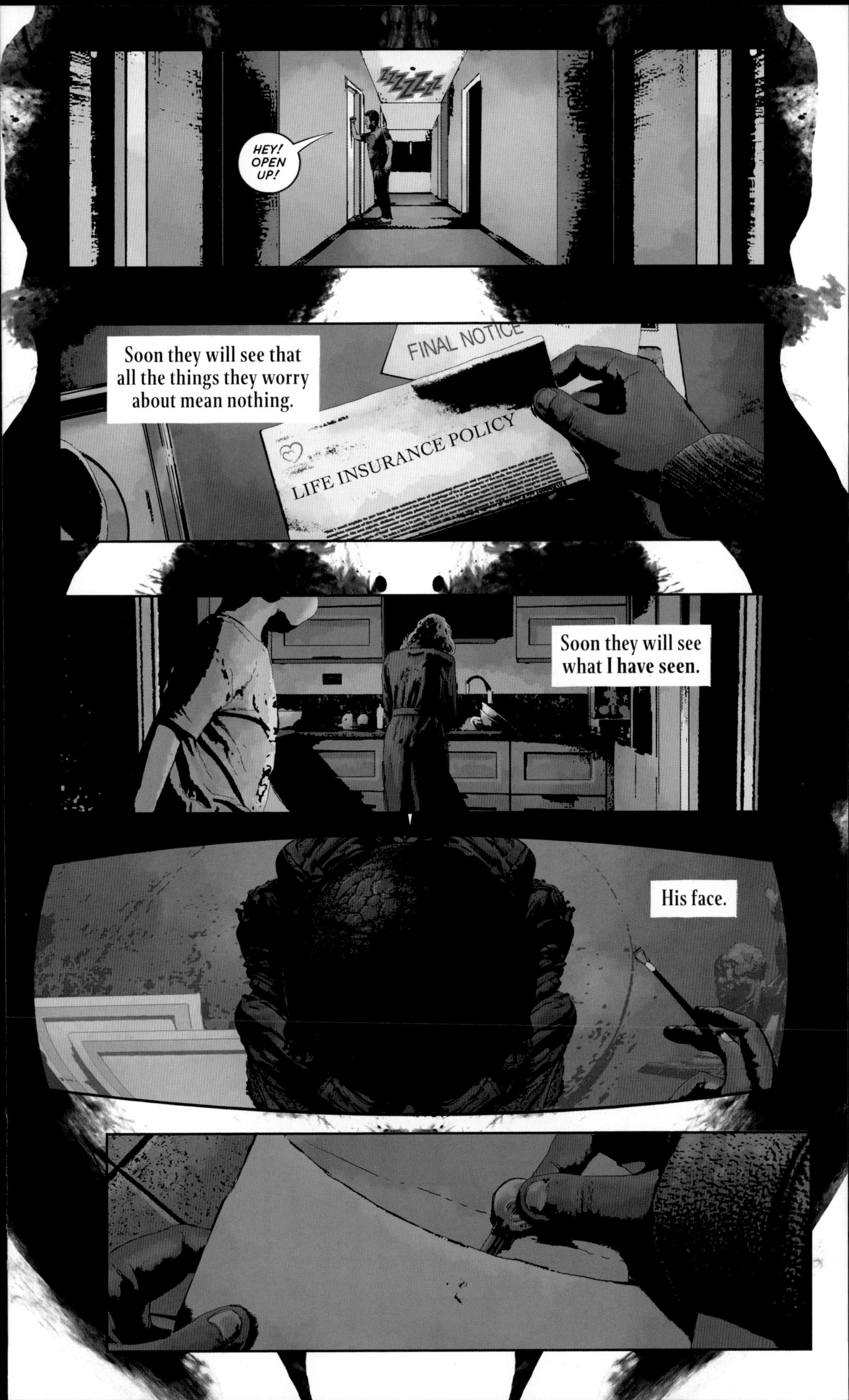

ZZZZZZZ
HEY! OPEN UP!
Soon they will see that all the things they worry about mean nothing.
FINAL NOTICE
LIFE INSURANCE POLICY
Soon they will see what I have seen.
His face.

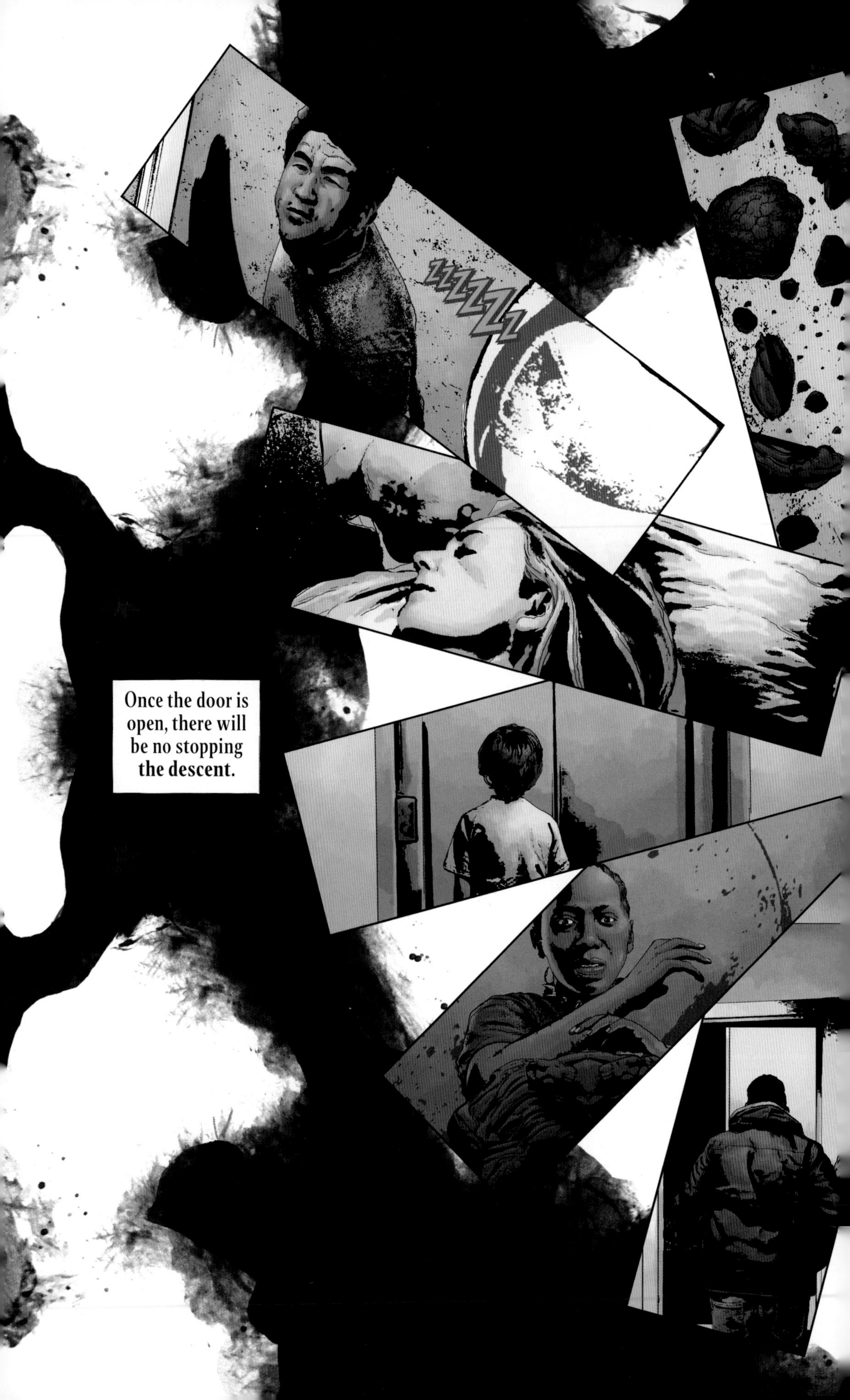
Once the door is open, there will be no stopping the descent.

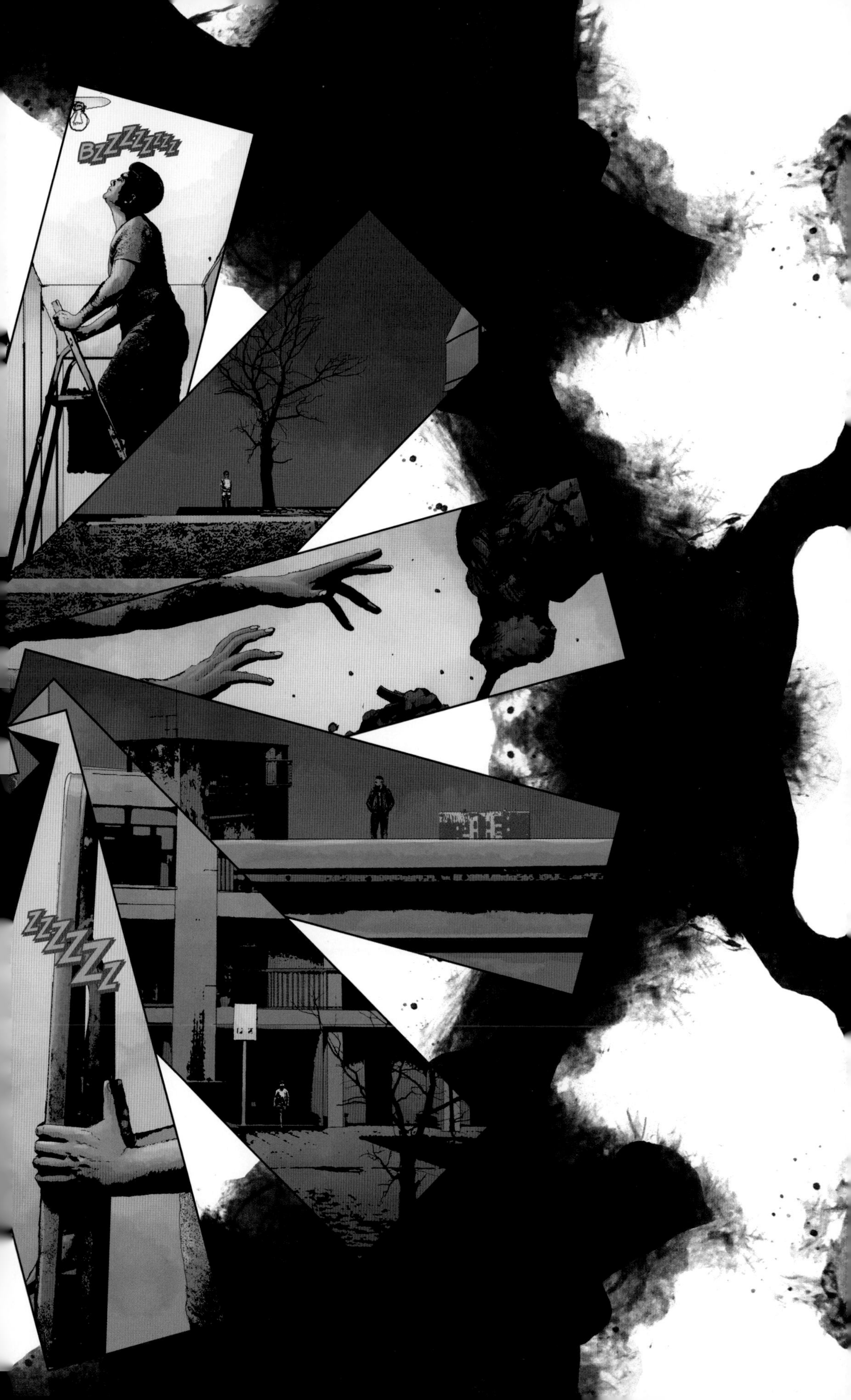

BZZZZZZZ
ZZZZZZ

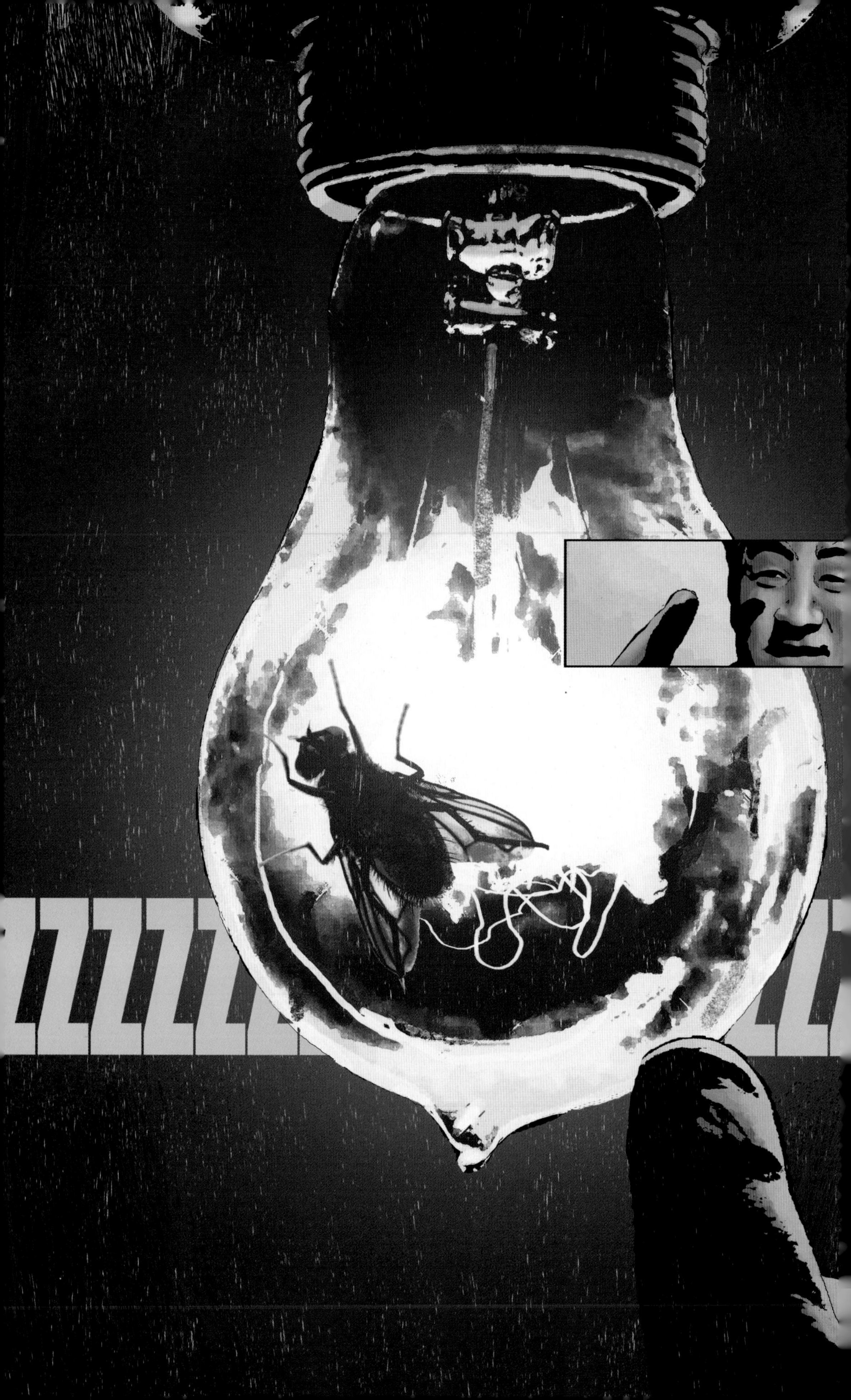

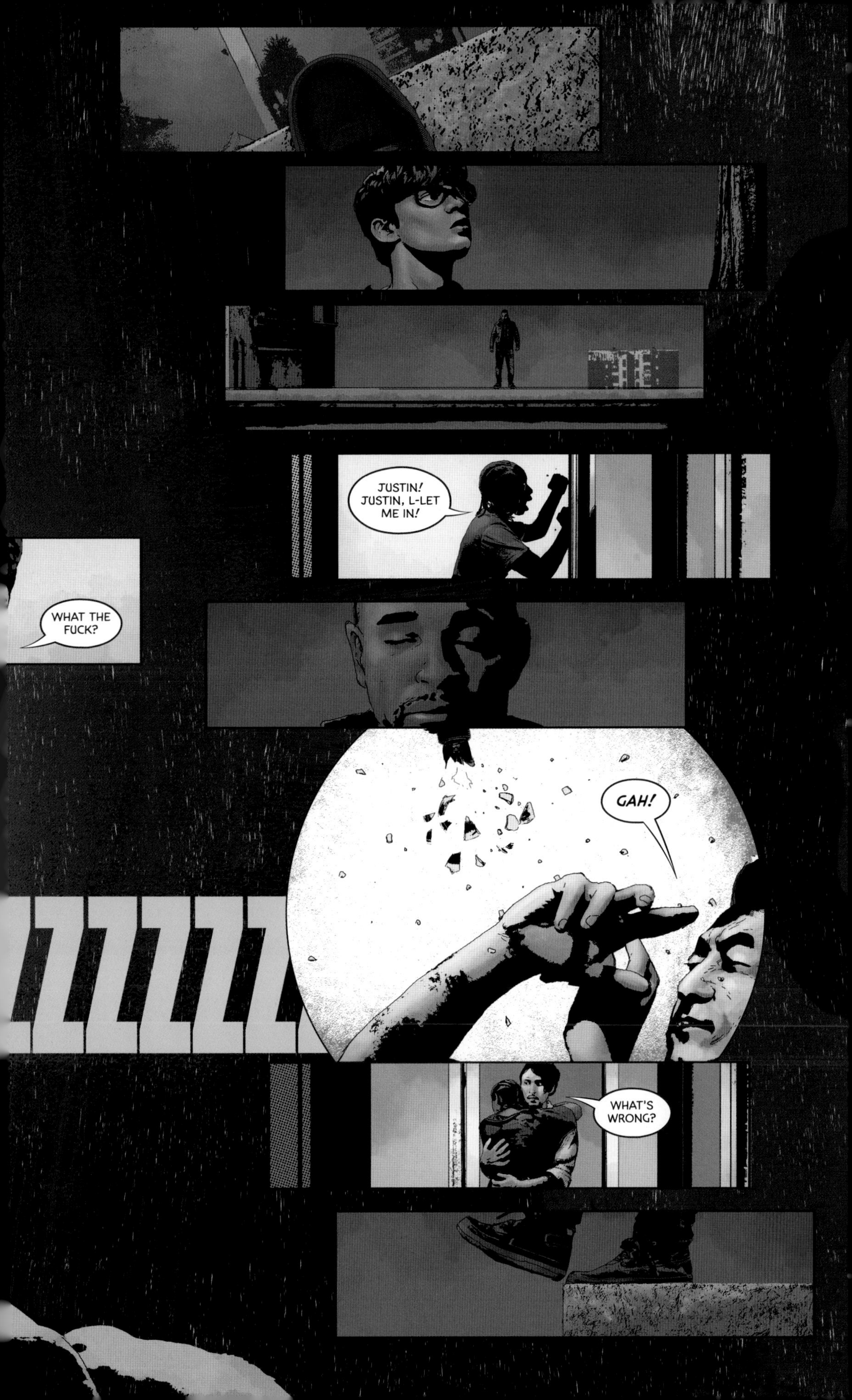
JUSTIN! JUSTIN, L-LET ME IN!
WHAT THE FUCK?
GAH!
ZZZZZ
WHAT'S WRONG?

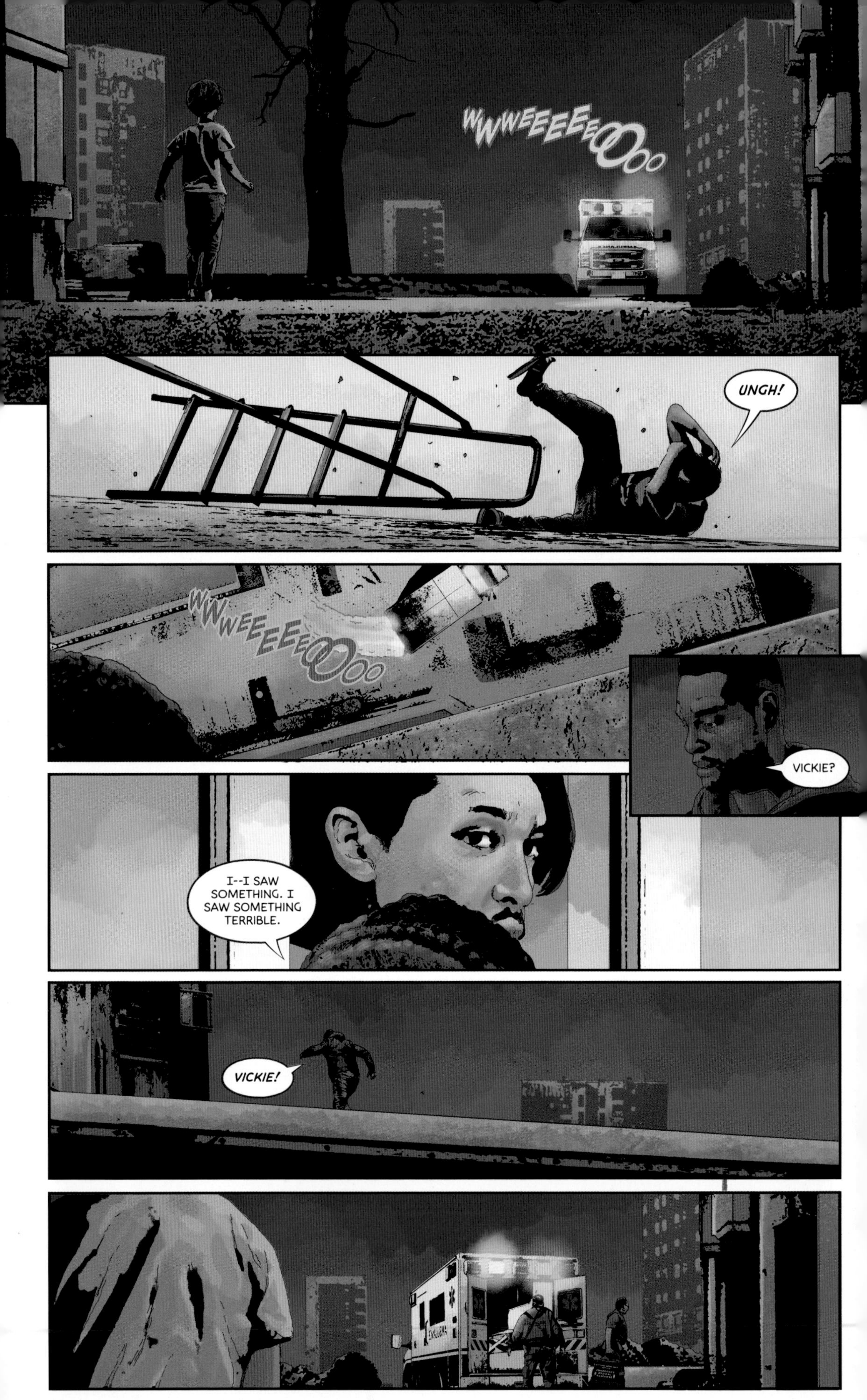
WWWEEEEEEOOOoo
UNGH!
WWWEEEEEOOOoo
VICKIE?
I--I SAW SOMETHING. I SAW SOMETHING TERRIBLE.
VICKIE!

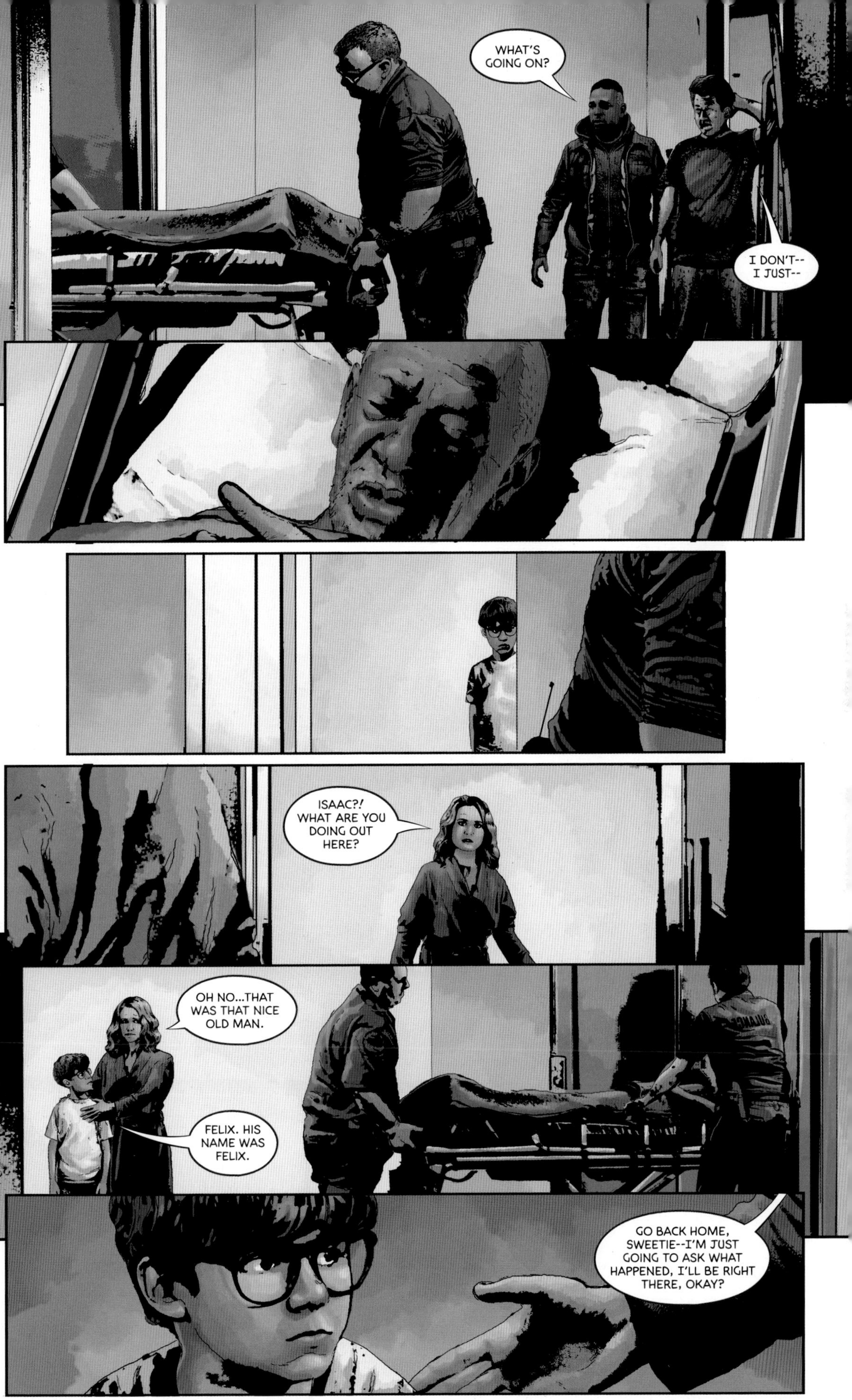
WHAT'S GOING ON?
I DON'T-- I JUST--
ISAAC?! WHAT ARE YOU DOING OUT HERE?
OH NO...THAT WAS THAT NICE OLD MAN.
FELIX. HIS NAME WAS FELIX.
GO BACK HOME, SWEETIE--I'M JUST GOING TO ASK WHAT HAPPENED, I'LL BE RIGHT THERE, OKAY?

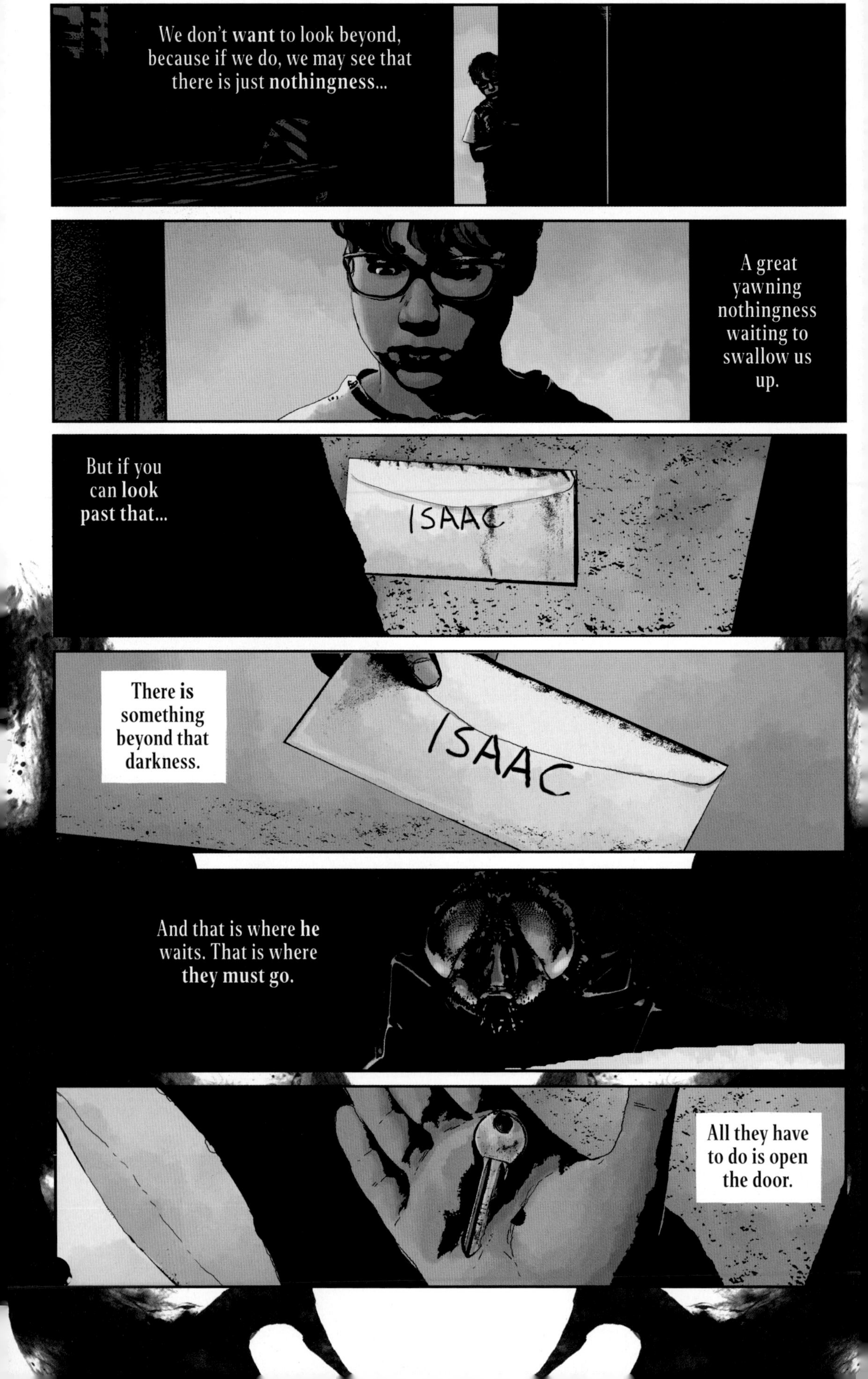
We don't **want** to look beyond, because if we do, we may see that there is just **nothingness**...
A great yawning nothingness waiting to swallow us up.
But if you can **look** past that...
ISAAC
There **is** something beyond that darkness.
ISAAC
And that is where **he** waits. That is where **they must** go.
All they have to do is open the door.

2

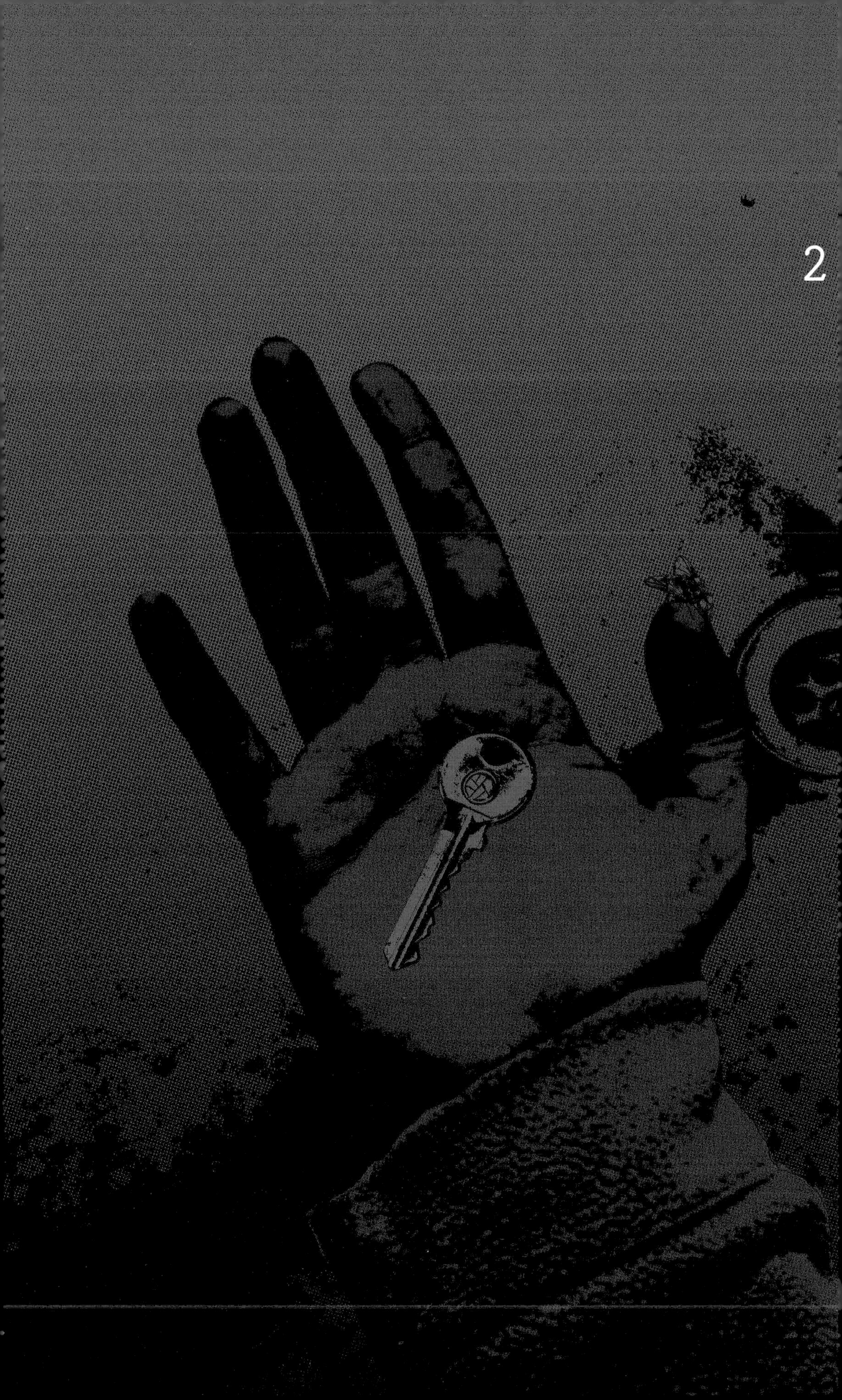

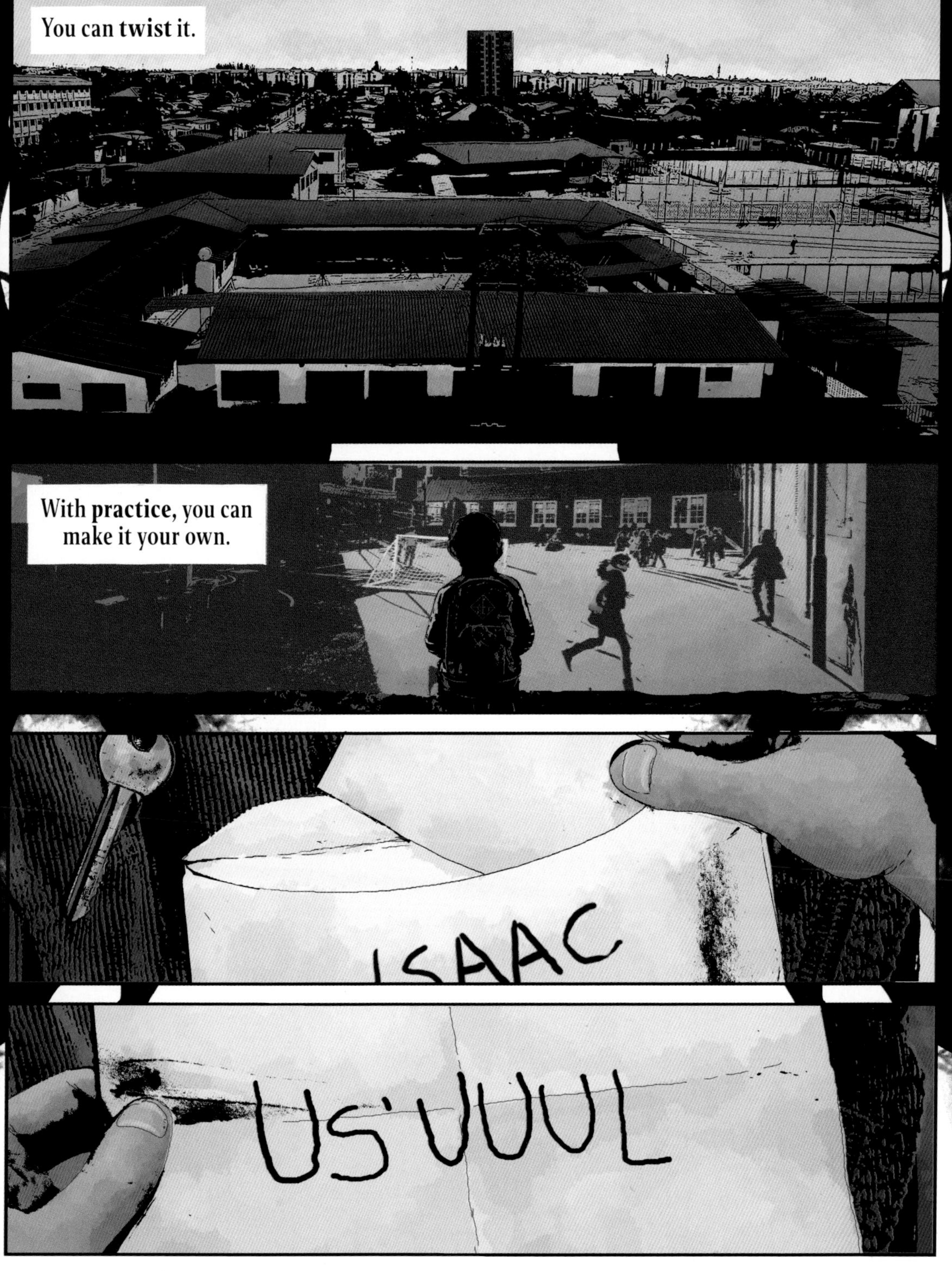
You can twist it.
With practice, you can make it your own.
ISAAC
US'UUL

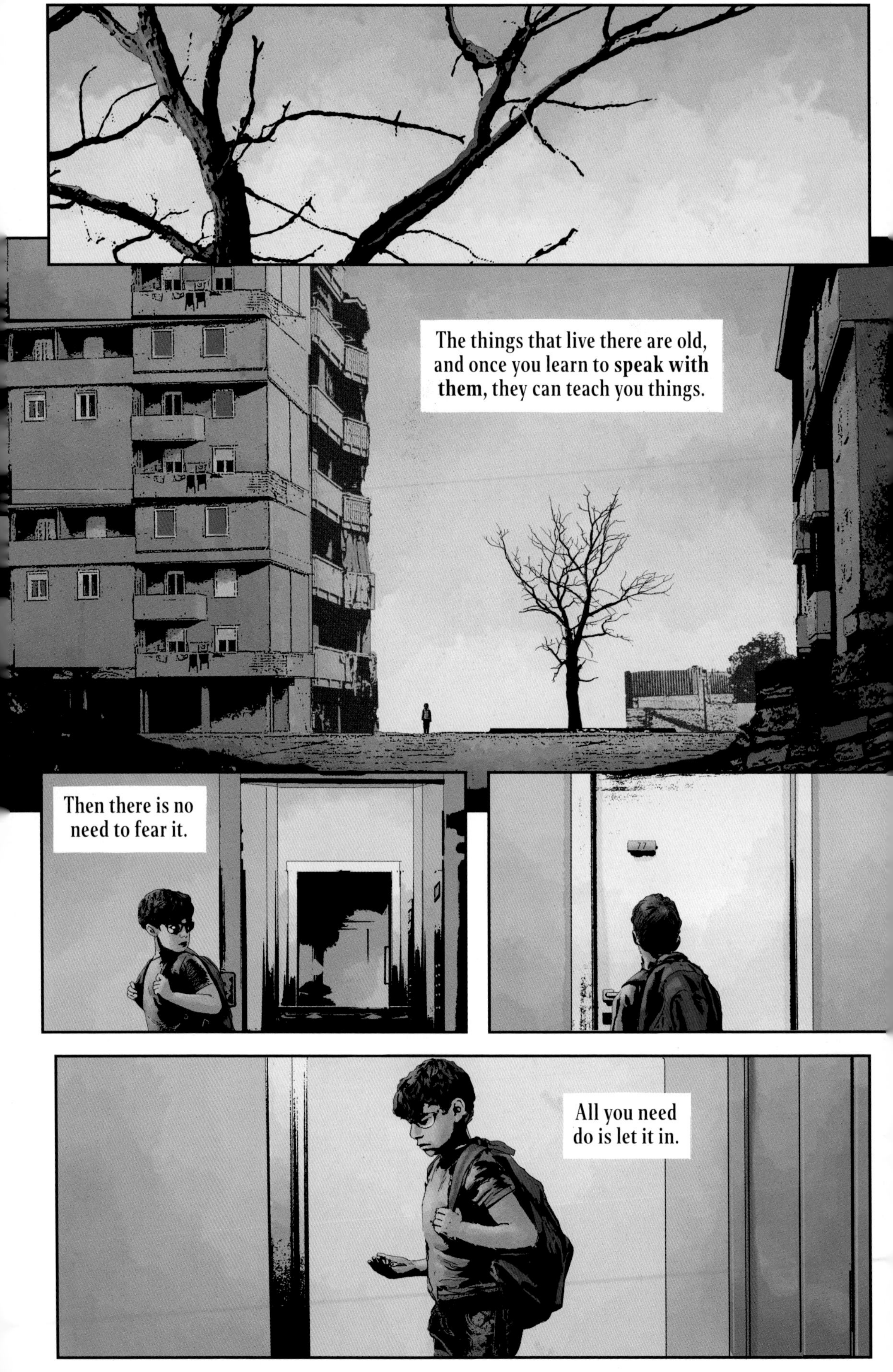
The things that live there are old, and once you learn to **speak with them**, they can teach you things.
Then there is no need to fear it.
77
All you need do is let it in.

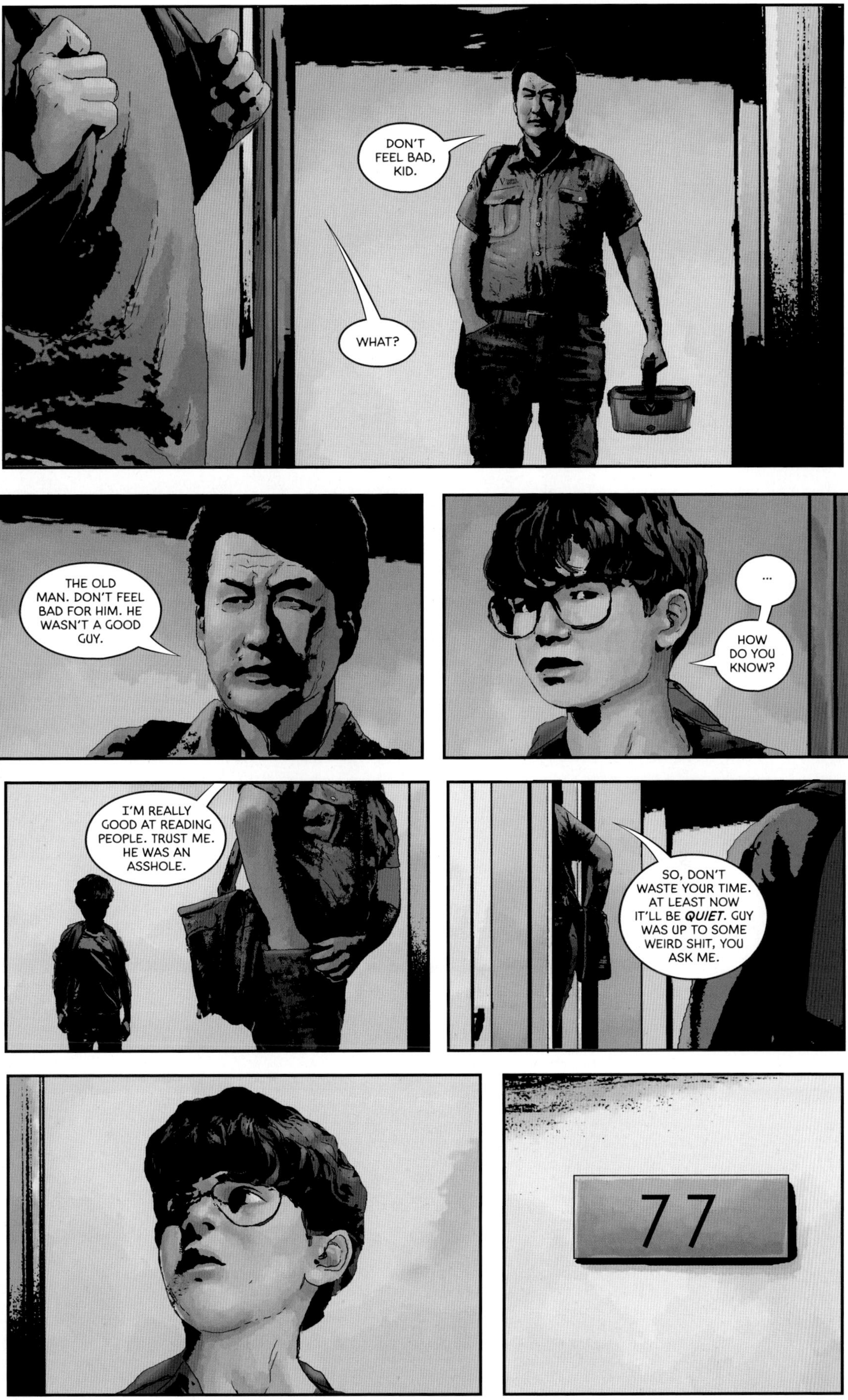
DON'T FEEL BAD, KID.
WHAT?
THE OLD MAN. DON'T FEEL BAD FOR HIM. HE WASN'T A GOOD GUY.
...
HOW DO YOU KNOW?
I'M REALLY GOOD AT READING PEOPLE. TRUST ME. HE WAS AN ASSHOLE.
SO, DON'T WASTE YOUR TIME. AT LEAST NOW IT'LL BE ***QUIET***. GUY WAS UP TO SOME WEIRD SHIT, YOU ASK ME.
77

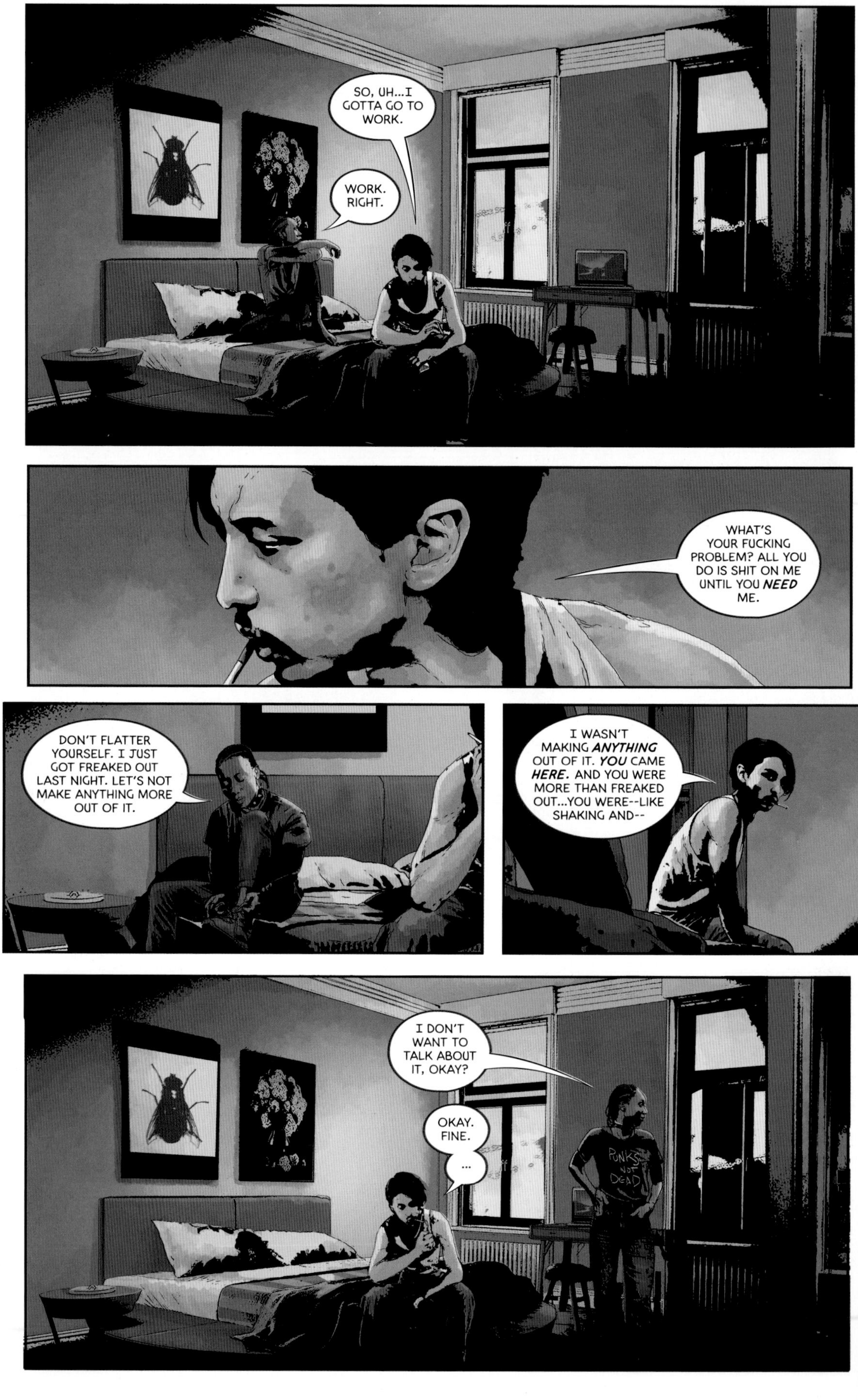
SO, UH...I GOTTA GO TO WORK.
WORK. RIGHT.
WHAT'S YOUR FUCKING PROBLEM? ALL YOU DO IS SHIT ON ME UNTIL YOU *NEED* ME.
DON'T FLATTER YOURSELF. I JUST GOT FREAKED OUT LAST NIGHT. LET'S NOT MAKE ANYTHING MORE OUT OF IT.
I WASN'T MAKING *ANYTHING* OUT OF IT. *YOU* CAME *HERE.* AND YOU WERE MORE THAN FREAKED OUT...YOU WERE--LIKE SHAKING AND--
I DON'T WANT TO TALK ABOUT IT, OKAY?
OKAY. FINE.
...
PUNKS NOT DEAD

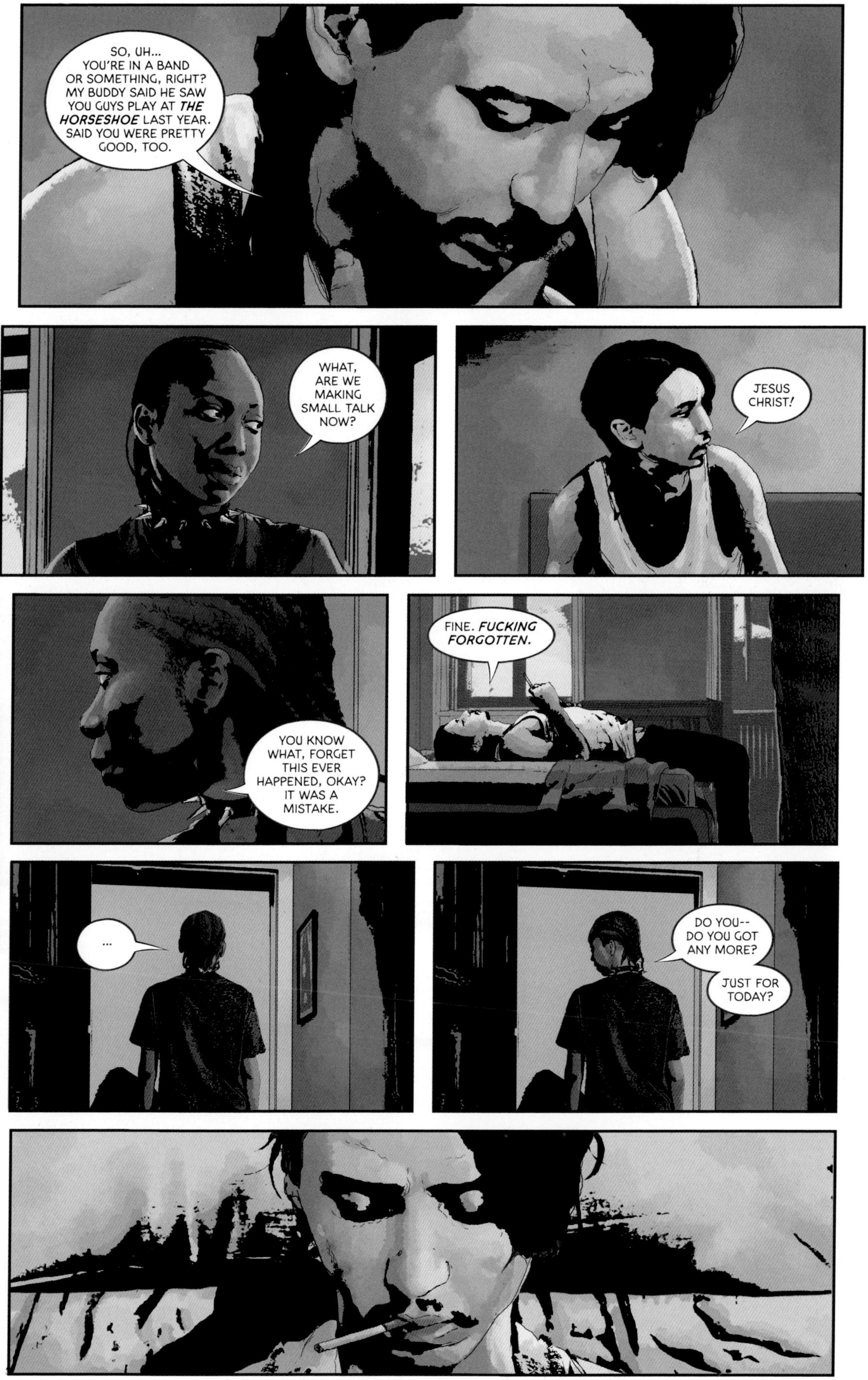
SO, UH... YOU'RE IN A BAND OR SOMETHING, RIGHT? MY BUDDY SAID HE SAW YOU GUYS PLAY AT *THE HORSESHOE* LAST YEAR. SAID YOU WERE PRETTY GOOD, TOO.
WHAT, ARE WE MAKING SMALL TALK NOW?
JESUS CHRIST!
YOU KNOW WHAT, FORGET THIS EVER HAPPENED, OKAY? IT WAS A MISTAKE.
FINE. *FUCKING FORGOTTEN.*
...
DO YOU-- DO YOU GOT ANY MORE?
JUST FOR TODAY?

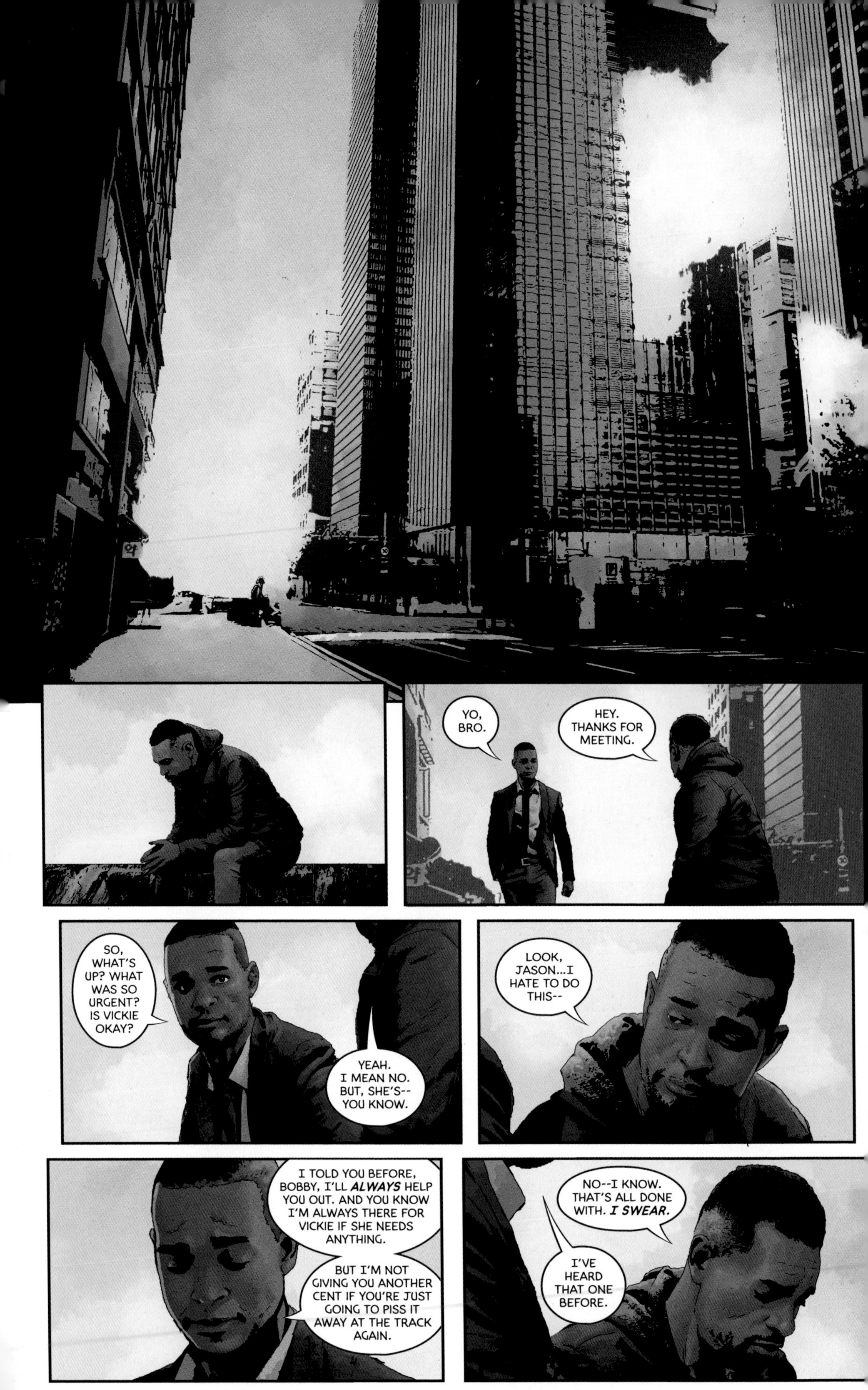

YO, BRO.
HEY. THANKS FOR MEETING.
SO, WHAT'S UP? WHAT WAS SO URGENT? IS VICKIE OKAY?
YEAH. I MEAN NO. BUT, SHE'S-- YOU KNOW.
LOOK, JASON...I HATE TO DO THIS--
I TOLD YOU BEFORE, BOBBY, I'LL ALWAYS HELP YOU OUT. AND YOU KNOW I'M ALWAYS THERE FOR VICKIE IF SHE NEEDS ANYTHING.
BUT I'M NOT GIVING YOU ANOTHER CENT IF YOU'RE JUST GOING TO PISS IT AWAY AT THE TRACK AGAIN.
NO--I KNOW. THAT'S ALL DONE WITH. I SWEAR.
I'VE HEARD THAT ONE BEFORE.

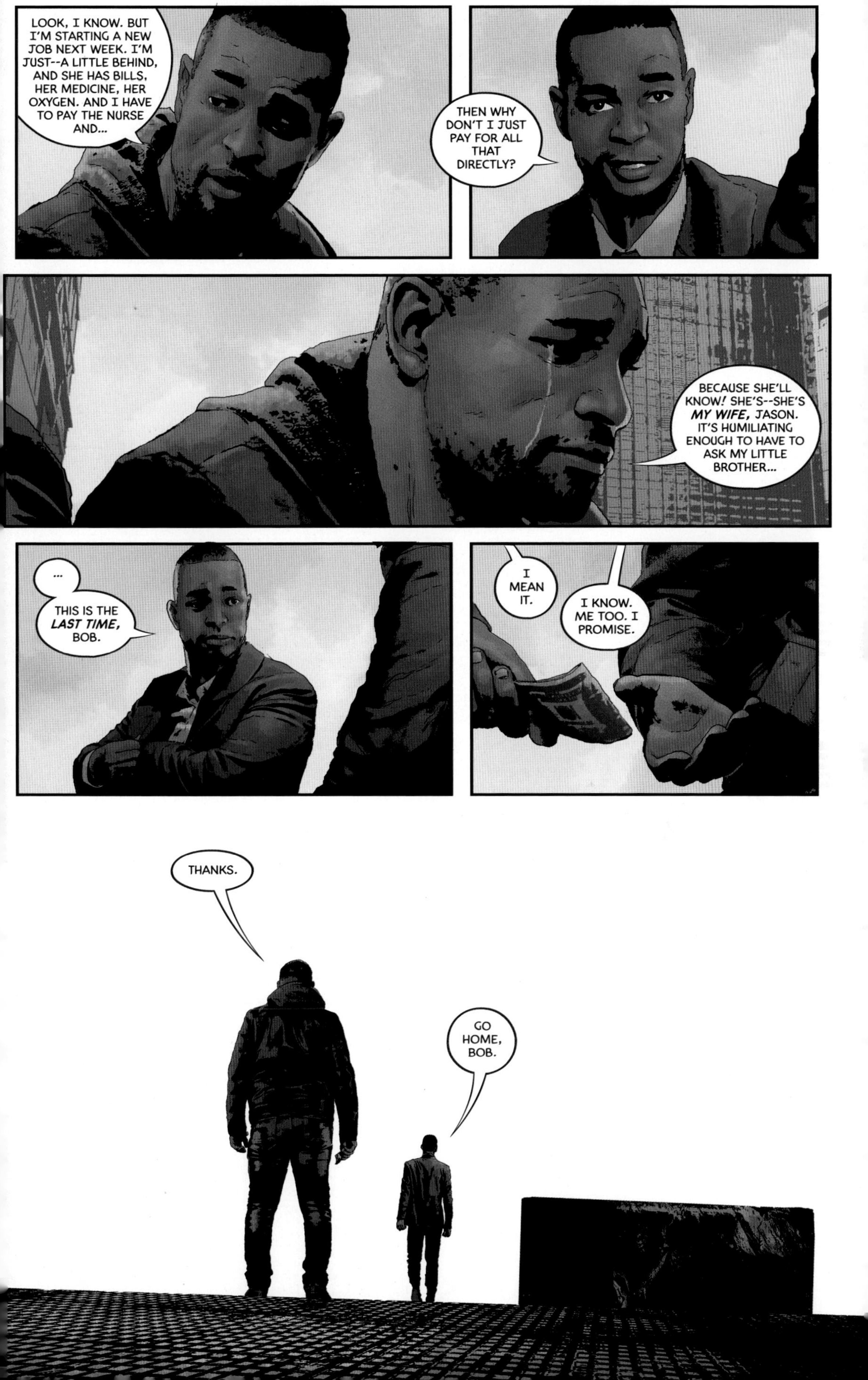
LOOK, I KNOW. BUT I'M STARTING A NEW JOB NEXT WEEK. I'M JUST--A LITTLE BEHIND, AND SHE HAS BILLS, HER MEDICINE, HER OXYGEN. AND I HAVE TO PAY THE NURSE AND...
THEN WHY DON'T I JUST PAY FOR ALL THAT DIRECTLY?
BECAUSE SHE'LL KNOW! SHE'S--SHE'S *MY WIFE,* JASON. IT'S HUMILIATING ENOUGH TO HAVE TO ASK MY LITTLE BROTHER...
...
THIS IS THE *LAST TIME,* BOB.
I MEAN IT.
I KNOW. ME TOO. I PROMISE.
THANKS.
GO HOME, BOB.

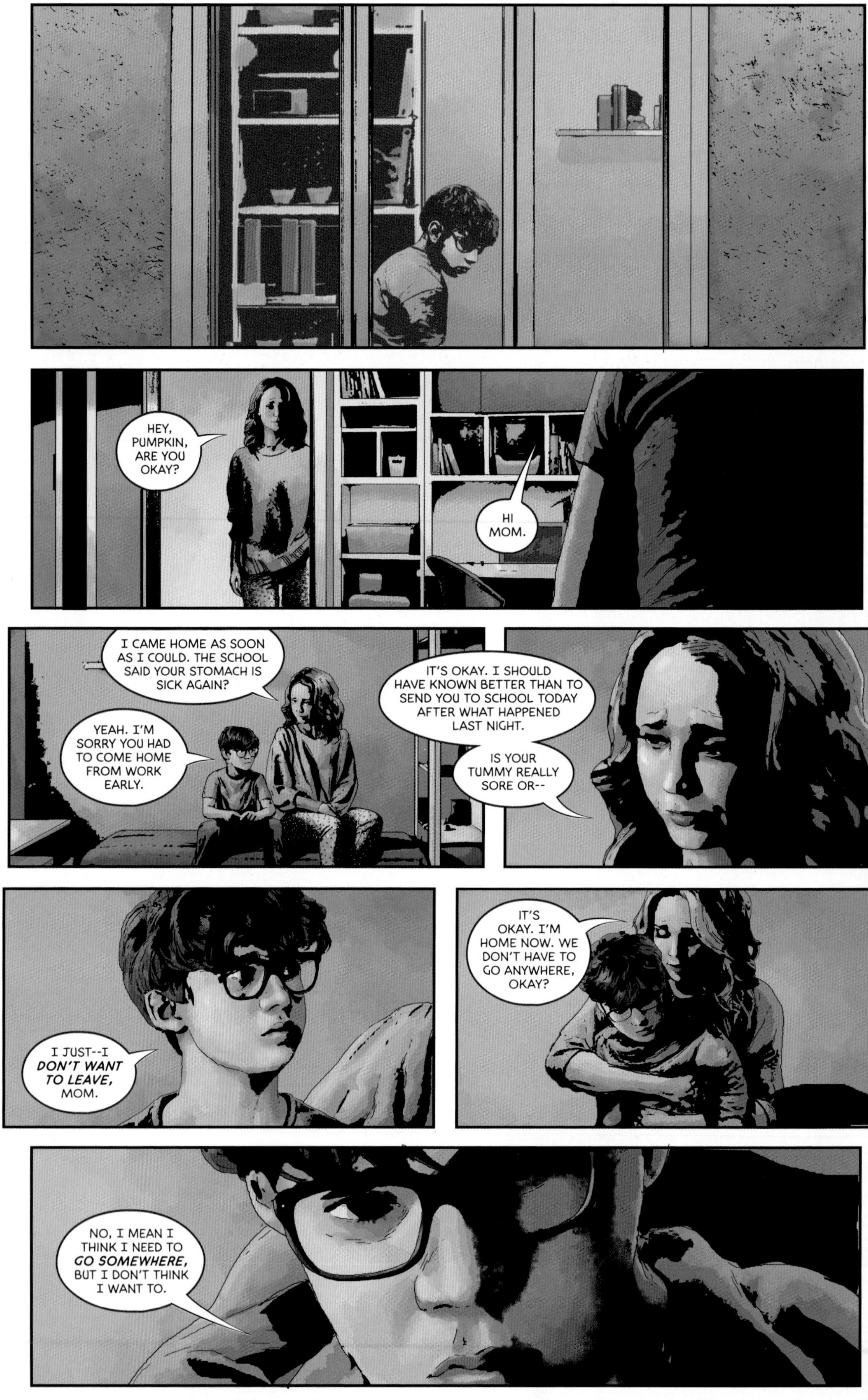
HEY, PUMPKIN, ARE YOU OKAY?
HI MOM.
I CAME HOME AS SOON AS I COULD. THE SCHOOL SAID YOUR STOMACH IS SICK AGAIN?
YEAH. I'M SORRY YOU HAD TO COME HOME FROM WORK EARLY.
IT'S OKAY. I SHOULD HAVE KNOWN BETTER THAN TO SEND YOU TO SCHOOL TODAY AFTER WHAT HAPPENED LAST NIGHT.
IS YOUR TUMMY REALLY SORE OR--
I JUST--I *DON'T WANT TO LEAVE,* MOM.
IT'S OKAY. I'M HOME NOW. WE DON'T HAVE TO GO ANYWHERE, OKAY?
NO, I MEAN I THINK I NEED TO *GO SOMEWHERE,* BUT I DON'T THINK I WANT TO.

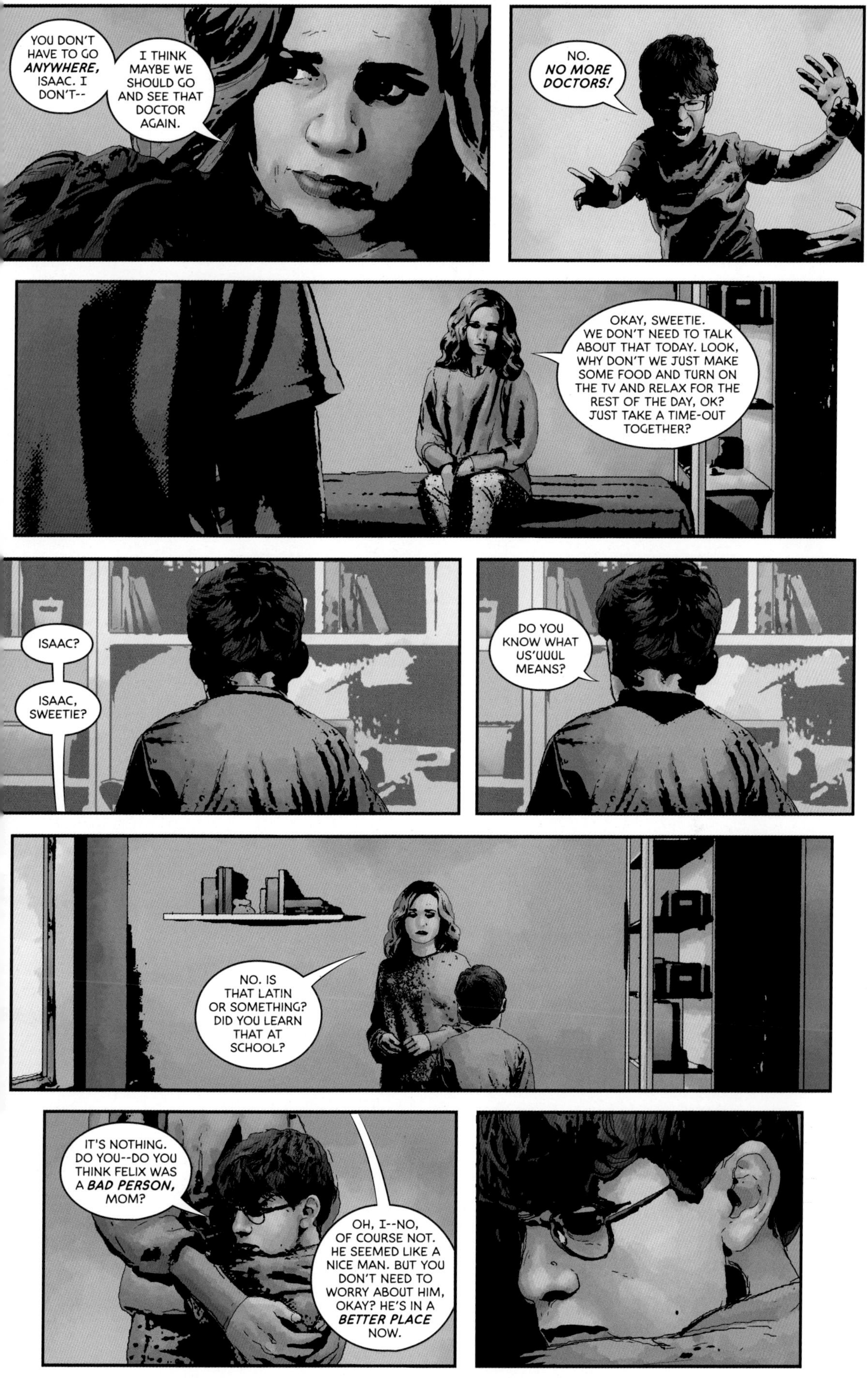
YOU DON'T HAVE TO GO *ANYWHERE,* ISAAC. I DON'T--
I THINK MAYBE WE SHOULD GO AND SEE THAT DOCTOR AGAIN.
NO. *NO MORE DOCTORS!*
OKAY, SWEETIE. WE DON'T NEED TO TALK ABOUT THAT TODAY. LOOK, WHY DON'T WE JUST MAKE SOME FOOD AND TURN ON THE TV AND RELAX FOR THE REST OF THE DAY, OK? JUST TAKE A TIME-OUT TOGETHER?
ISAAC?
ISAAC, SWEETIE?
DO YOU KNOW WHAT US'UUUL MEANS?
NO. IS THAT LATIN OR SOMETHING? DID YOU LEARN THAT AT SCHOOL?
IT'S NOTHING. DO YOU--DO YOU THINK FELIX WAS A *BAD PERSON,* MOM?
OH, I--NO, OF COURSE NOT. HE SEEMED LIKE A NICE MAN. BUT YOU DON'T NEED TO WORRY ABOUT HIM, OKAY? HE'S IN A *BETTER PLACE* NOW.

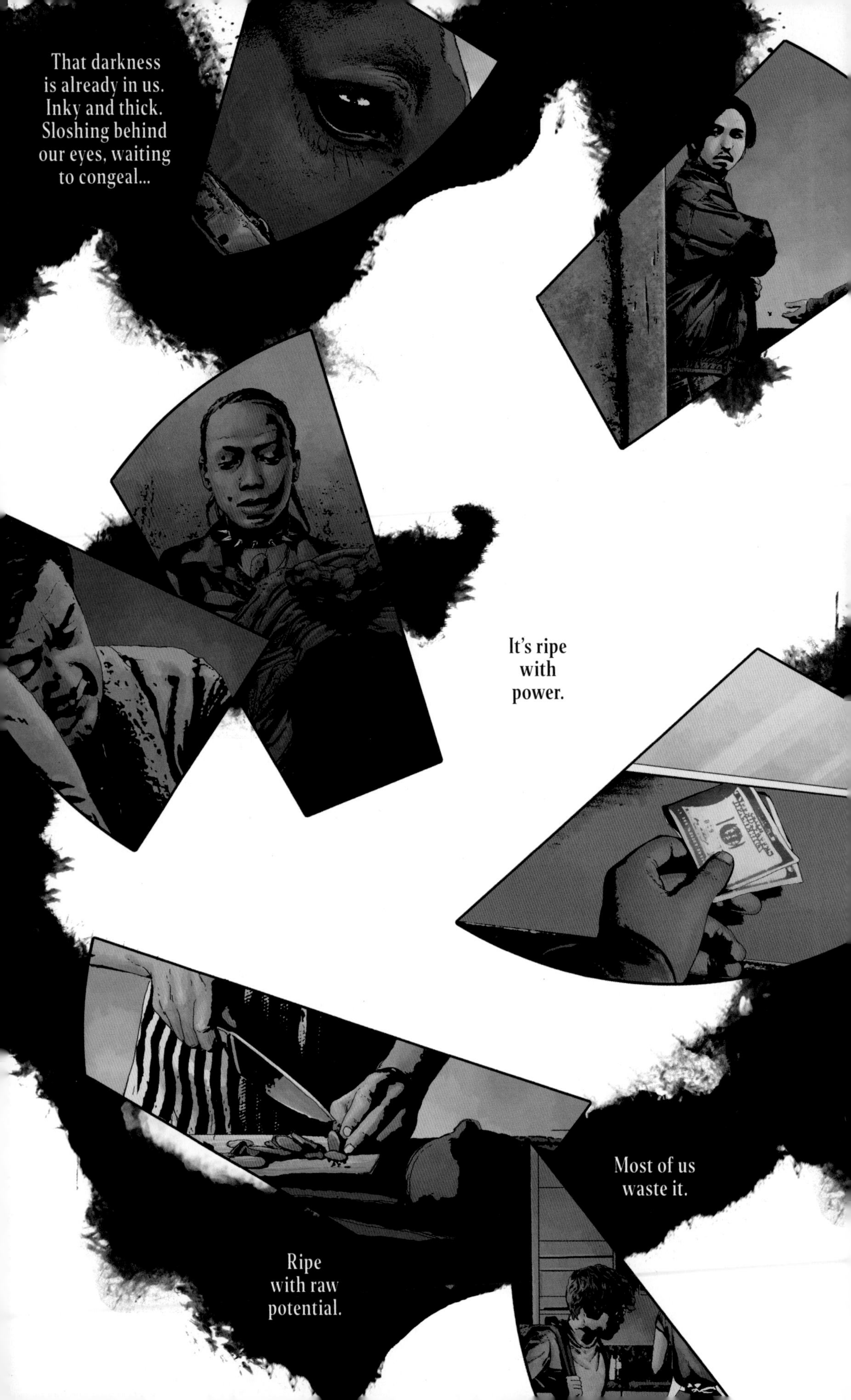
That darkness is already in us. Inky and thick. Sloshing behind our eyes, waiting to congeal...
It's ripe with power.
Ripe with raw potential.
Most of us waste it.

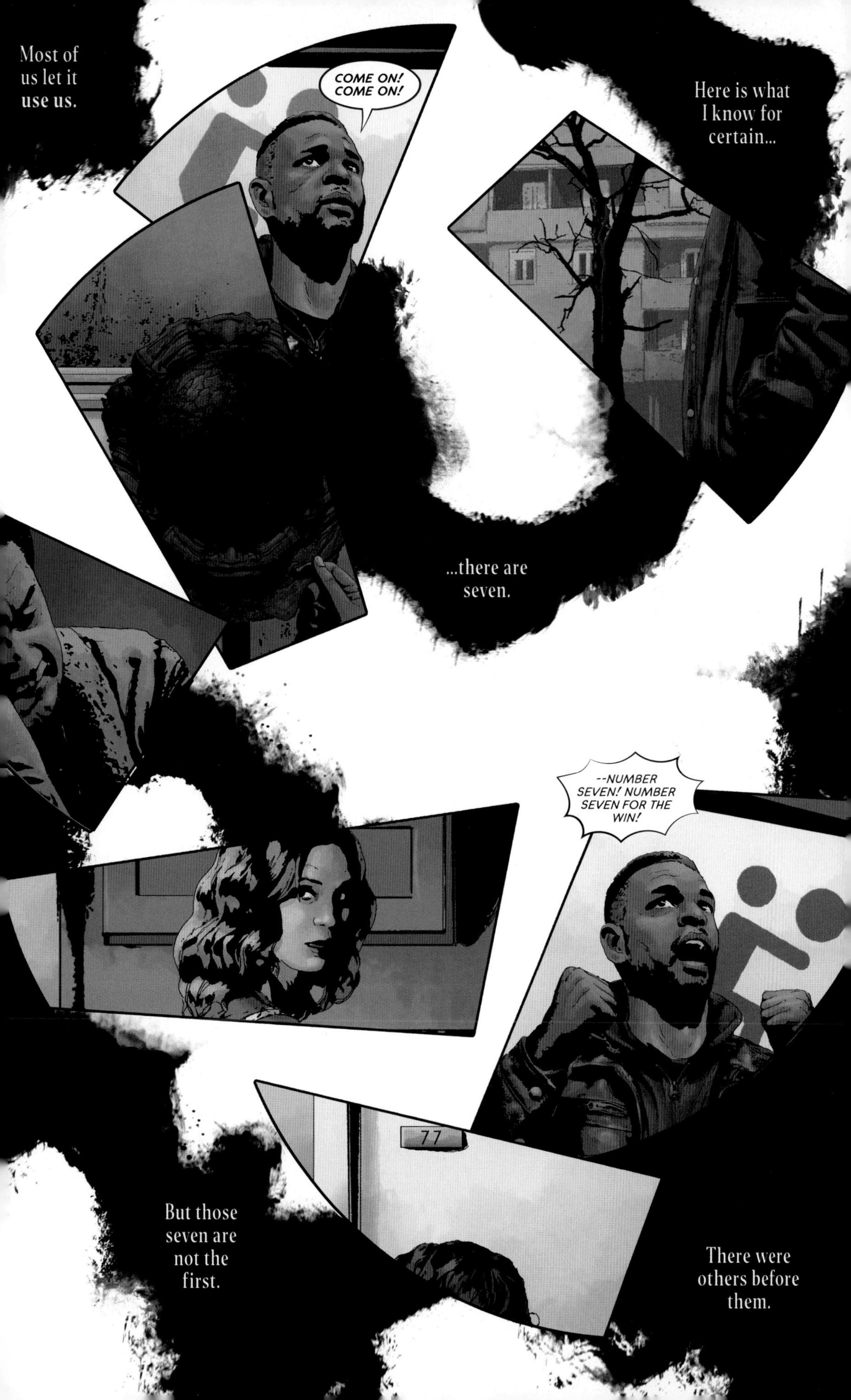
Most of us let it use us.
COME ON! COME ON!
Here is what I know for certain...
...there are seven.
--NUMBER SEVEN! NUMBER SEVEN FOR THE WIN!
77
But those seven are not the first.
There were others before them.

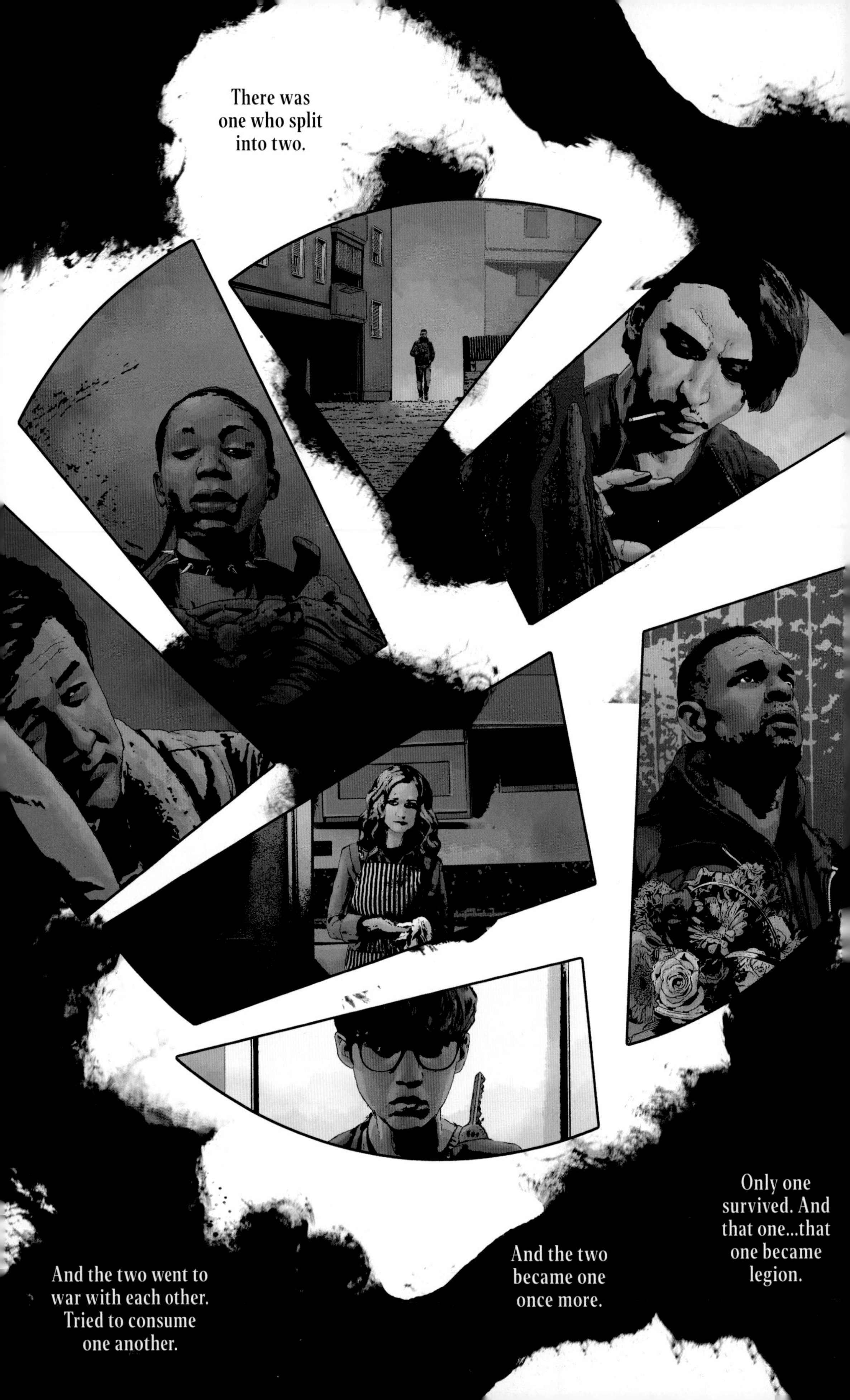
There was one who split into two.
And the two went to war with each other. Tried to consume one another.
And the two became one once more.
Only one survived. And that one...that one became legion.

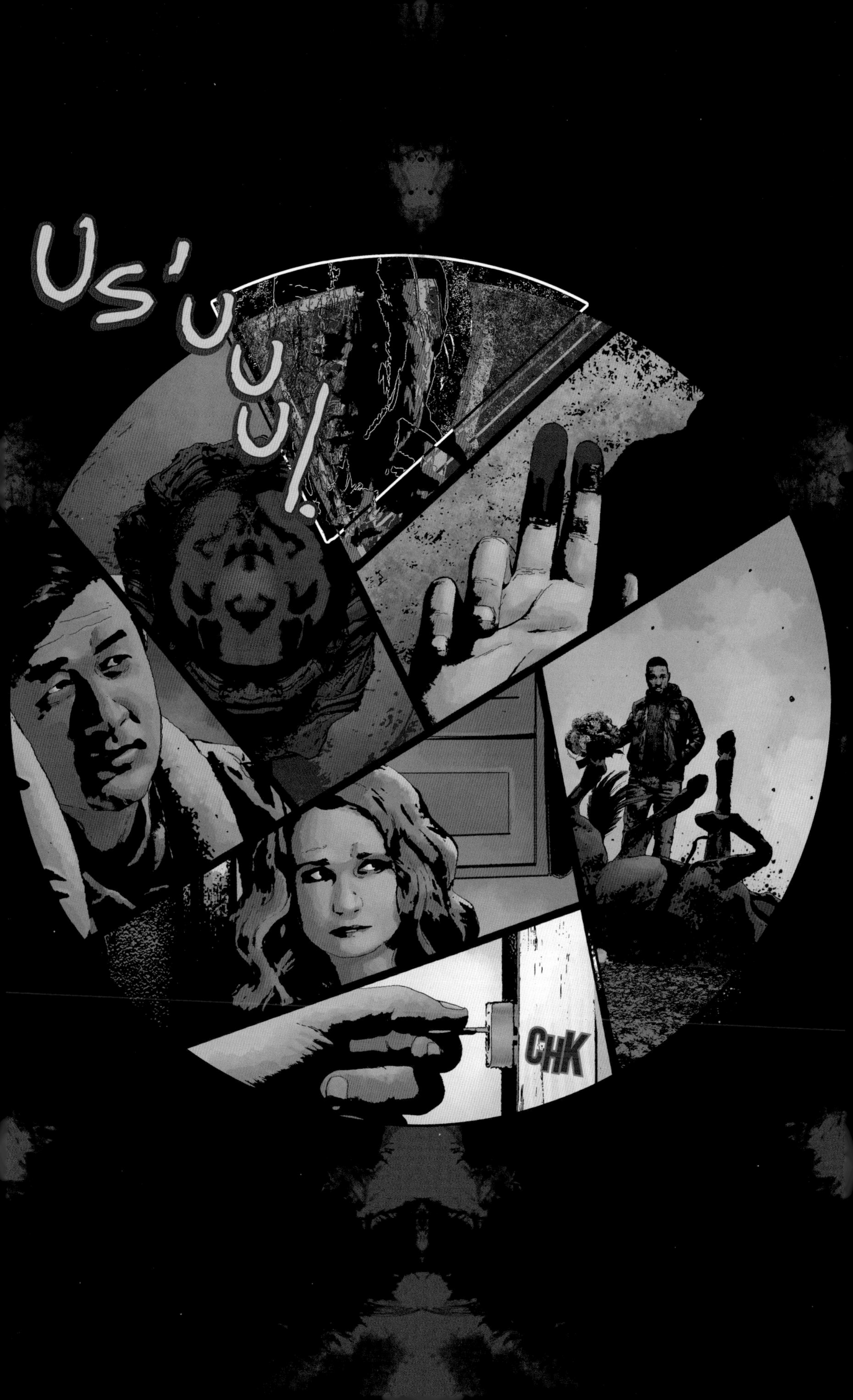
Us'uuu!
CHK

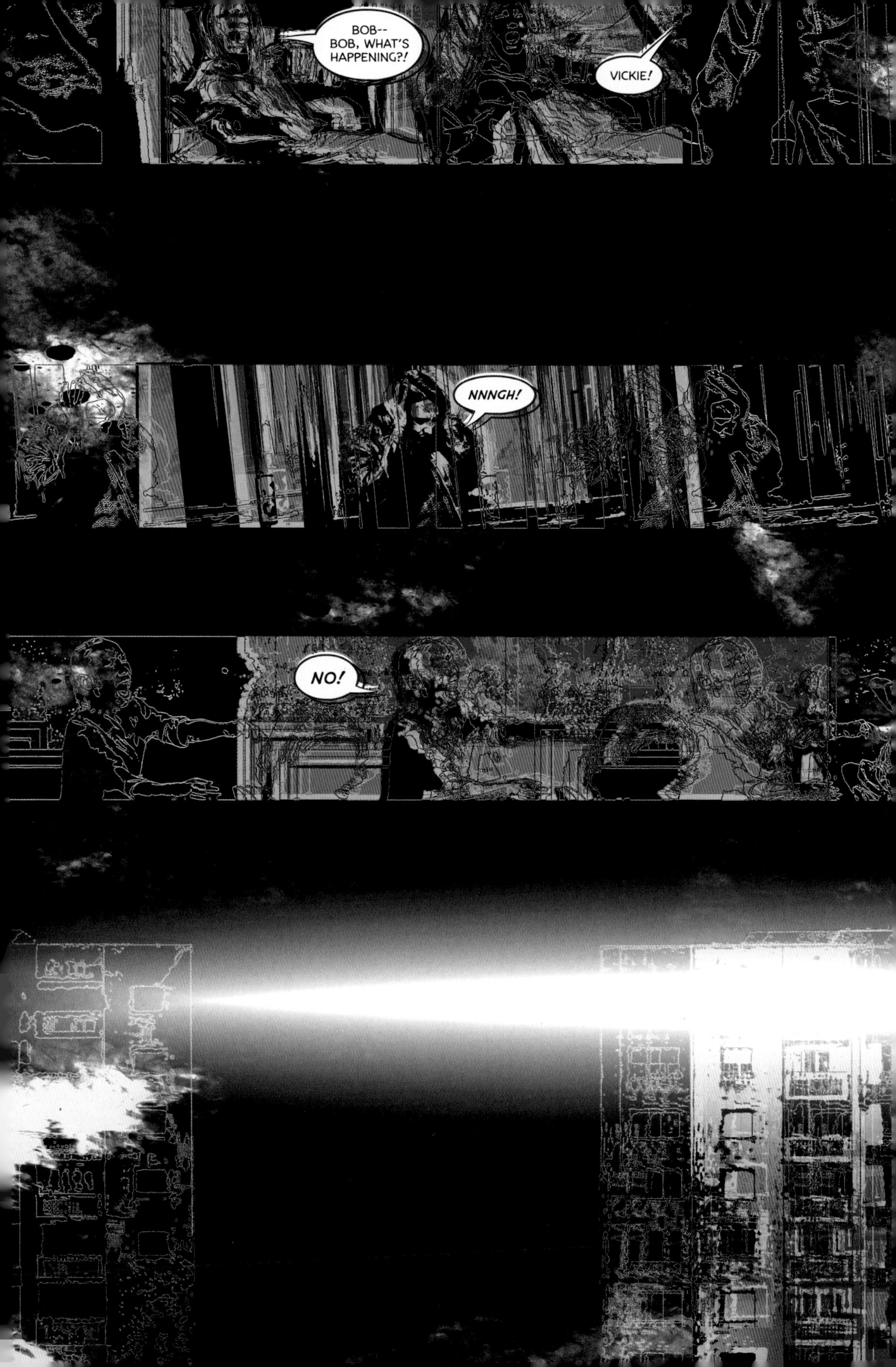
BOB--
BOB, WHAT'S HAPPENING?!
VICKIE!
NNNGH!
NO!

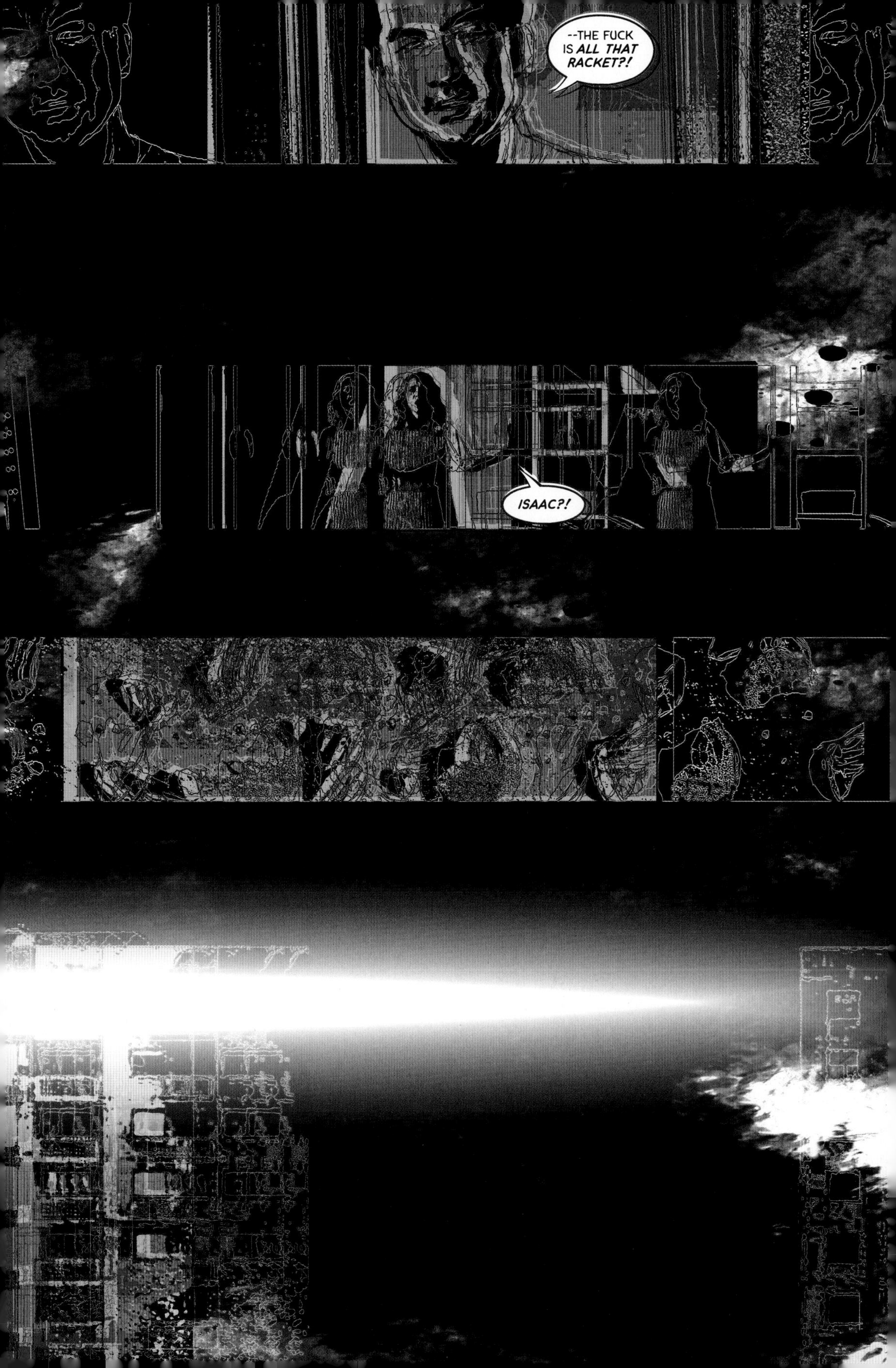
--THE FUCK IS ALL THAT RACKET?!
ISAAC?!

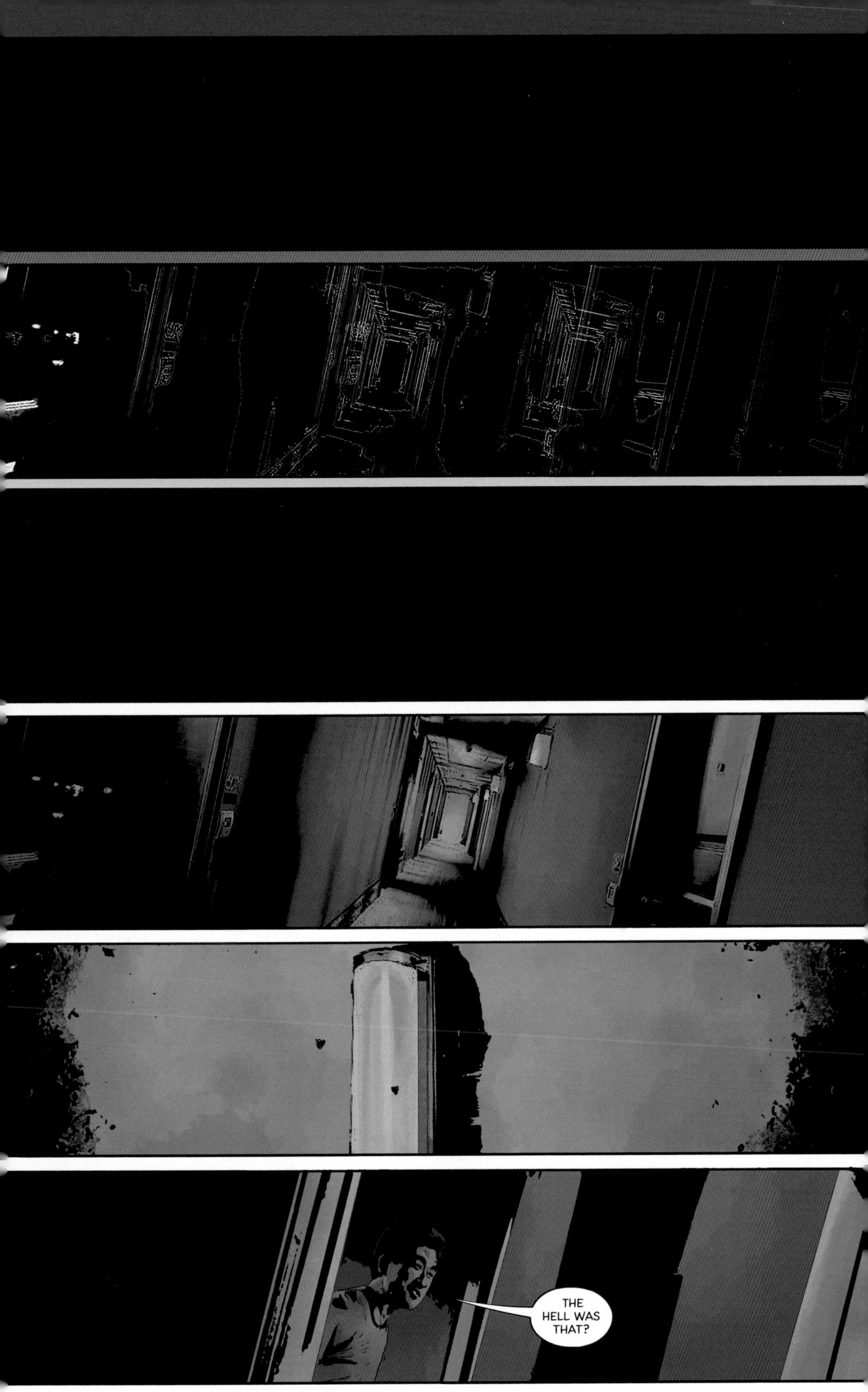
THE HELL WAS THAT?

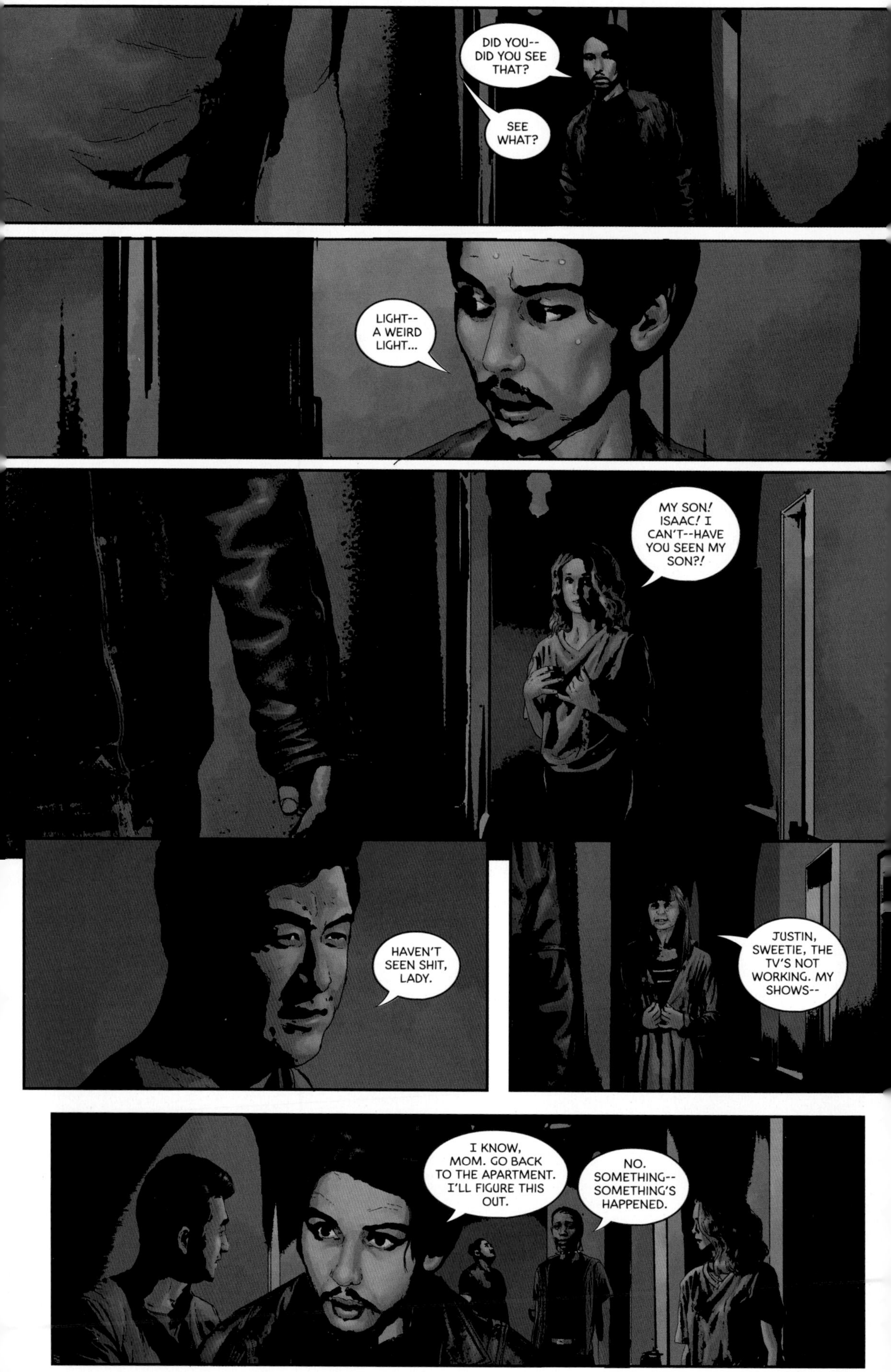

DID YOU-- DID YOU SEE THAT?
SEE WHAT?
LIGHT-- A WEIRD LIGHT...
MY SON! ISAAC! I CAN'T--HAVE YOU SEEN MY SON?!
HAVEN'T SEEN SHIT, LADY.
JUSTIN, SWEETIE, THE TV'S NOT WORKING. MY SHOWS--
I KNOW, MOM. GO BACK TO THE APARTMENT. I'LL FIGURE THIS OUT.
NO. SOMETHING-- SOMETHING'S HAPPENED.

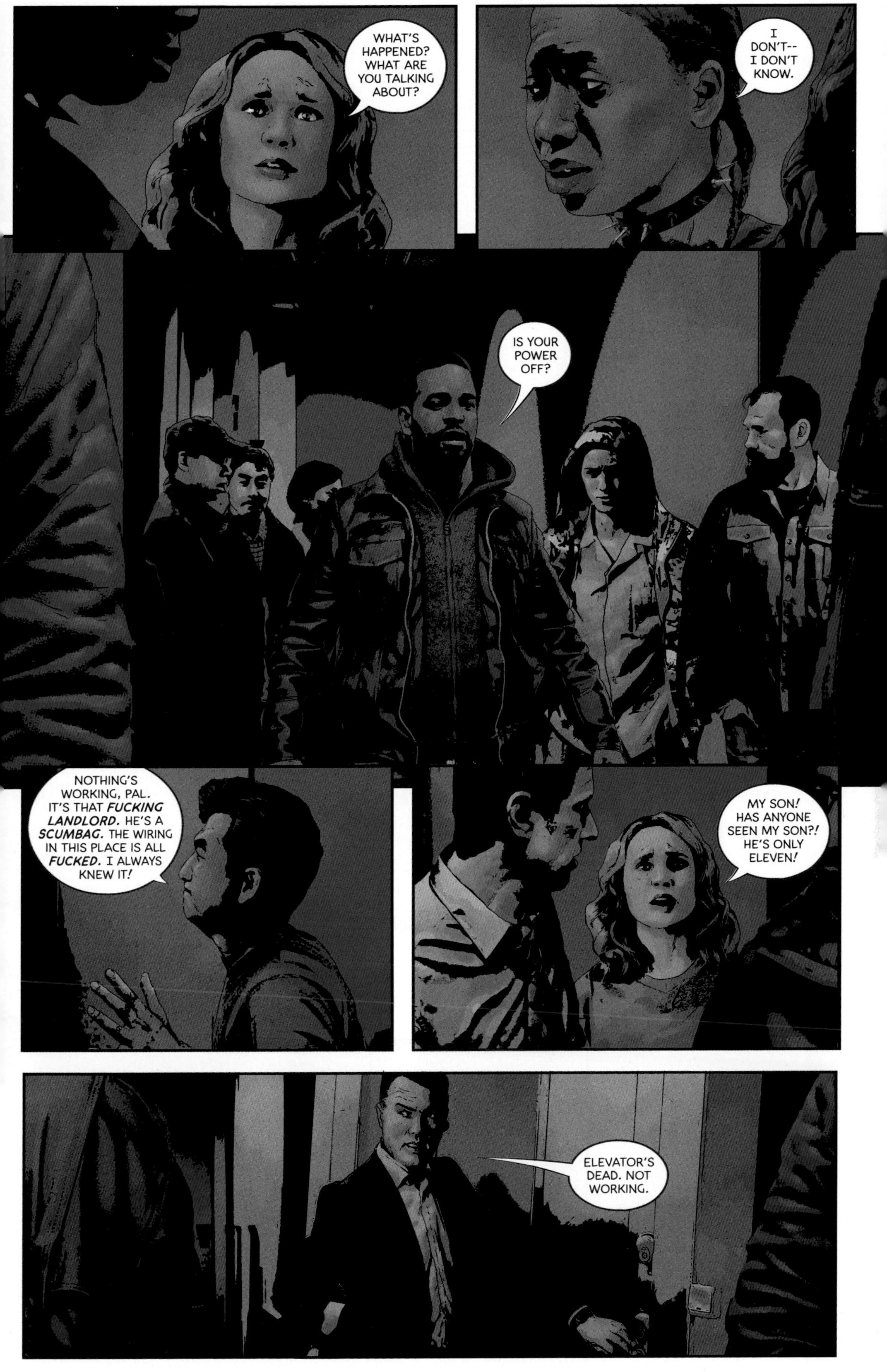
WHAT'S HAPPENED? WHAT ARE YOU TALKING ABOUT?
I DON'T-- I DON'T KNOW.
IS YOUR POWER OFF?
NOTHING'S WORKING, PAL. IT'S THAT *FUCKING LANDLORD.* HE'S A *SCUMBAG.* THE WIRING IN THIS PLACE IS ALL *FUCKED.* I ALWAYS KNEW IT!
MY SON! HAS ANYONE SEEN MY SON?! HE'S ONLY ELEVEN!
ELEVATOR'S DEAD. NOT WORKING.

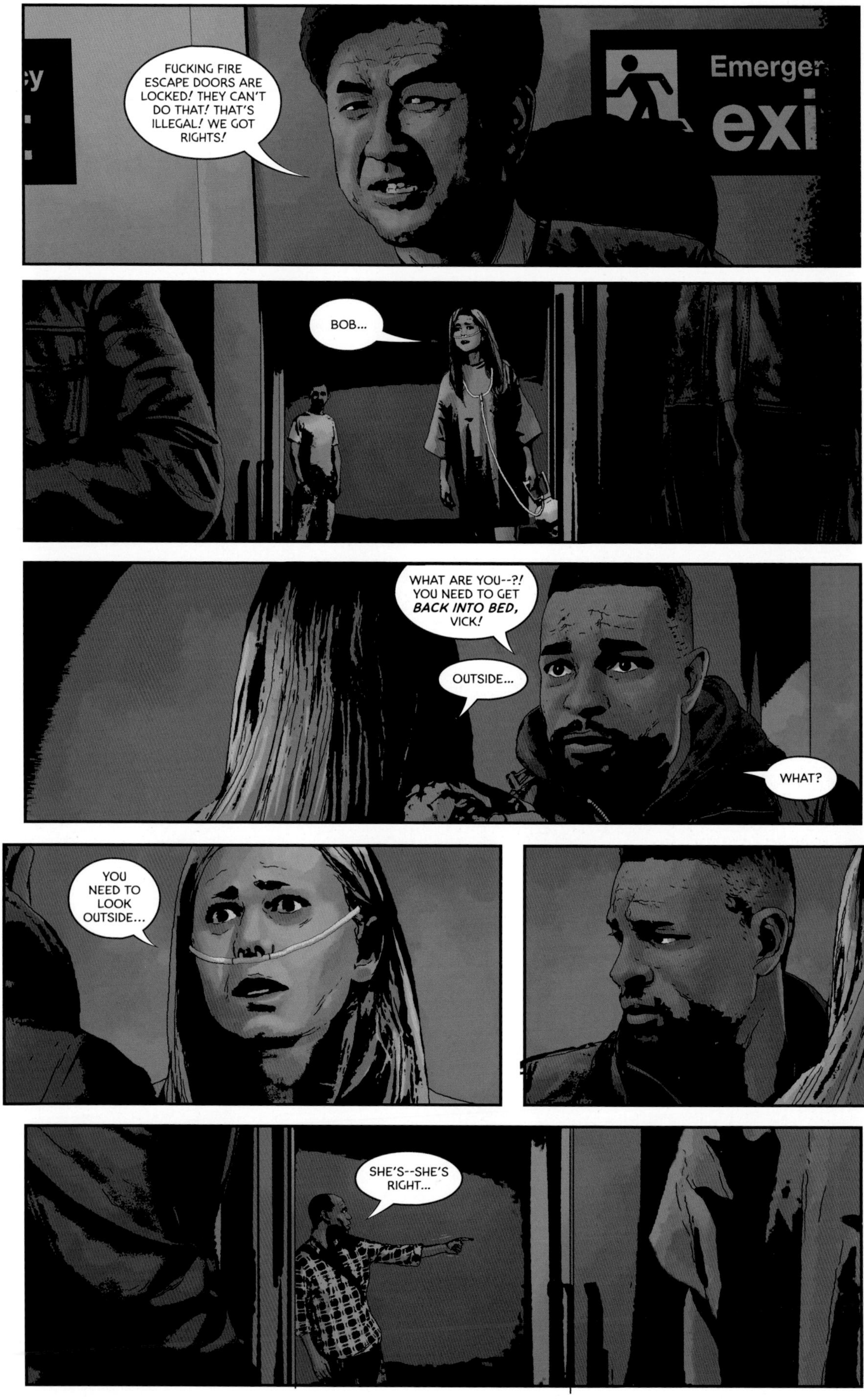
FUCKING FIRE ESCAPE DOORS ARE LOCKED! THEY CAN'T DO THAT! THAT'S ILLEGAL! WE GOT RIGHTS!
Emergen
exi
BOB...
WHAT ARE YOU--?! YOU NEED TO GET *BACK INTO BED,* VICK!
OUTSIDE...
WHAT?
YOU NEED TO LOOK OUTSIDE...
SHE'S--SHE'S RIGHT...

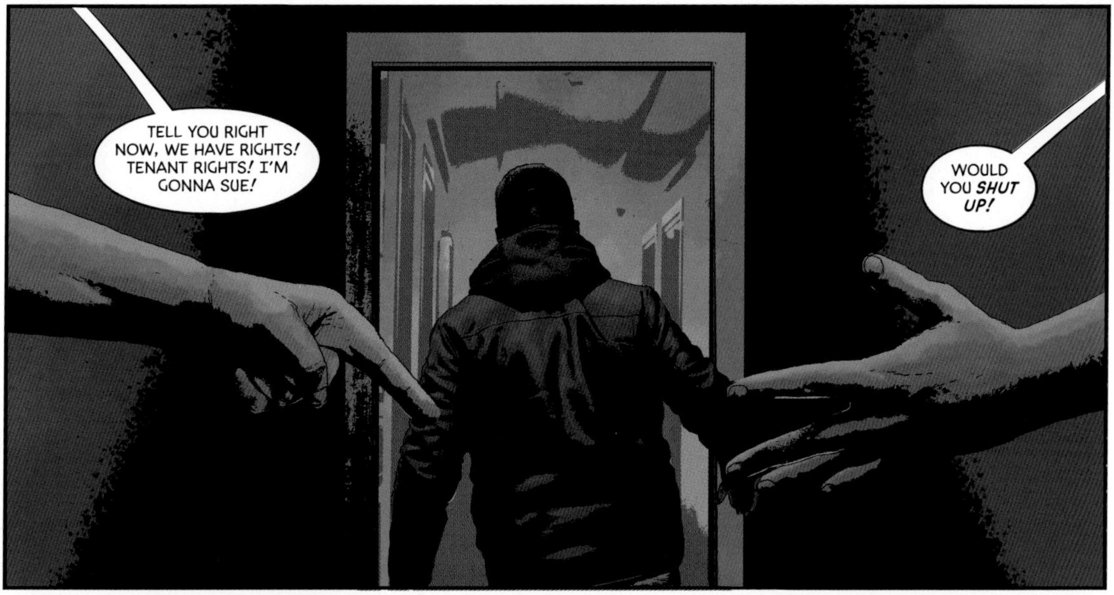
TELL YOU RIGHT NOW, WE HAVE RIGHTS! TENANT RIGHTS! I'M GONNA SUE!
WOULD YOU *SHUT UP!*

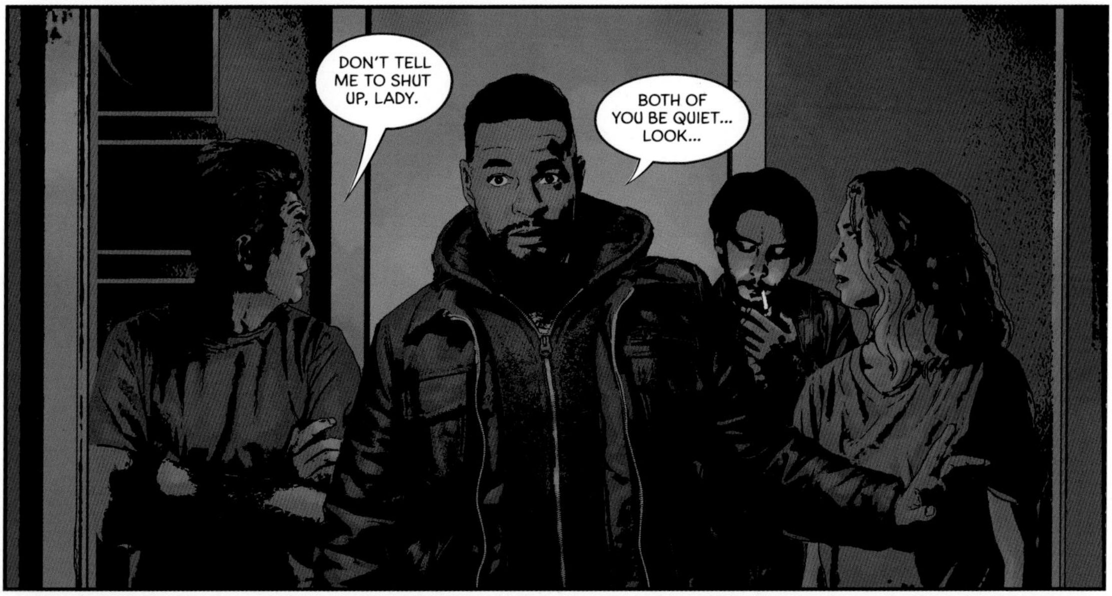
DON'T TELL ME TO SHUT UP, LADY.
BOTH OF YOU BE QUIET... LOOK...

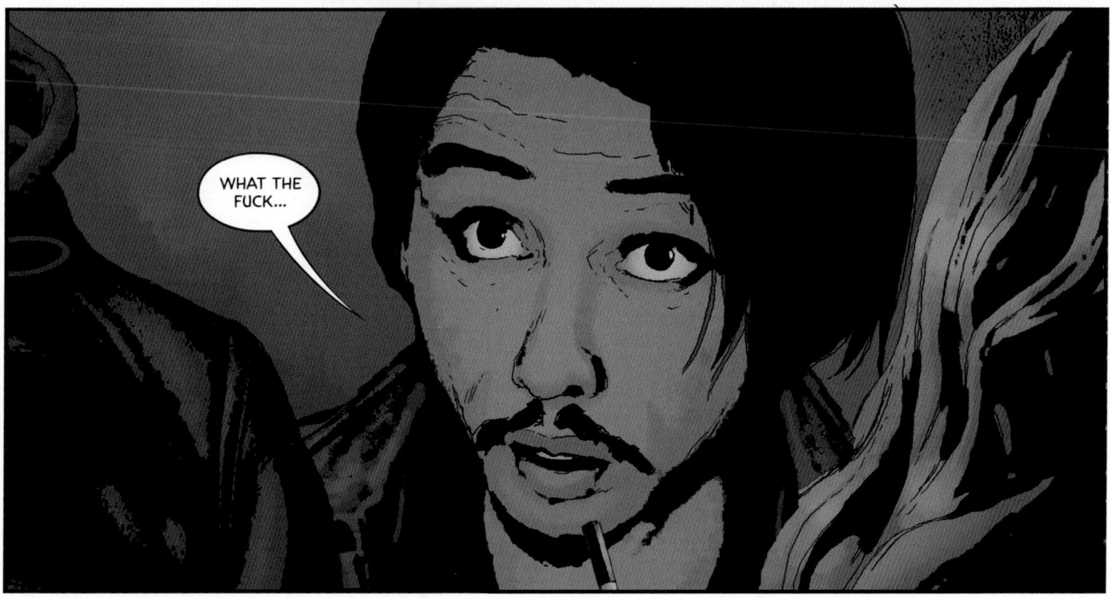
WHAT THE FUCK...

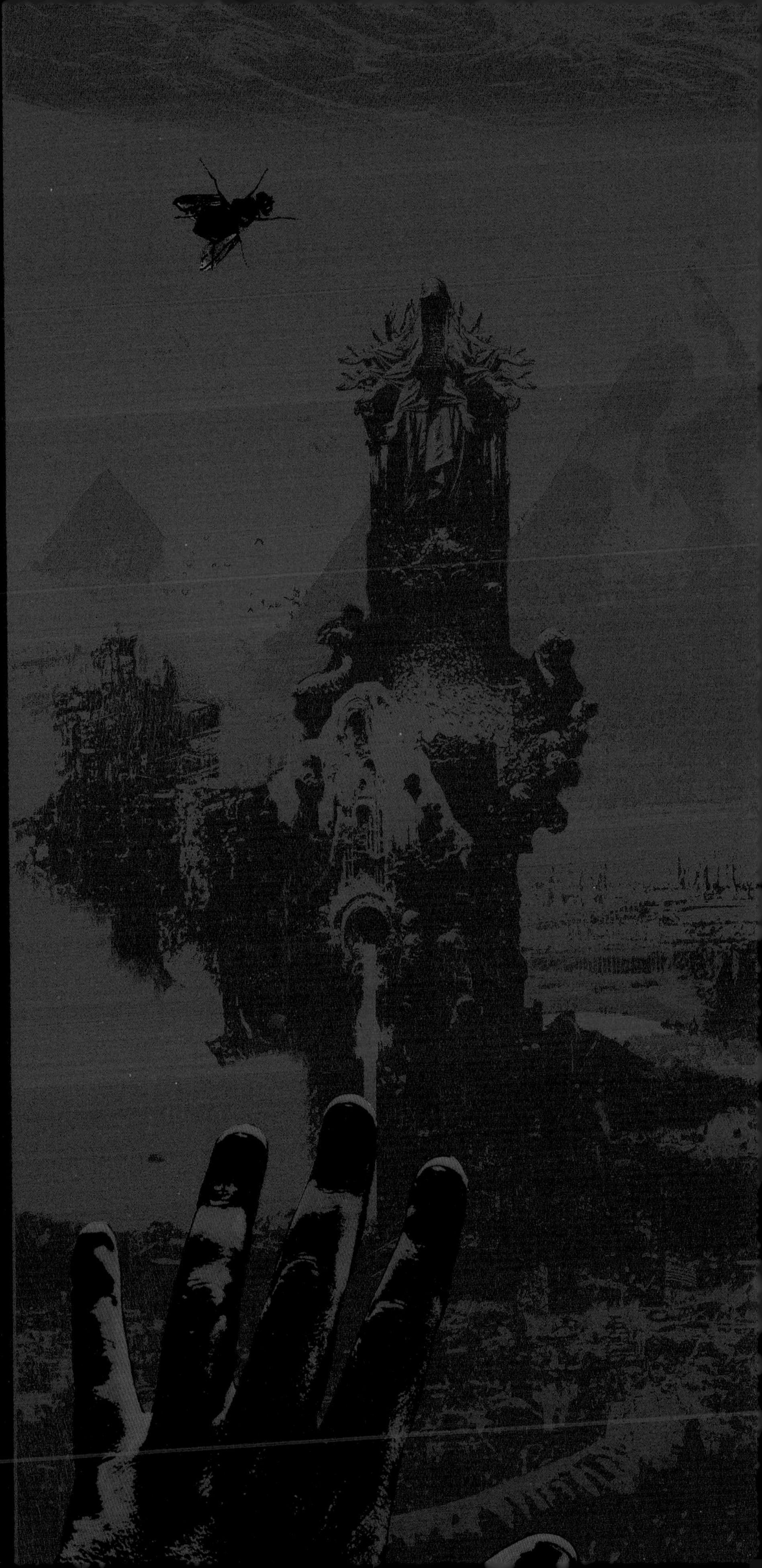

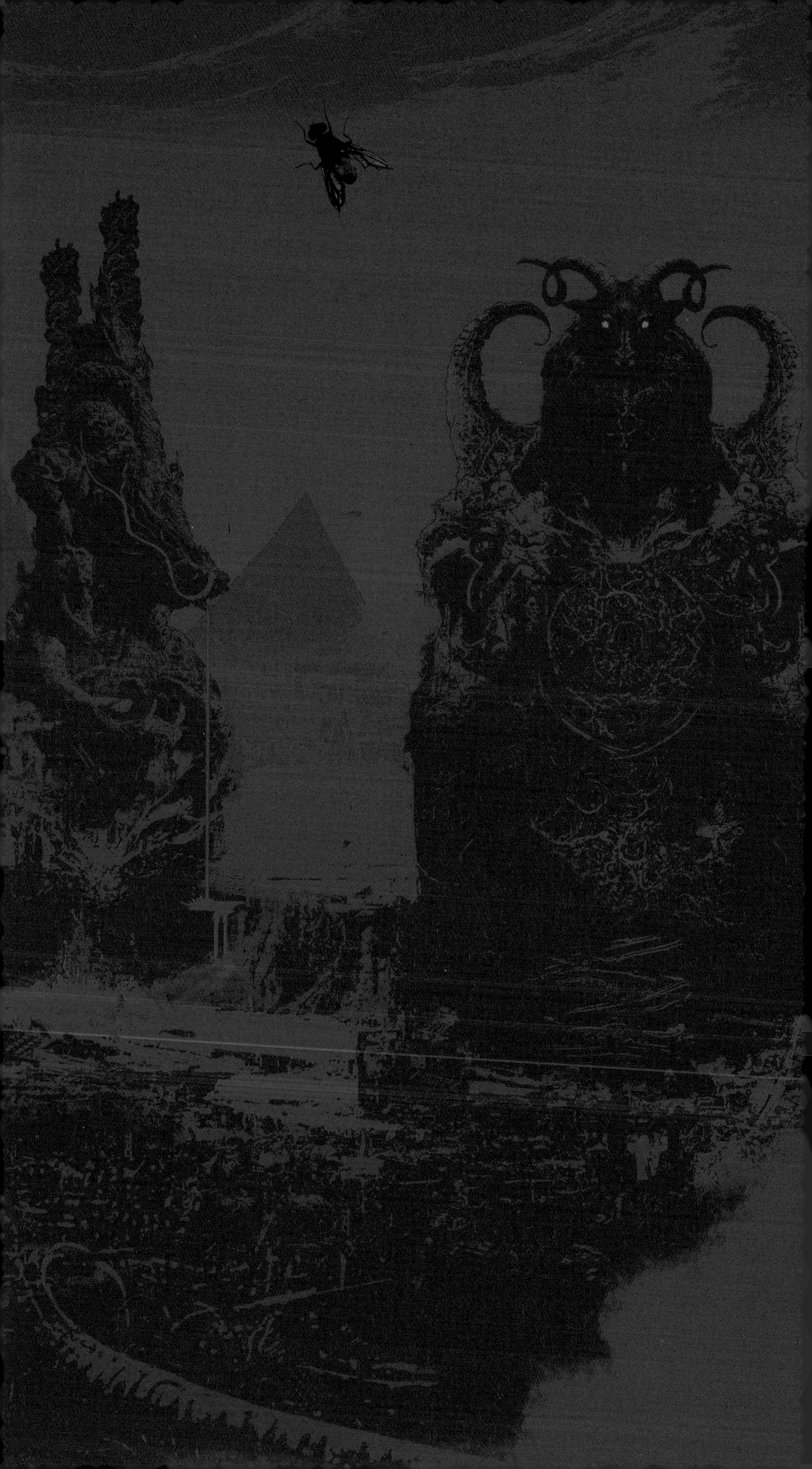

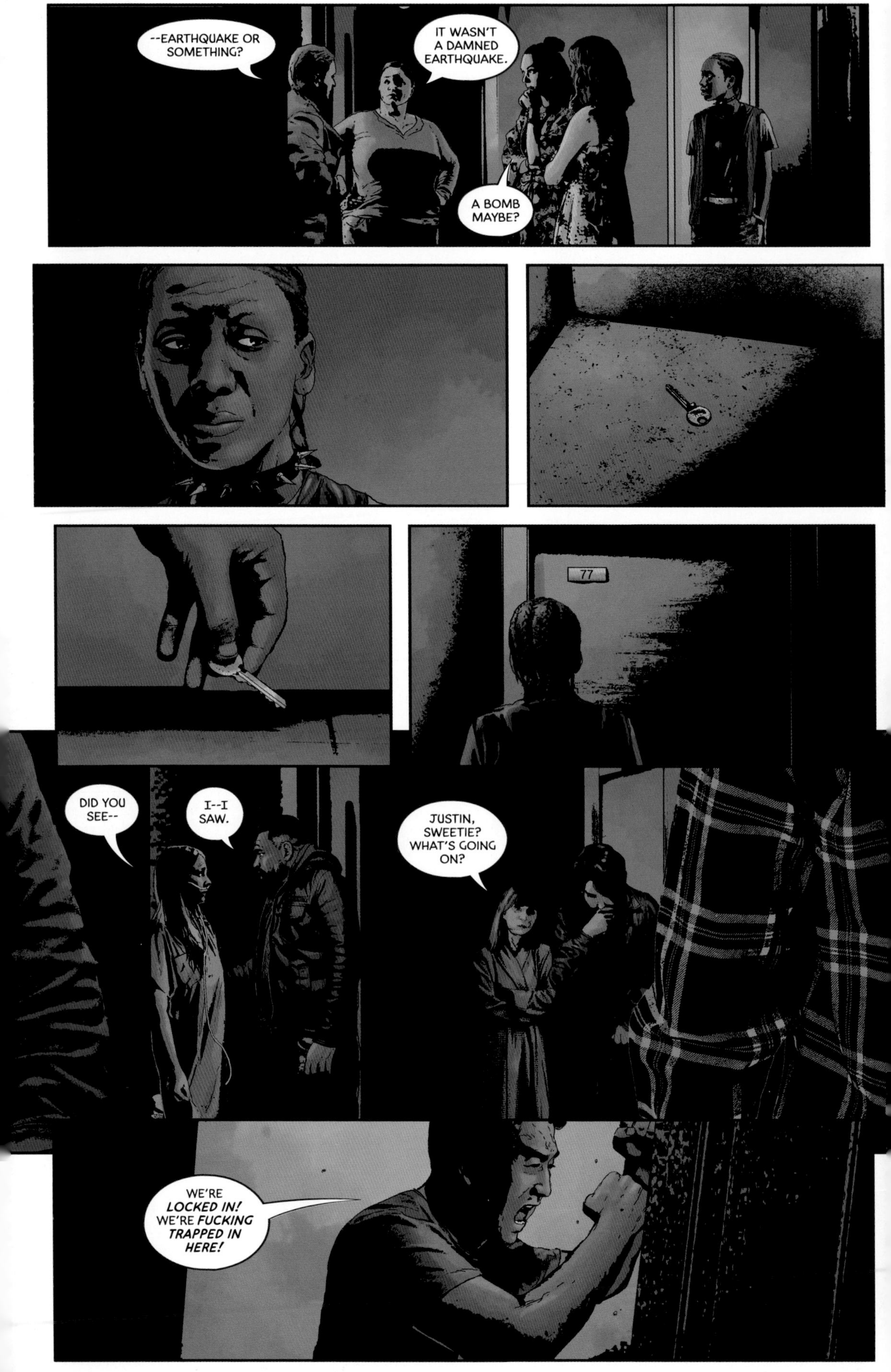
--EARTHQUAKE OR SOMETHING?
IT WASN'T A DAMNED EARTHQUAKE.
A BOMB MAYBE?
77
DID YOU SEE--
I--I SAW.
JUSTIN, SWEETIE? WHAT'S GOING ON?
WE'RE *LOCKED IN!* WE'RE *FUCKING TRAPPED IN HERE!*

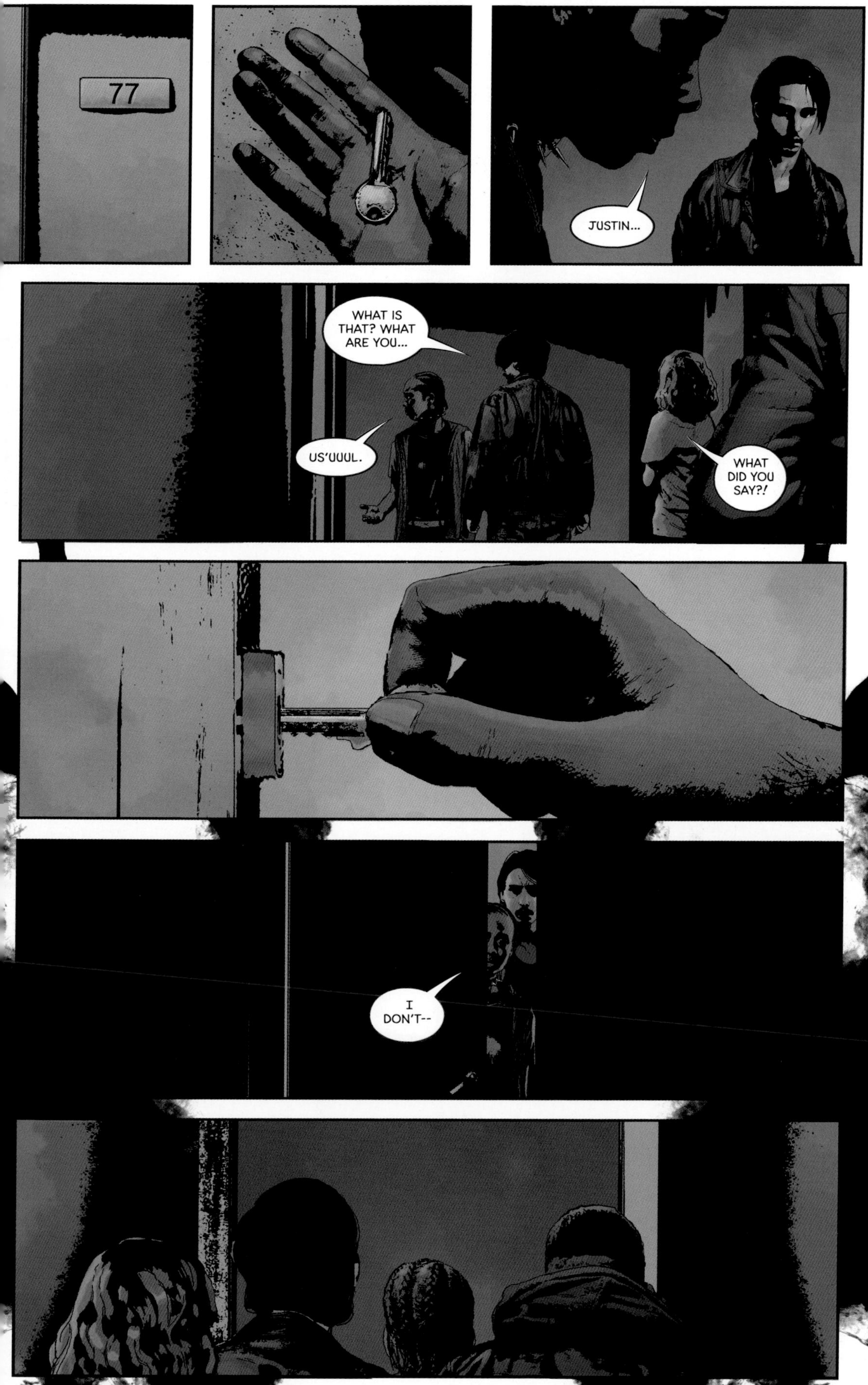
JUSTIN...
WHAT IS THAT? WHAT ARE YOU...
US'UUUL.
WHAT DID YOU SAY?!
I DON'T--

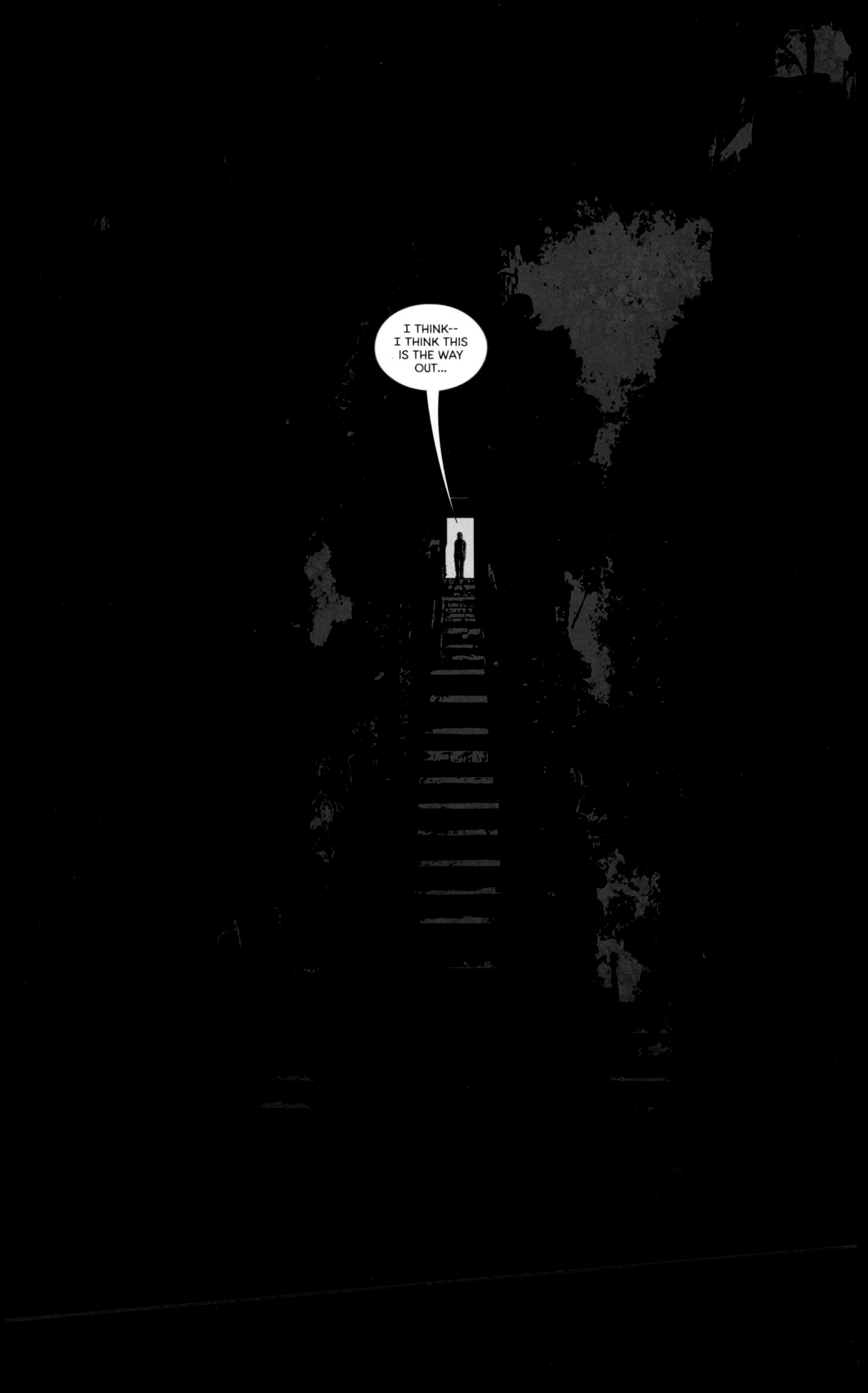
I THINK-- I THINK THIS IS THE WAY OUT...

3

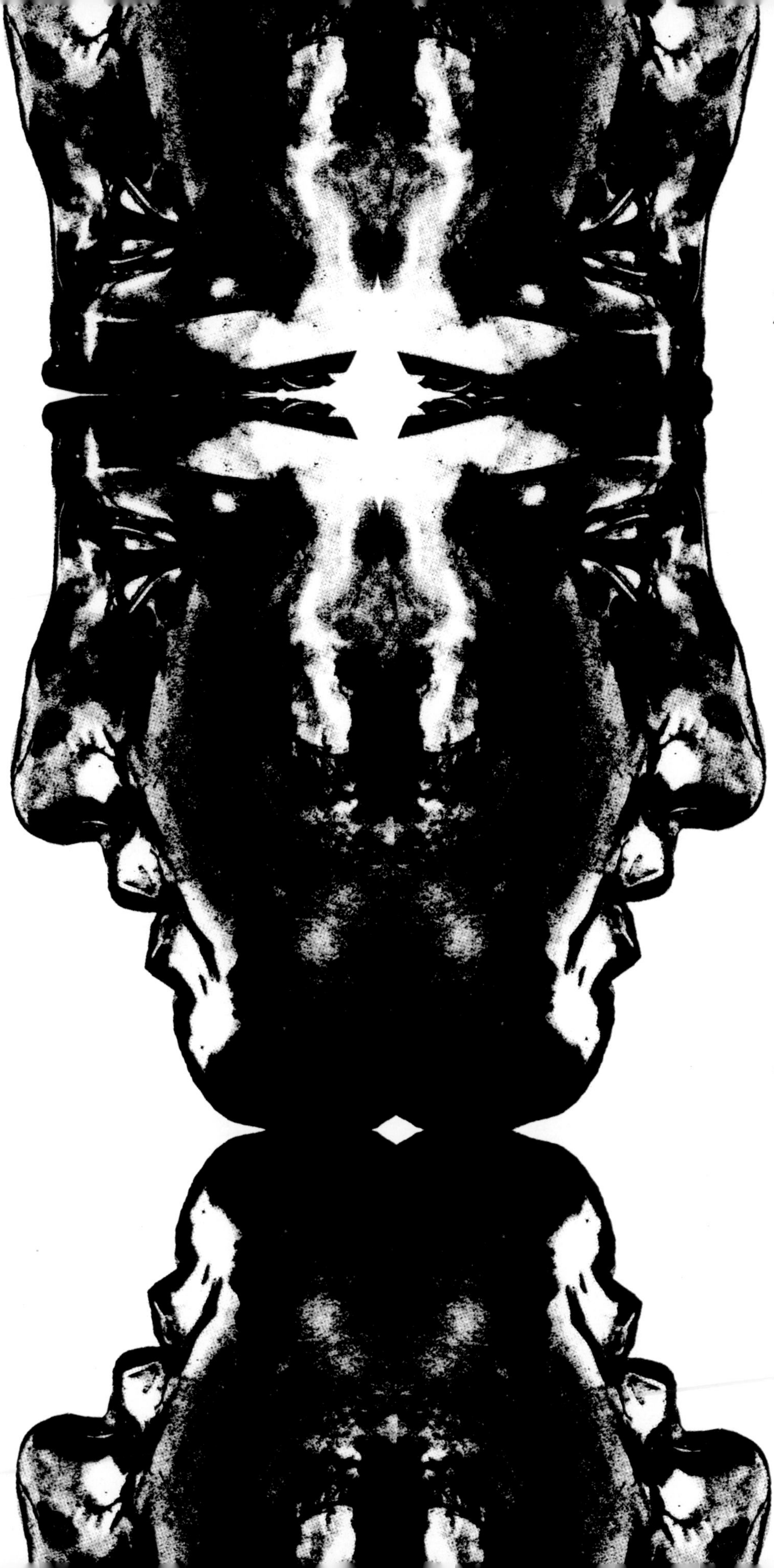

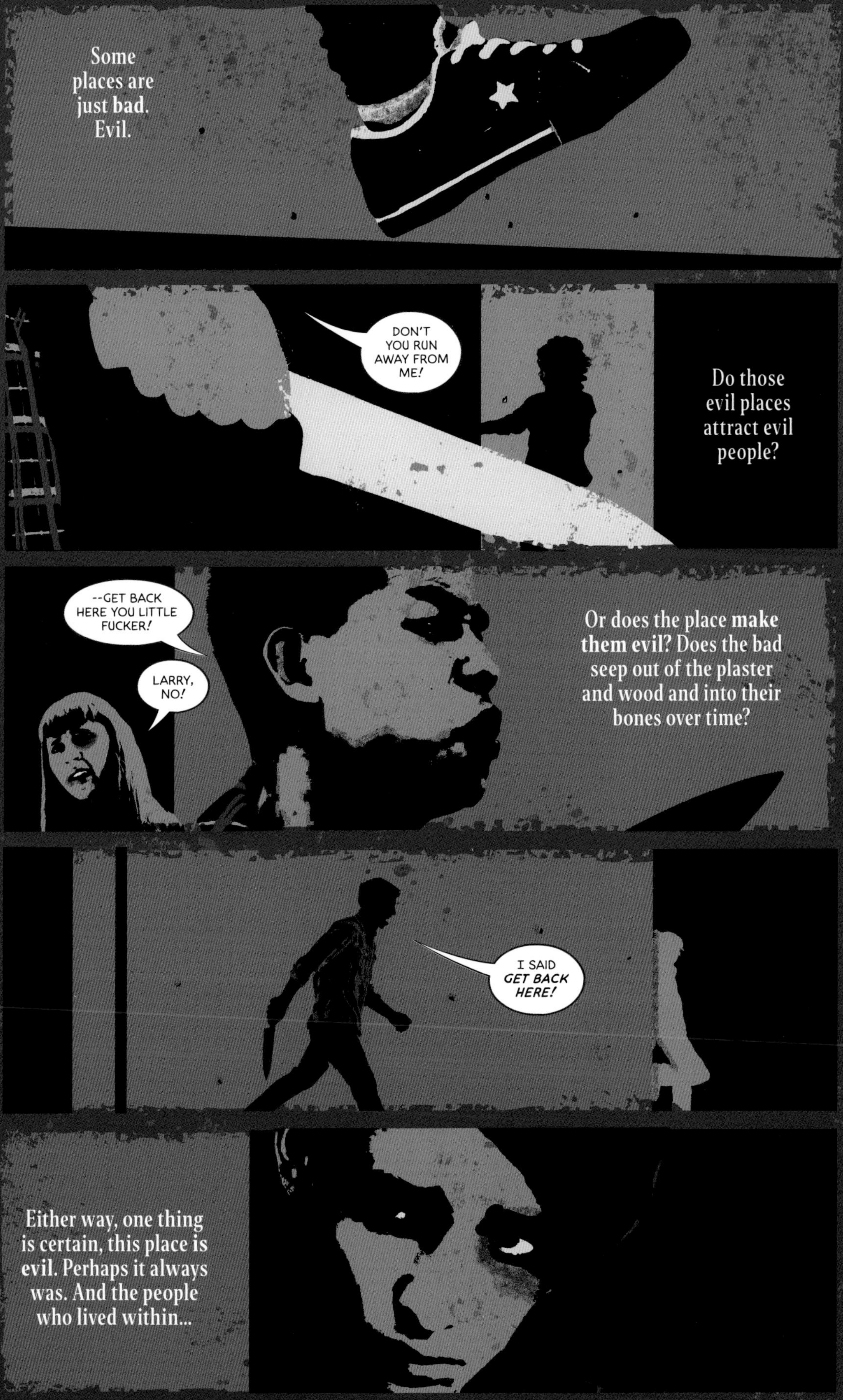

Some places are just **bad**. Evil.
DON'T YOU RUN AWAY FROM ME!
Do those evil places attract evil people?
--GET BACK HERE YOU LITTLE FUCKER!
LARRY, NO!
Or does the place **make them evil**? Does the bad seep out of the plaster and wood and into their bones over time?
I SAID *GET BACK HERE!*
Either way, one thing is certain, this place is **evil**. Perhaps it always was. And the people who lived within...

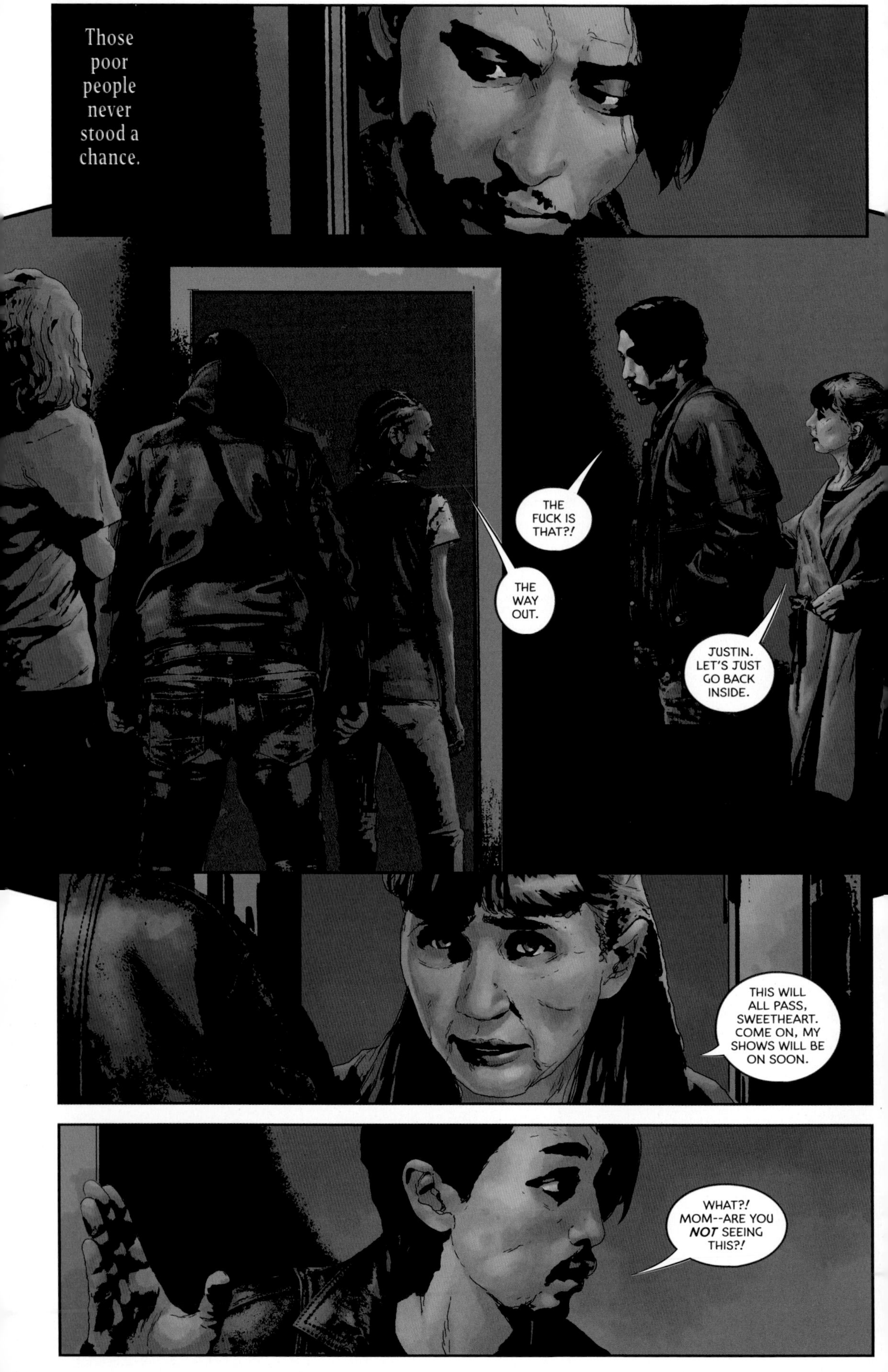
Those poor people never stood a chance.
THE FUCK IS THAT?!
THE WAY OUT.
JUSTIN. LET'S JUST GO BACK INSIDE.
THIS WILL ALL PASS, SWEETHEART. COME ON, MY SHOWS WILL BE ON SOON.
WHAT?! MOM--ARE YOU *NOT* SEEING THIS?!

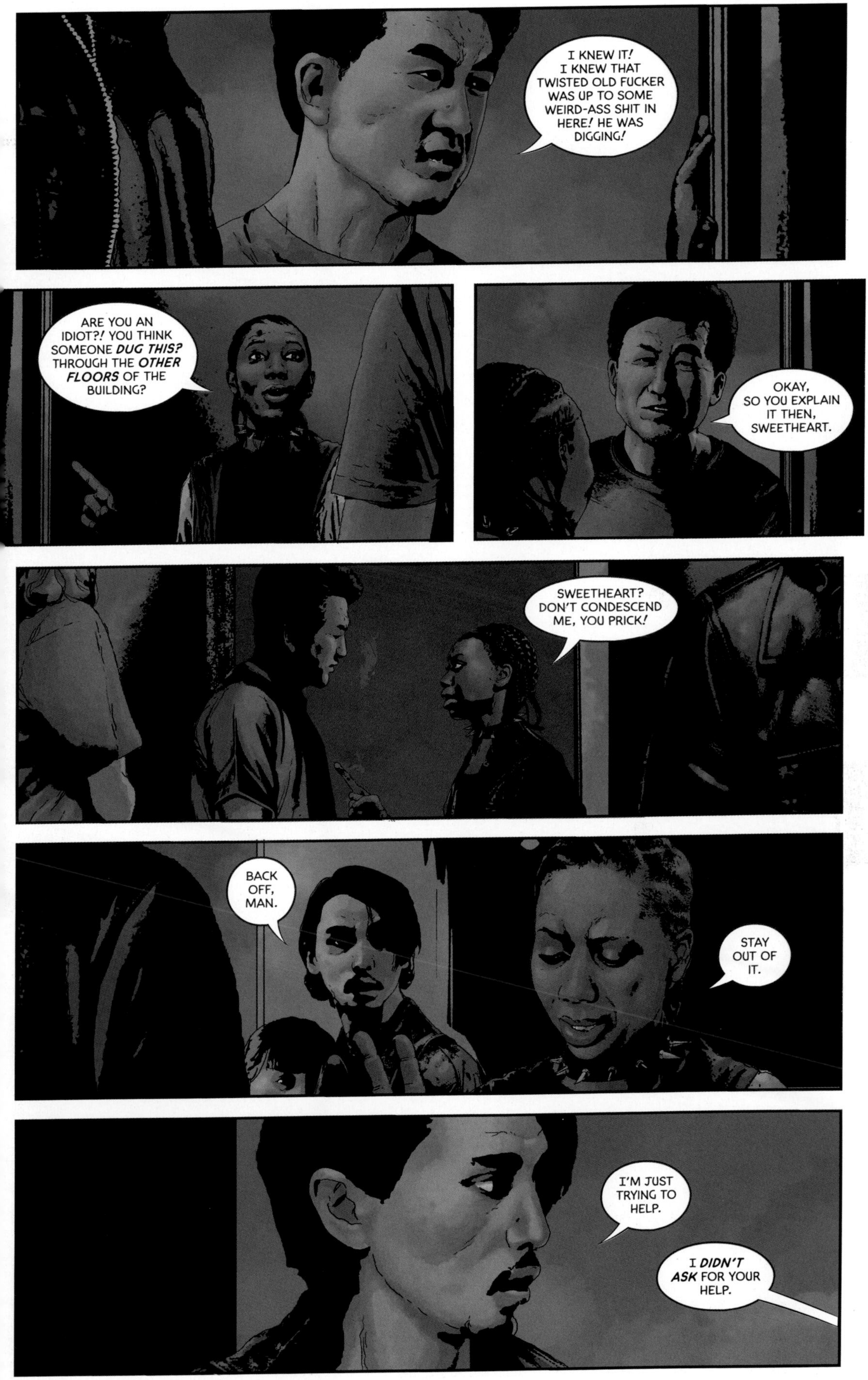
I KNEW IT! I KNEW THAT TWISTED OLD FUCKER WAS UP TO SOME WEIRD-ASS SHIT IN HERE! HE WAS DIGGING!
ARE YOU AN IDIOT?! YOU THINK SOMEONE DUG THIS? THROUGH THE OTHER FLOORS OF THE BUILDING?
OKAY, SO YOU EXPLAIN IT THEN, SWEETHEART.
SWEETHEART? DON'T CONDESCEND ME, YOU PRICK!
BACK OFF, MAN.
STAY OUT OF IT.
I'M JUST TRYING TO HELP.
I DIDN'T ASK FOR YOUR HELP.

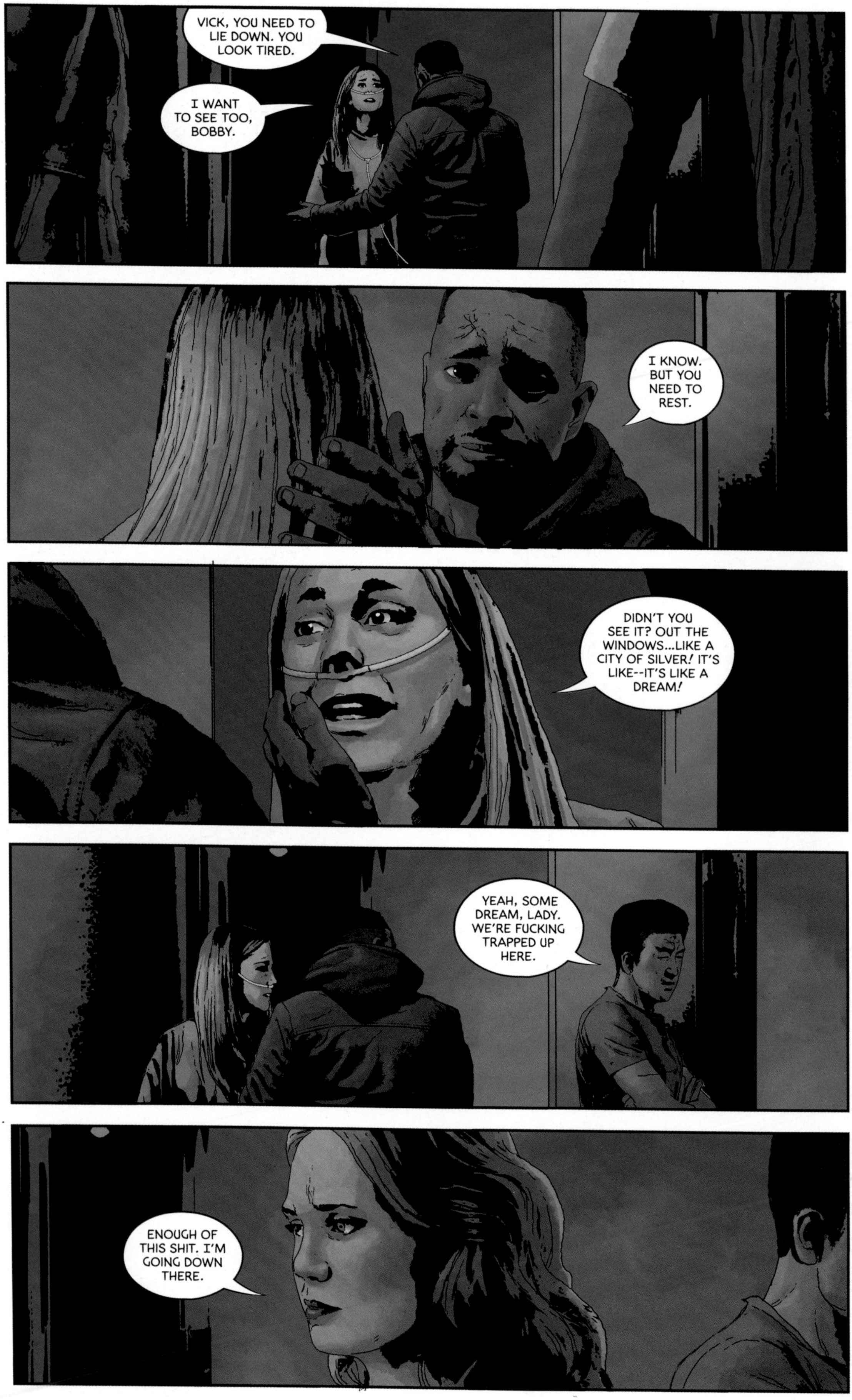
VICK, YOU NEED TO LIE DOWN. YOU LOOK TIRED.
I WANT TO SEE TOO, BOBBY.
I KNOW. BUT YOU NEED TO REST.
DIDN'T YOU SEE IT? OUT THE WINDOWS...LIKE A CITY OF SILVER! IT'S LIKE--IT'S LIKE A DREAM!
YEAH, SOME DREAM, LADY. WE'RE FUCKING TRAPPED UP HERE.
ENOUGH OF THIS SHIT. I'M GOING DOWN THERE.

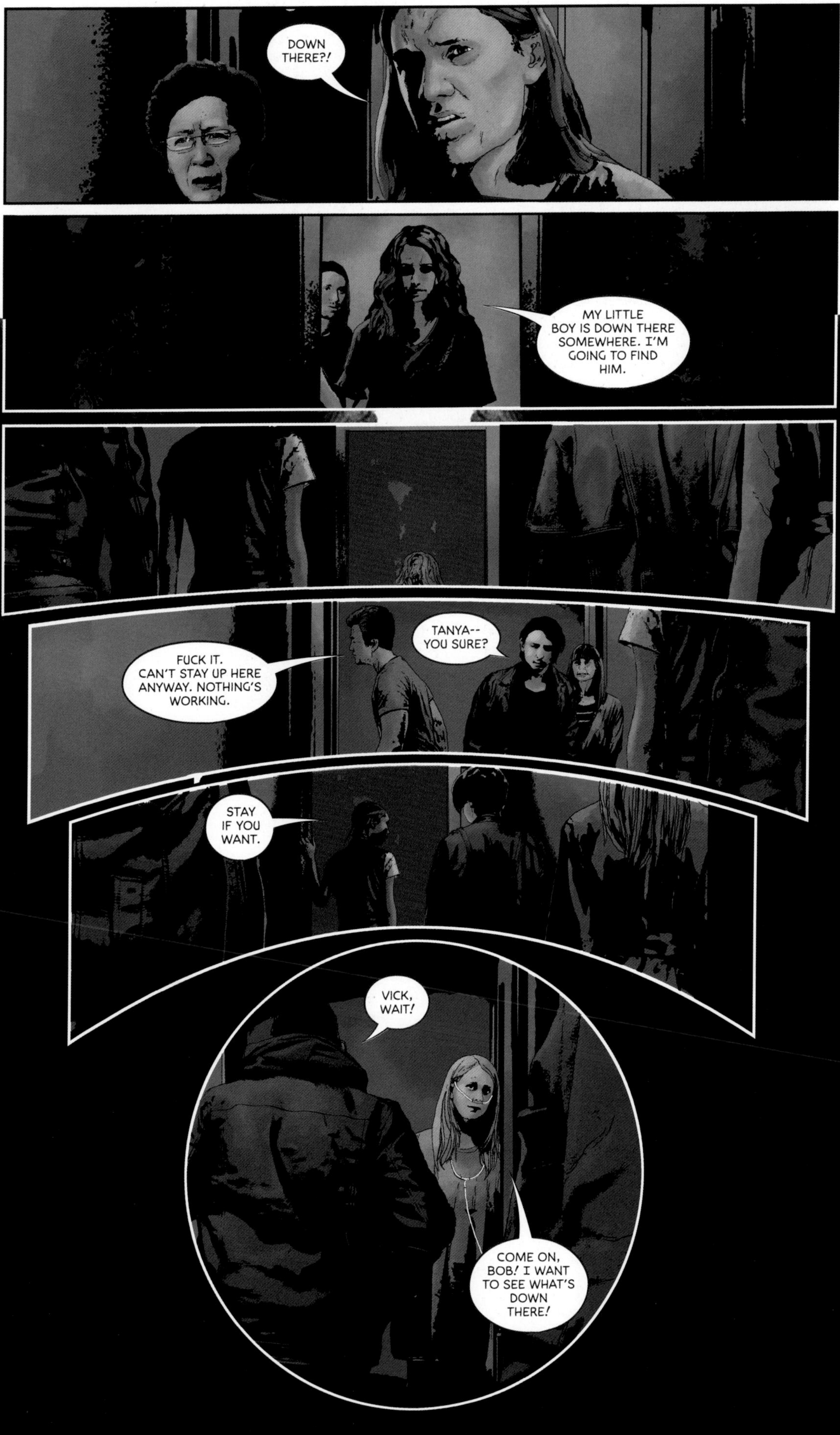
DOWN THERE?!
MY LITTLE BOY IS DOWN THERE SOMEWHERE. I'M GOING TO FIND HIM.
FUCK IT. CAN'T STAY UP HERE ANYWAY. NOTHING'S WORKING.
TANYA-- YOU SURE?
STAY IF YOU WANT.
VICK, WAIT!
COME ON, BOB! I WANT TO SEE WHAT'S DOWN THERE!

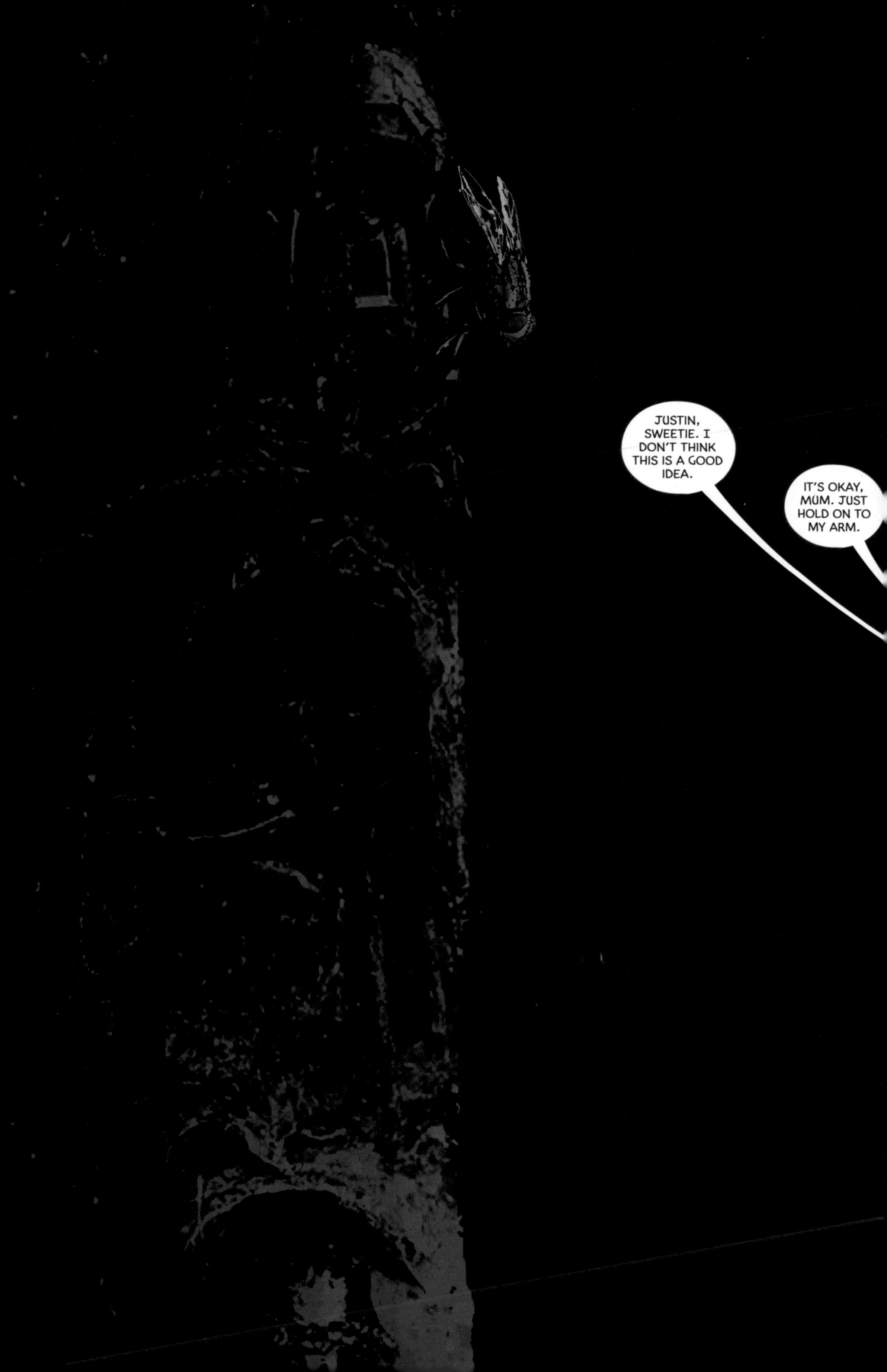
JUSTIN, SWEETIE. I DON'T THINK THIS IS A GOOD IDEA.
IT'S OKAY, MUM. JUST HOLD ON TO MY ARM.

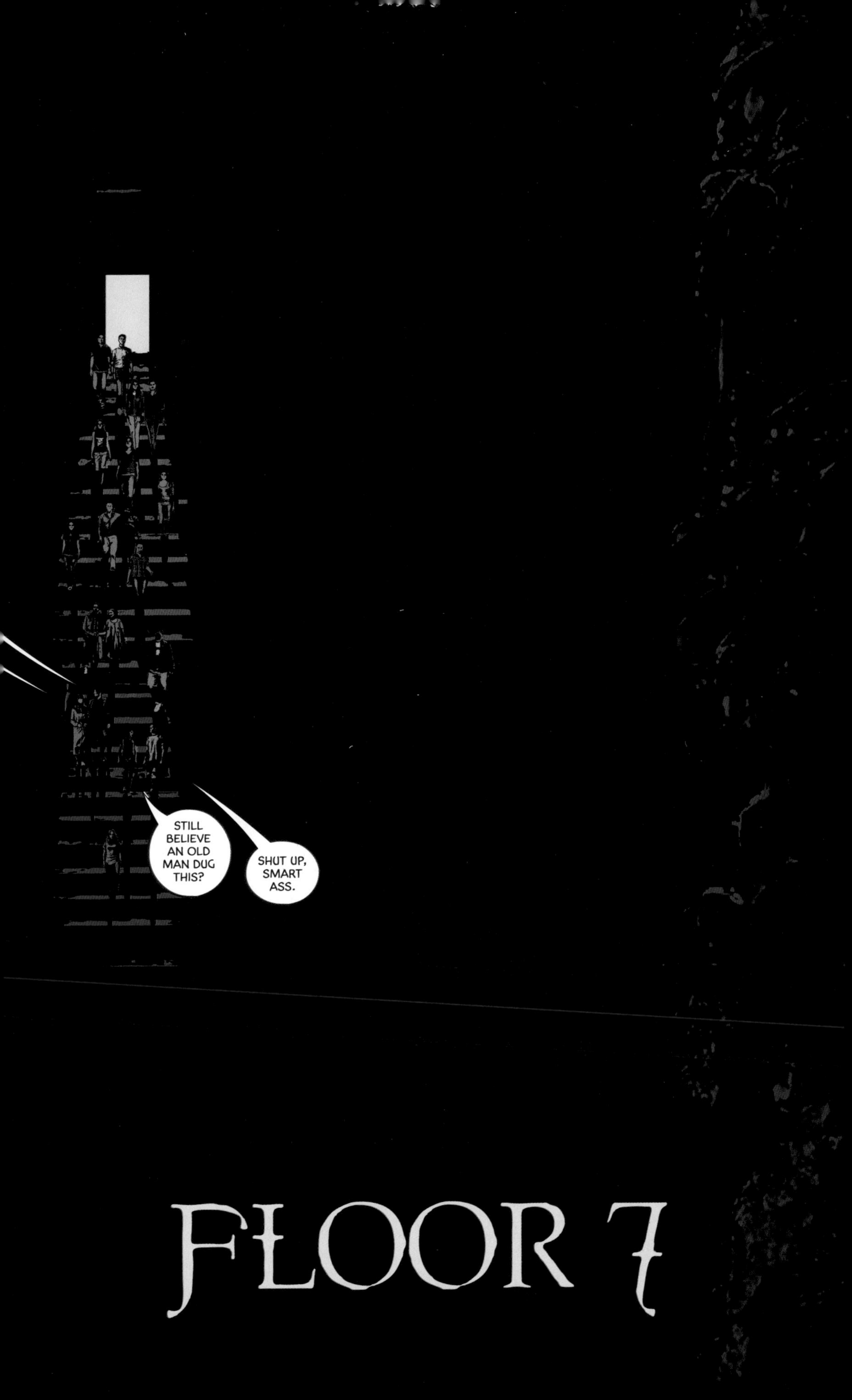
STILL BELIEVE AN OLD MAN DUG THIS?
SHUT UP, SMART ASS.
FLOOR 7

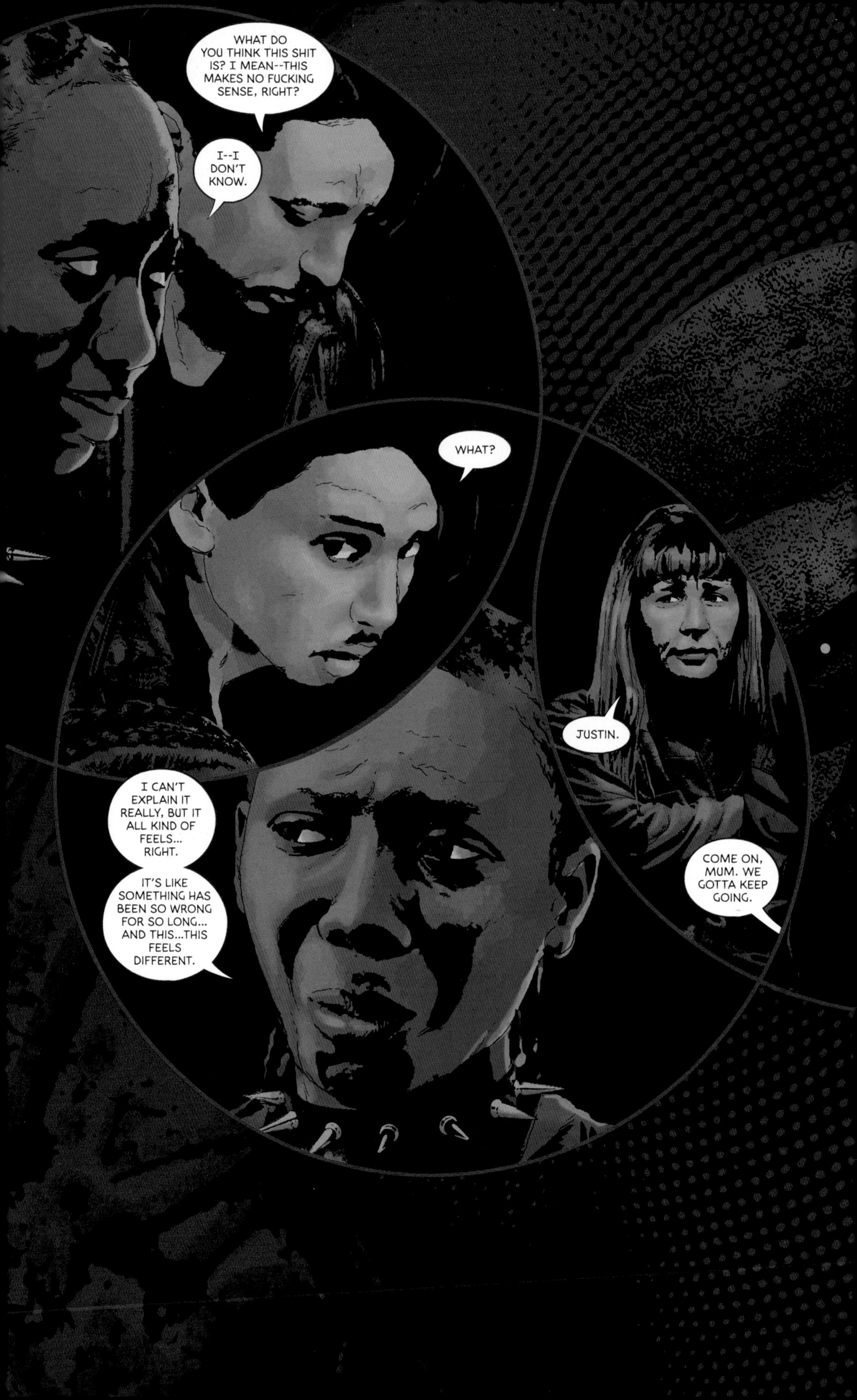
WHAT DO YOU THINK THIS SHIT IS? I MEAN--THIS MAKES NO FUCKING SENSE, RIGHT?
I--I DON'T KNOW.
WHAT?
JUSTIN.
I CAN'T EXPLAIN IT REALLY, BUT IT ALL KIND OF FEELS... RIGHT.
IT'S LIKE SOMETHING HAS BEEN SO WRONG FOR SO LONG... AND THIS...THIS FEELS DIFFERENT.
COME ON, MUM. WE GOTTA KEEP GOING.

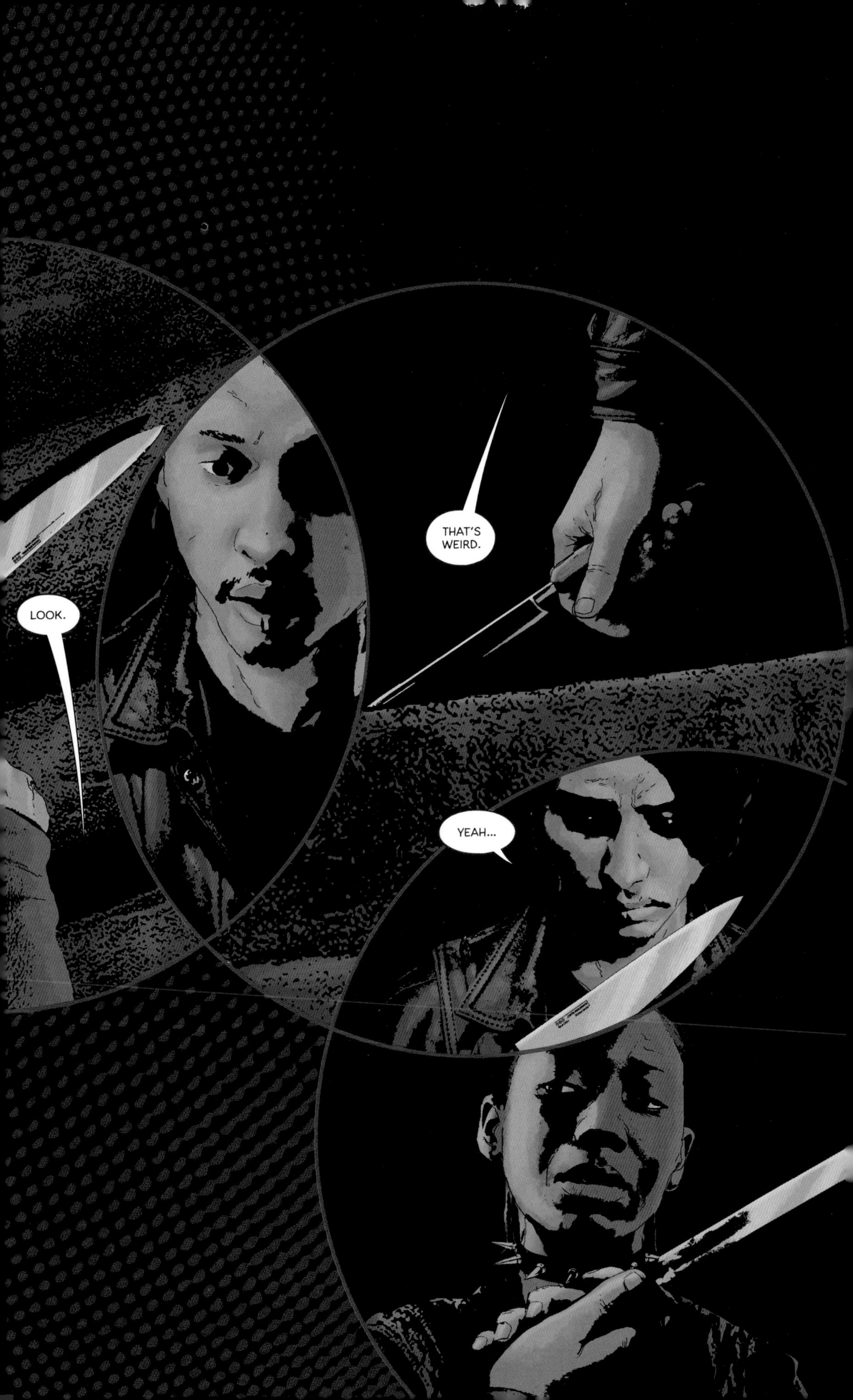
LOOK.
THAT'S
WEIRD.
YEAH...

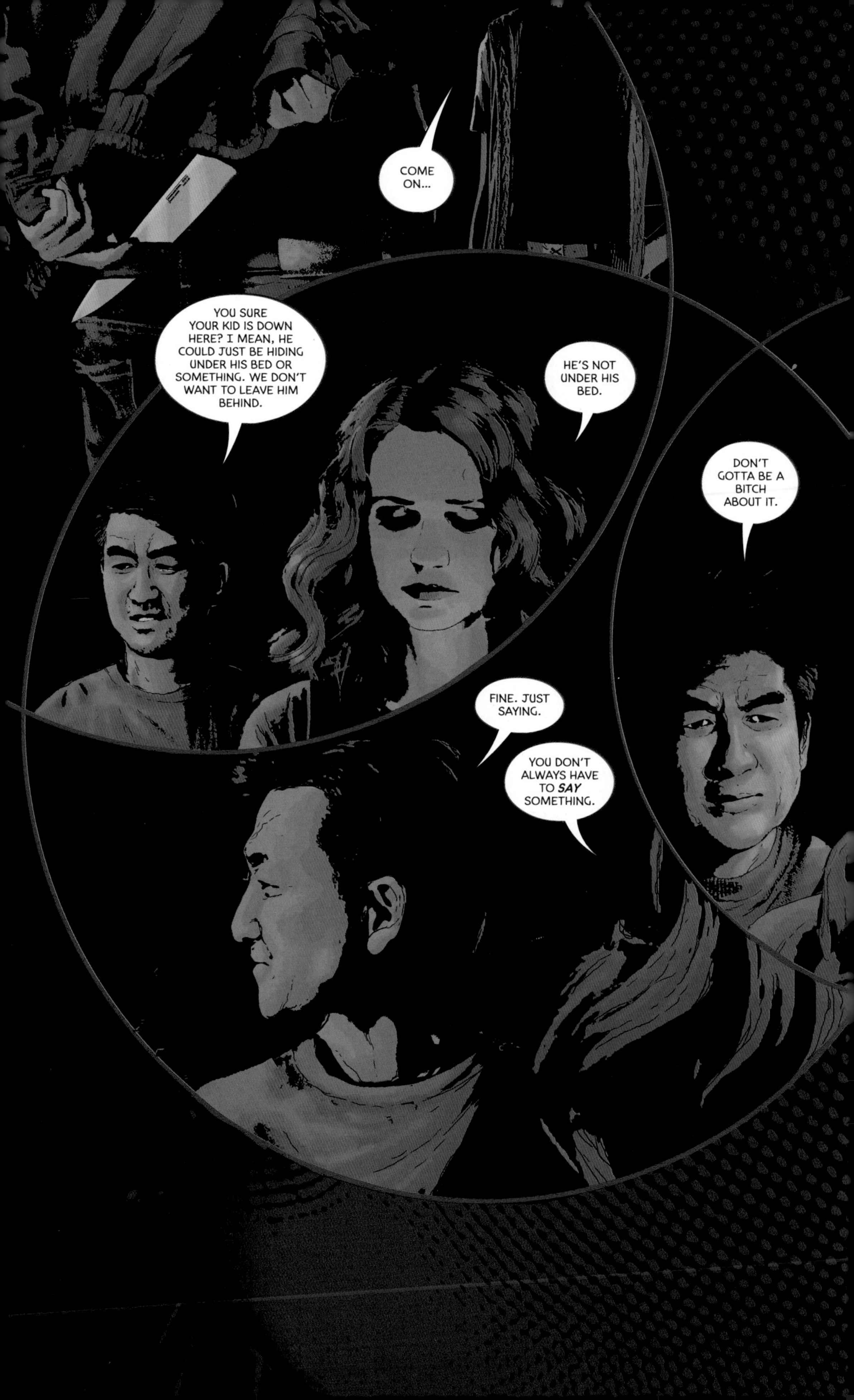
COME ON...
YOU SURE YOUR KID IS DOWN HERE? I MEAN, HE COULD JUST BE HIDING UNDER HIS BED OR SOMETHING. WE DON'T WANT TO LEAVE HIM BEHIND.
HE'S NOT UNDER HIS BED.
DON'T GOTTA BE A BITCH ABOUT IT.
FINE. JUST SAYING.
YOU DON'T ALWAYS HAVE TO *SAY* SOMETHING.

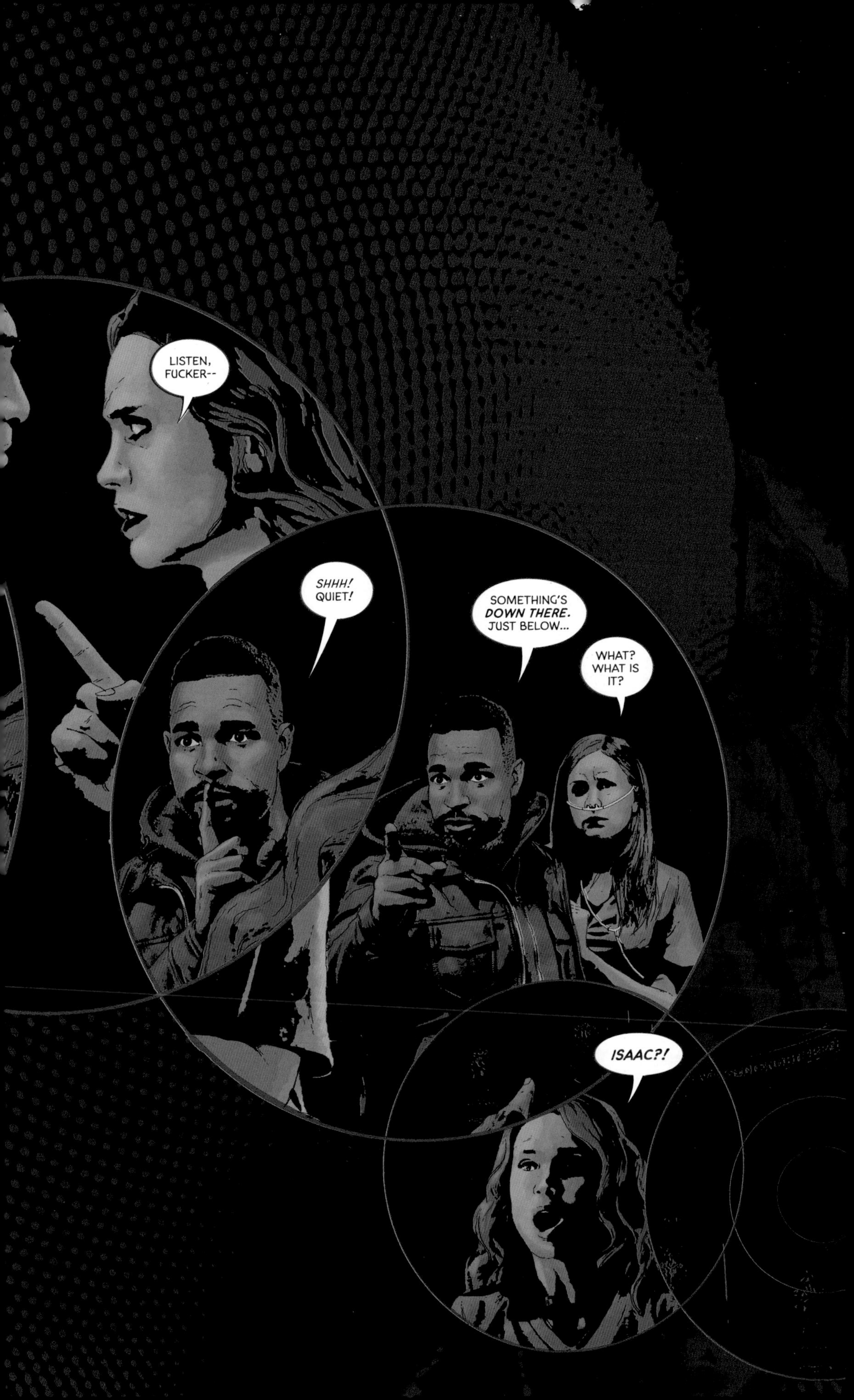
LISTEN, FUCKER--
SHHH! QUIET!
SOMETHING'S DOWN THERE. JUST BELOW...
WHAT? WHAT IS IT?
ISAAC?!

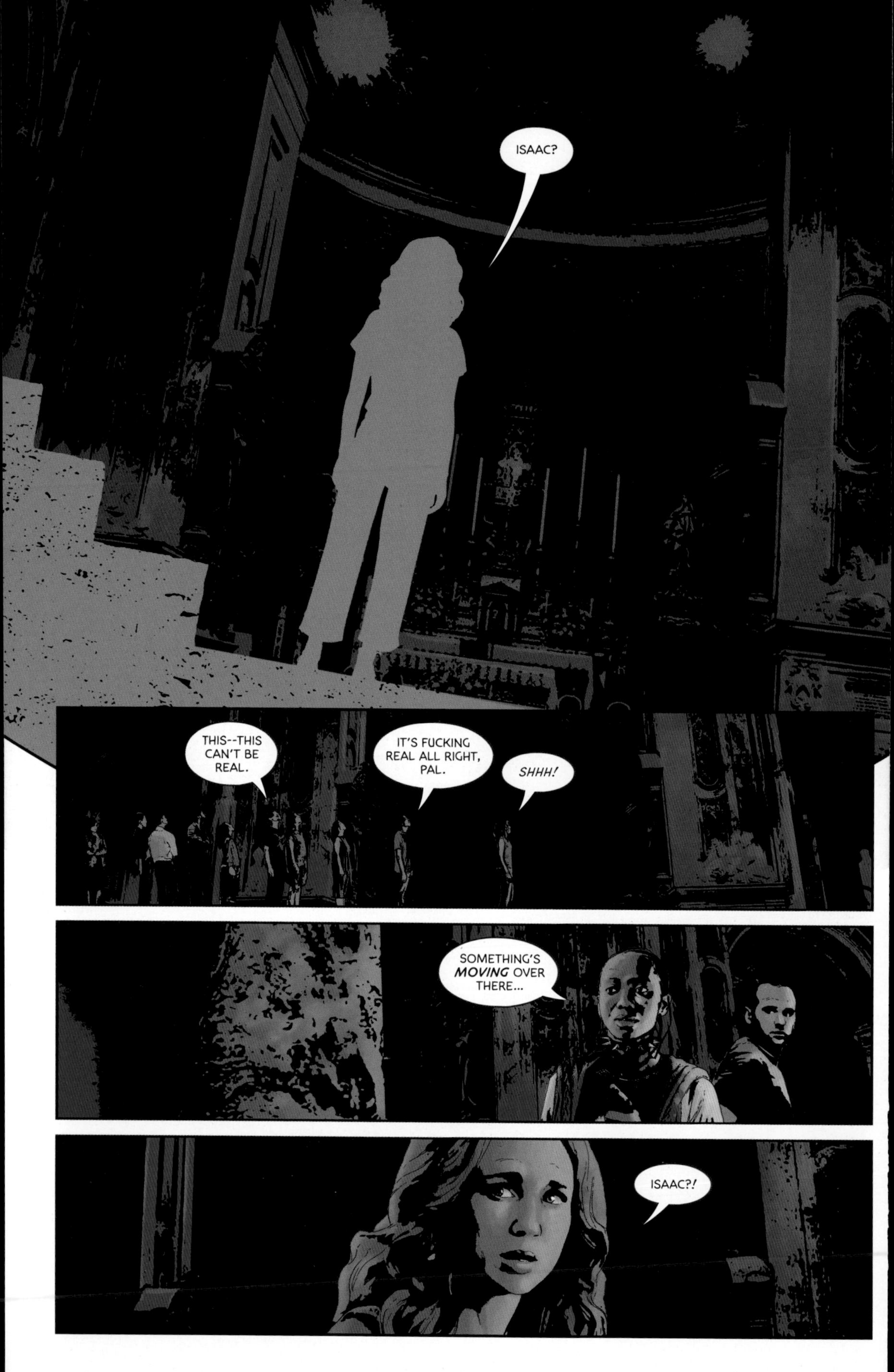
ISAAC?
THIS--THIS CAN'T BE REAL.
IT'S FUCKING REAL ALL RIGHT, PAL.
SHHH!
SOMETHING'S ***MOVING*** OVER THERE...
ISAAC?*!*

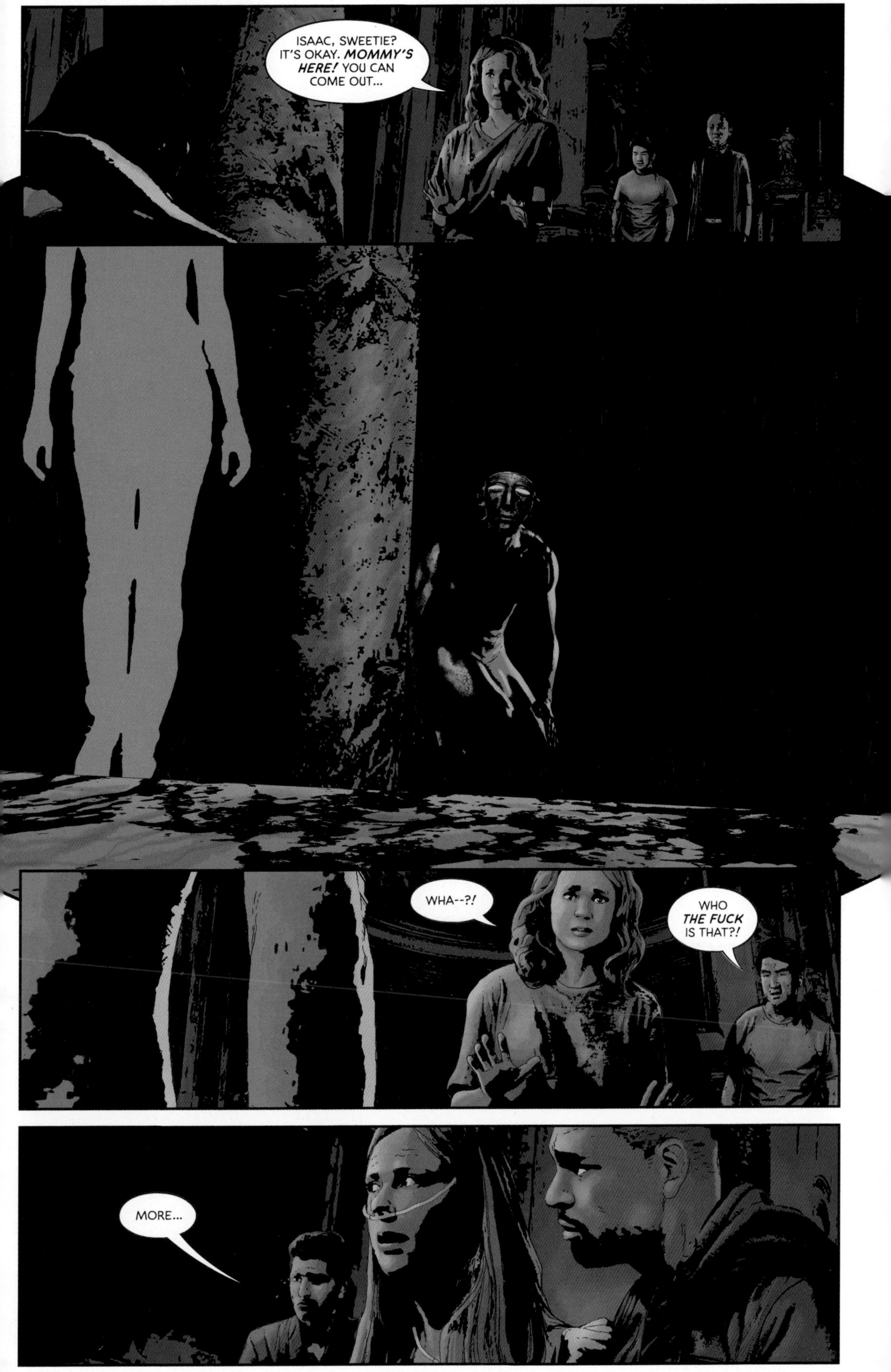
ISAAC, SWEETIE? IT'S OKAY. ***MOMMY'S HERE!*** YOU CAN COME OUT...
WHA--?!
WHO ***THE FUCK*** IS THAT?!
MORE...

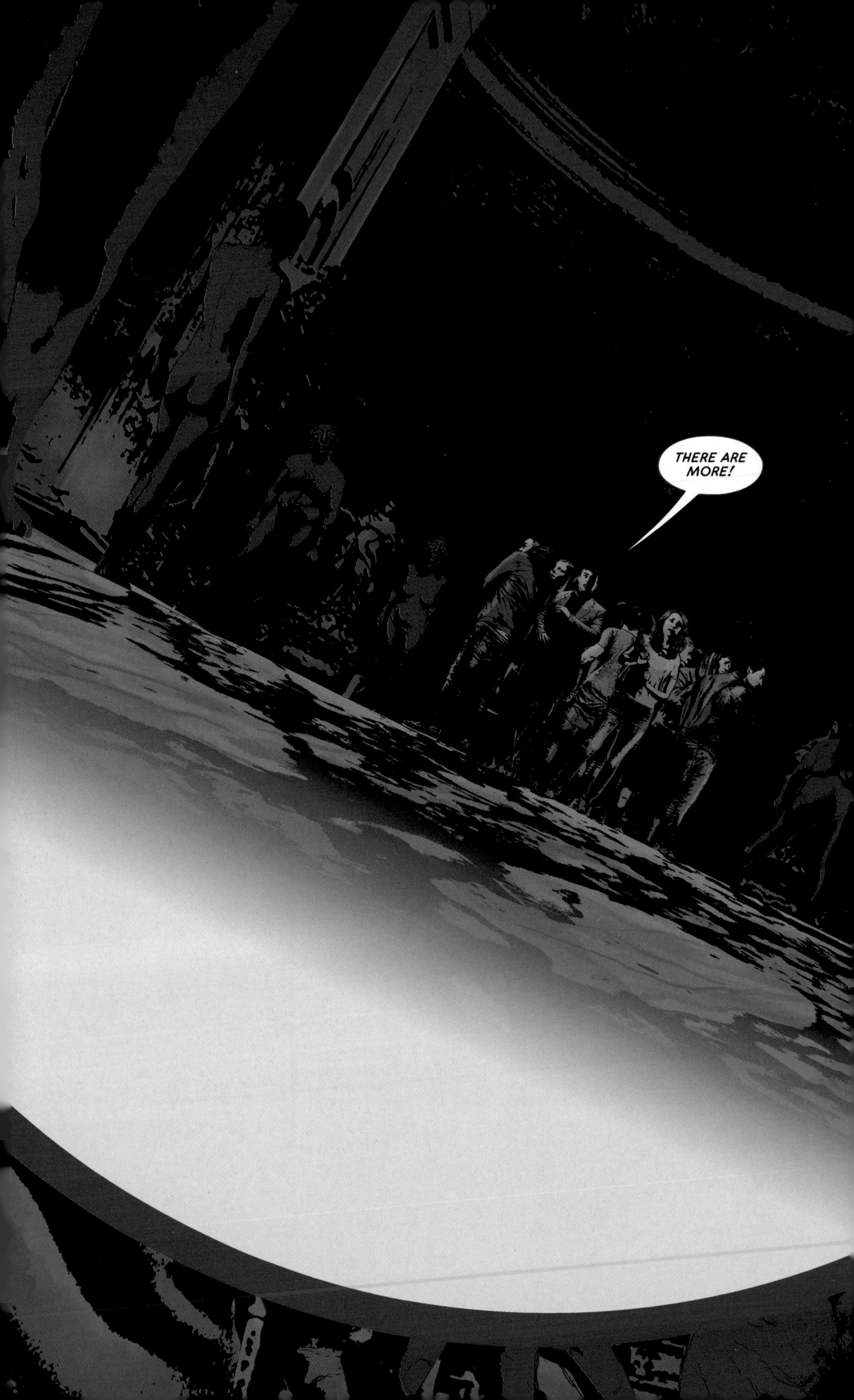
THERE ARE MORE!

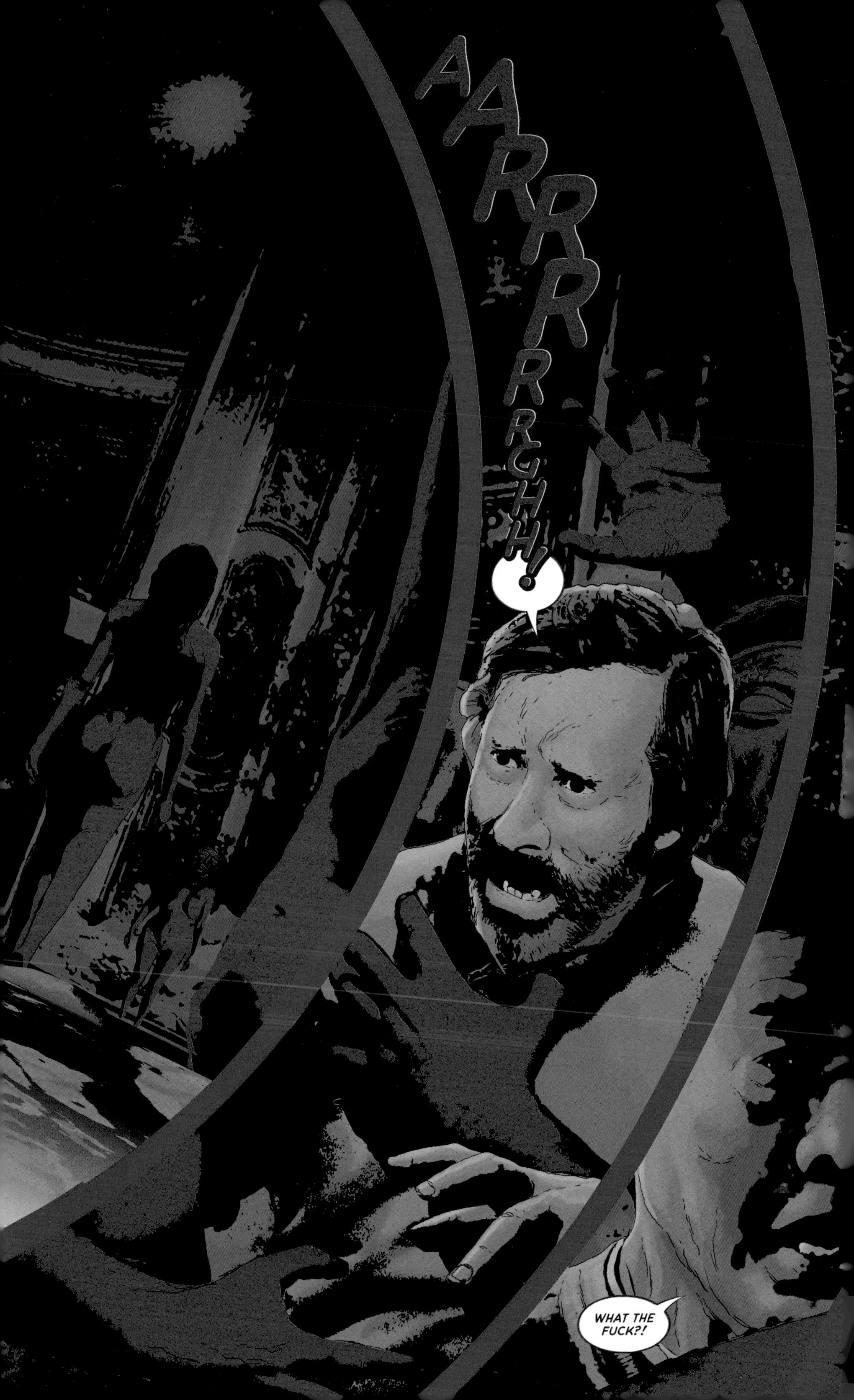
AARRRRRRGHH!
WHAT THE FUCK?!

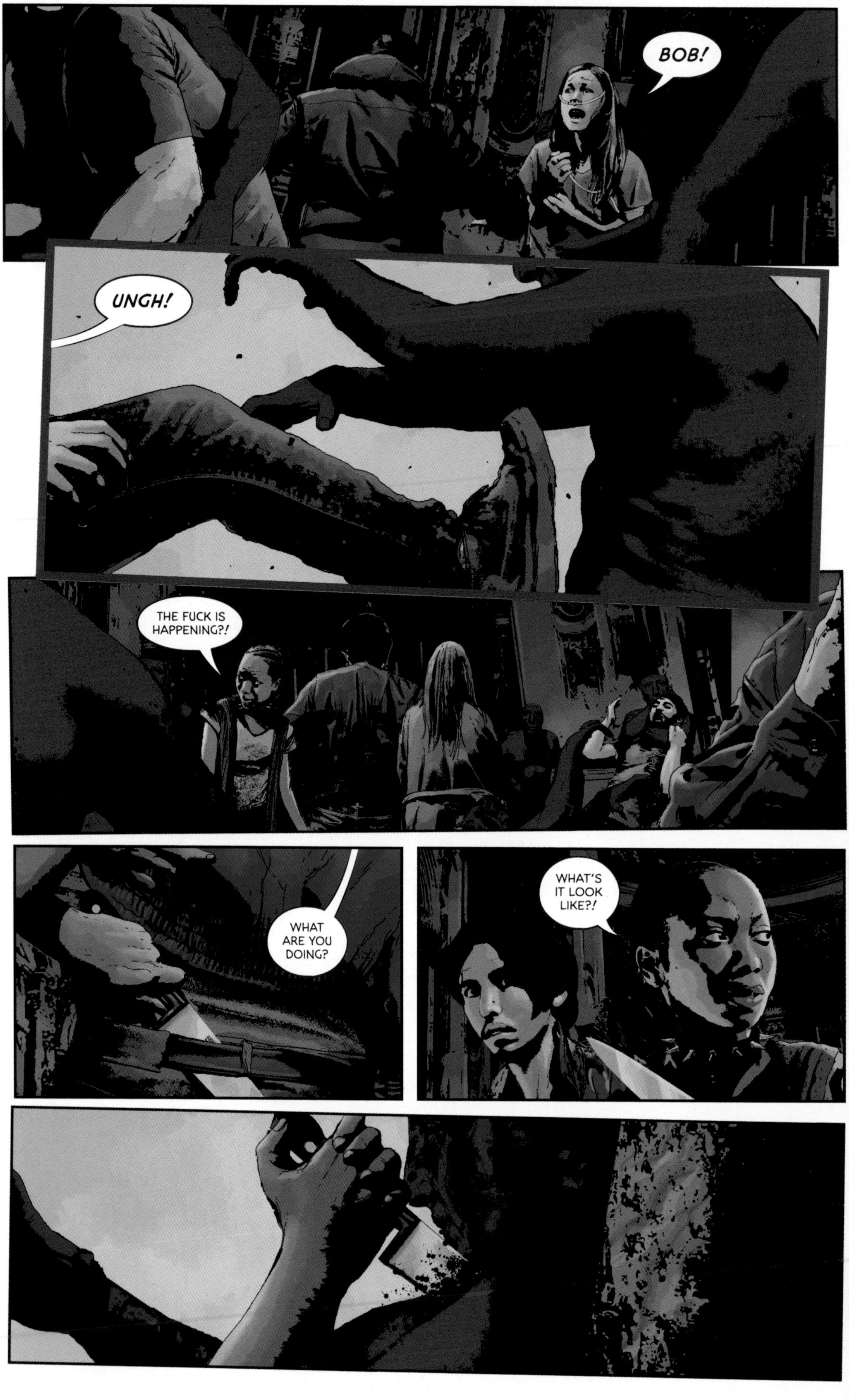
BOB!
UNGH!
THE FUCK IS HAPPENING?!
WHAT ARE YOU DOING?
WHAT'S IT LOOK LIKE?!

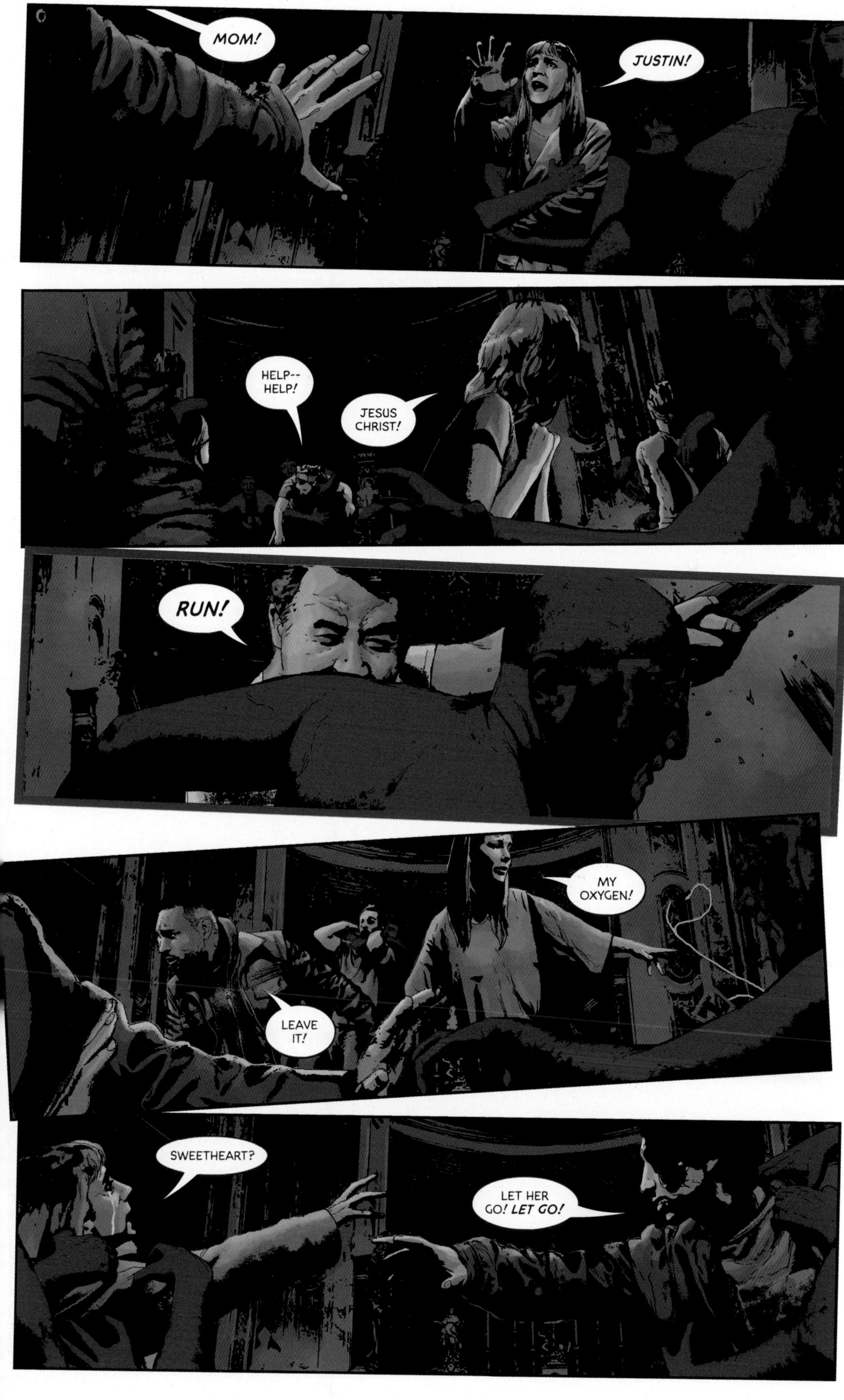
MOM!
JUSTIN!
HELP--
HELP!
JESUS
CHRIST!
RUN!
MY
OXYGEN!
LEAVE
IT!
SWEETHEART?
LET HER
GO! LET GO!

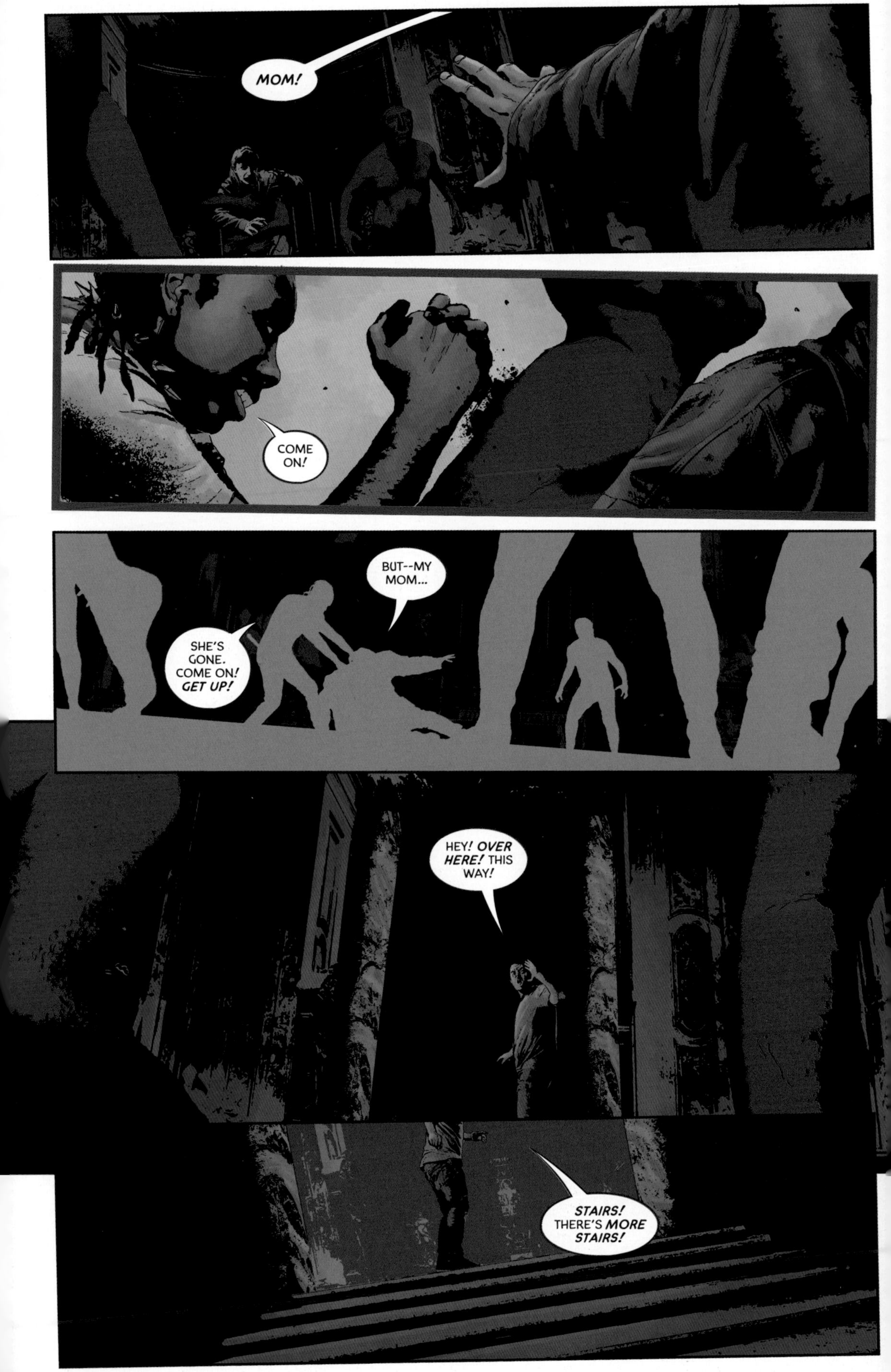
MOM!
COME ON!
SHE'S GONE. COME ON! GET UP!
BUT--MY MOM...
HEY! OVER HERE! THIS WAY!
STAIRS! THERE'S MORE STAIRS!

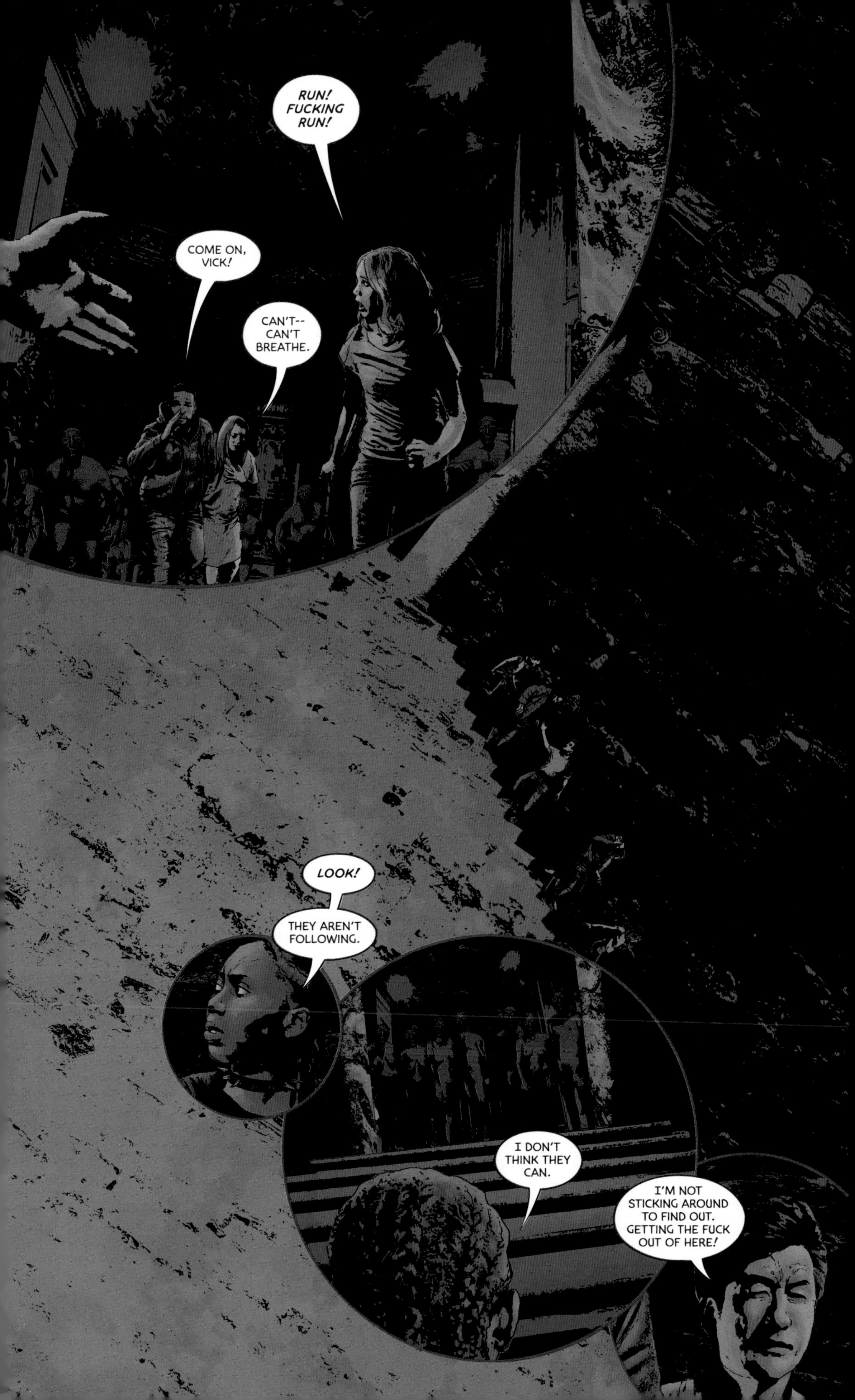
RUN! FUCKING RUN!
COME ON, VICK!
CAN'T-- CAN'T BREATHE.
LOOK!
THEY AREN'T FOLLOWING.
I DON'T THINK THEY CAN.
I'M NOT STICKING AROUND TO FIND OUT. GETTING THE FUCK OUT OF HERE!

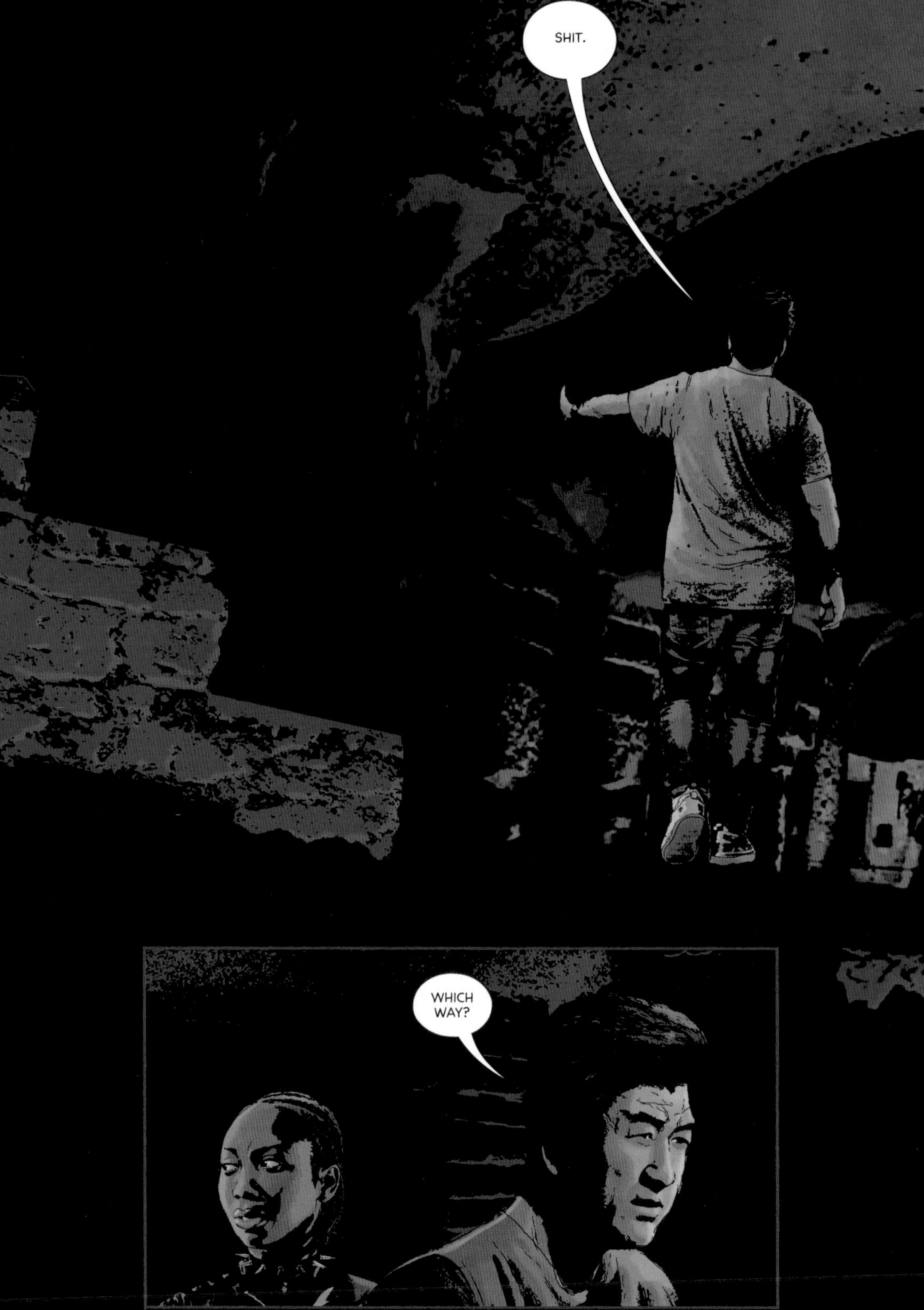
SHIT.
WHICH WAY?

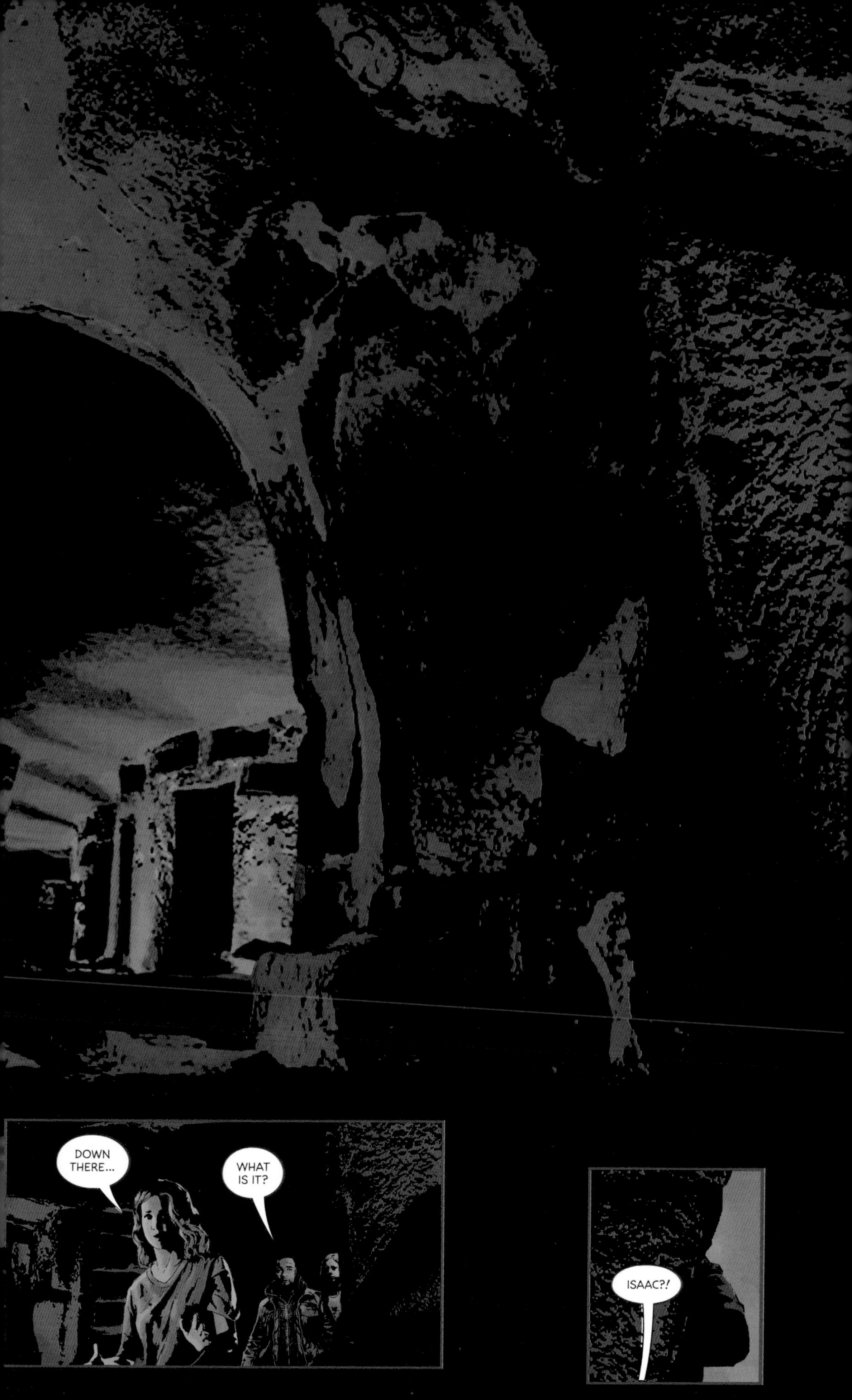
DOWN THERE...
WHAT IS IT?
ISAAC?!

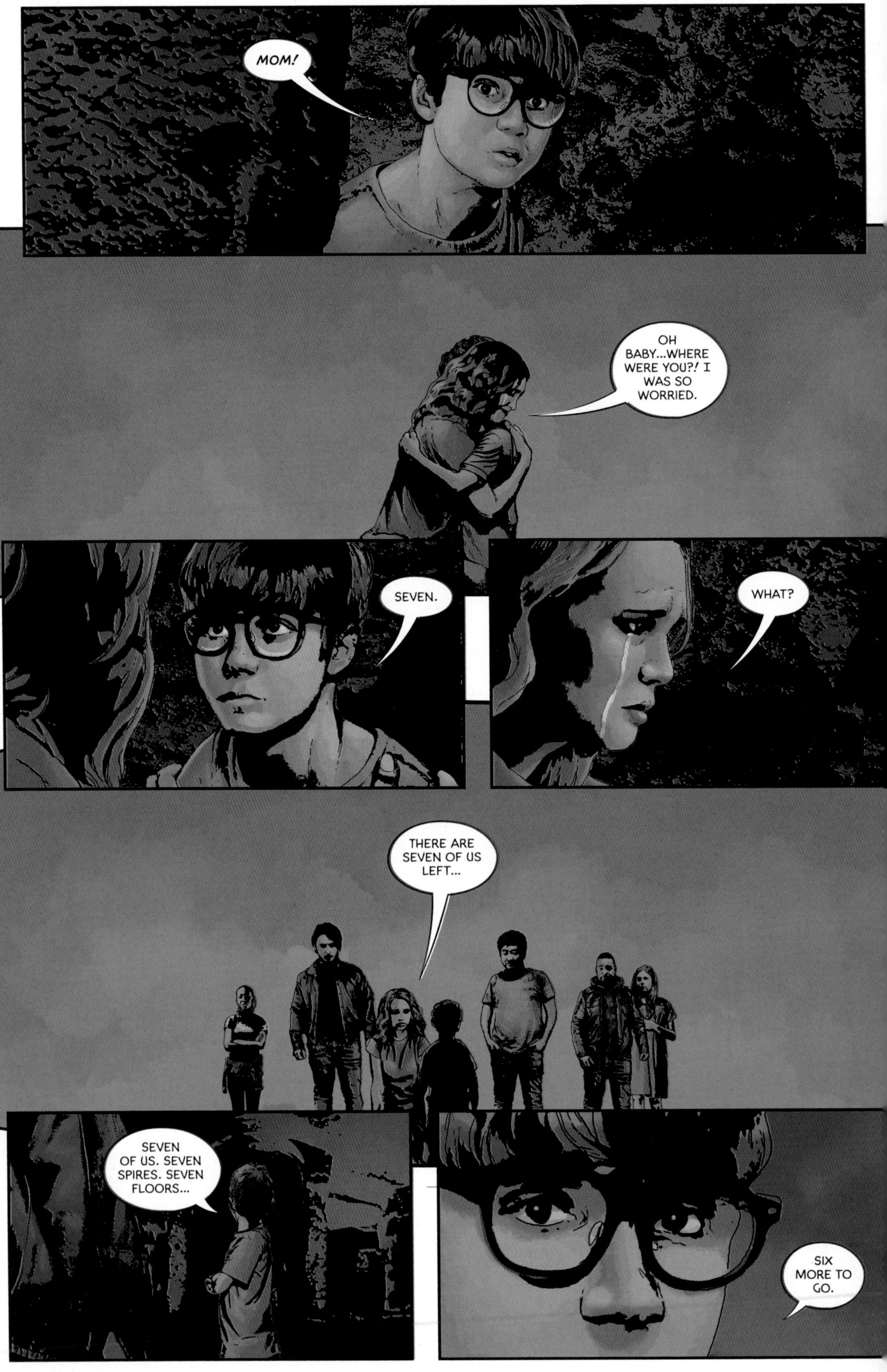
MOM!
OH BABY...WHERE WERE YOU?! I WAS SO WORRIED.
SEVEN.
WHAT?
THERE ARE SEVEN OF US LEFT...
SEVEN OF US. SEVEN SPIRES. SEVEN FLOORS...
SIX MORE TO GO.

4

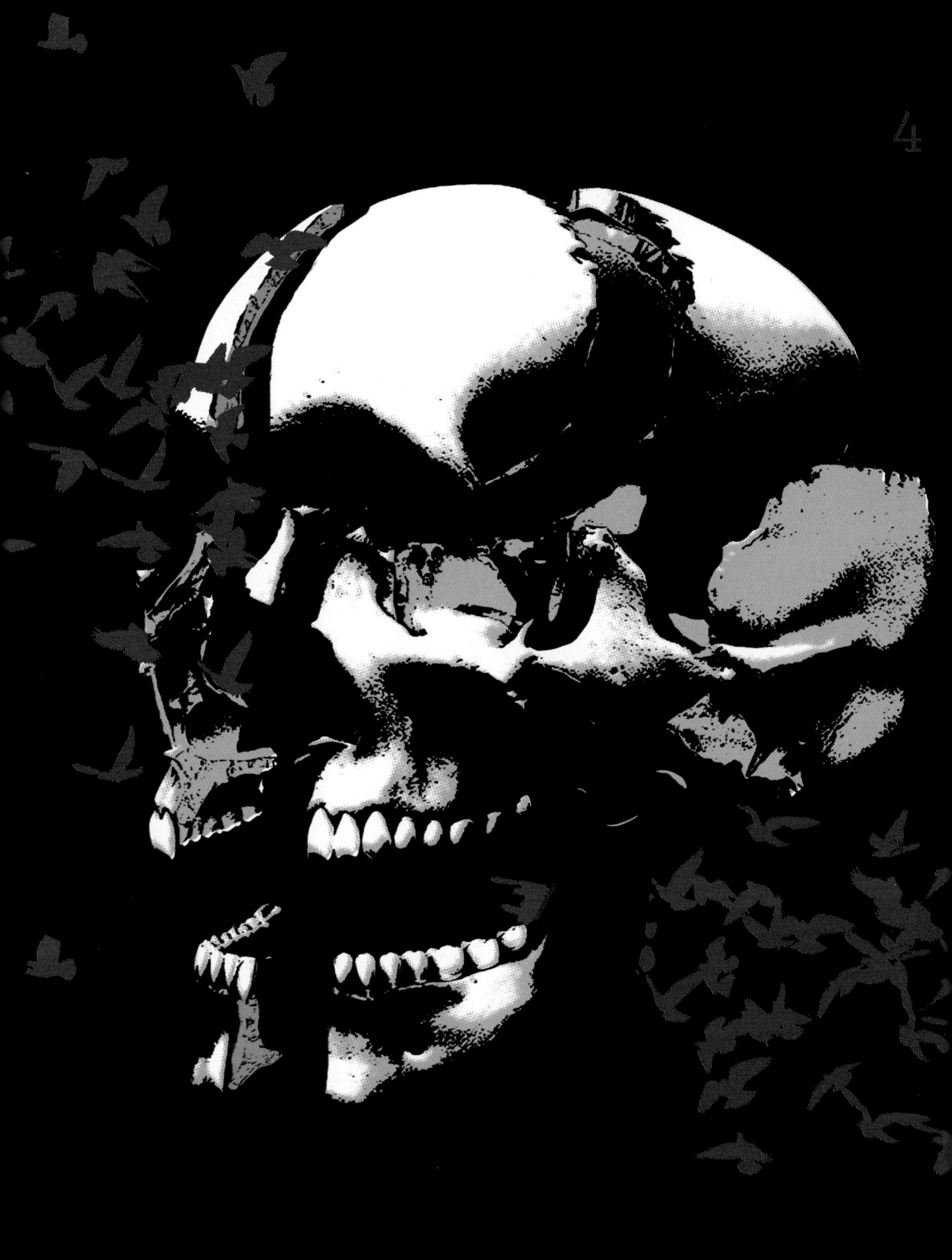

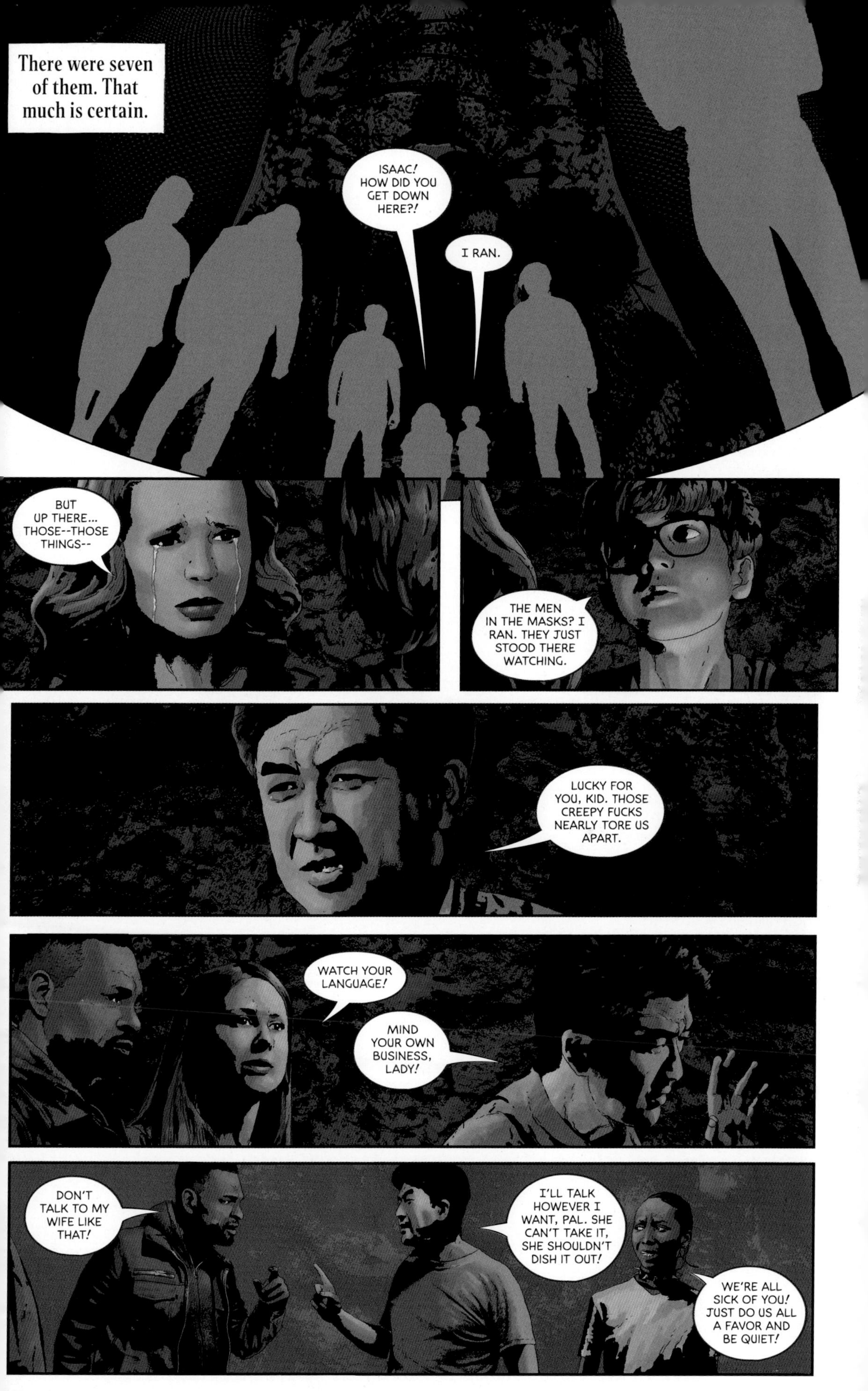

There were seven of them. That much is certain.
ISAAC! HOW DID YOU GET DOWN HERE?!
I RAN.
BUT UP THERE... THOSE--THOSE THINGS--
THE MEN IN THE MASKS? I RAN. THEY JUST STOOD THERE WATCHING.
LUCKY FOR YOU, KID. THOSE CREEPY FUCKS NEARLY TORE US APART.
WATCH YOUR LANGUAGE!
MIND YOUR OWN BUSINESS, LADY!
DON'T TALK TO MY WIFE LIKE THAT!
I'LL TALK HOWEVER I WANT, PAL. SHE CAN'T TAKE IT, SHE SHOULDN'T DISH IT OUT!
WE'RE ALL SICK OF YOU! JUST DO US ALL A FAVOR AND BE QUIET!

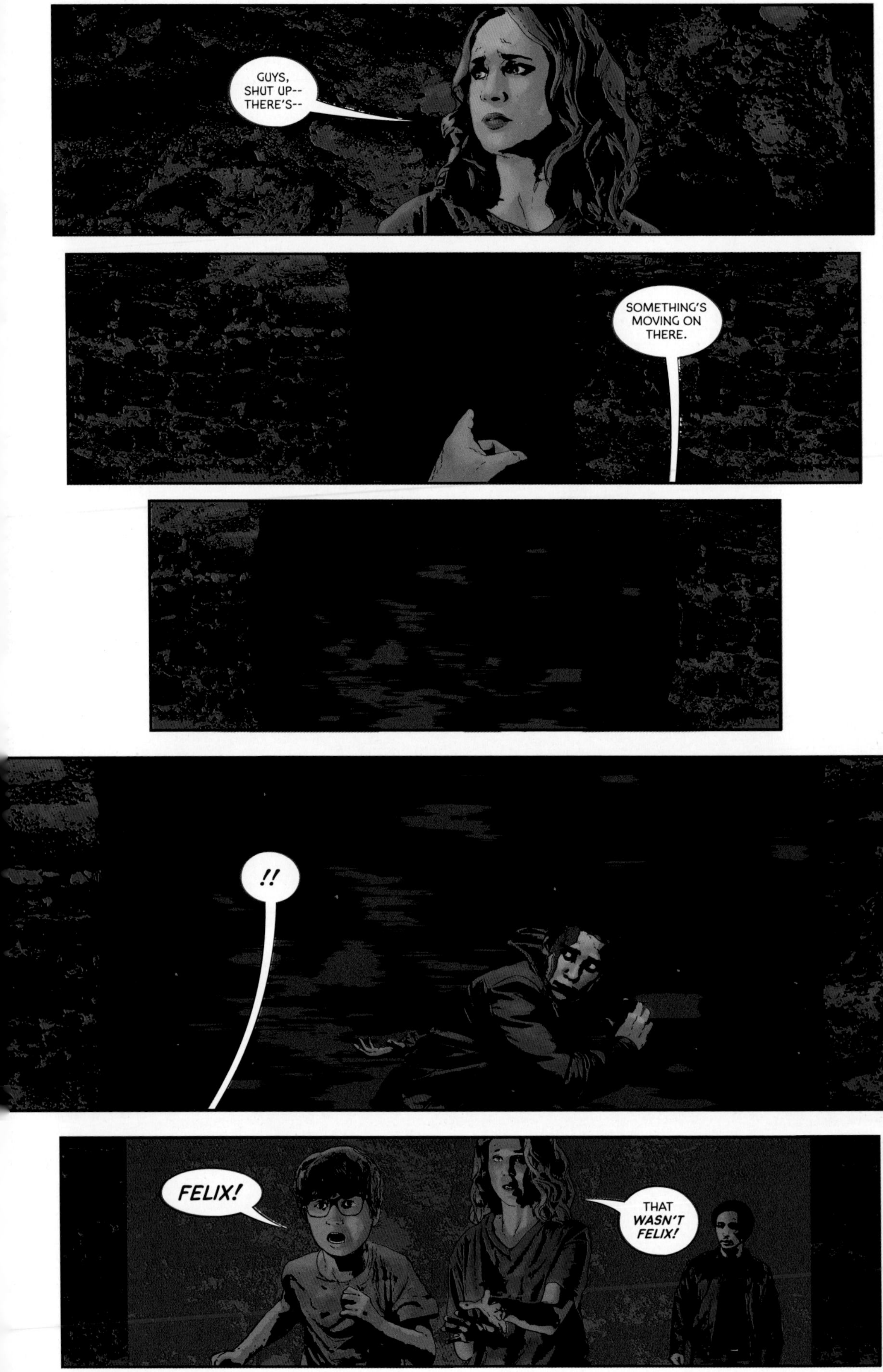
GUYS, SHUT UP-- THERE'S--
SOMETHING'S MOVING ON THERE.
!!
FELIX!
THAT *WASN'T* FELIX!

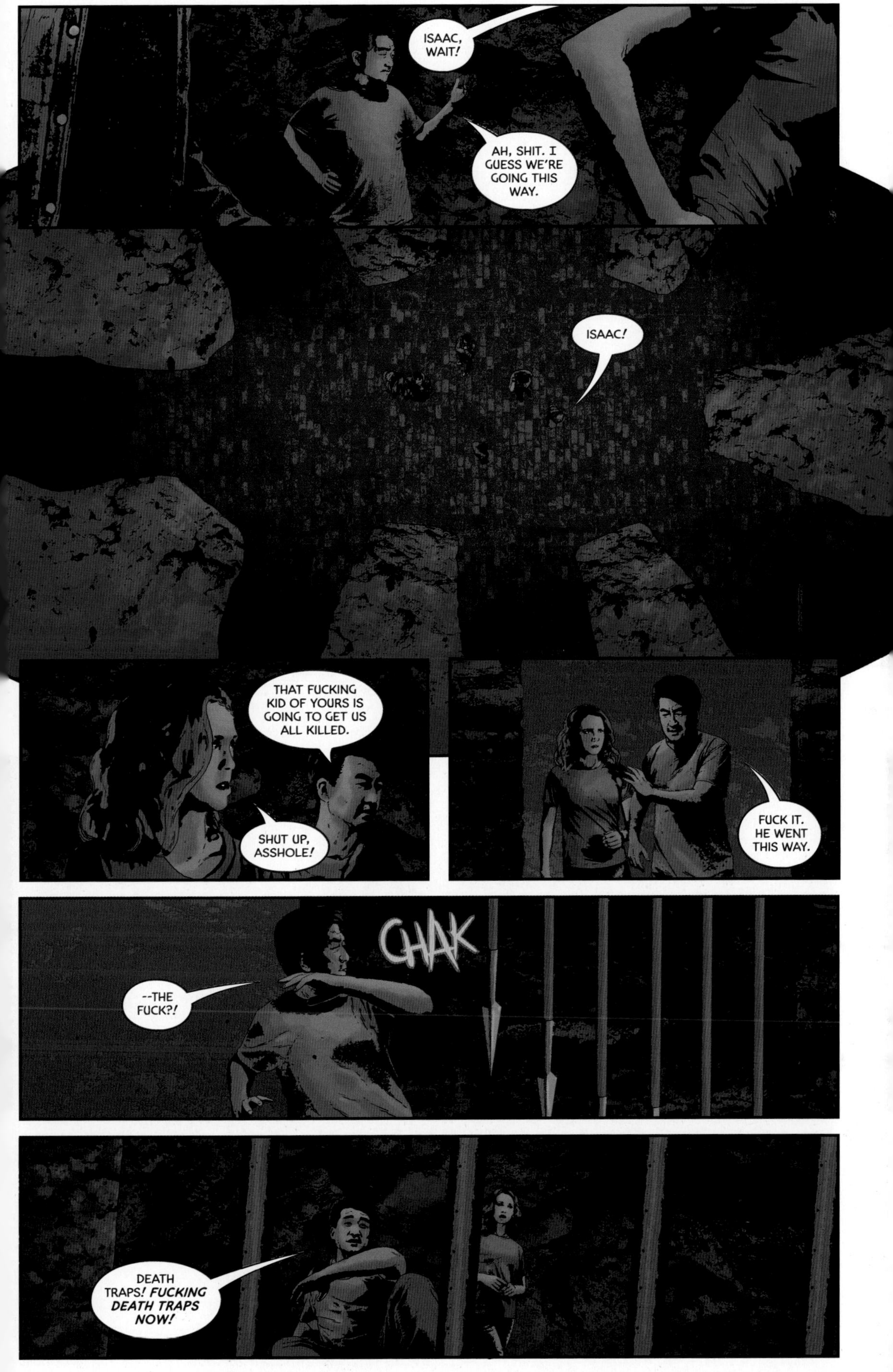
ISAAC, WAIT!
AH, SHIT. I GUESS WE'RE GOING THIS WAY.
ISAAC!
THAT FUCKING KID OF YOURS IS GOING TO GET US ALL KILLED.
SHUT UP, ASSHOLE!
FUCK IT. HE WENT THIS WAY.
CHAK
--THE FUCK?!
DEATH TRAPS! FUCKING DEATH TRAPS NOW!

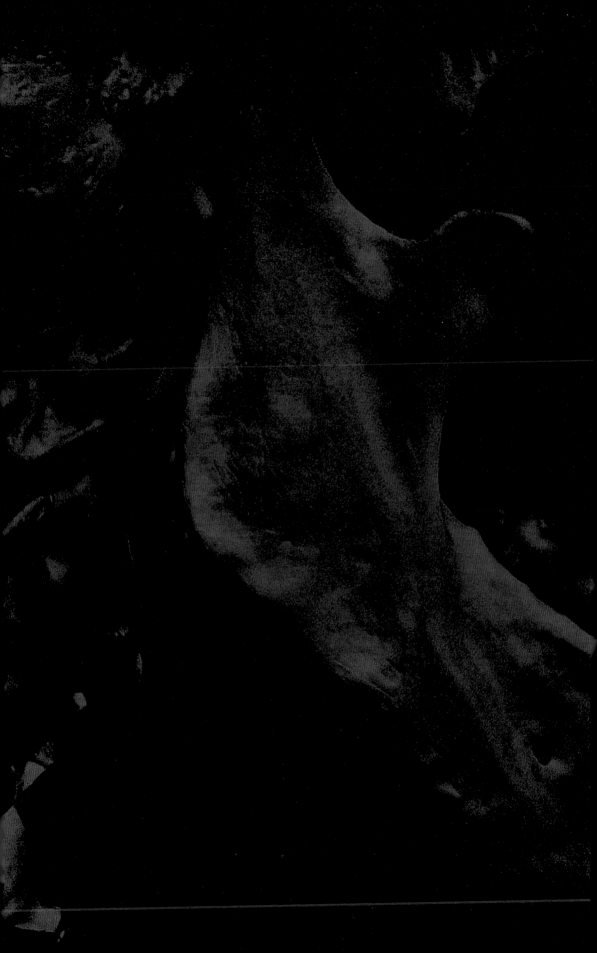

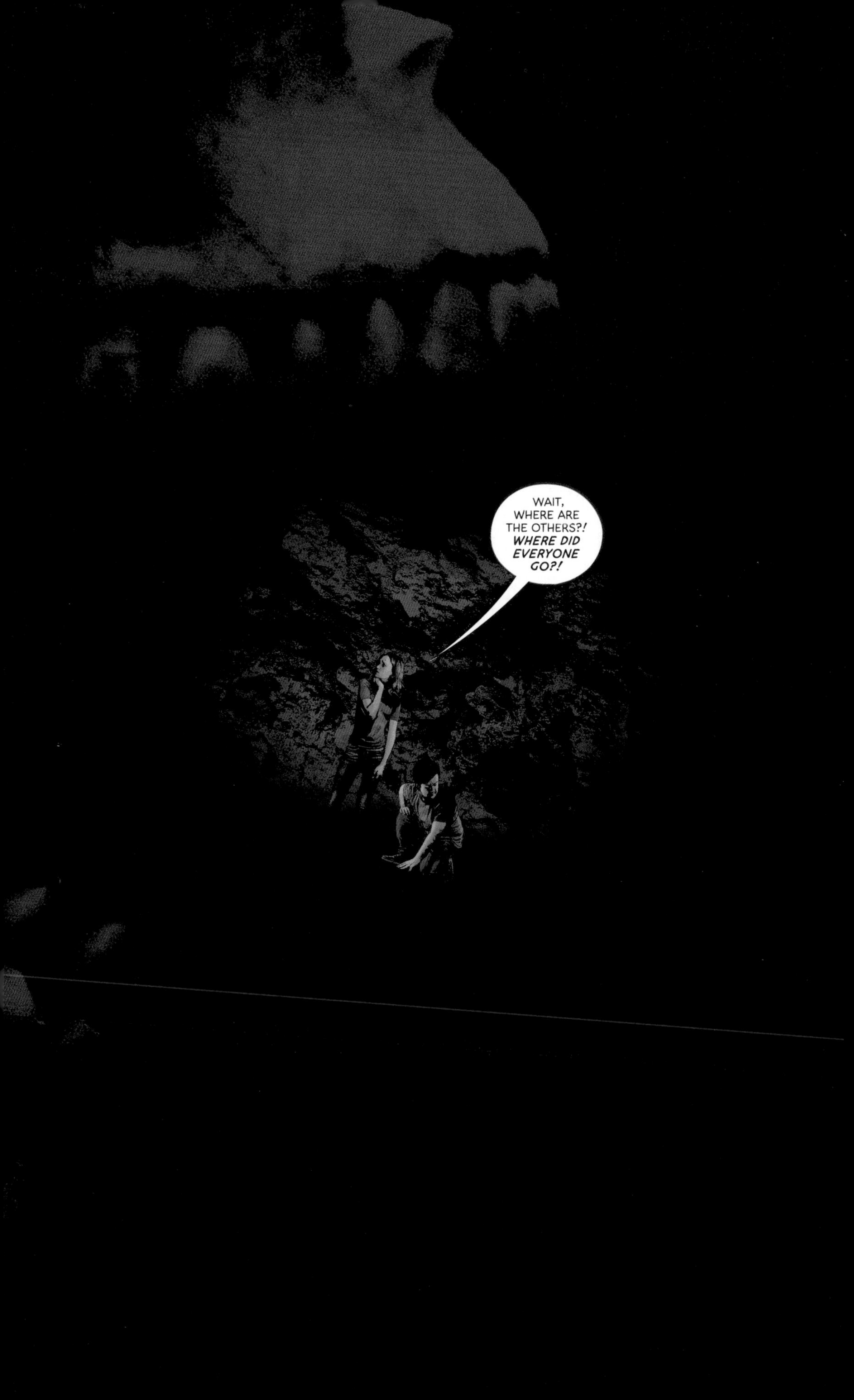
WAIT, WHERE ARE THE OTHERS?! *WHERE DID EVERYONE GO?!*

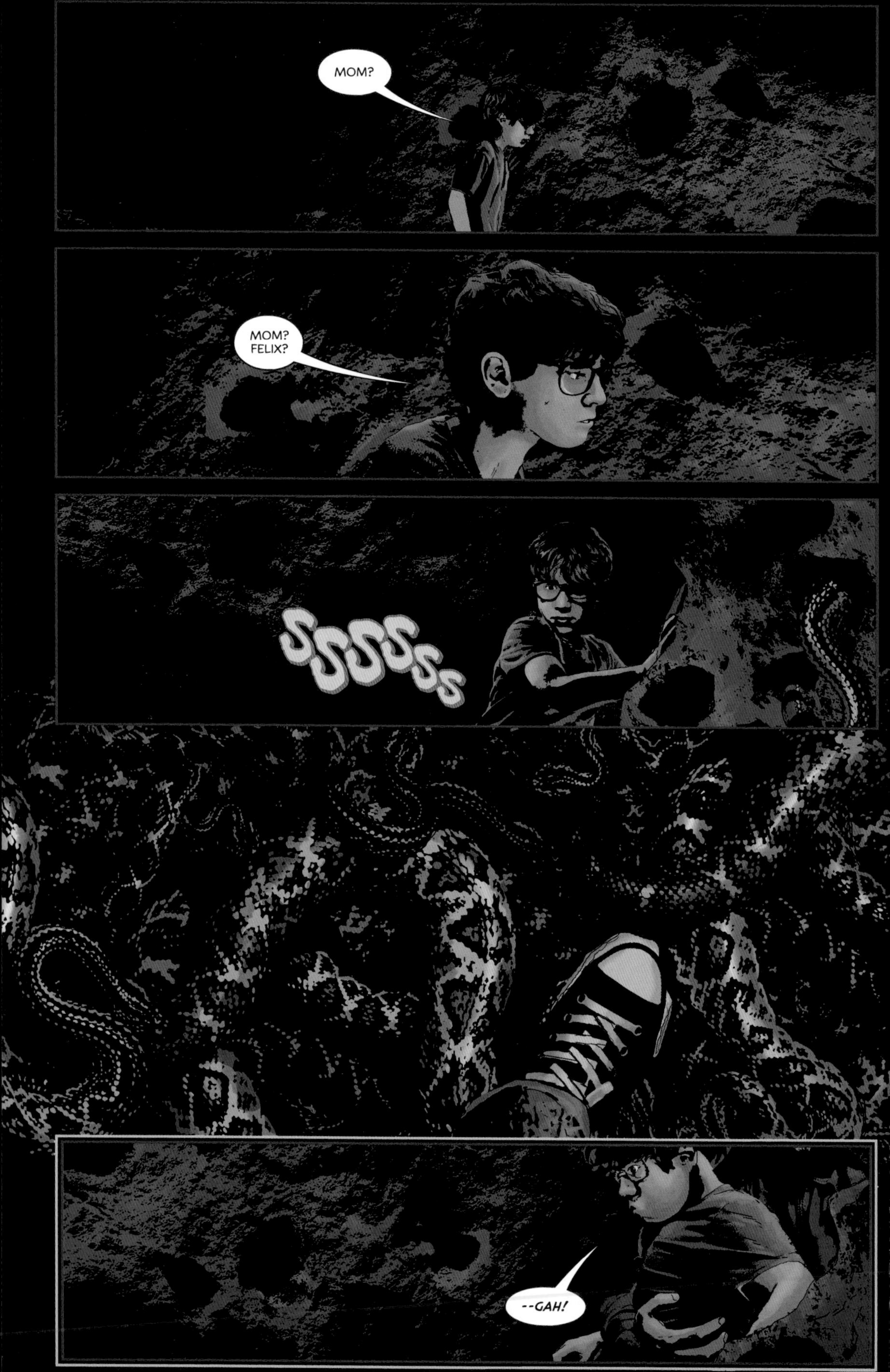

MOM?
MOM? FELIX?
SSSSSS
--GAH!

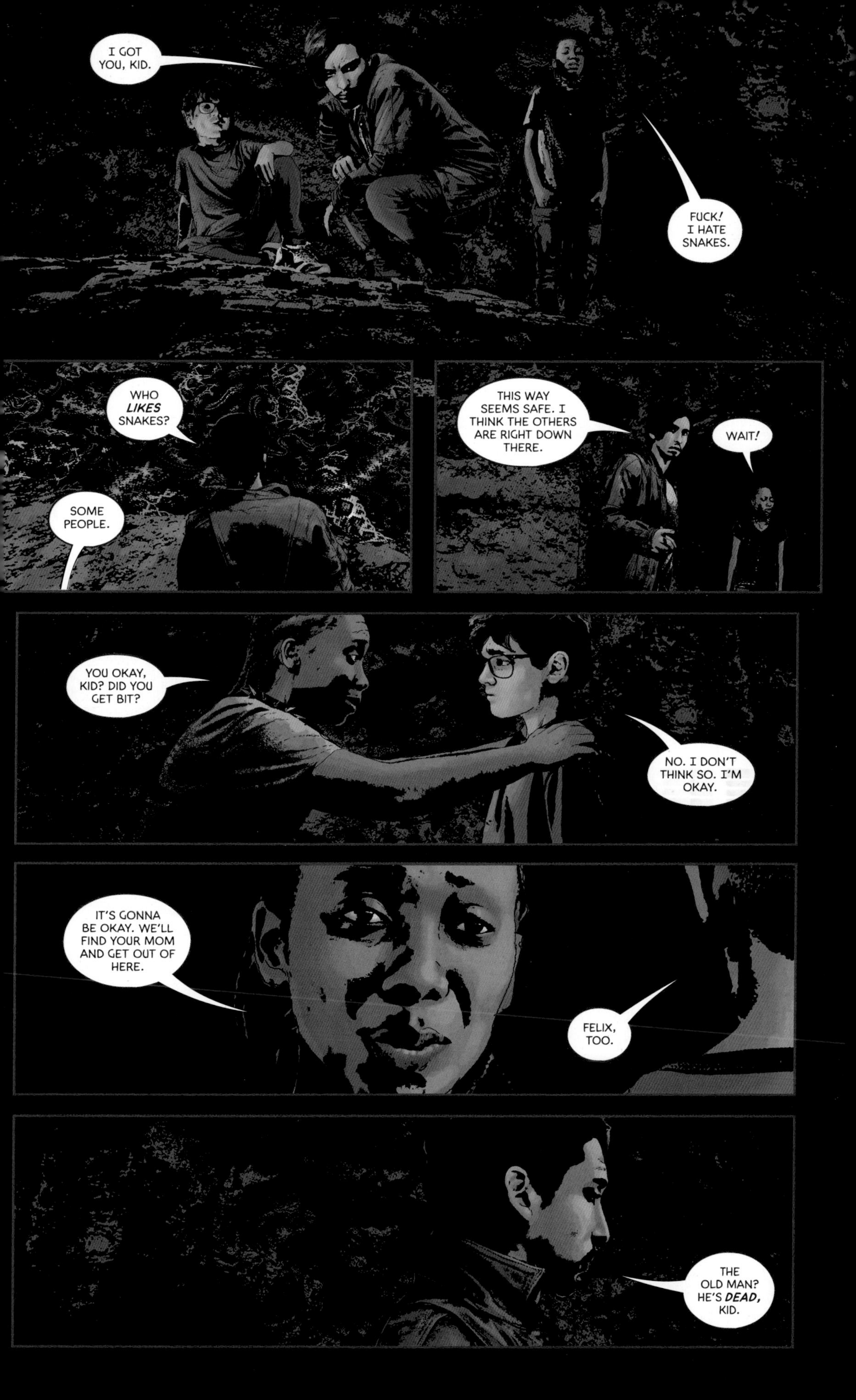

I GOT YOU, KID.
FUCK! I HATE SNAKES.
WHO *LIKES* SNAKES?
SOME PEOPLE.
THIS WAY SEEMS SAFE. I THINK THE OTHERS ARE RIGHT DOWN THERE.
WAIT!
YOU OKAY, KID? DID YOU GET BIT?
NO. I DON'T THINK SO. I'M OKAY.
IT'S GONNA BE OKAY. WE'LL FIND YOUR MOM AND GET OUT OF HERE.
FELIX, TOO.
THE OLD MAN? HE'S *DEAD,* KID.

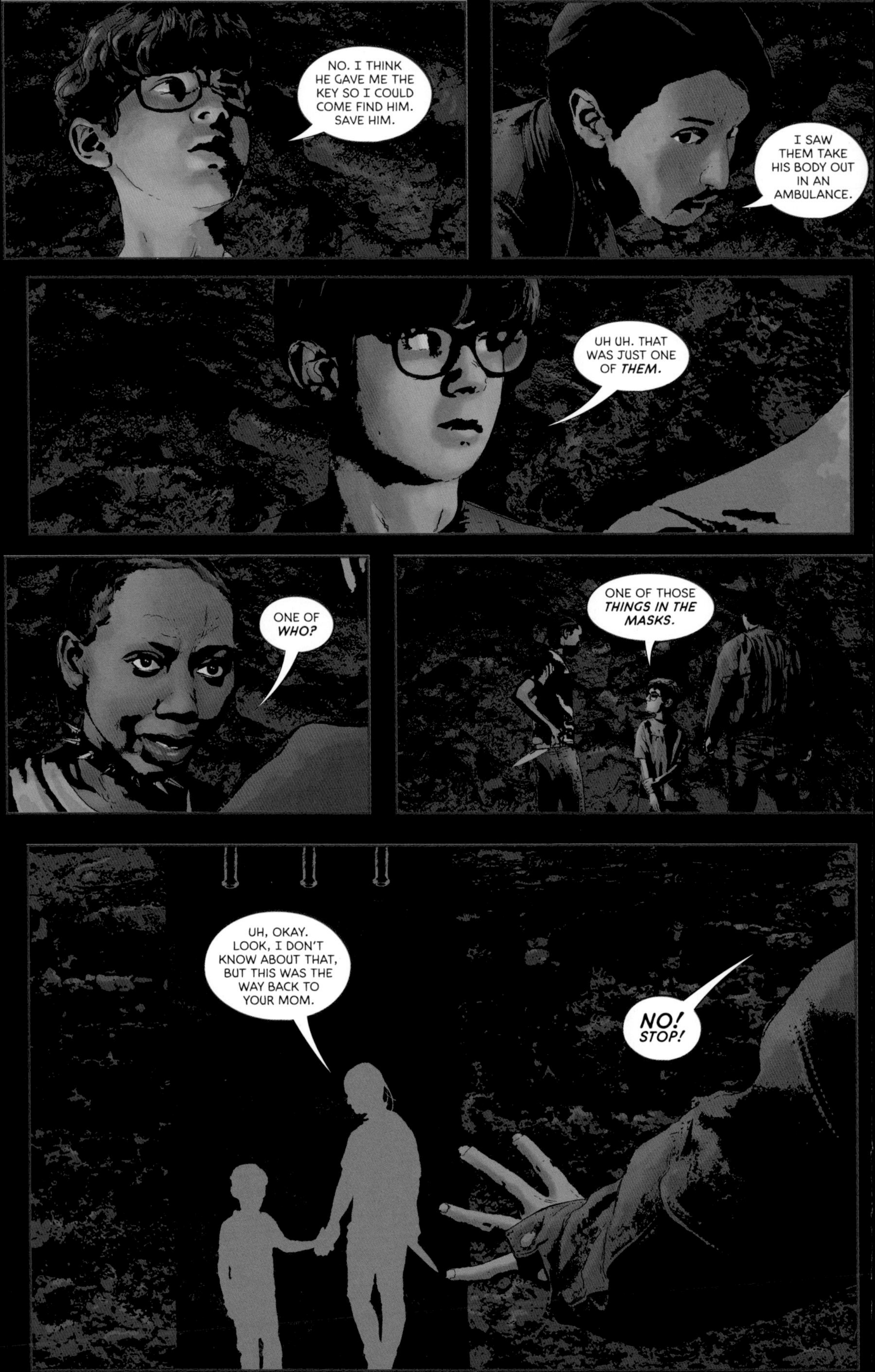
NO. I THINK HE GAVE ME THE KEY SO I COULD COME FIND HIM. SAVE HIM.
I SAW THEM TAKE HIS BODY OUT IN AN AMBULANCE.
UH UH. THAT WAS JUST ONE OF *THEM.*
ONE OF *WHO?*
ONE OF THOSE *THINGS IN THE MASKS.*
UH, OKAY. LOOK, I DON'T KNOW ABOUT THAT, BUT THIS WAS THE WAY BACK TO YOUR MOM.
NO! STOP!

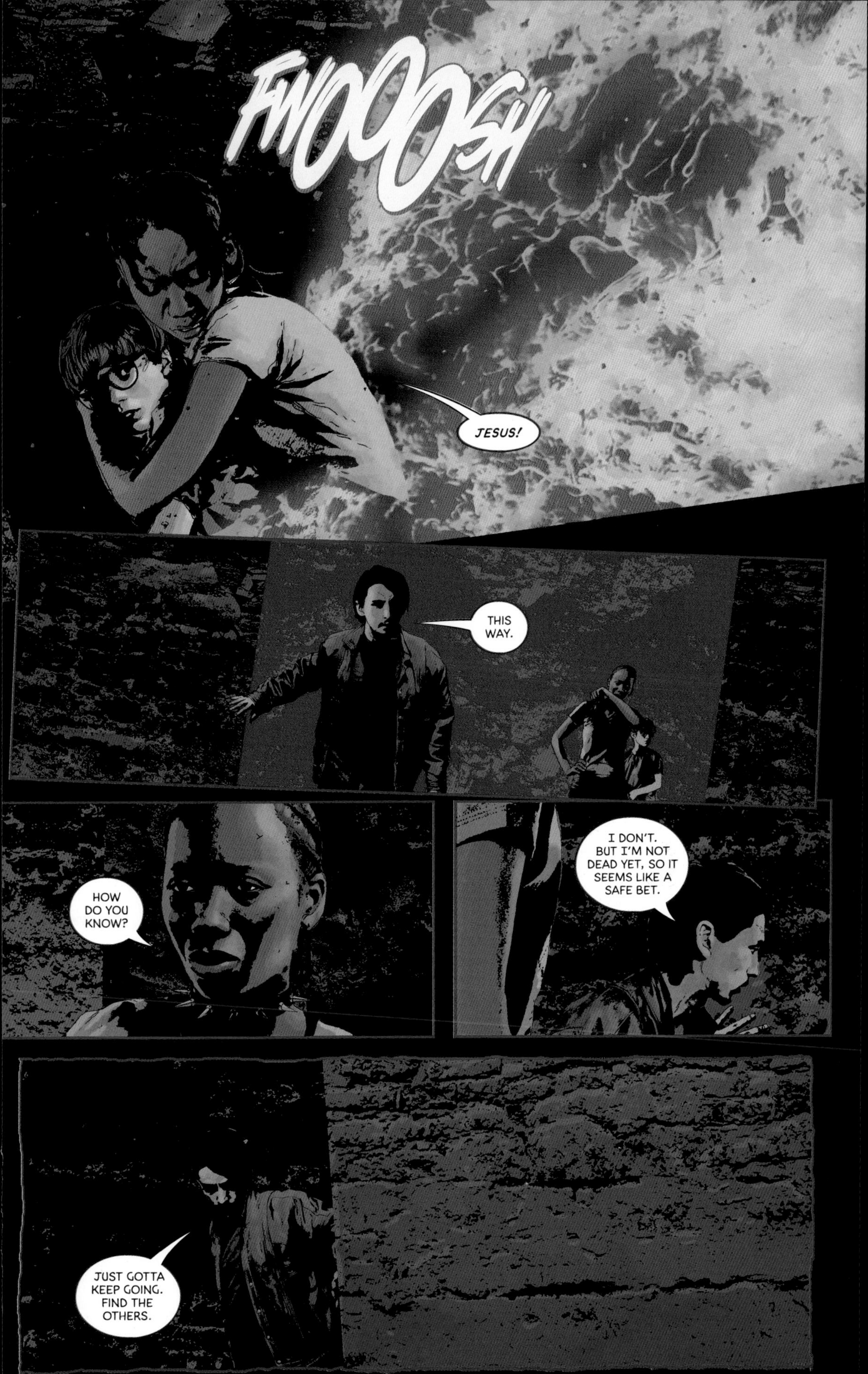
FWOOOOSH
JESUS!
THIS WAY.
HOW DO YOU KNOW?
I DON'T. BUT I'M NOT DEAD YET, SO IT SEEMS LIKE A SAFE BET.
JUST GOTTA KEEP GOING. FIND THE OTHERS.

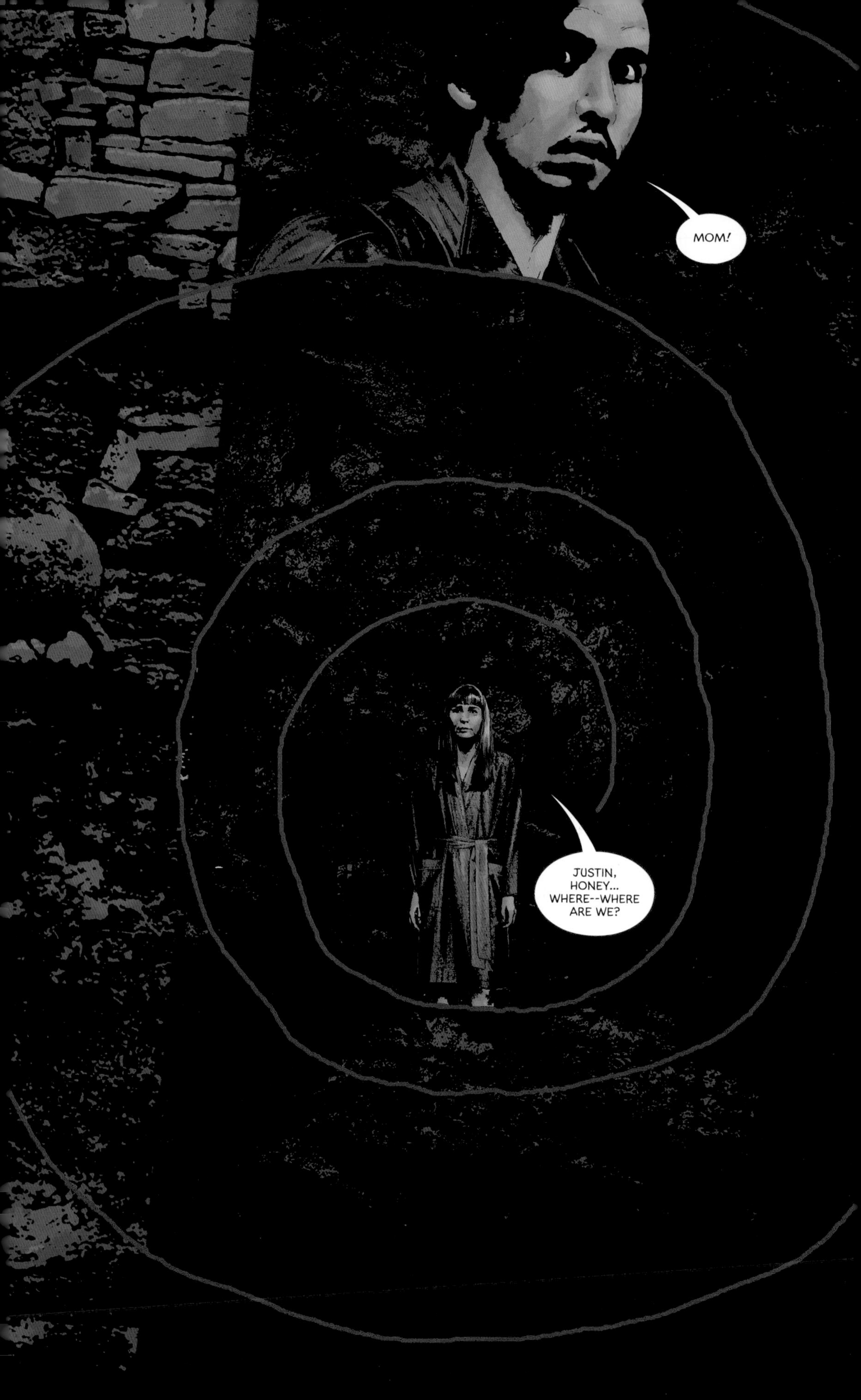
MOM!
JUSTIN, HONEY... WHERE--WHERE ARE WE?

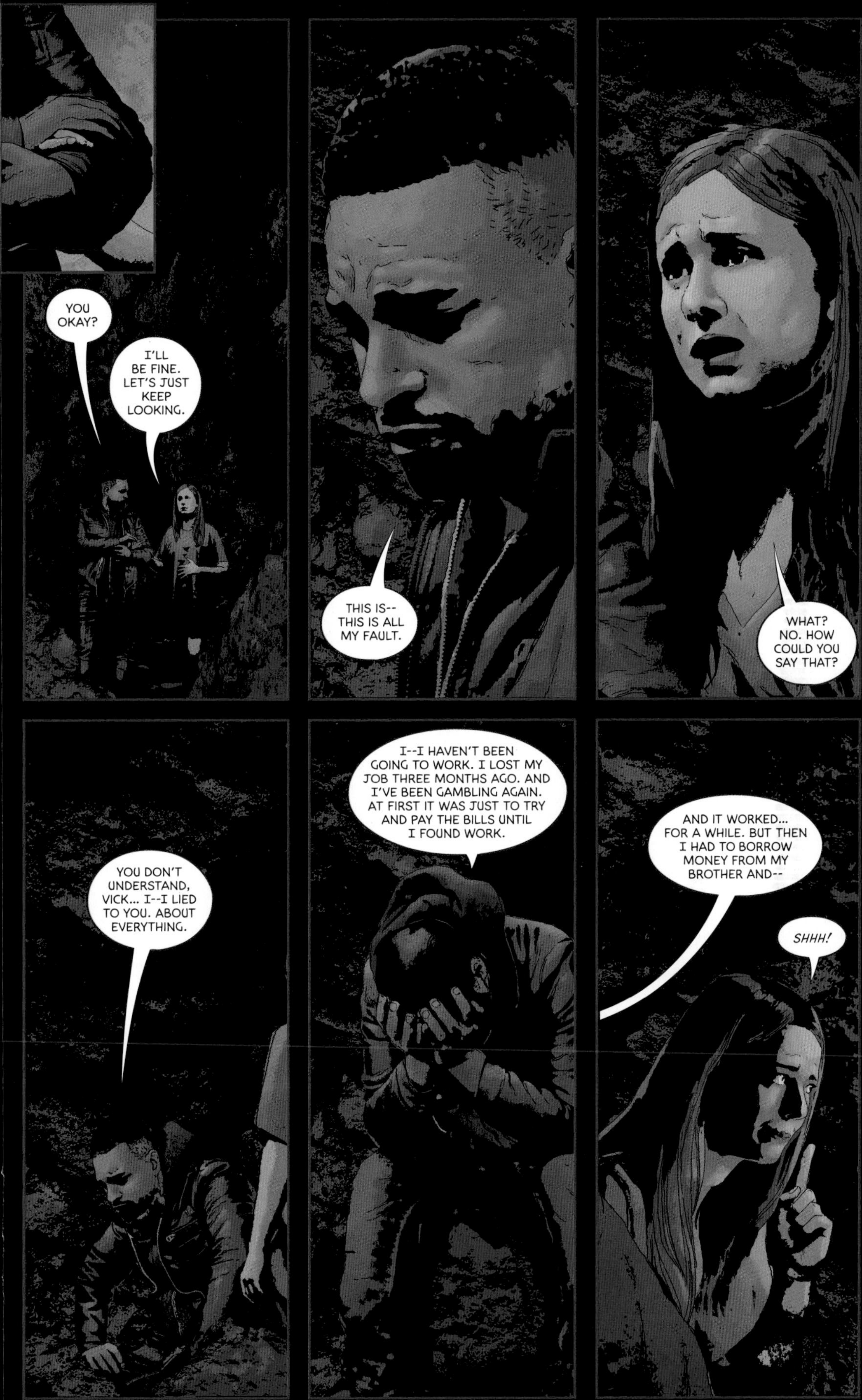
YOU OKAY?
I'LL BE FINE. LET'S JUST KEEP LOOKING.
THIS IS-- THIS IS ALL MY FAULT.
WHAT? NO. HOW COULD YOU SAY THAT?
YOU DON'T UNDERSTAND, VICK... I--I LIED TO YOU. ABOUT EVERYTHING.
I--I HAVEN'T BEEN GOING TO WORK. I LOST MY JOB THREE MONTHS AGO. AND I'VE BEEN GAMBLING AGAIN. AT FIRST IT WAS JUST TO TRY AND PAY THE BILLS UNTIL I FOUND WORK.
AND IT WORKED... FOR A WHILE. BUT THEN I HAD TO BORROW MONEY FROM MY BROTHER AND--
SHHH!

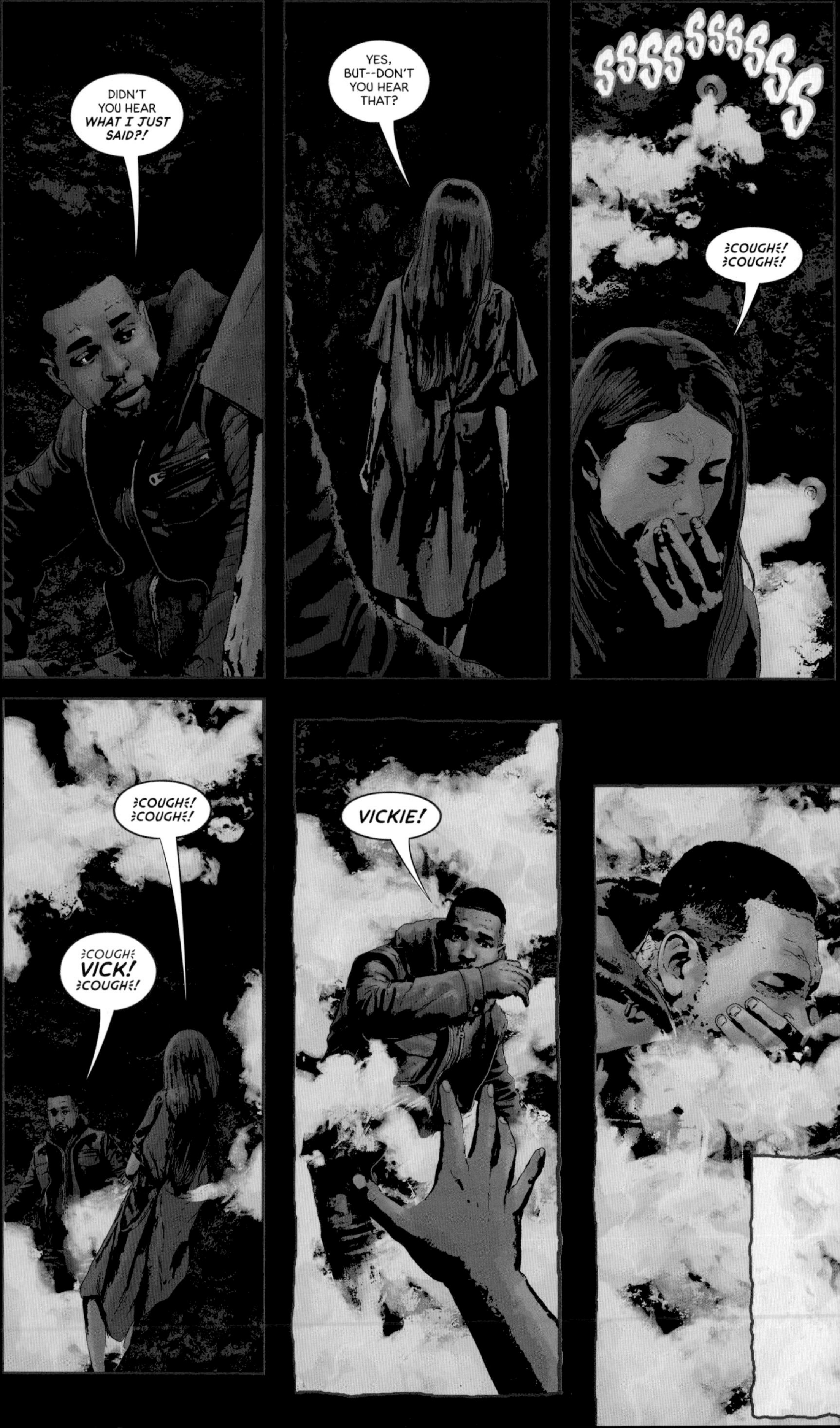
DIDN'T YOU HEAR WHAT I JUST SAID?!
YES, BUT--DON'T YOU HEAR THAT?
SSSSSSSSSSS
COUGH! COUGH!
COUGH! COUGH!
COUGH VICK! COUGH!
VICKIE!

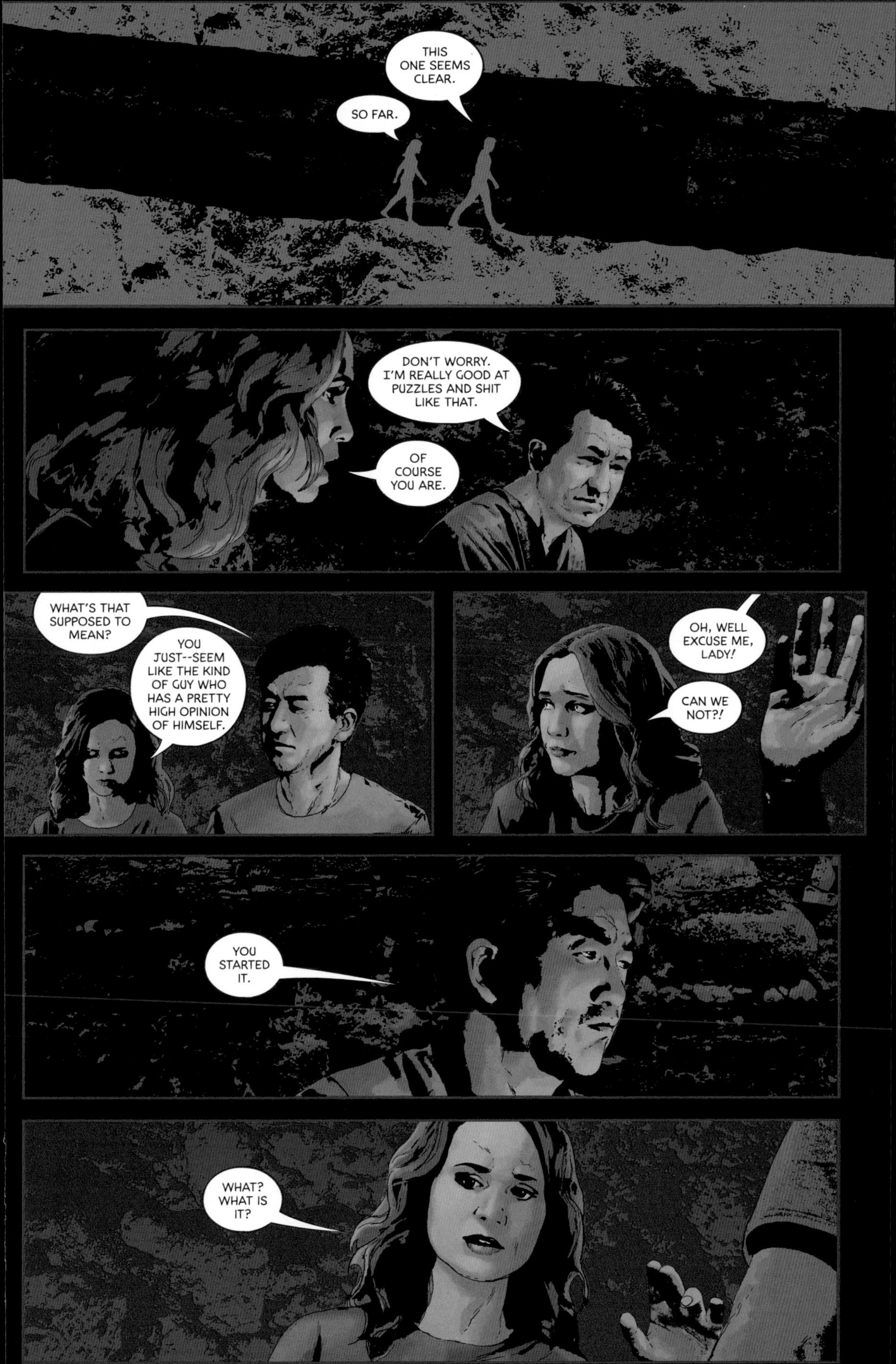
THIS ONE SEEMS CLEAR.
SO FAR.
DON'T WORRY. I'M REALLY GOOD AT PUZZLES AND SHIT LIKE THAT.
OF COURSE YOU ARE.
WHAT'S THAT SUPPOSED TO MEAN?
YOU JUST--SEEM LIKE THE KIND OF GUY WHO HAS A PRETTY HIGH OPINION OF HIMSELF.
OH, WELL EXCUSE ME, LADY!
CAN WE NOT?!
YOU STARTED IT.
WHAT? WHAT IS IT?

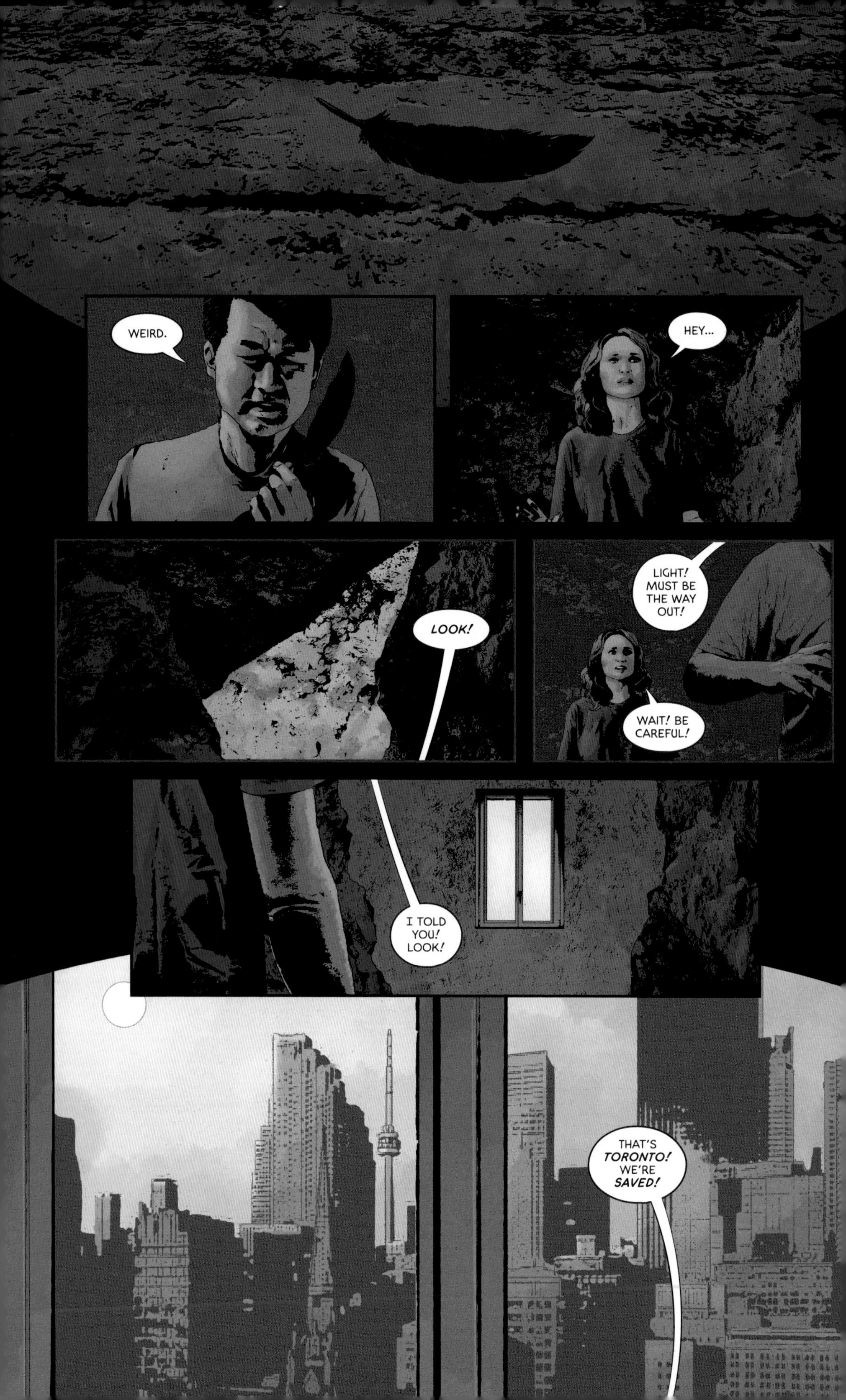
WEIRD.
HEY...
LOOK!
LIGHT! MUST BE THE WAY OUT!
WAIT! BE CAREFUL!
I TOLD YOU! LOOK!
THAT'S TORONTO! WE'RE SAVED!

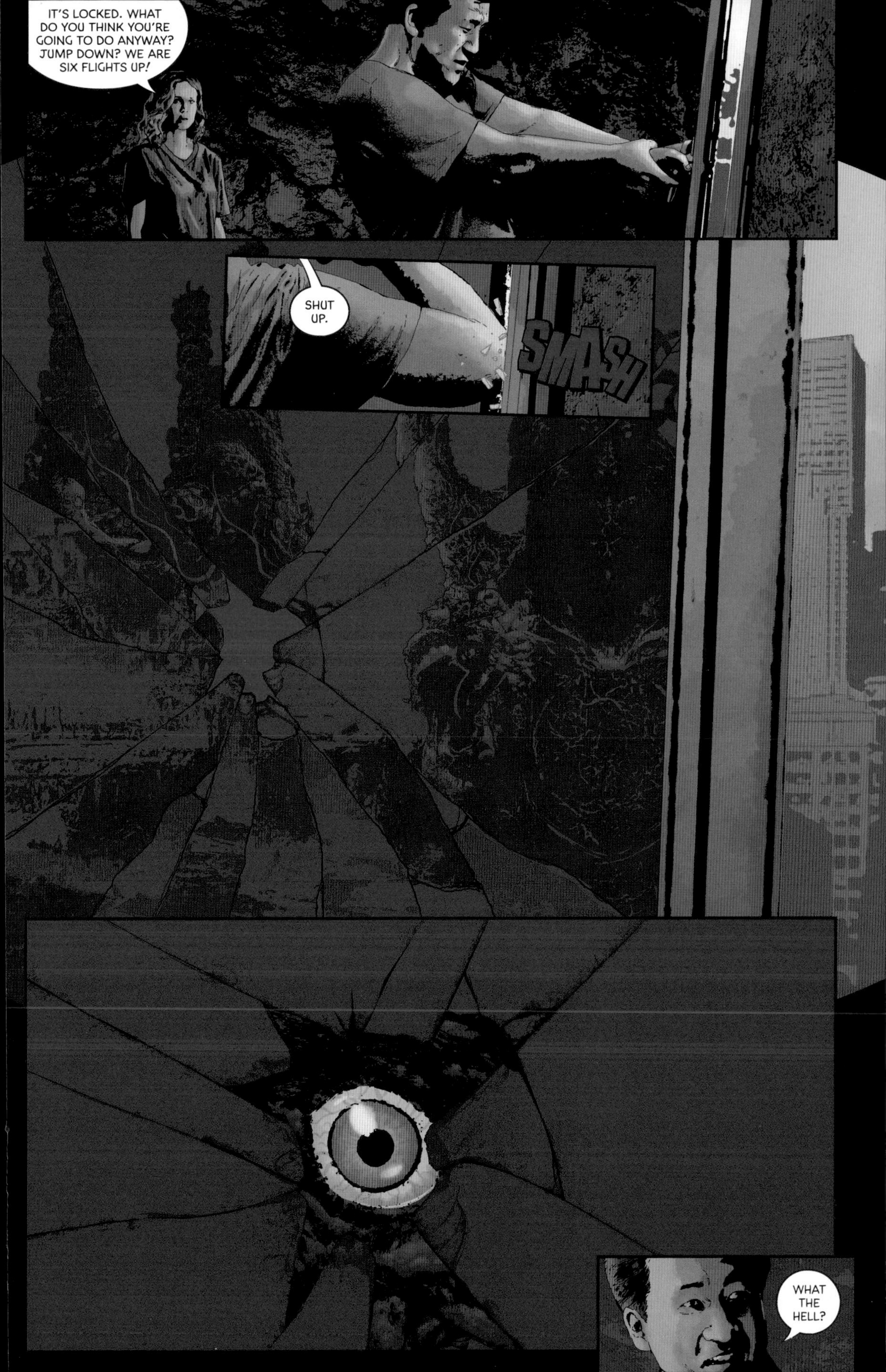
IT'S LOCKED. WHAT DO YOU THINK YOU'RE GOING TO DO ANYWAY? JUMP DOWN? WE ARE SIX FLIGHTS UP!
SHUT UP.
SMASH
WHAT THE HELL?

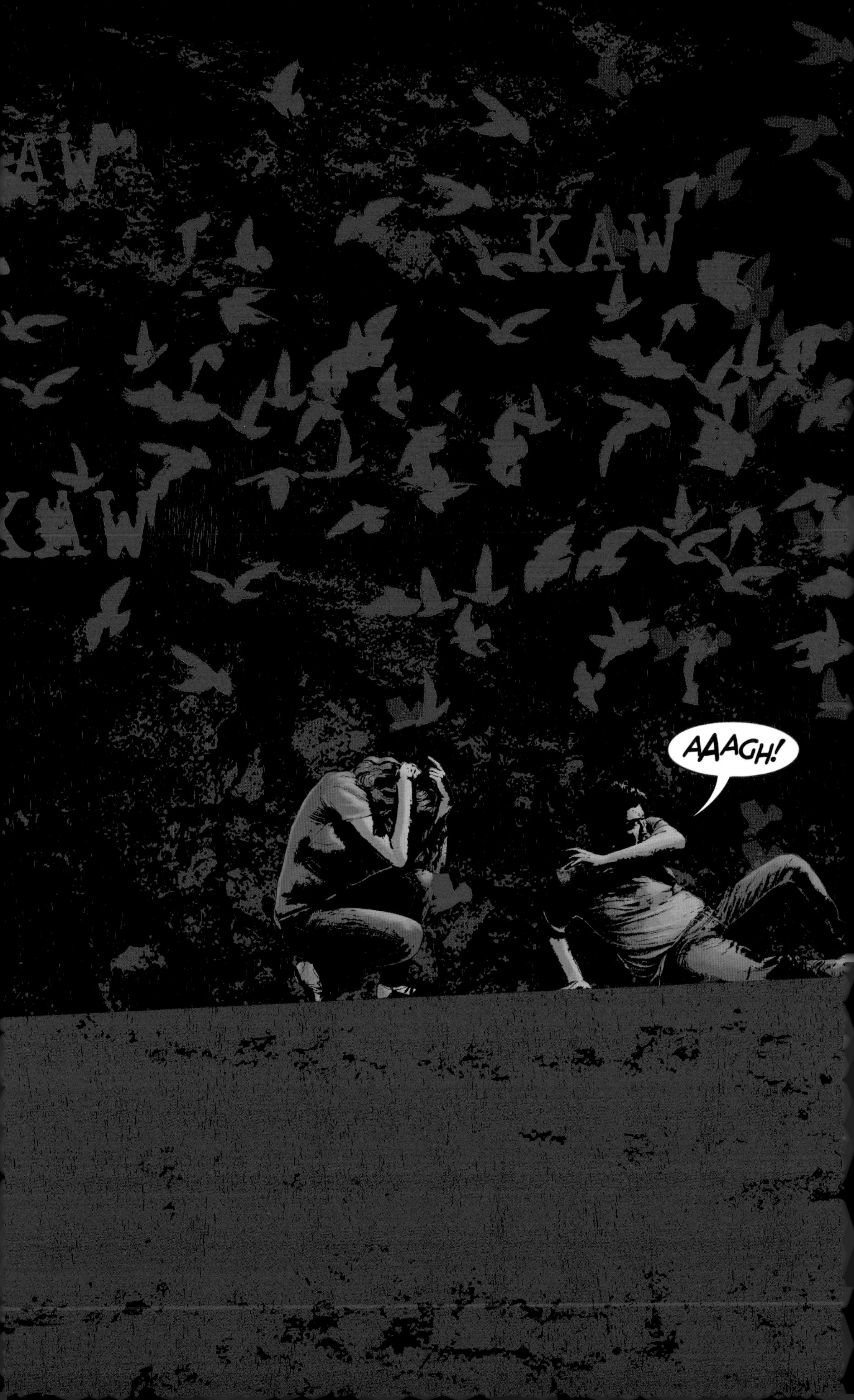
KAW
KAW
AAAGH!

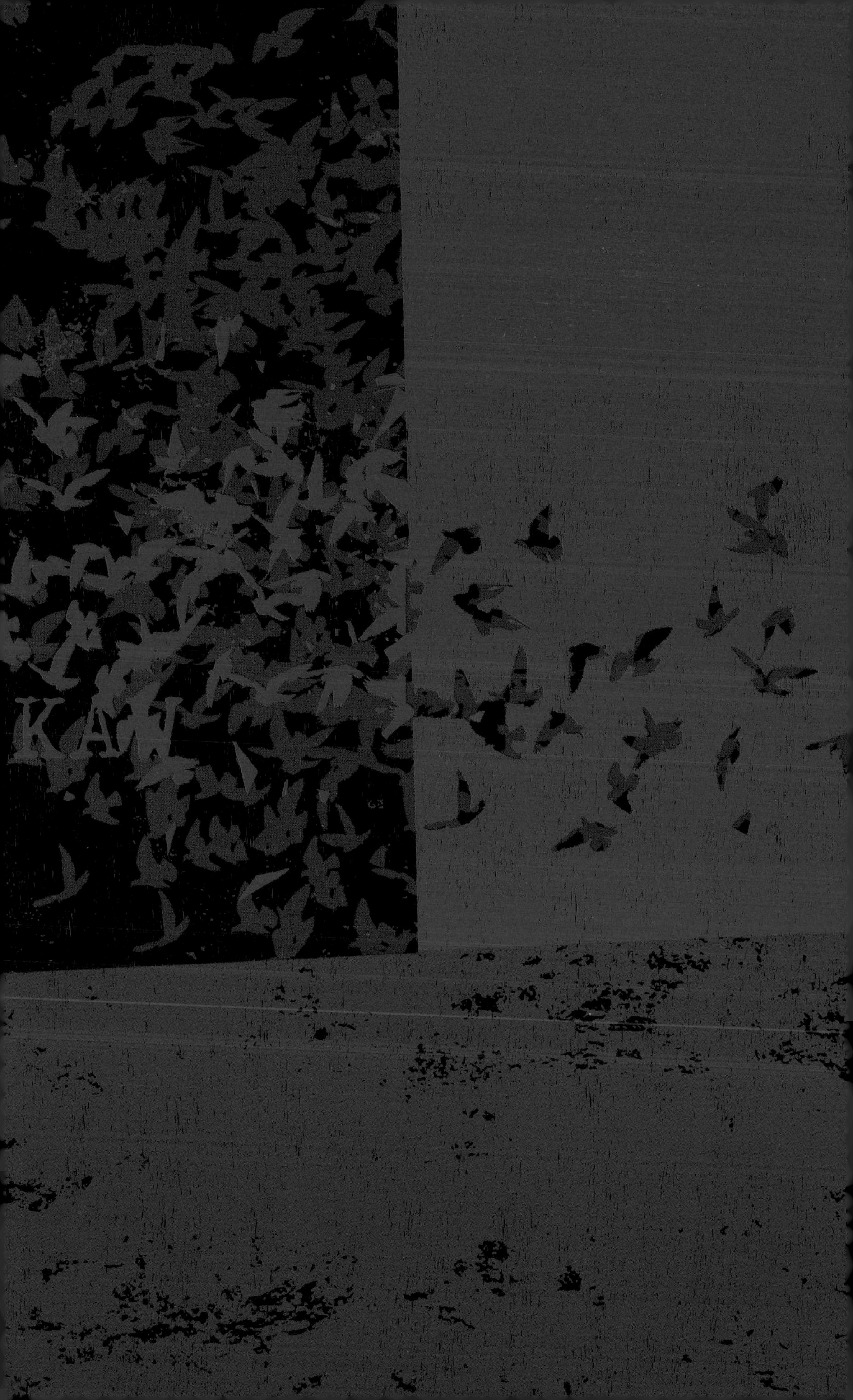

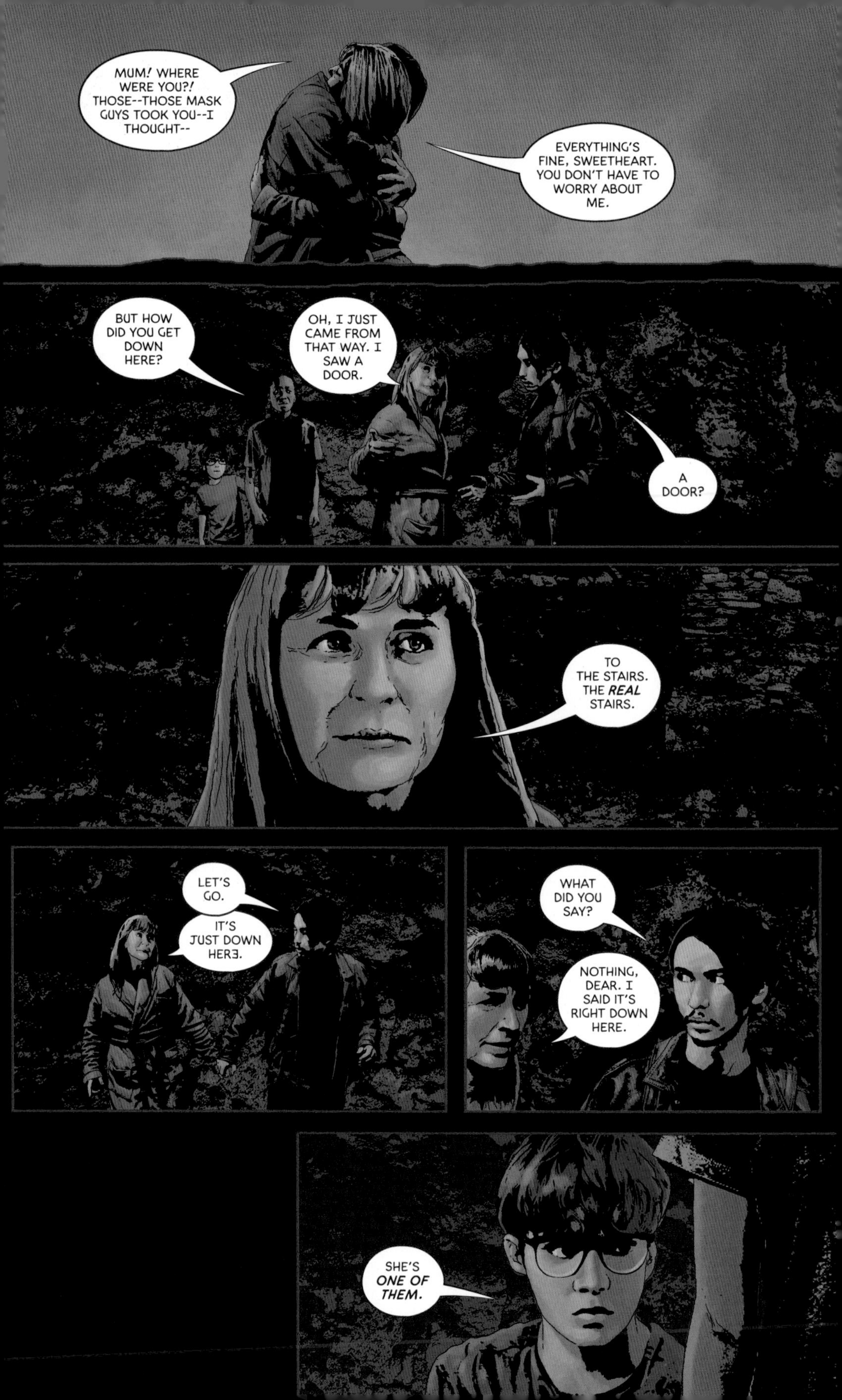
MUM! WHERE WERE YOU?! THOSE--THOSE MASK GUYS TOOK YOU--I THOUGHT--
EVERYTHING'S FINE, SWEETHEART. YOU DON'T HAVE TO WORRY ABOUT ME.
BUT HOW DID YOU GET DOWN HERE?
OH, I JUST CAME FROM THAT WAY. I SAW A DOOR.
A DOOR?
TO THE STAIRS. THE REAL STAIRS.
LET'S GO.
IT'S JUST DOWN HERƎ.
WHAT DID YOU SAY?
NOTHING, DEAR. I SAID IT'S RIGHT DOWN HERE.
SHE'S ONE OF THEM.

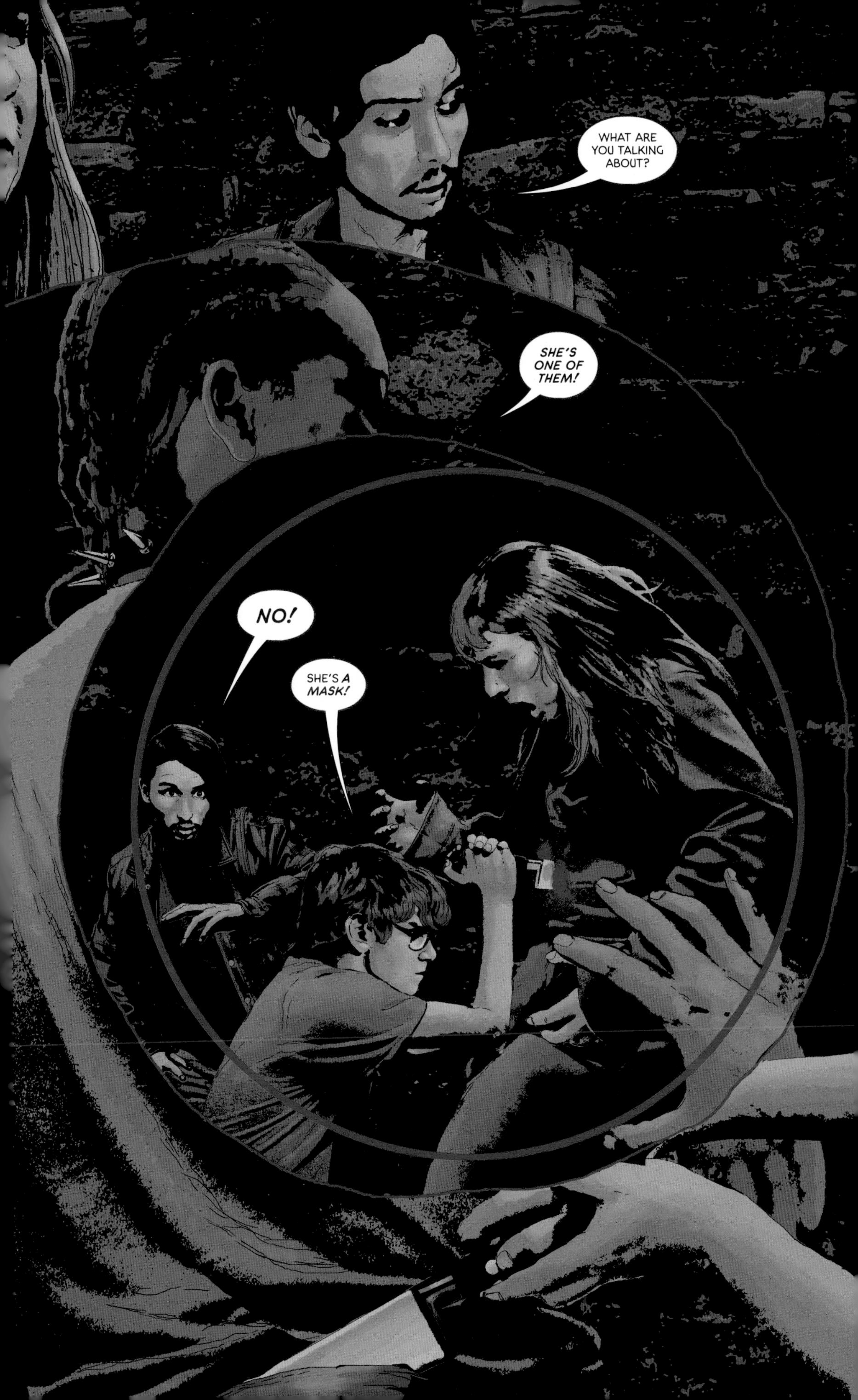
WHAT ARE YOU TALKING ABOUT?
SHE'S ONE OF THEM!
NO!
SHE'S A MASK!

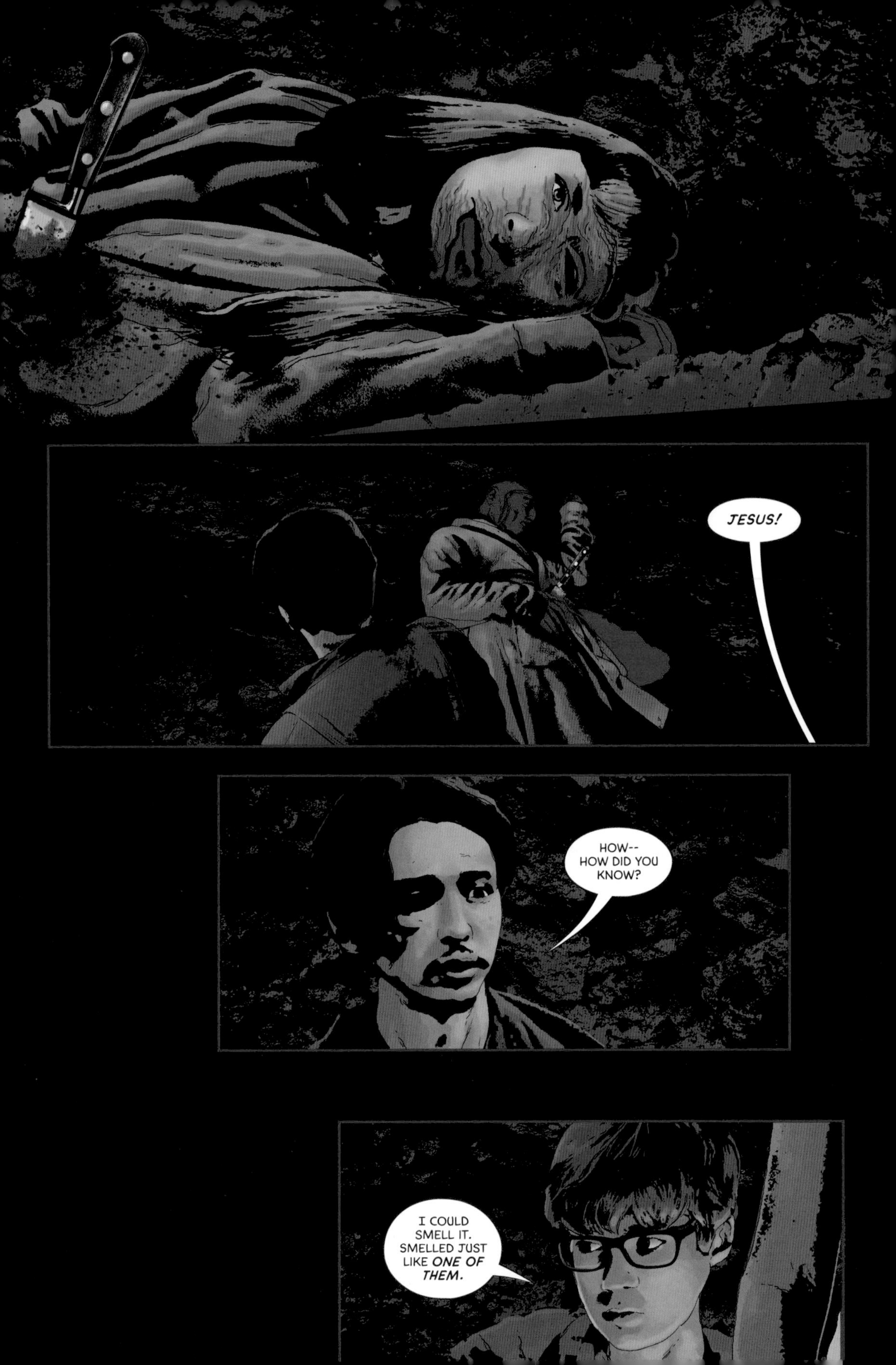
JESUS!
HOW-- HOW DID YOU KNOW?
I COULD SMELL IT. SMELLED JUST LIKE *ONE OF THEM*.

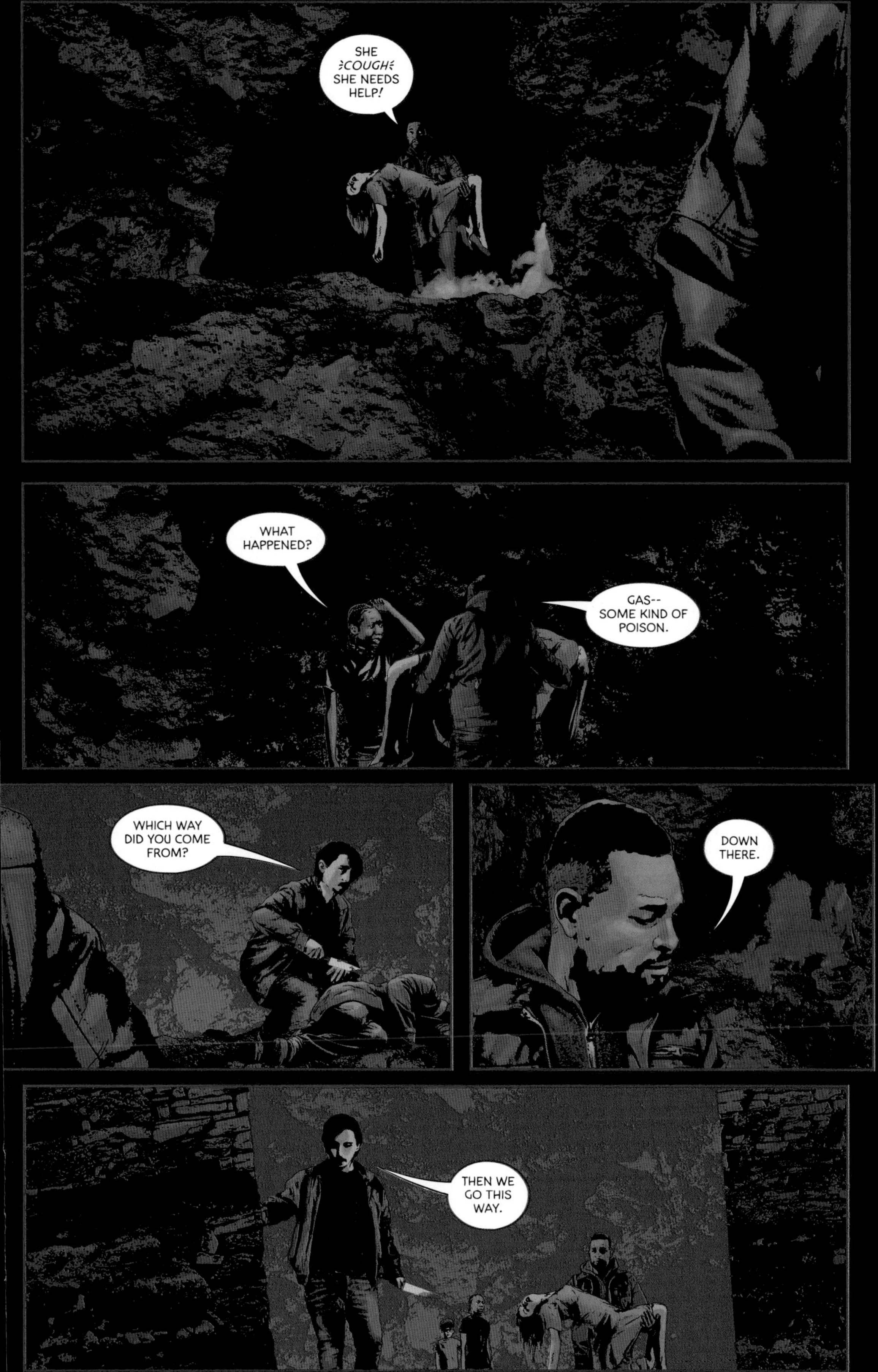
SHE *COUGH* SHE NEEDS HELP!
WHAT HAPPENED?
GAS-- SOME KIND OF POISON.
WHICH WAY DID YOU COME FROM?
DOWN THERE.
THEN WE GO THIS WAY.

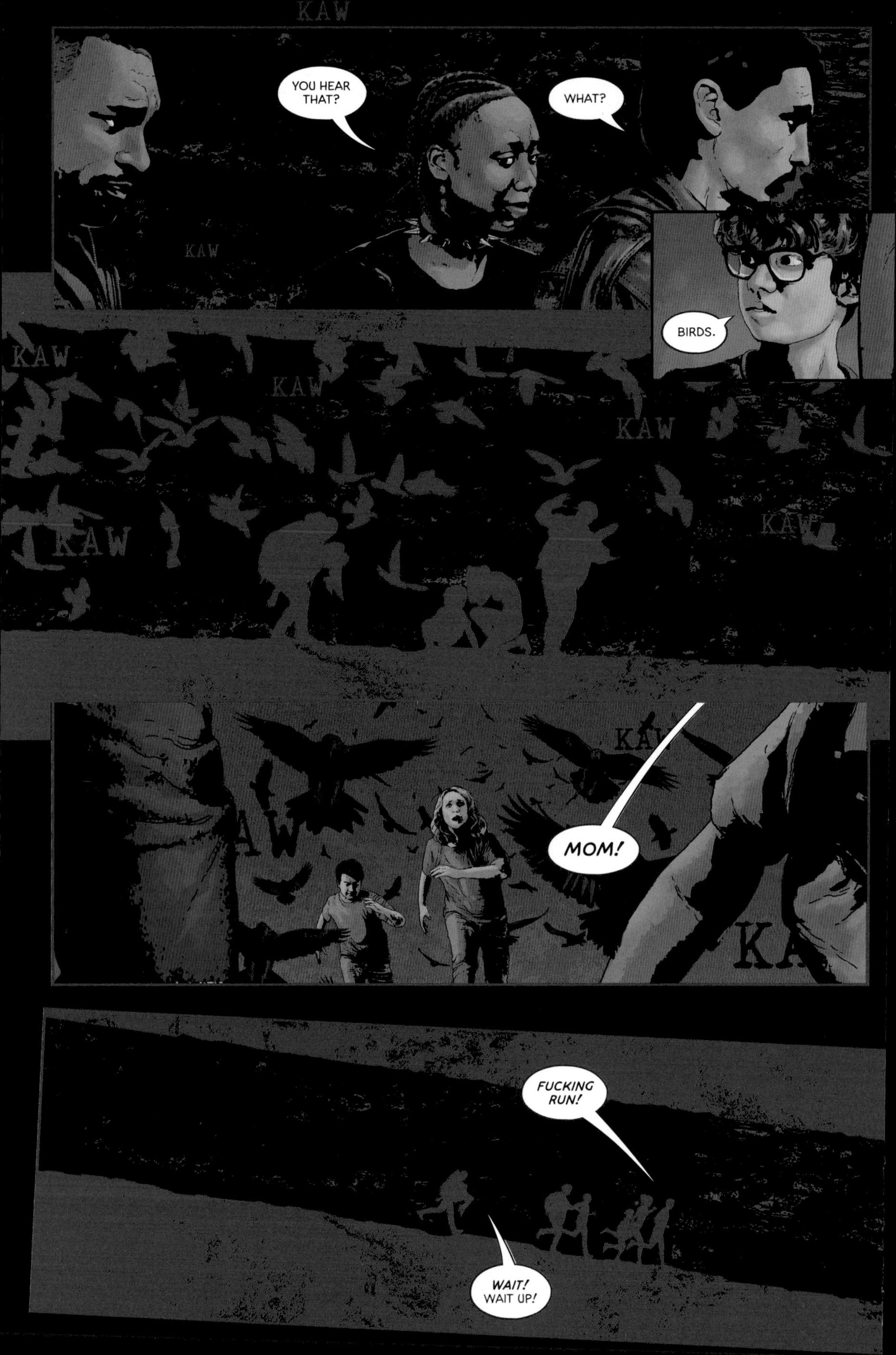
KAW
YOU HEAR THAT?
WHAT?
KAW
BIRDS.
KAW
KAW
KAW
KAW
KAW
KAW
MOM!
KA
FUCKING RUN!
WAIT! WAIT UP!

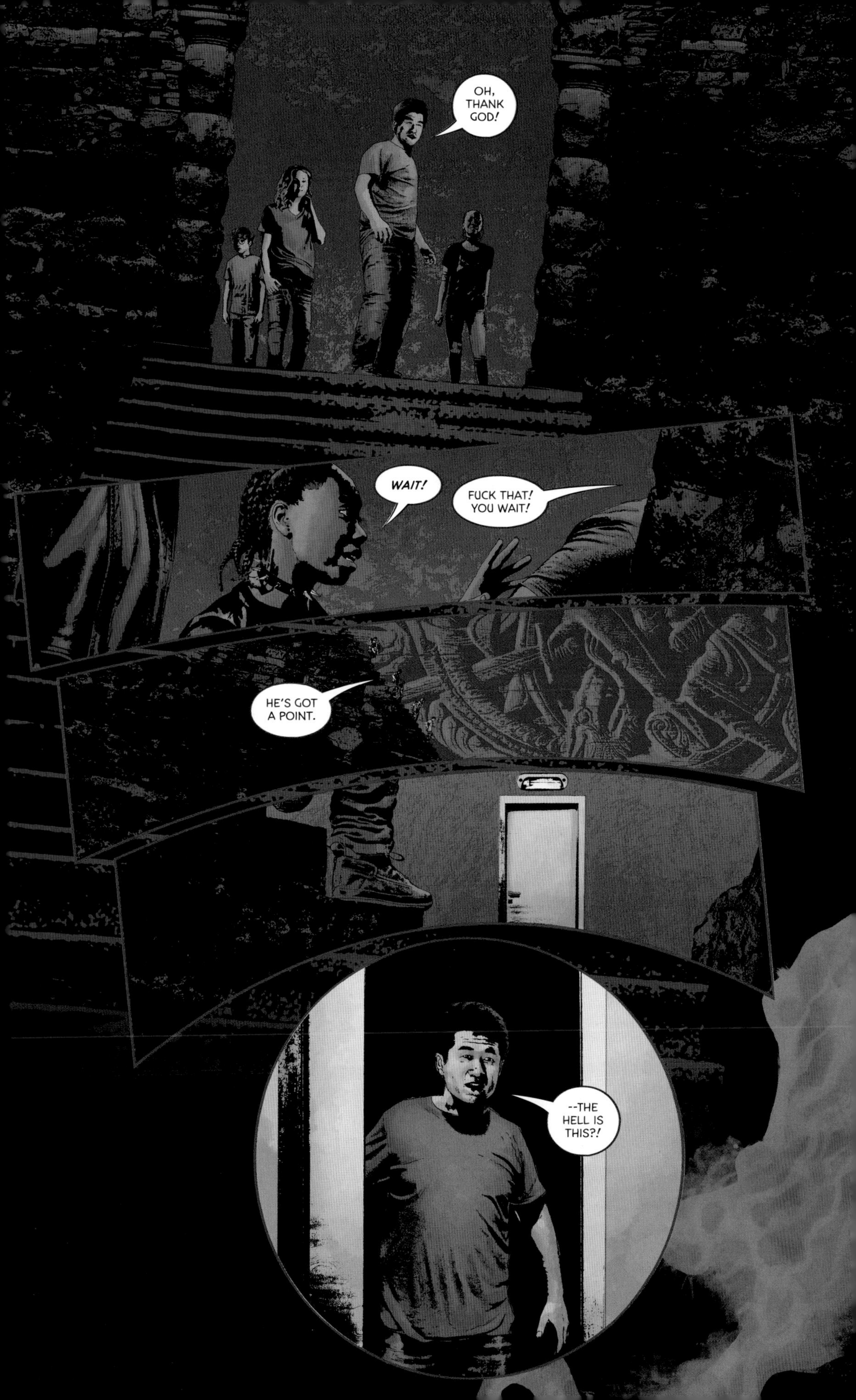
OH, THANK GOD!
WAIT!
FUCK THAT! YOU WAIT!
HE'S GOT A POINT.
--THE HELL IS THIS?!

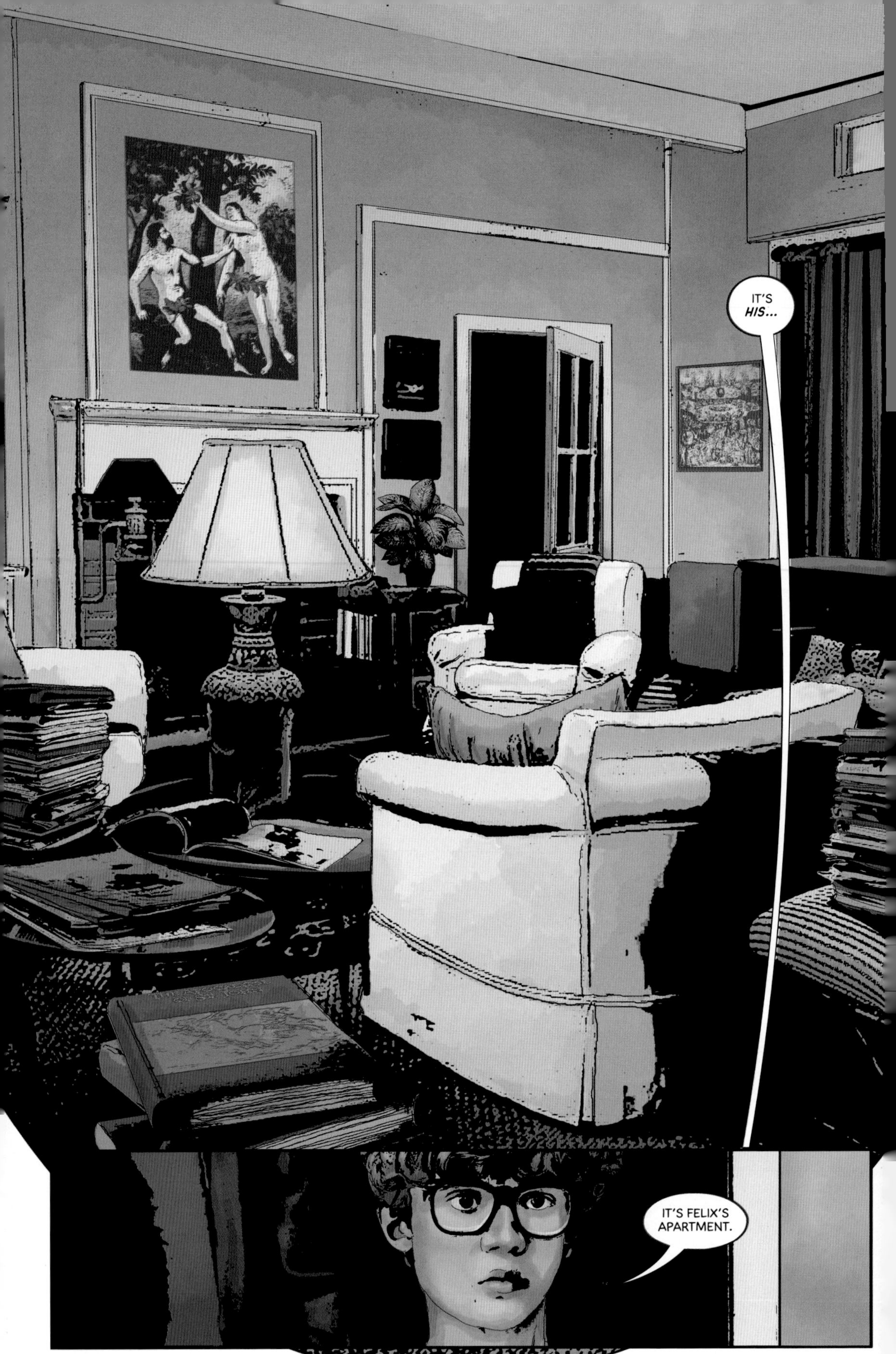
IT'S HIS...
IT'S FELIX'S APARTMENT.

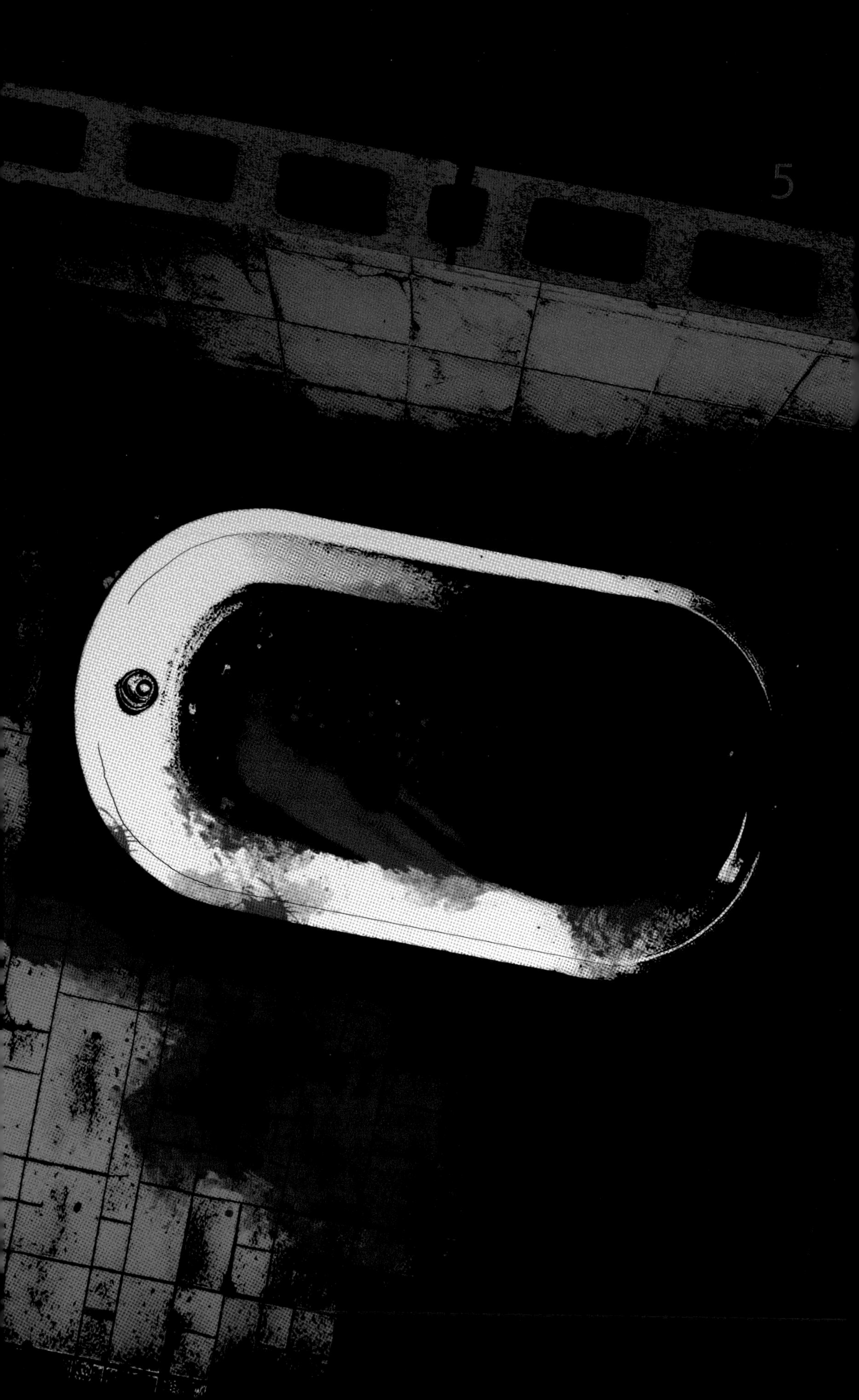
5

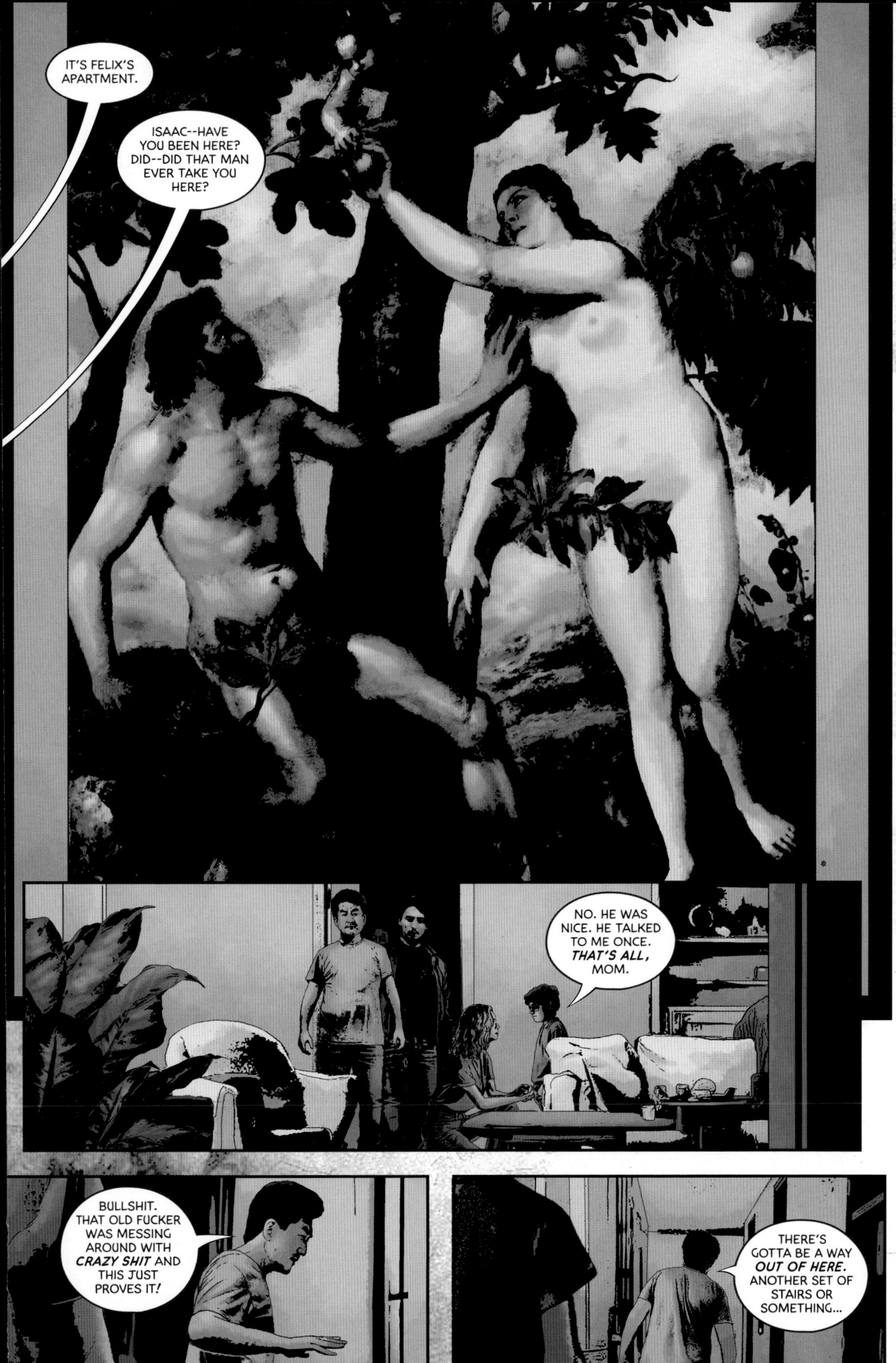

IT'S FELIX'S APARTMENT.
ISAAC--HAVE YOU BEEN HERE? DID--DID THAT MAN EVER TAKE YOU HERE?
*
NO. HE WAS NICE. HE TALKED TO ME ONCE. ***THAT'S ALL,*** MOM.
BULLSHIT. THAT OLD FUCKER WAS MESSING AROUND WITH ***CRAZY SHIT*** AND THIS JUST PROVES IT!
THERE'S GOTTA BE A WAY ***OUT OF HERE.*** ANOTHER SET OF STAIRS OR SOMETHING...

*The Fall of Man by Tiziano

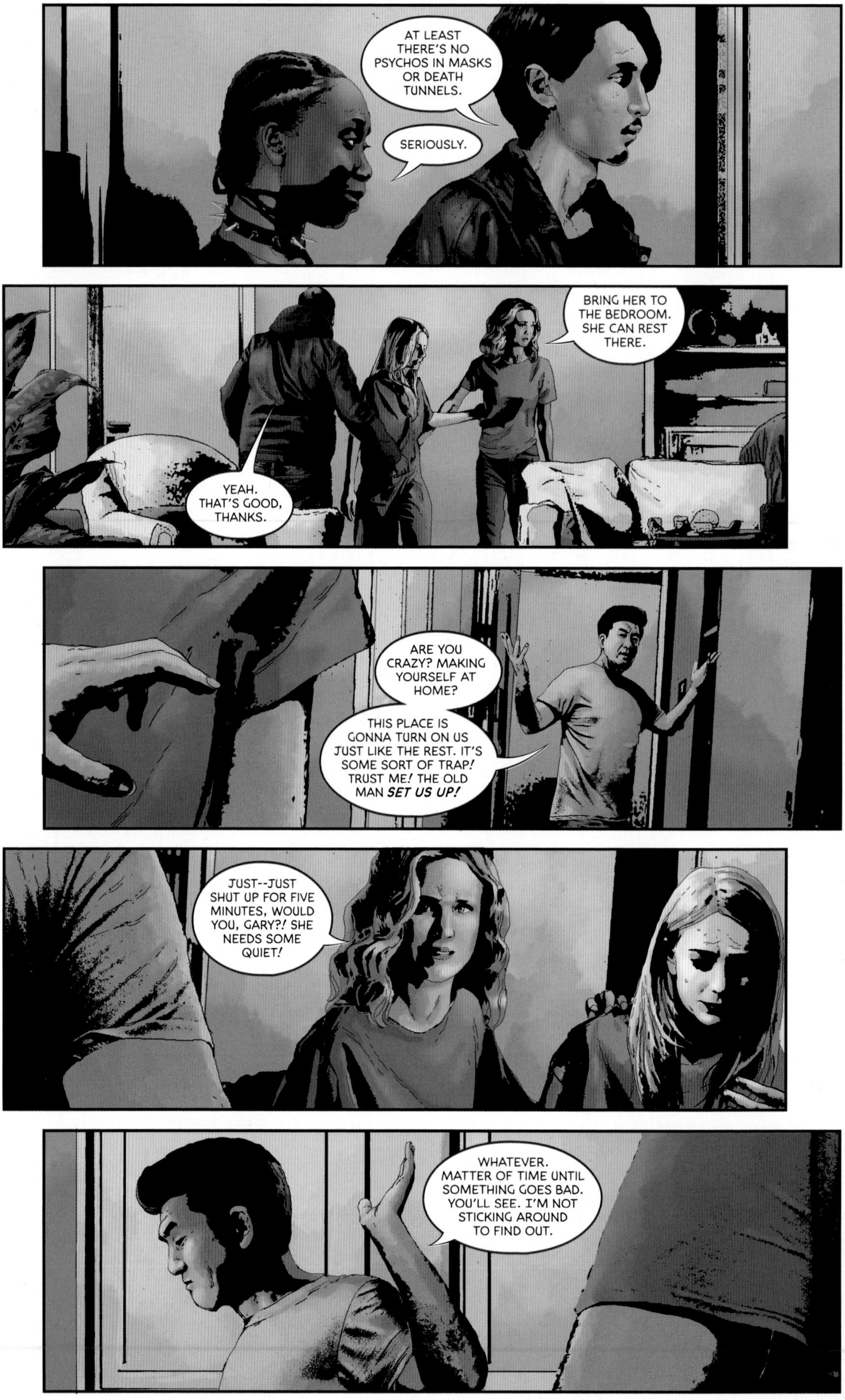
AT LEAST THERE'S NO PSYCHOS IN MASKS OR DEATH TUNNELS.
SERIOUSLY.
BRING HER TO THE BEDROOM. SHE CAN REST THERE.
YEAH. THAT'S GOOD, THANKS.
ARE YOU CRAZY? MAKING YOURSELF AT HOME?
THIS PLACE IS GONNA TURN ON US JUST LIKE THE REST. IT'S SOME SORT OF TRAP! TRUST ME! THE OLD MAN SET US UP!
JUST--JUST SHUT UP FOR FIVE MINUTES, WOULD YOU, GARY?! SHE NEEDS SOME QUIET!
WHATEVER. MATTER OF TIME UNTIL SOMETHING GOES BAD. YOU'LL SEE. I'M NOT STICKING AROUND TO FIND OUT.

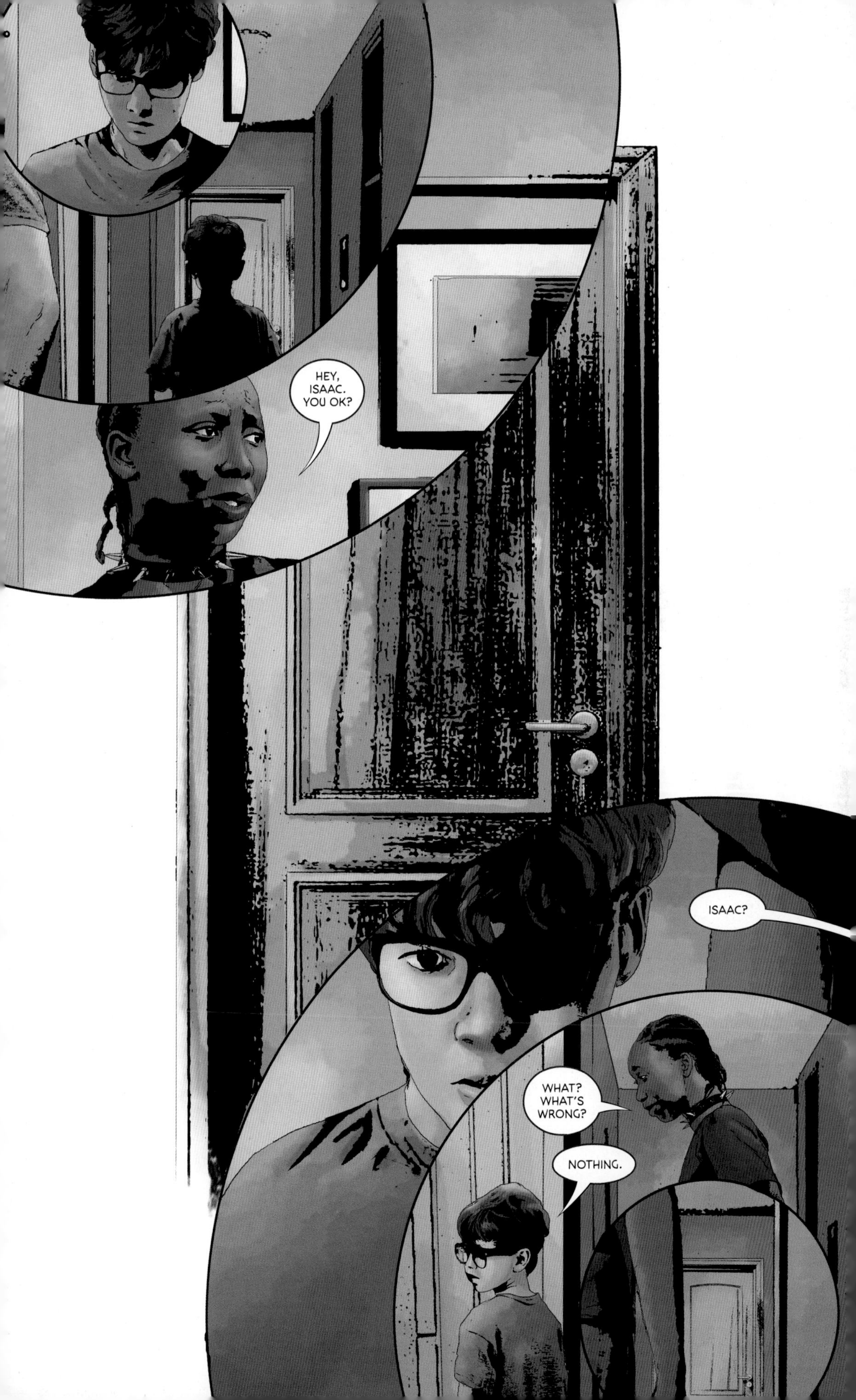
HEY, ISAAC. YOU OK?
ISAAC?
WHAT? WHAT'S WRONG?
NOTHING.

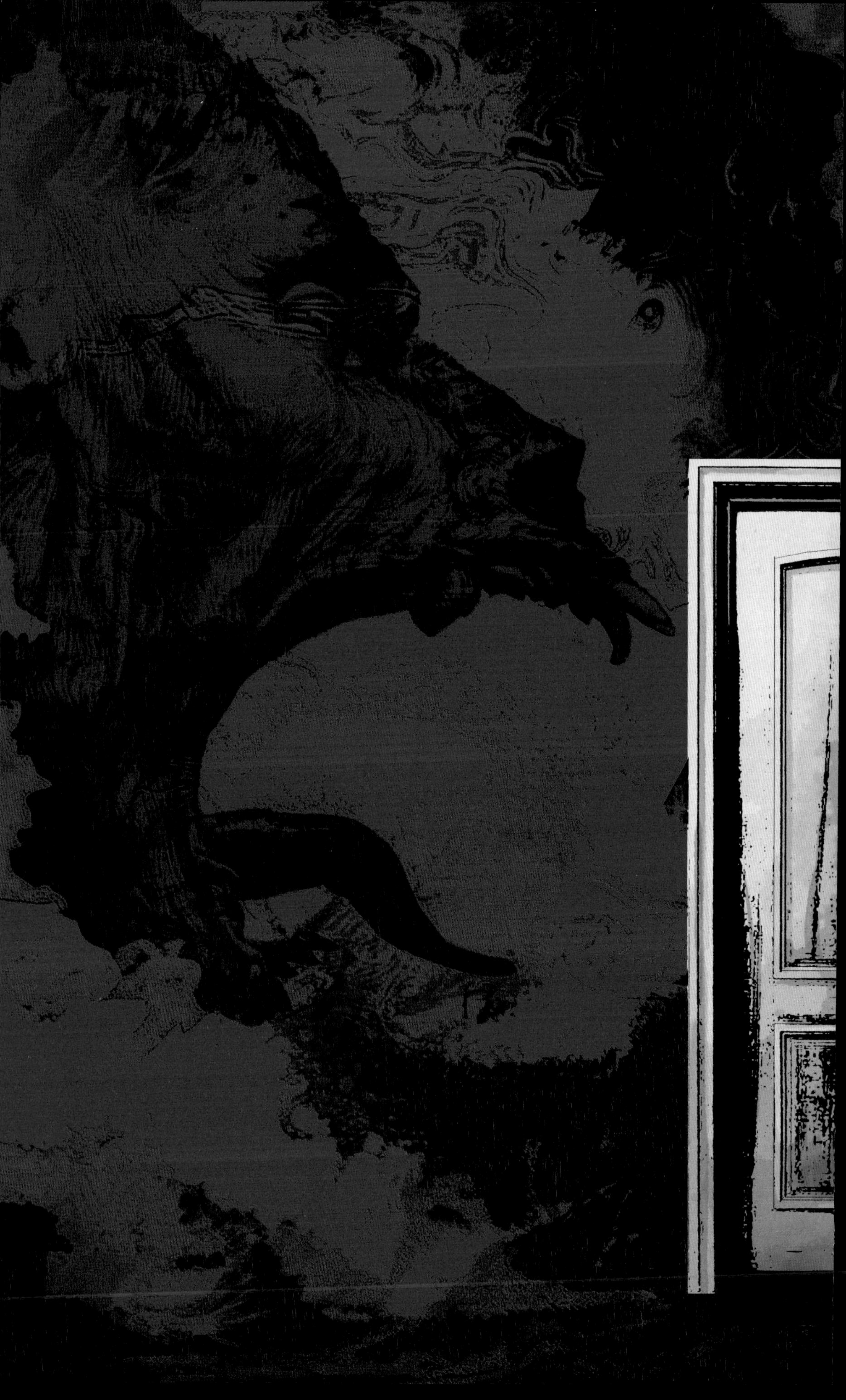

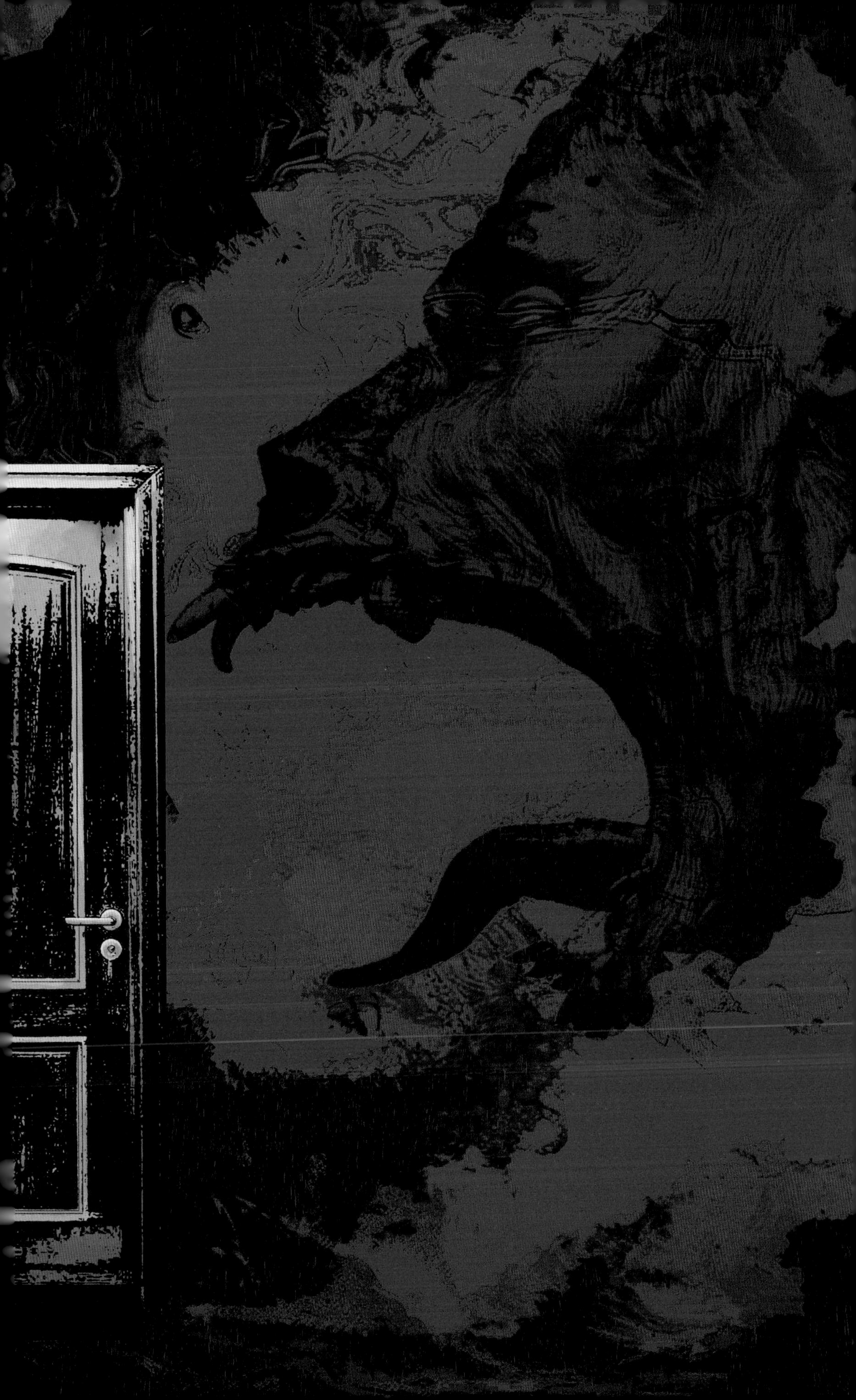

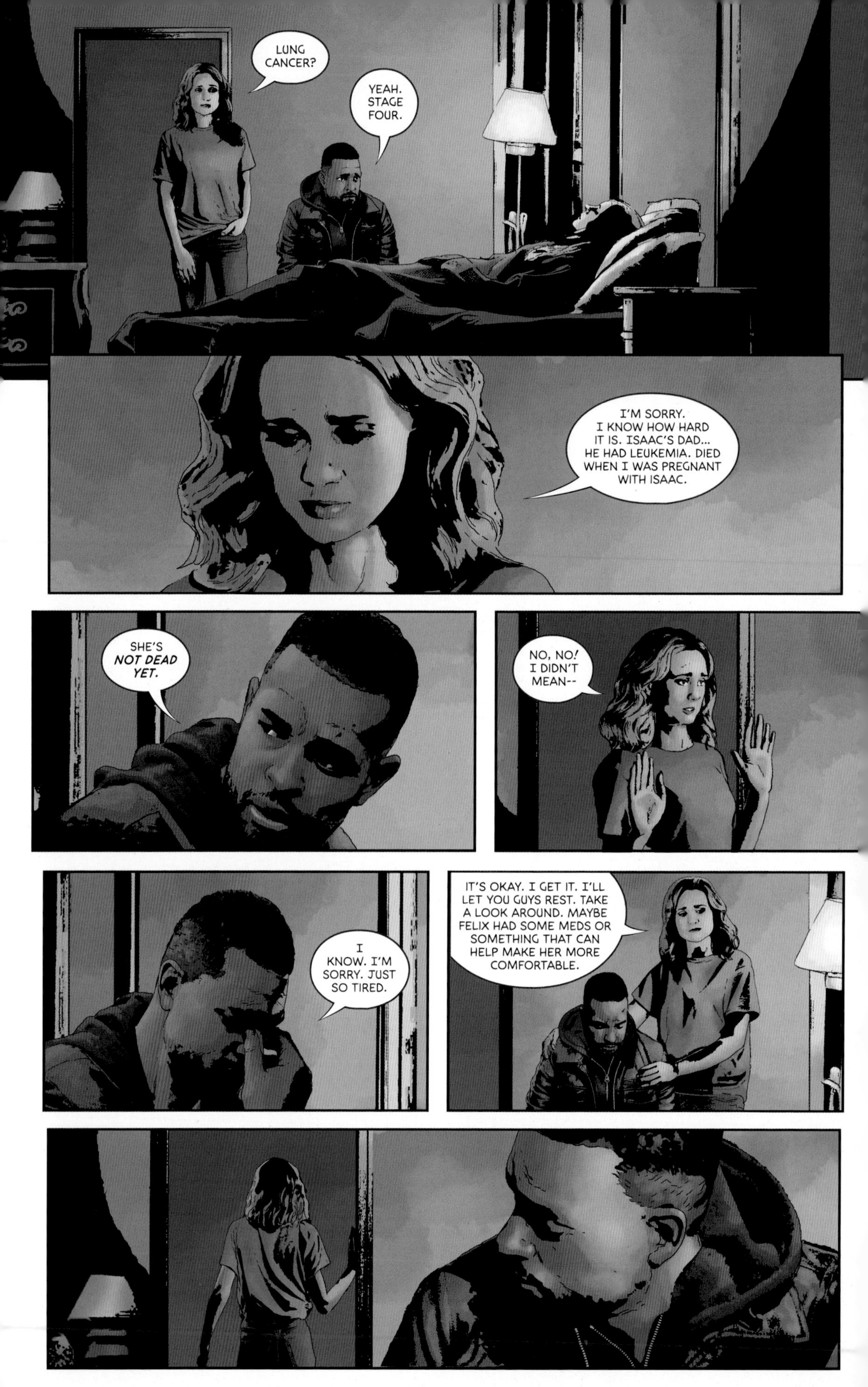
LUNG CANCER?
YEAH. STAGE FOUR.
I'M SORRY. I KNOW HOW HARD IT IS. ISAAC'S DAD... HE HAD LEUKEMIA. DIED WHEN I WAS PREGNANT WITH ISAAC.
SHE'S *NOT DEAD YET.*
NO, NO! I DIDN'T MEAN--
I KNOW. I'M SORRY. JUST SO TIRED.
IT'S OKAY. I GET IT. I'LL LET YOU GUYS REST. TAKE A LOOK AROUND. MAYBE FELIX HAD SOME MEDS OR SOMETHING THAT CAN HELP MAKE HER MORE COMFORTABLE.

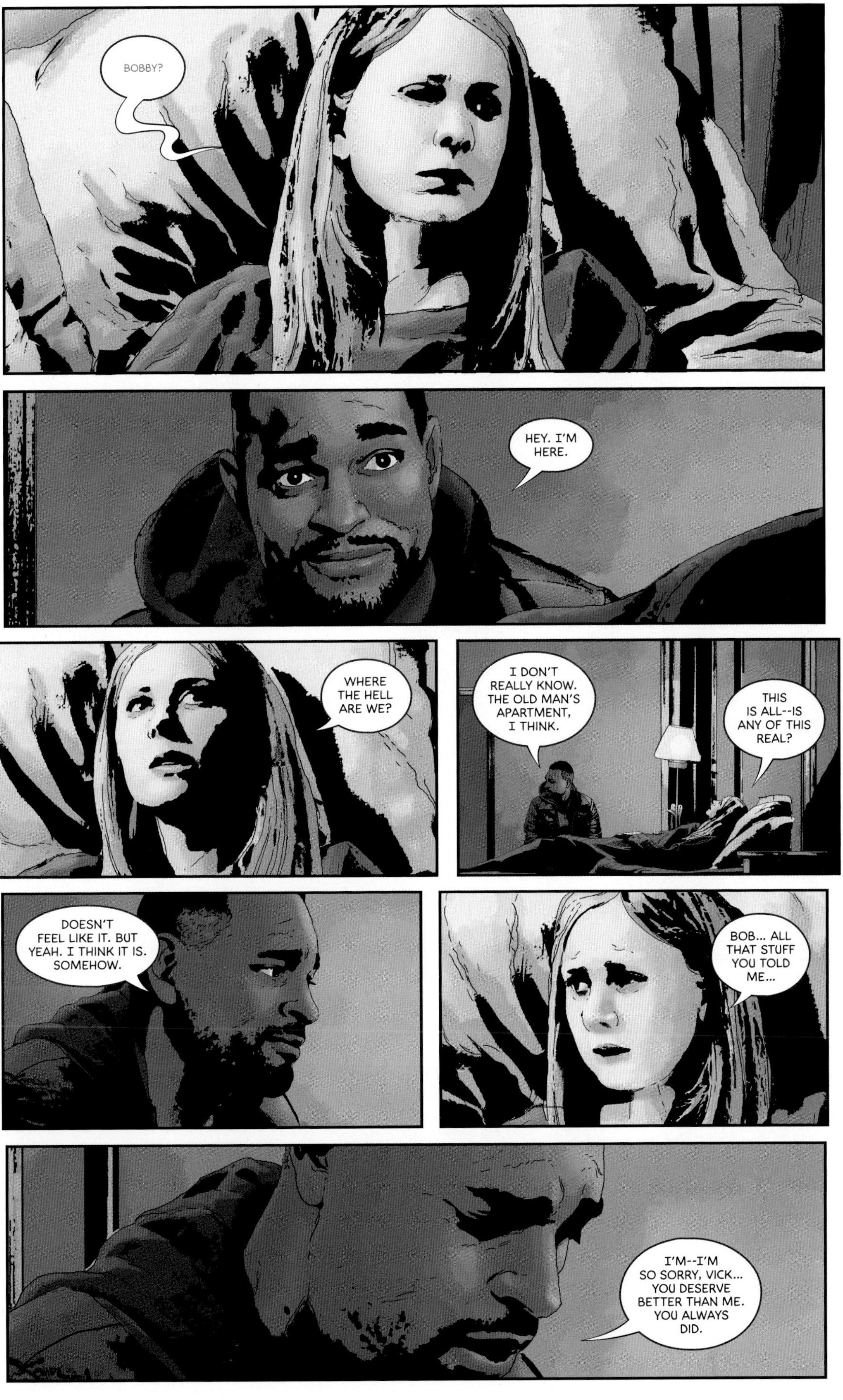
BOBBY?
HEY. I'M HERE.
WHERE THE HELL ARE WE?
I DON'T REALLY KNOW. THE OLD MAN'S APARTMENT, I THINK.
THIS IS ALL--IS ANY OF THIS REAL?
DOESN'T FEEL LIKE IT. BUT YEAH. I THINK IT IS. SOMEHOW.
BOB... ALL THAT STUFF YOU TOLD ME...
I'M--I'M SO SORRY, VICK... YOU DESERVE BETTER THAN ME. YOU ALWAYS DID.

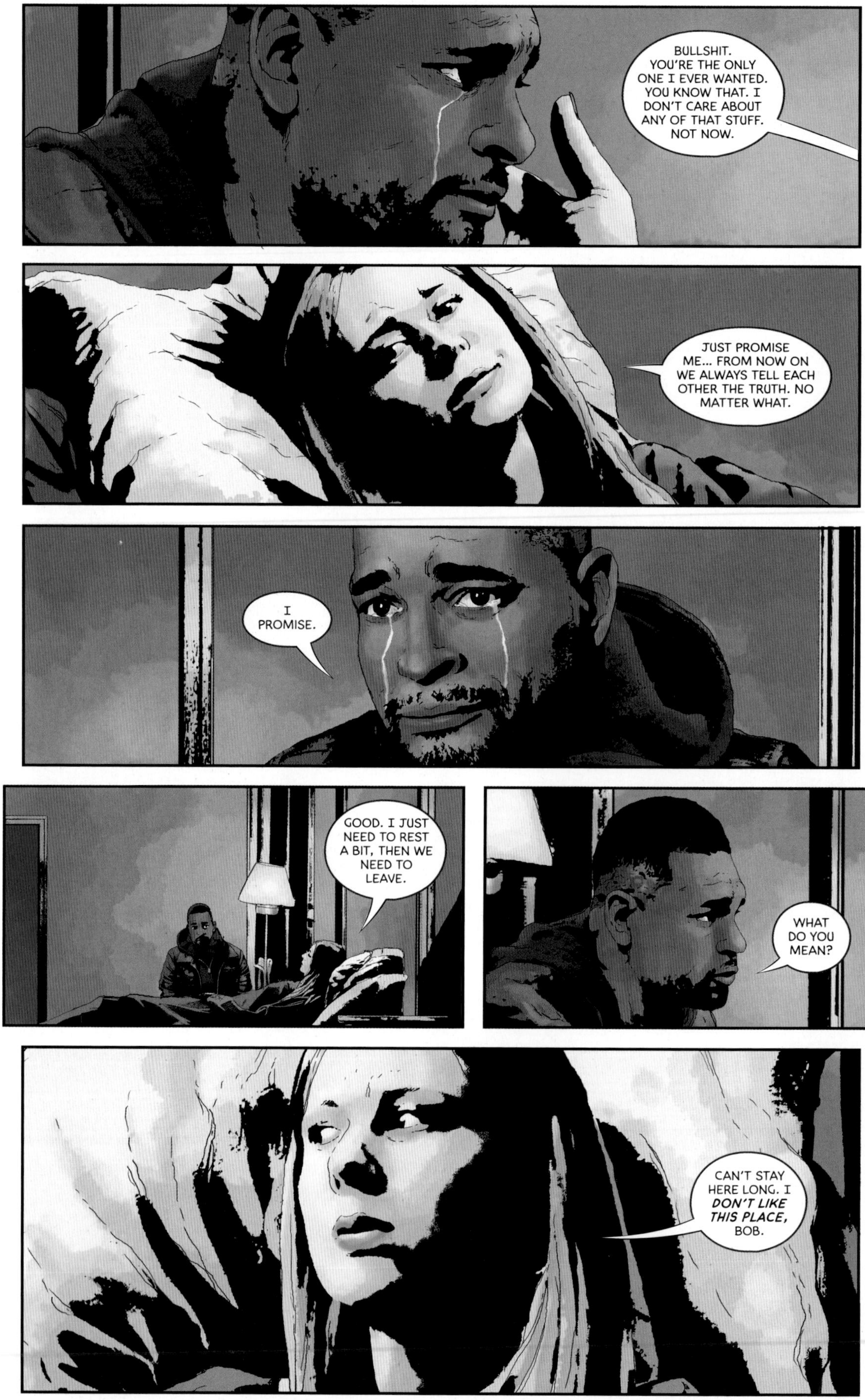
BULLSHIT. YOU'RE THE ONLY ONE I EVER WANTED. YOU KNOW THAT. I DON'T CARE ABOUT ANY OF THAT STUFF. NOT NOW.
JUST PROMISE ME... FROM NOW ON WE ALWAYS TELL EACH OTHER THE TRUTH. NO MATTER WHAT.
I PROMISE.
GOOD. I JUST NEED TO REST A BIT, THEN WE NEED TO LEAVE.
WHAT DO YOU MEAN?
CAN'T STAY HERE LONG. I *DON'T LIKE THIS PLACE,* BOB.

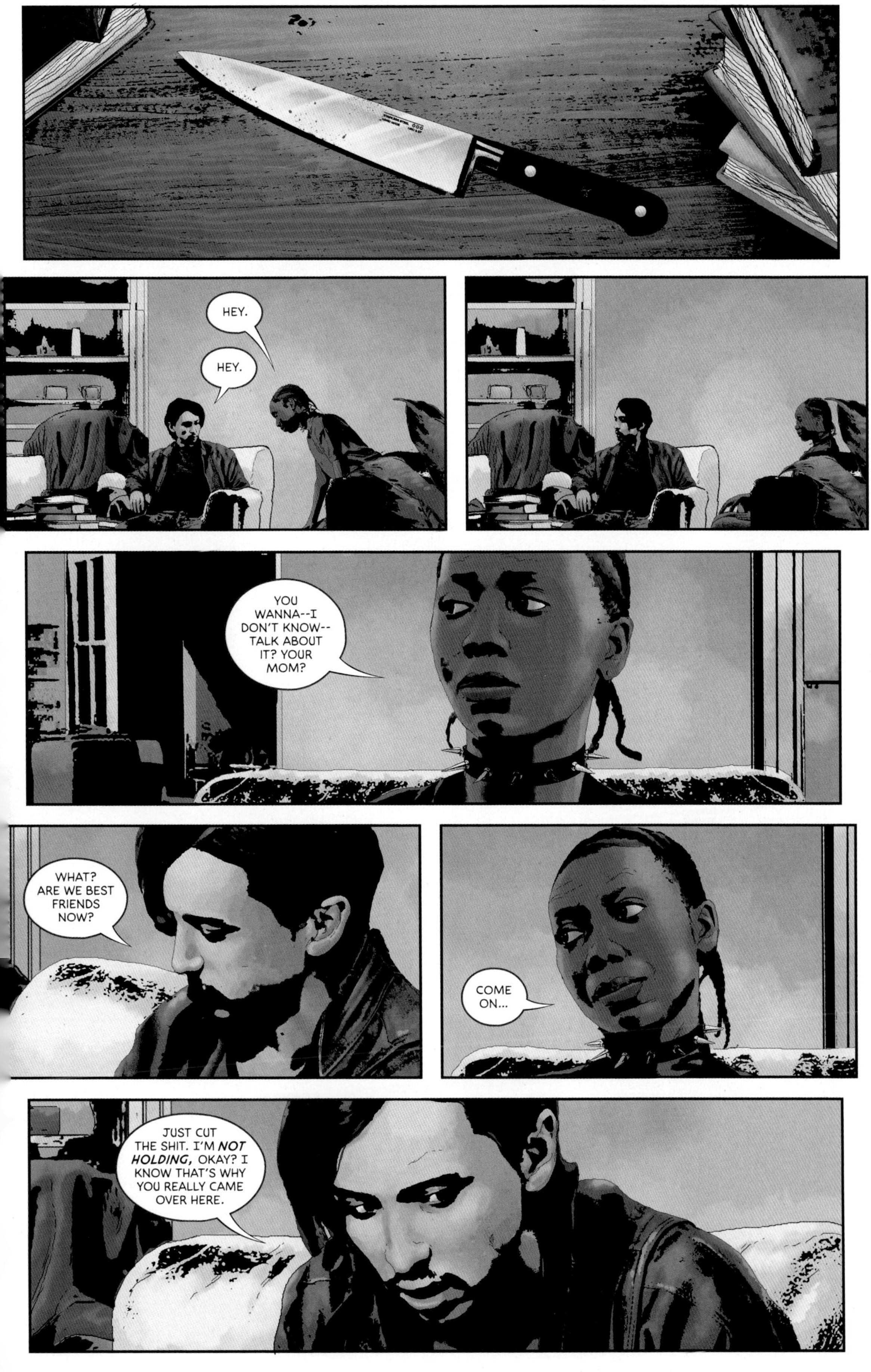
HEY.
HEY.
YOU WANNA--I DON'T KNOW--TALK ABOUT IT? YOUR MOM?
WHAT? ARE WE BEST FRIENDS NOW?
COME ON...
JUST CUT THE SHIT. I'M ***NOT HOLDING,*** OKAY? I KNOW THAT'S WHY YOU REALLY CAME OVER HERE.

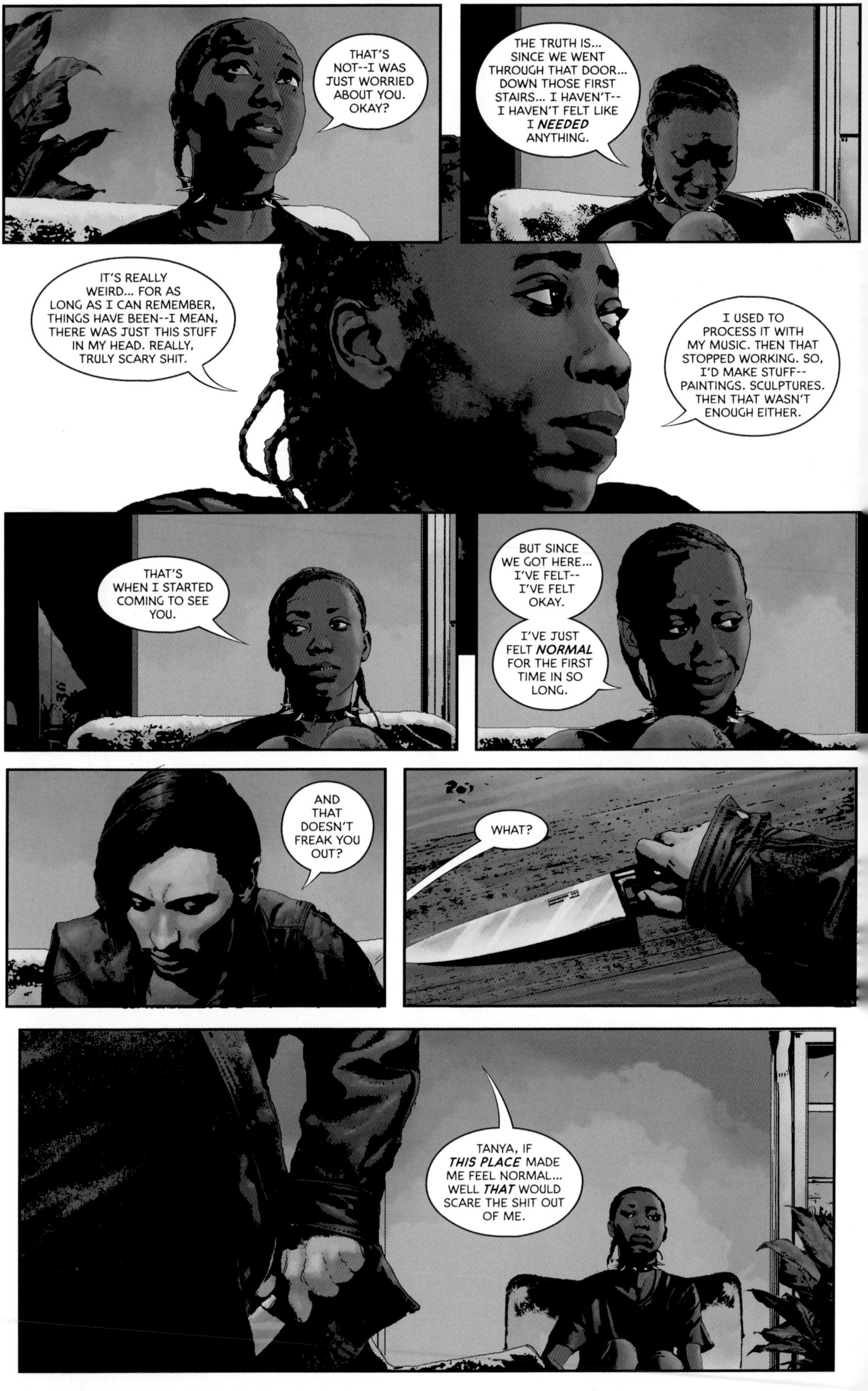
THAT'S NOT--I WAS JUST WORRIED ABOUT YOU. OKAY?
THE TRUTH IS... SINCE WE WENT THROUGH THAT DOOR... DOWN THOSE FIRST STAIRS... I HAVEN'T-- I HAVEN'T FELT LIKE I *NEEDED* ANYTHING.
IT'S REALLY WEIRD... FOR AS LONG AS I CAN REMEMBER, THINGS HAVE BEEN--I MEAN, THERE WAS JUST THIS STUFF IN MY HEAD. REALLY, TRULY SCARY SHIT.
I USED TO PROCESS IT WITH MY MUSIC. THEN THAT STOPPED WORKING. SO, I'D MAKE STUFF-- PAINTINGS. SCULPTURES. THEN THAT WASN'T ENOUGH EITHER.
THAT'S WHEN I STARTED COMING TO SEE YOU.
BUT SINCE WE GOT HERE... I'VE FELT-- I'VE FELT OKAY.
I'VE JUST FELT **NORMAL** FOR THE FIRST TIME IN SO LONG.
AND THAT DOESN'T FREAK YOU OUT?
WHAT?
TANYA, IF ***THIS PLACE*** MADE ME FEEL NORMAL... WELL ***THAT*** WOULD SCARE THE SHIT OUT OF ME.

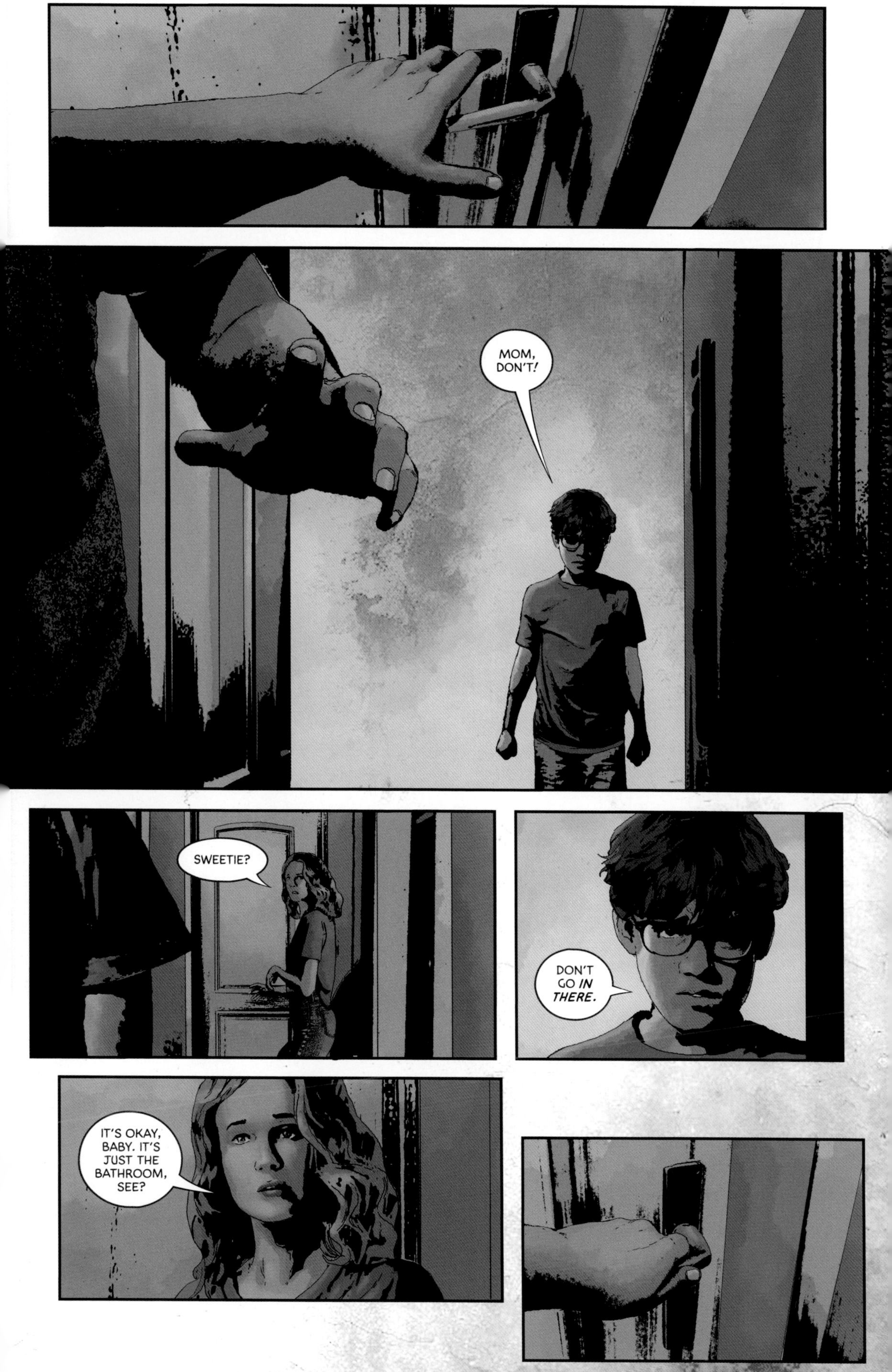
MOM, DON'T!
SWEETIE?
DON'T GO IN THERE.
IT'S OKAY, BABY. IT'S JUST THE BATHROOM, SEE?

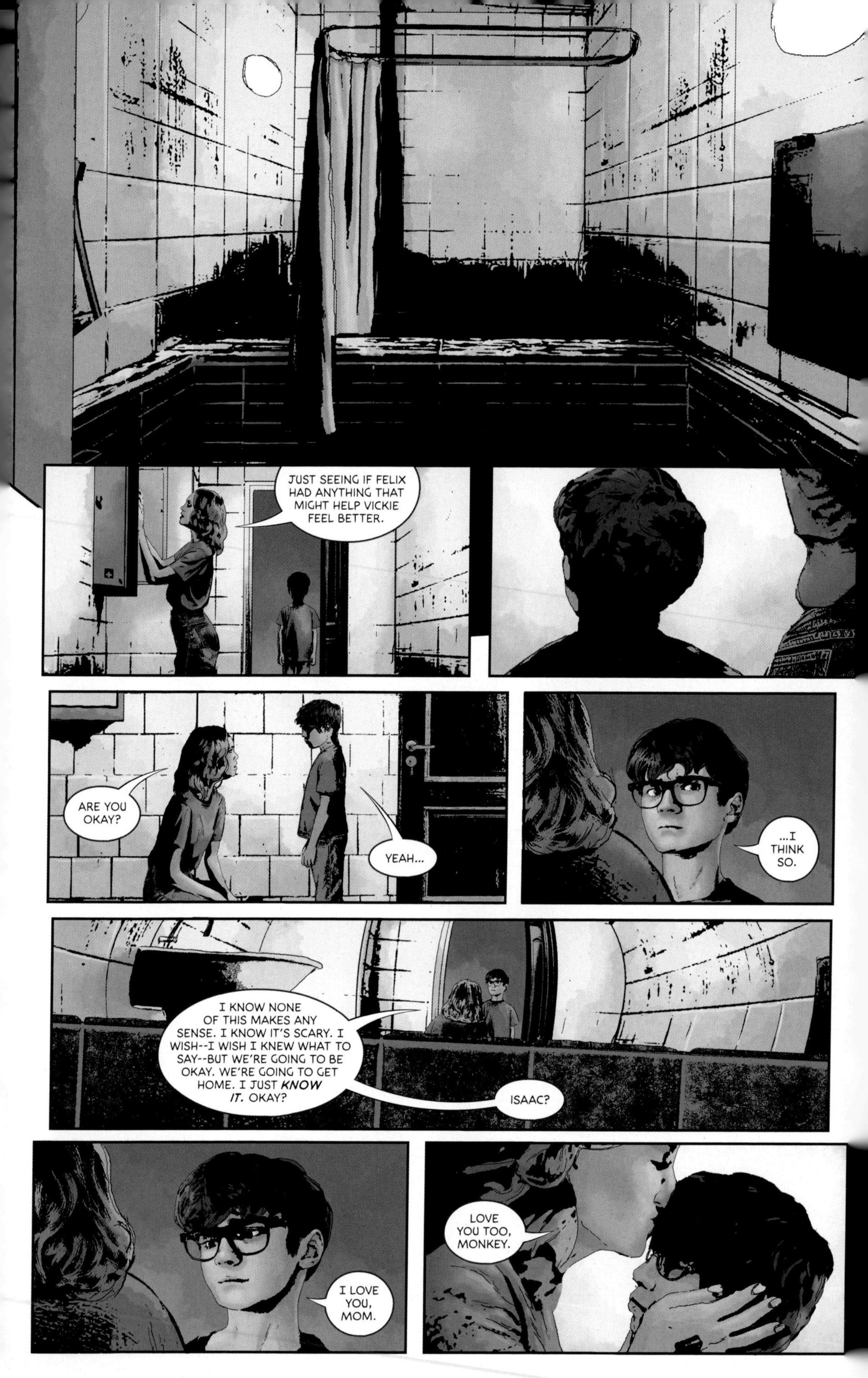
JUST SEEING IF FELIX HAD ANYTHING THAT MIGHT HELP VICKIE FEEL BETTER.
ARE YOU OKAY?
YEAH...
...I THINK SO.
I KNOW NONE OF THIS MAKES ANY SENSE. I KNOW IT'S SCARY. I WISH--I WISH I KNEW WHAT TO SAY--BUT WE'RE GOING TO BE OKAY. WE'RE GOING TO GET HOME. I JUST *KNOW IT.* OKAY?
ISAAC?
I LOVE YOU, MOM.
LOVE YOU TOO, MONKEY.

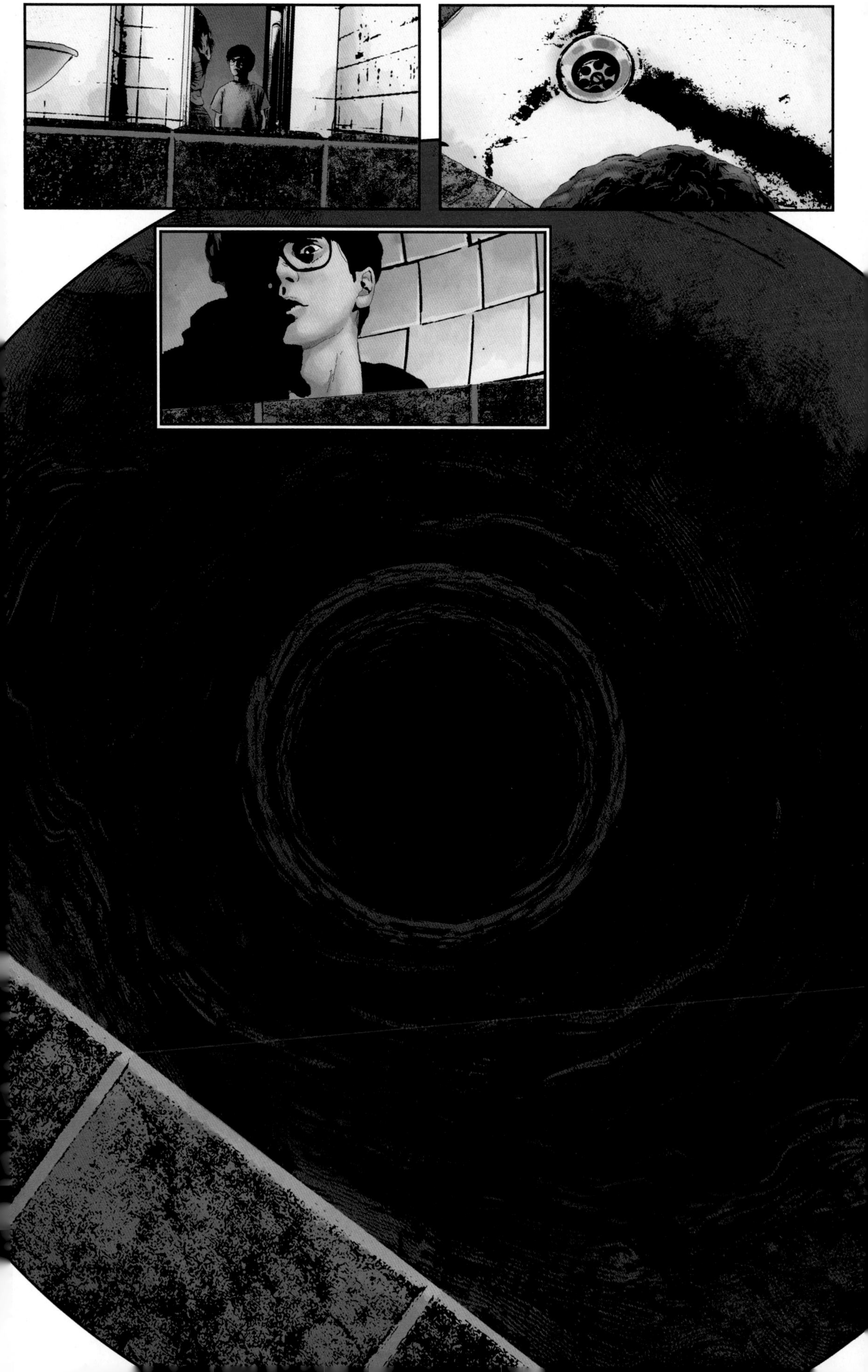

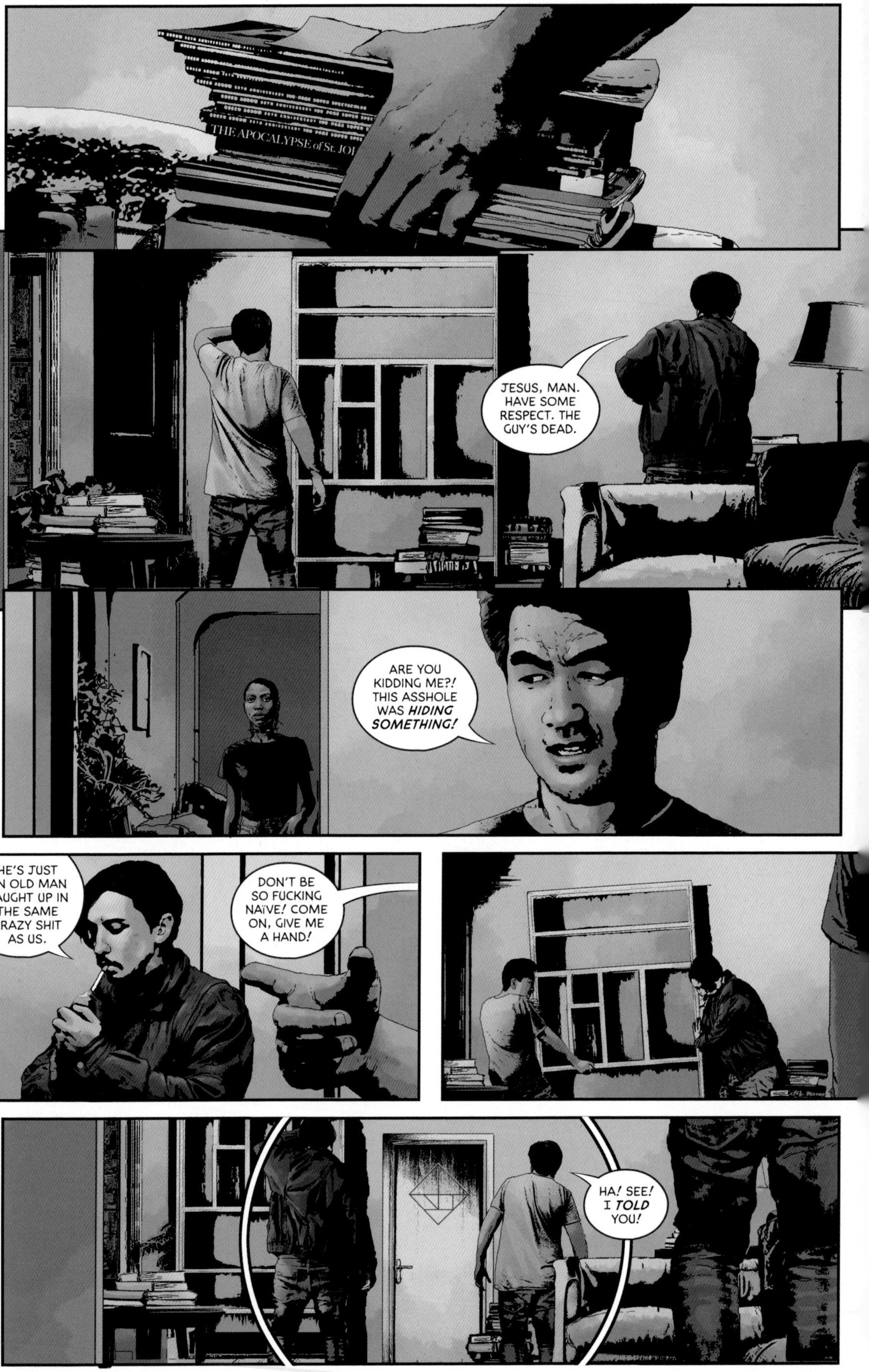
THE APOCALYPSE of St. JOH
JESUS, MAN. HAVE SOME RESPECT. THE GUY'S DEAD.
ARE YOU KIDDING ME?! THIS ASSHOLE WAS *HIDING SOMETHING!*
HE'S JUST AN OLD MAN CAUGHT UP IN THE SAME CRAZY SHIT AS US.
DON'T BE SO FUCKING NAÏVE! COME ON, GIVE ME A HAND!
HA! SEE! I *TOLD* YOU!

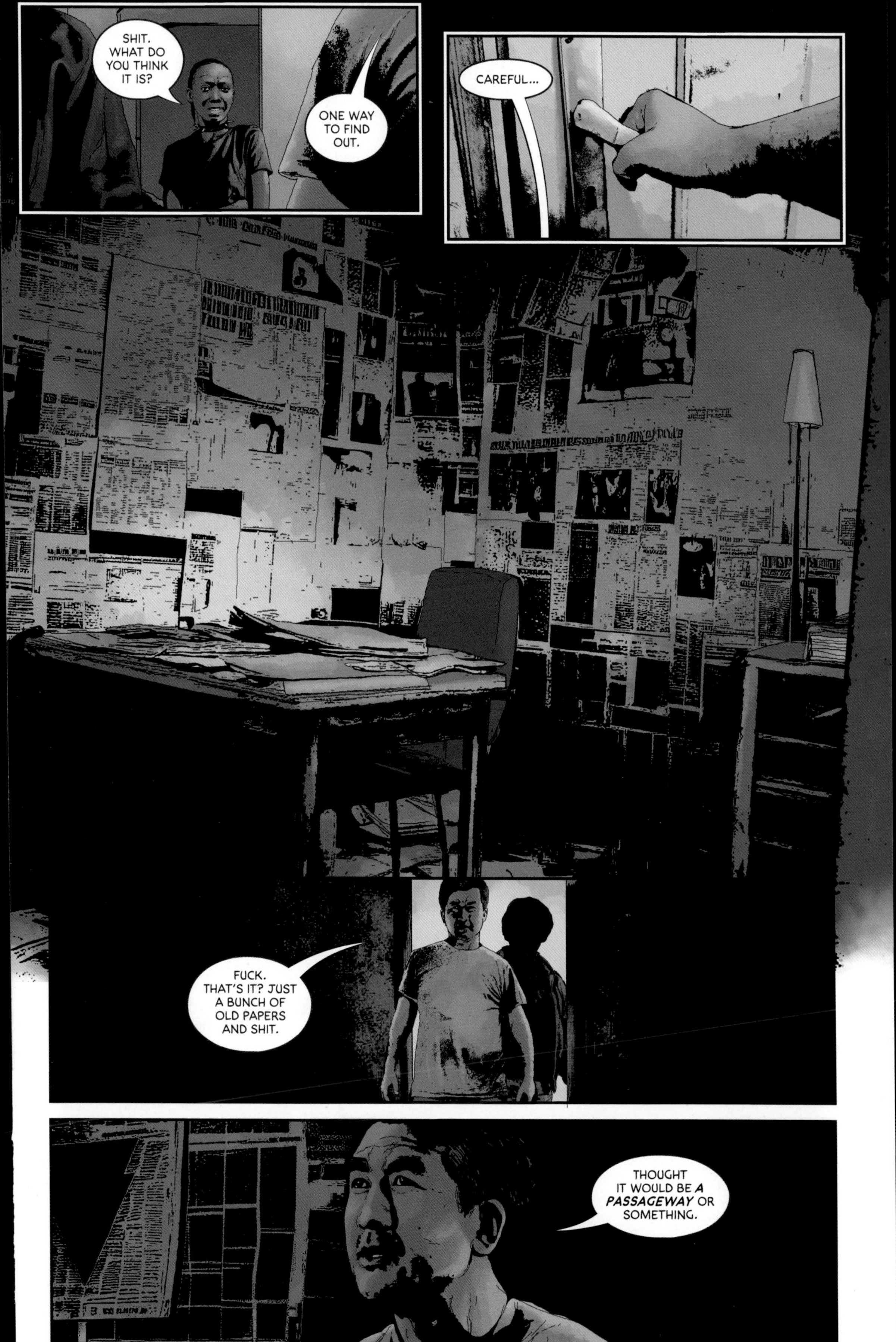
SHIT. WHAT DO YOU THINK IT IS?
ONE WAY TO FIND OUT.
CAREFUL...
FUCK. THAT'S IT? JUST A BUNCH OF OLD PAPERS AND SHIT.
THOUGHT IT WOULD BE *A PASSAGEWAY* OR SOMETHING.

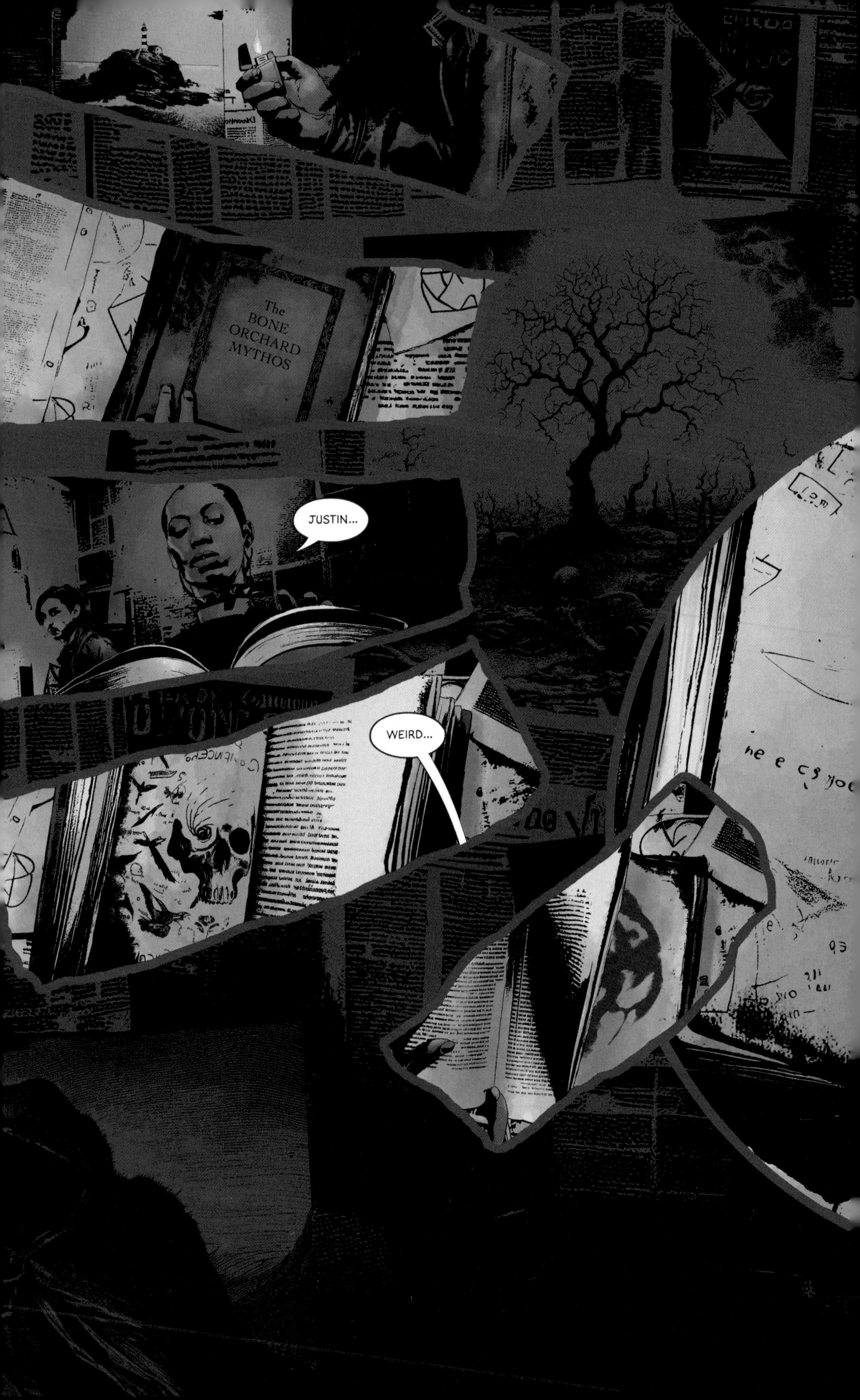
The
BONE
ORCHARD
MYTHOS
JUSTIN...
WEIRD...

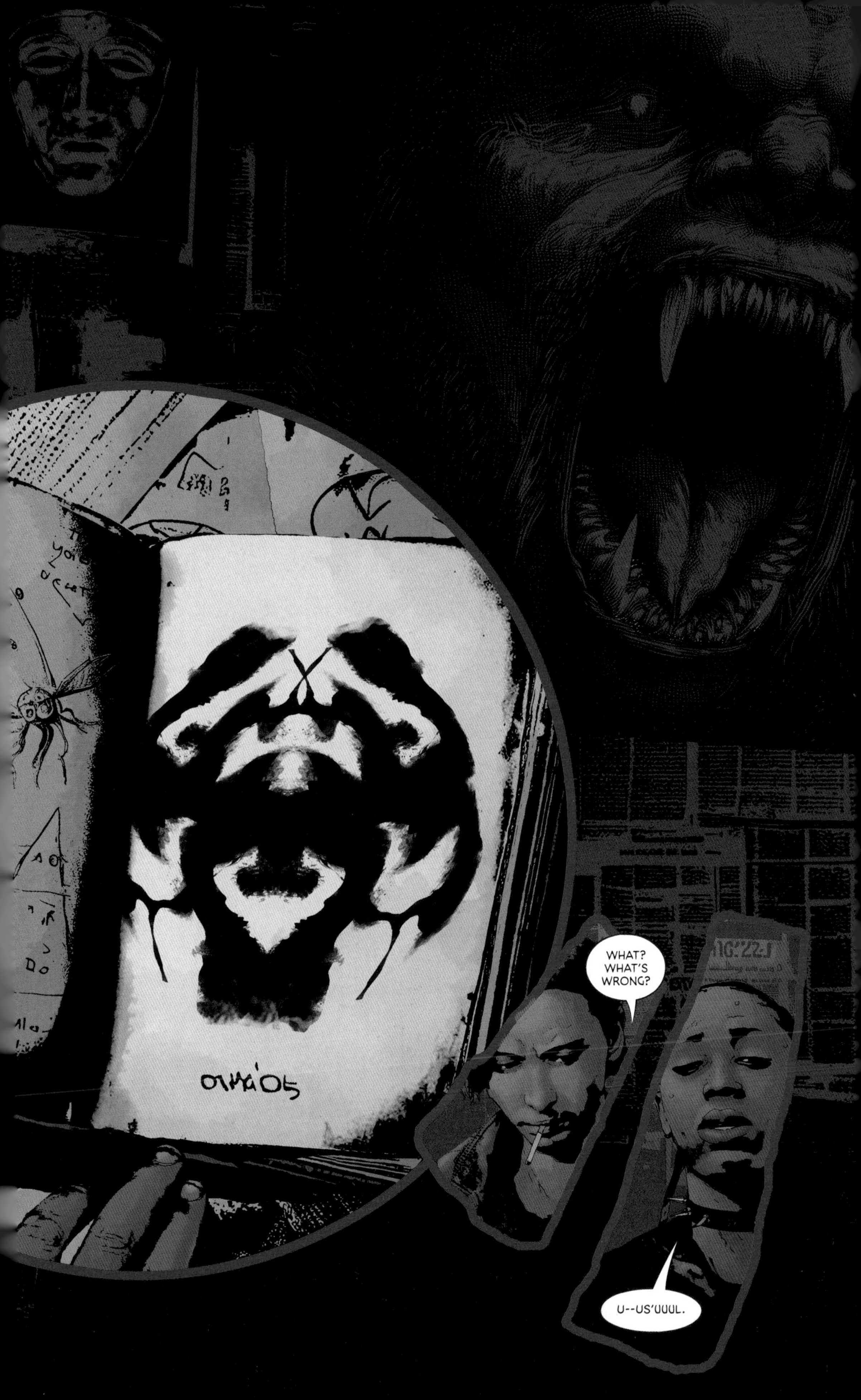
WHAT? WHAT'S WRONG?
U--US'UUUL.

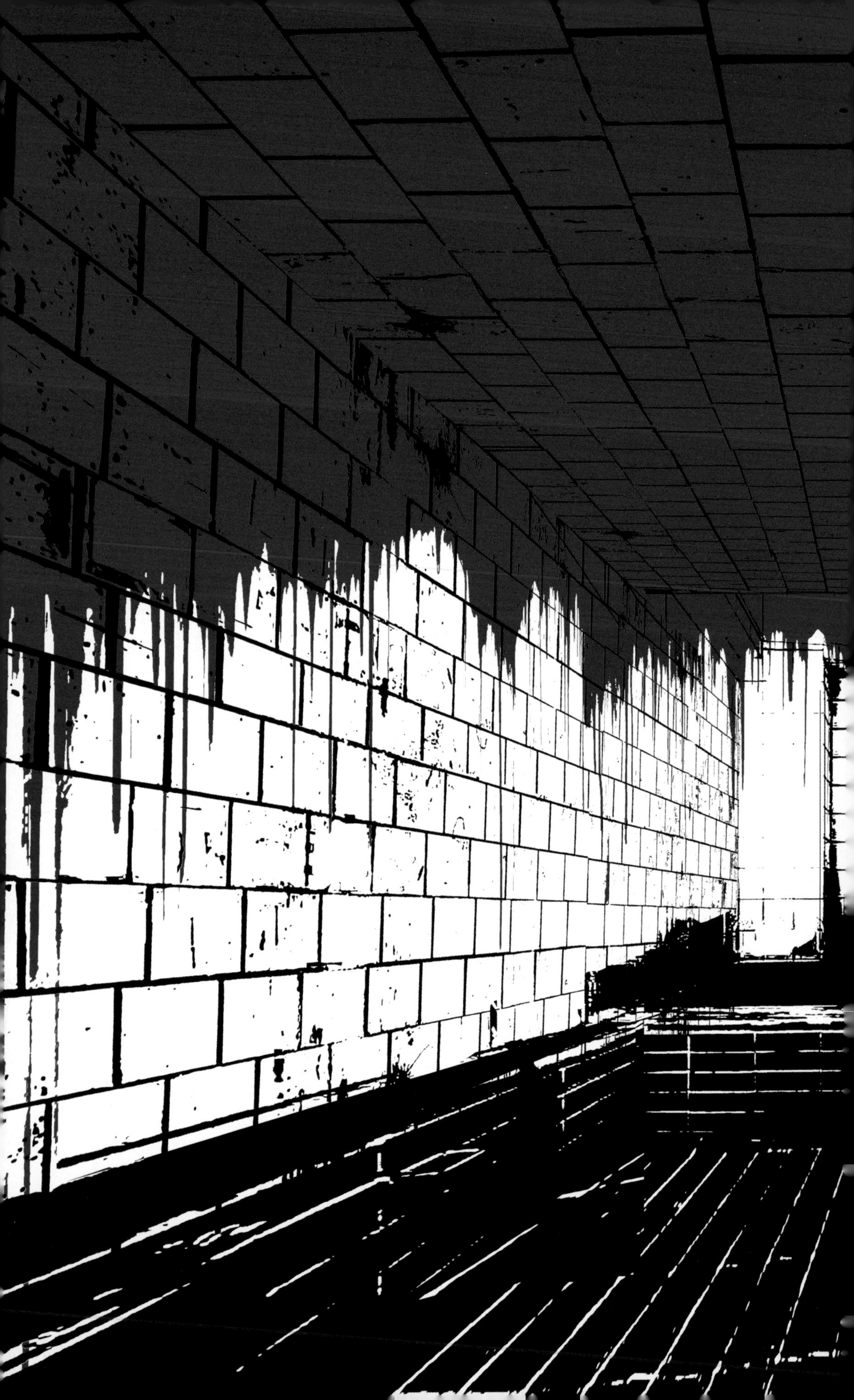

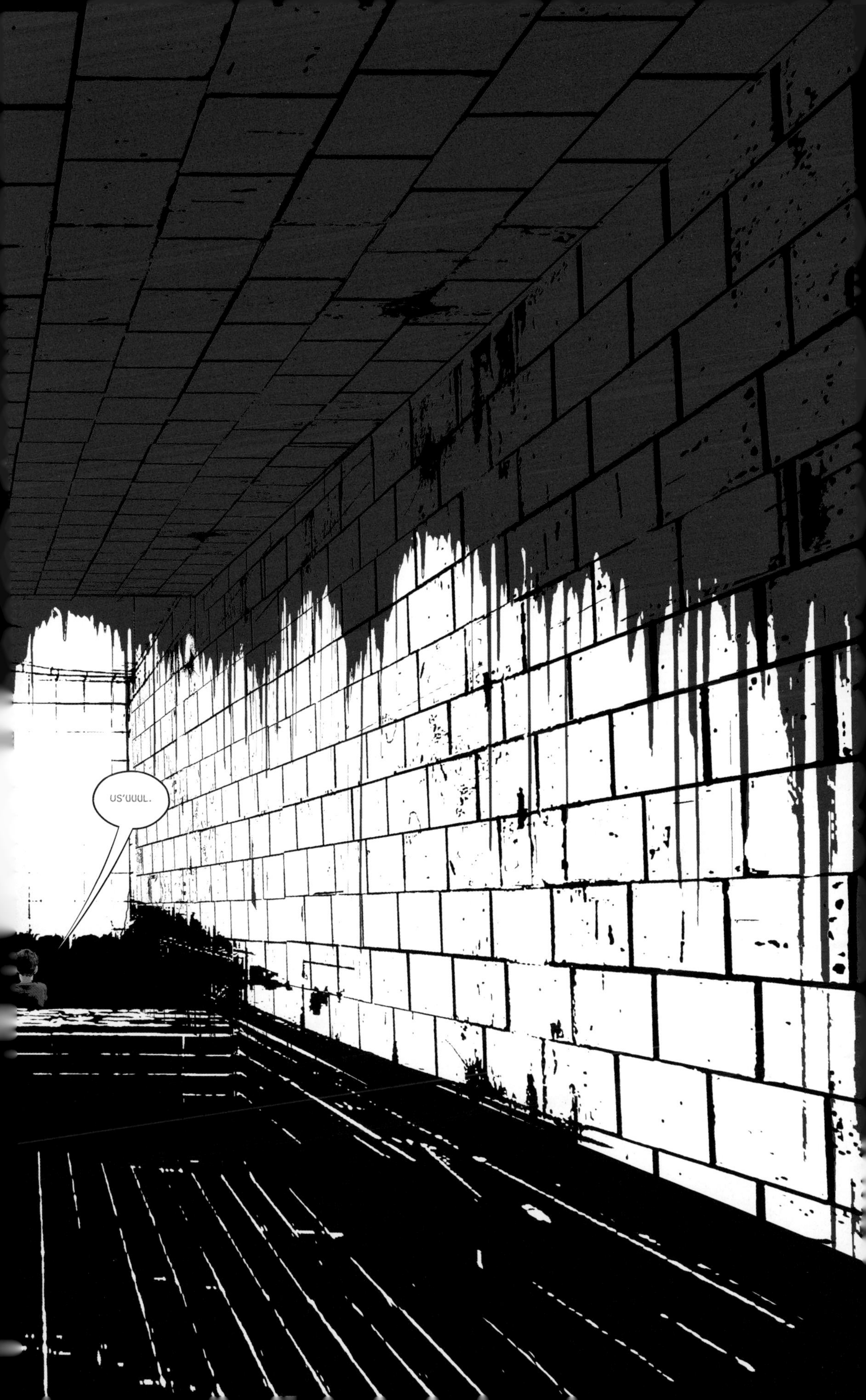
US'UUUL.

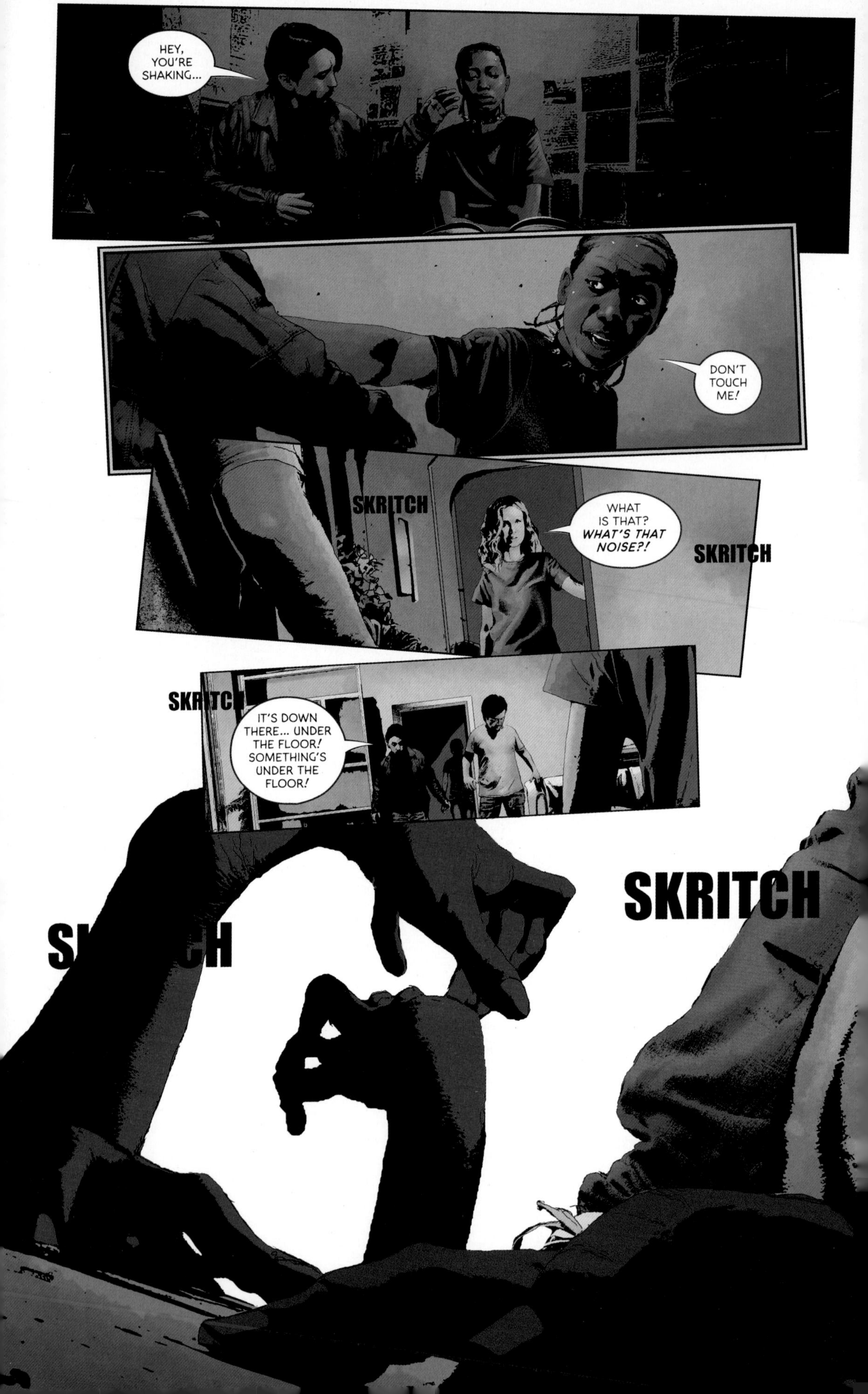
HEY, YOU'RE SHAKING...
DON'T TOUCH ME!
SKRITCH
WHAT IS THAT? WHAT'S THAT NOISE?!
SKRITCH
SKRITCH
IT'S DOWN THERE... UNDER THE FLOOR! SOMETHING'S UNDER THE FLOOR!
SKRITCH

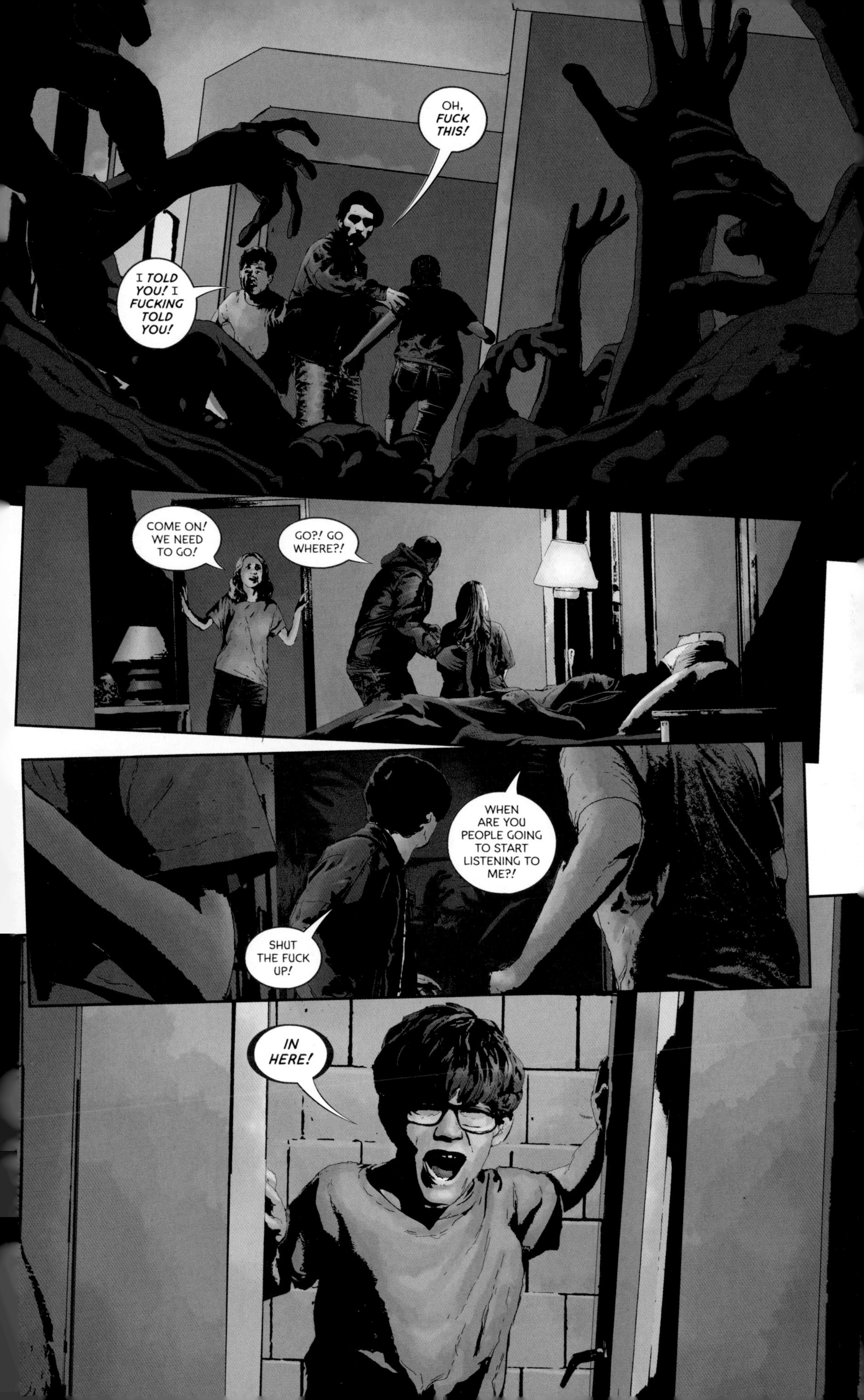
OH, FUCK THIS!
I TOLD YOU! I FUCKING TOLD YOU!
COME ON! WE NEED TO GO!
GO?! GO WHERE?!
WHEN ARE YOU PEOPLE GOING TO START LISTENING TO ME?!
SHUT THE FUCK UP!
IN HERE!

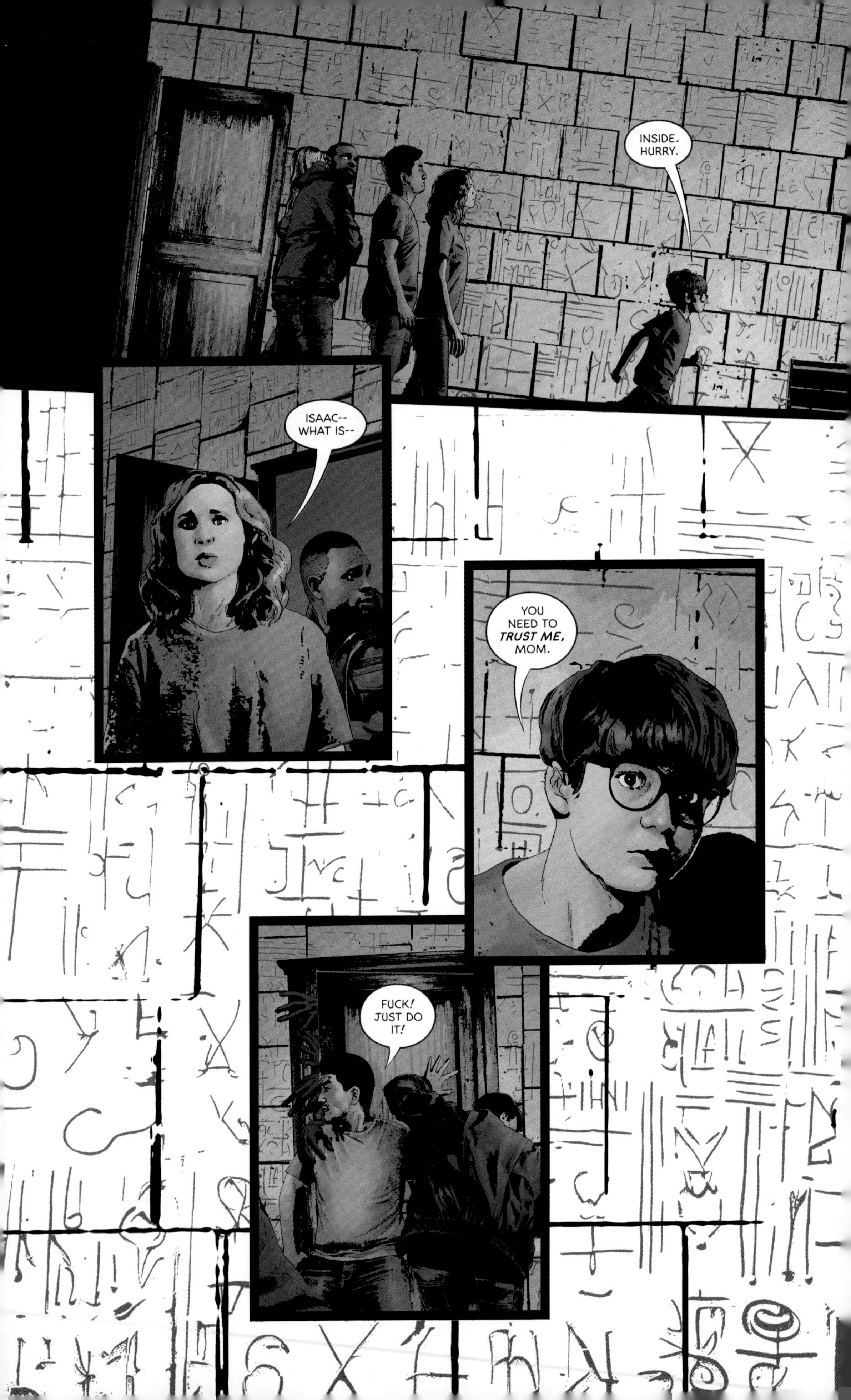
INSIDE. HURRY.
ISAAC-- WHAT IS--
YOU NEED TO *TRUST ME,* MOM.
FUCK! JUST DO IT!

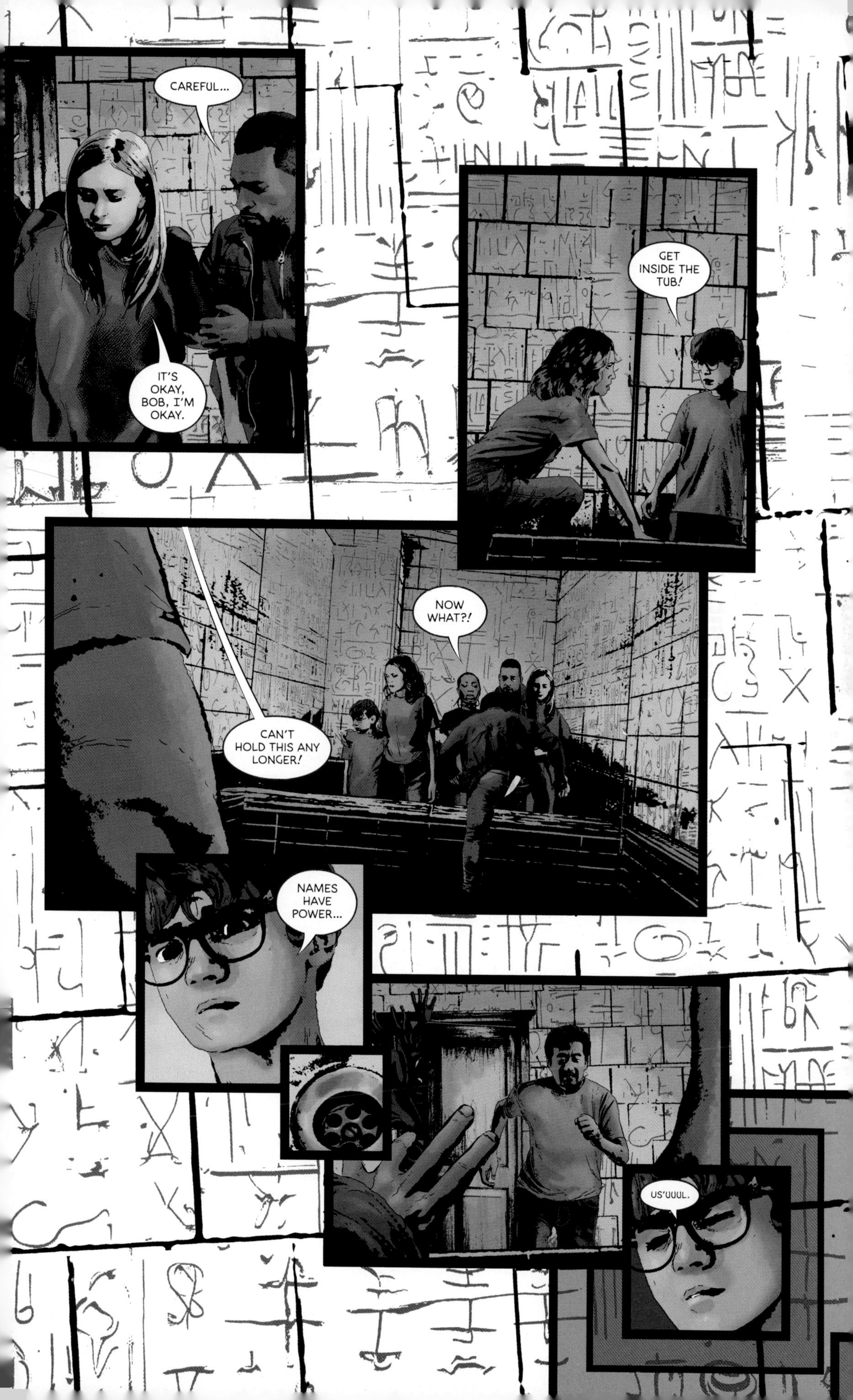
CAREFUL...
IT'S OKAY, BOB, I'M OKAY.
GET INSIDE THE TUB!
NOW WHAT?!
CAN'T HOLD THIS ANY LONGER!
NAMES HAVE POWER...
US'UUUL.

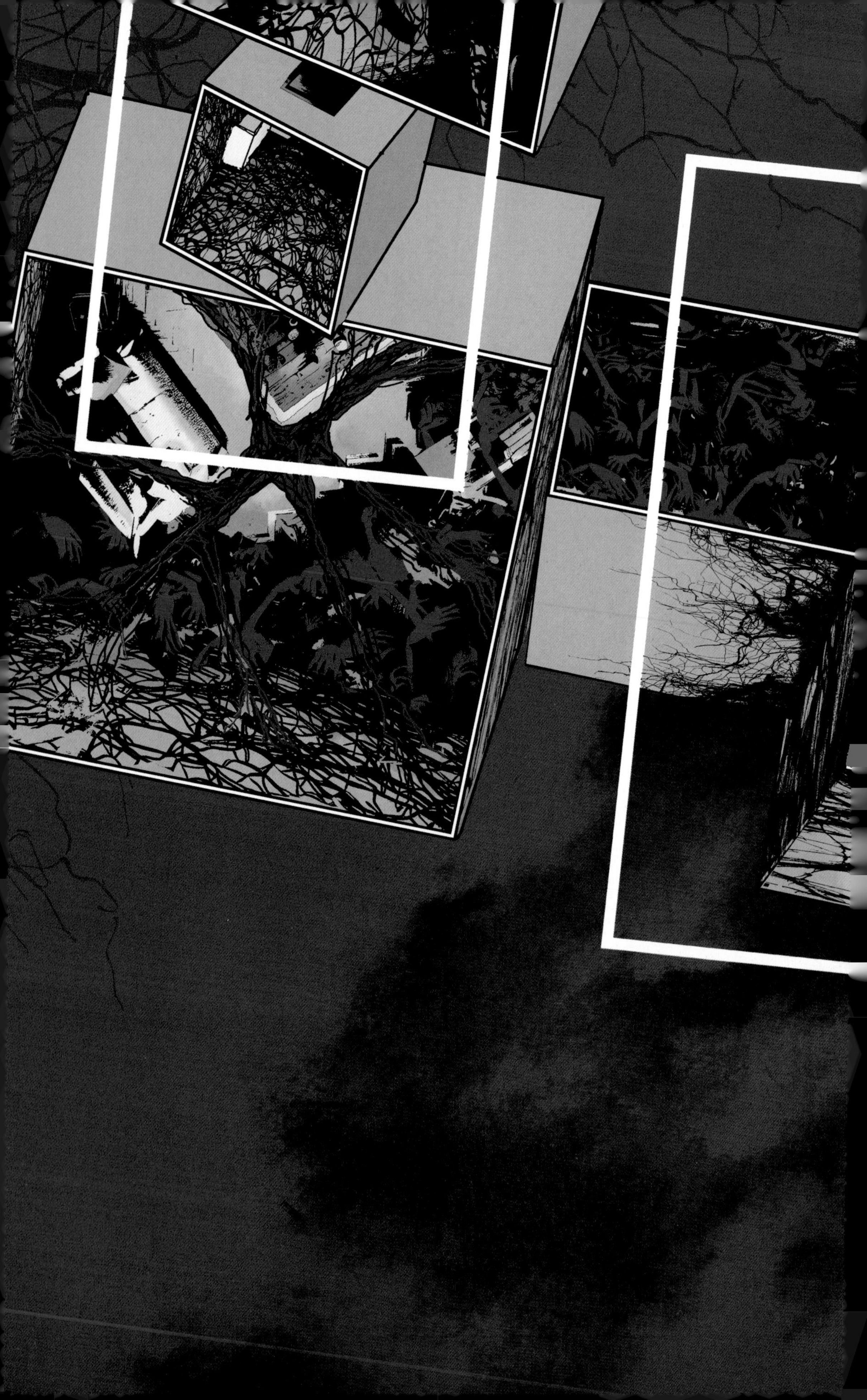

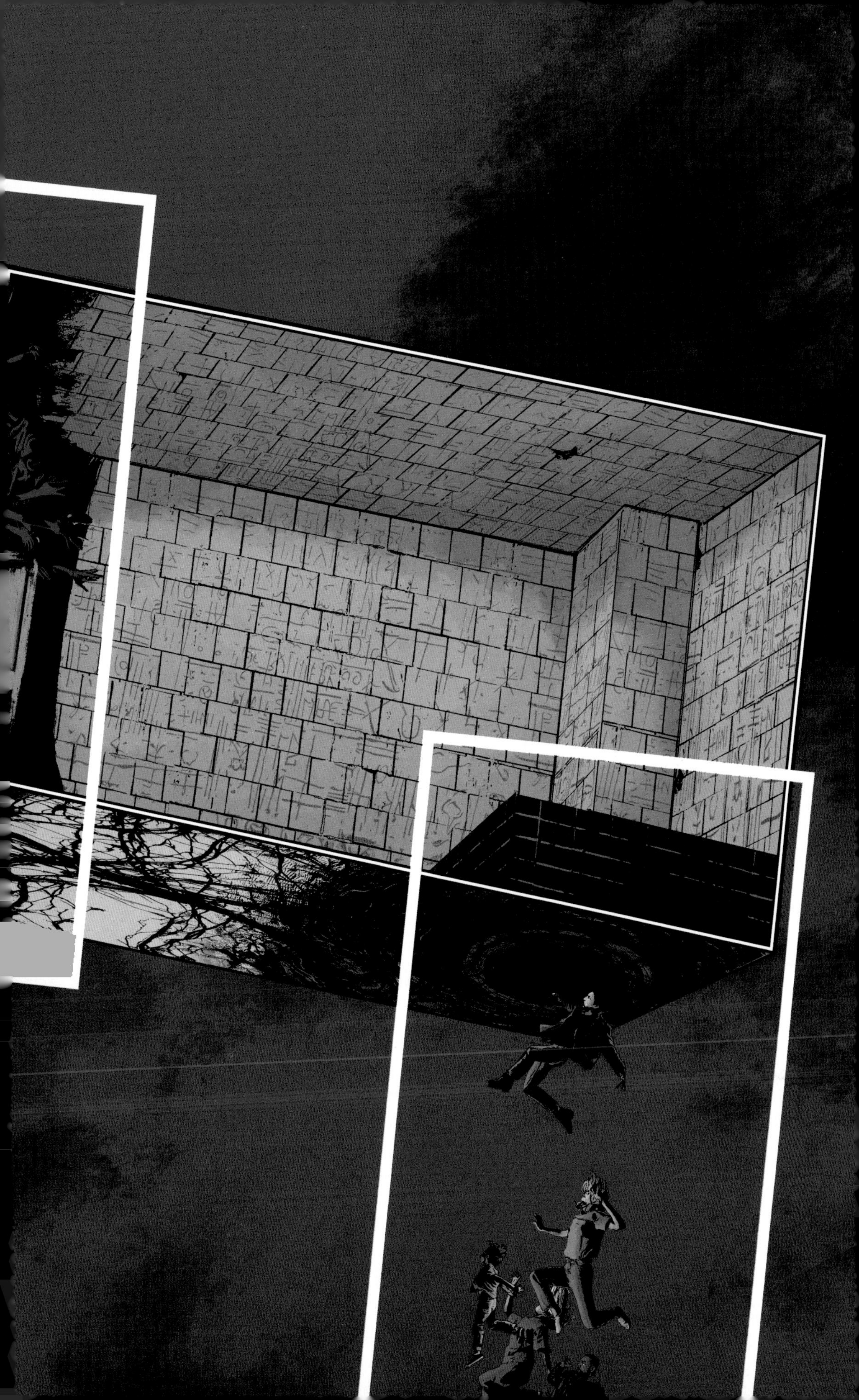

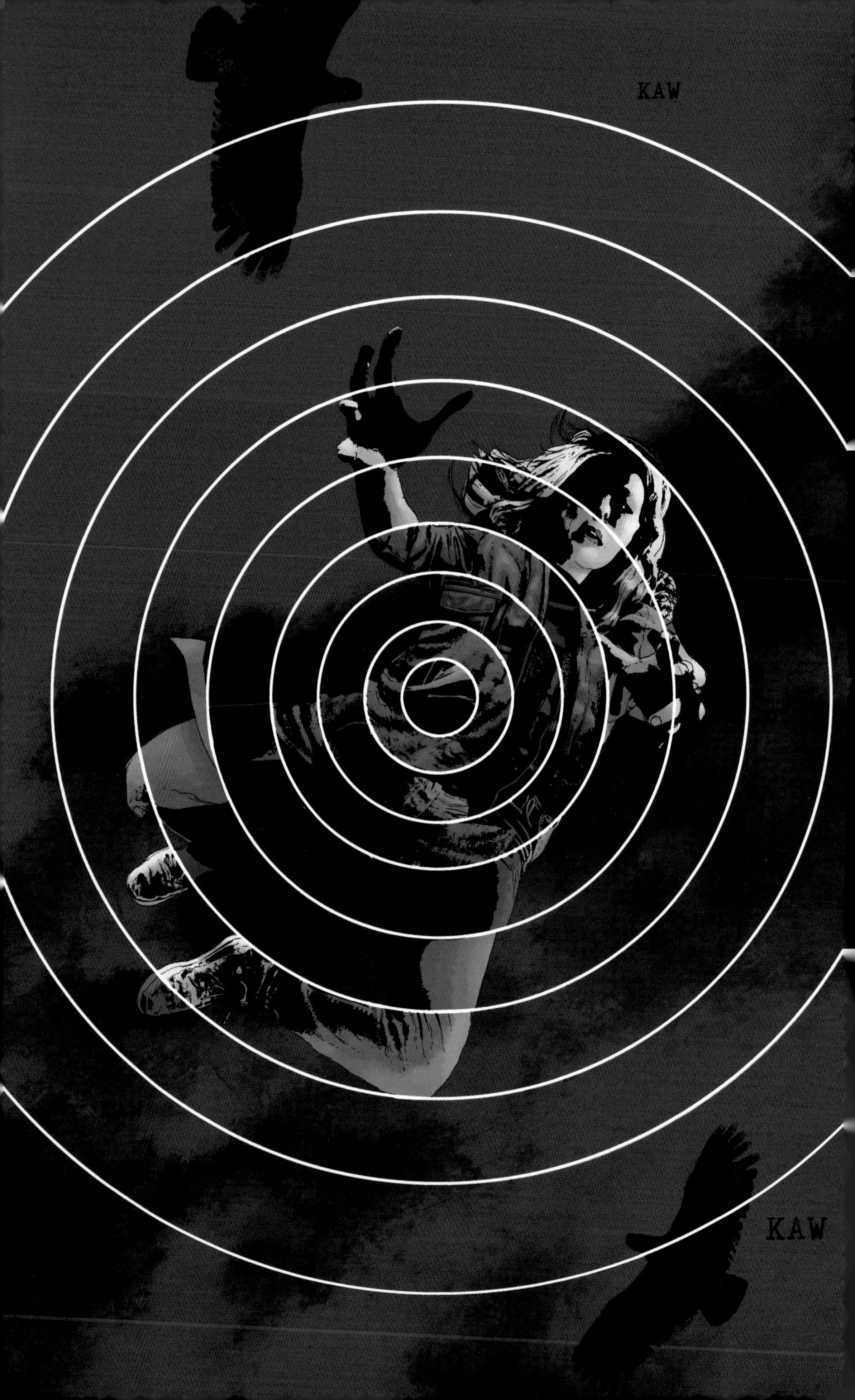
KAW
KAW

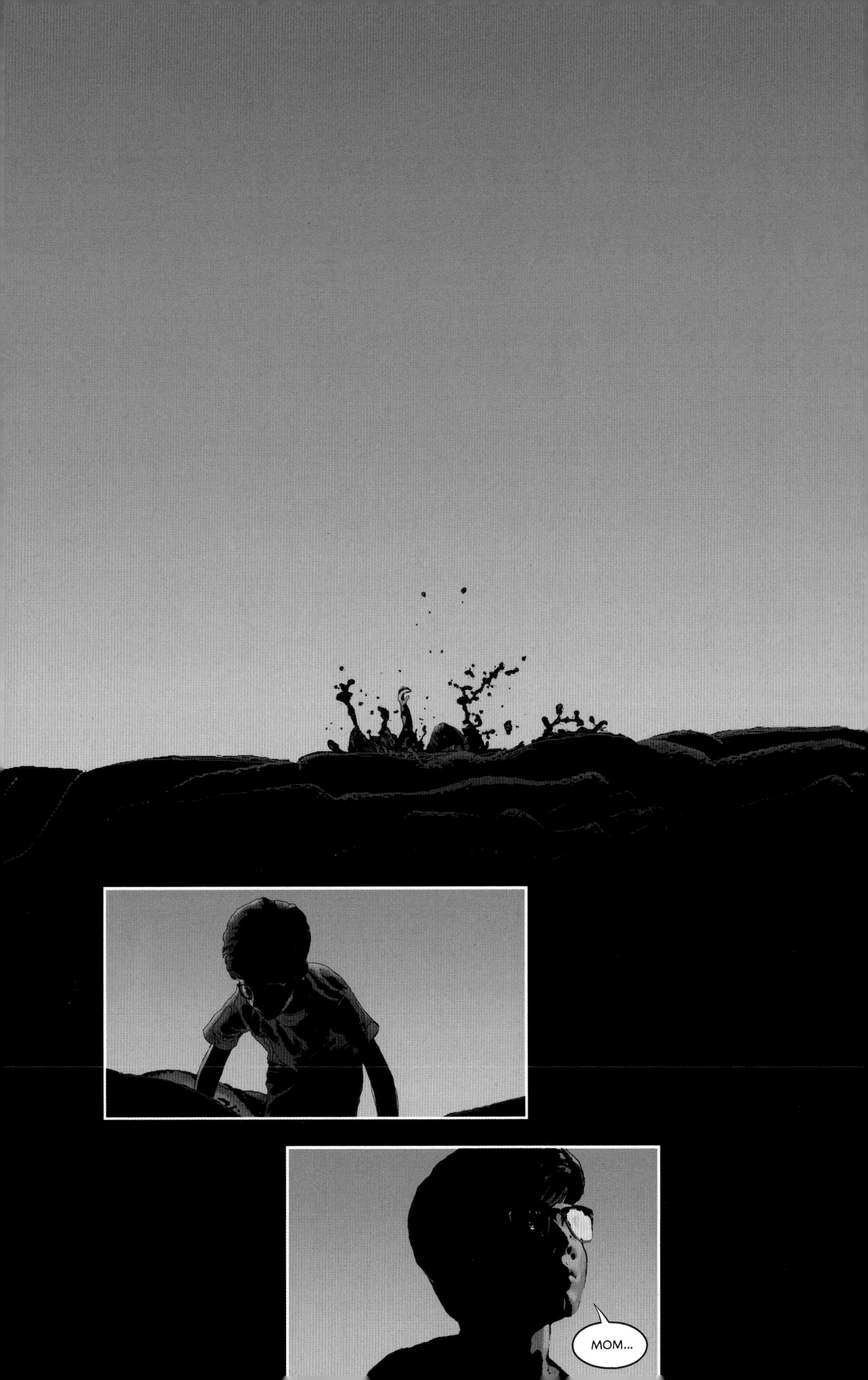
MOM...

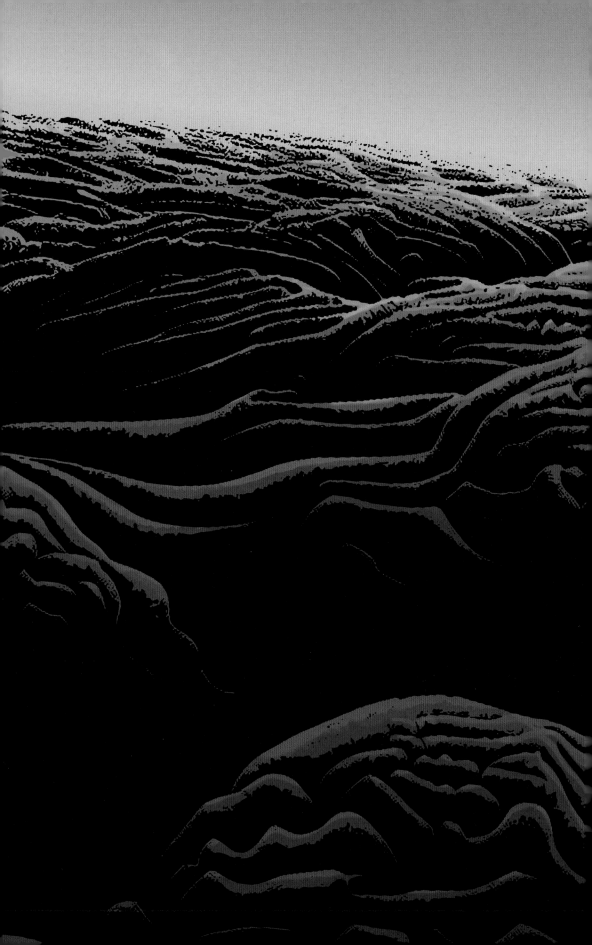

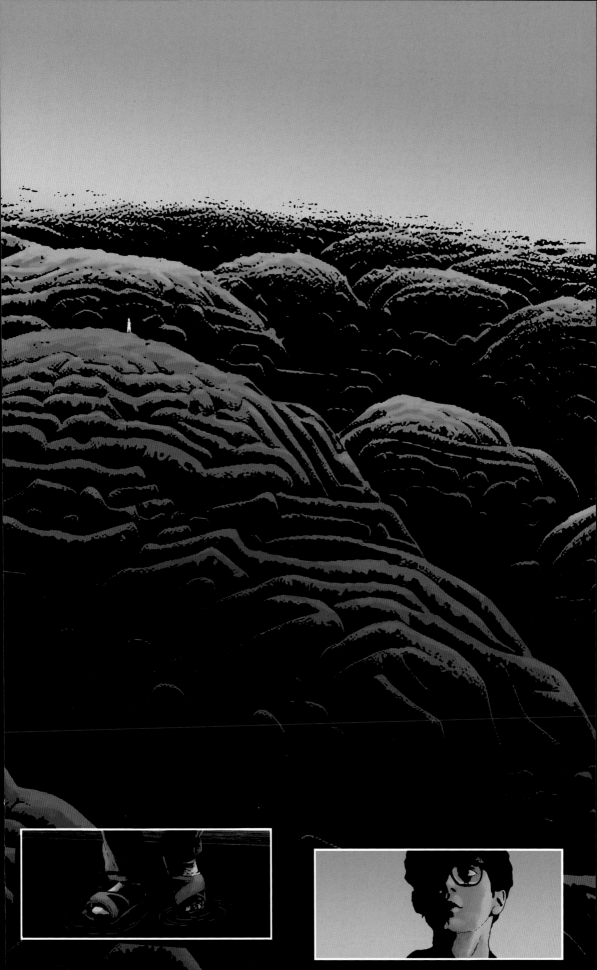

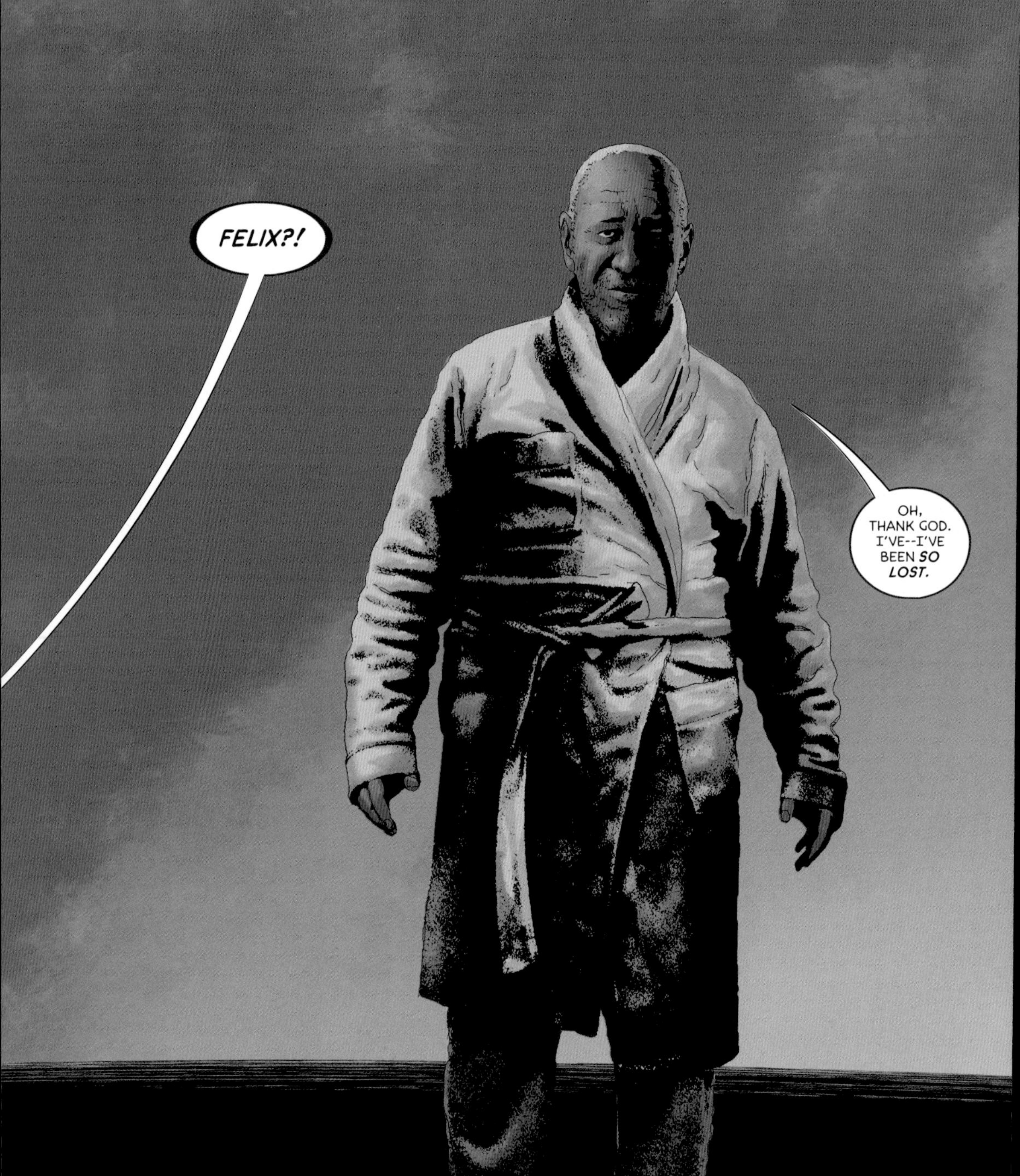
FELIX?!
OH, THANK GOD. I'VE--I'VE BEEN SO LOST.

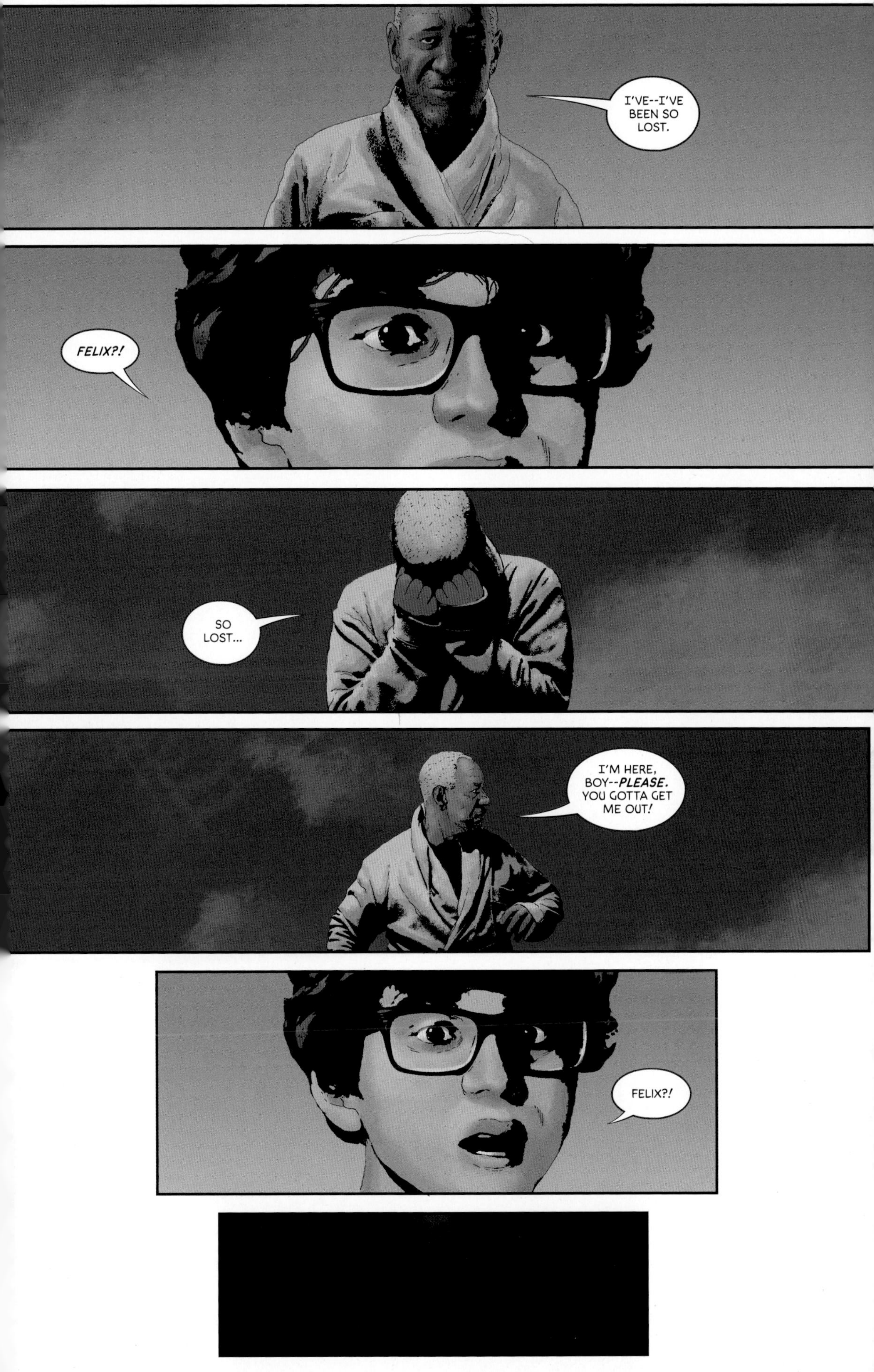
I'VE--I'VE BEEN SO LOST.
FELIX?!
SO LOST...
I'M HERE, BOY--PLEASE. YOU GOTTA GET ME OUT!
FELIX?!

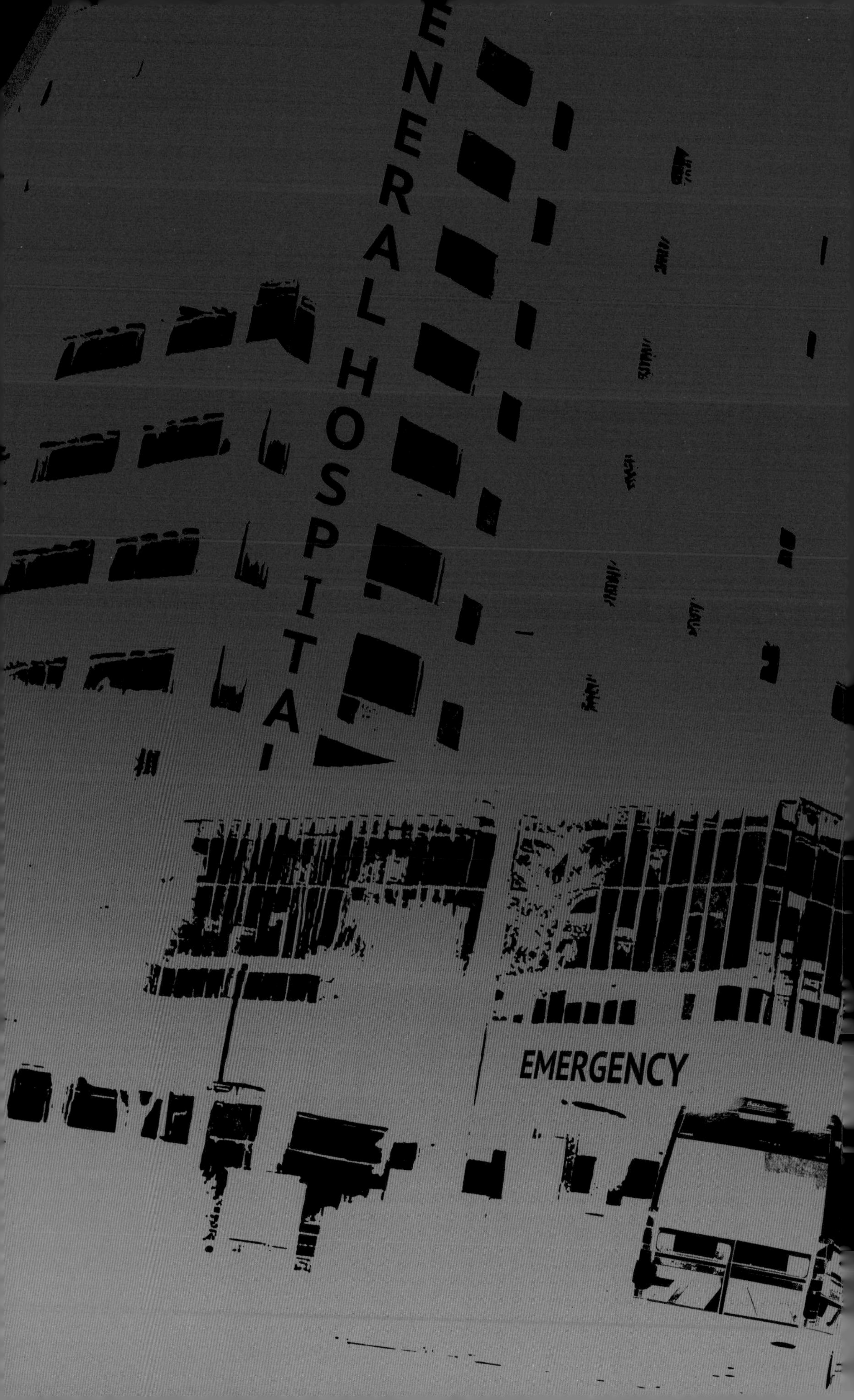
ENERAL HOSPITA
EMERGENCY

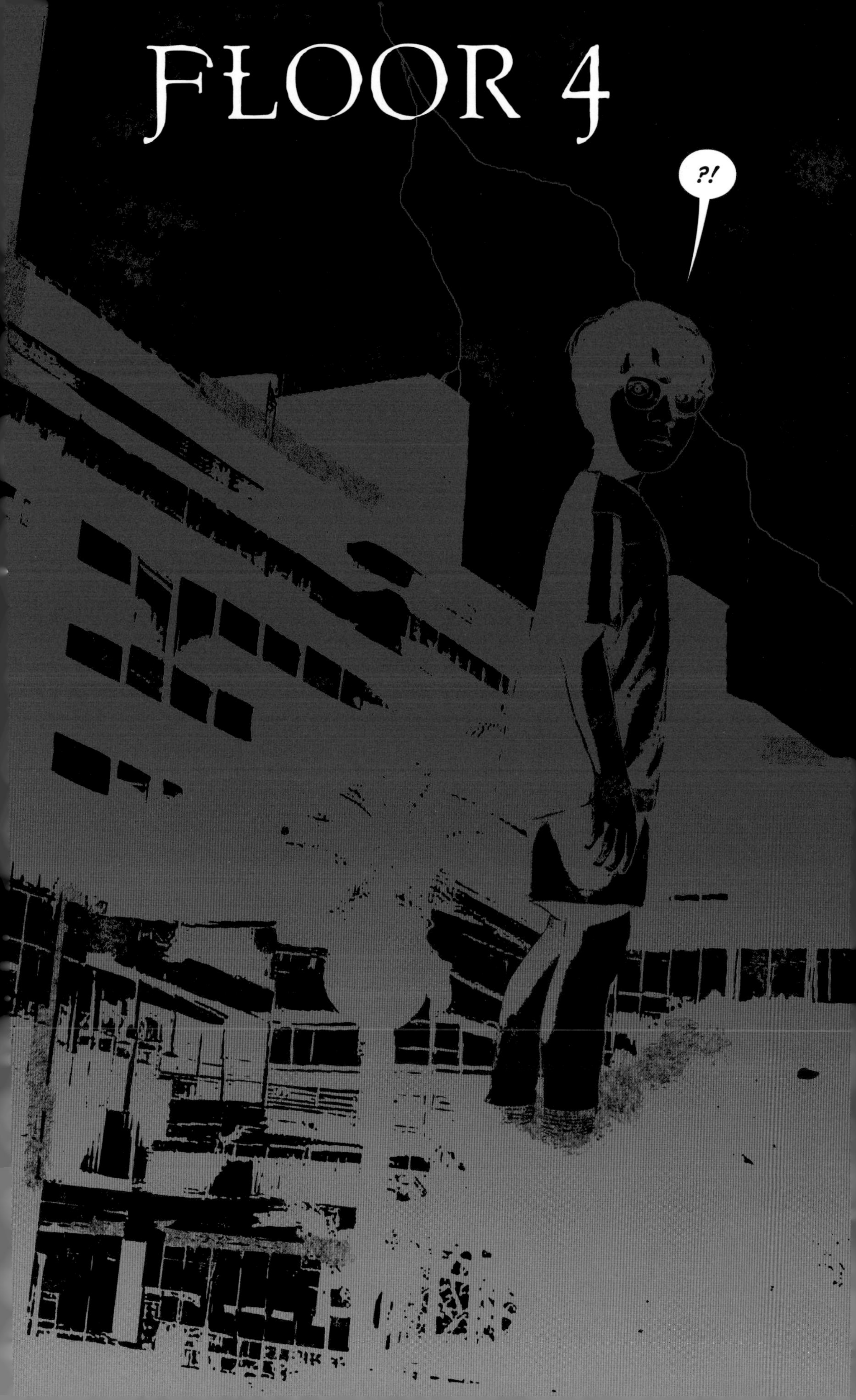
FLOOR 4
?!

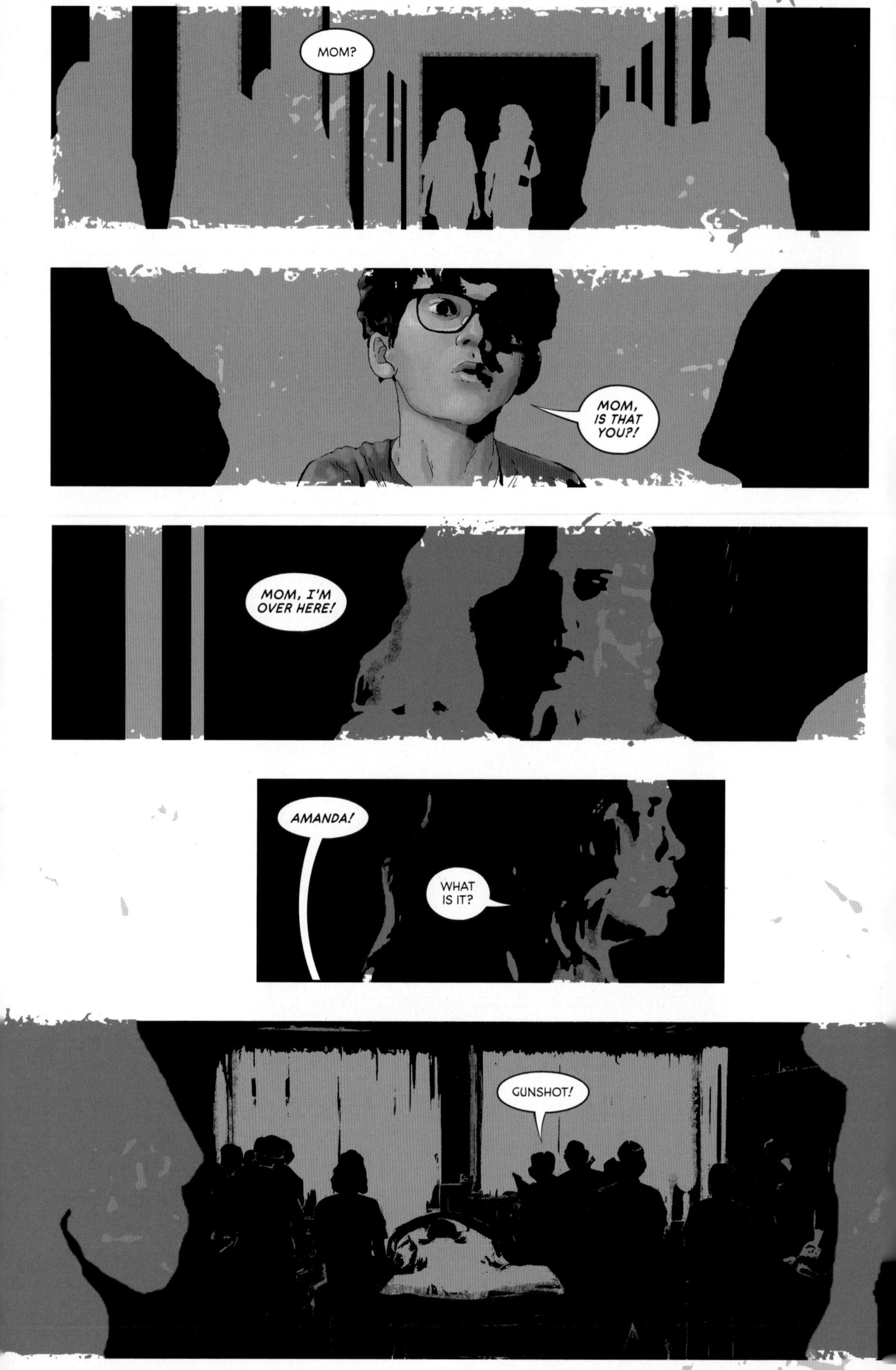
MOM?
MOM, IS THAT YOU?!
MOM, I'M OVER HERE!
AMANDA!
WHAT IS IT?
GUNSHOT!

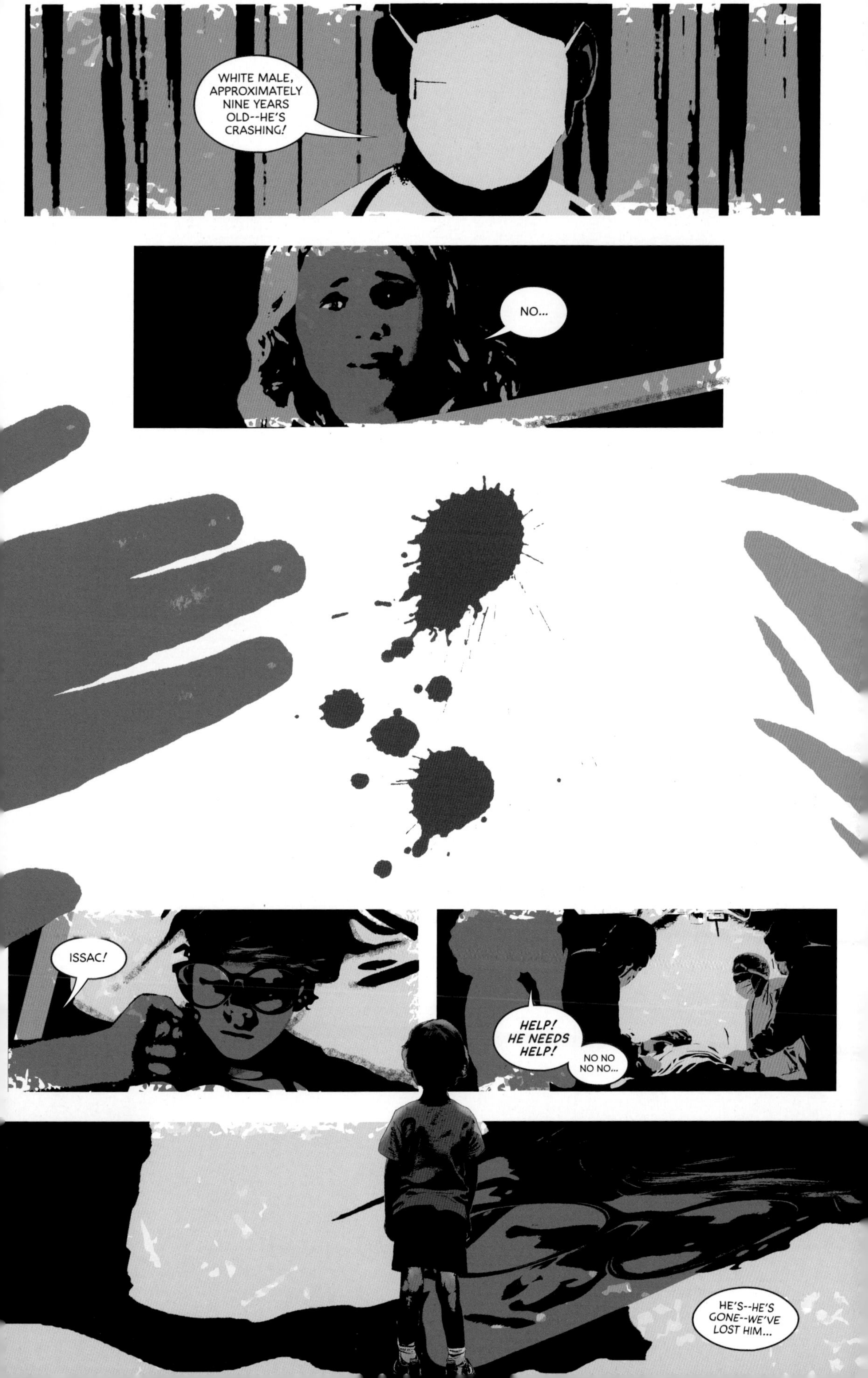
WHITE MALE, APPROXIMATELY NINE YEARS OLD--HE'S CRASHING!
NO...
ISSAC!
HELP! HE NEEDS HELP!
NO NO NO NO...
HE'S--HE'S GONE--WE'VE LOST HIM...

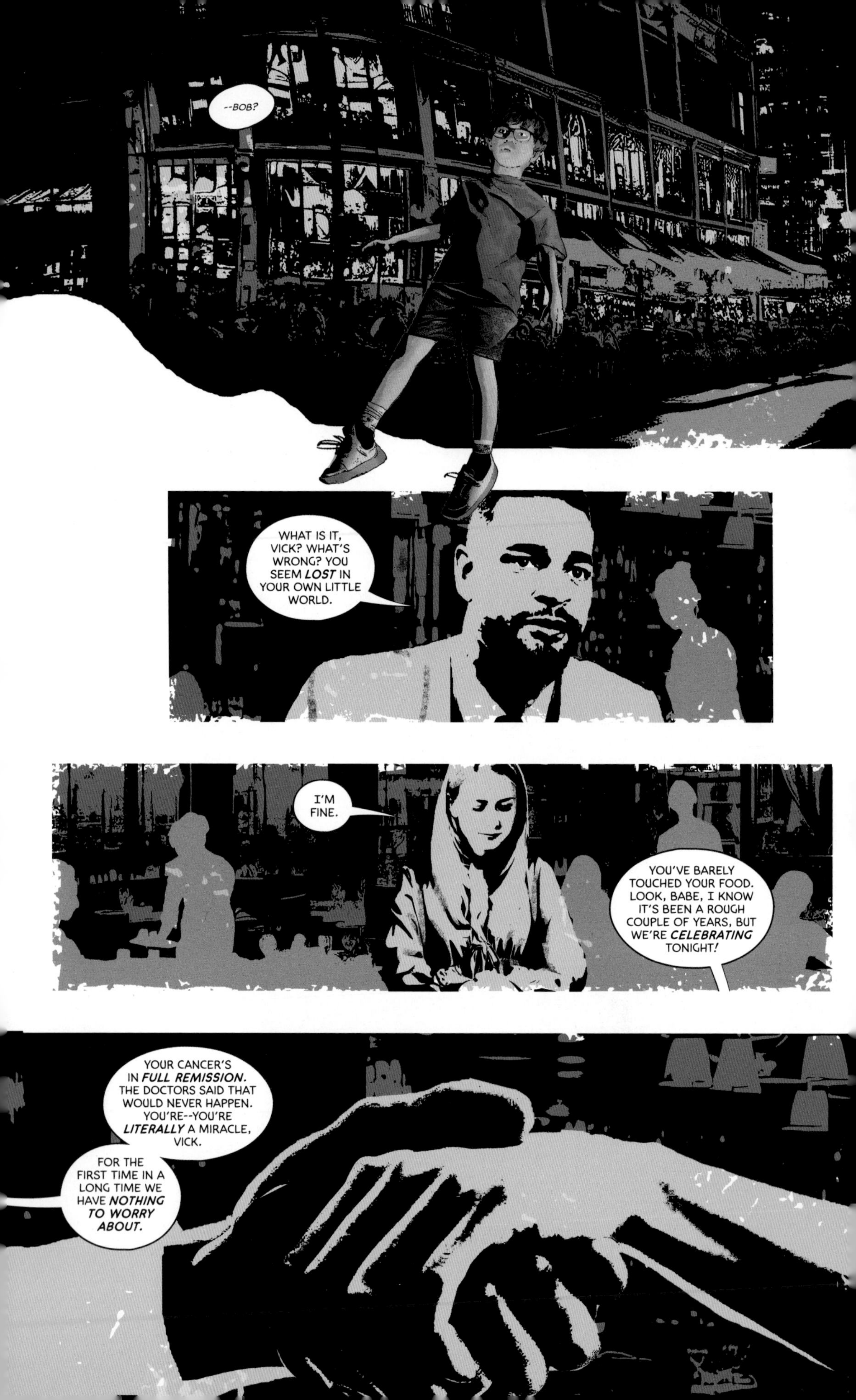
--BOB?
WHAT IS IT, VICK? WHAT'S WRONG? YOU SEEM LOST IN YOUR OWN LITTLE WORLD.
I'M FINE.
YOU'VE BARELY TOUCHED YOUR FOOD. LOOK, BABE, I KNOW IT'S BEEN A ROUGH COUPLE OF YEARS, BUT WE'RE CELEBRATING TONIGHT!
YOUR CANCER'S IN FULL REMISSION. THE DOCTORS SAID THAT WOULD NEVER HAPPEN. YOU'RE--YOU'RE LITERALLY A MIRACLE, VICK.
FOR THE FIRST TIME IN A LONG TIME WE HAVE NOTHING TO WORRY ABOUT.

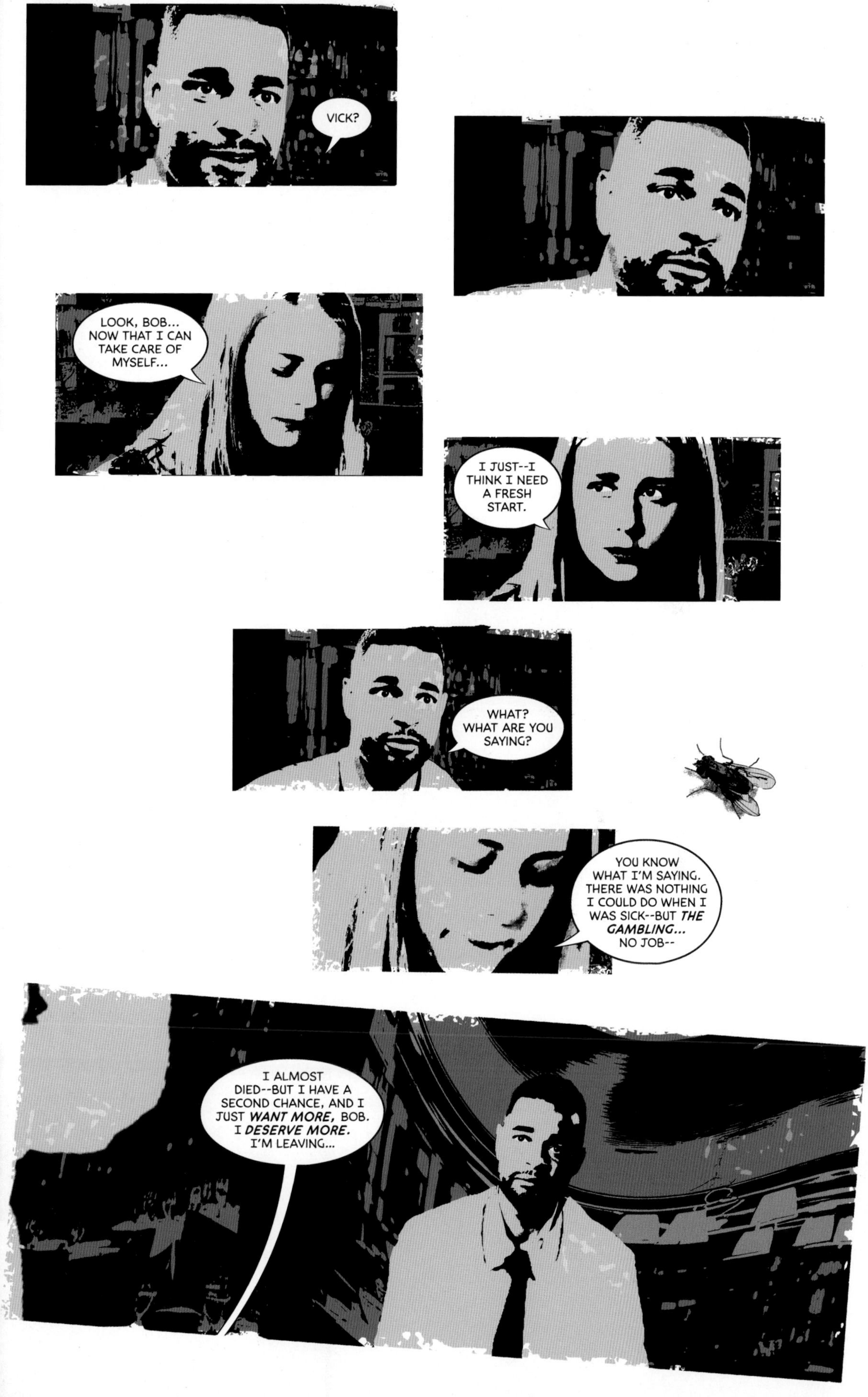
VICK?
LOOK, BOB... NOW THAT I CAN TAKE CARE OF MYSELF...
I JUST--I THINK I NEED A FRESH START.
WHAT? WHAT ARE YOU SAYING?
YOU KNOW WHAT I'M SAYING. THERE WAS NOTHING I COULD DO WHEN I WAS SICK--BUT ***THE GAMBLING...*** NO JOB--
I ALMOST DIED--BUT I HAVE A SECOND CHANCE, AND I JUST ***WANT MORE,*** BOB. I ***DESERVE MORE.*** I'M LEAVING...

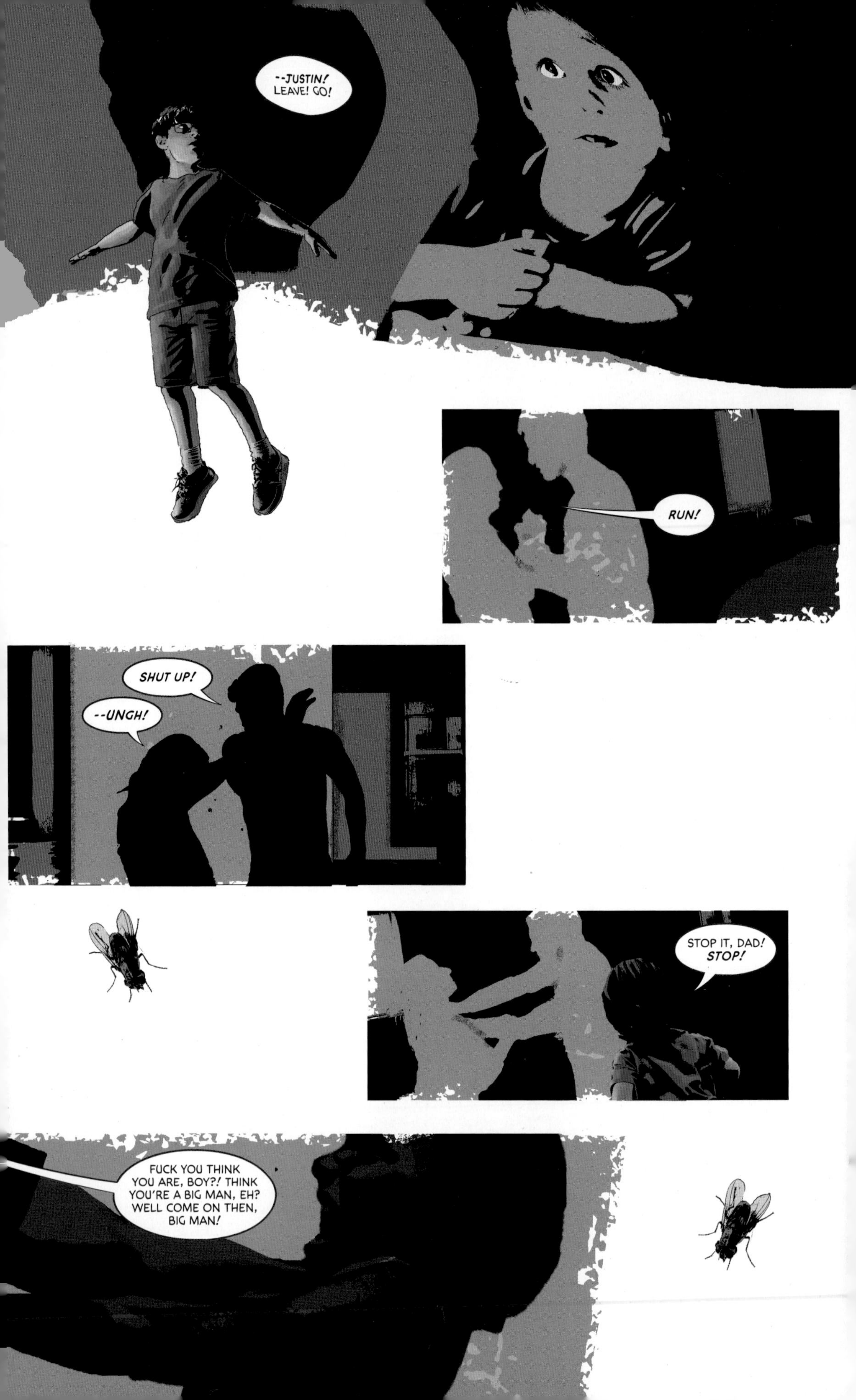
--JUSTIN! LEAVE! GO!
RUN!
SHUT UP!
--UNGH!
STOP IT, DAD! STOP!
FUCK YOU THINK YOU ARE, BOY?! THINK YOU'RE A BIG MAN, EH? WELL COME ON THEN, BIG MAN!

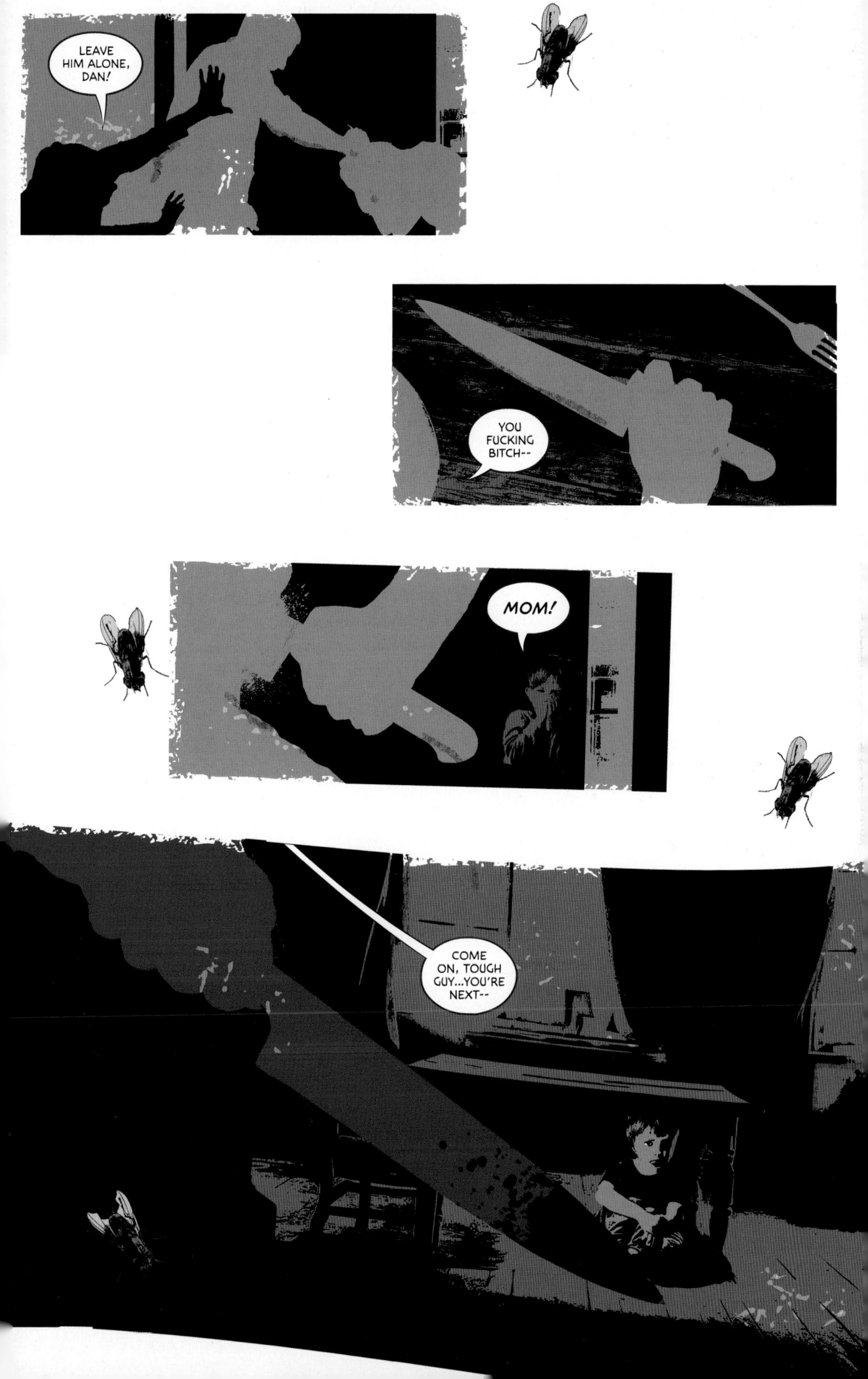
LEAVE HIM ALONE, DAN!
YOU FUCKING BITCH--
MOM!
COME ON, TOUGH GUY...YOU'RE NEXT--

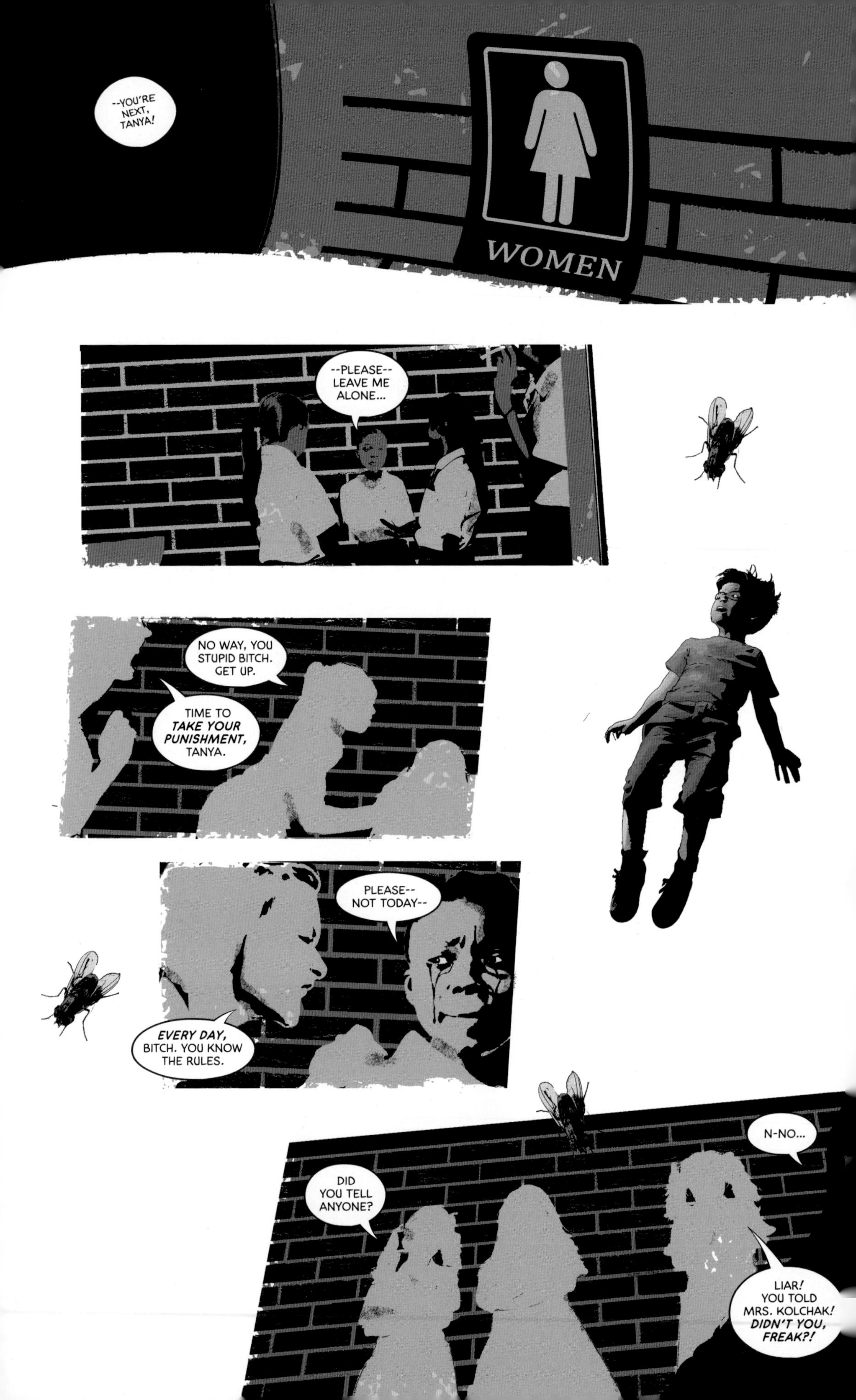
--YOU'RE NEXT, TANYA!
WOMEN
--PLEASE-- LEAVE ME ALONE...
NO WAY, YOU STUPID BITCH. GET UP.
TIME TO *TAKE YOUR PUNISHMENT,* TANYA.
PLEASE-- NOT TODAY--
EVERY DAY, BITCH. YOU KNOW THE RULES.
DID YOU TELL ANYONE?
N-NO...
LIAR! YOU TOLD MRS. KOLCHAK! *DIDN'T YOU, FREAK?!*

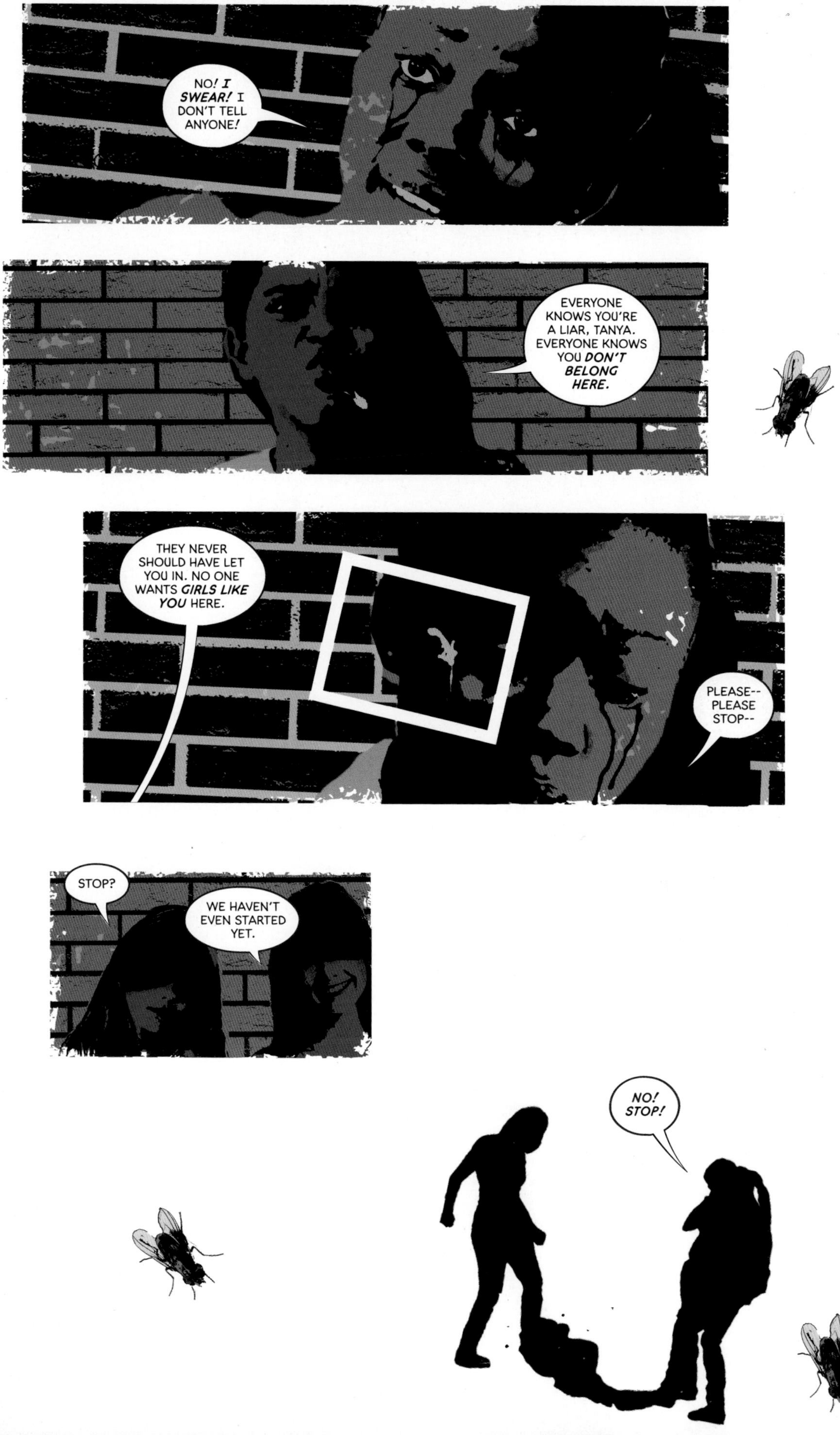
NO! I SWEAR! I DON'T TELL ANYONE!
EVERYONE KNOWS YOU'RE A LIAR, TANYA. EVERYONE KNOWS YOU DON'T BELONG HERE.
THEY NEVER SHOULD HAVE LET YOU IN. NO ONE WANTS GIRLS LIKE YOU HERE.
PLEASE-- PLEASE STOP--
STOP?
WE HAVEN'T EVEN STARTED YET.
NO! STOP!

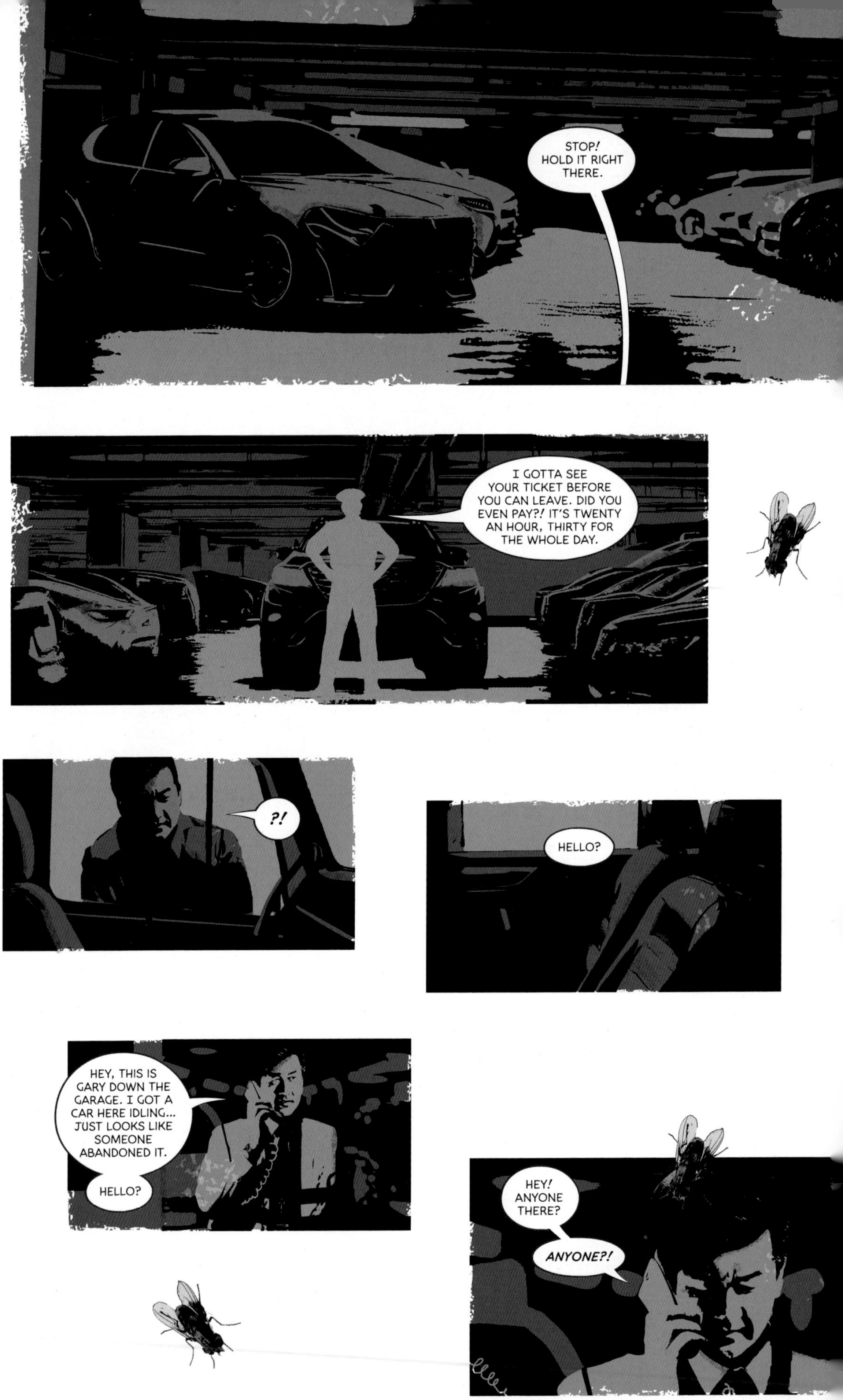

STOP! HOLD IT RIGHT THERE.
I GOTTA SEE YOUR TICKET BEFORE YOU CAN LEAVE. DID YOU EVEN PAY?! IT'S TWENTY AN HOUR, THIRTY FOR THE WHOLE DAY.
?!
HELLO?
HEY, THIS IS GARY DOWN THE GARAGE. I GOT A CAR HERE IDLING... JUST LOOKS LIKE SOMEONE ABANDONED IT.
HELLO?
HEY! ANYONE THERE?
ANYONE?!

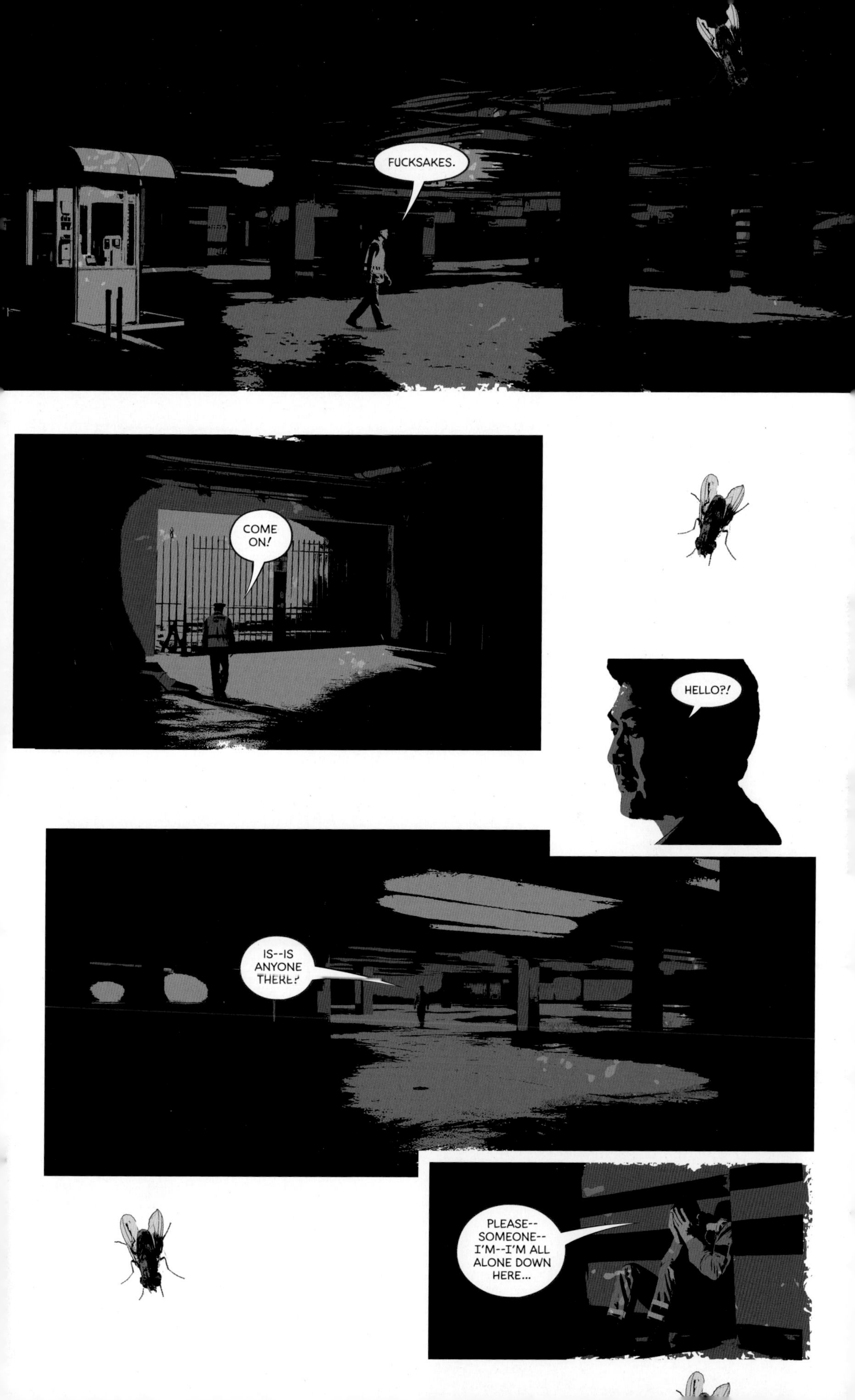
FUCKSAKES.
COME ON!
HELLO?!
IS--IS ANYONE THERE?
PLEASE-- SOMEONE-- I'M--I'M ALL ALONE DOWN HERE...

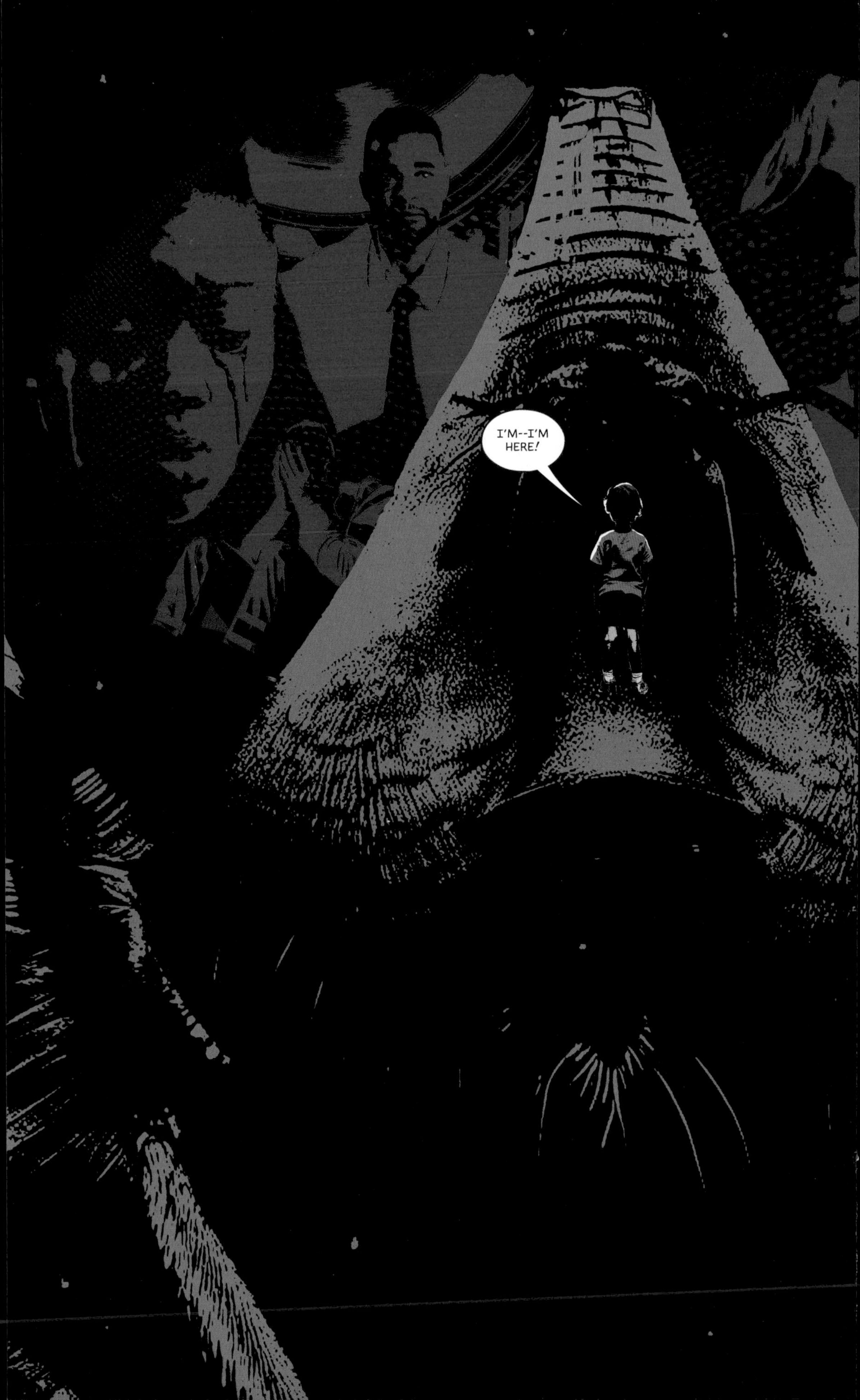
I'M--I'M HERE!

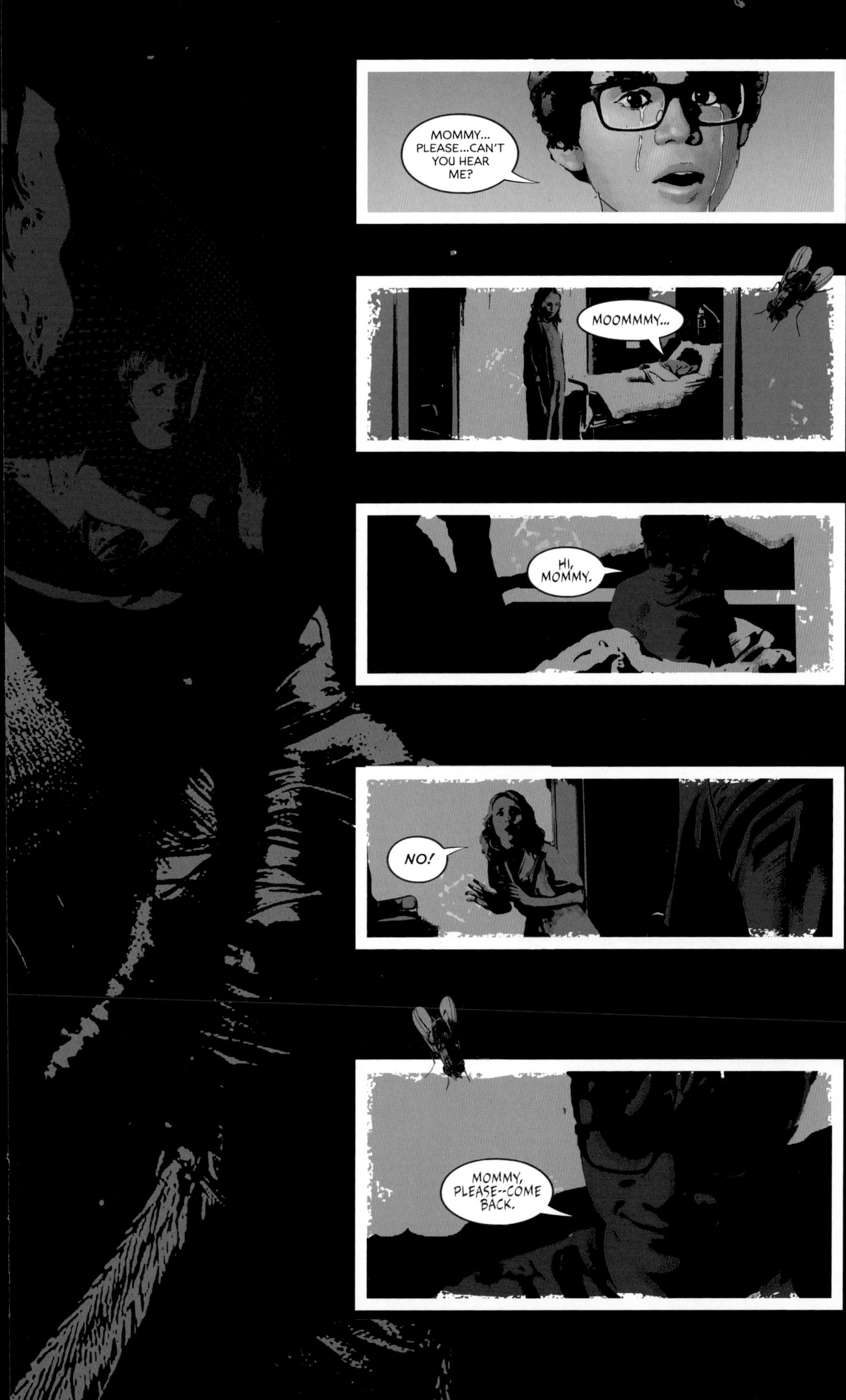
MOMMY... PLEASE...CAN'T YOU HEAR ME?
MOOMMMY...
HI, MOMMY.
NO!
MOMMY, PLEASE--COME BACK.

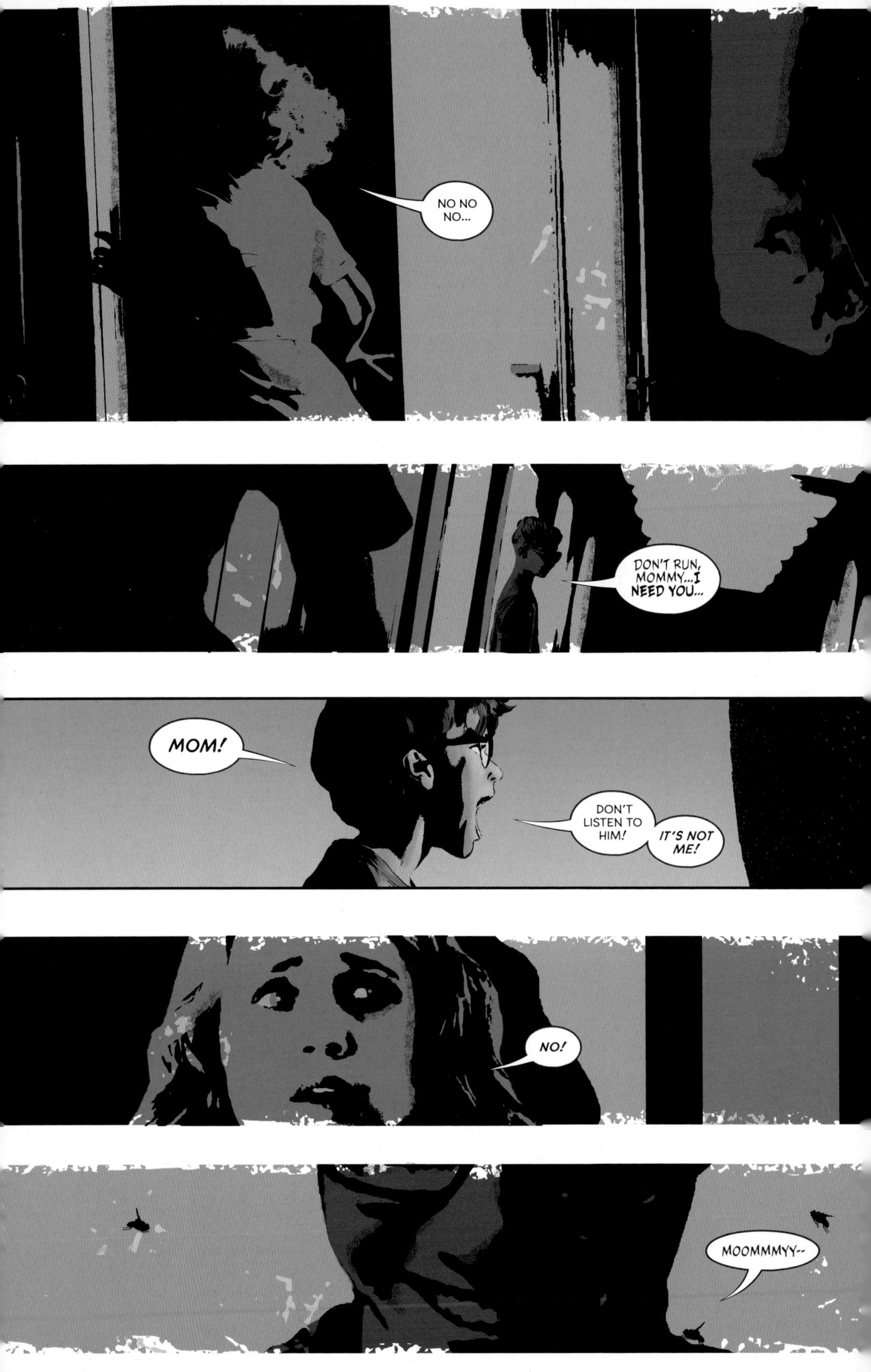
NO NO NO...
DON'T RUN, MOMMY...I NEED YOU...
MOM!
DON'T LISTEN TO HIM!
IT'S NOT ME!
NO!
MOOMMMYY--

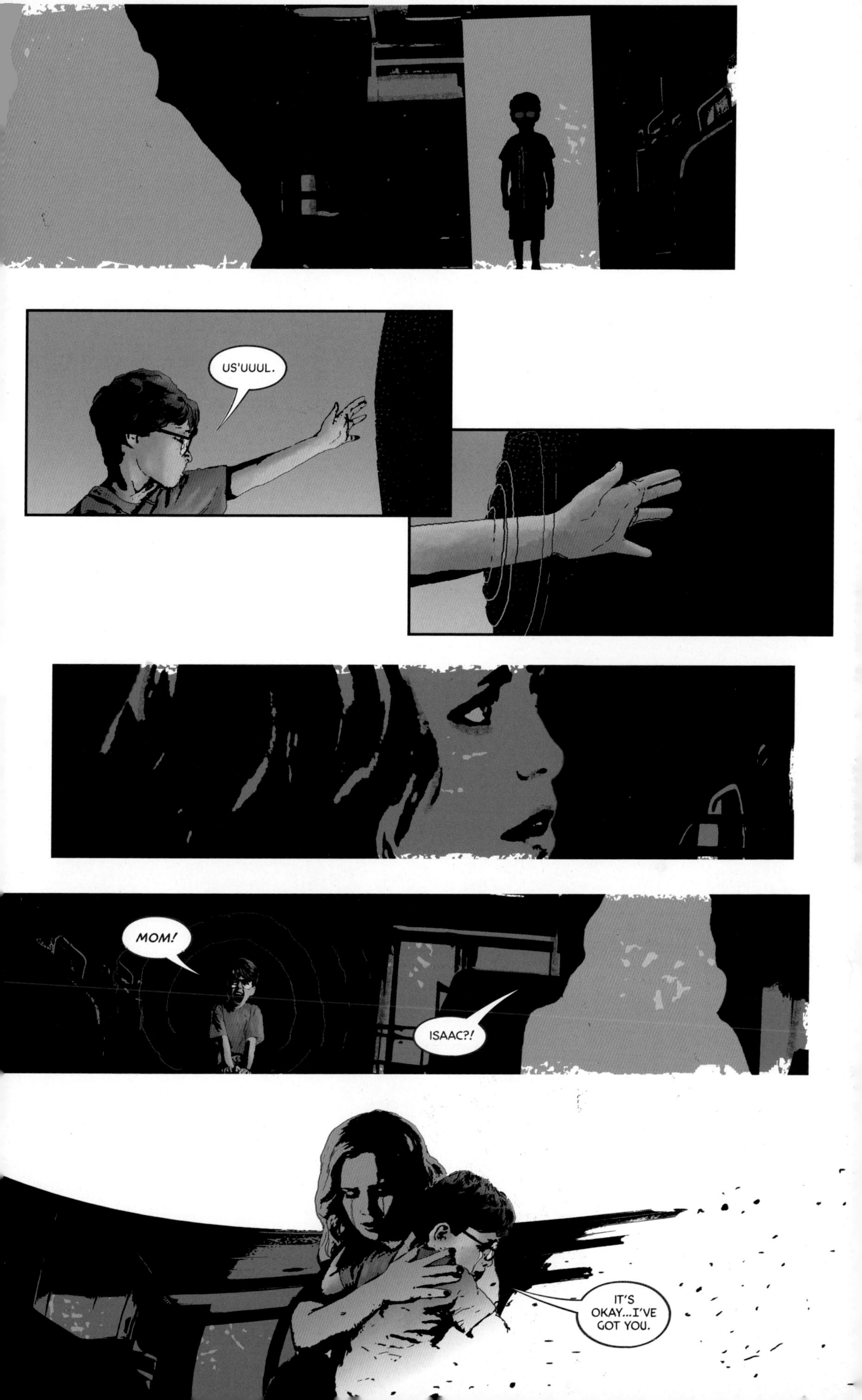
US'UUUL.
MOM!
ISAAC?!
IT'S OKAY...I'VE GOT YOU.

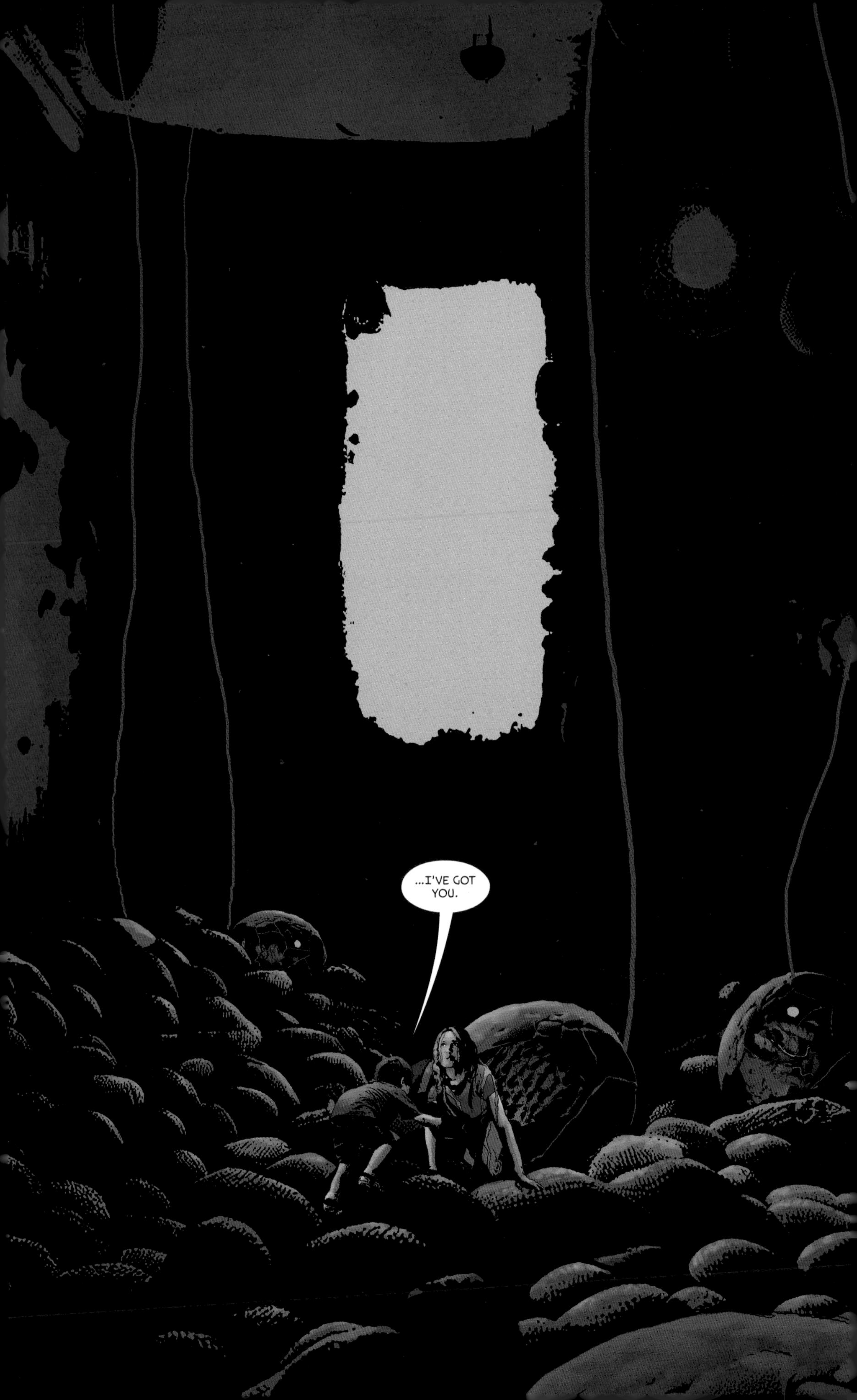
...I'VE GOT YOU.

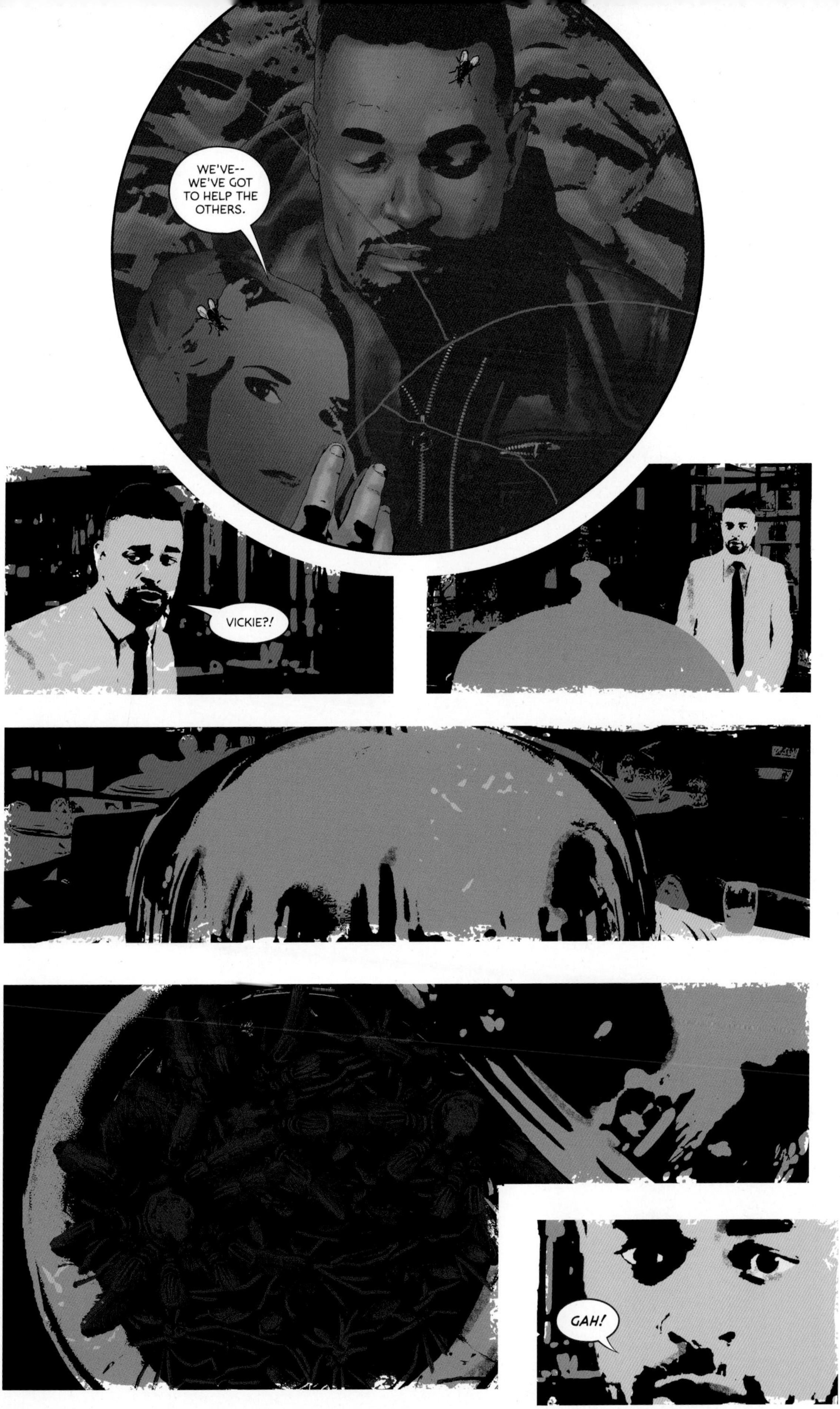
WE'VE--
WE'VE GOT TO HELP THE OTHERS.
VICKIE?!
GAH!

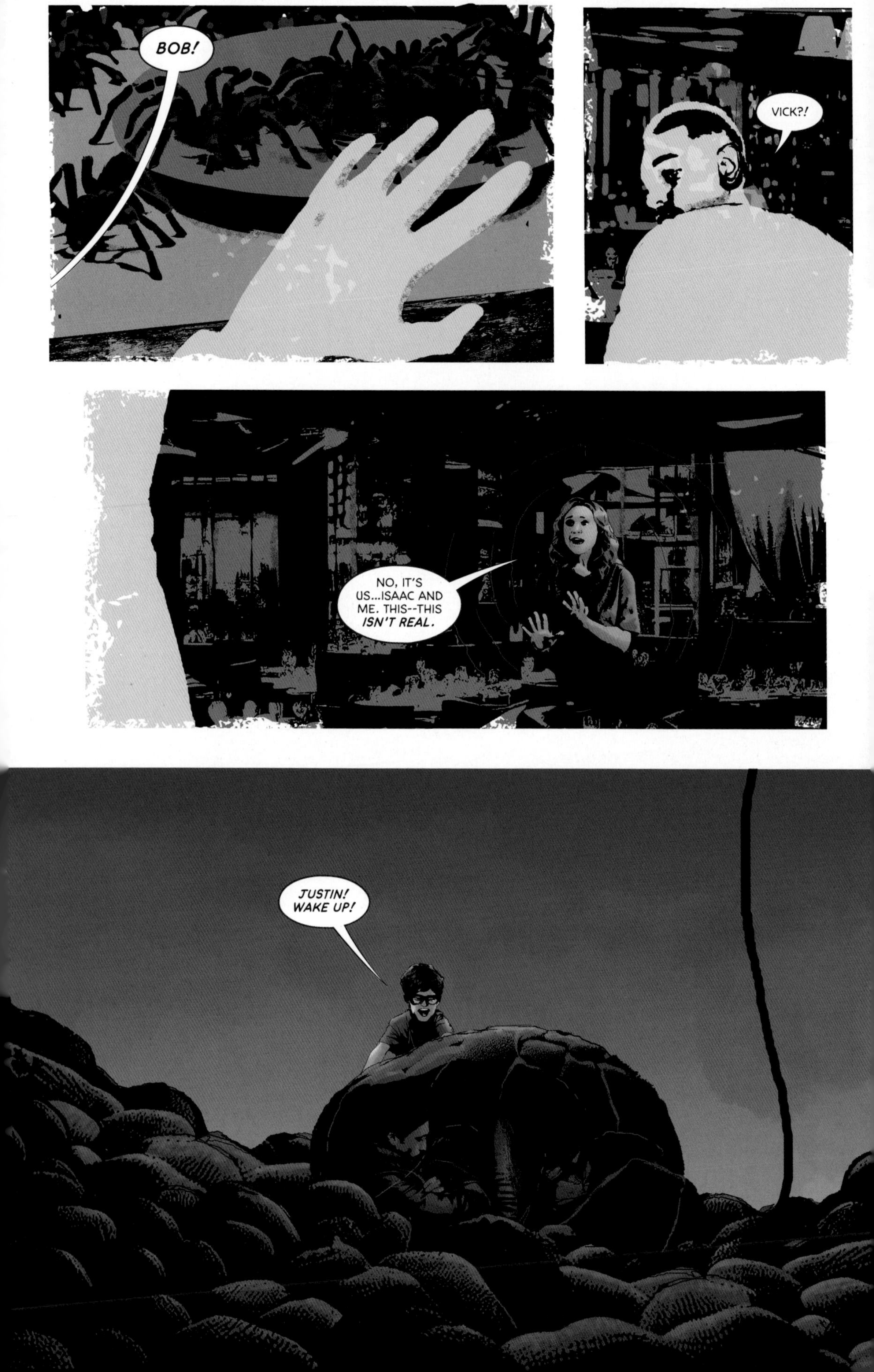
BOB!
VICK?!
NO, IT'S US...ISAAC AND ME. THIS--THIS ISN'T REAL.
JUSTIN! WAKE UP!

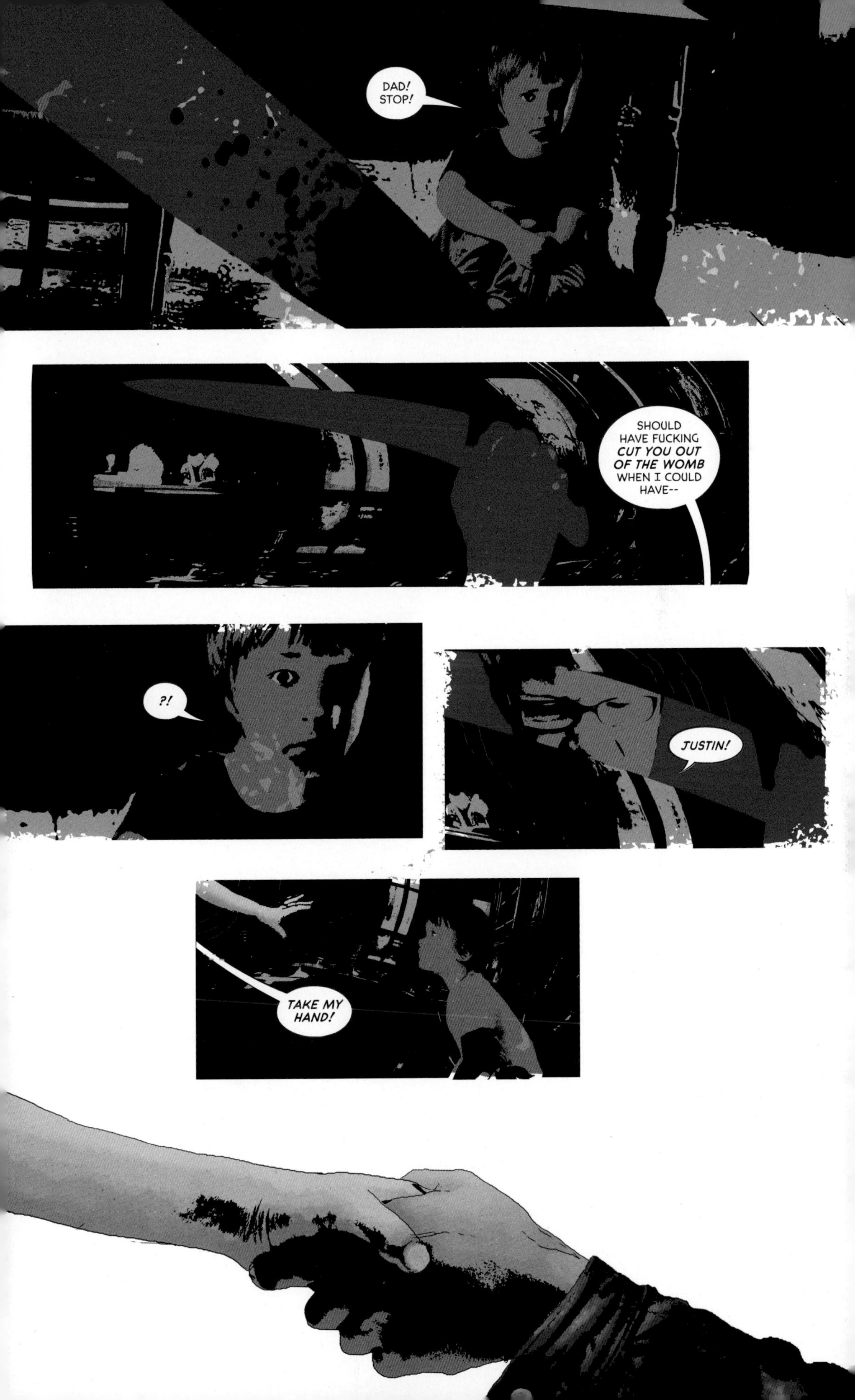
DAD! STOP!
SHOULD HAVE FUCKING CUT YOU OUT OF THE WOMB WHEN I COULD HAVE--
?!
JUSTIN!
TAKE MY HAND!

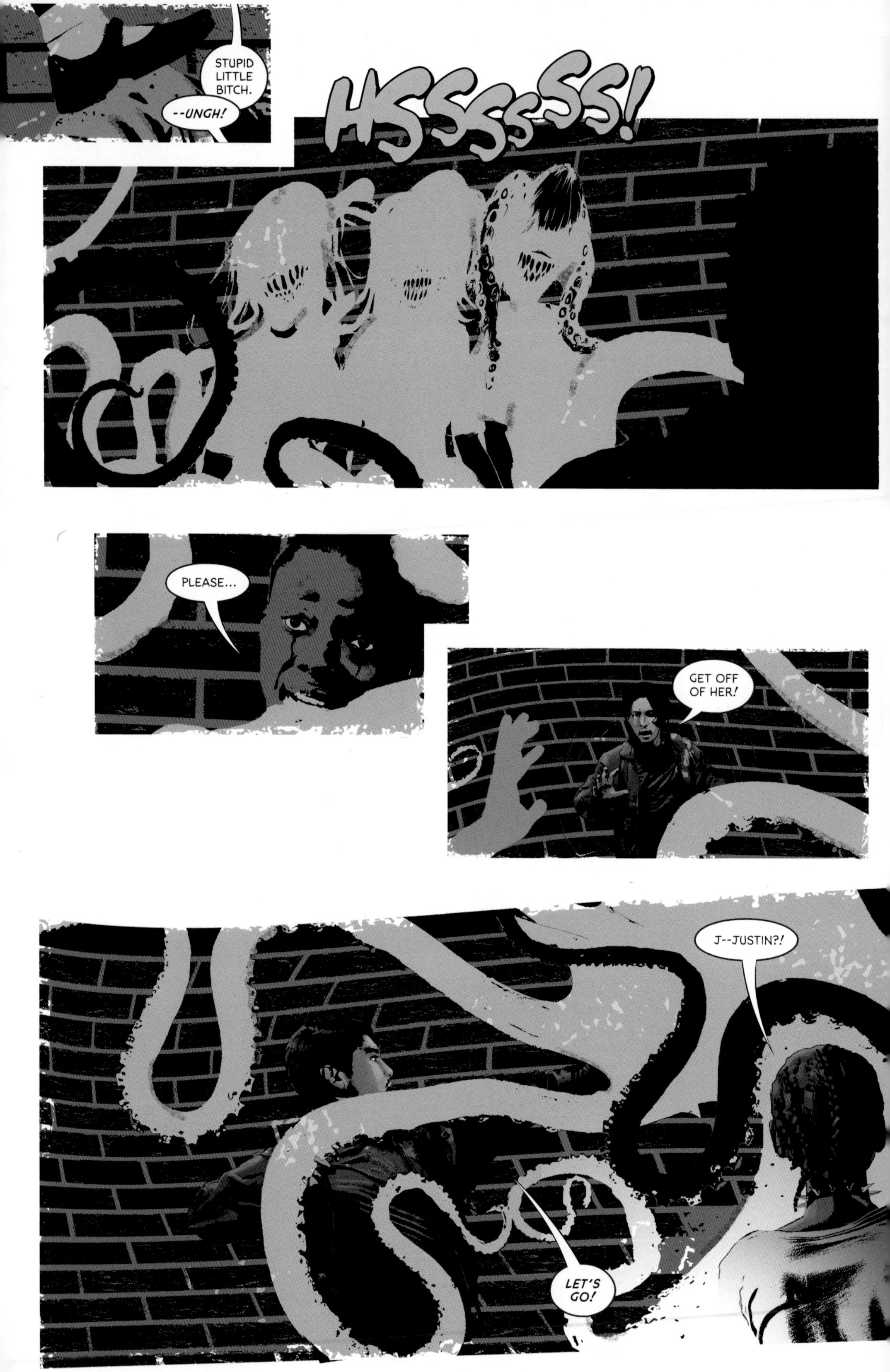
STUPID LITTLE BITCH.
--UNGH!
HSSSSSS!
PLEASE...
GET OFF OF HER!
J--JUSTIN?!
LET'S GO!

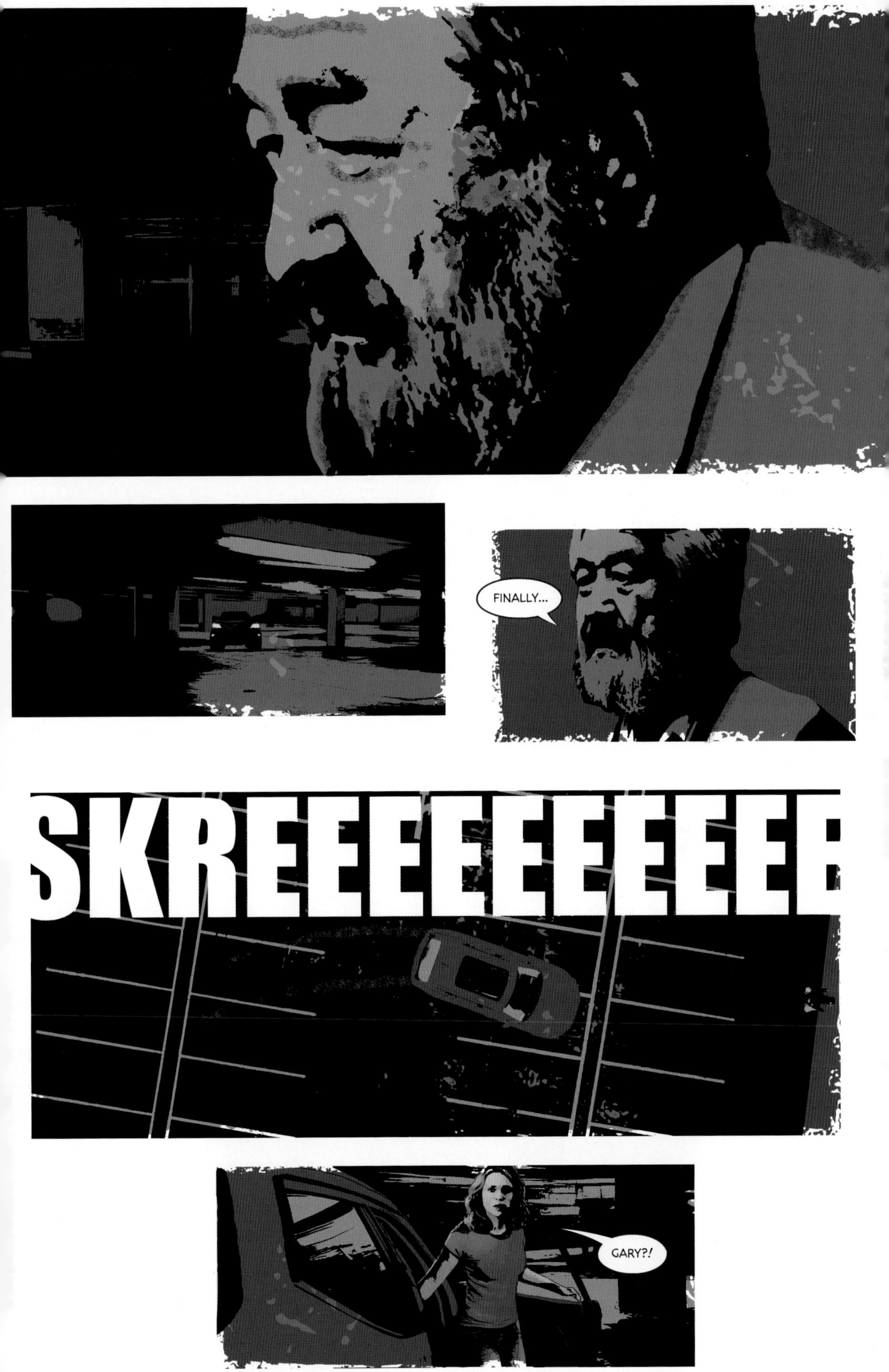
FINALLY...
SKREEEEEEEEEEE
GARY?!

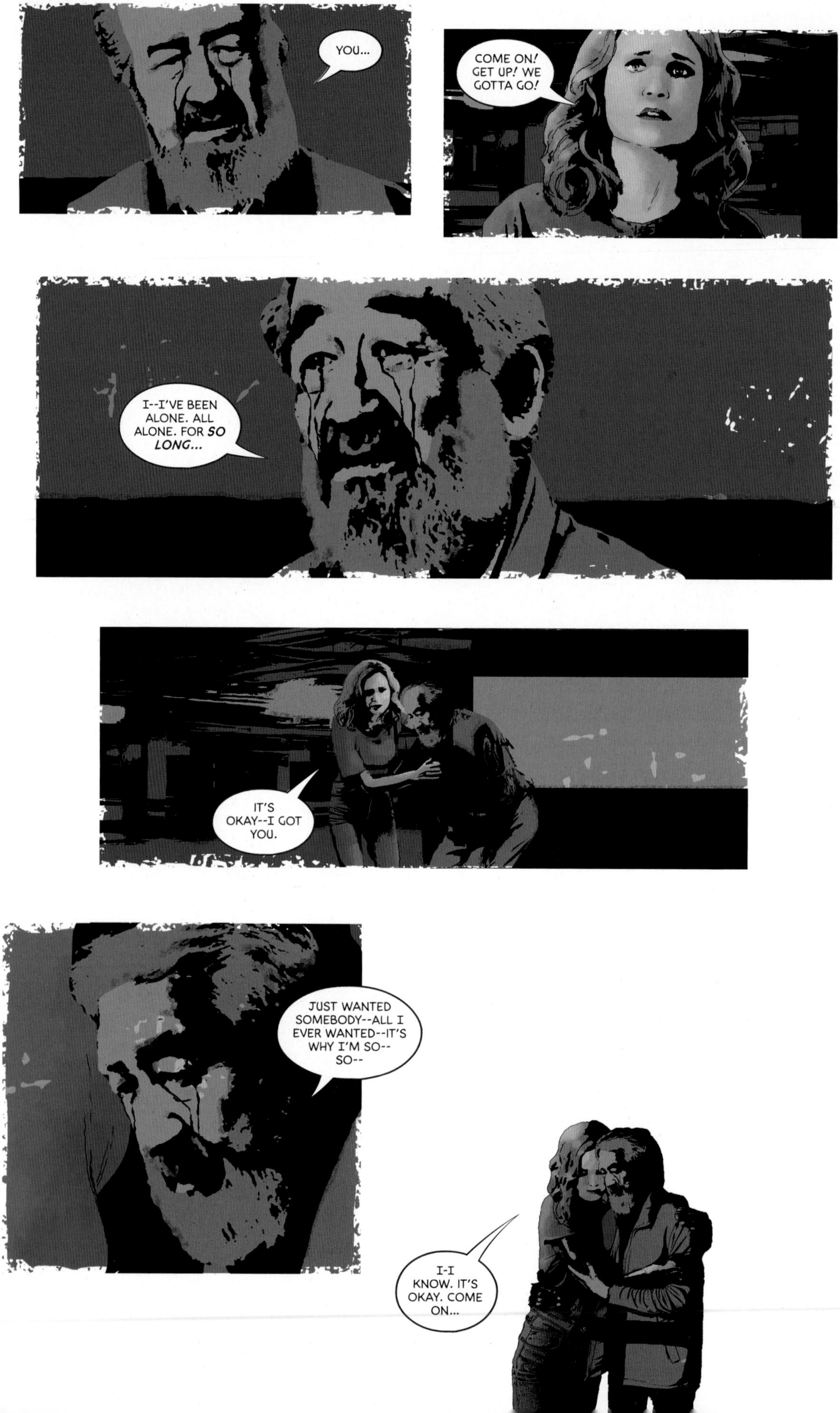
YOU...
COME ON! GET UP! WE GOTTA GO!
I--I'VE BEEN ALONE. ALL ALONE. FOR SO LONG...
IT'S OKAY--I GOT YOU.
JUST WANTED SOMEBODY--ALL I EVER WANTED--IT'S WHY I'M SO-- SO--
I-I KNOW. IT'S OKAY. COME ON...

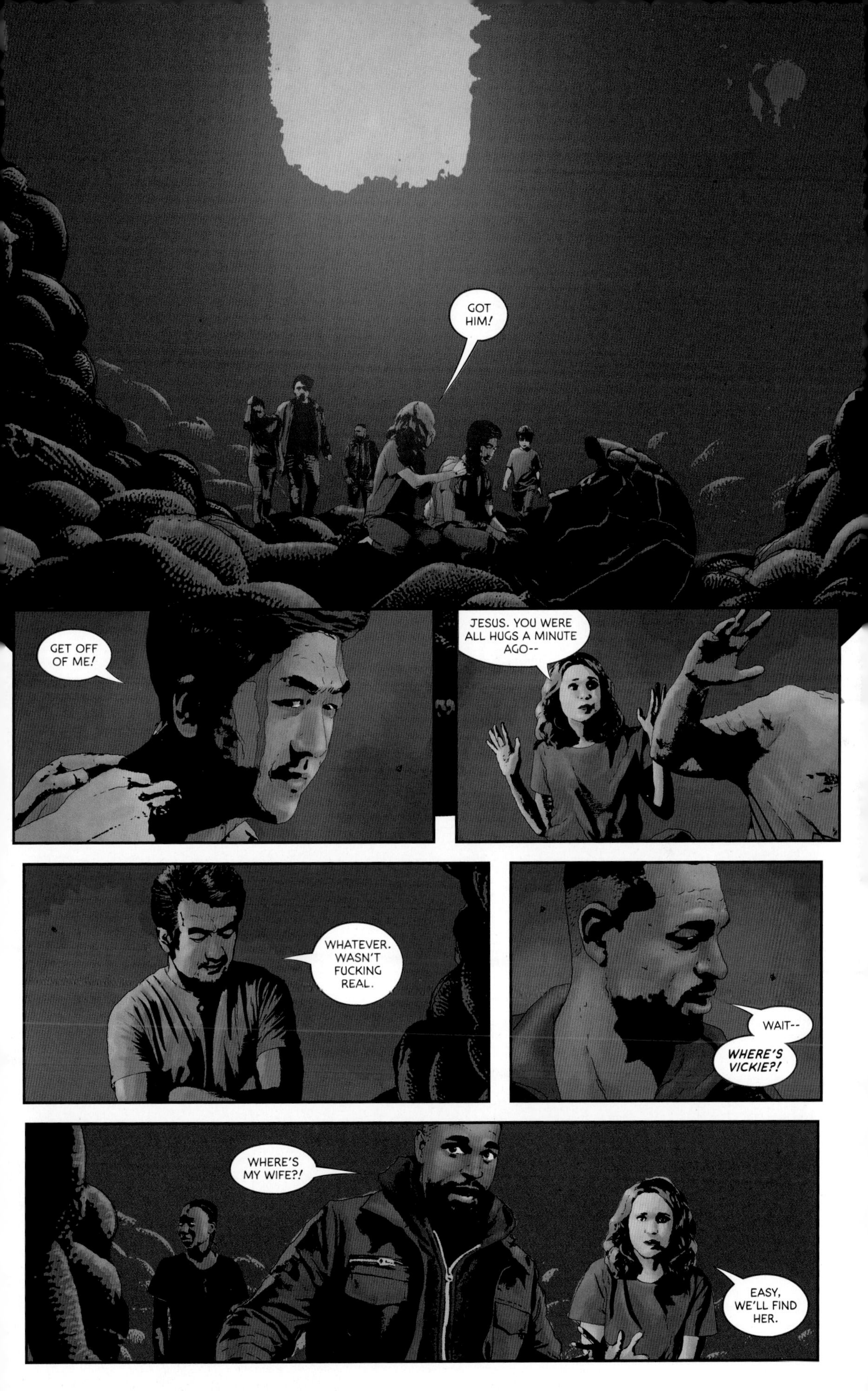
GOT HIM!
GET OFF OF ME!
JESUS. YOU WERE ALL HUGS A MINUTE AGO--
WHATEVER. WASN'T FUCKING REAL.
WAIT--
WHERE'S VICKIE?!
WHERE'S MY WIFE?!
EASY, WE'LL FIND HER.

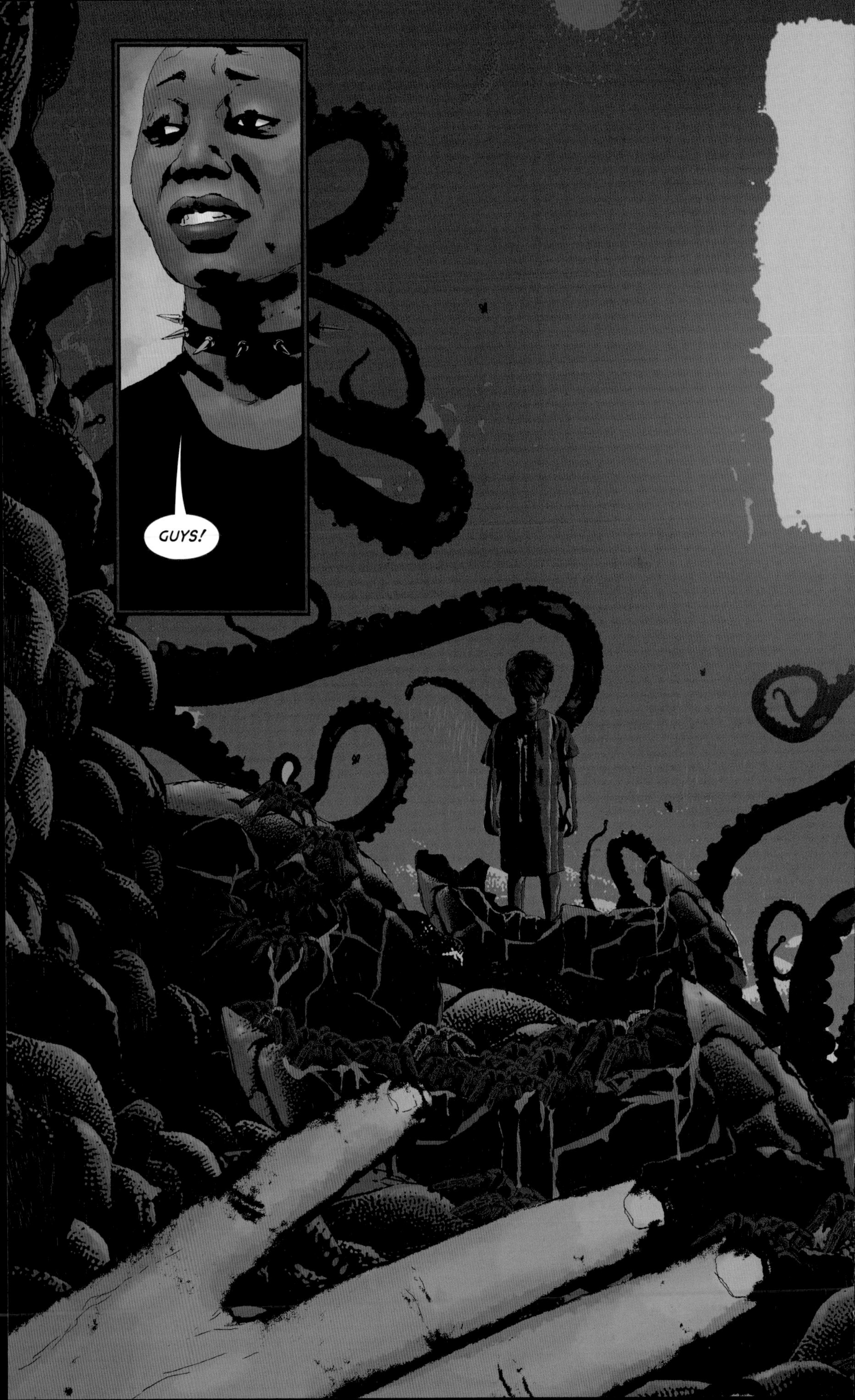
GUYS!

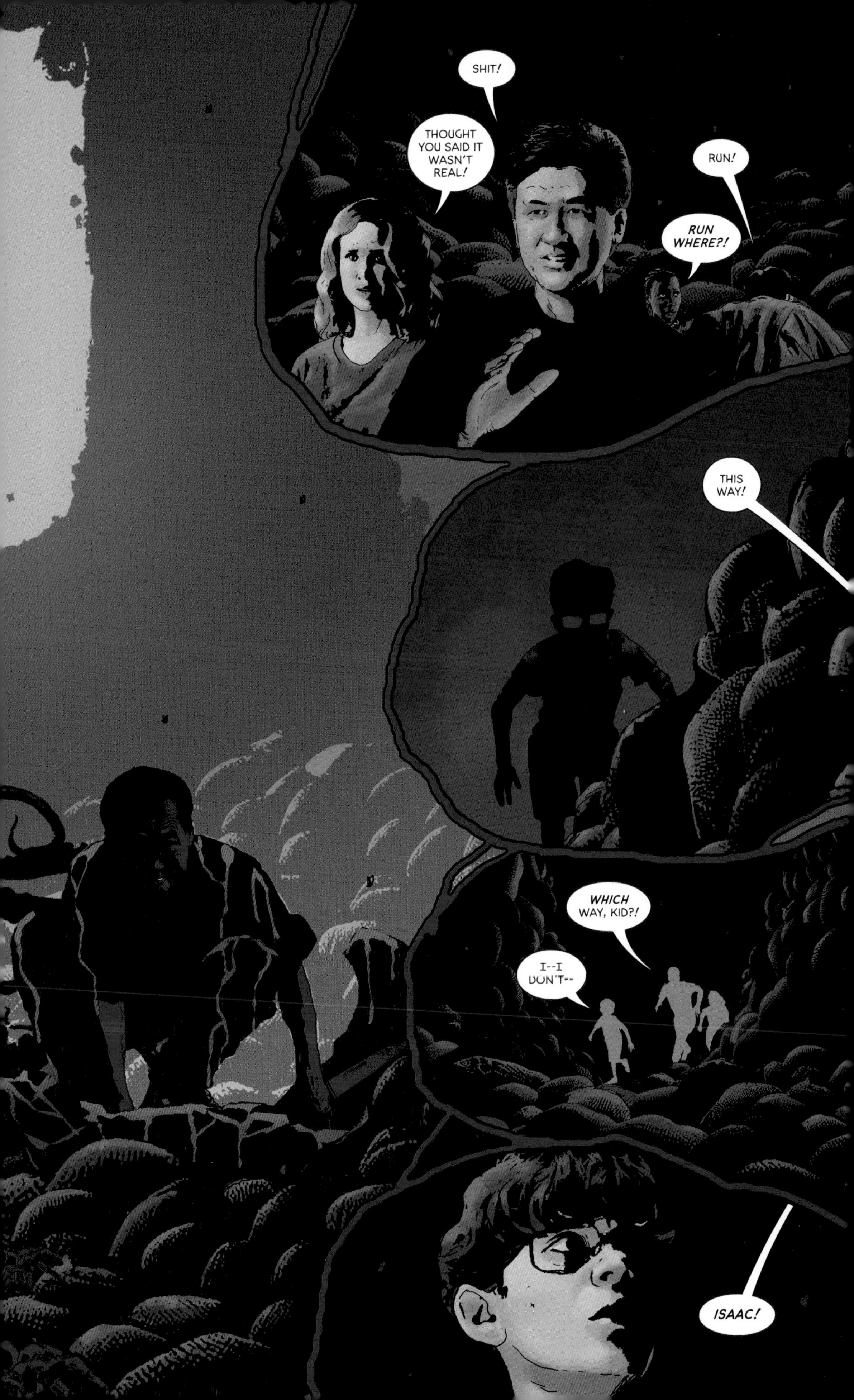
SHIT!
THOUGHT YOU SAID IT WASN'T REAL!
RUN!
RUN WHERE?!
THIS WAY!
WHICH WAY, KID?!
I--I DON'T--
ISAAC!

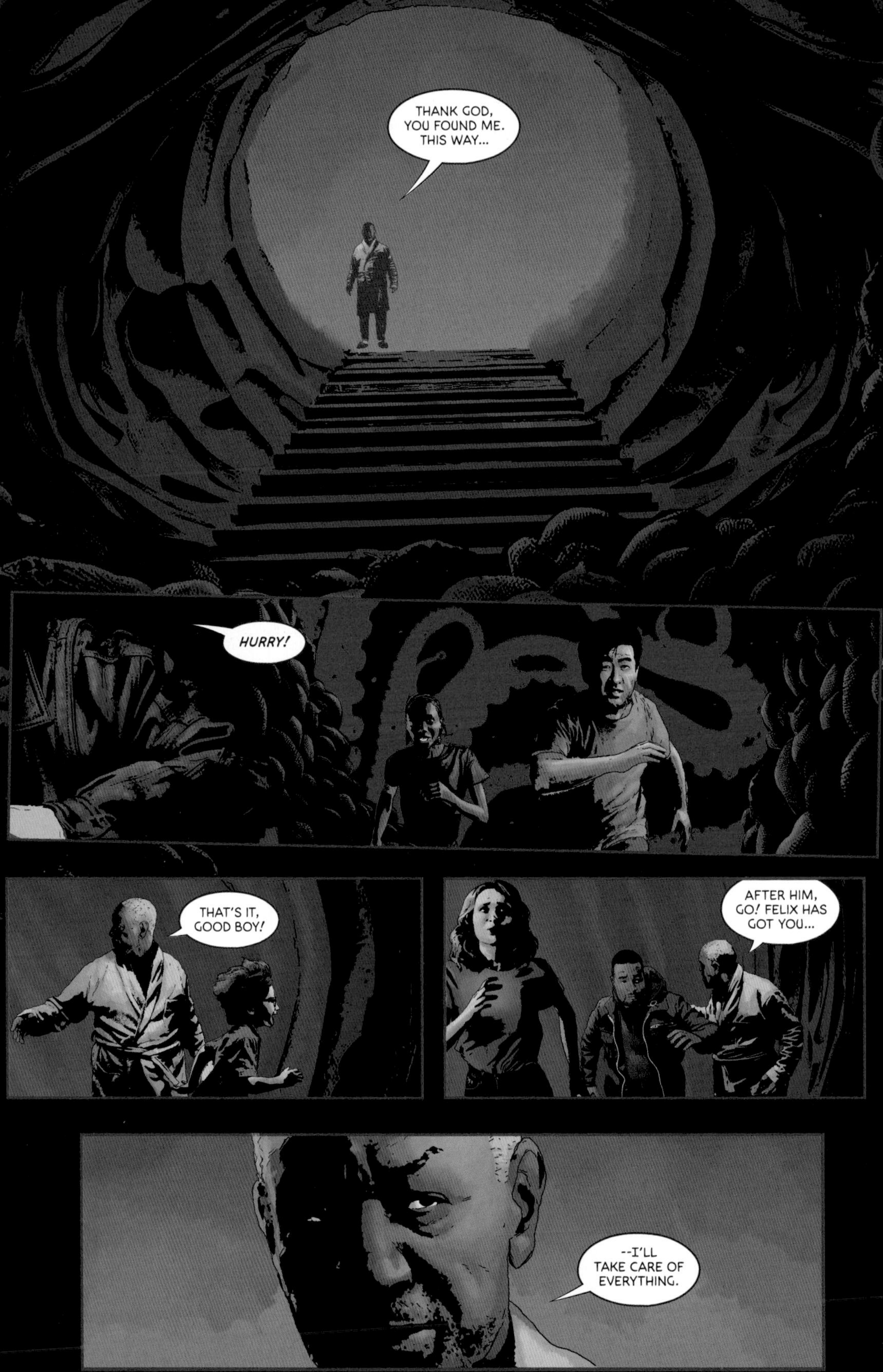
THANK GOD, YOU FOUND ME. THIS WAY...
HURRY!
THAT'S IT, GOOD BOY!
AFTER HIM, GO! FELIX HAS GOT YOU...
--I'LL TAKE CARE OF EVERYTHING.

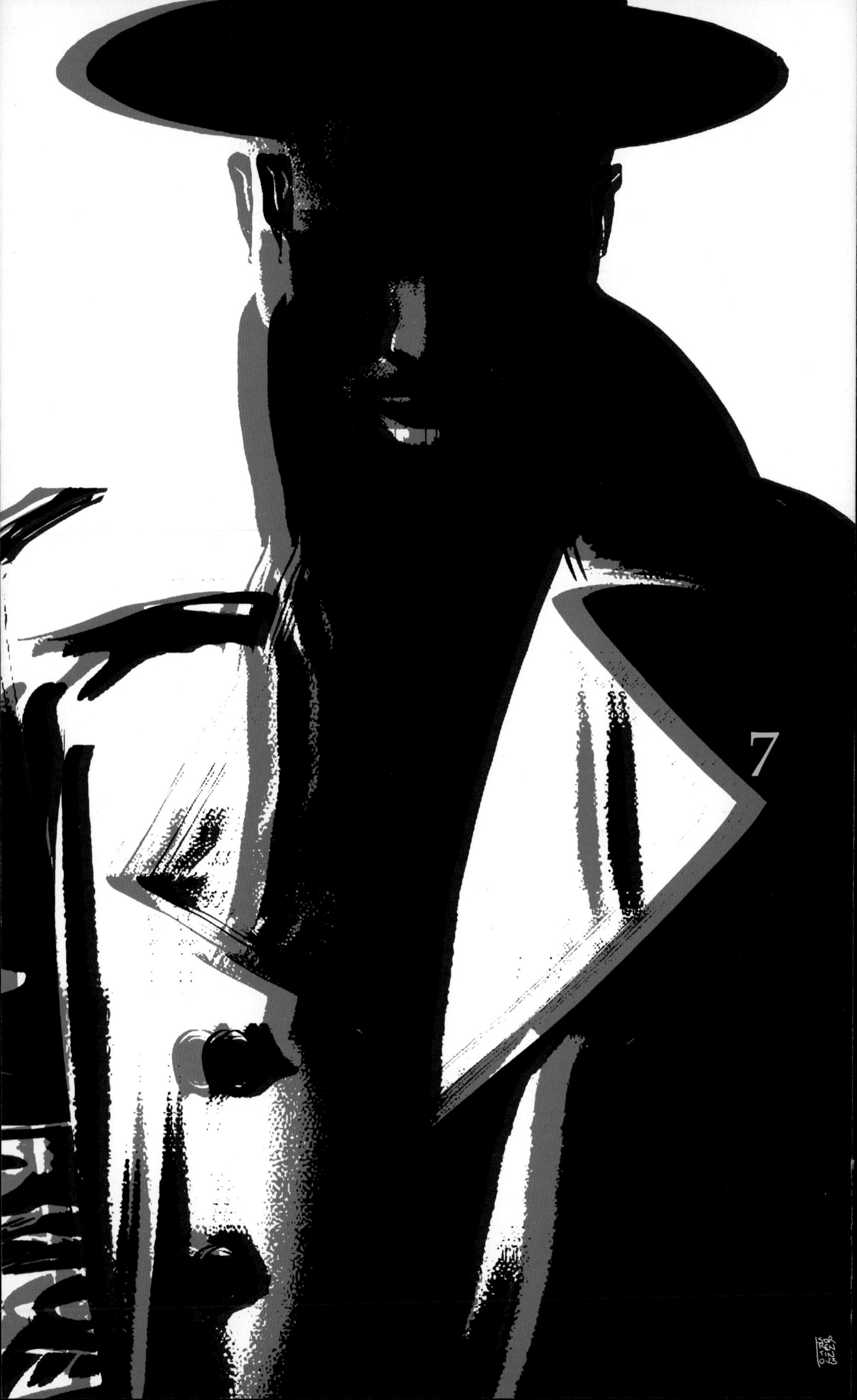
7

Som... s taken thei... ...ve of scary mov... one step too far.
...ving this mystery is going to be murder.

1996

June 21, 1996. Woke up with the shittiest hangover. I need to slow down. Could barely get out of bed this morning. Then again, maybe I shouldn't have.

City is going to hell. Fucking disgusting. Maybe I should leave. Move to the country somewhere. Maybe near a lake or something.

But what the fuck would I do in the country? I guess those are my options, live here surrounded by shit or live alone but be lonely and bored out of my skull.

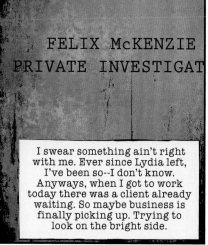

FELIX McKENZIE
PRIVATE INVESTIGAT...

I swear something ain't right with me. Ever since Lydia left, I've been so--I don't know. Anyways, when I got to work today there was a client already waiting. So maybe business is finally picking up. Trying to look on the bright side.

One look at this poor bastard and I already knew, but I went through the motions anyway, playing my role...

WHAT CAN I DO FOR YOU, MR.--?

HADLEY. *VINCENT HADLEY.* IT'S--IT'S MY WIFE.

Yep. Knew it. Fuck, I hate this job.

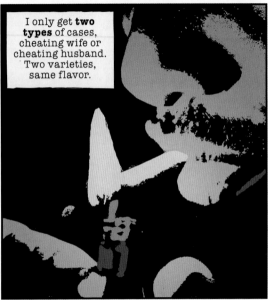

I only get **two types** of cases, cheating wife or cheating husband. Two varieties, same flavor.

Hadley's wife Terri had been coming home late a couple nights a month.

She works at an accounting firm downtown and they live out in the suburbs.

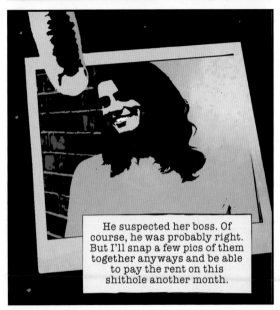

He suspected her boss. Of course, he was probably right. But I'll snap a few pics of them together anyways and be able to pay the rent on this shithole another month.

I don't know what I expected when I left the force. Something **more exciting,** I guess...

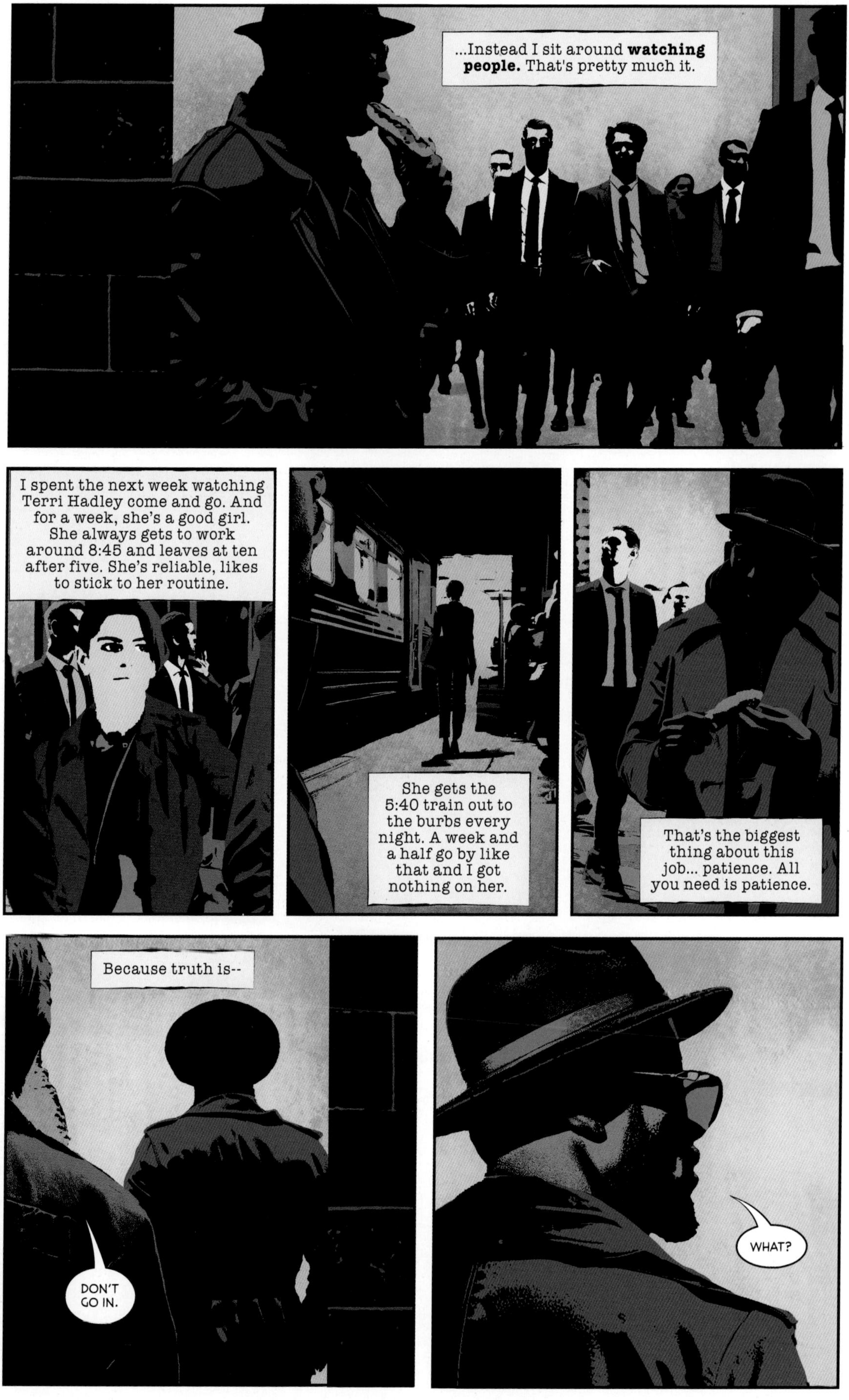
...Instead I sit around **watching people.** That's pretty much it.
I spent the next week watching Terri Hadley come and go. And for a week, she's a good girl. She always gets to work around 8:45 and leaves at ten after five. She's reliable, likes to stick to her routine.
She gets the 5:40 train out to the burbs every night. A week and a half go by like that and I got nothing on her.
That's the biggest thing about this job... patience. All you need is patience.
Because truth is--
DON'T GO IN.
WHAT?

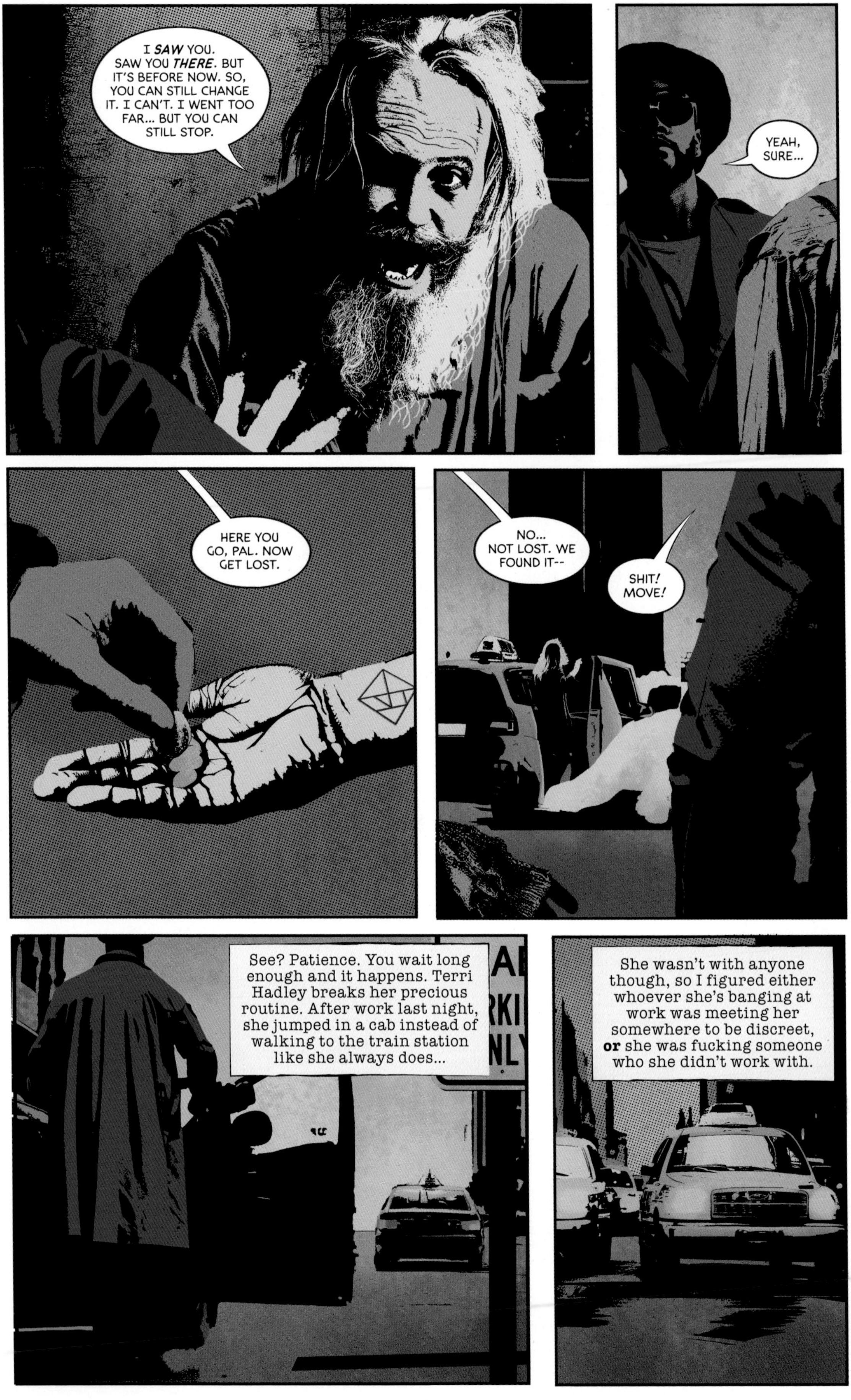
I SAW YOU. SAW YOU THERE. BUT IT'S BEFORE NOW. SO, YOU CAN STILL CHANGE IT. I CAN'T. I WENT TOO FAR... BUT YOU CAN STILL STOP.
YEAH, SURE...
HERE YOU GO, PAL. NOW GET LOST.
NO... NOT LOST. WE FOUND IT--
SHIT! MOVE!
See? Patience. You wait long enough and it happens. Terri Hadley breaks her precious routine. After work last night, she jumped in a cab instead of walking to the train station like she always does...
She wasn't with anyone though, so I figured either whoever she's banging at work was meeting her somewhere to be discreet, or she was fucking someone who she didn't work with.

Either way, I thought I was onto her. I trailed her to Parkdale where she ditched the cab and walked three blocks...

This case--reminds me of Lydia. But then again, they **all do.**

When I **caught her,** it was in a neighborhood like this.

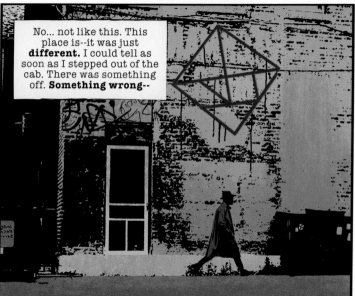

No... not like this. This place is--it was just **different.** I could tell as soon as I stepped out of the cab. There was something off. **Something wrong--**

I don't usually go in for superstitions or any of that bullshit. But I swear... something was weird here.

I followed her three blocks and then I **found it.**

I found where she was going...

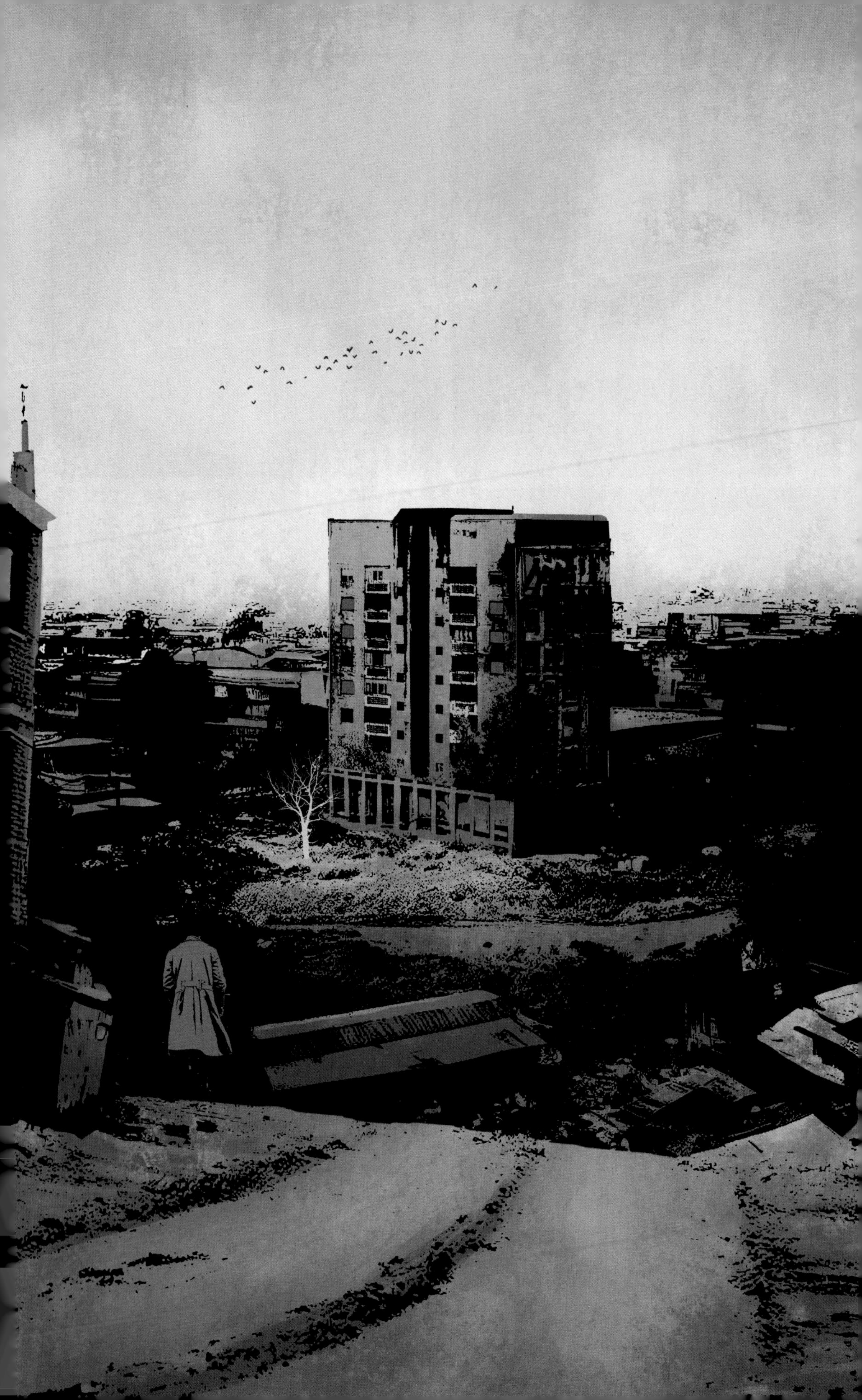

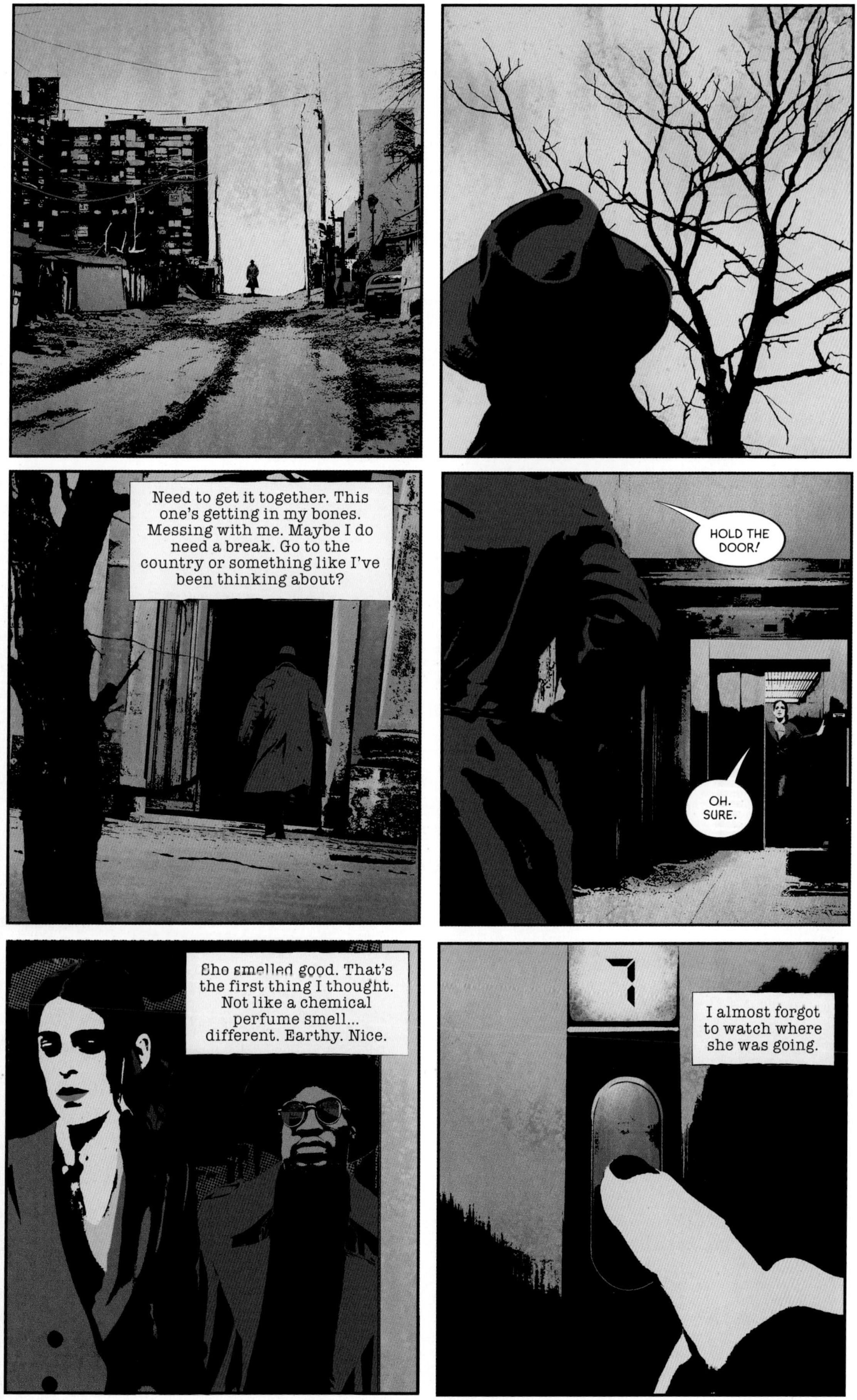
Need to get it together. This one's getting in my bones. Messing with me. Maybe I do need a break. Go to the country or something like I've been thinking about?
HOLD THE DOOR!
OH. SURE.
She smelled good. That's the first thing I thought. Not like a chemical perfume smell... different. Earthy. Nice.
7
I almost forgot to watch where she was going.

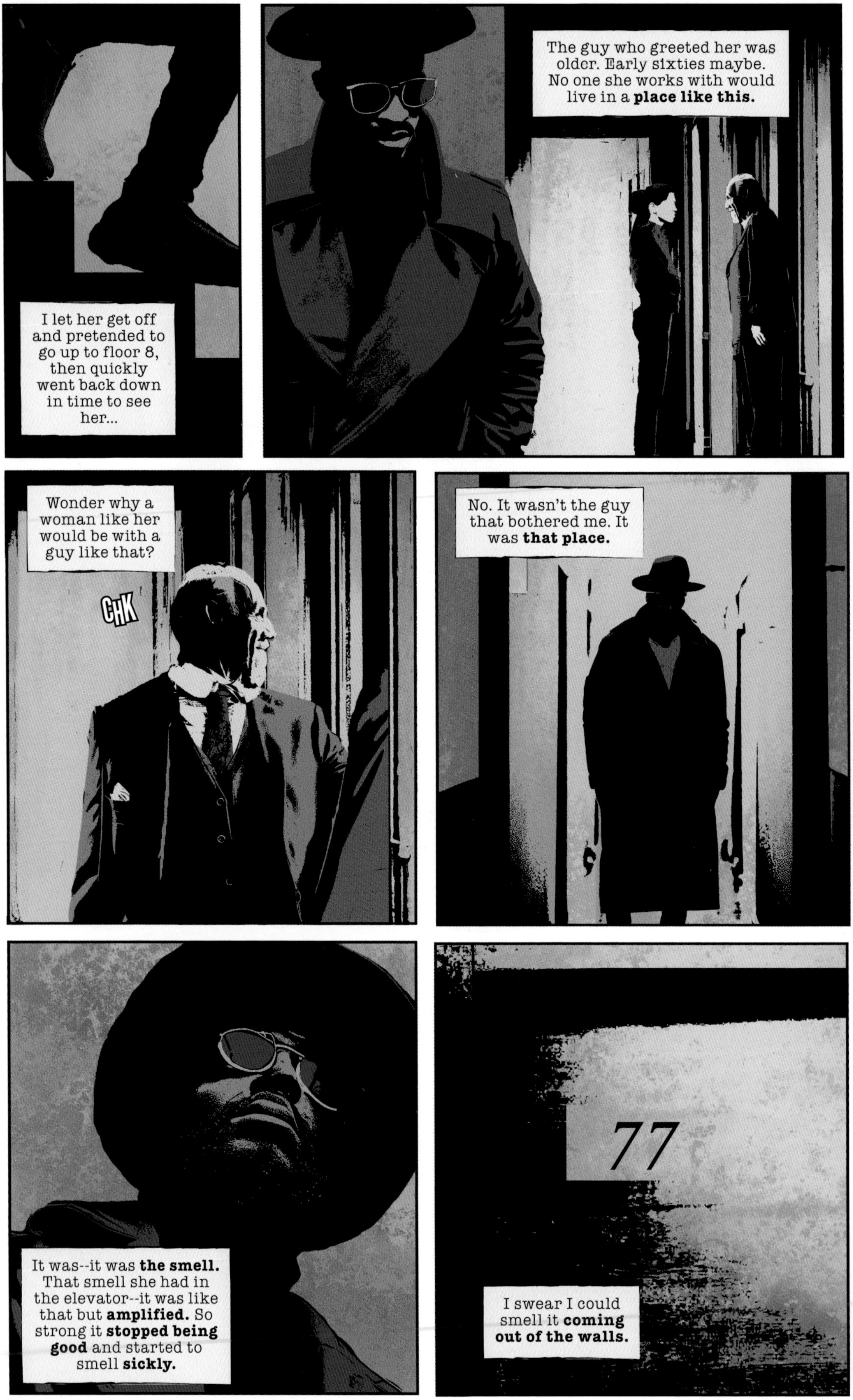
I let her get off and pretended to go up to floor 8, then quickly went back down in time to see her...
The guy who greeted her was older. Early sixties maybe. No one she works with would live in a **place like this.**
Wonder why a woman like her would be with a guy like that?
CHK
No. It wasn't the guy that bothered me. It was **that place.**
It was--it was **the smell.** That smell she had in the elevator--it was like that but **amplified.** So strong it **stopped being good** and started to smell **sickly.**
77
I swear I could smell it **coming out of the walls.**

Then things got weirder. **Two more** people went into the apartment about ten minutes after Terri Hadley.

Then, twenty minutes later, **another guy** showed up and went in. What the fuck is **going on** in there?!

Two more people went in before the night was over. Seven in all.

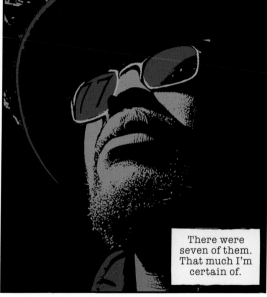

There were seven of them. That much I'm certain of.

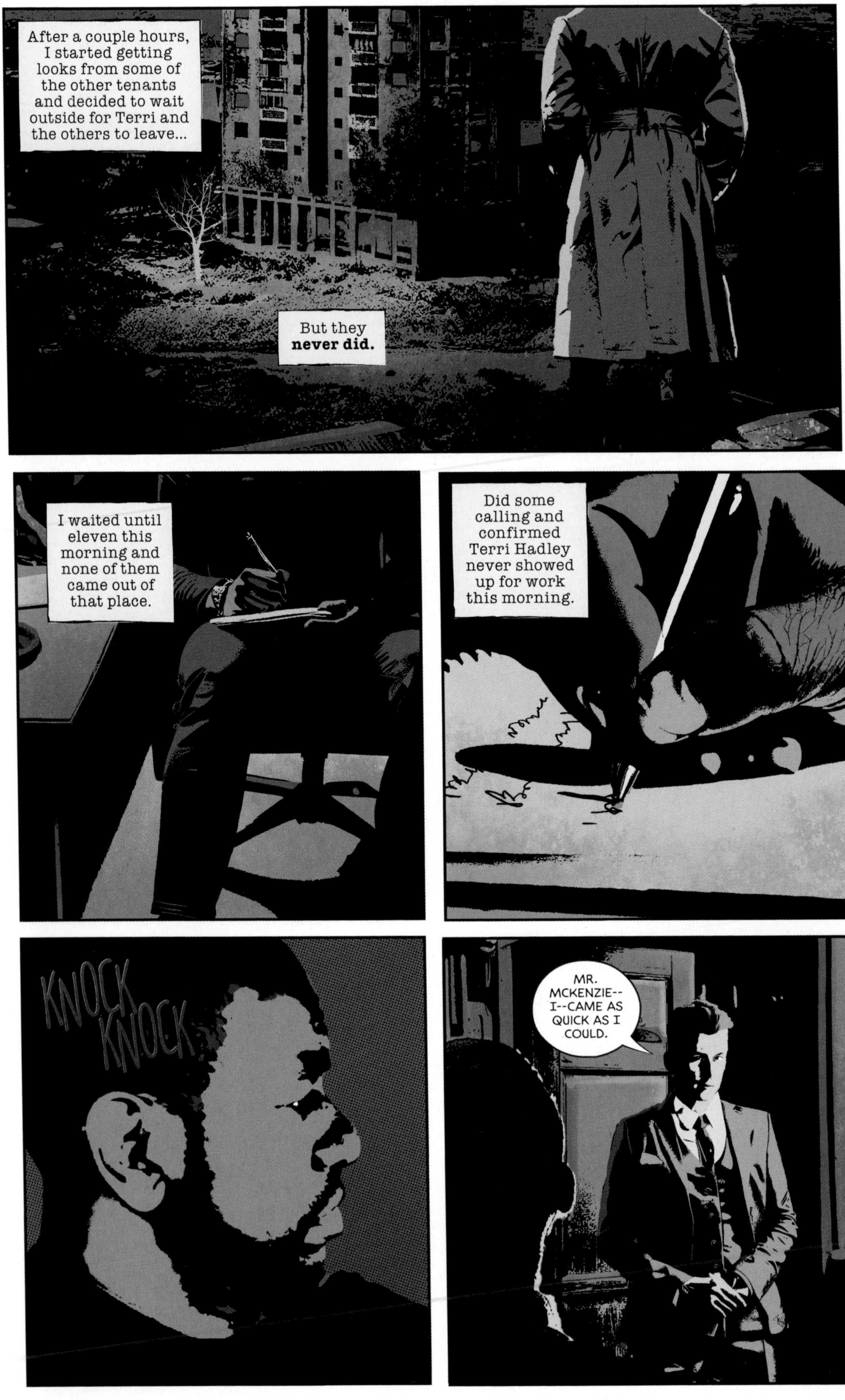
After a couple hours, I started getting looks from some of the other tenants and decided to wait outside for Terri and the others to leave...
But they **never did.**
I waited until eleven this morning and none of them came out of that place.
Did some calling and confirmed Terri Hadley never showed up for work this morning.
KNOCK KNOCK
MR. MCKENZIE-- I--CAME AS QUICK AS I COULD.

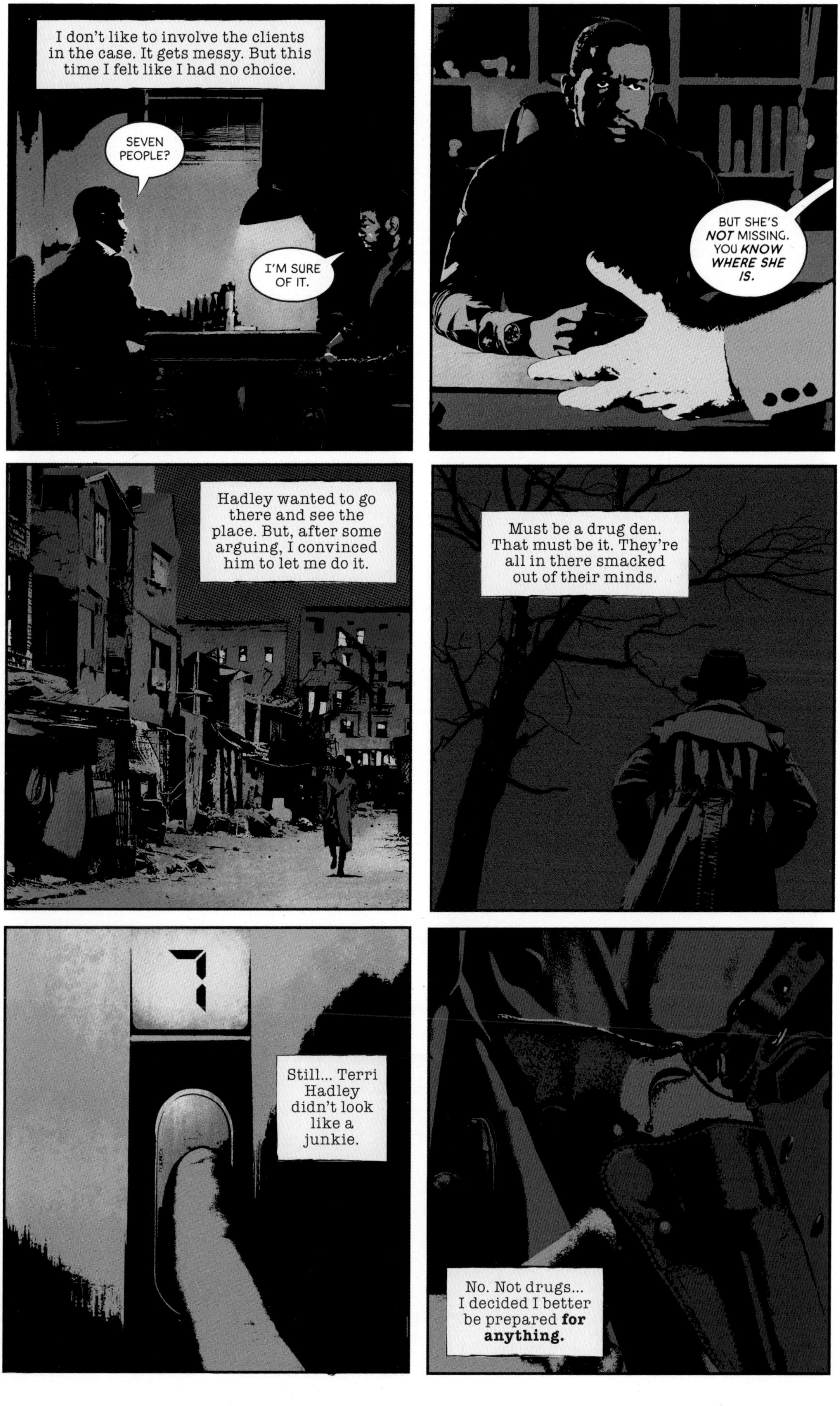

I don't like to involve the clients in the case. It gets messy. But this time I felt like I had no choice.
SEVEN PEOPLE?
I'M SURE OF IT.
BUT SHE'S *NOT* MISSING. YOU *KNOW WHERE SHE IS.*
Hadley wanted to go there and see the place. But, after some arguing, I convinced him to let me do it.
Must be a drug den. That must be it. They're all in there smacked out of their minds.
7
Still... Terri Hadley didn't look like a junkie.
No. Not drugs... I decided I better be prepared **for anything.**

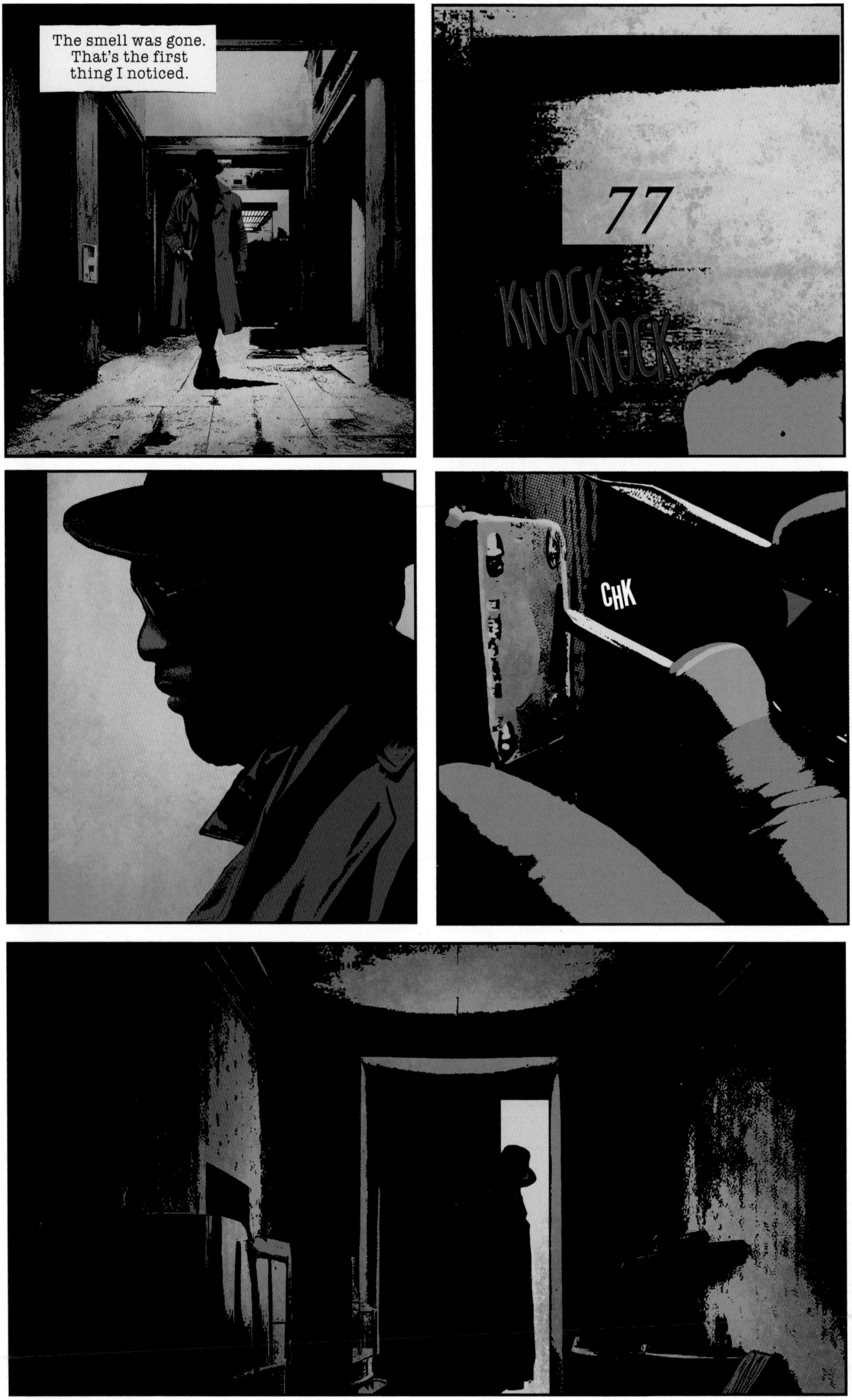
The smell was gone. That's the first thing I noticed.
77
KNOCK KNOCK
CHK

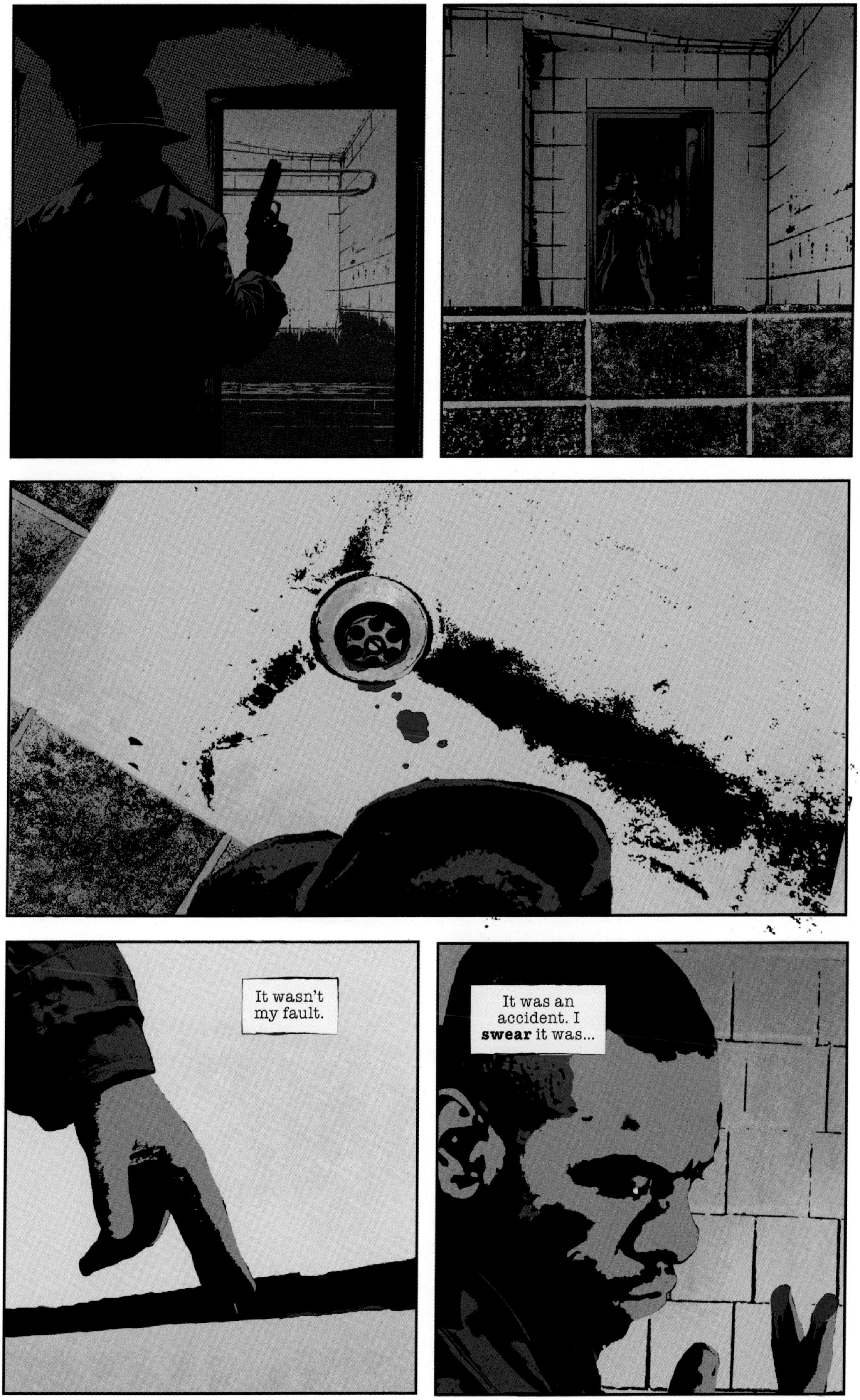
It wasn't my fault.
It was an accident. I **swear** it was...

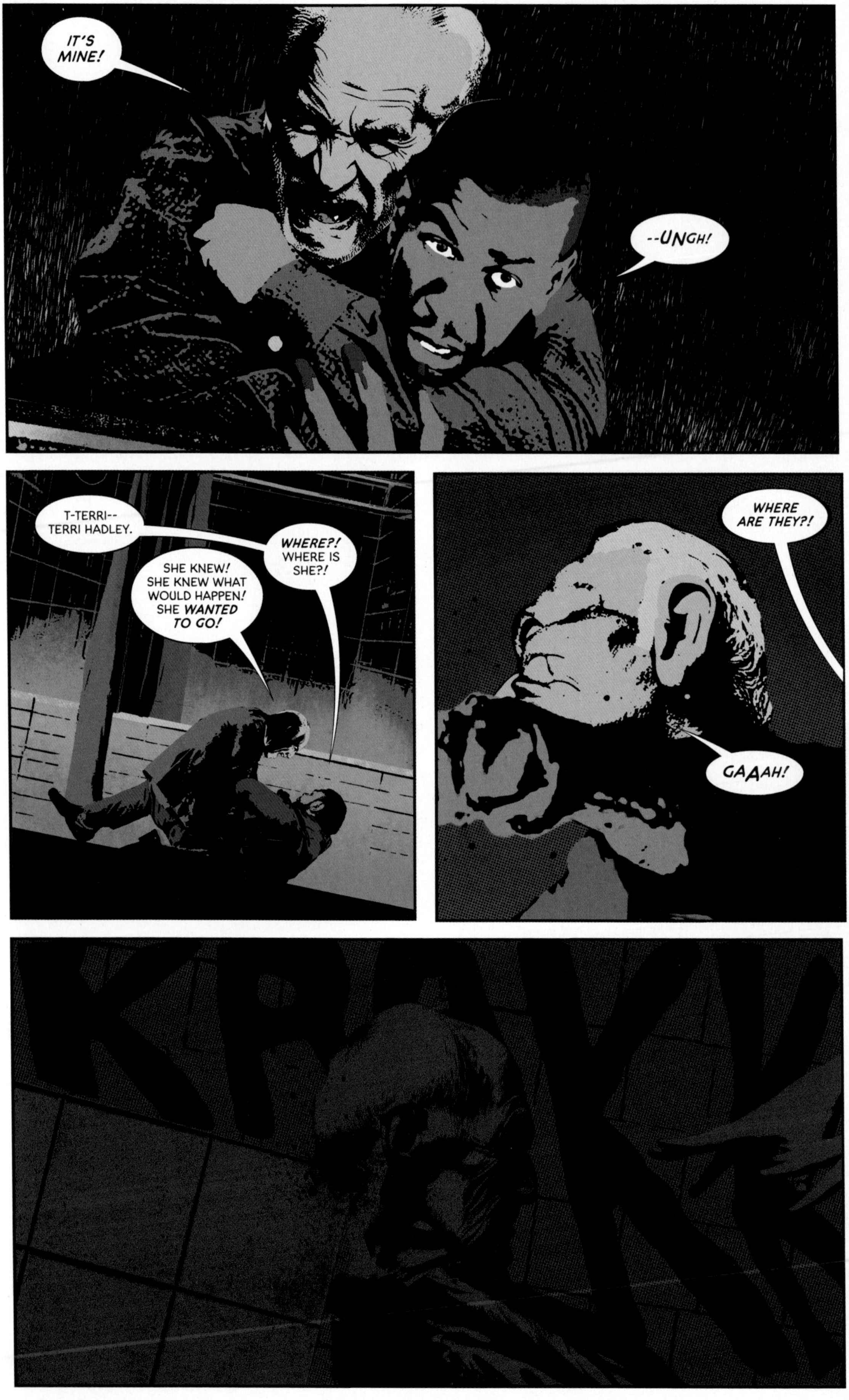
IT'S MINE!
--UNGH!
T-TERRI-- TERRI HADLEY.
WHERE?! WHERE IS SHE?!
SHE KNEW! SHE KNEW WHAT WOULD HAPPEN! SHE WANTED TO GO!
WHERE ARE THEY?!
GAAAH!
KRAK!

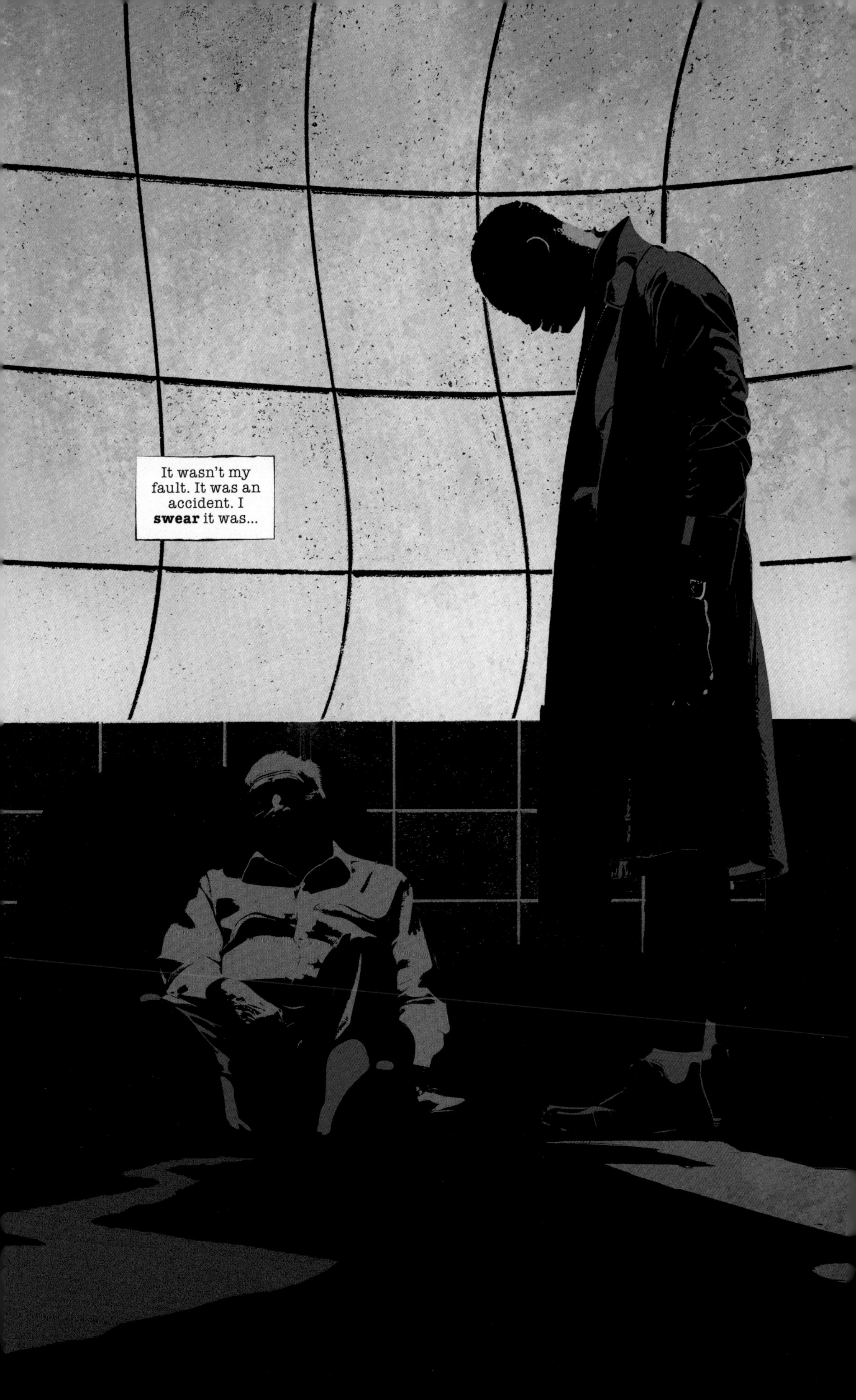
It wasn't my fault. It was an accident. I **swear** it was...

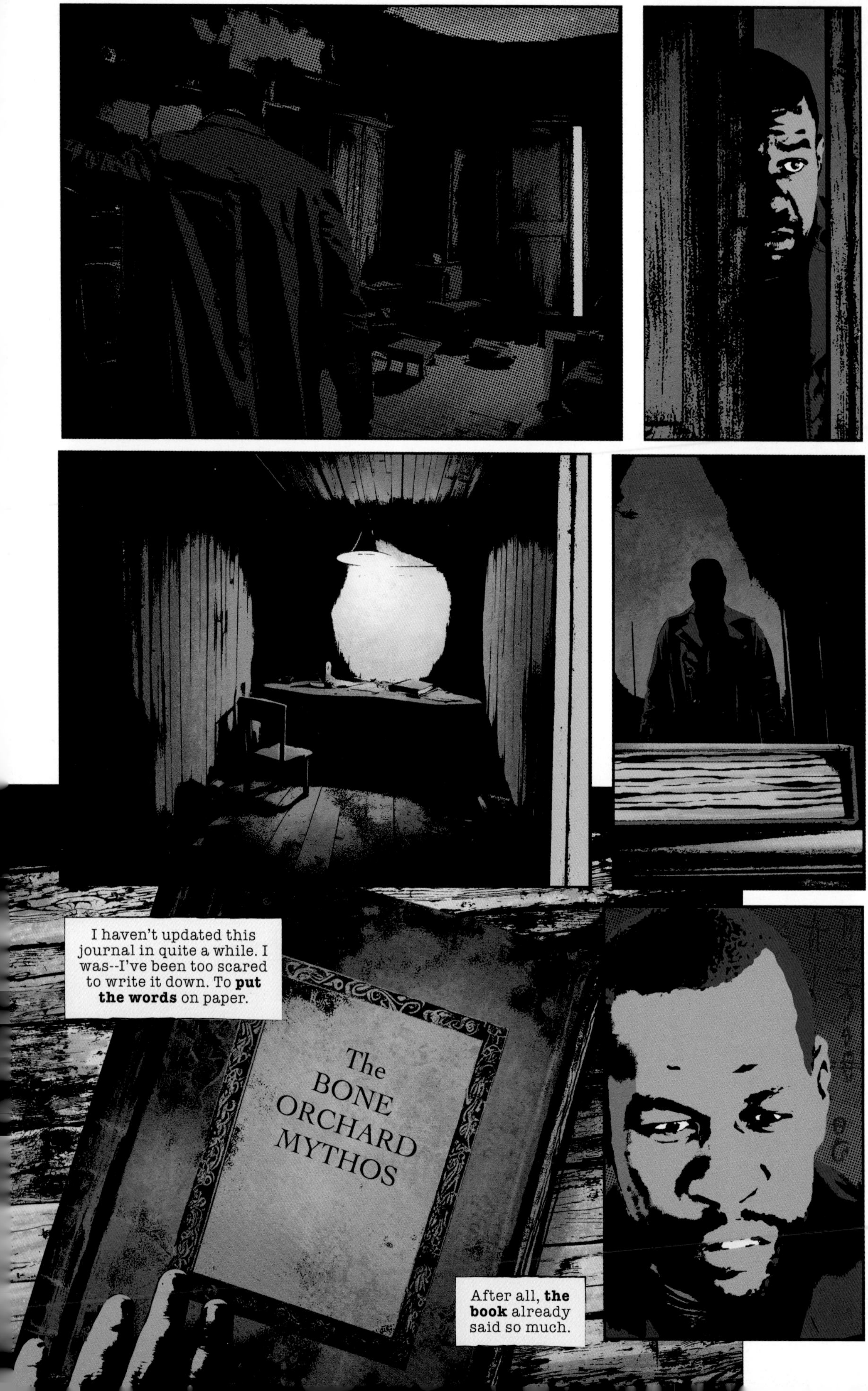
I haven't updated this journal in quite a while. I was--I've been too scared to write it down. To **put the words** on paper.
The BONE ORCHARD MYTHOS
After all, **the book** already said so much.

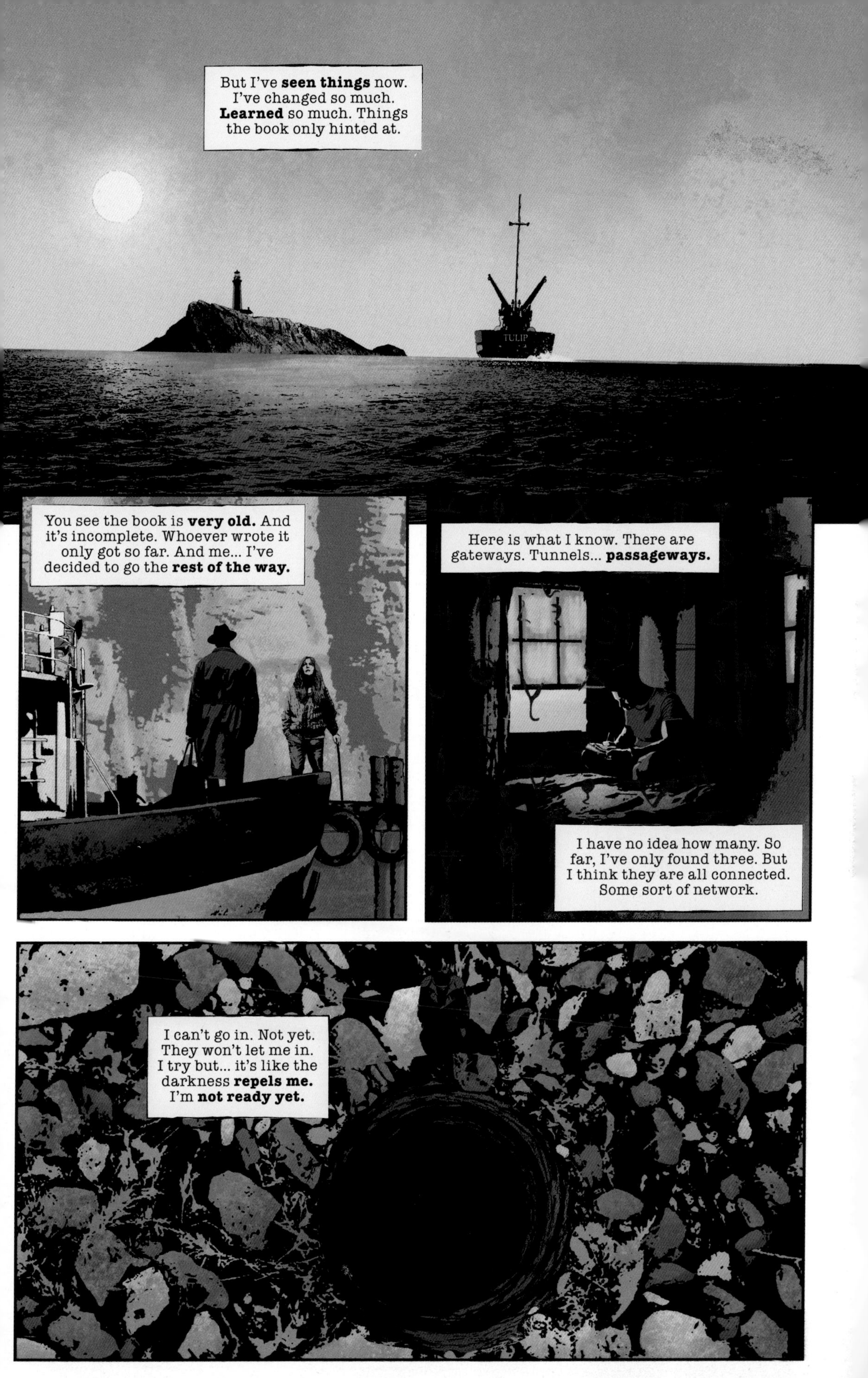
But I've **seen things** now. I've changed so much. **Learned** so much. Things the book only hinted at.
TULIP
You see the book is **very old.** And it's incomplete. Whoever wrote it only got so far. And me... I've decided to go the **rest of the way.**
Here is what I know. There are gateways. Tunnels... **passageways.**
I have no idea how many. So far, I've only found three. But I think they are all connected. Some sort of network.
I can't go in. Not yet. They won't let me in. I try but... it's like the darkness **repels me.** I'm **not ready yet.**

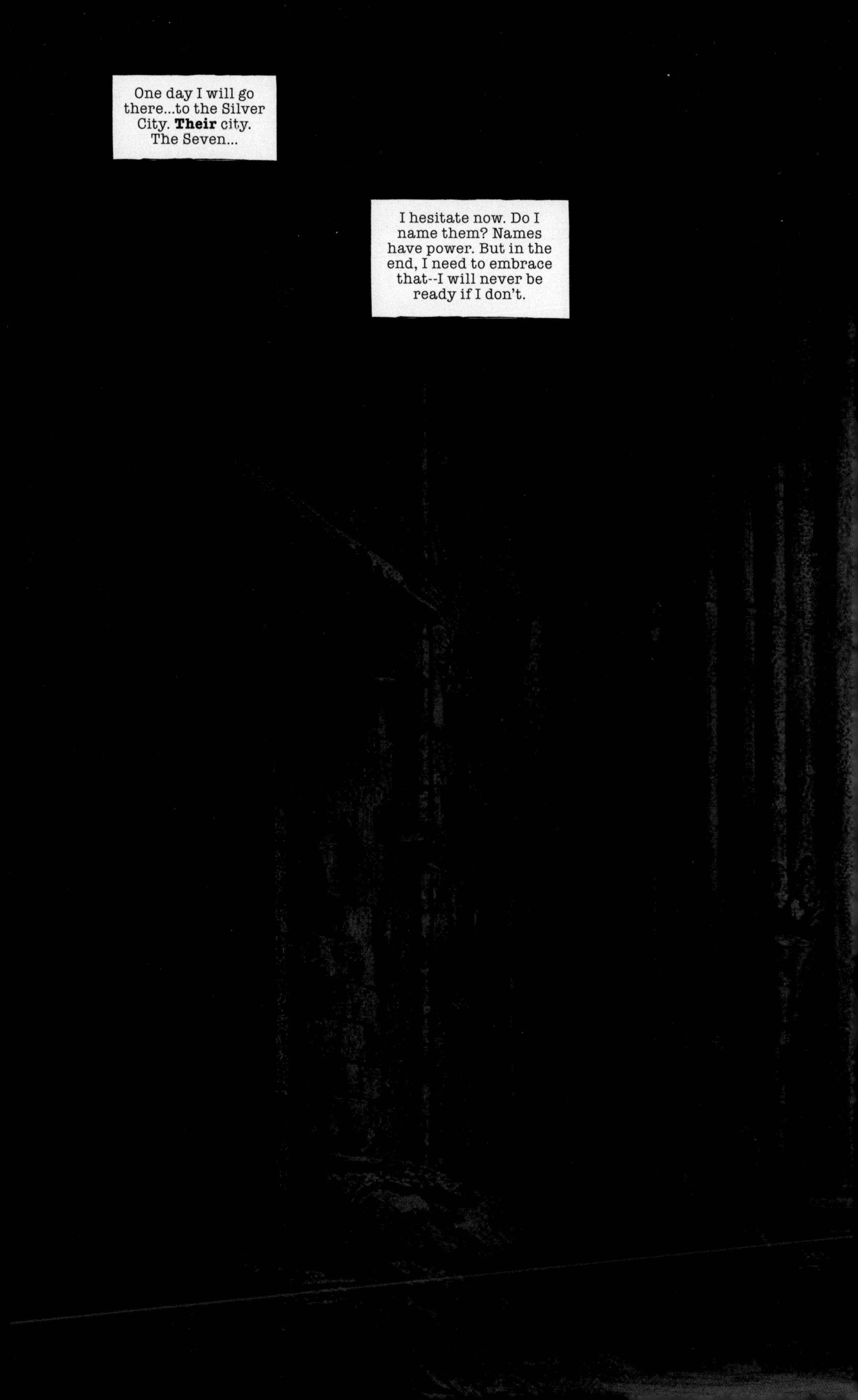
One day I will go there...to the Silver City. **Their** city. The Seven...
I hesitate now. Do I name them? Names have power. But in the end, I need to embrace that--I will never be ready if I don't.

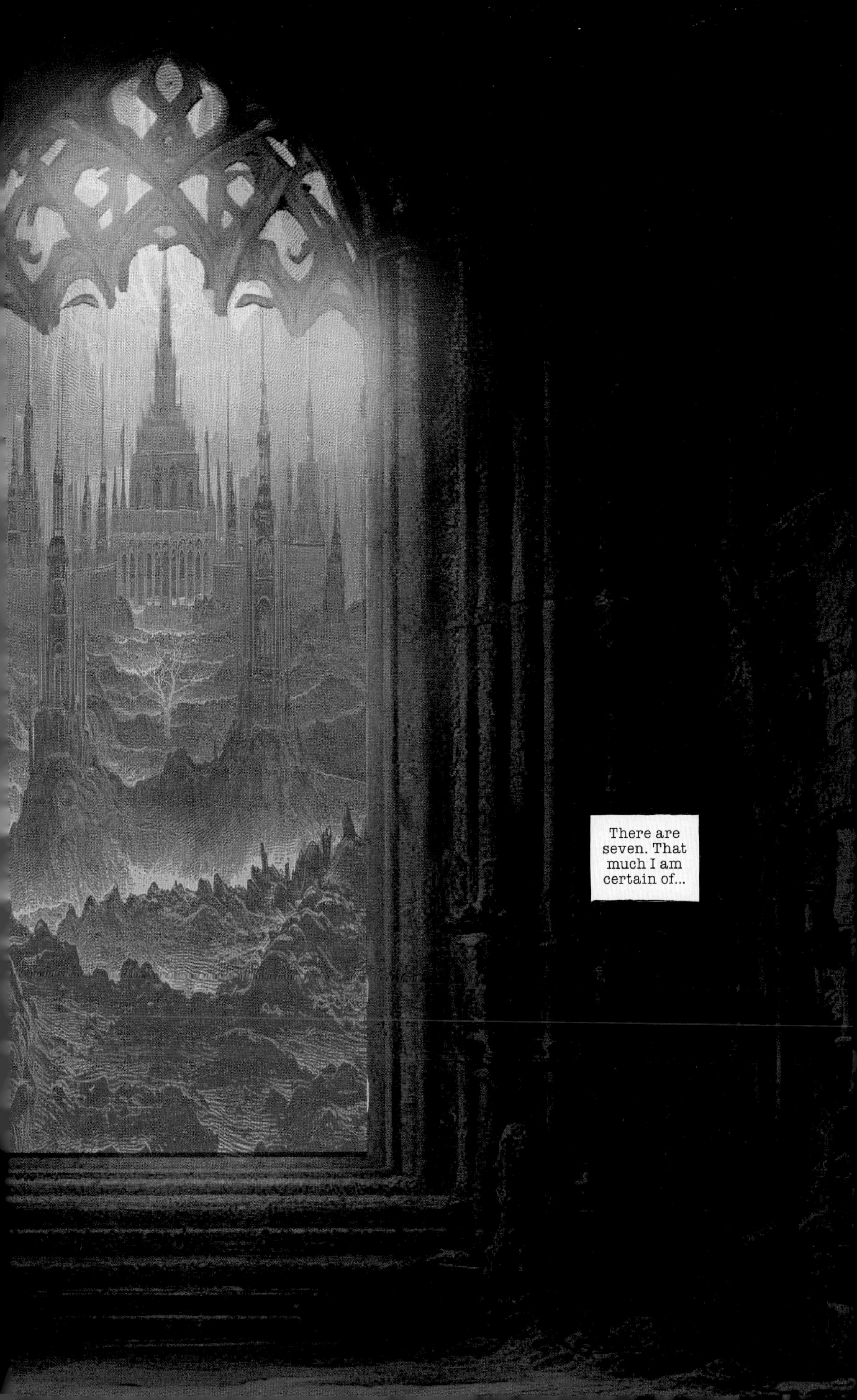
There are seven. That much I am certain of...

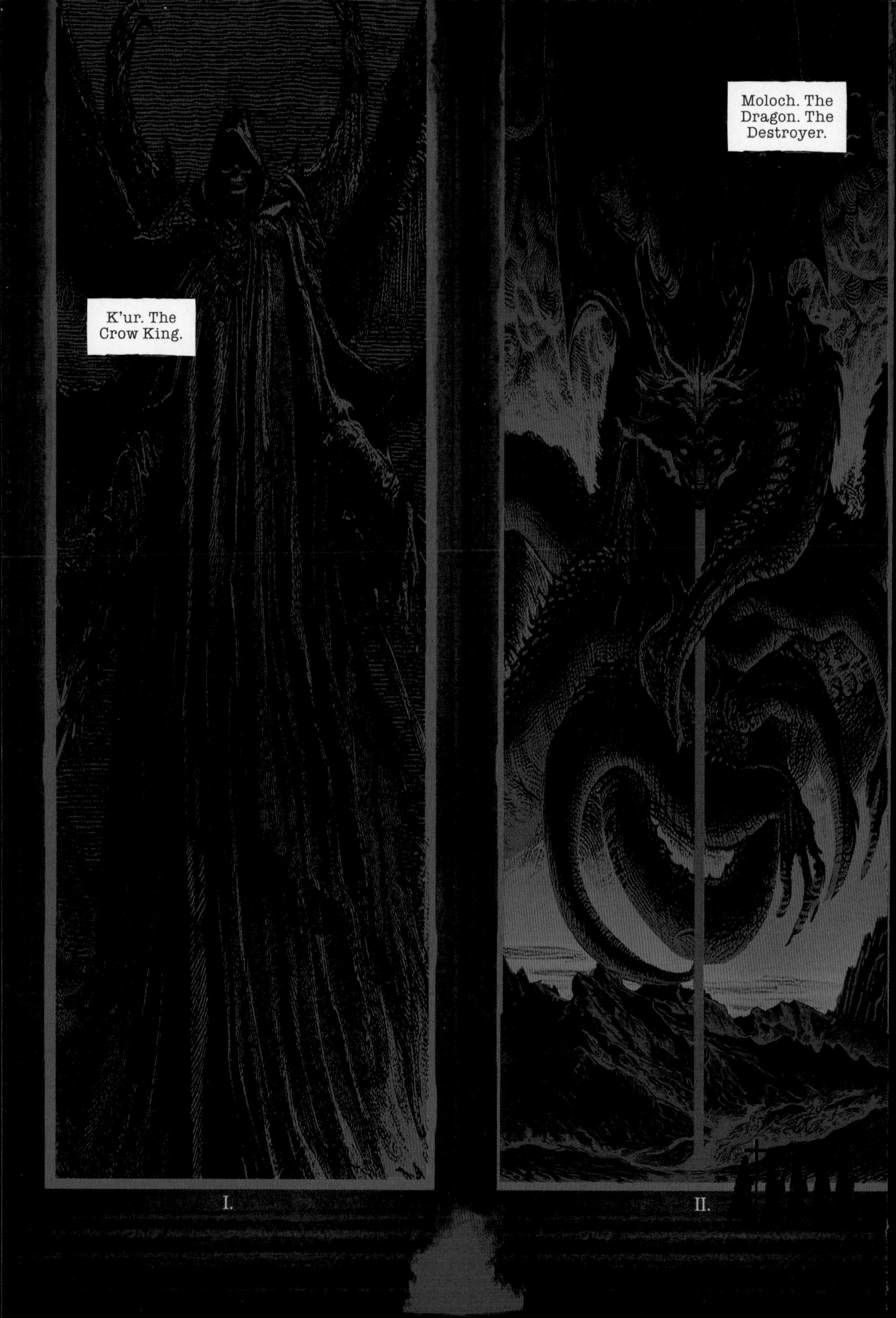
K'ur. The
Crow King.
I.
Moloch. The
Dragon. The
Destroyer.
II.

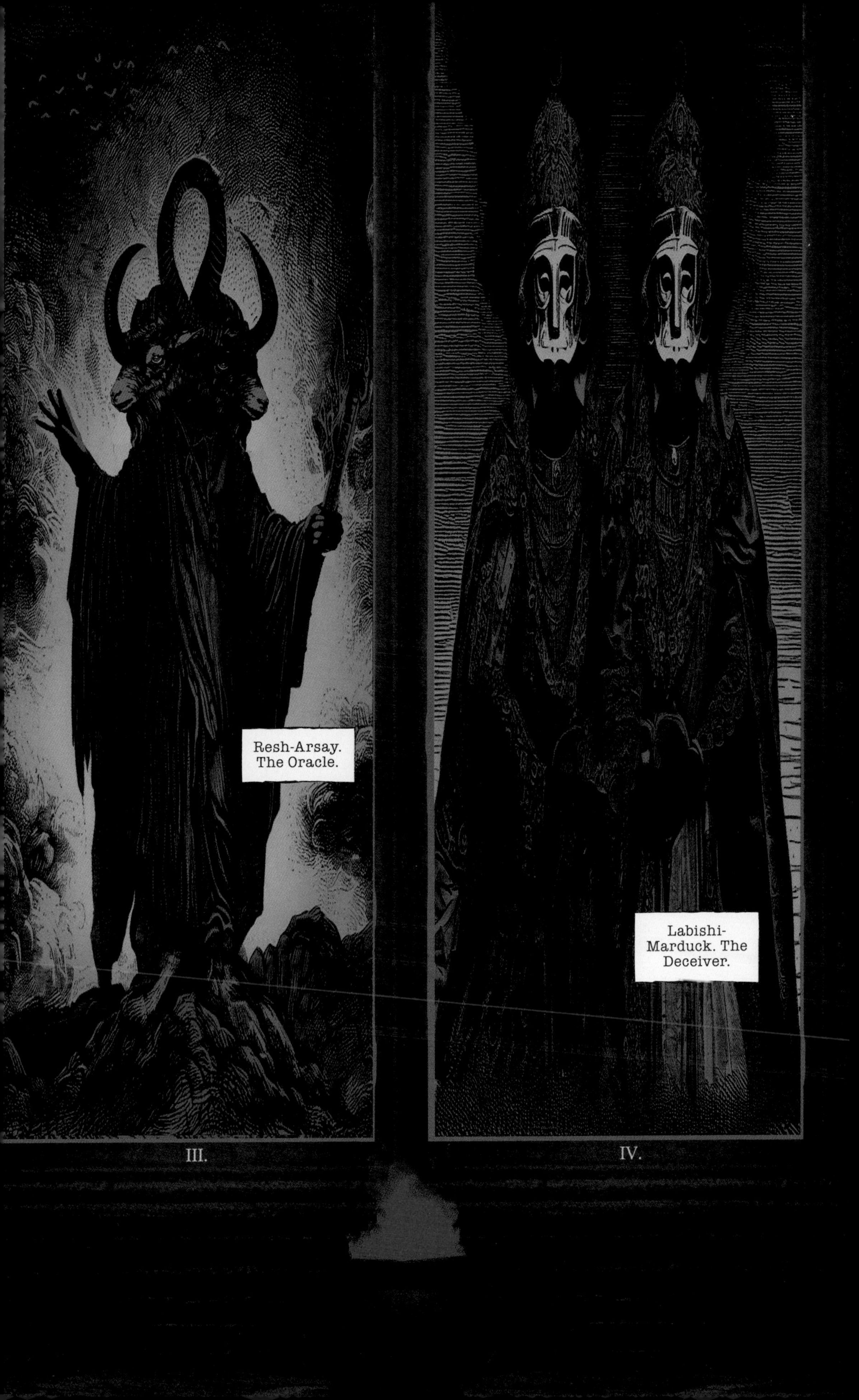
Resh-Arsay.
The Oracle.
III.
Labishi-
Marduck. The
Deceiver.
IV.

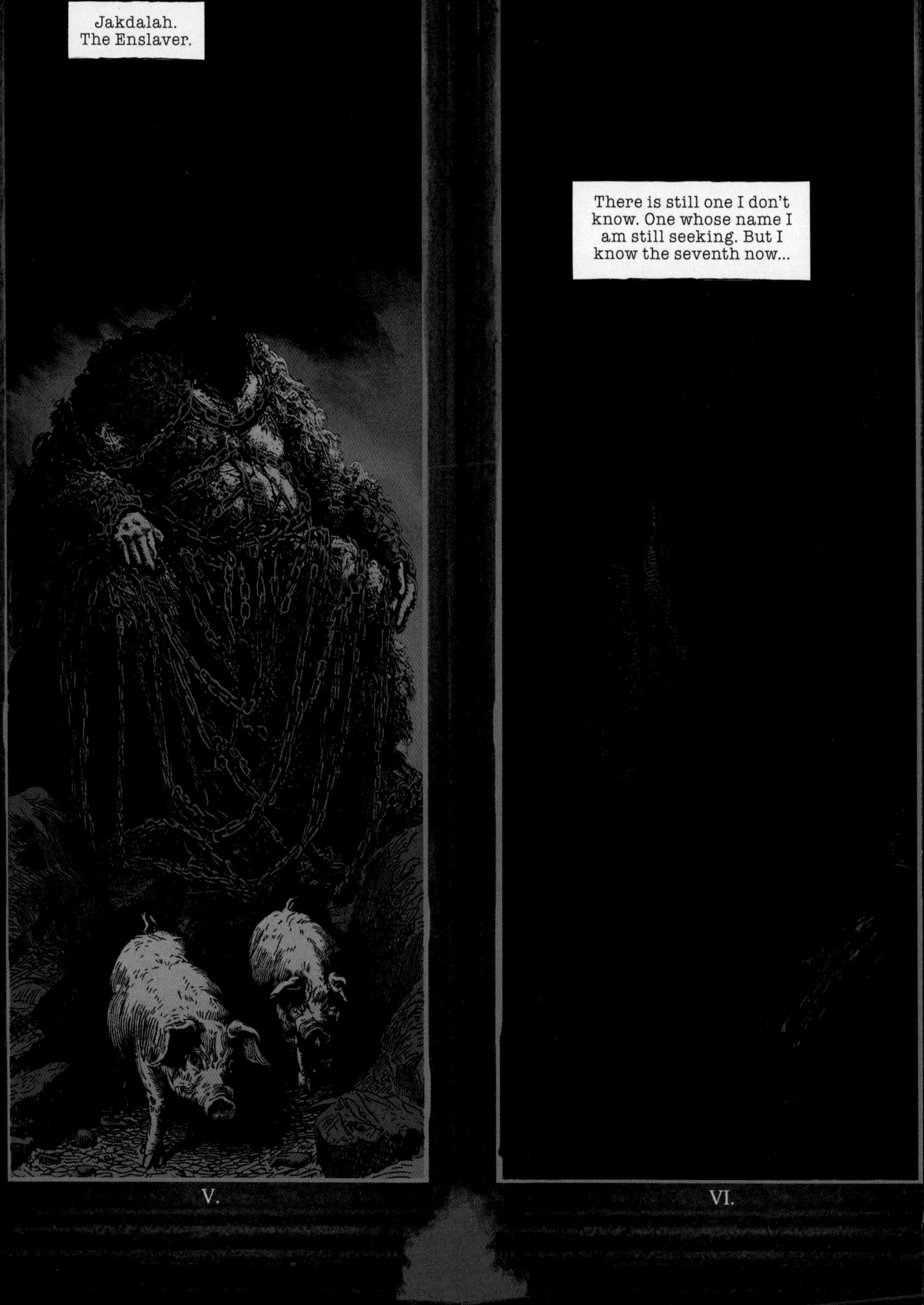
Jakdalah.
The Enslaver.
There is still one I don't know. One whose name I am still seeking. But I know the seventh now...
V.
VI.

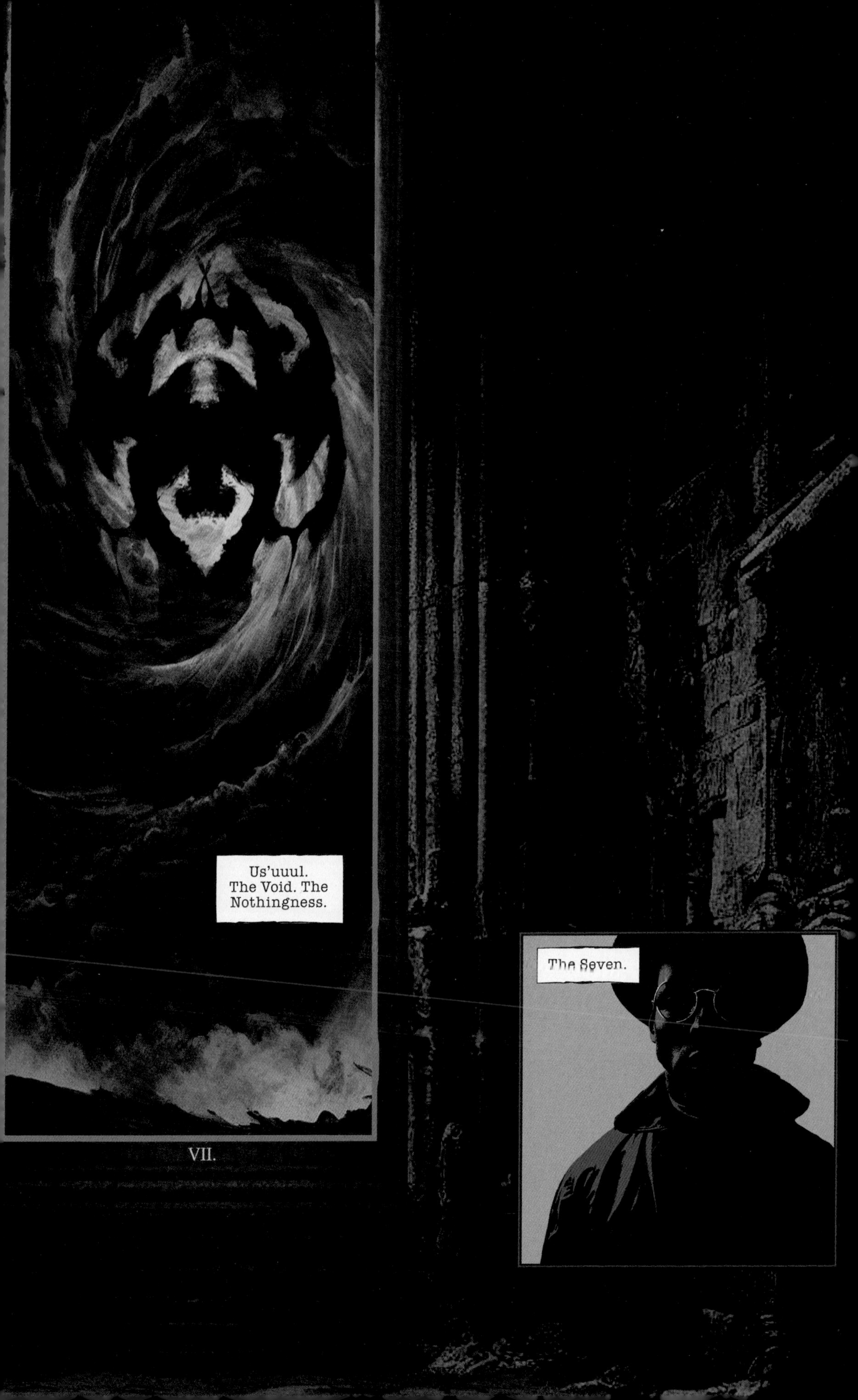
Us'uuul.
The Void. The Nothingness.
VII.
The Seven.

But that's just it, isn't it? We don't **want** to look beyond, because if we do, we may see that there is only **nothingness** beyond...

A great yawning abyss waiting to swallow us up.

And that is too terrifying to think about, so we force order and meaning on them to get us through.

That false meaning will unravel. It always does eventually.

But if you **keep looking,** you'll see there is something beyond that darkness...

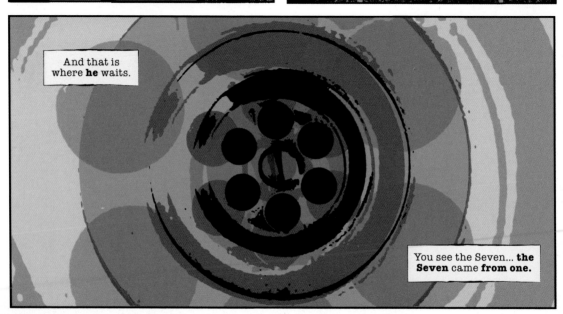

And that is where **he** waits.

You see the Seven... **the Seven** came **from one.**

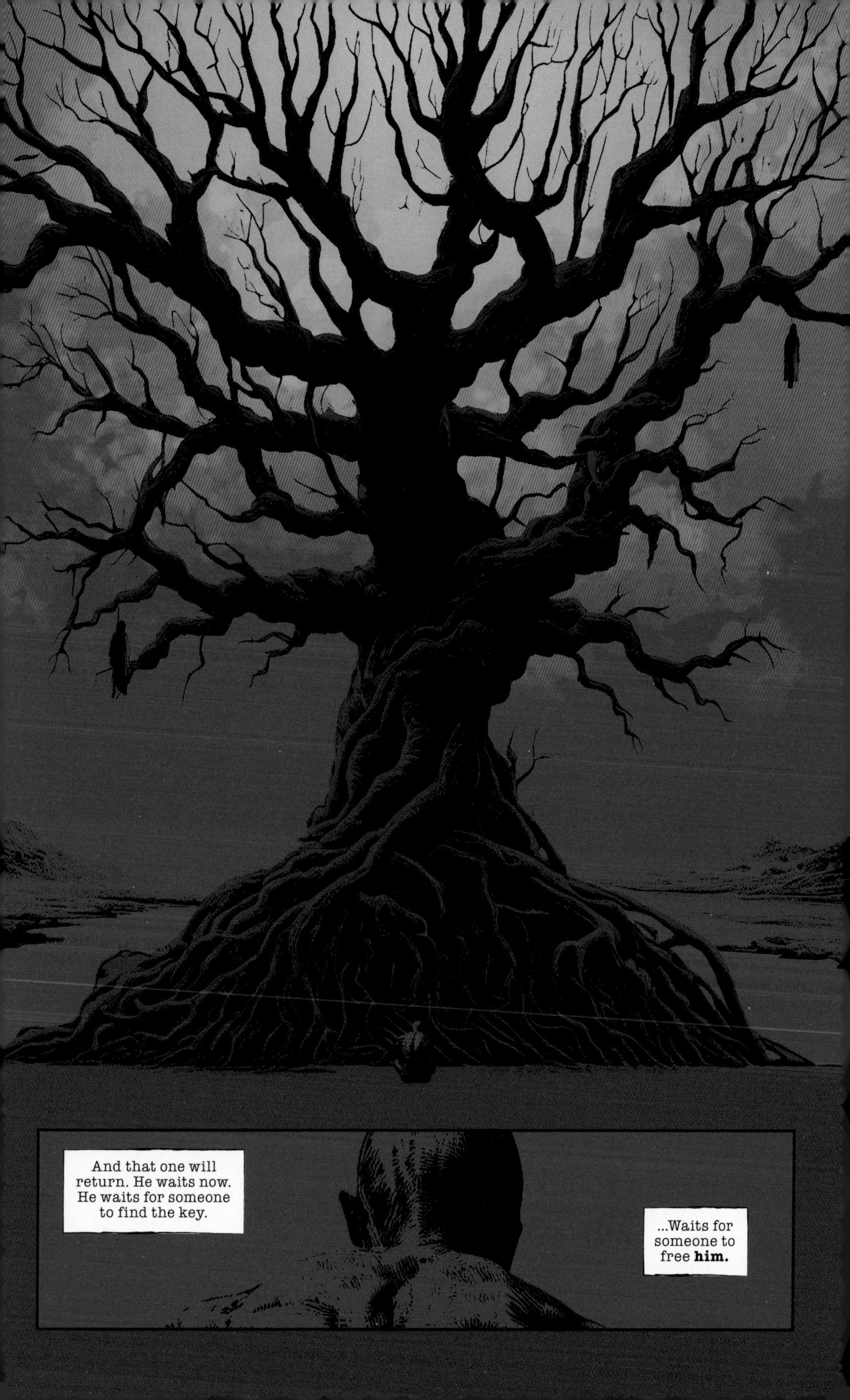
And that one will return. He waits now. He waits for someone to find the key.
...Waits for someone to free **him.**

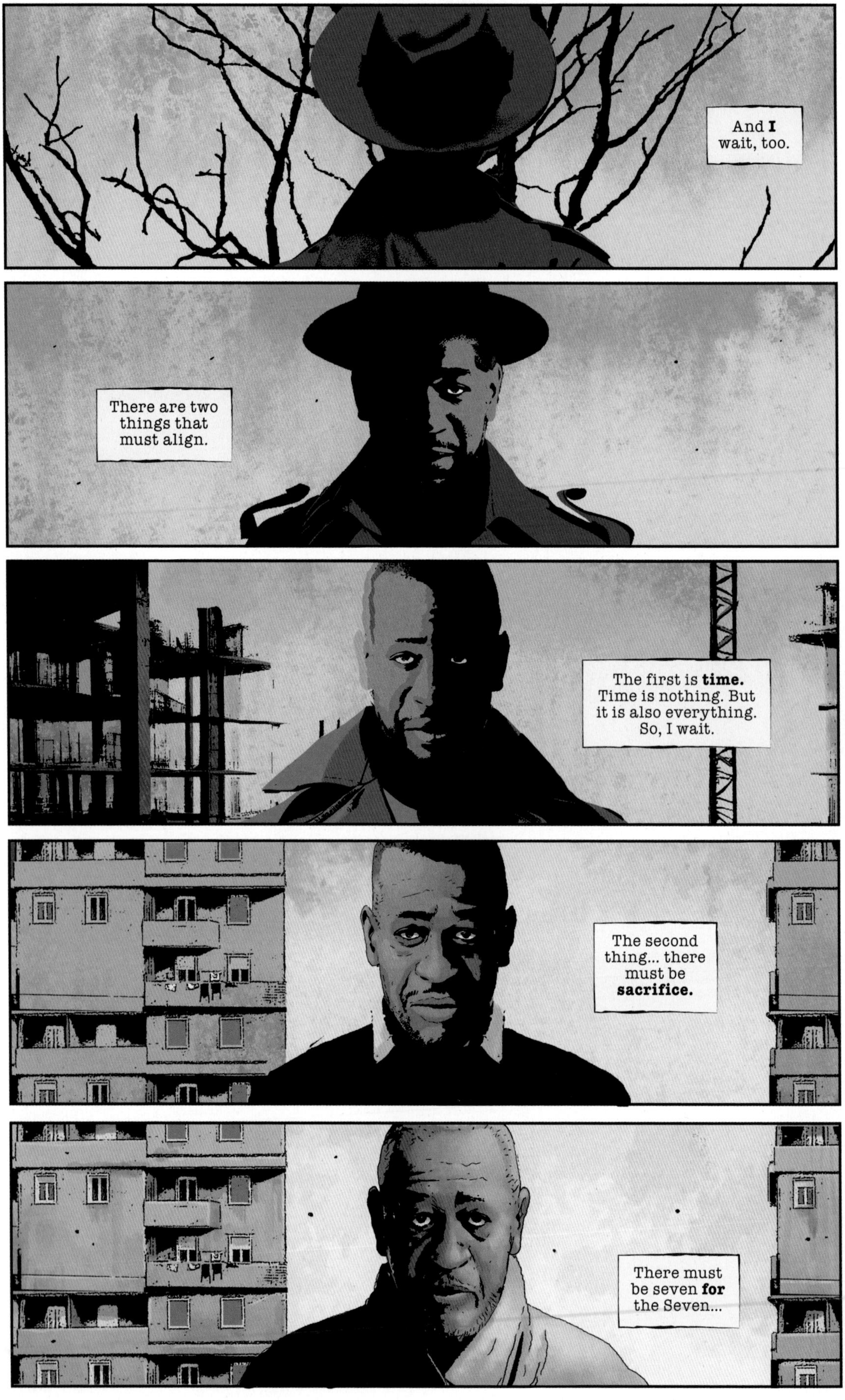
And **I** wait, too.
There are two things that must align.
The first is **time.** Time is nothing. But it is also everything. So, I wait.
The second thing... there must be **sacrifice.**
There must be seven **for** the Seven...

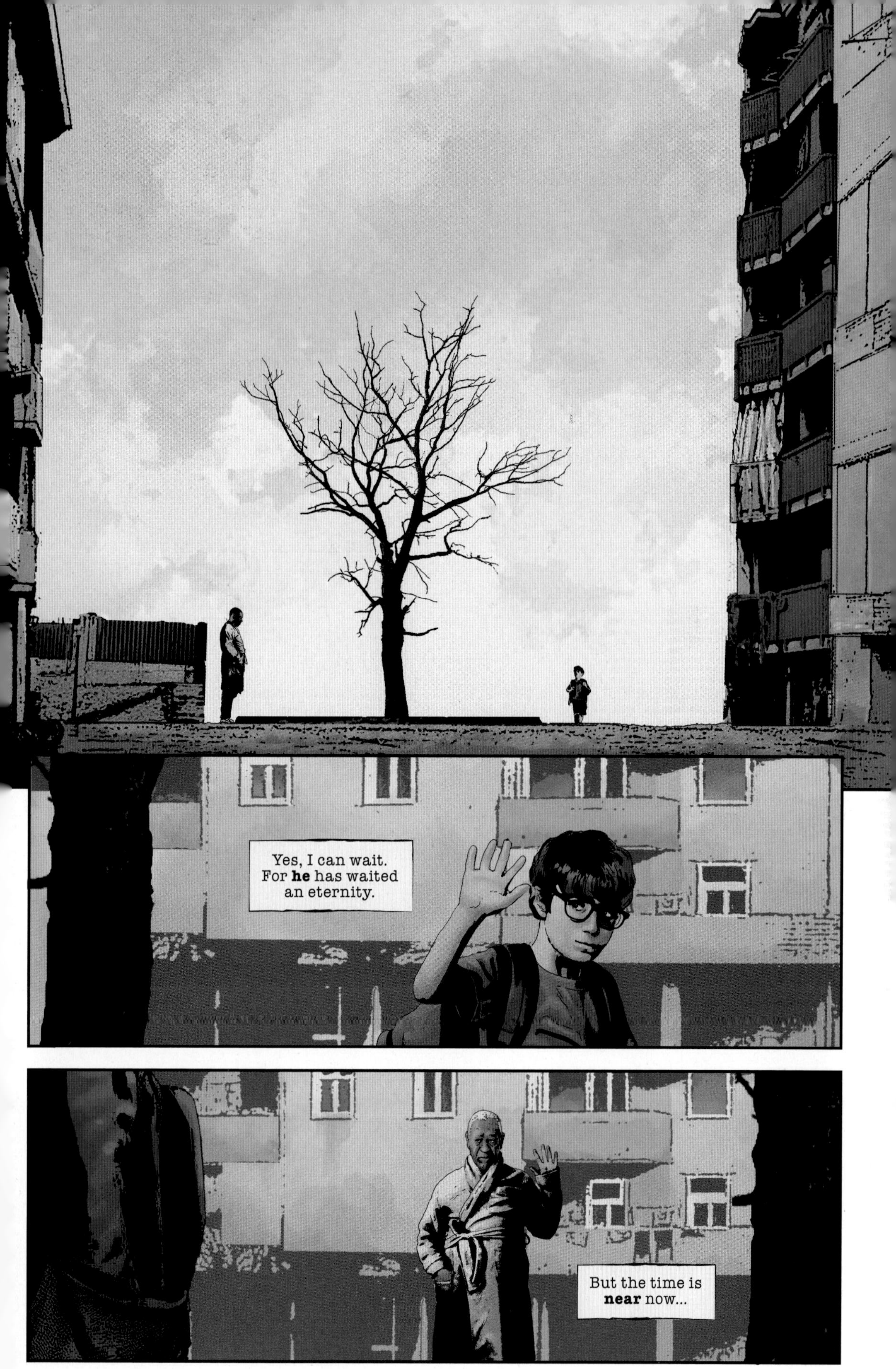
Yes, I can wait. For **he** has waited an eternity.
But the time is **near** now...

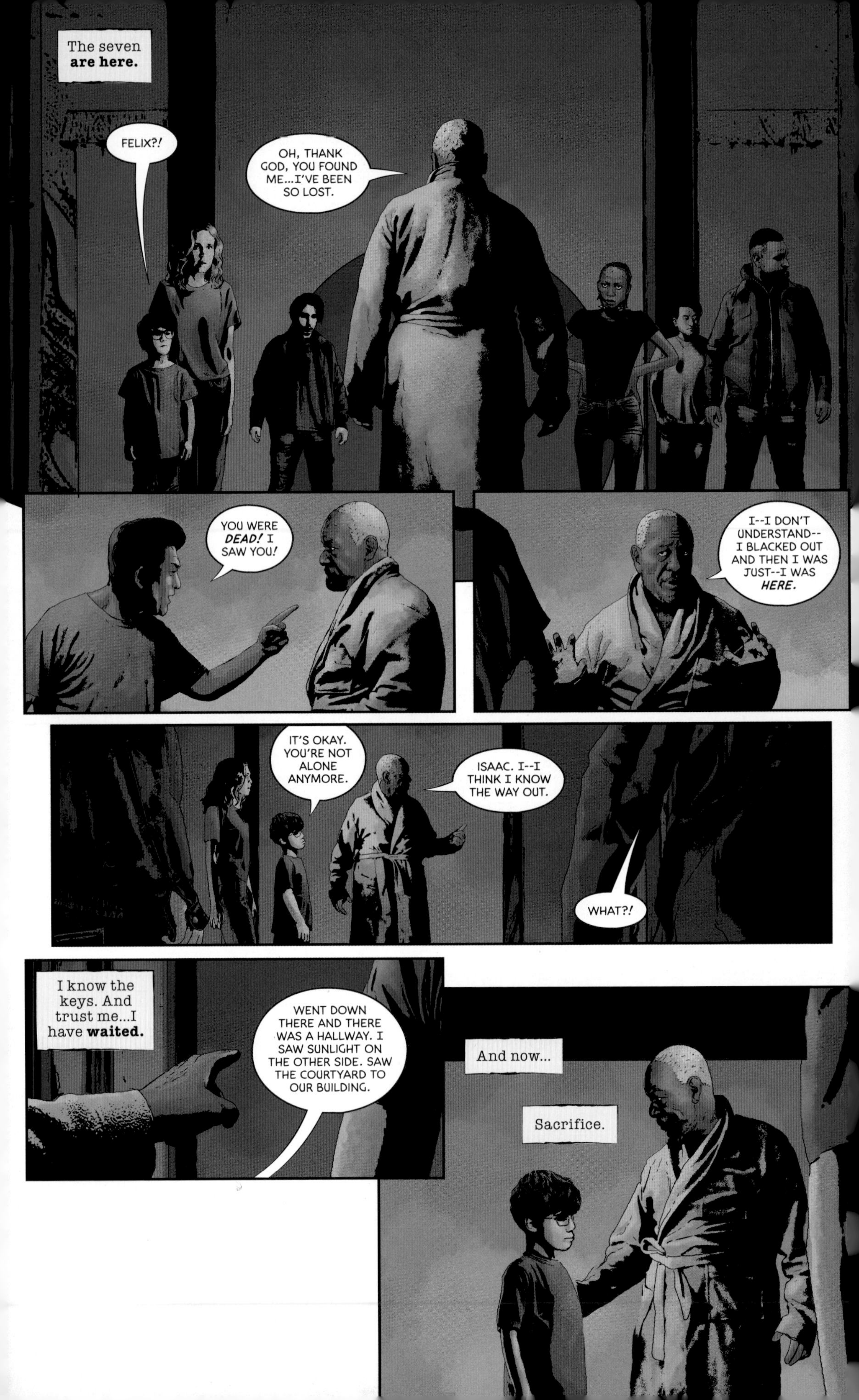

The seven are here.
FELIX?!
OH, THANK GOD, YOU FOUND ME...I'VE BEEN SO LOST.
YOU WERE DEAD! I SAW YOU!
I--I DON'T UNDERSTAND-- I BLACKED OUT AND THEN I WAS JUST--I WAS HERE.
IT'S OKAY. YOU'RE NOT ALONE ANYMORE.
ISAAC. I--I THINK I KNOW THE WAY OUT.
WHAT?!
I know the keys. And trust me...I have waited.
WENT DOWN THERE AND THERE WAS A HALLWAY. I SAW SUNLIGHT ON THE OTHER SIDE. SAW THE COURTYARD TO OUR BUILDING.
And now...
Sacrifice.

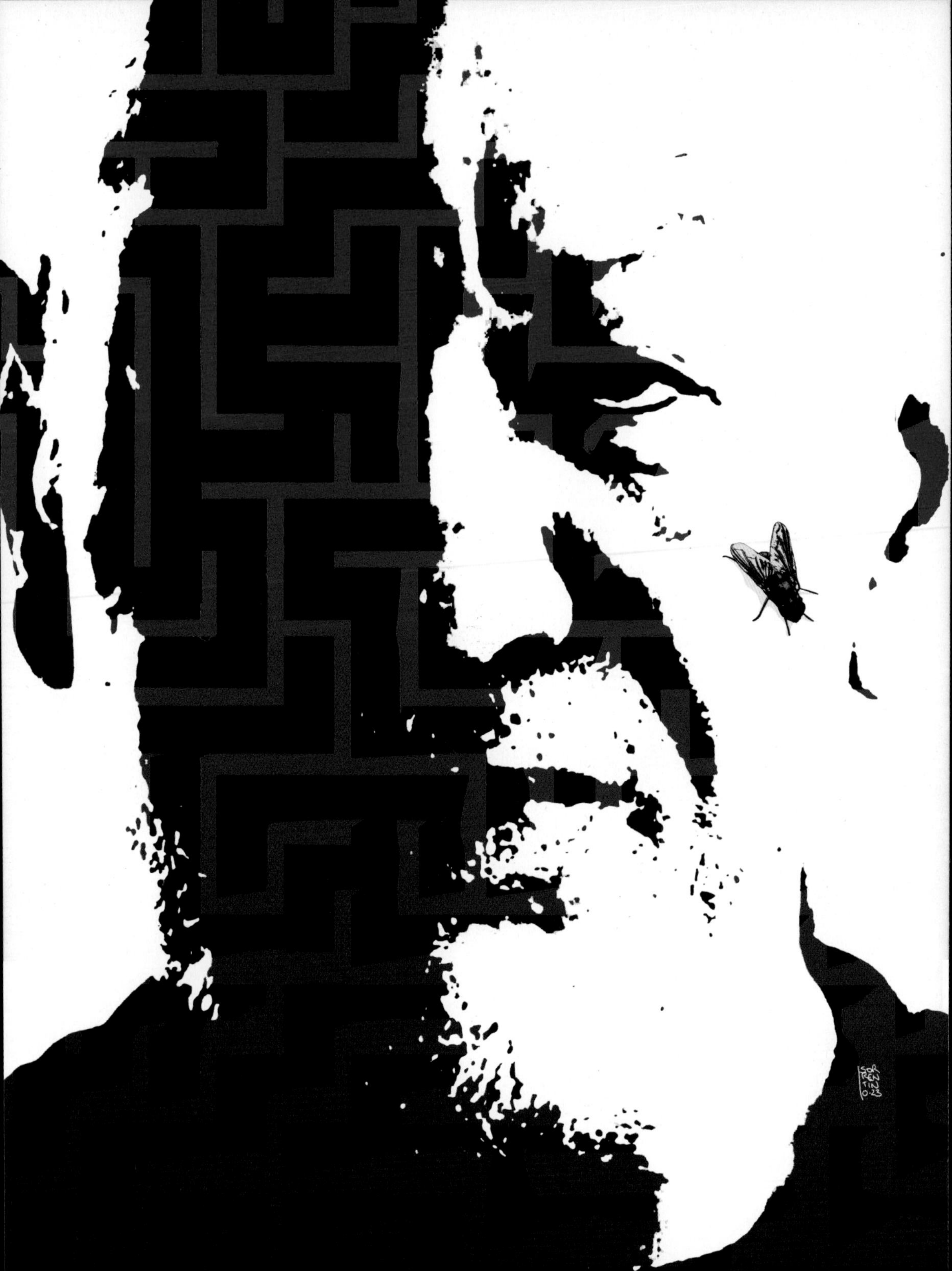

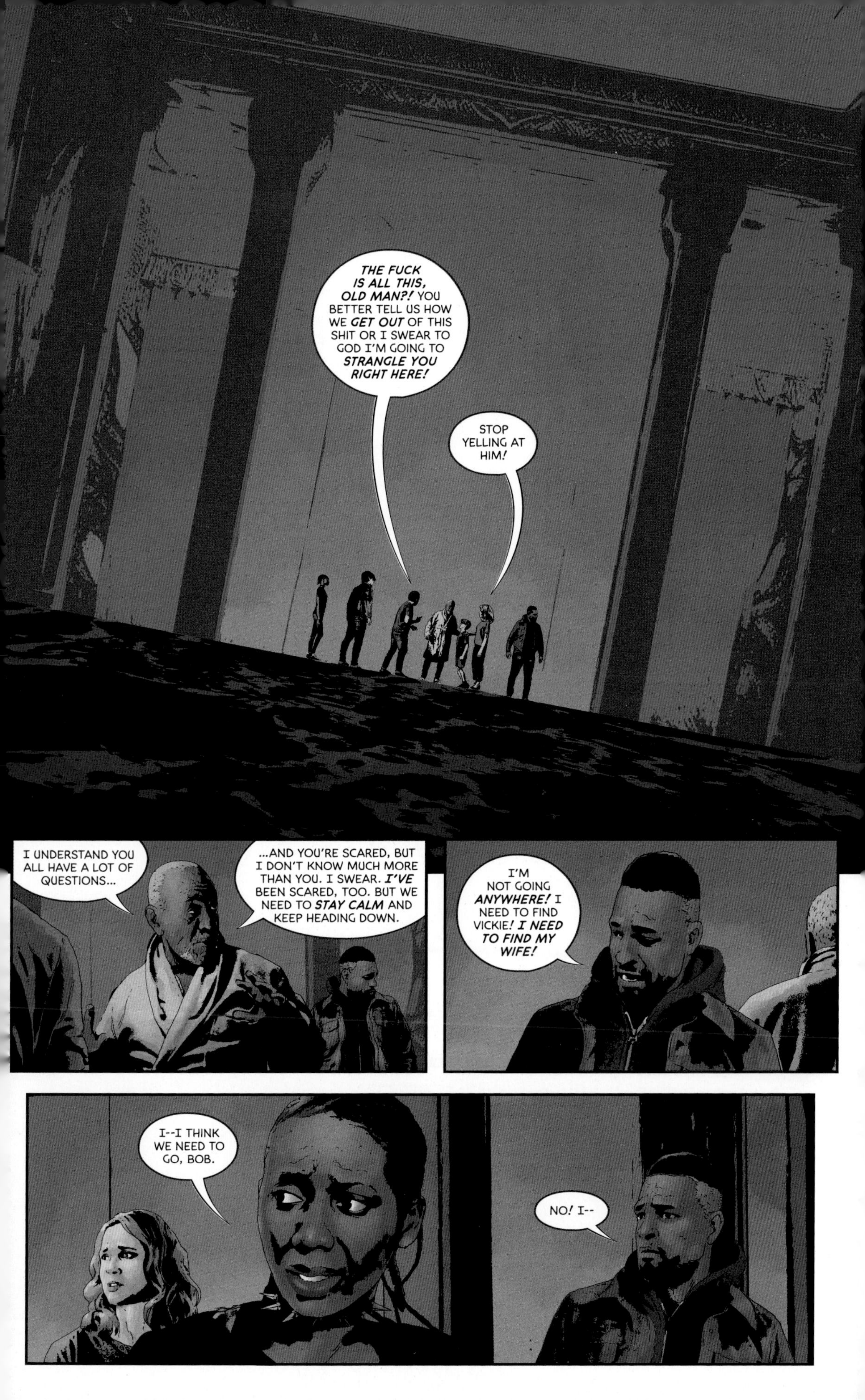
THE FUCK IS ALL THIS, OLD MAN?! YOU BETTER TELL US HOW WE GET OUT OF THIS SHIT OR I SWEAR TO GOD I'M GOING TO STRANGLE YOU RIGHT HERE!
STOP YELLING AT HIM!
I UNDERSTAND YOU ALL HAVE A LOT OF QUESTIONS...
...AND YOU'RE SCARED, BUT I DON'T KNOW MUCH MORE THAN YOU. I SWEAR. I'VE BEEN SCARED, TOO. BUT WE NEED TO STAY CALM AND KEEP HEADING DOWN.
I'M NOT GOING ANYWHERE! I NEED TO FIND VICKIE! I NEED TO FIND MY WIFE!
I--I THINK WE NEED TO GO, BOB.
NO! I--

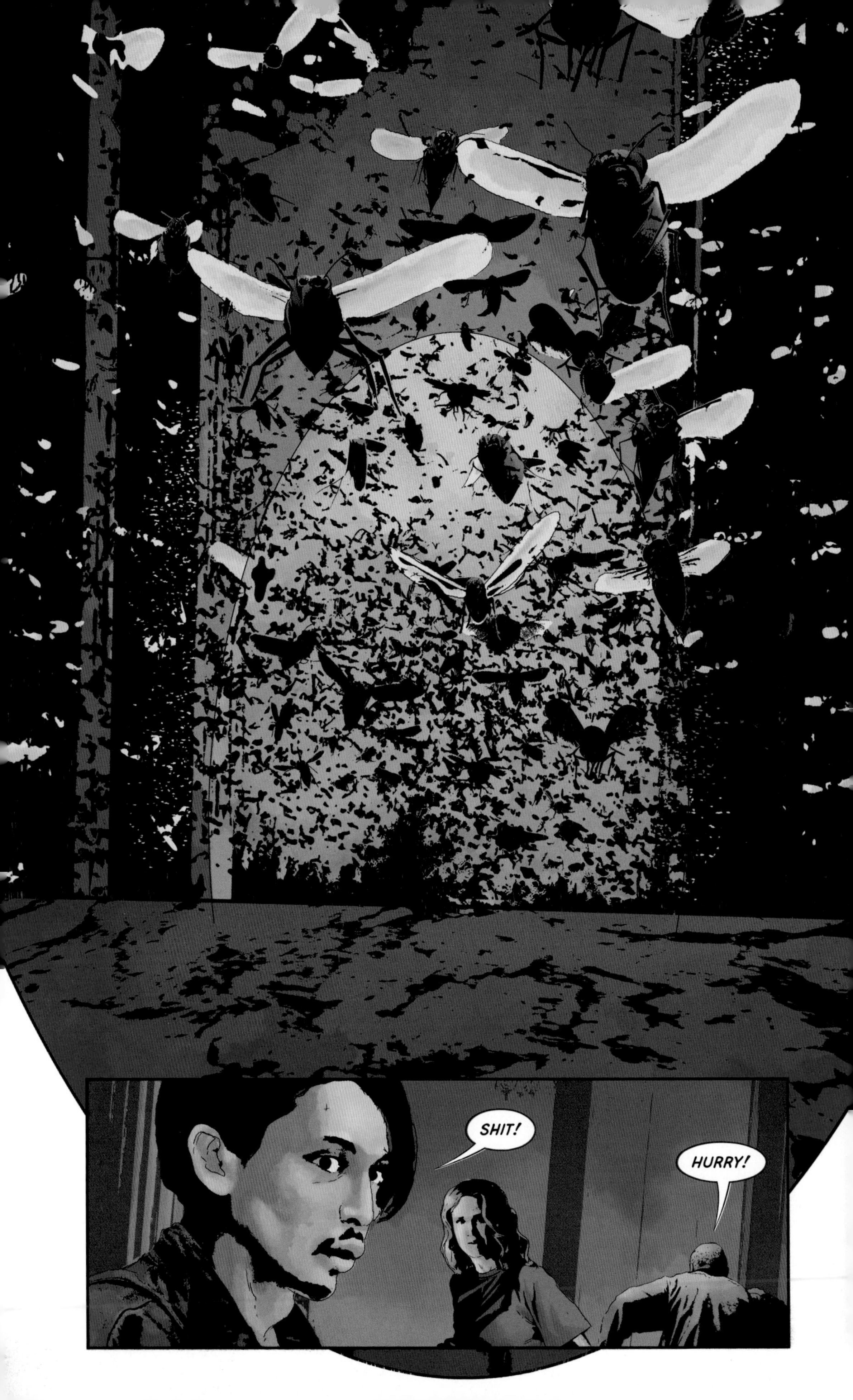
SHIT!
HURRY!

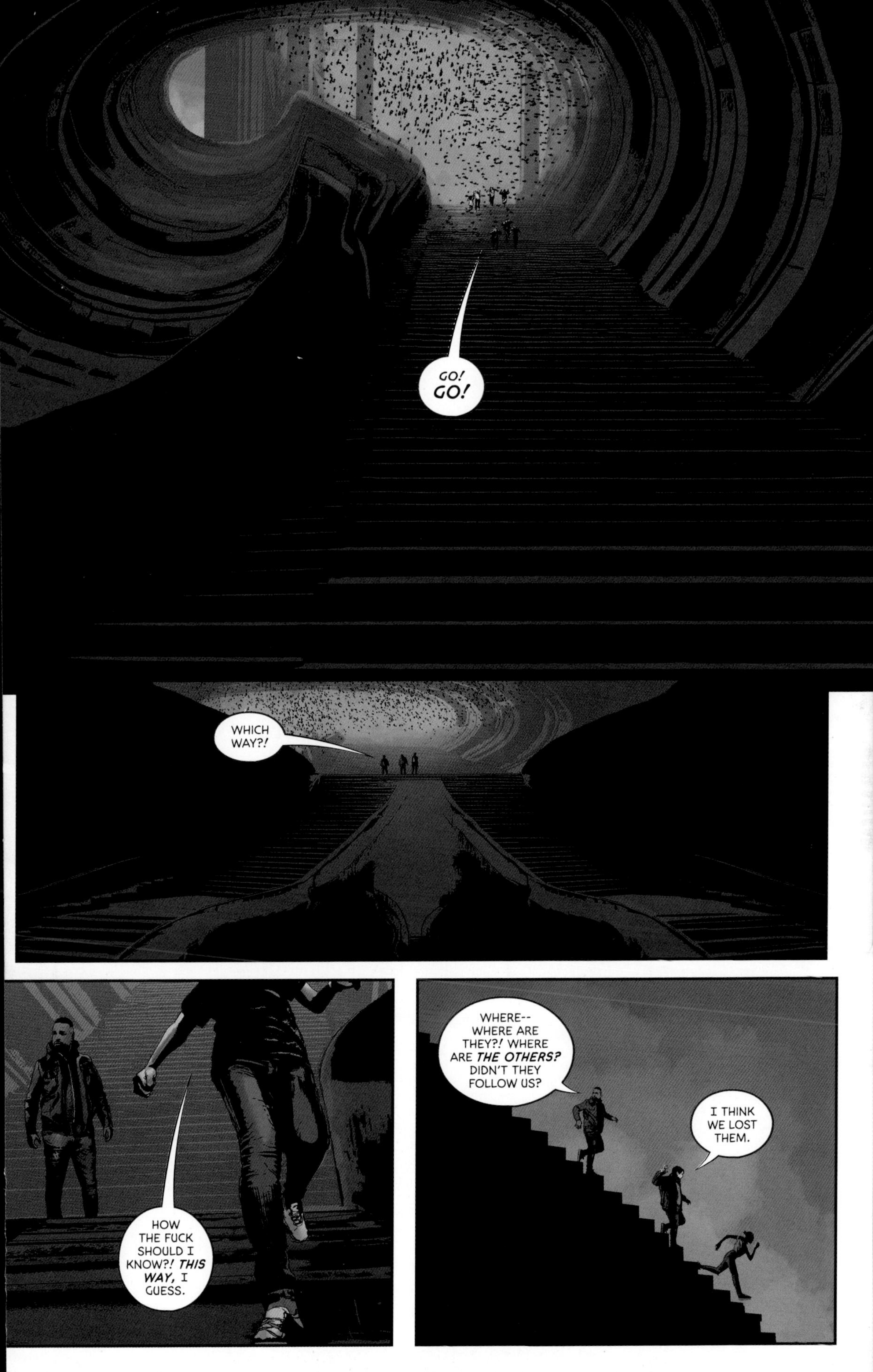
GO!
GO!
WHICH WAY?!
HOW THE FUCK SHOULD I KNOW?! THIS WAY, I GUESS.
WHERE-- WHERE ARE THEY?! WHERE ARE THE OTHERS? DIDN'T THEY FOLLOW US?
I THINK WE LOST THEM.

FLOOR 3

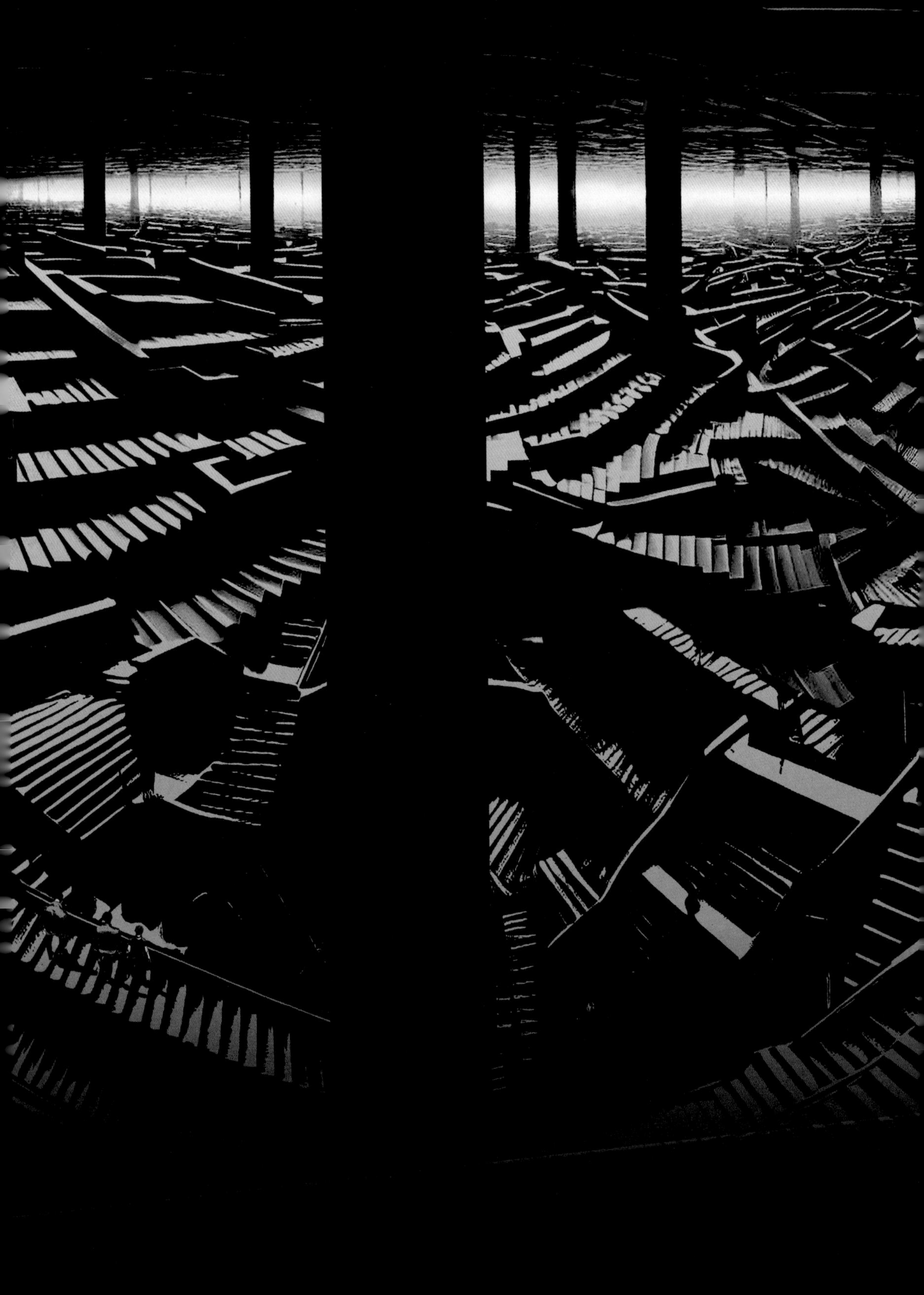

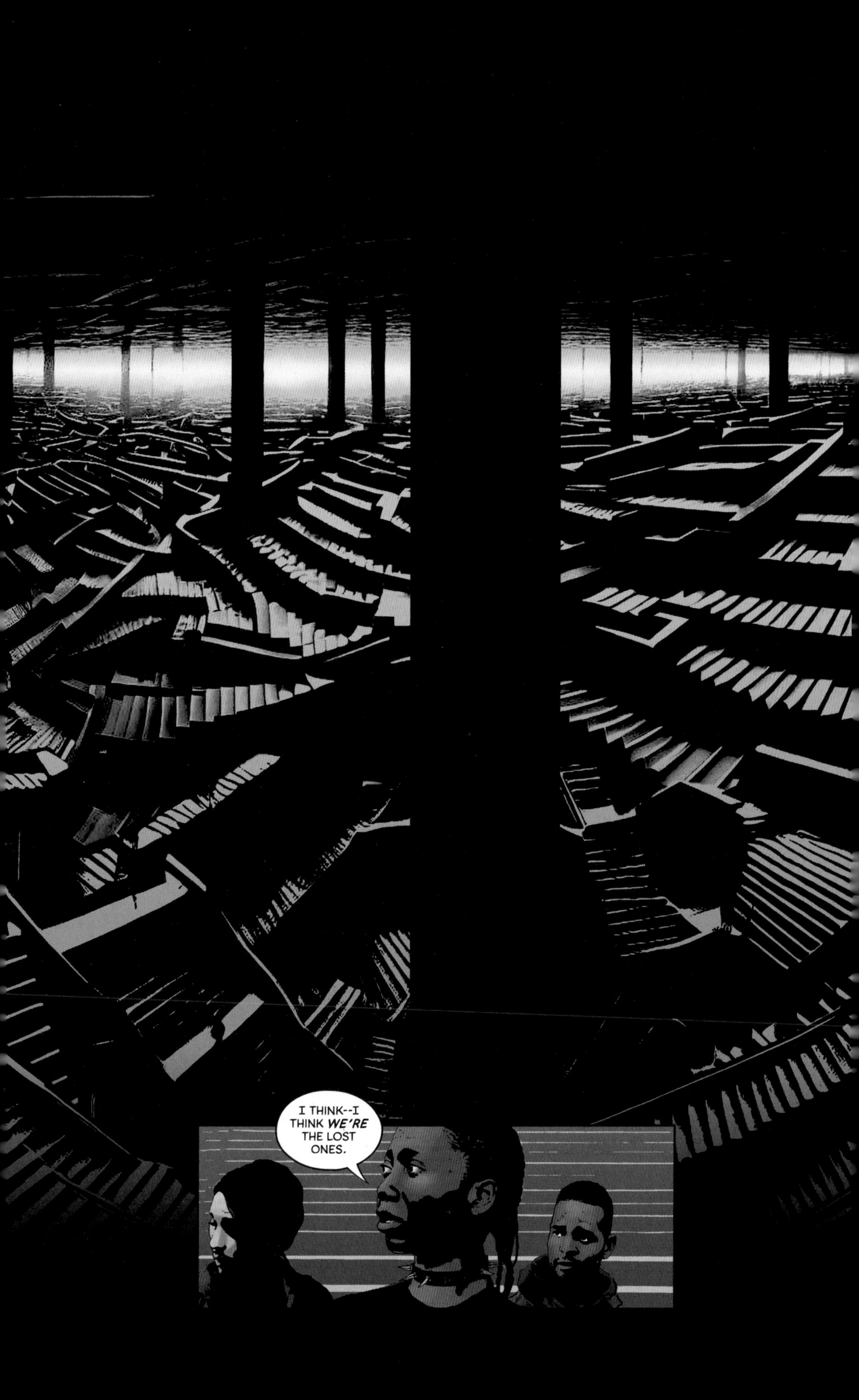
I THINK--I THINK WE'RE THE LOST ONES.

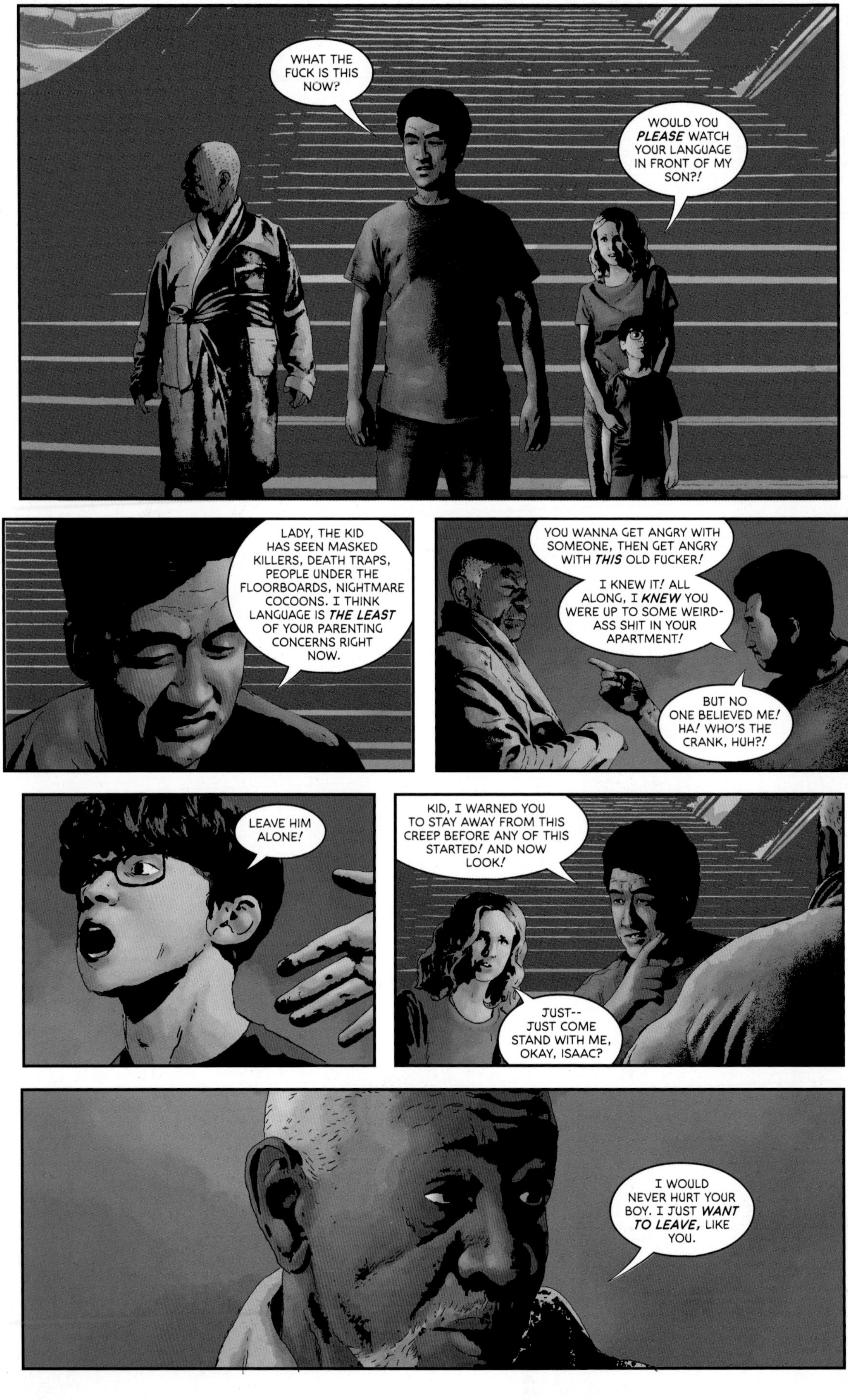
WHAT THE FUCK IS THIS NOW?
WOULD YOU *PLEASE* WATCH YOUR LANGUAGE IN FRONT OF MY SON?!
LADY, THE KID HAS SEEN MASKED KILLERS, DEATH TRAPS, PEOPLE UNDER THE FLOORBOARDS, NIGHTMARE COCOONS. I THINK LANGUAGE IS *THE LEAST* OF YOUR PARENTING CONCERNS RIGHT NOW.
YOU WANNA GET ANGRY WITH SOMEONE, THEN GET ANGRY WITH *THIS* OLD FUCKER!
I KNEW IT! ALL ALONG, I *KNEW* YOU WERE UP TO SOME WEIRD-ASS SHIT IN YOUR APARTMENT!
BUT NO ONE BELIEVED ME! HA! WHO'S THE CRANK, HUH?!
LEAVE HIM ALONE!
KID, I WARNED YOU TO STAY AWAY FROM THIS CREEP BEFORE ANY OF THIS STARTED! AND NOW LOOK!
JUST-- JUST COME STAND WITH ME, OKAY, ISAAC?
I WOULD NEVER HURT YOUR BOY. I JUST *WANT TO LEAVE,* LIKE YOU.

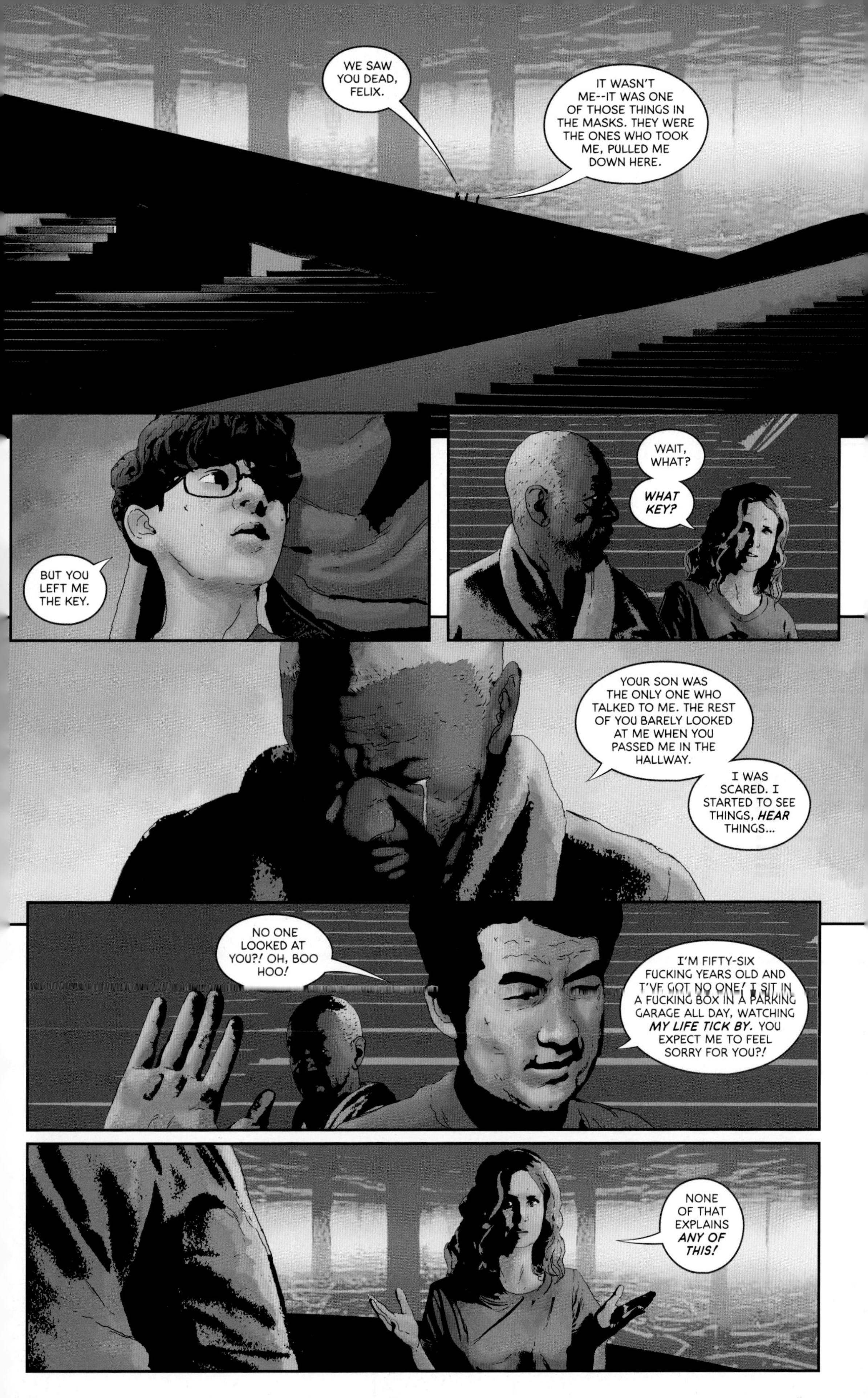

WE SAW YOU DEAD, FELIX.
IT WASN'T ME--IT WAS ONE OF THOSE THINGS IN THE MASKS. THEY WERE THE ONES WHO TOOK ME, PULLED ME DOWN HERE.
BUT YOU LEFT ME THE KEY.
WAIT, WHAT?
WHAT KEY?
YOUR SON WAS THE ONLY ONE WHO TALKED TO ME. THE REST OF YOU BARELY LOOKED AT ME WHEN YOU PASSED ME IN THE HALLWAY.
I WAS SCARED. I STARTED TO SEE THINGS, *HEAR* THINGS...
NO ONE LOOKED AT YOU?! OH, BOO HOO!
I'M FIFTY-SIX FUCKING YEARS OLD AND I'VE GOT NO ONE! I SIT IN A FUCKING BOX IN A PARKING GARAGE ALL DAY, WATCHING *MY LIFE TICK BY.* YOU EXPECT ME TO FEEL SORRY FOR YOU?!
NONE OF THAT EXPLAINS *ANY OF THIS!*

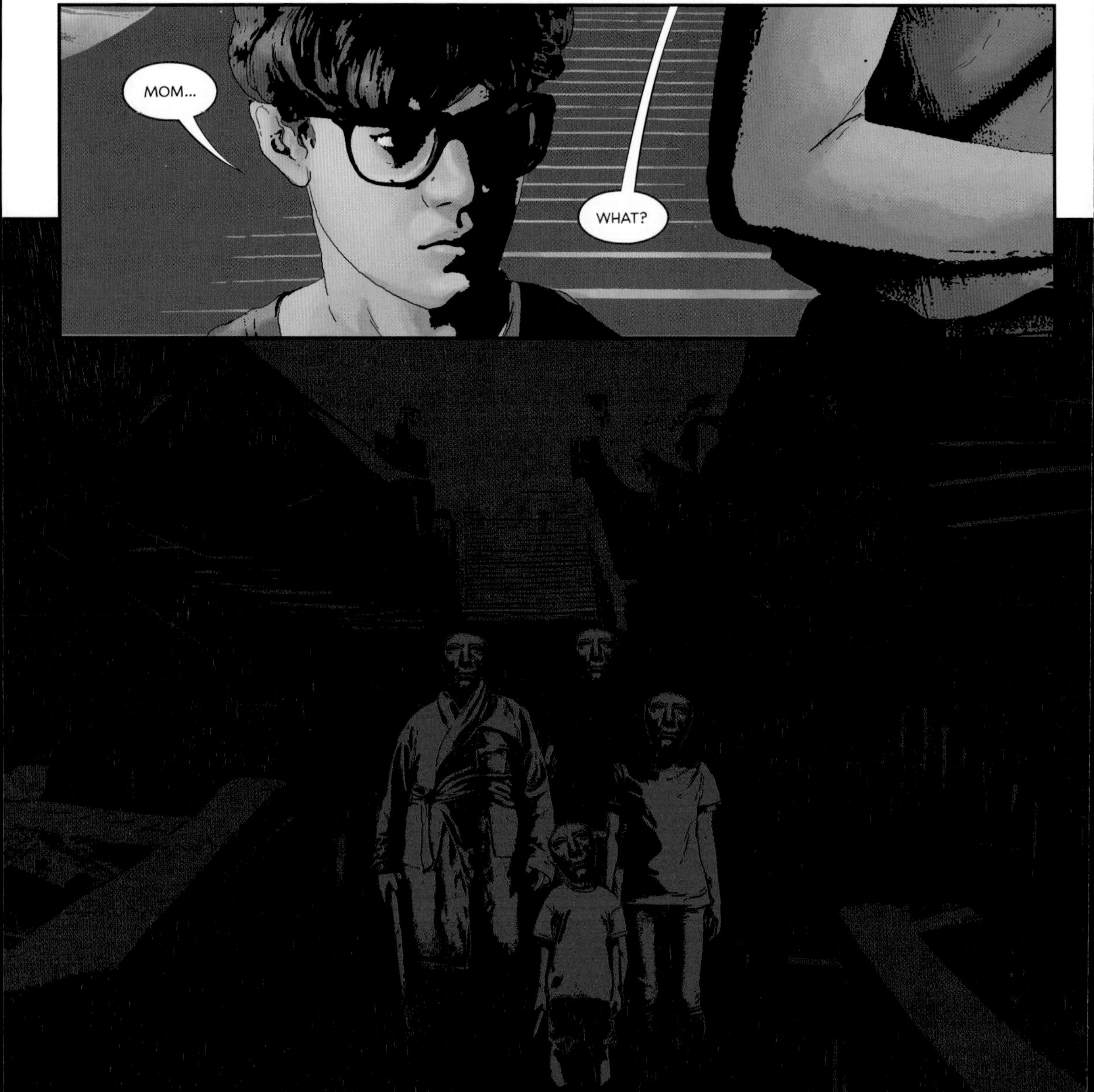
MOM...
WHAT?

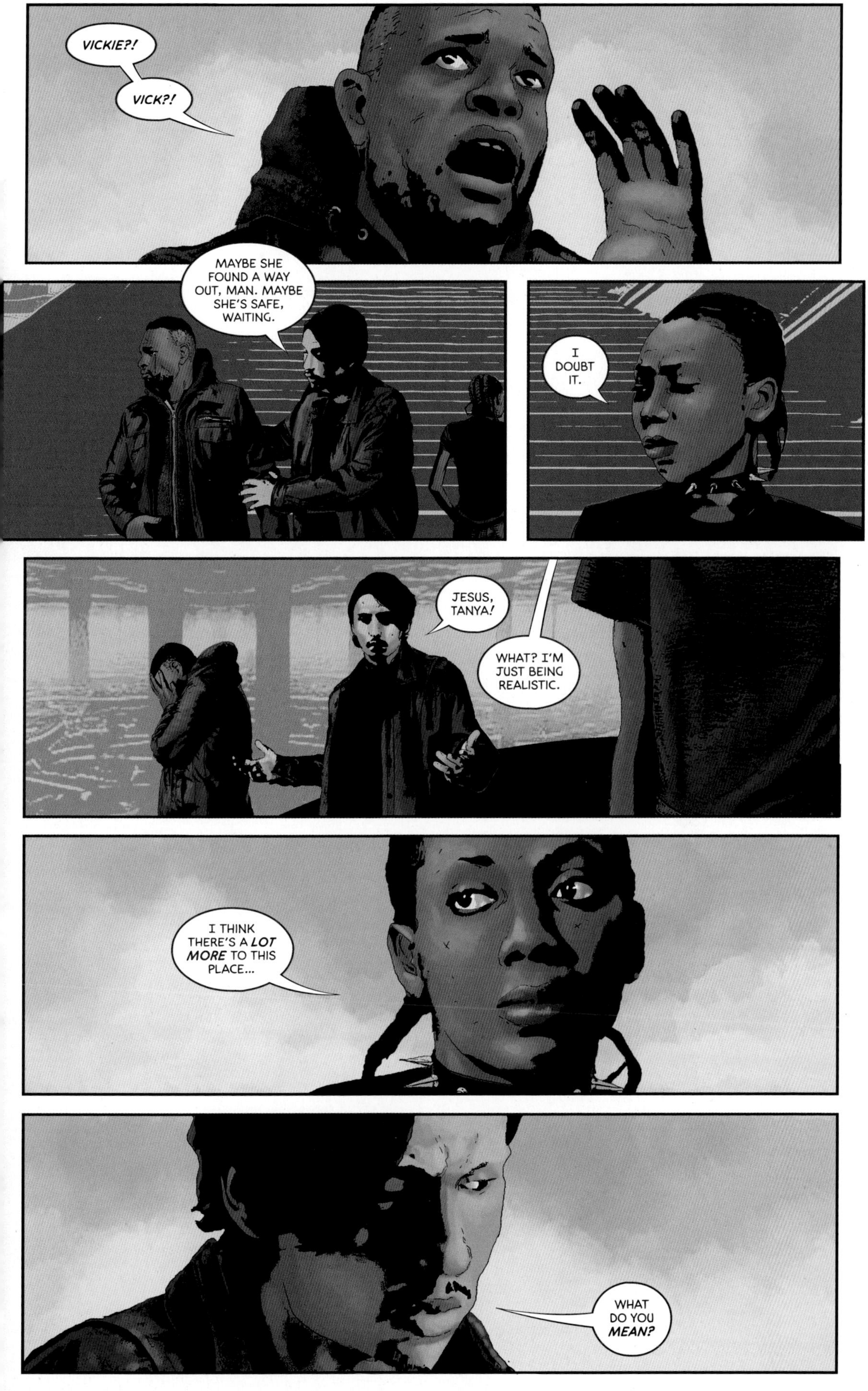
VICKIE?!
VICK?!
MAYBE SHE FOUND A WAY OUT, MAN. MAYBE SHE'S SAFE, WAITING.
I DOUBT IT.
JESUS, TANYA!
WHAT? I'M JUST BEING REALISTIC.
I THINK THERE'S A *LOT MORE* TO THIS PLACE...
WHAT DO YOU *MEAN?*

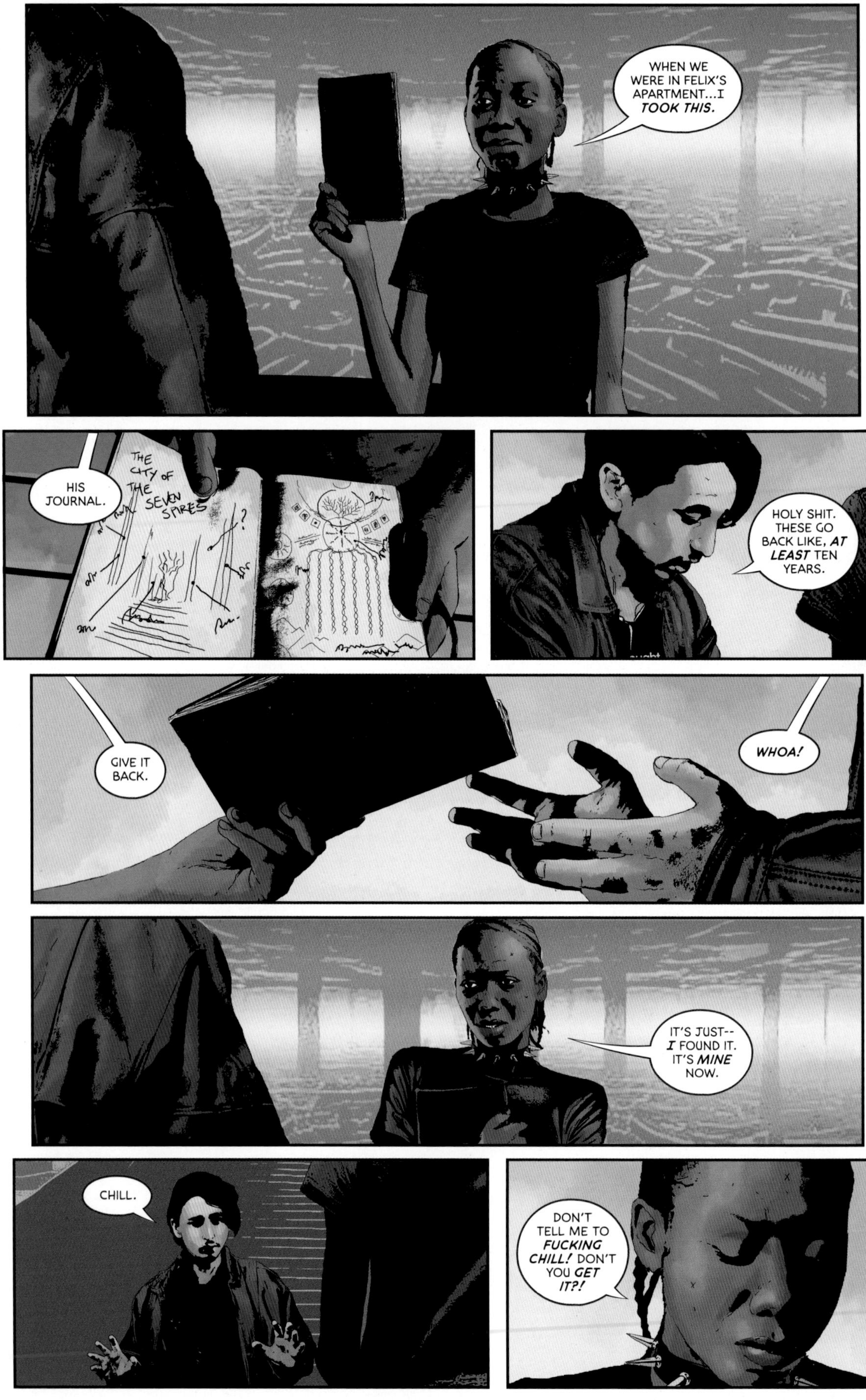
WHEN WE WERE IN FELIX'S APARTMENT...I *TOOK THIS.*
HIS JOURNAL.
THE CITY OF THE SEVEN SPIRES
HOLY SHIT. THESE GO BACK LIKE, *AT LEAST* TEN YEARS.
GIVE IT BACK.
WHOA!
IT'S JUST-- *I* FOUND IT. IT'S *MINE* NOW.
CHILL.
DON'T TELL ME TO *FUCKING CHILL!* DON'T YOU *GET IT?!*

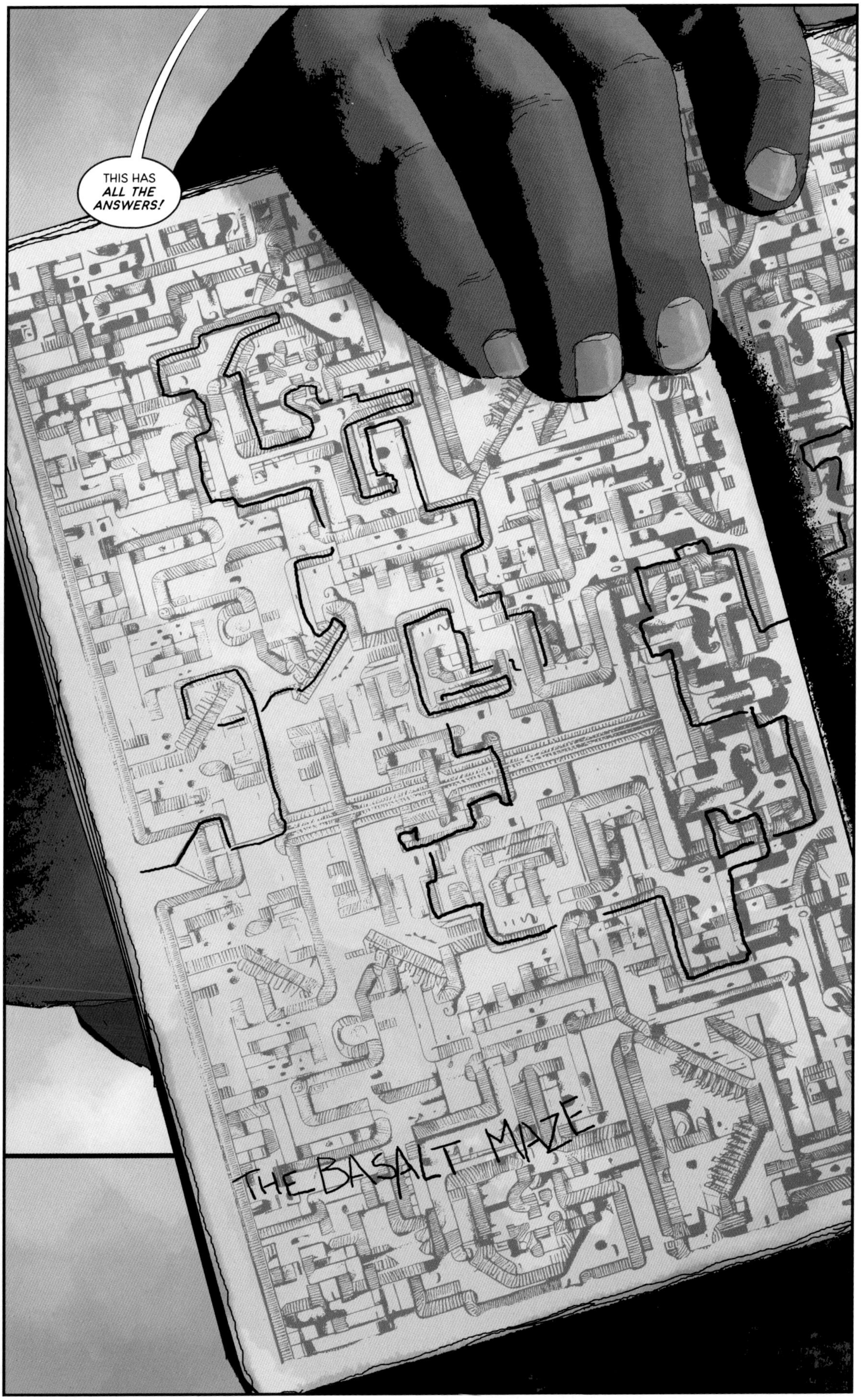
THIS HAS ALL THE ANSWERS!
THE BASALT MAZE

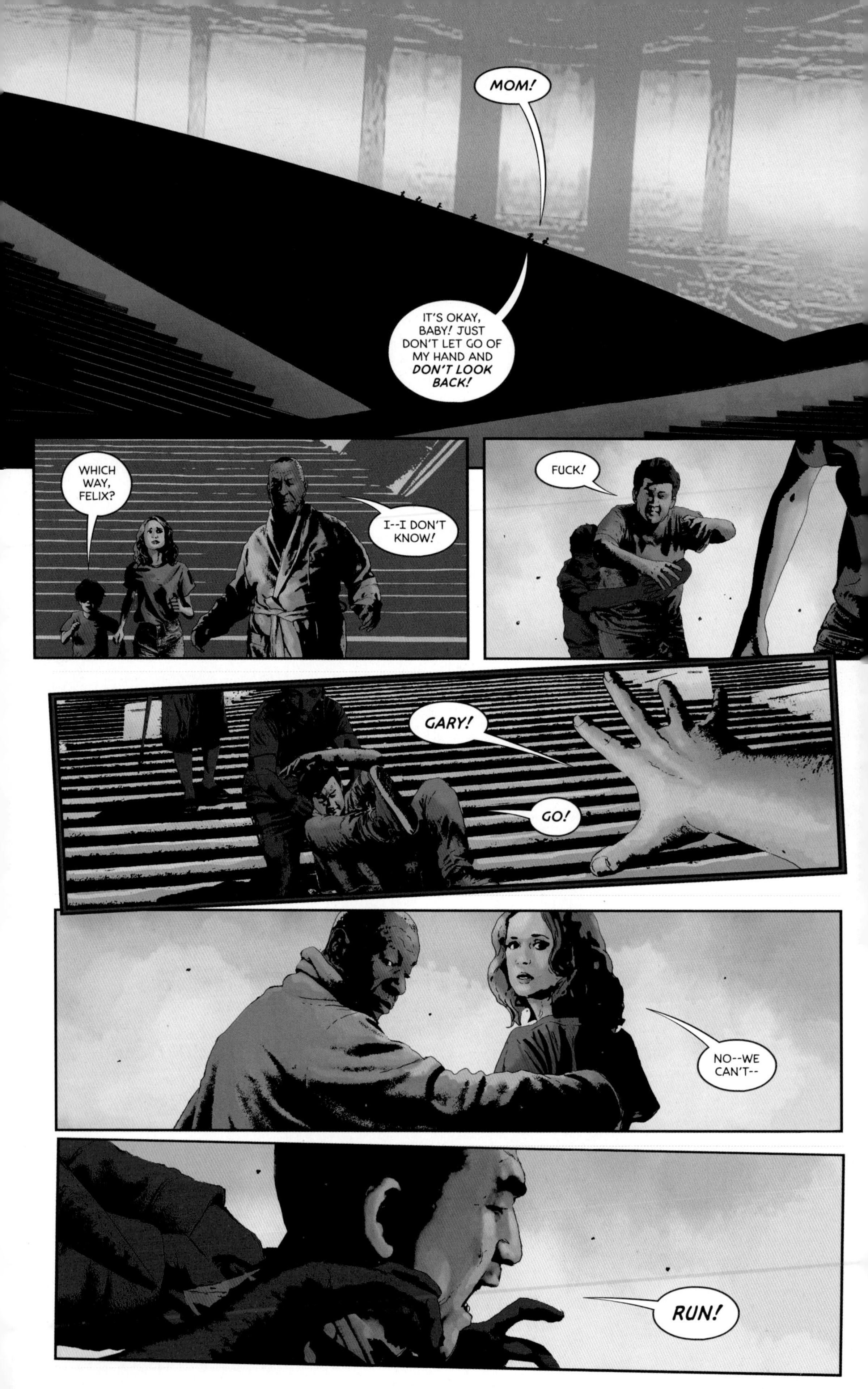
MOM!
IT'S OKAY, BABY! JUST DON'T LET GO OF MY HAND AND DON'T LOOK BACK!
WHICH WAY, FELIX?
I--I DON'T KNOW!
FUCK!
GARY!
GO!
NO--WE CAN'T--
RUN!

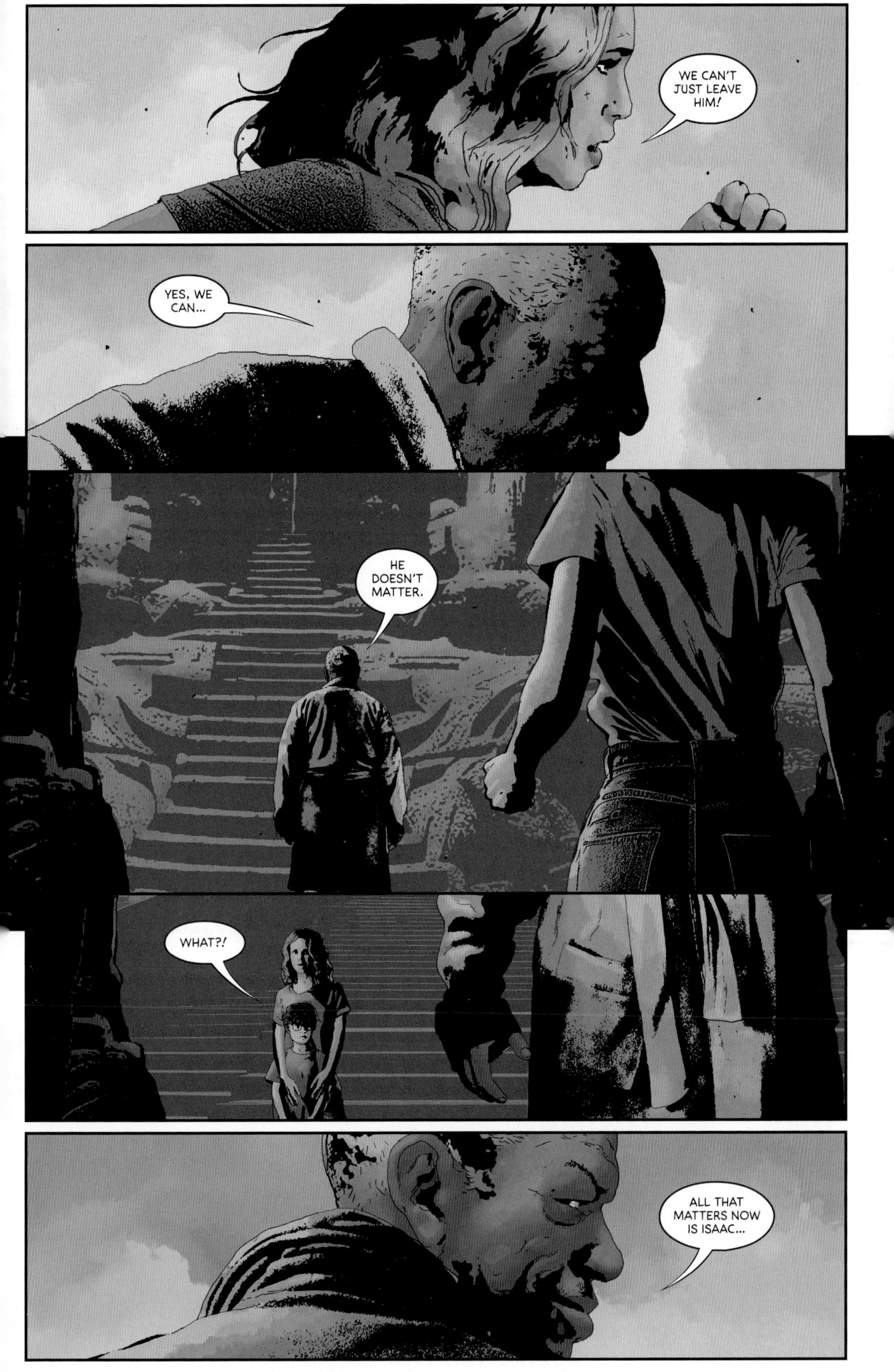
WE CAN'T JUST LEAVE HIM!
YES, WE CAN...
HE DOESN'T MATTER.
WHAT?!
ALL THAT MATTERS NOW IS ISAAC...

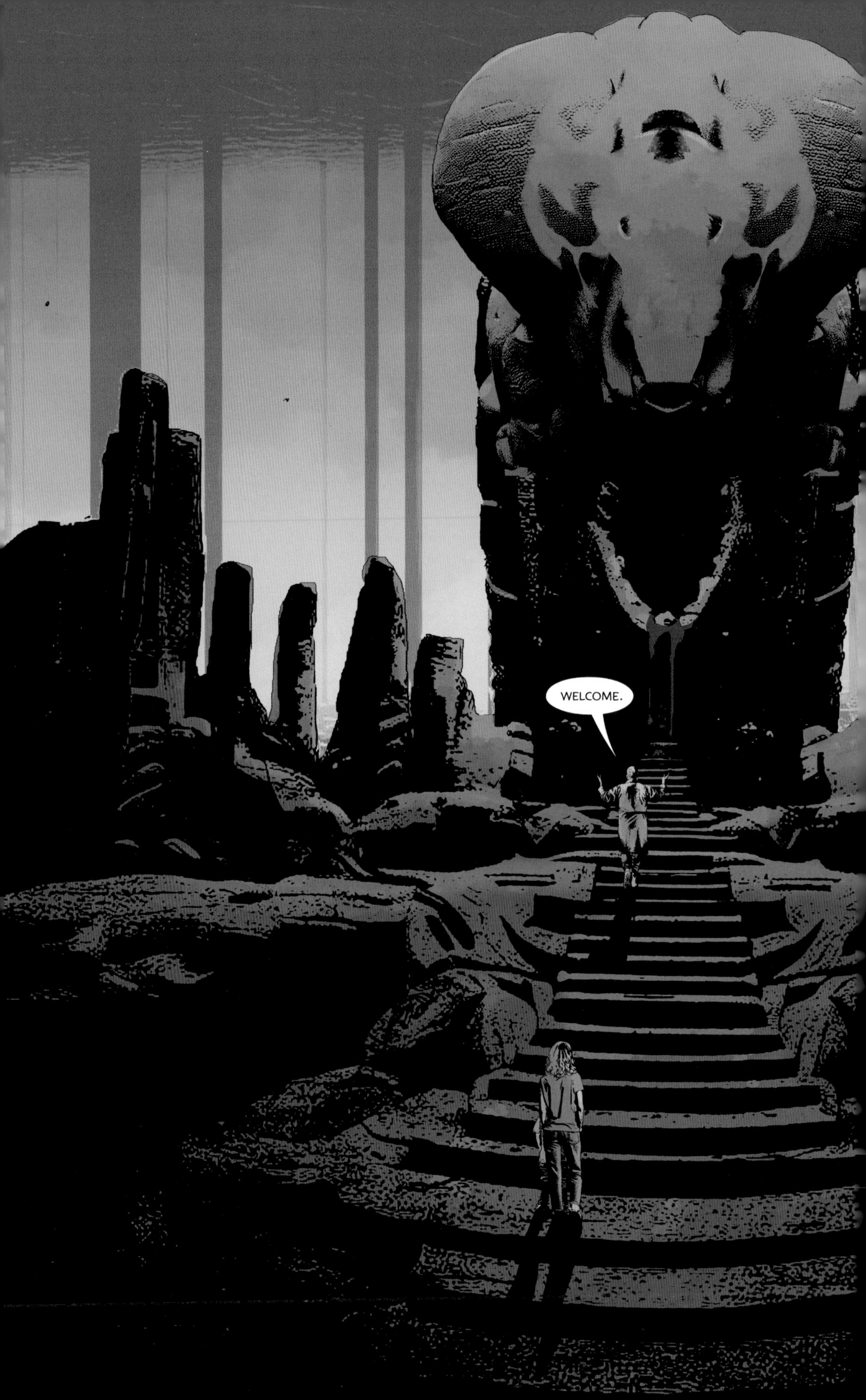
WELCOME.

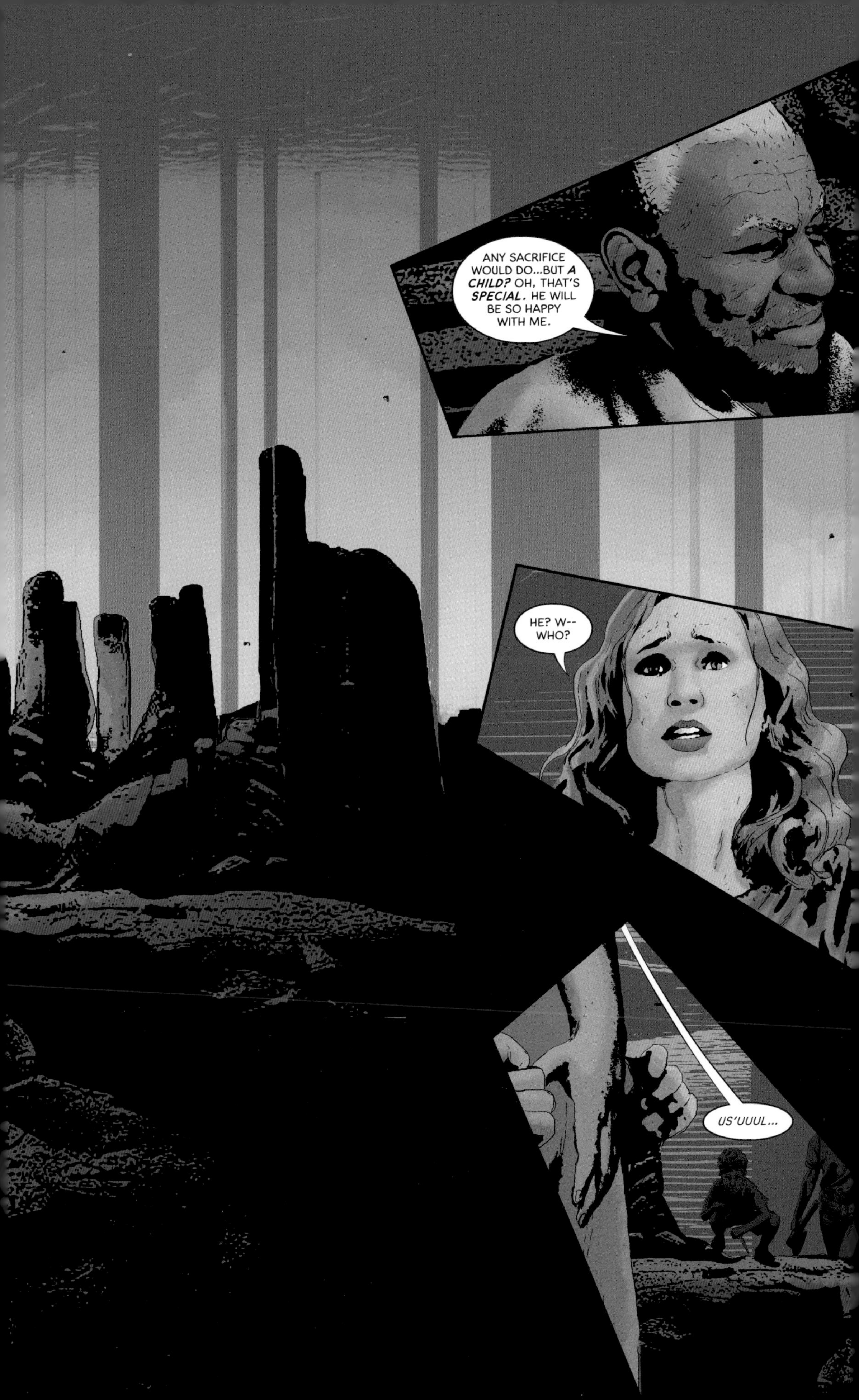
ANY SACRIFICE WOULD DO...BUT *A CHILD?* OH, THAT'S *SPECIAL.* HE WILL BE SO HAPPY WITH ME.
HE? W-- WHO?
US'UUUL...

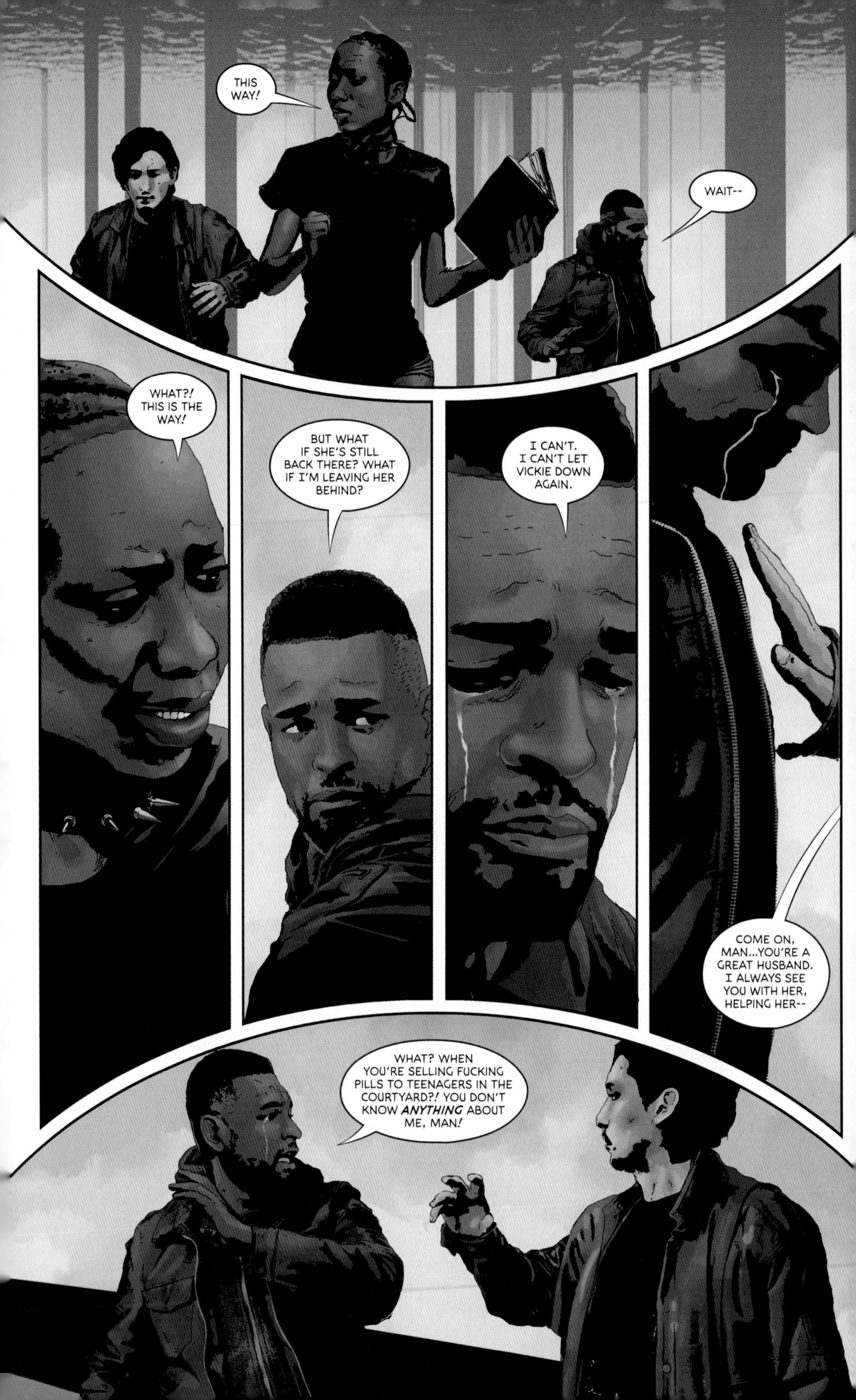
THIS WAY!
WAIT--
WHAT?! THIS IS THE WAY!
BUT WHAT IF SHE'S STILL BACK THERE? WHAT IF I'M LEAVING HER BEHIND?
I CAN'T. I CAN'T LET VICKIE DOWN AGAIN.
COME ON, MAN...YOU'RE A GREAT HUSBAND. I ALWAYS SEE YOU WITH HER, HELPING HER--
WHAT? WHEN YOU'RE SELLING FUCKING PILLS TO TEENAGERS IN THE COURTYARD?! YOU DON'T KNOW ***ANYTHING*** ABOUT ME, MAN!

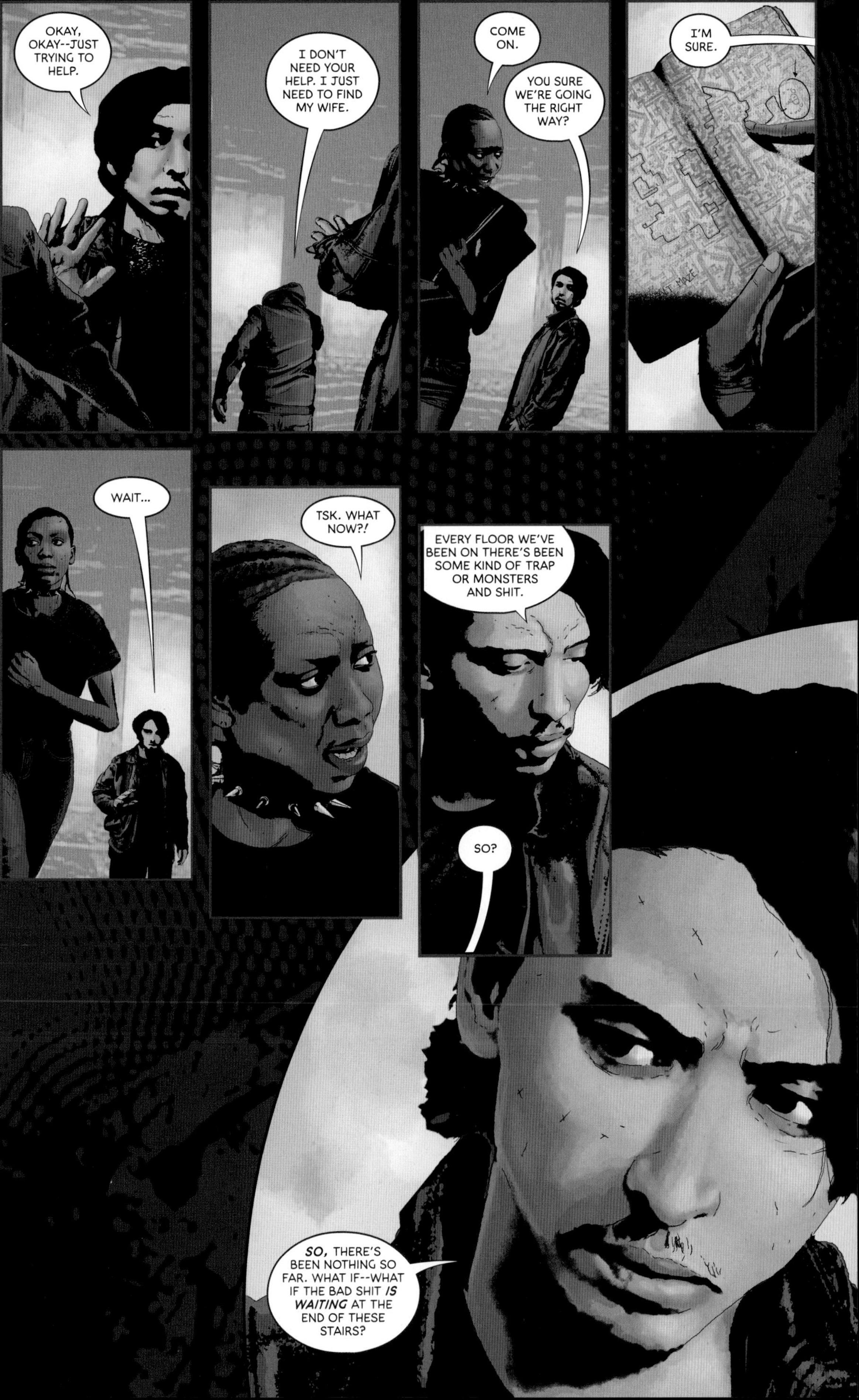
OKAY, OKAY--JUST TRYING TO HELP.
I DON'T NEED YOUR HELP. I JUST NEED TO FIND MY WIFE.
COME ON.
YOU SURE WE'RE GOING THE RIGHT WAY?
I'M SURE.
WAIT...
TSK. WHAT NOW?!
EVERY FLOOR WE'VE BEEN ON THERE'S BEEN SOME KIND OF TRAP OR MONSTERS AND SHIT.
SO?
SO, THERE'S BEEN NOTHING SO FAR. WHAT IF--WHAT IF THE BAD SHIT *IS WAITING* AT THE END OF THESE STAIRS?

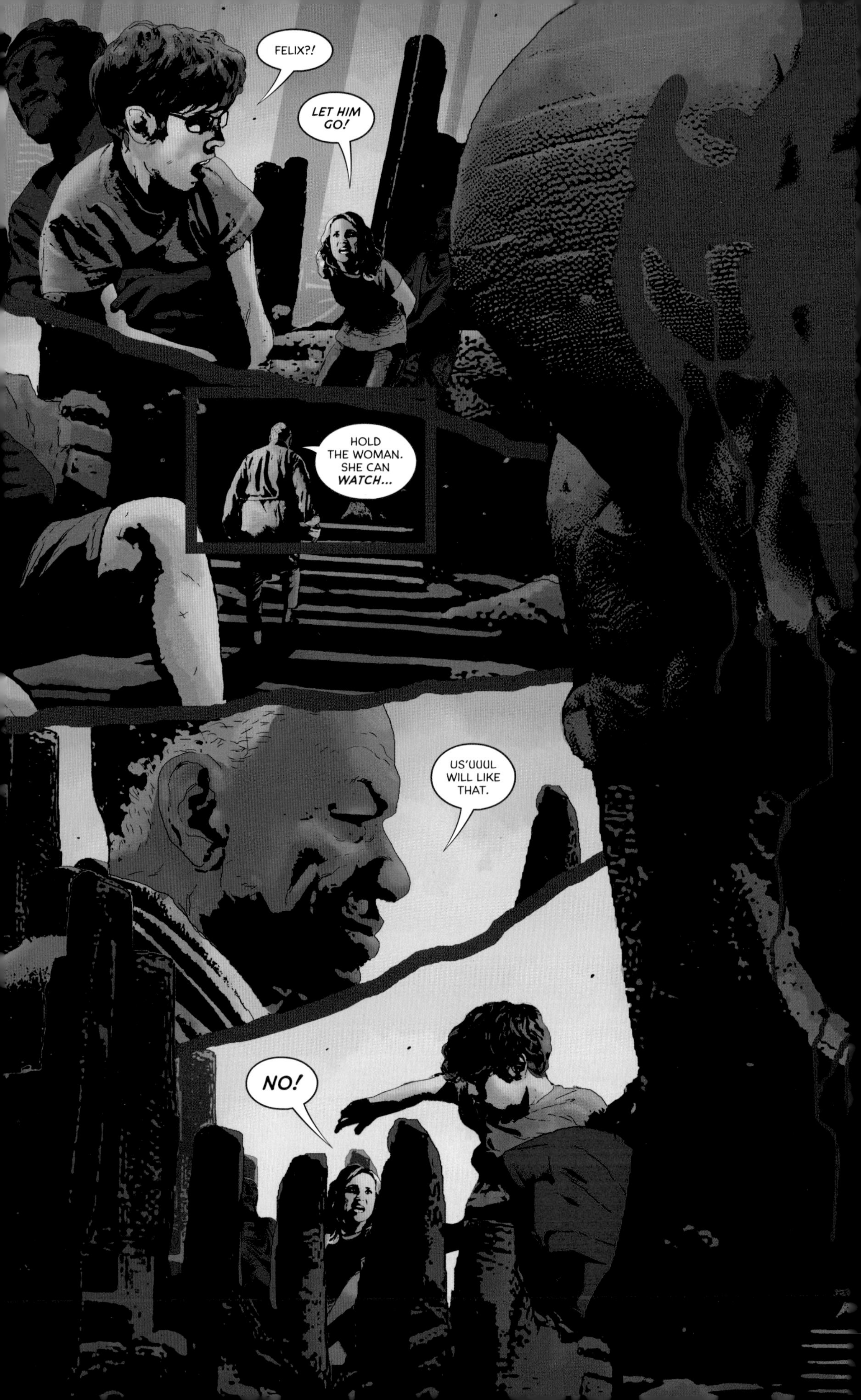
FELIX?!
LET HIM GO!
HOLD THE WOMAN. SHE CAN WATCH...
US'UUUL WILL LIKE THAT.
NO!

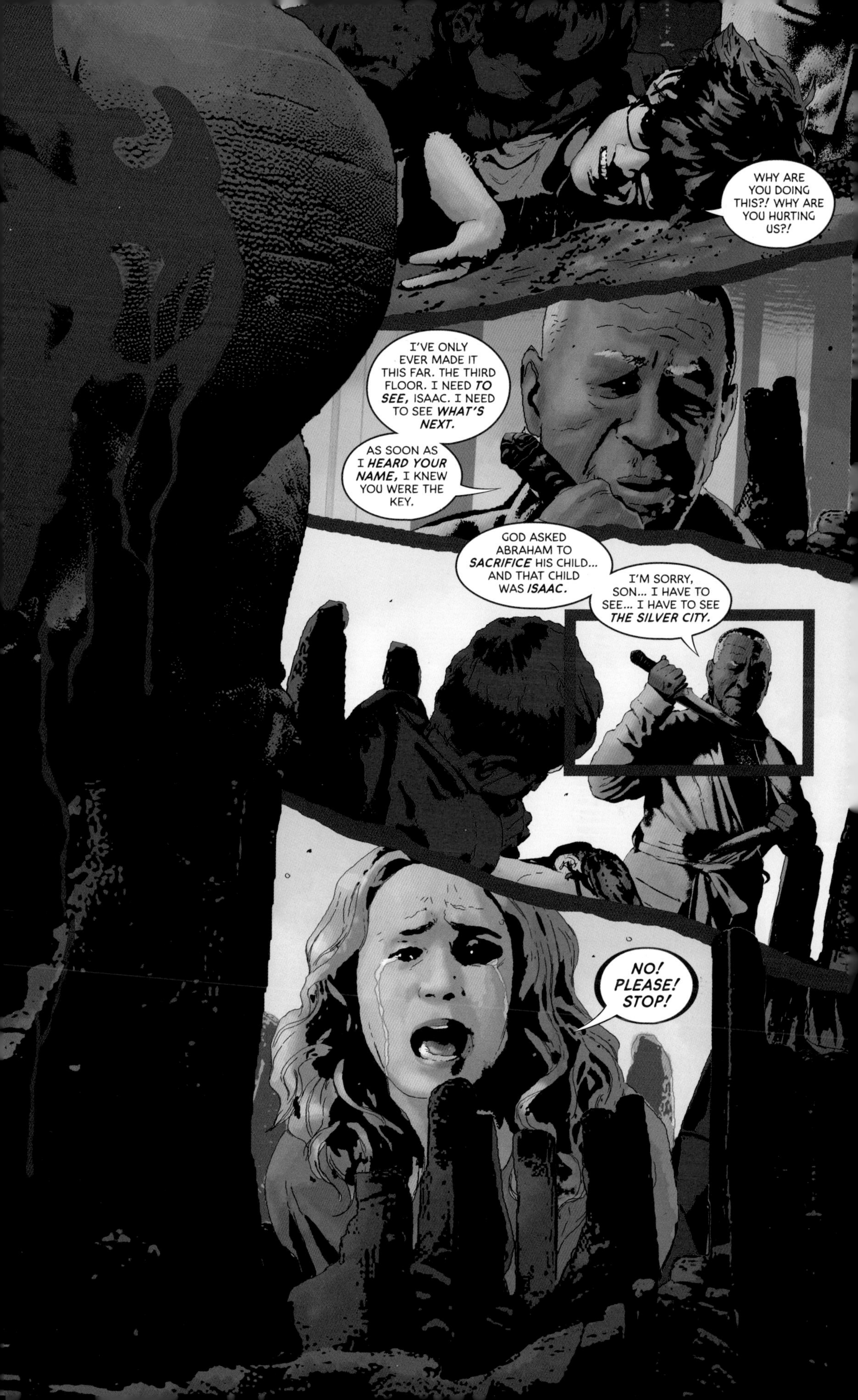
WHY ARE YOU DOING THIS?! WHY ARE YOU HURTING US?!
I'VE ONLY EVER MADE IT THIS FAR. THE THIRD FLOOR. I NEED TO SEE, ISAAC. I NEED TO SEE WHAT'S NEXT.
AS SOON AS I HEARD YOUR NAME, I KNEW YOU WERE THE KEY.
GOD ASKED ABRAHAM TO SACRIFICE HIS CHILD... AND THAT CHILD WAS ISAAC.
I'M SORRY, SON... I HAVE TO SEE... I HAVE TO SEE THE SILVER CITY.
NO! PLEASE! STOP!

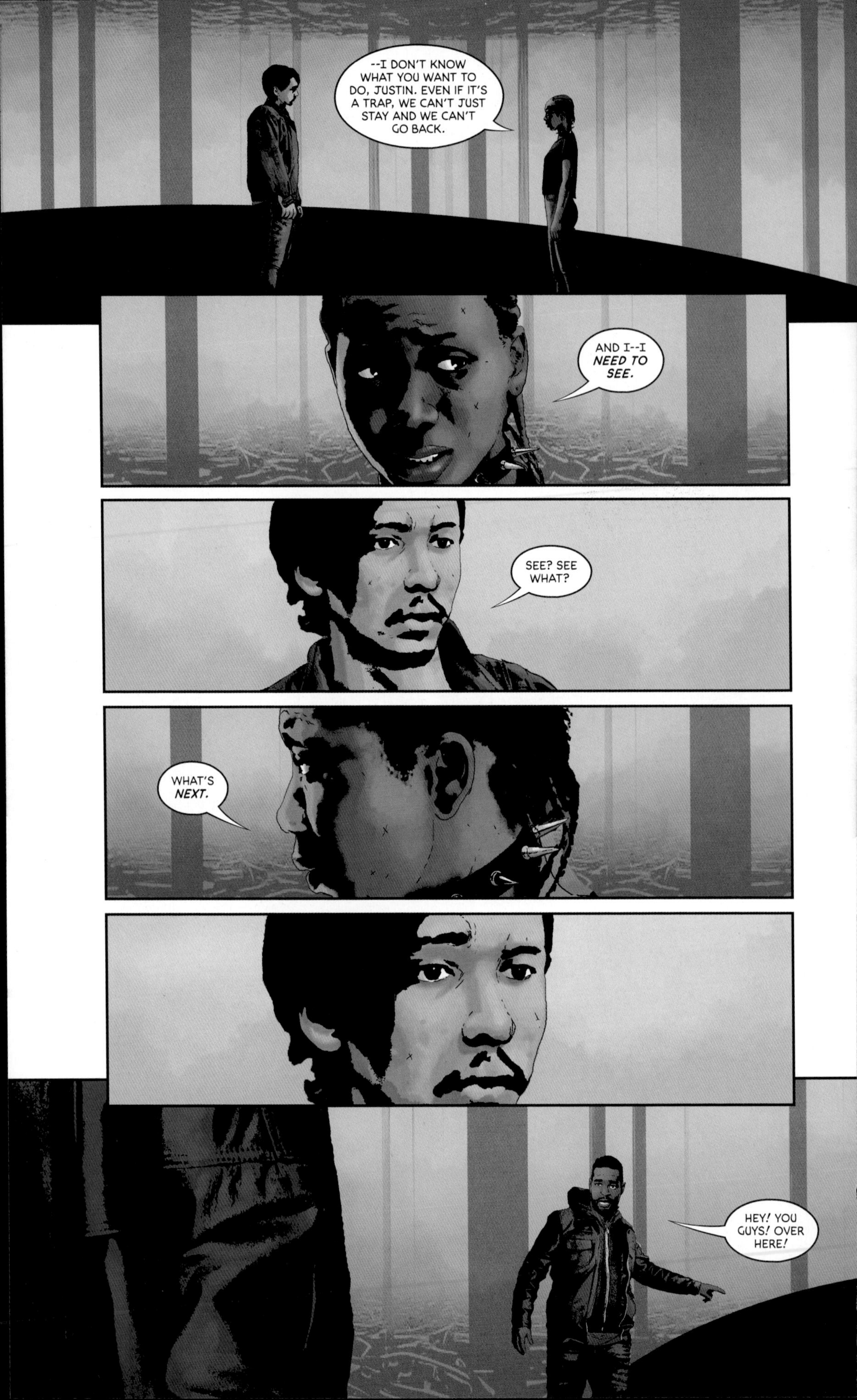
--I DON'T KNOW WHAT YOU WANT TO DO, JUSTIN. EVEN IF IT'S A TRAP, WE CAN'T JUST STAY AND WE CAN'T GO BACK.
AND I--I *NEED TO SEE.*
SEE? SEE WHAT?
WHAT'S *NEXT.*
HEY! YOU GUYS! OVER HERE!

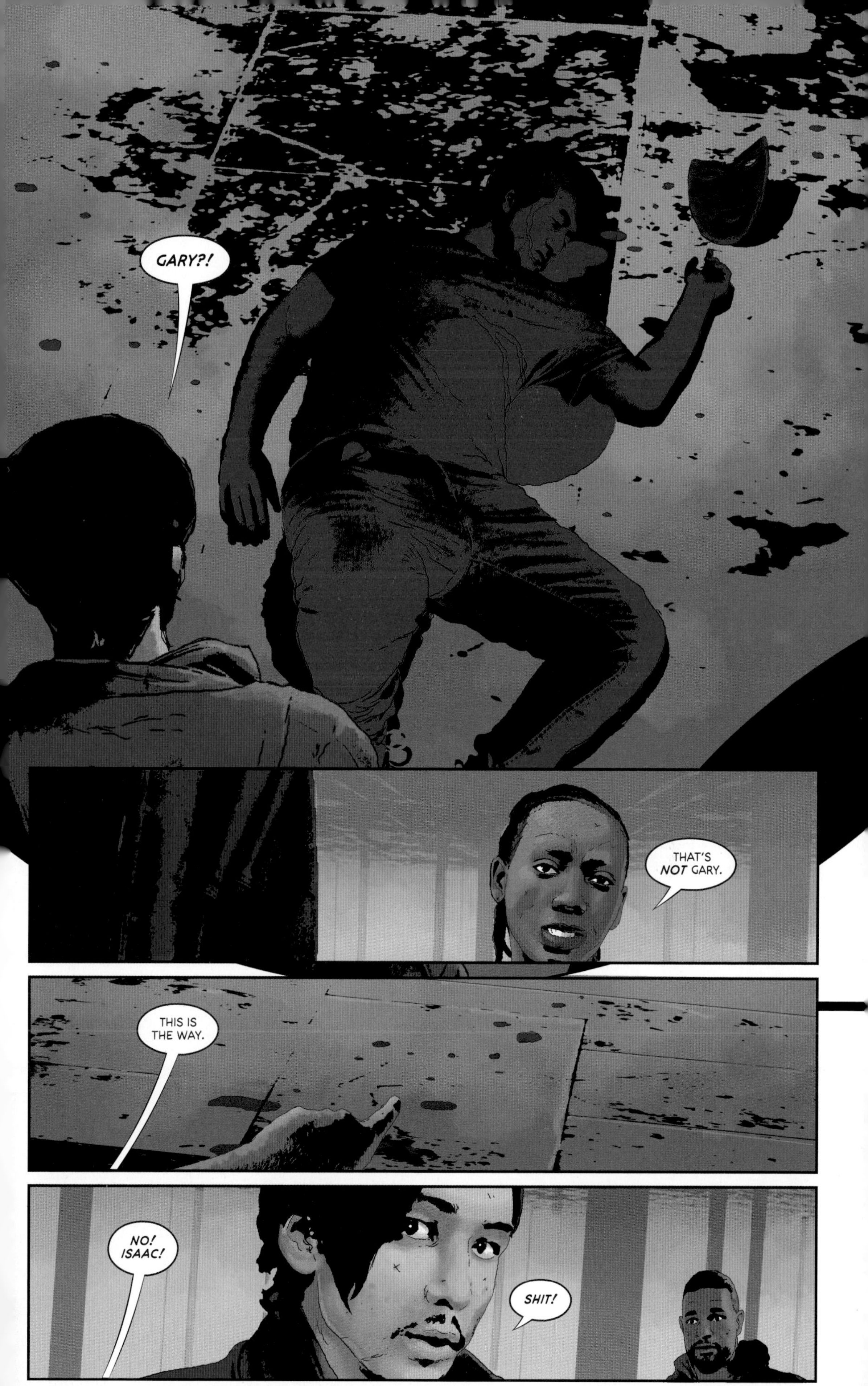
GARY?!
THAT'S NOT GARY.
THIS IS THE WAY.
NO! ISAAC!
SHIT!

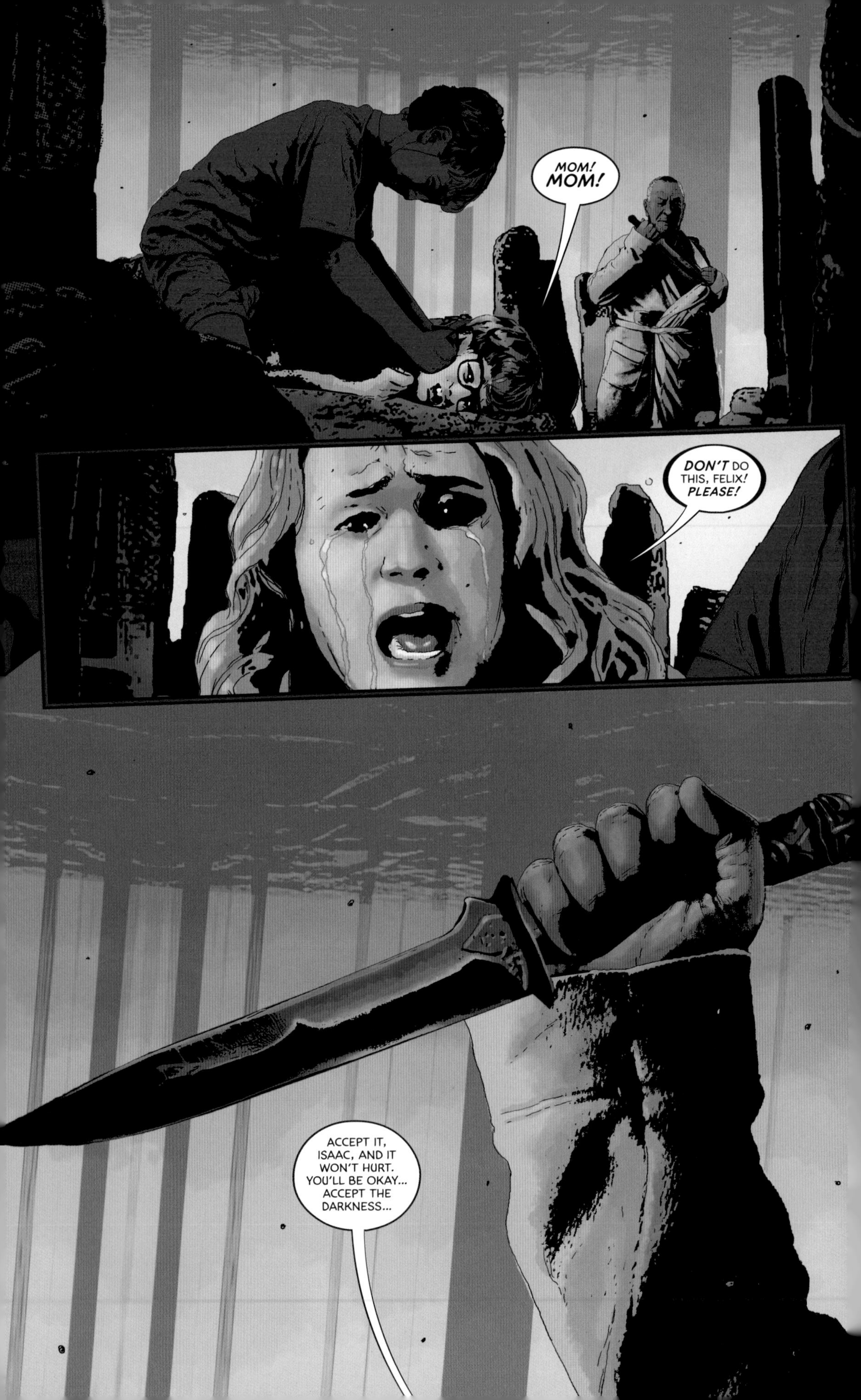
MOM! MOM!
DON'T DO THIS, FELIX! PLEASE!
ACCEPT IT, ISAAC, AND IT WON'T HURT. YOU'LL BE OKAY... ACCEPT THE DARKNESS...

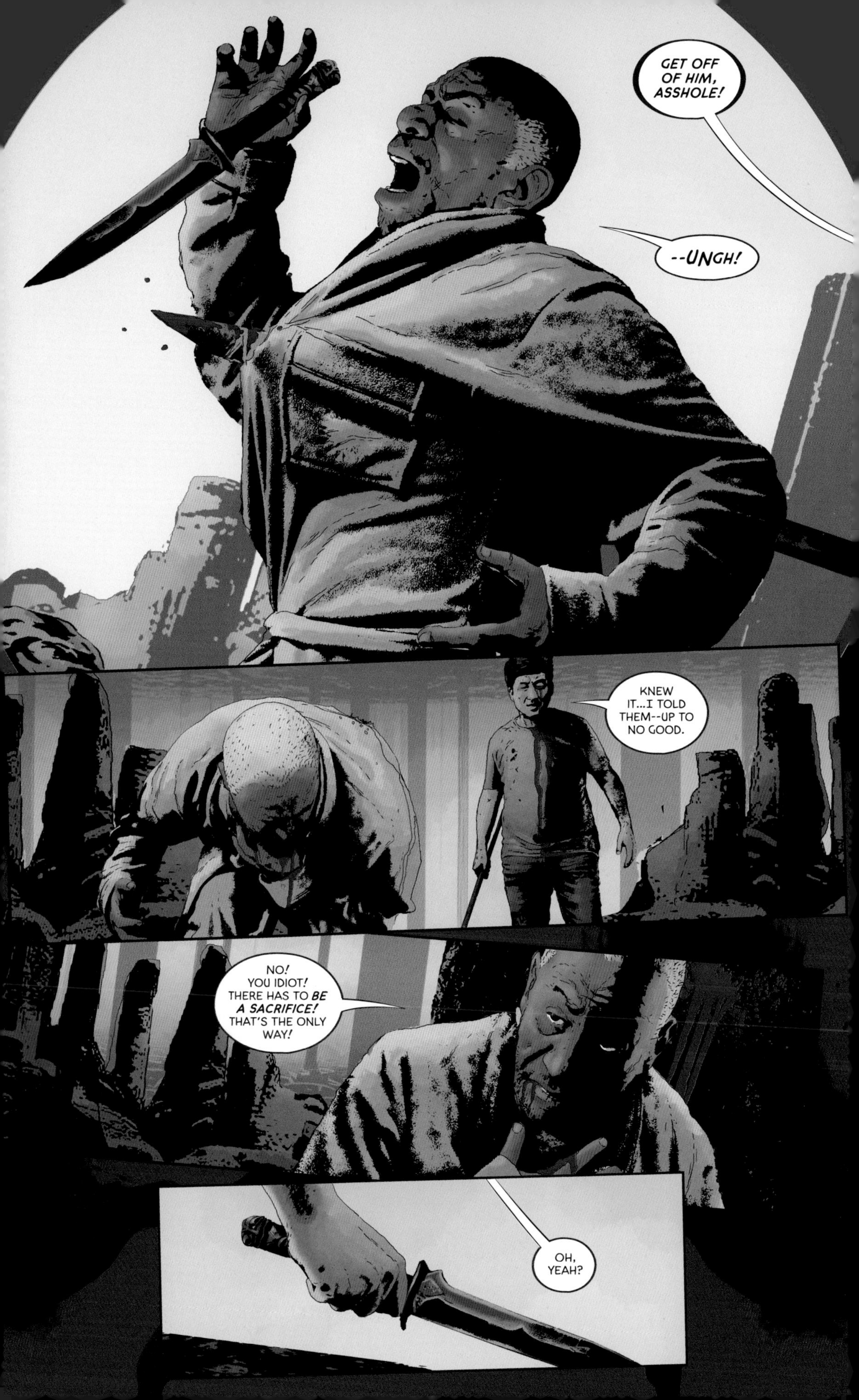
GET OFF OF HIM, ASSHOLE!
--UNGH!
KNEW IT...I TOLD THEM--UP TO NO GOOD.
NO! YOU IDIOT! THERE HAS TO BE A SACRIFICE! THAT'S THE ONLY WAY!
OH, YEAH?

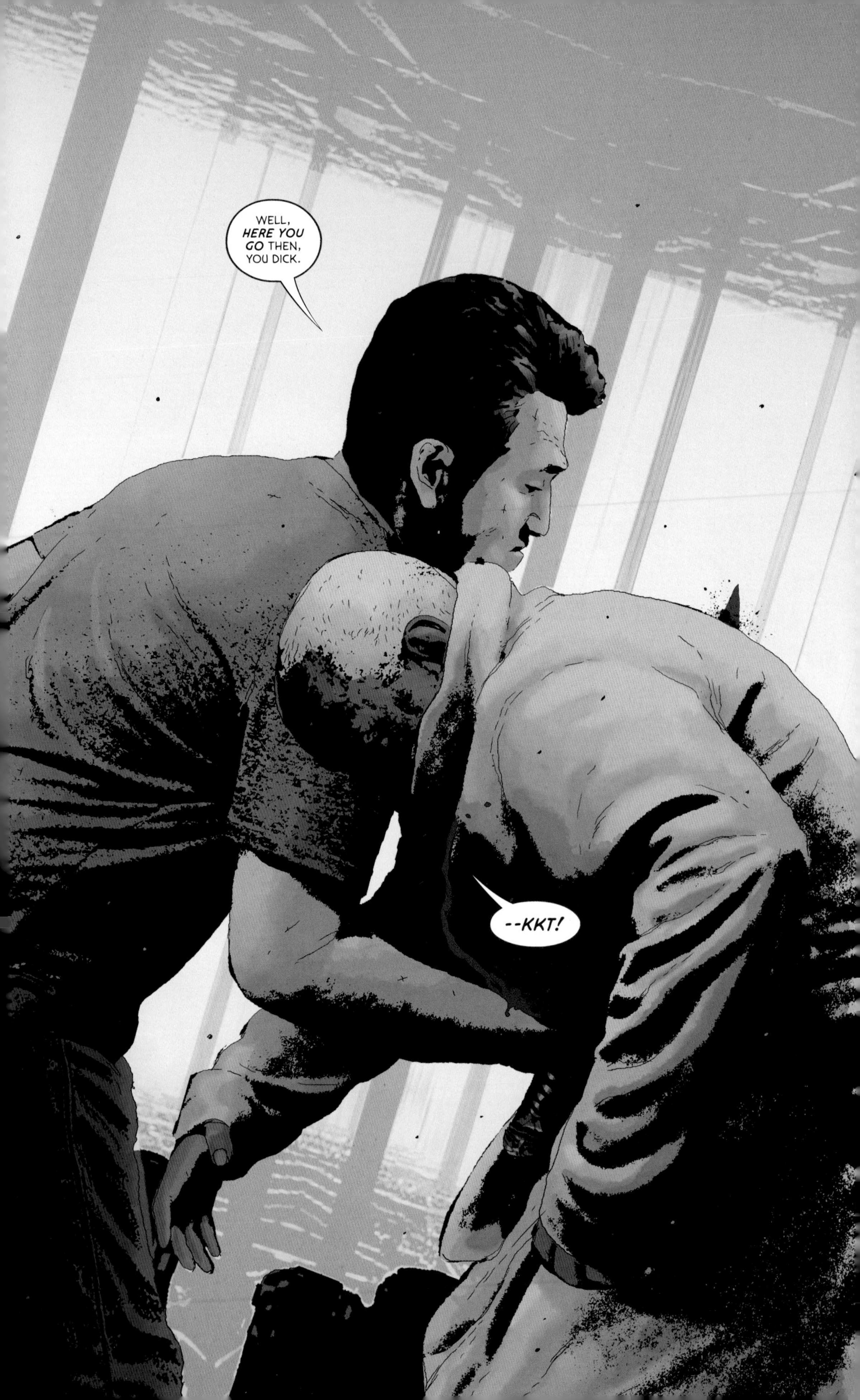
WELL, HERE YOU GO THEN, YOU DICK.
--KKT!

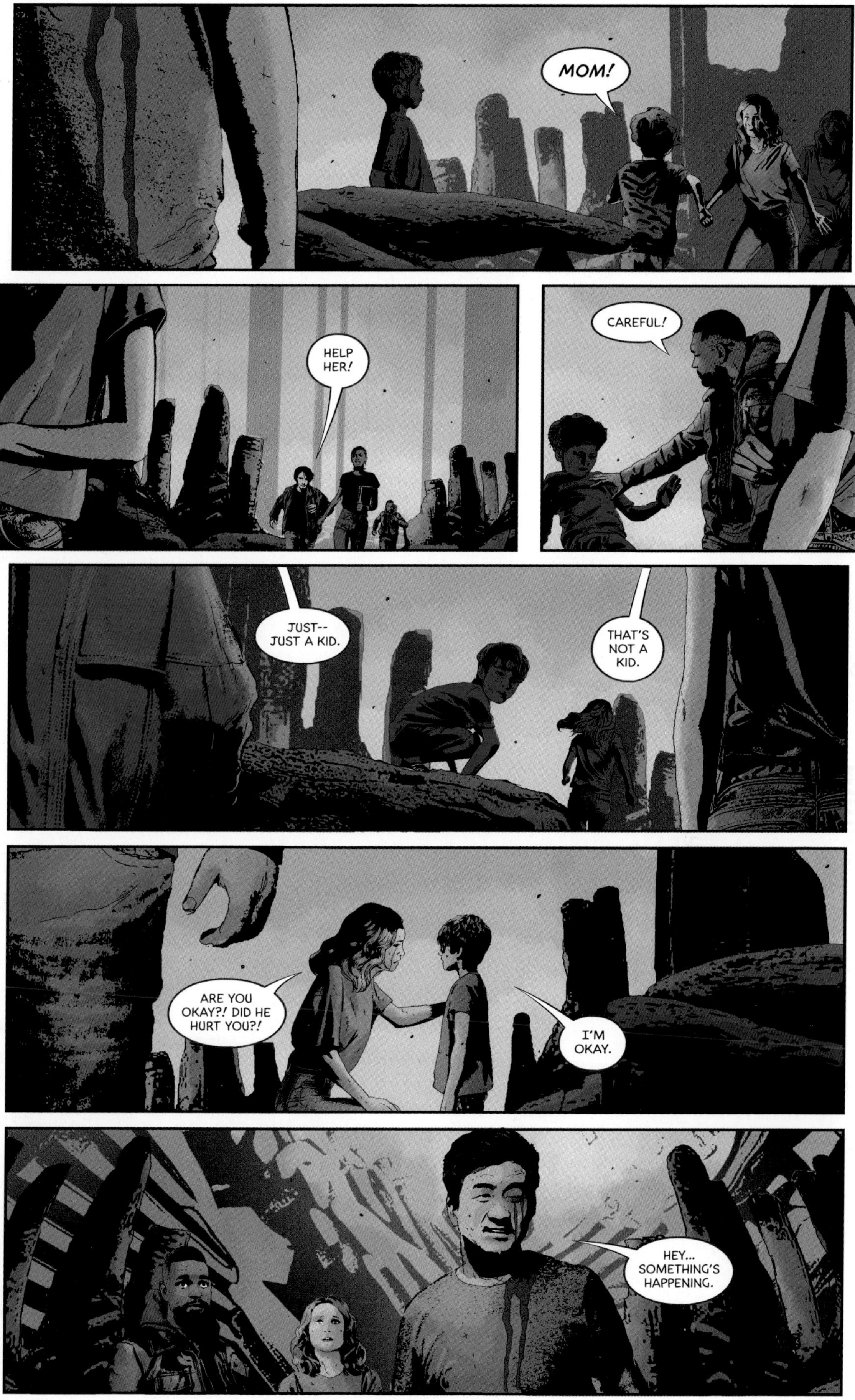
MOM!
HELP HER!
CAREFUL!
JUST-- JUST A KID.
THAT'S NOT A KID.
ARE YOU OKAY?! DID HE HURT YOU?!
I'M OKAY.
HEY... SOMETHING'S HAPPENING.

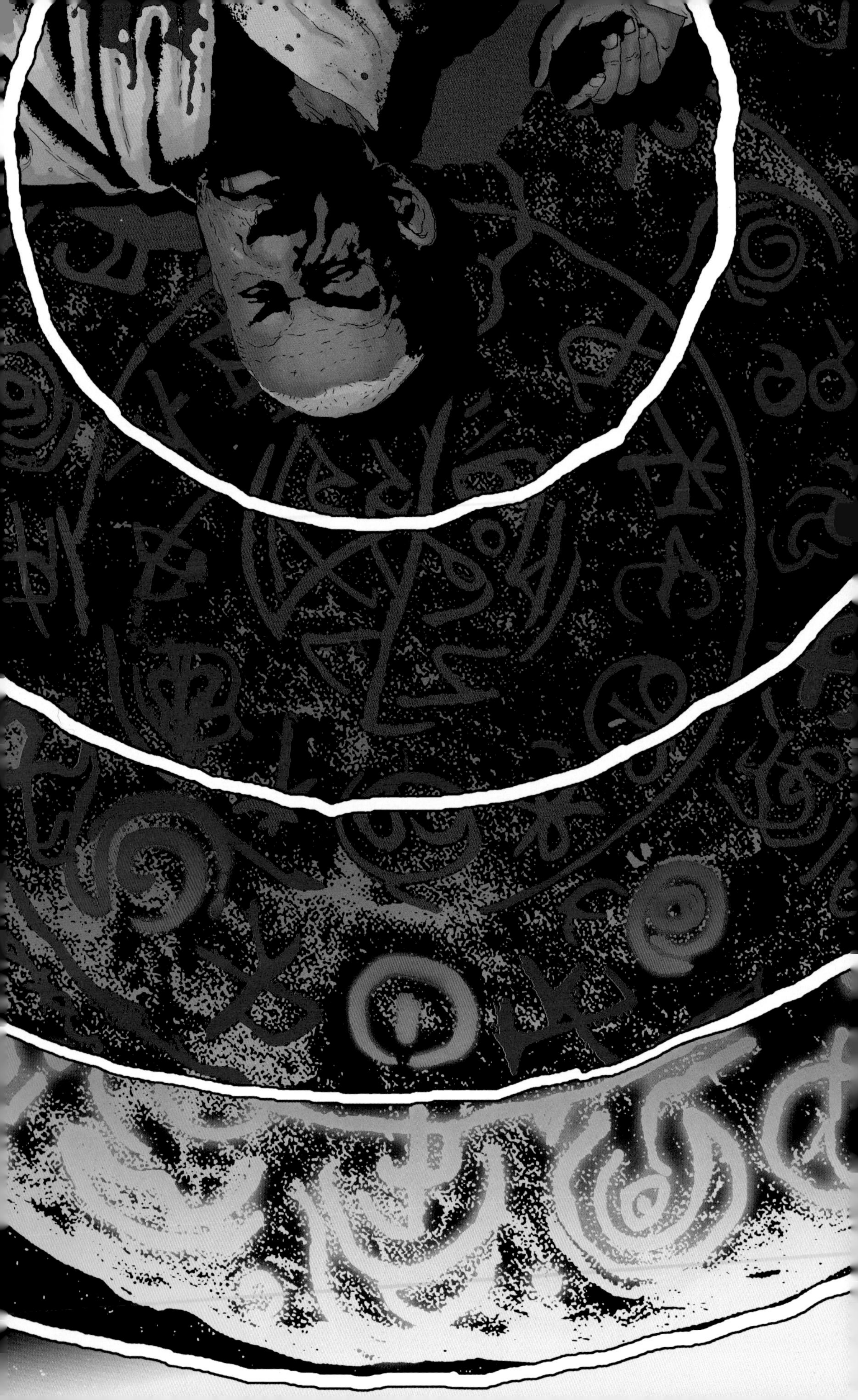

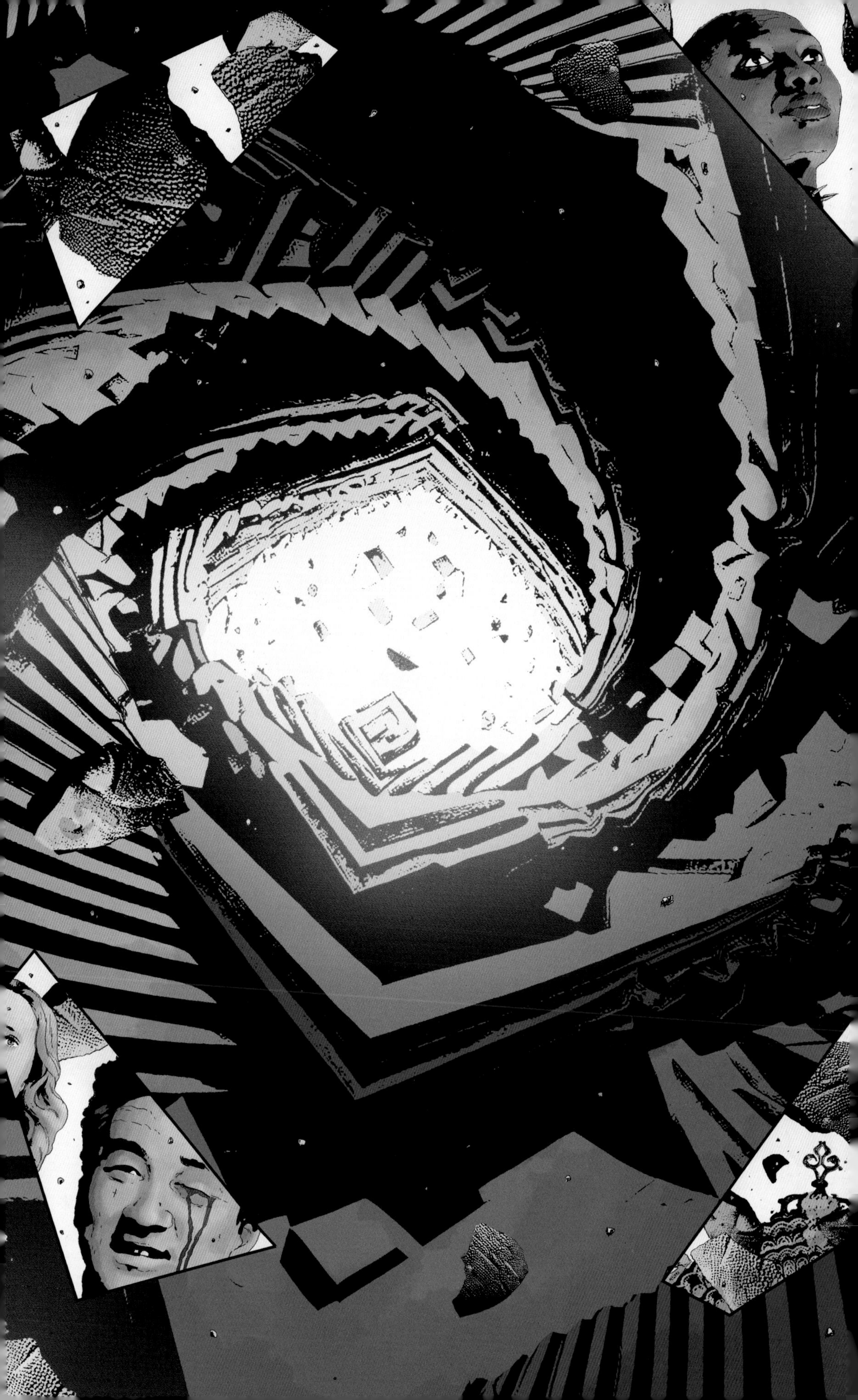

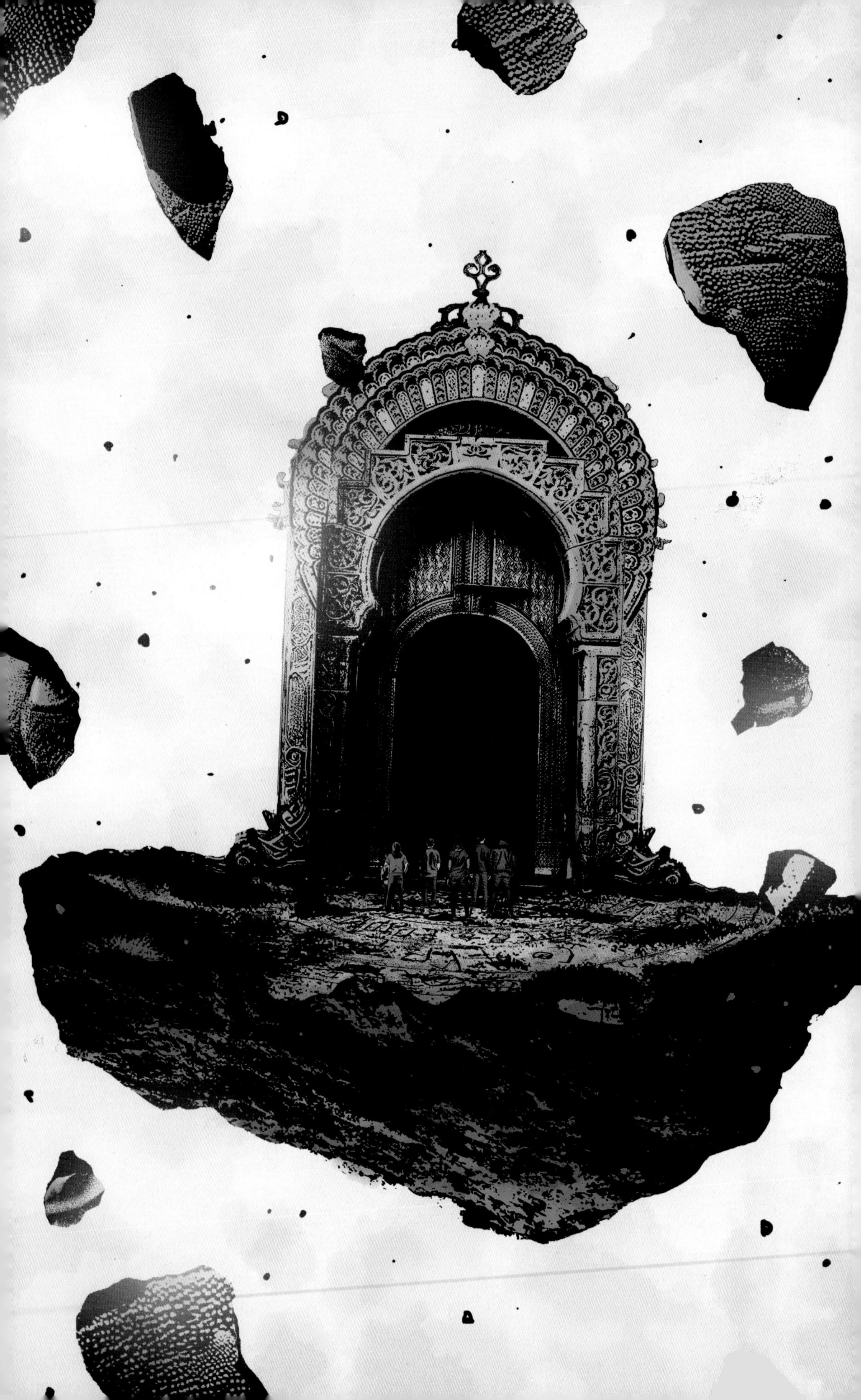

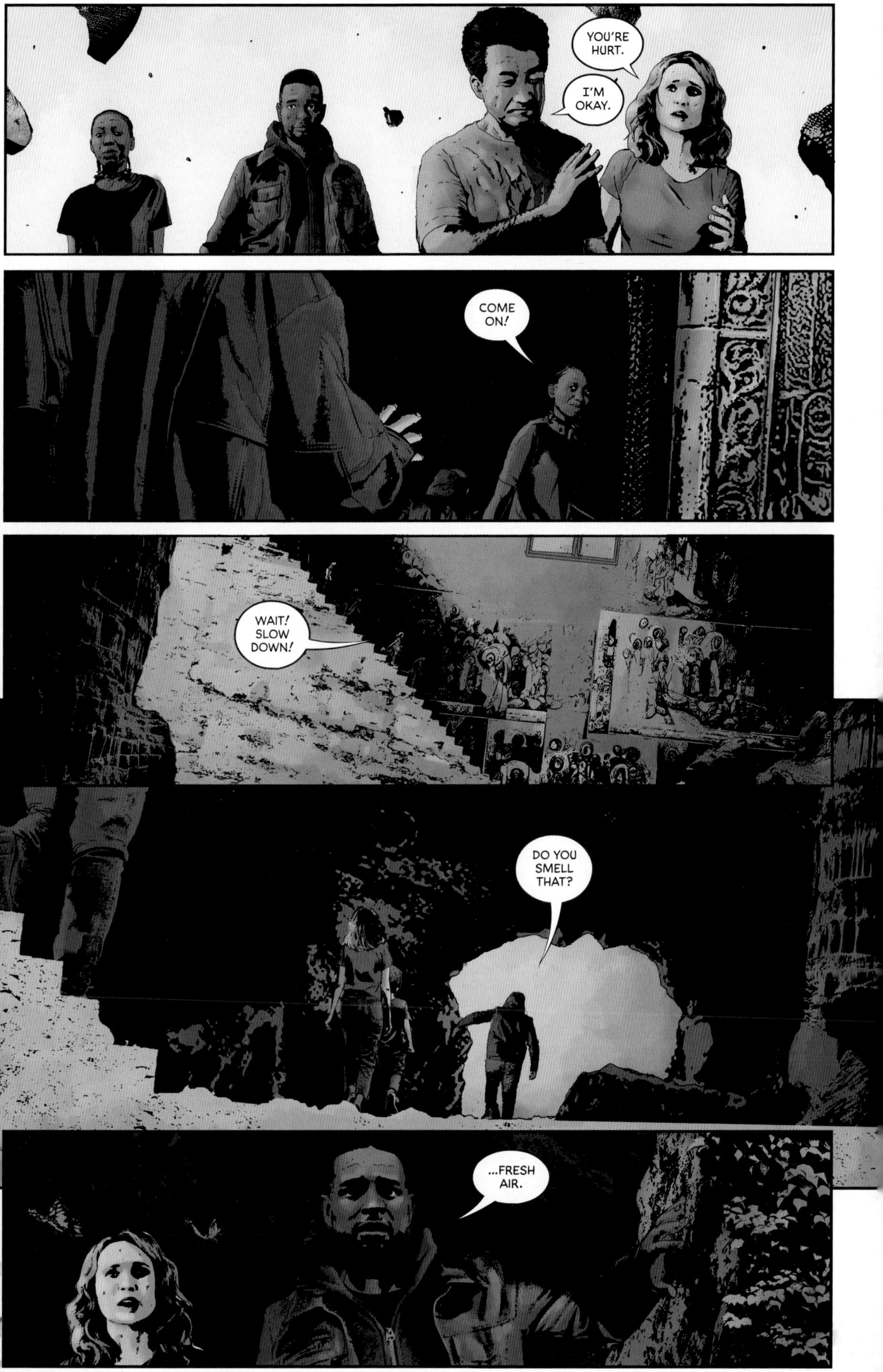
YOU'RE HURT.
I'M OKAY.
COME ON!
WAIT! SLOW DOWN!
DO YOU SMELL THAT?
...FRESH AIR.

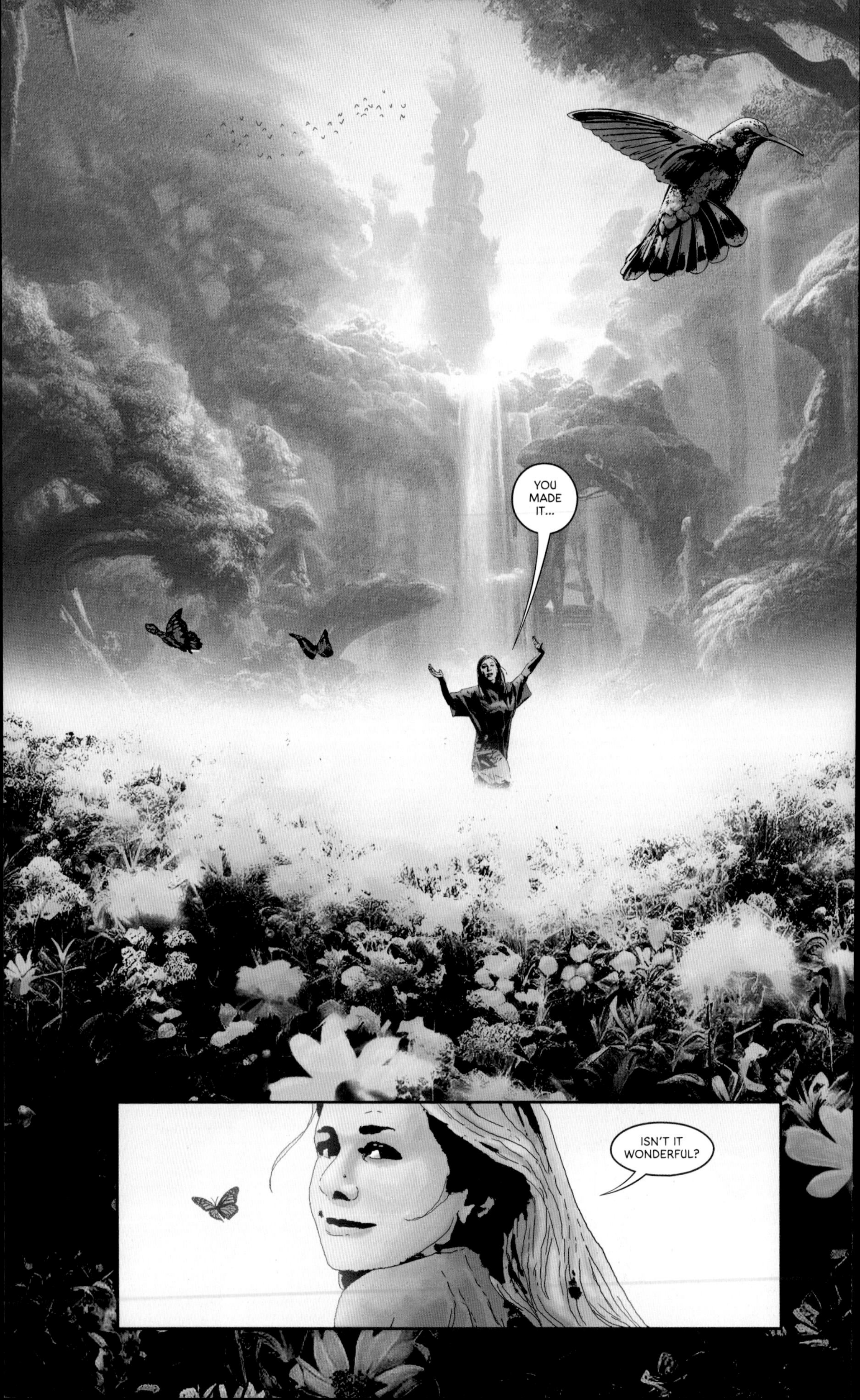
YOU MADE IT...
ISN'T IT WONDERFUL?

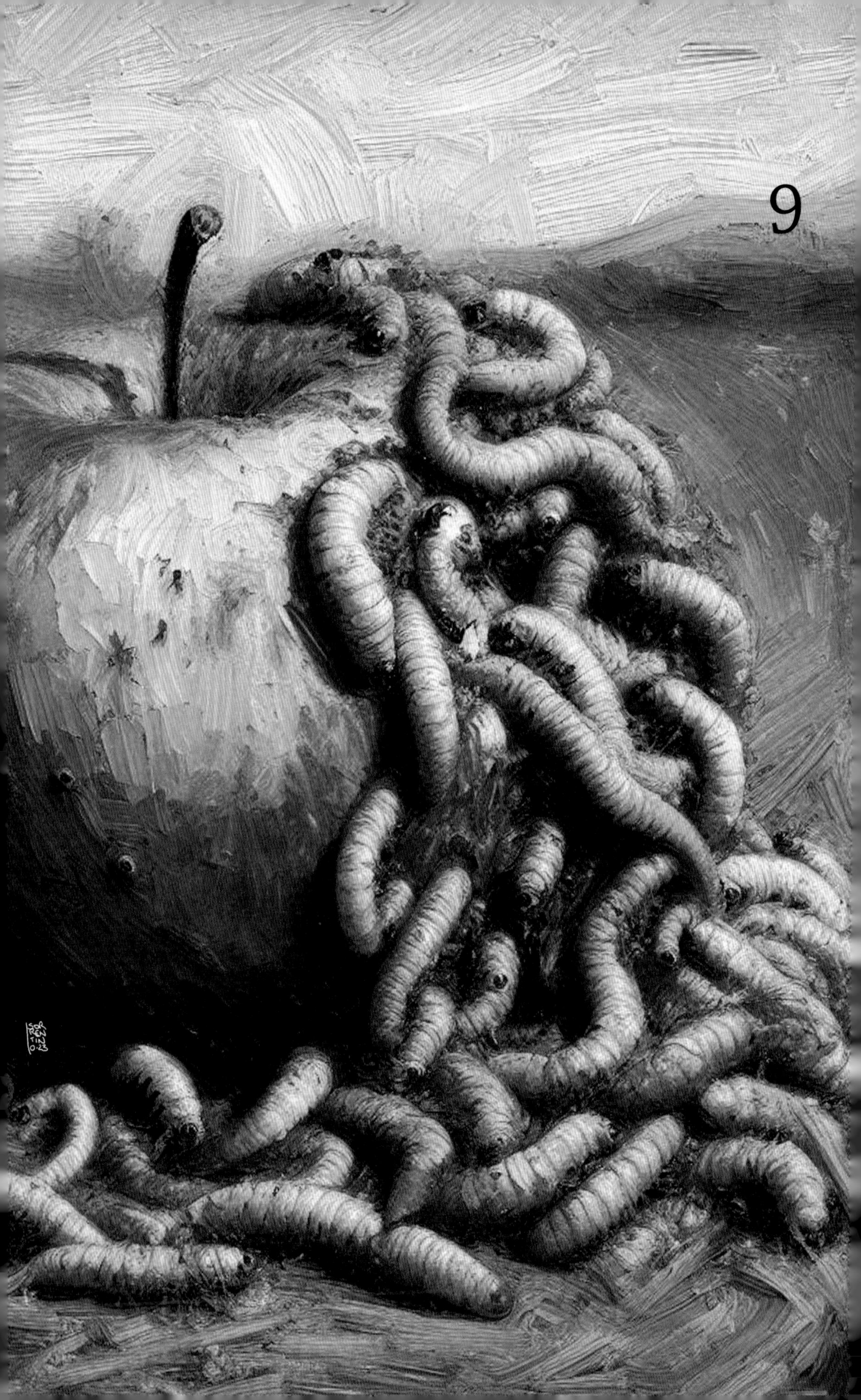
9

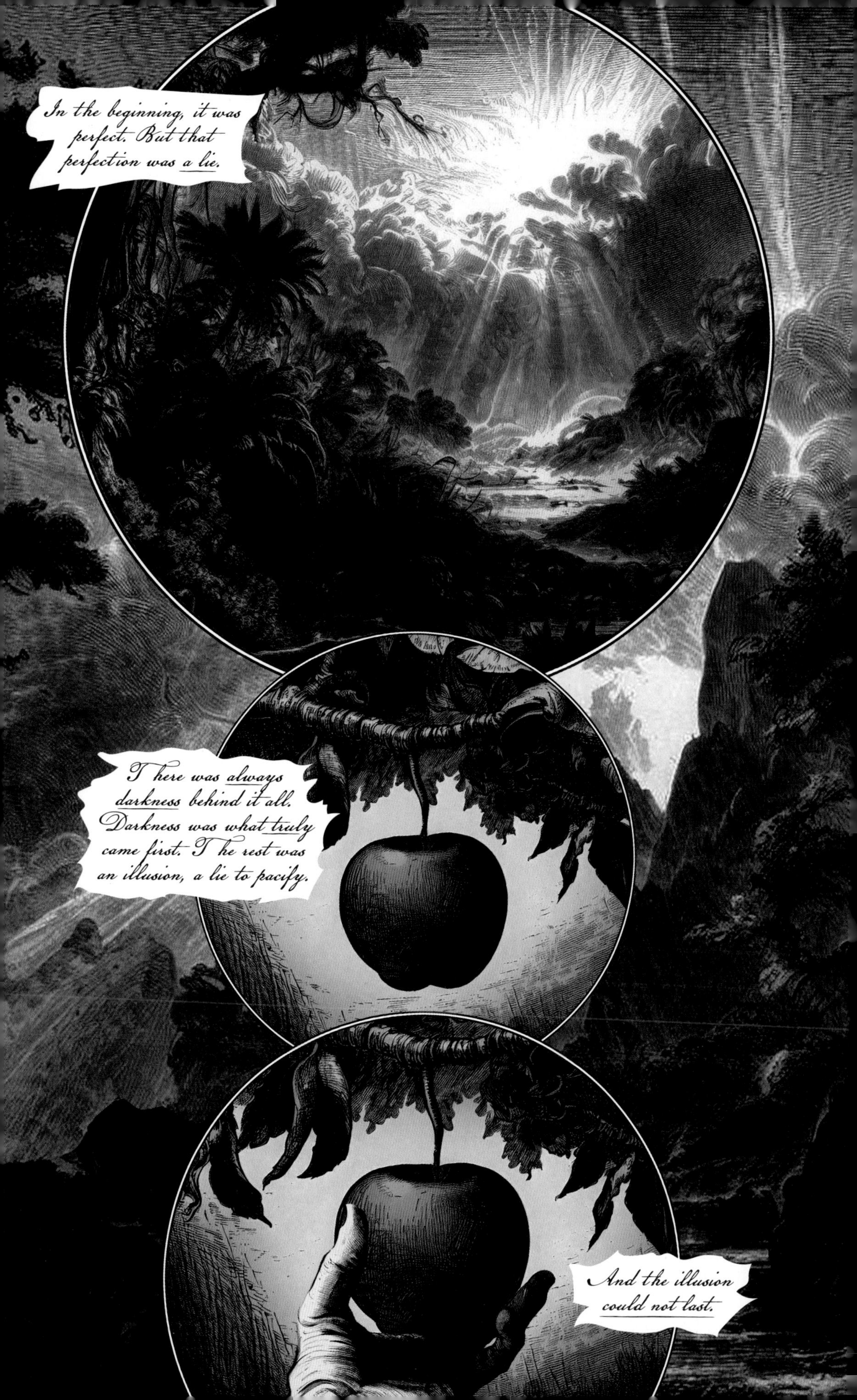
In the beginning, it was perfect. But that perfection was a lie.
There was always darkness behind it all. Darkness was what truly came first. The rest was an illusion, a lie to pacify.
And the illusion could not last.

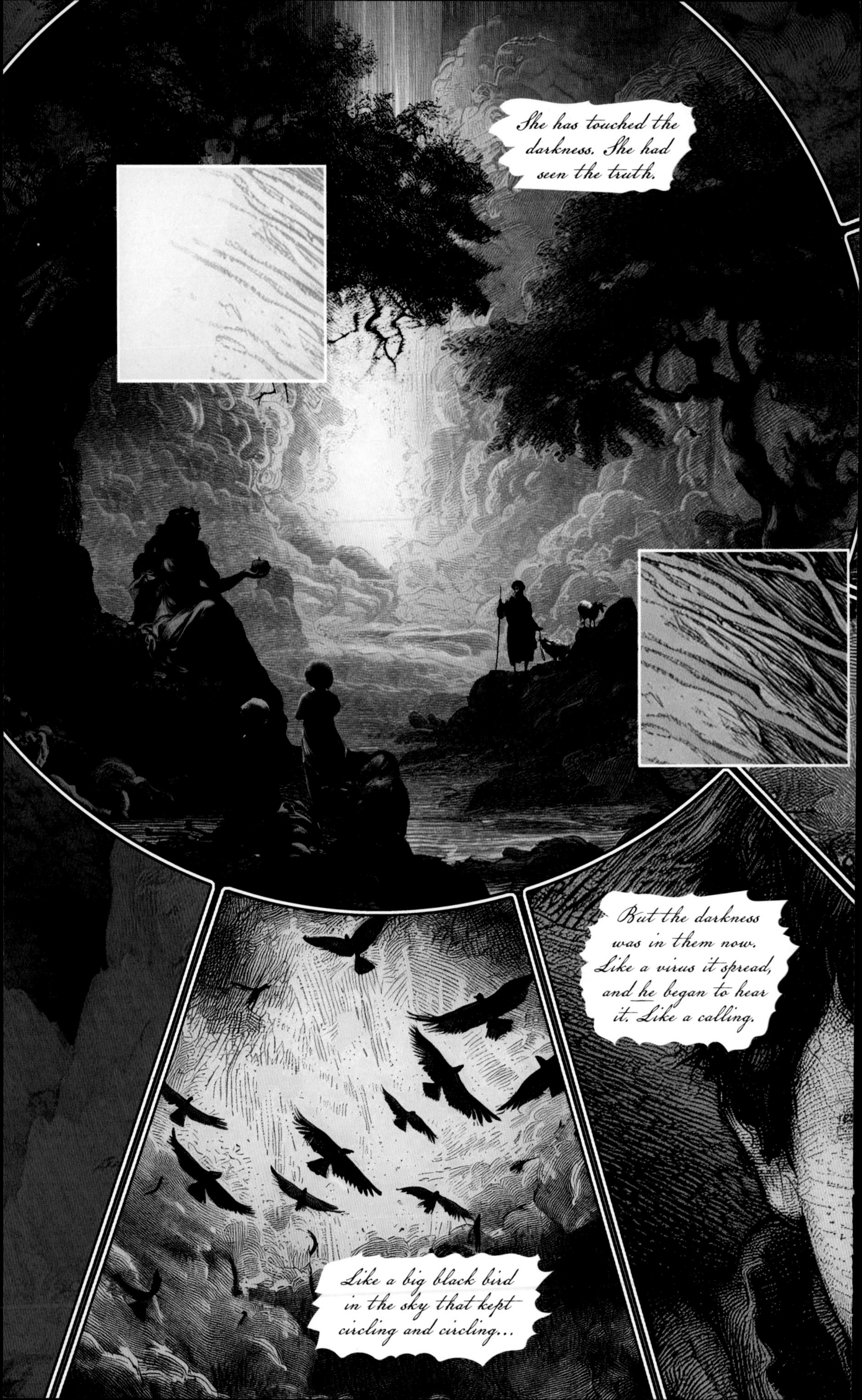

She has touched the darkness. She had seen the truth.
But the darkness was in them now. Like a virus it spread, and he began to hear it. Like a calling.
Like a big black bird in the sky that kept circling and circling...

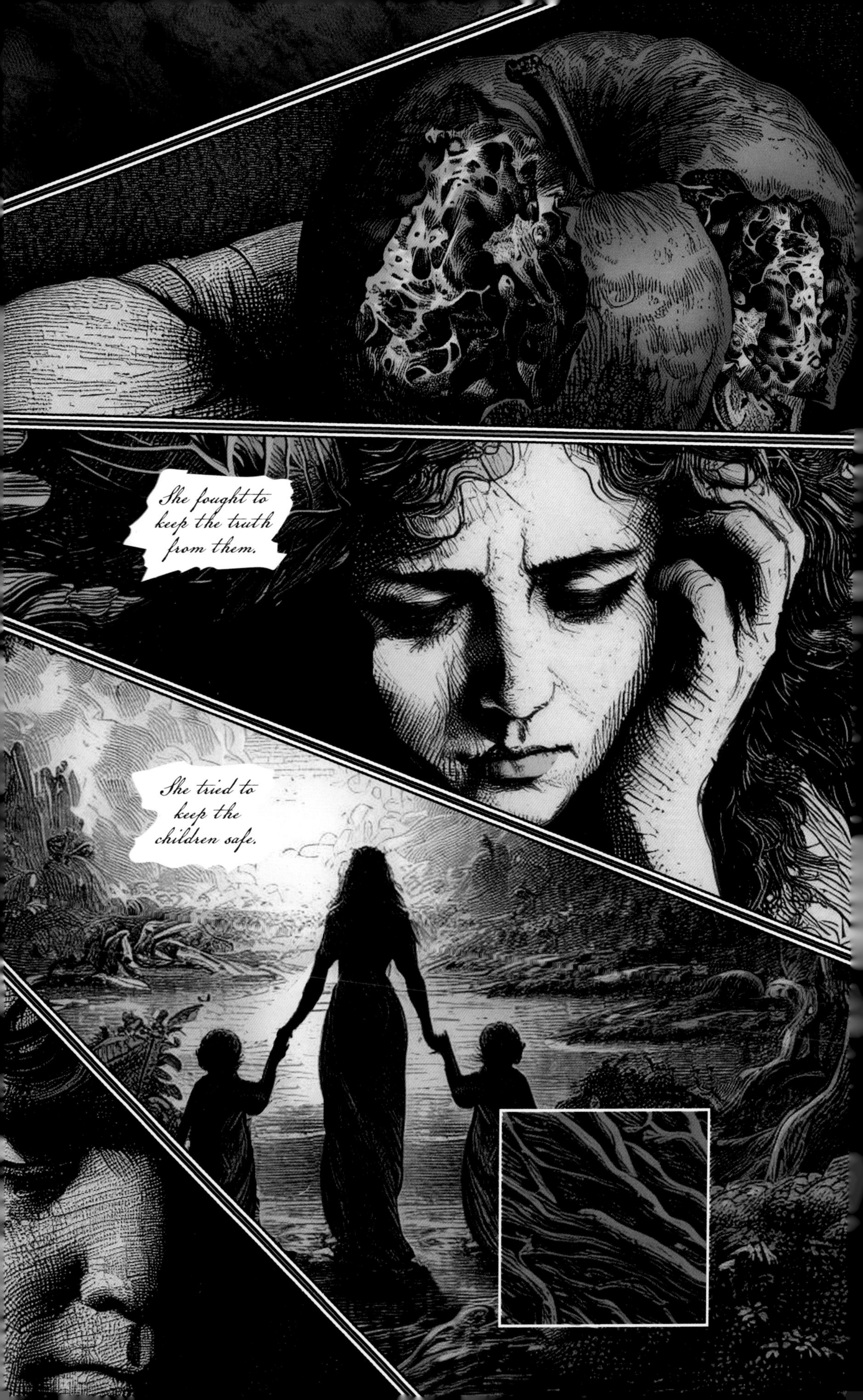
She fought to keep the truth from them.
She tried to keep the children safe.

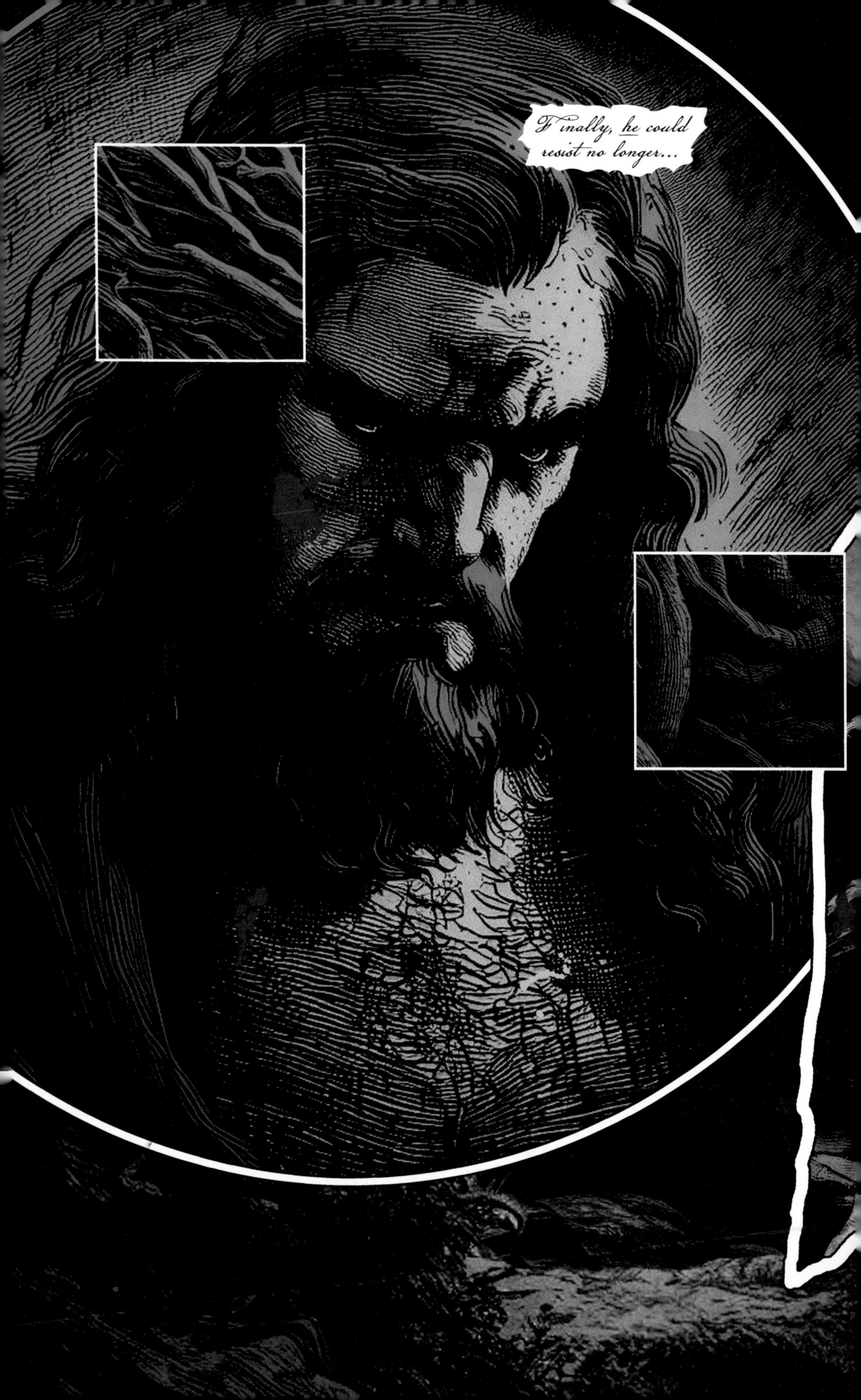
Finally, he could resist no longer...

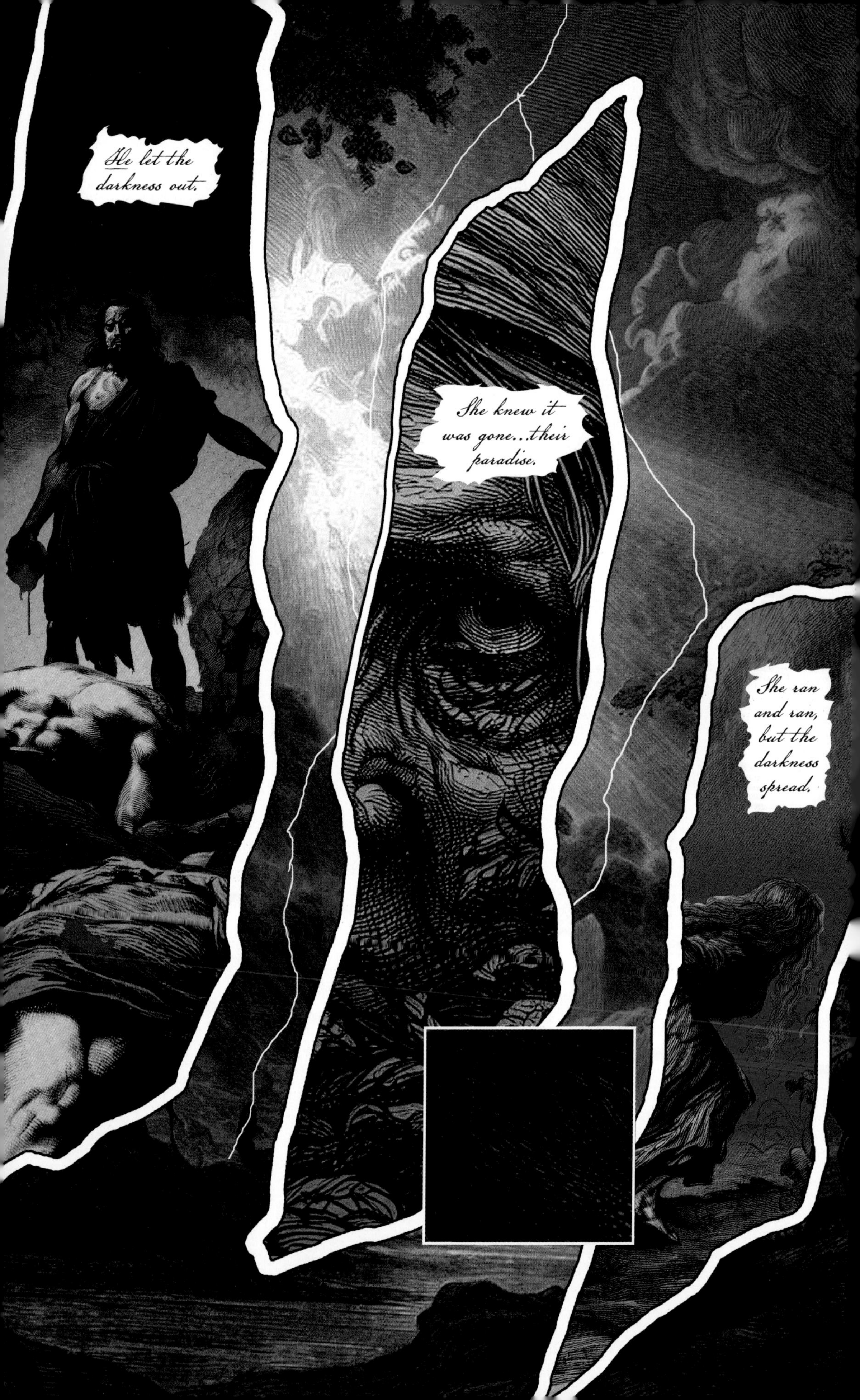
He let the darkness out.
She knew it was gone...their paradise.
She ran and ran, but the darkness spread.

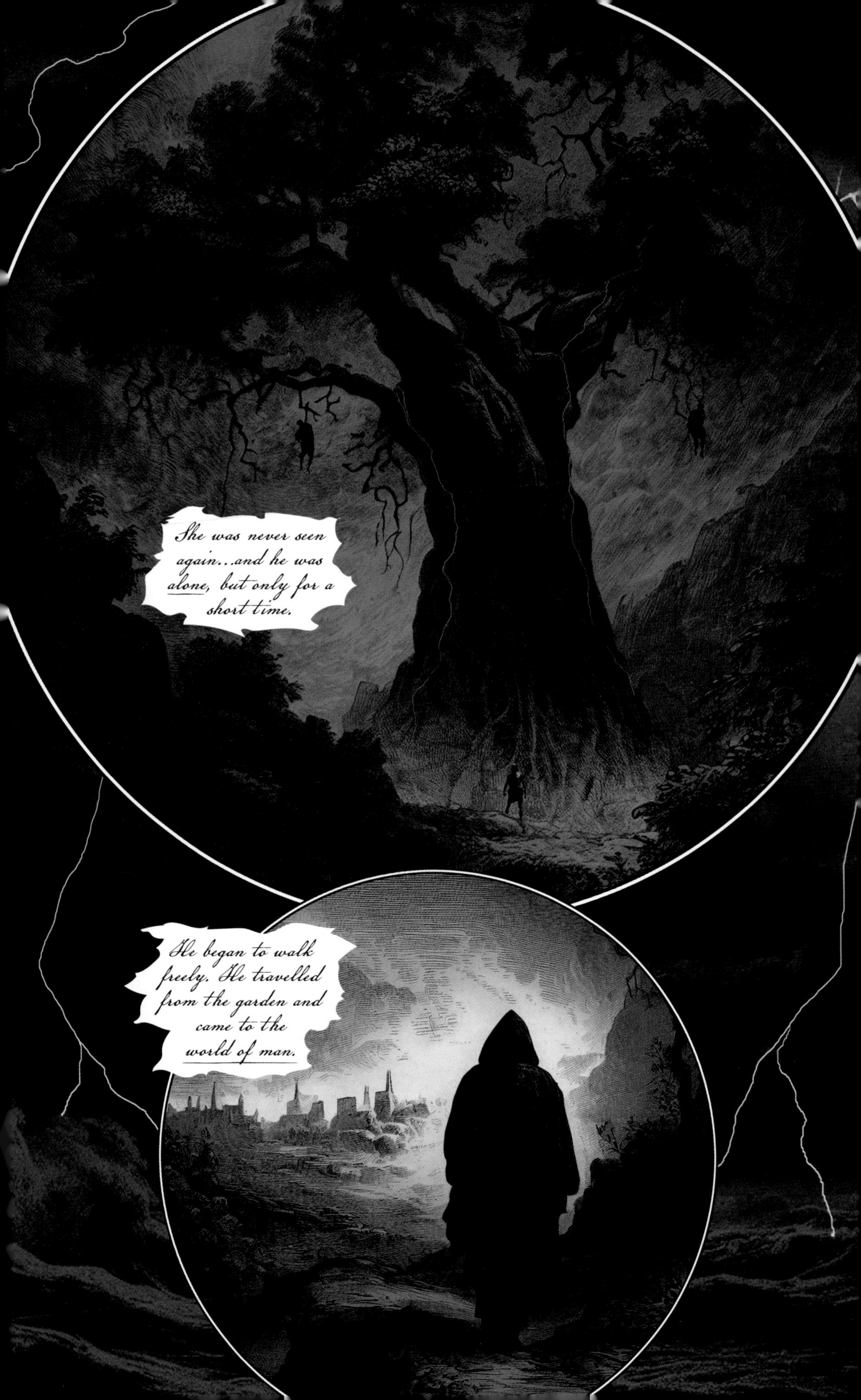
She was never seen again...and he was alone, but only for a short time.
He began to walk freely. He travelled from the garden and came to the world of man.

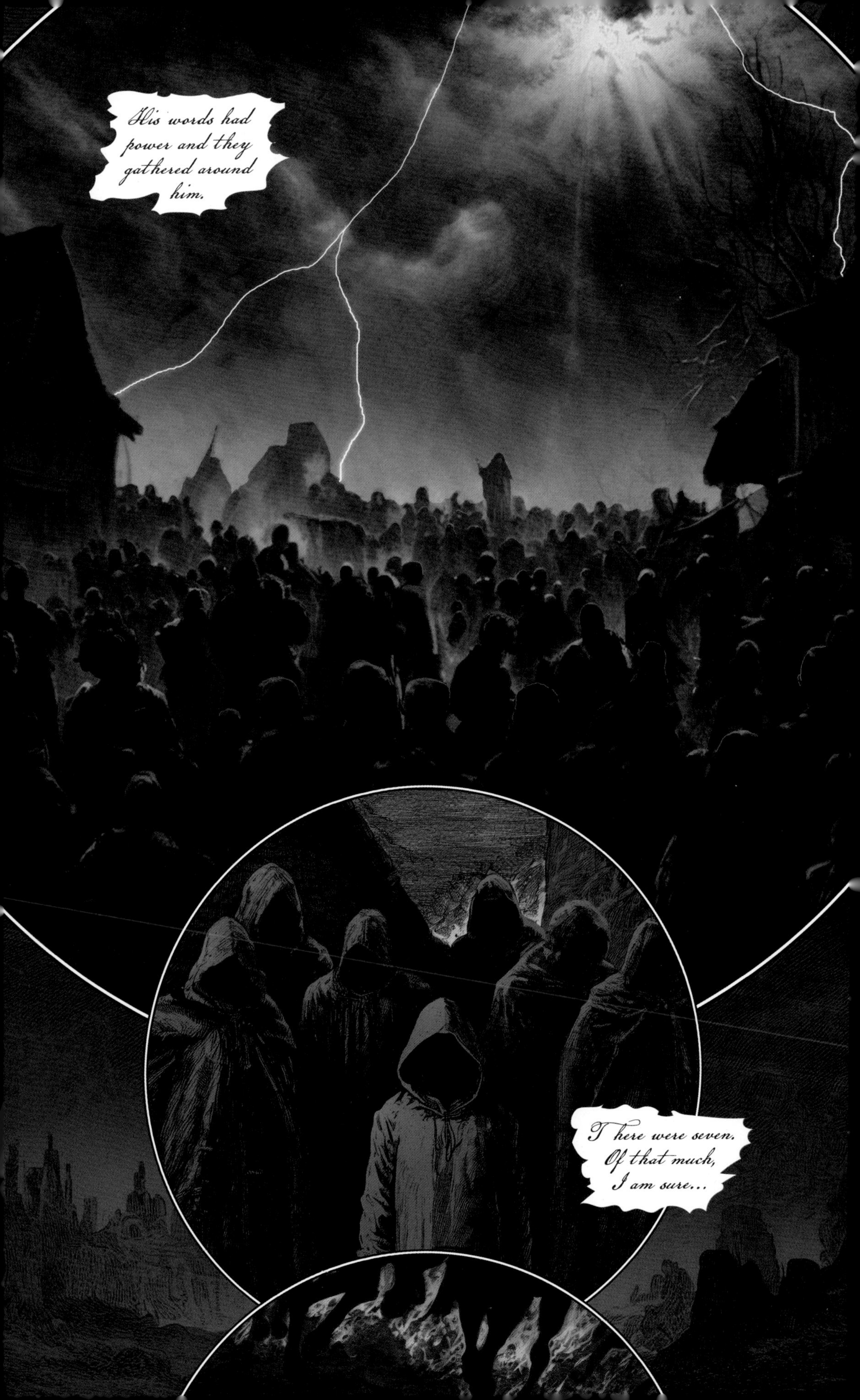
His words had power and they gathered around him.
There were seven. Of that much, I am sure...

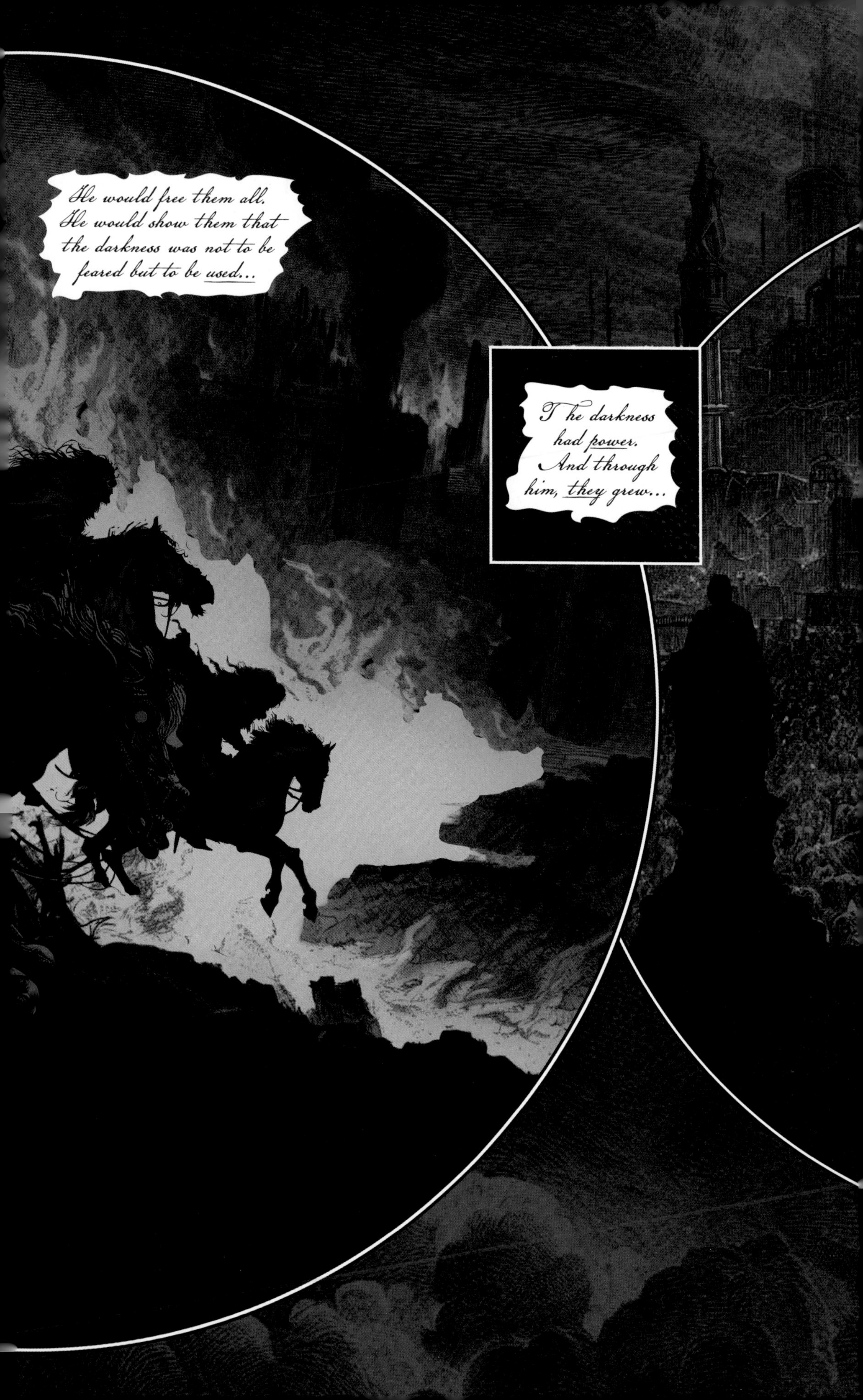
He would free them all. He would show them that the darkness was not to be feared but to be used...
The darkness had power. And through him, they grew...

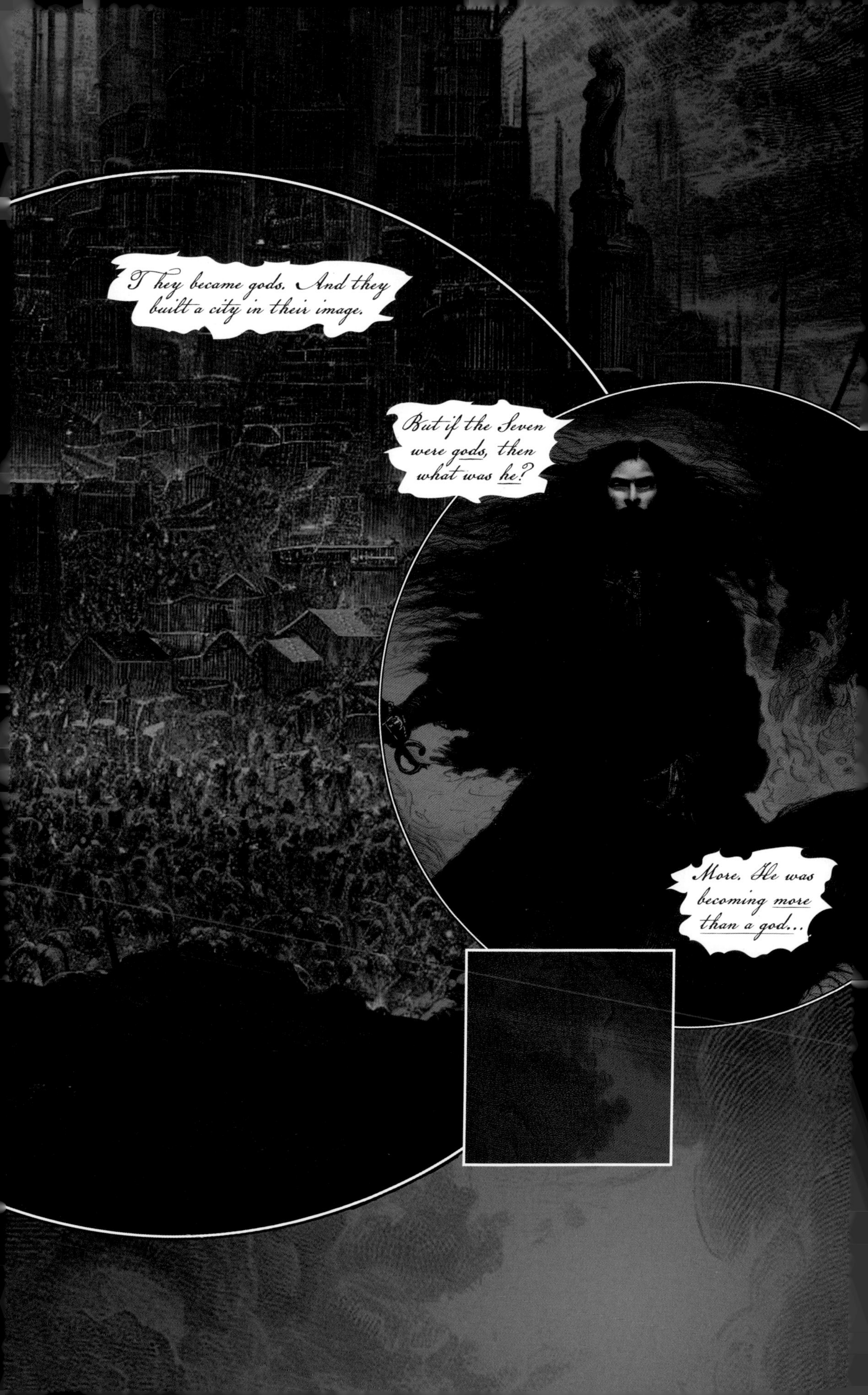
They became gods. And they built a city in their image.
But if the Seven were gods, then what was he?
More. He was becoming more than a god...

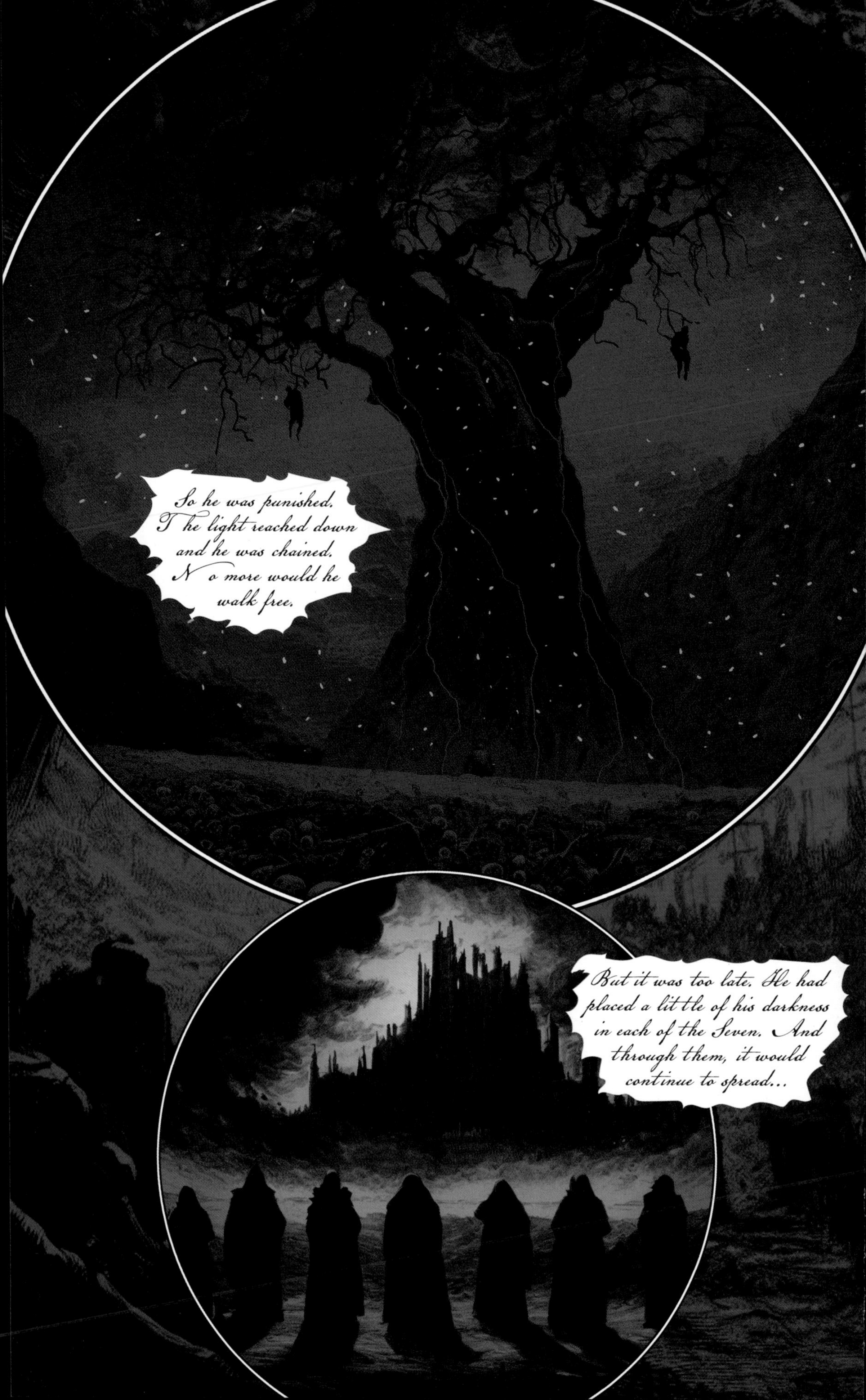
So he was punished. The light reached down and he was chained. No more would he walk free.
But it was too late. He had placed a little of his darkness in each of the Seven. And through them, it would continue to spread...

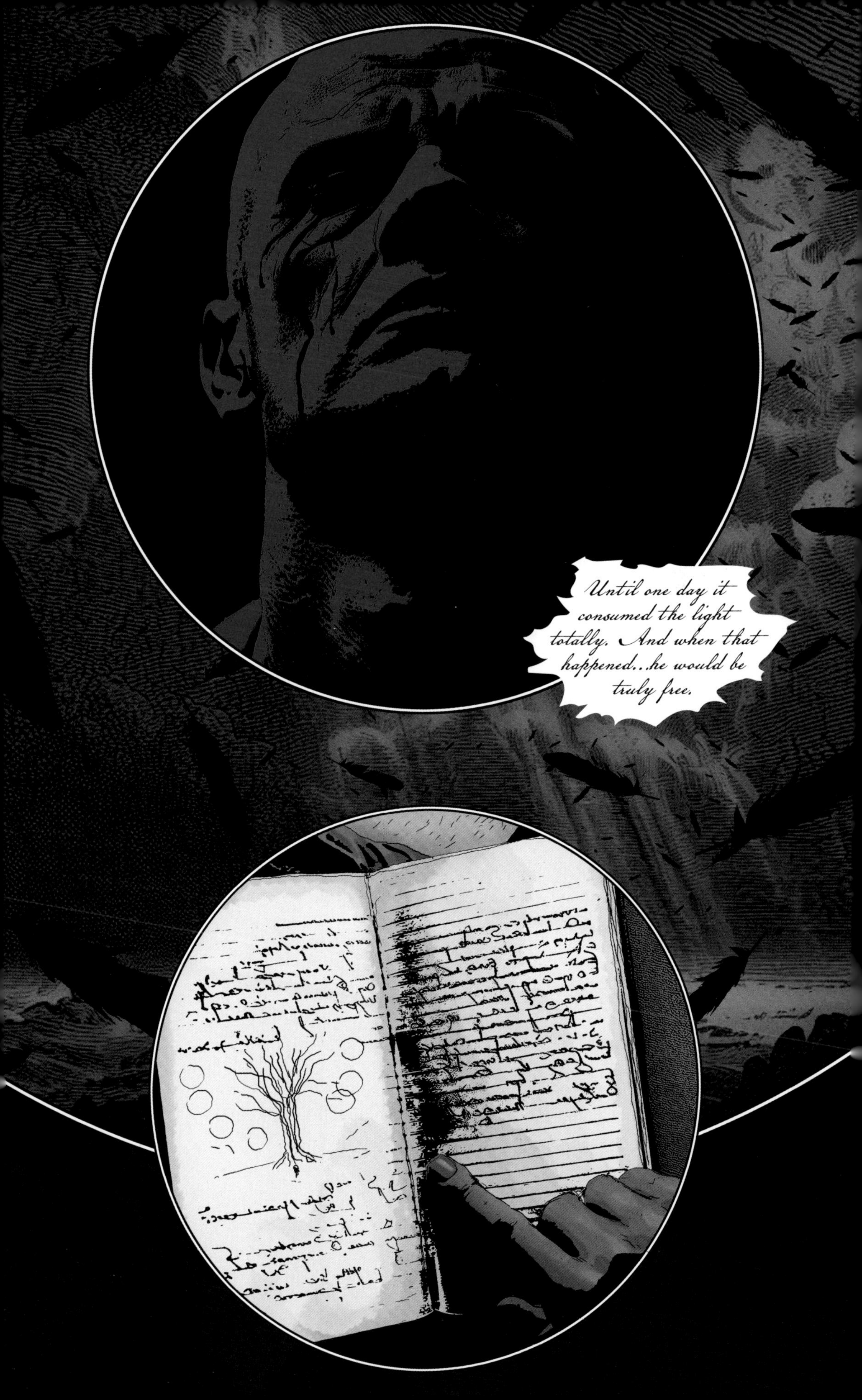
Until one day it consumed the light totally. And when that happened...he would be truly free.

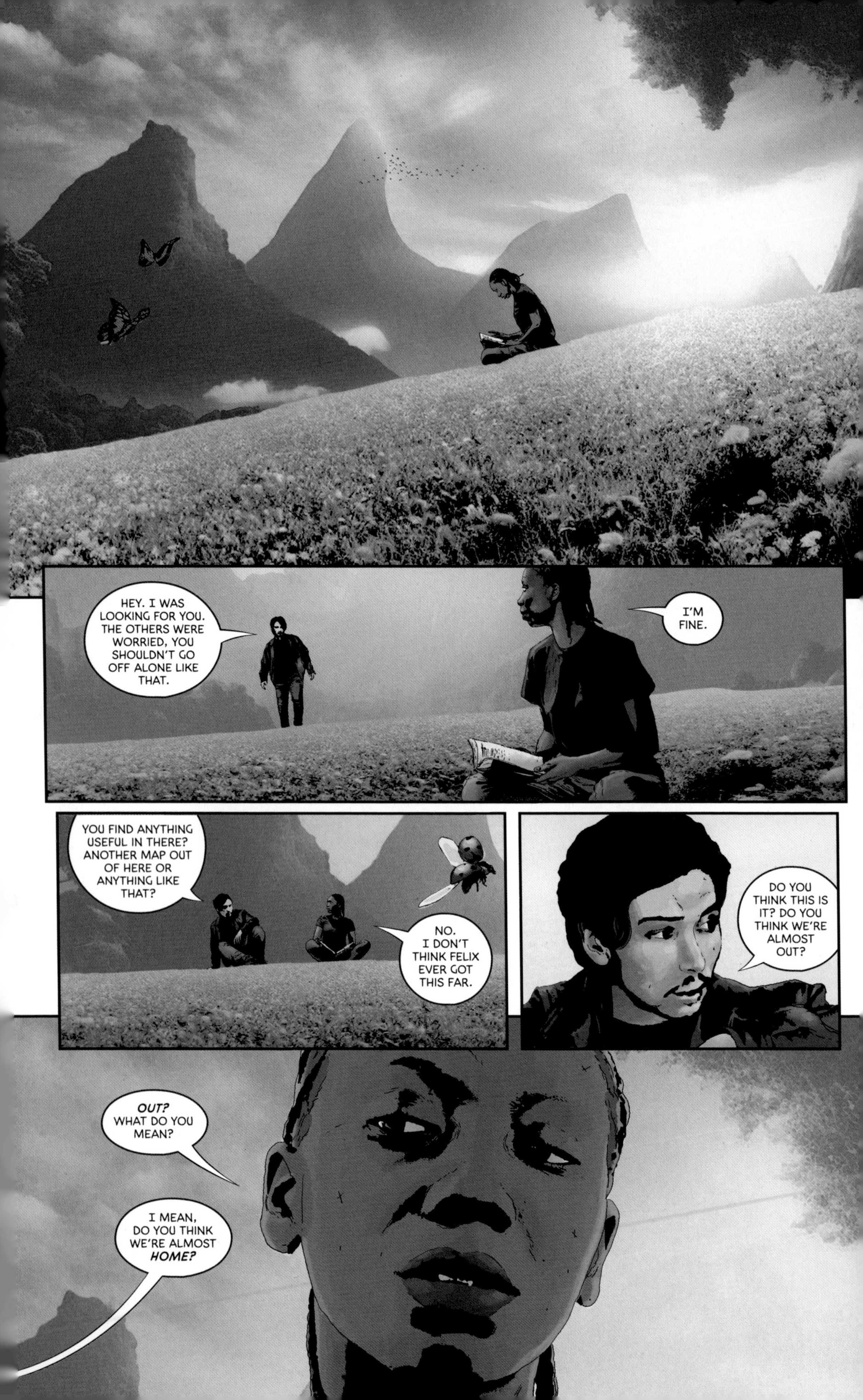
HEY. I WAS LOOKING FOR YOU. THE OTHERS WERE WORRIED, YOU SHOULDN'T GO OFF ALONE LIKE THAT.
I'M FINE.
YOU FIND ANYTHING USEFUL IN THERE? ANOTHER MAP OUT OF HERE OR ANYTHING LIKE THAT?
NO. I DON'T THINK FELIX EVER GOT THIS FAR.
DO YOU THINK THIS IS IT? DO YOU THINK WE'RE ALMOST OUT?
OUT? WHAT DO YOU MEAN?
I MEAN, DO YOU THINK WE'RE ALMOST *HOME?*

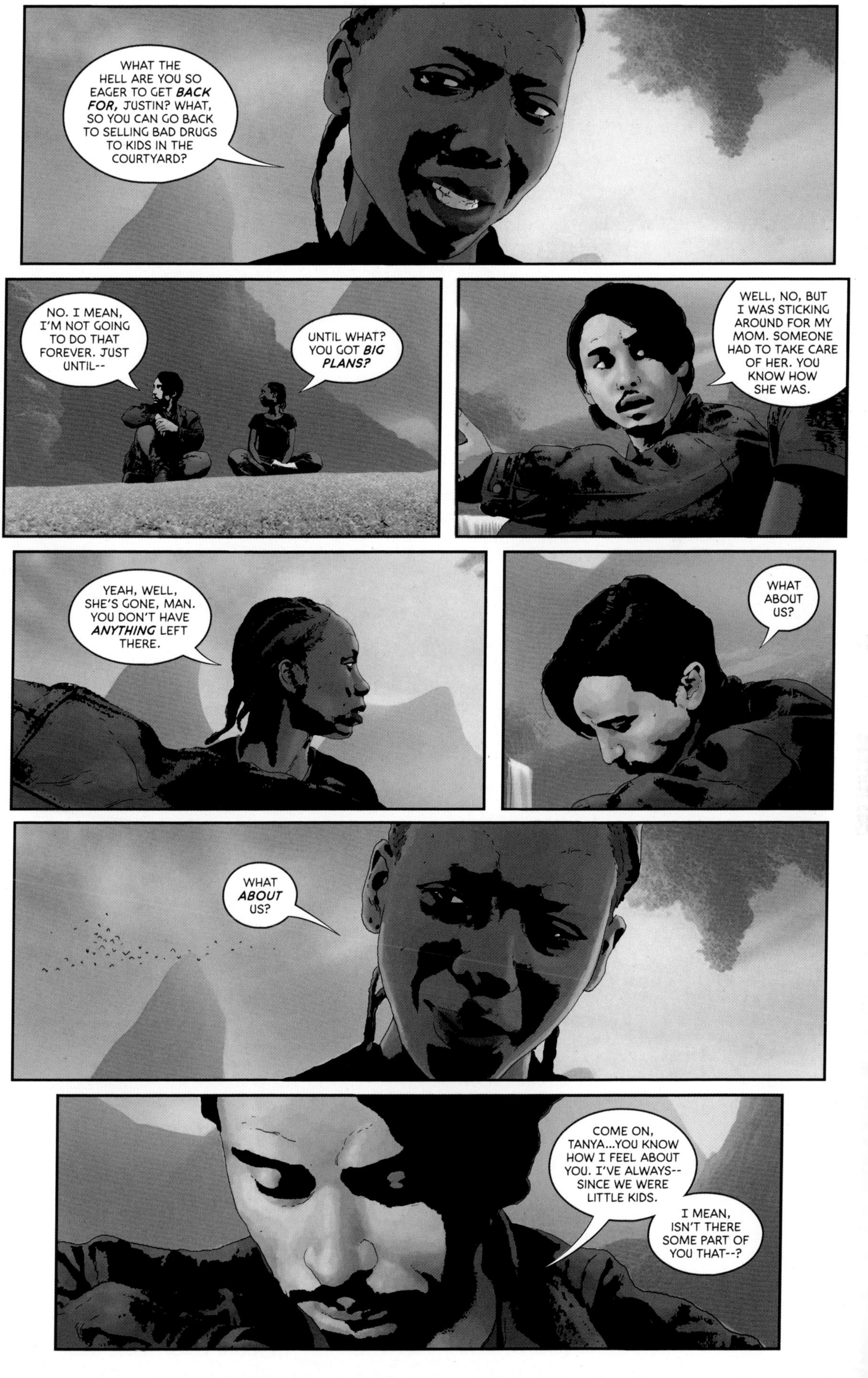
WHAT THE HELL ARE YOU SO EAGER TO GET BACK FOR, JUSTIN? WHAT, SO YOU CAN GO BACK TO SELLING BAD DRUGS TO KIDS IN THE COURTYARD?
NO. I MEAN, I'M NOT GOING TO DO THAT FOREVER. JUST UNTIL--
UNTIL WHAT? YOU GOT BIG PLANS?
WELL, NO, BUT I WAS STICKING AROUND FOR MY MOM. SOMEONE HAD TO TAKE CARE OF HER. YOU KNOW HOW SHE WAS.
YEAH, WELL, SHE'S GONE, MAN. YOU DON'T HAVE ANYTHING LEFT THERE.
WHAT ABOUT US?
WHAT ABOUT US?
COME ON, TANYA...YOU KNOW HOW I FEEL ABOUT YOU. I'VE ALWAYS-- SINCE WE WERE LITTLE KIDS.
I MEAN, ISN'T THERE SOME PART OF YOU THAT--?

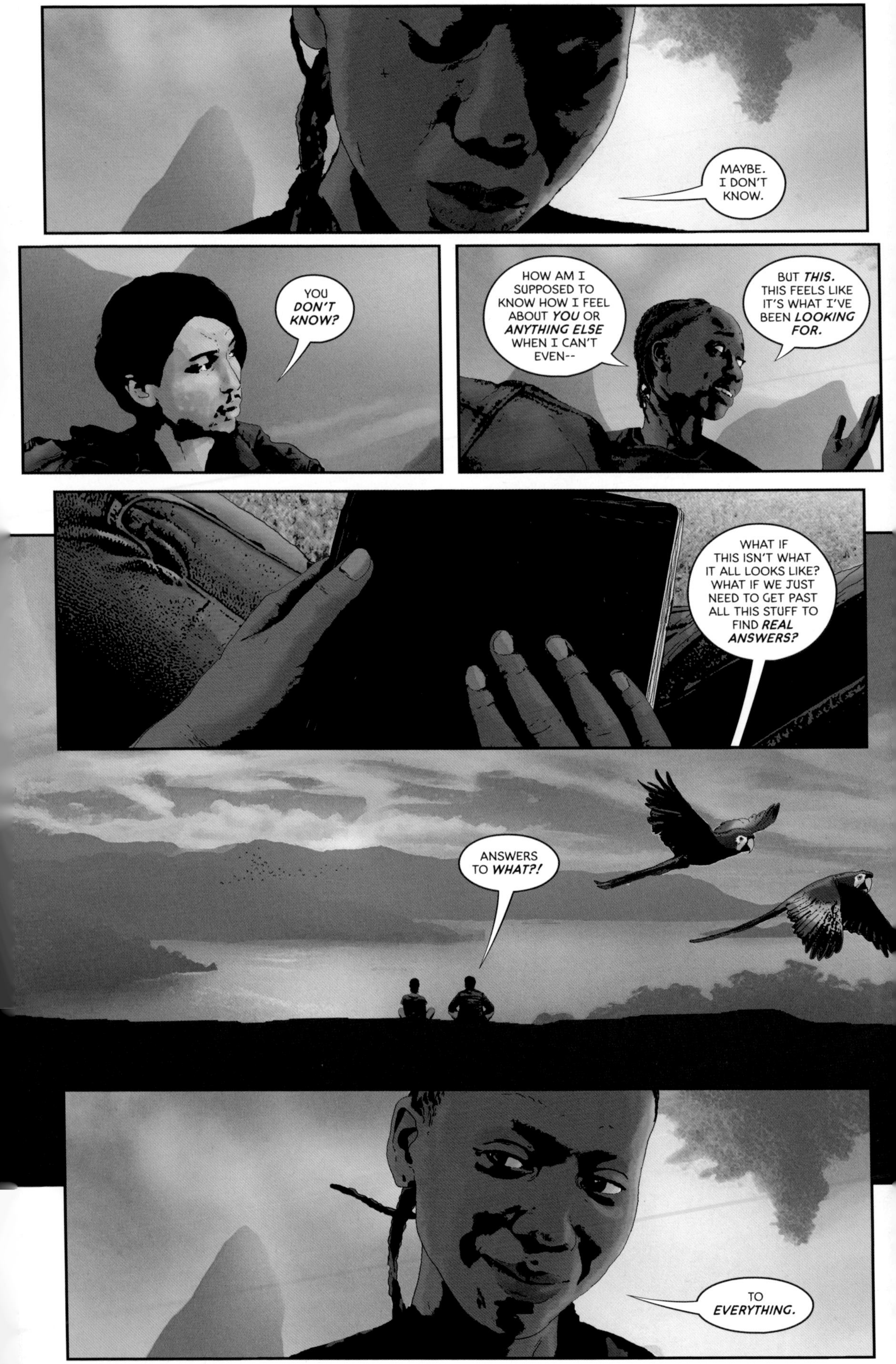
MAYBE. I DON'T KNOW.
YOU *DON'T KNOW?*
HOW AM I SUPPOSED TO KNOW HOW I FEEL ABOUT *YOU* OR *ANYTHING ELSE* WHEN I CAN'T EVEN--
BUT *THIS.* THIS FEELS LIKE IT'S WHAT I'VE BEEN *LOOKING FOR.*
WHAT IF THIS ISN'T WHAT IT ALL LOOKS LIKE? WHAT IF WE JUST NEED TO GET PAST ALL THIS STUFF TO FIND *REAL ANSWERS?*
ANSWERS TO *WHAT?!*
TO *EVERYTHING.*

FLOOR 2

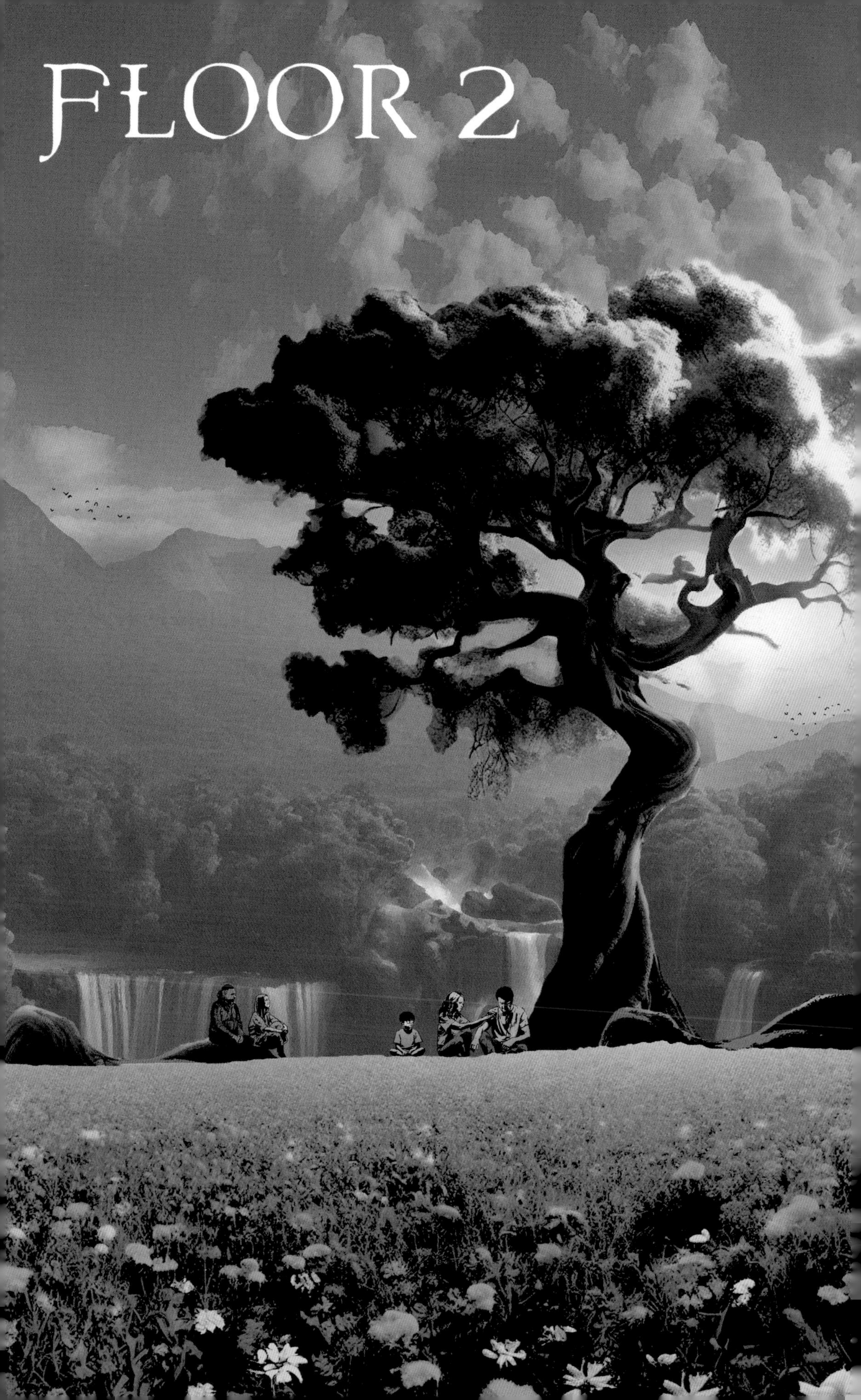

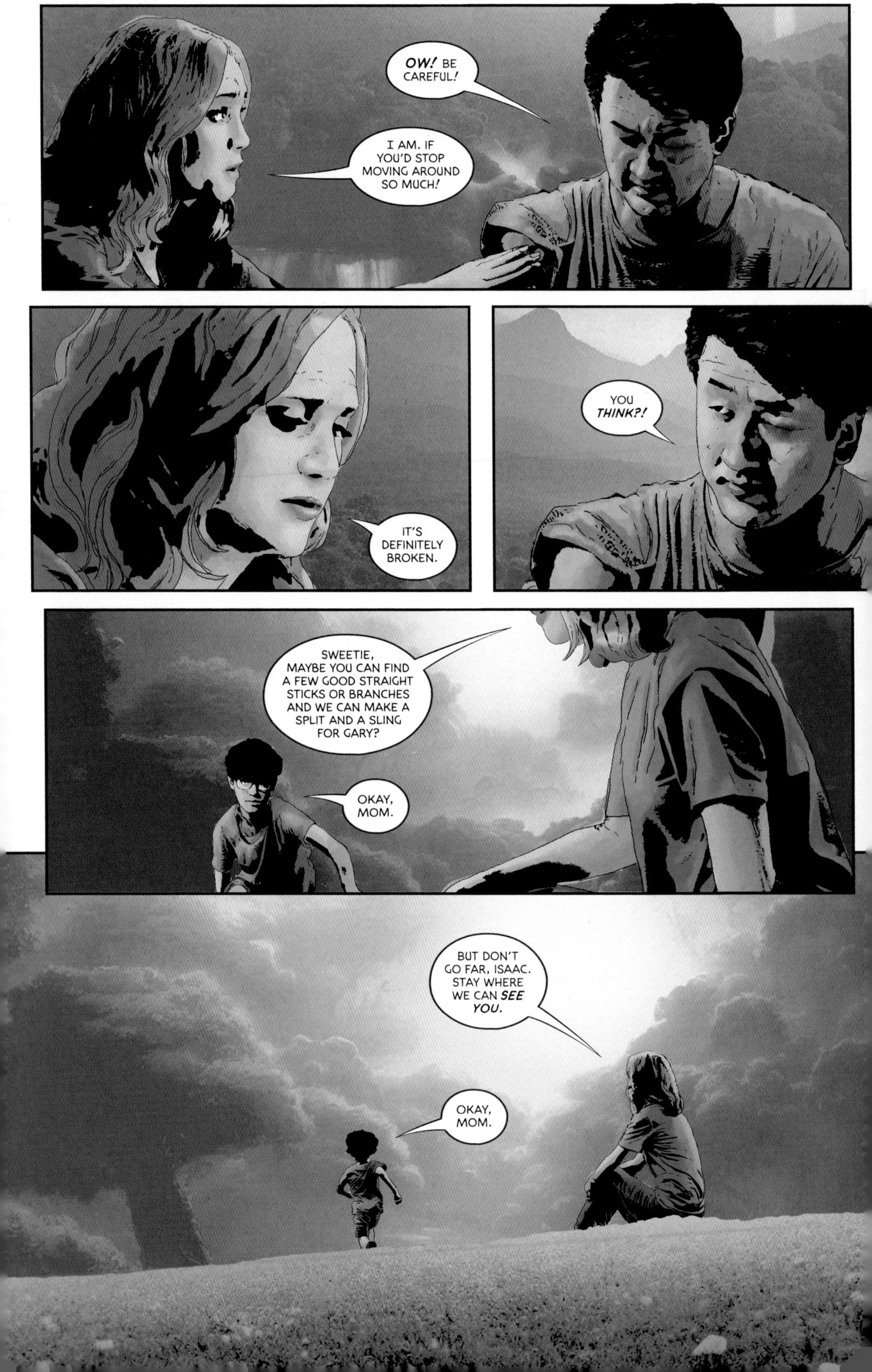
OW! BE CAREFUL!
I AM. IF YOU'D STOP MOVING AROUND SO MUCH!
IT'S DEFINITELY BROKEN.
YOU THINK?!
SWEETIE, MAYBE YOU CAN FIND A FEW GOOD STRAIGHT STICKS OR BRANCHES AND WE CAN MAKE A SPLIT AND A SLING FOR GARY?
OKAY, MOM.
BUT DON'T GO FAR, ISAAC. STAY WHERE WE CAN SEE YOU.
OKAY, MOM.

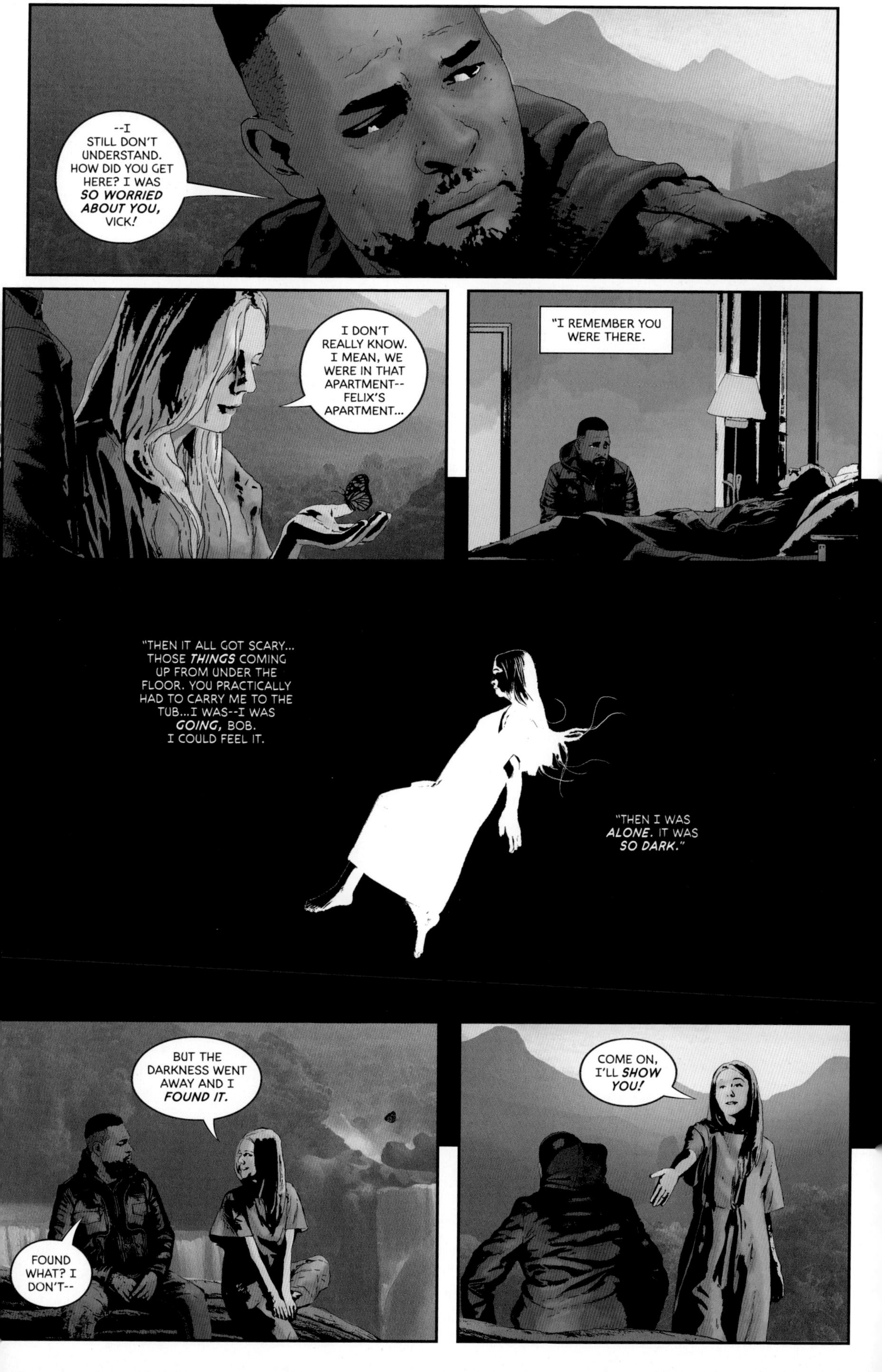
--I STILL DON'T UNDERSTAND. HOW DID YOU GET HERE? I WAS SO WORRIED ABOUT YOU, VICK!
I DON'T REALLY KNOW. I MEAN, WE WERE IN THAT APARTMENT-- FELIX'S APARTMENT...
"I REMEMBER YOU WERE THERE.
"THEN IT ALL GOT SCARY... THOSE THINGS COMING UP FROM UNDER THE FLOOR. YOU PRACTICALLY HAD TO CARRY ME TO THE TUB...I WAS--I WAS GOING, BOB. I COULD FEEL IT.
"THEN I WAS ALONE. IT WAS SO DARK."
BUT THE DARKNESS WENT AWAY AND I FOUND IT.
FOUND WHAT? I DON'T--
COME ON, I'LL SHOW YOU!

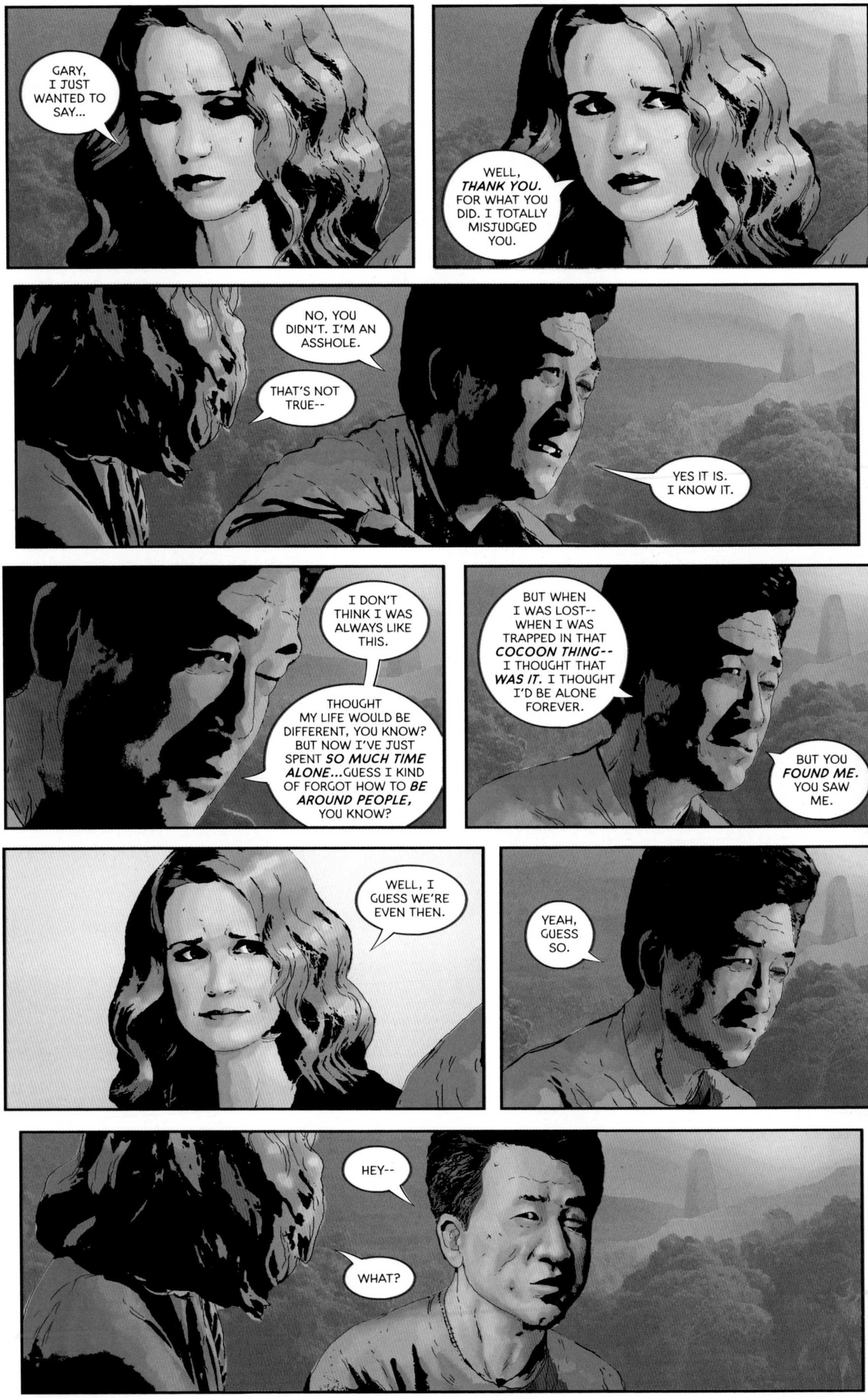
GARY, I JUST WANTED TO SAY...
WELL, THANK YOU. FOR WHAT YOU DID. I TOTALLY MISJUDGED YOU.
NO, YOU DIDN'T. I'M AN ASSHOLE.
THAT'S NOT TRUE--
YES IT IS. I KNOW IT.
I DON'T THINK I WAS ALWAYS LIKE THIS.
THOUGHT MY LIFE WOULD BE DIFFERENT, YOU KNOW? BUT NOW I'VE JUST SPENT SO MUCH TIME ALONE...GUESS I KIND OF FORGOT HOW TO BE AROUND PEOPLE, YOU KNOW?
BUT WHEN I WAS LOST-- WHEN I WAS TRAPPED IN THAT COCOON THING-- I THOUGHT THAT WAS IT. I THOUGHT I'D BE ALONE FOREVER.
BUT YOU FOUND ME. YOU SAW ME.
WELL, I GUESS WE'RE EVEN THEN.
YEAH, GUESS SO.
HEY--
WHAT?

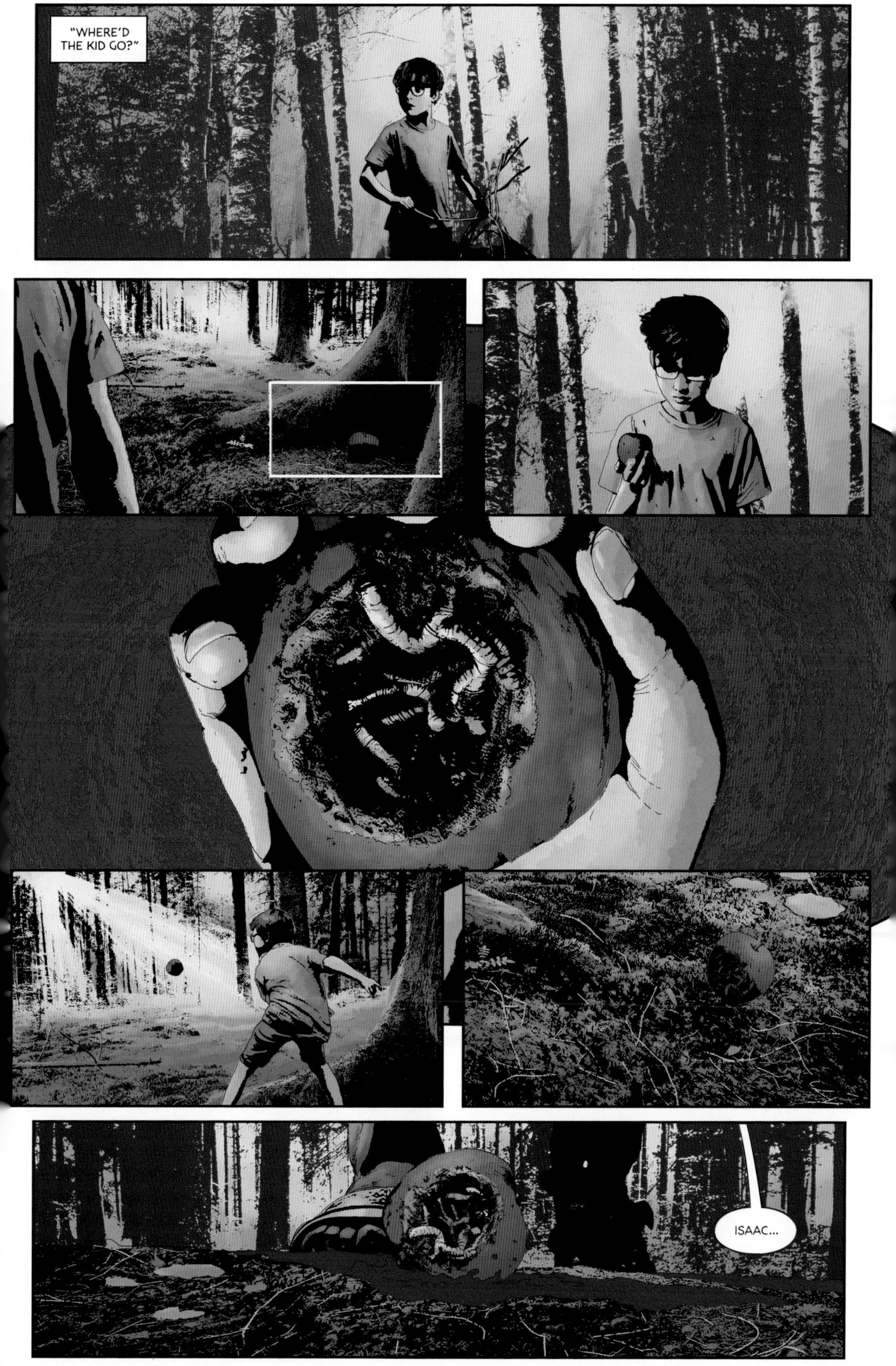
"WHERE'D THE KID GO?"
ISAAC...

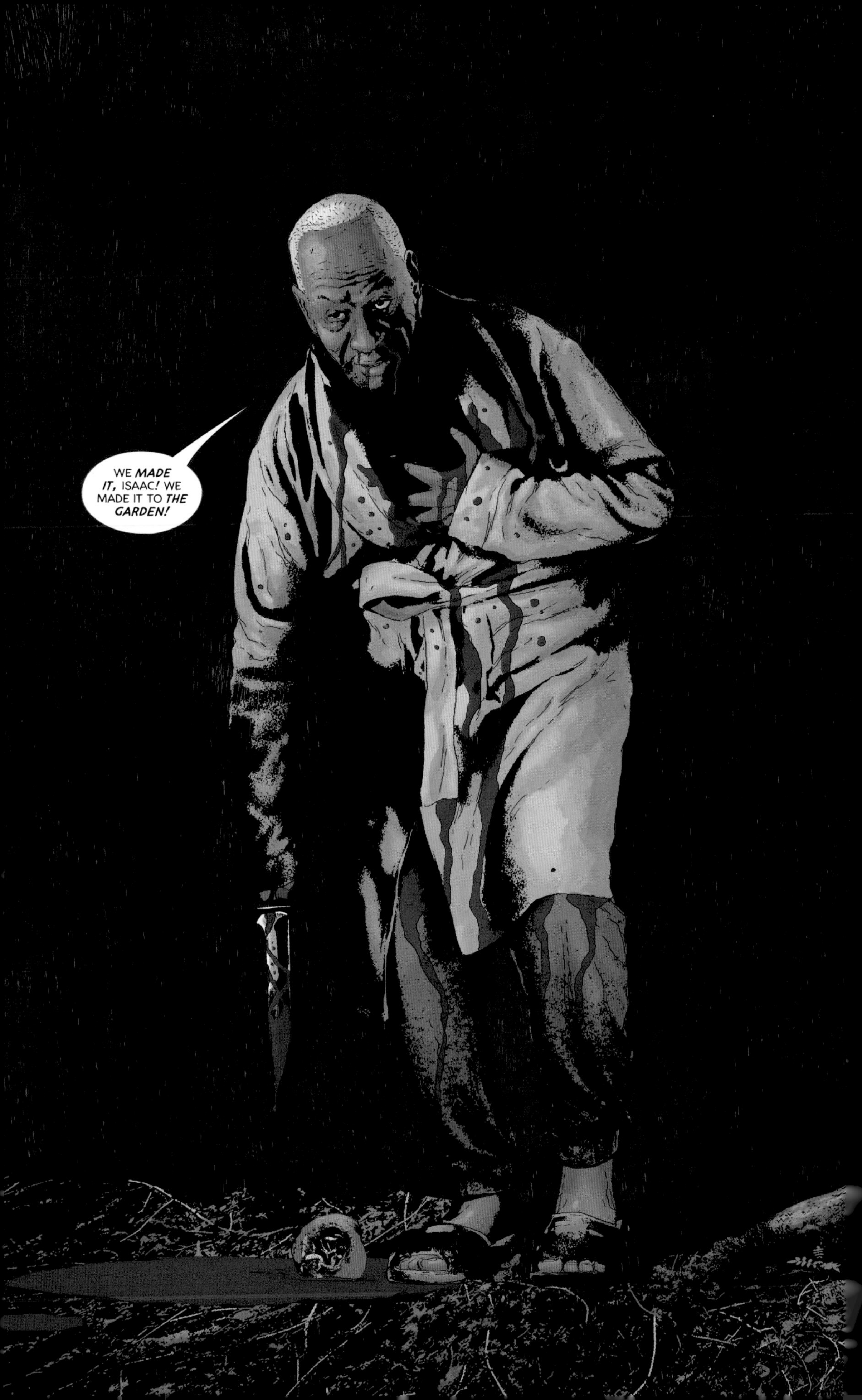
WE *MADE IT,* ISAAC! WE MADE IT TO *THE GARDEN!*

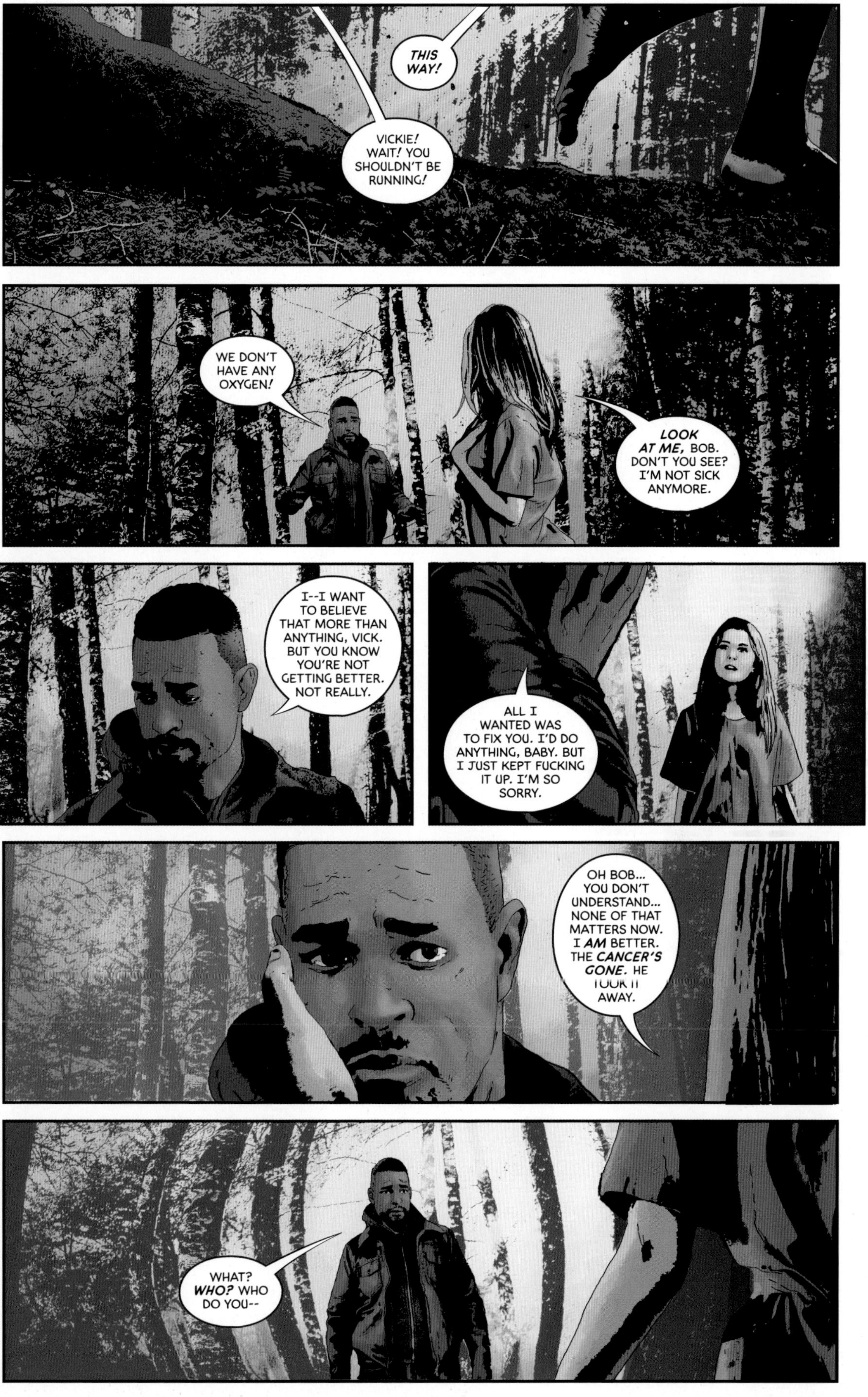
THIS WAY!
VICKIE! WAIT! YOU SHOULDN'T BE RUNNING!
WE DON'T HAVE ANY OXYGEN!
LOOK AT ME, BOB. DON'T YOU SEE? I'M NOT SICK ANYMORE.
I--I WANT TO BELIEVE THAT MORE THAN ANYTHING, VICK. BUT YOU KNOW YOU'RE NOT GETTING BETTER. NOT REALLY.
ALL I WANTED WAS TO FIX YOU. I'D DO ANYTHING, BABY. BUT I JUST KEPT FUCKING IT UP. I'M SO SORRY.
OH BOB... YOU DON'T UNDERSTAND... NONE OF THAT MATTERS NOW. I AM BETTER. THE CANCER'S GONE. HE TOOK IT AWAY.
WHAT? WHO? WHO DO YOU--

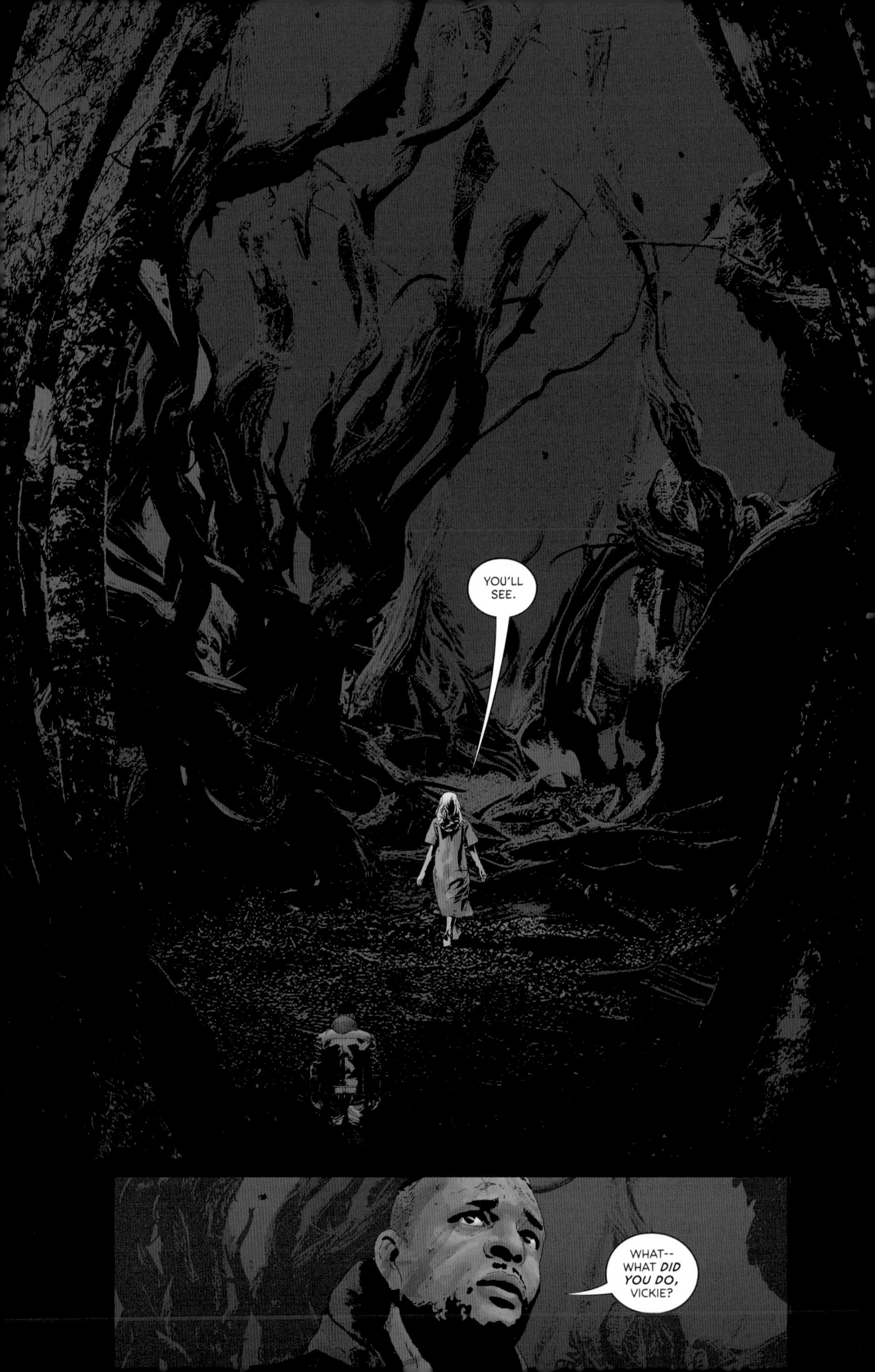
YOU'LL SEE.
WHAT-- WHAT *DID YOU DO,* VICKIE?

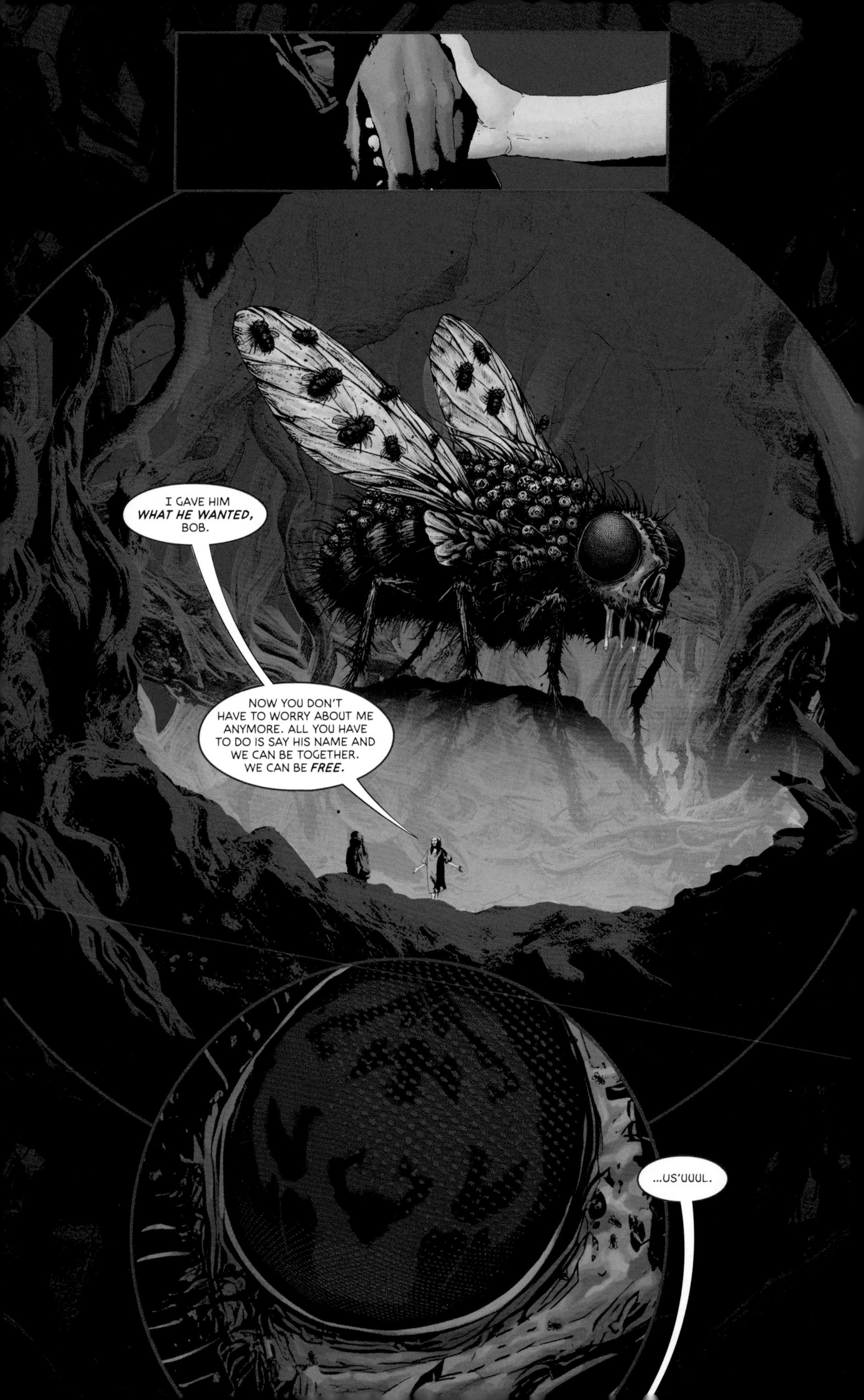
I GAVE HIM *WHAT HE WANTED,* BOB.
NOW YOU DON'T HAVE TO WORRY ABOUT ME ANYMORE. ALL YOU HAVE TO DO IS SAY HIS NAME AND WE CAN BE TOGETHER. WE CAN BE *FREE.*
...US'UUUL.

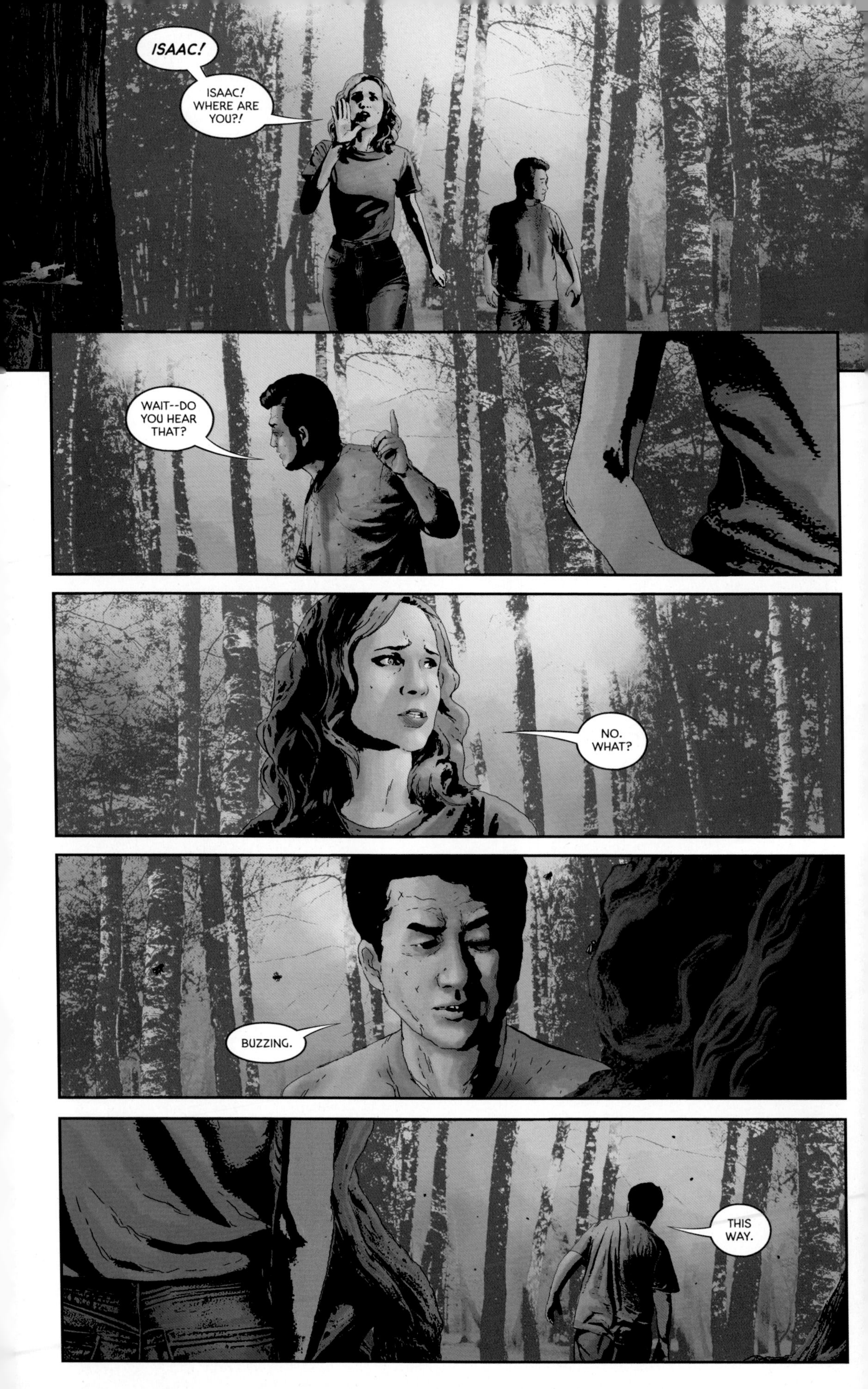
ISAAC!
ISAAC! WHERE ARE YOU?!
WAIT--DO YOU HEAR THAT?
NO. WHAT?
BUZZING.
THIS WAY.

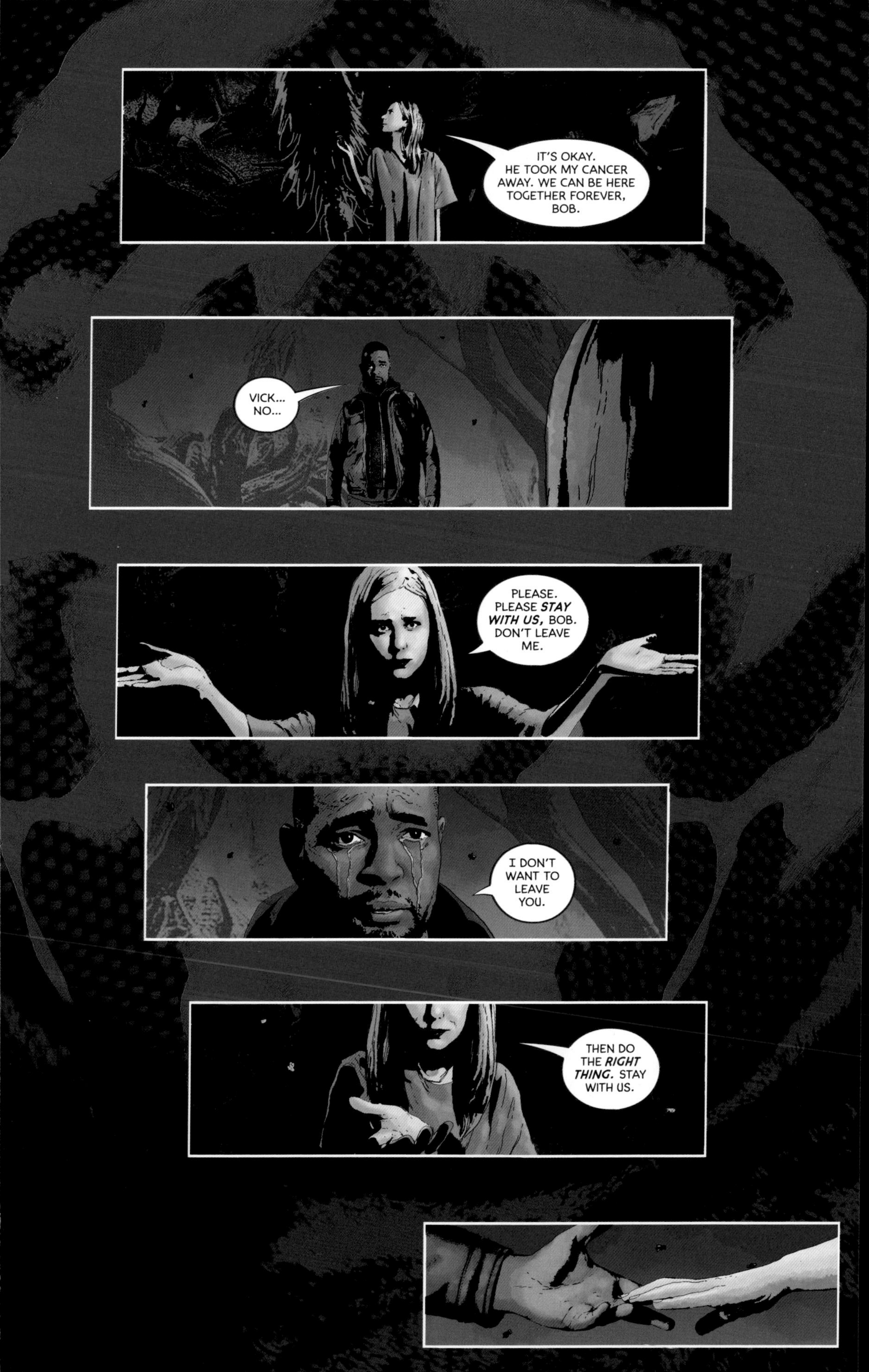
IT'S OKAY. HE TOOK MY CANCER AWAY. WE CAN BE HERE TOGETHER FOREVER, BOB.
VICK... NO...
PLEASE. PLEASE *STAY WITH US,* BOB. DON'T LEAVE ME.
I DON'T WANT TO LEAVE YOU.
THEN DO THE *RIGHT THING.* STAY WITH US.

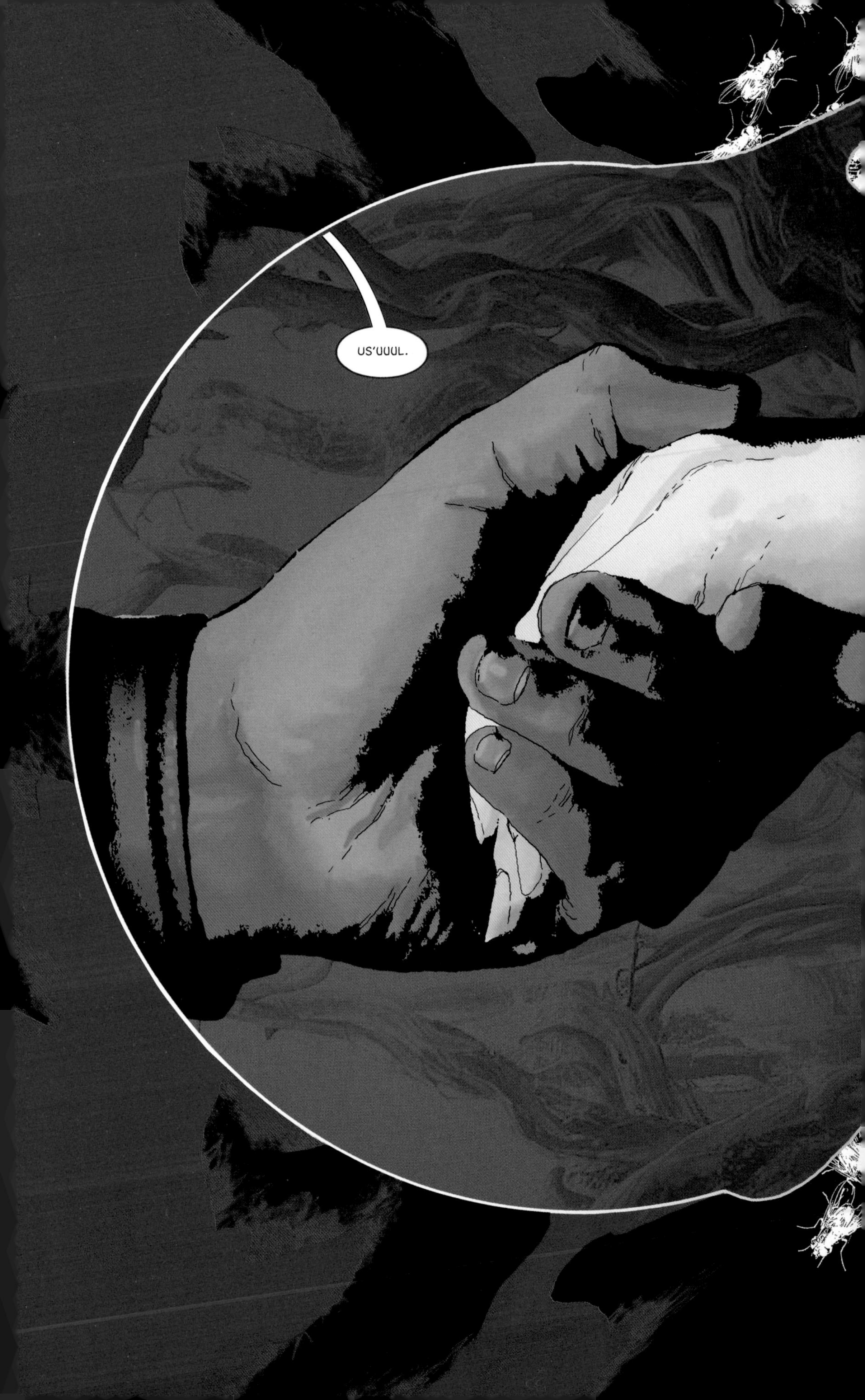
US'UUUL.

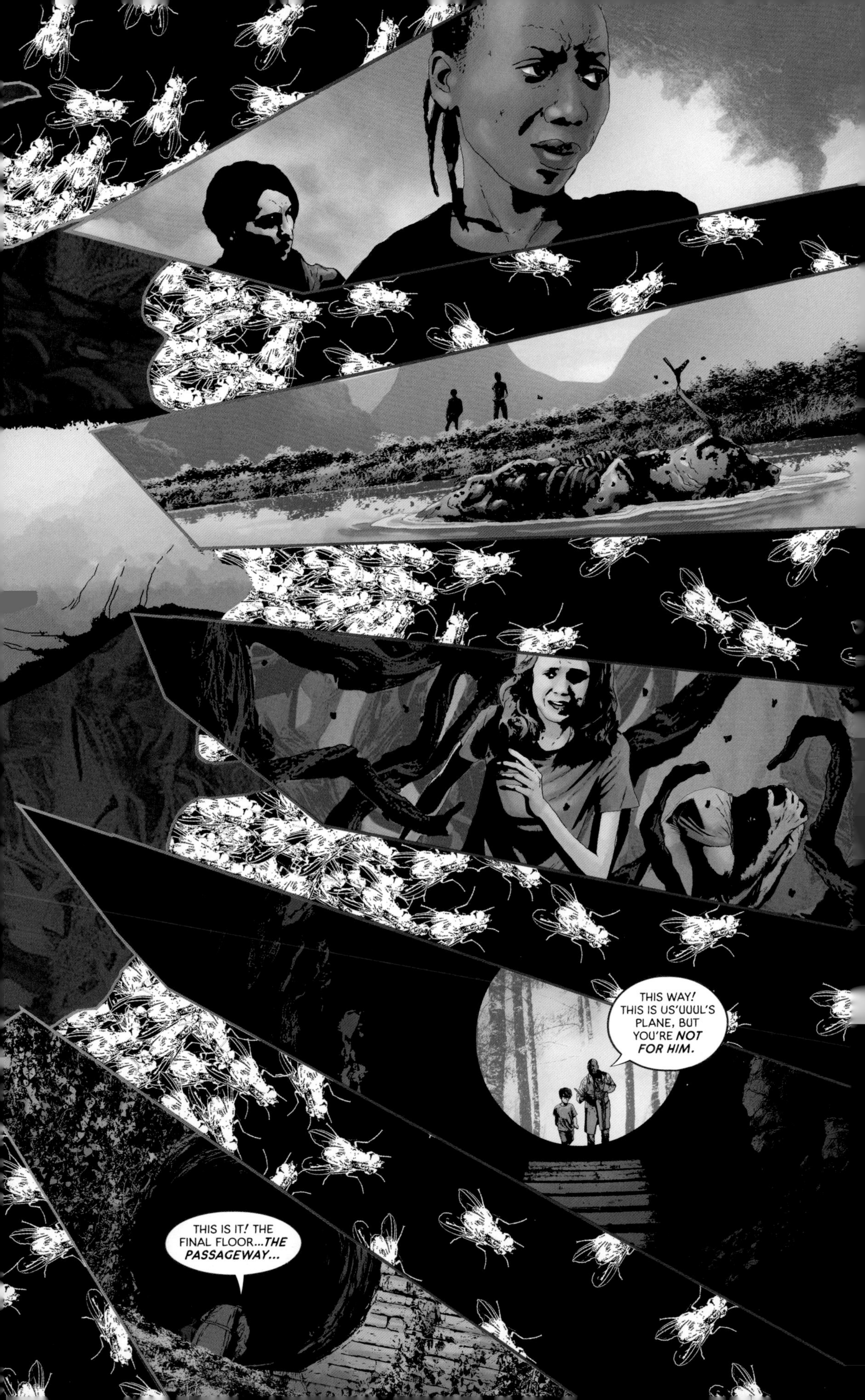
THIS WAY! THIS IS US'UUUL'S PLANE, BUT YOU'RE NOT FOR HIM.
THIS IS IT! THE FINAL FLOOR...THE PASSAGEWAY...

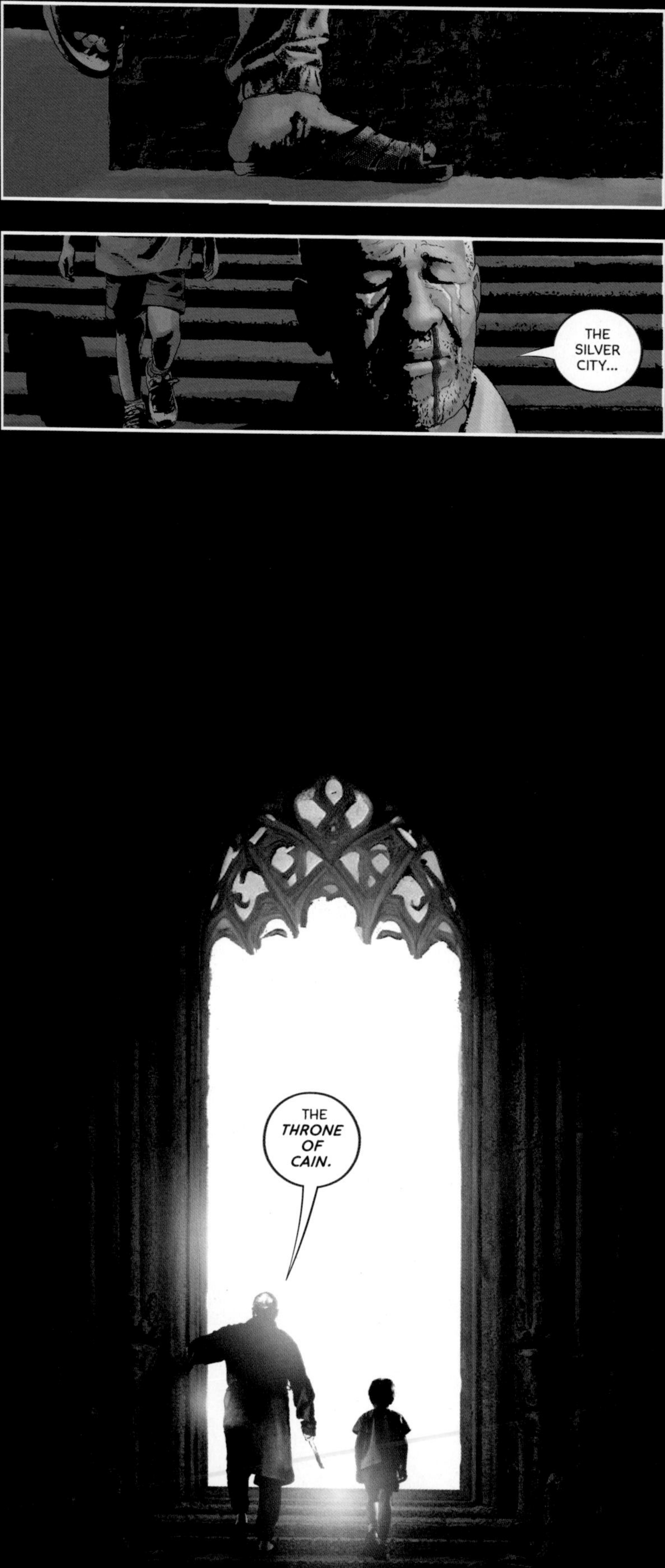
THE SILVER CITY...
THE *THRONE OF CAIN.*

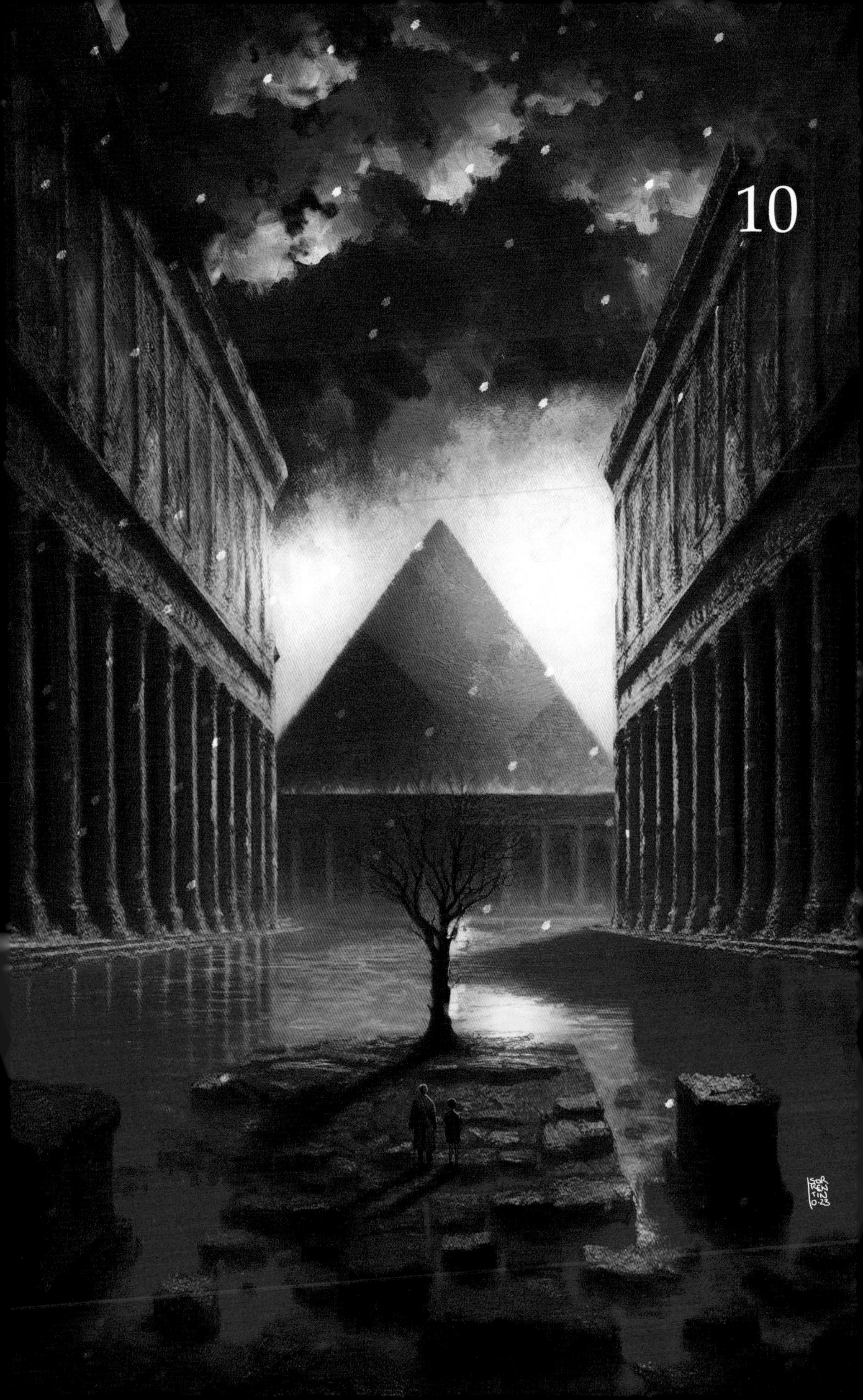
10

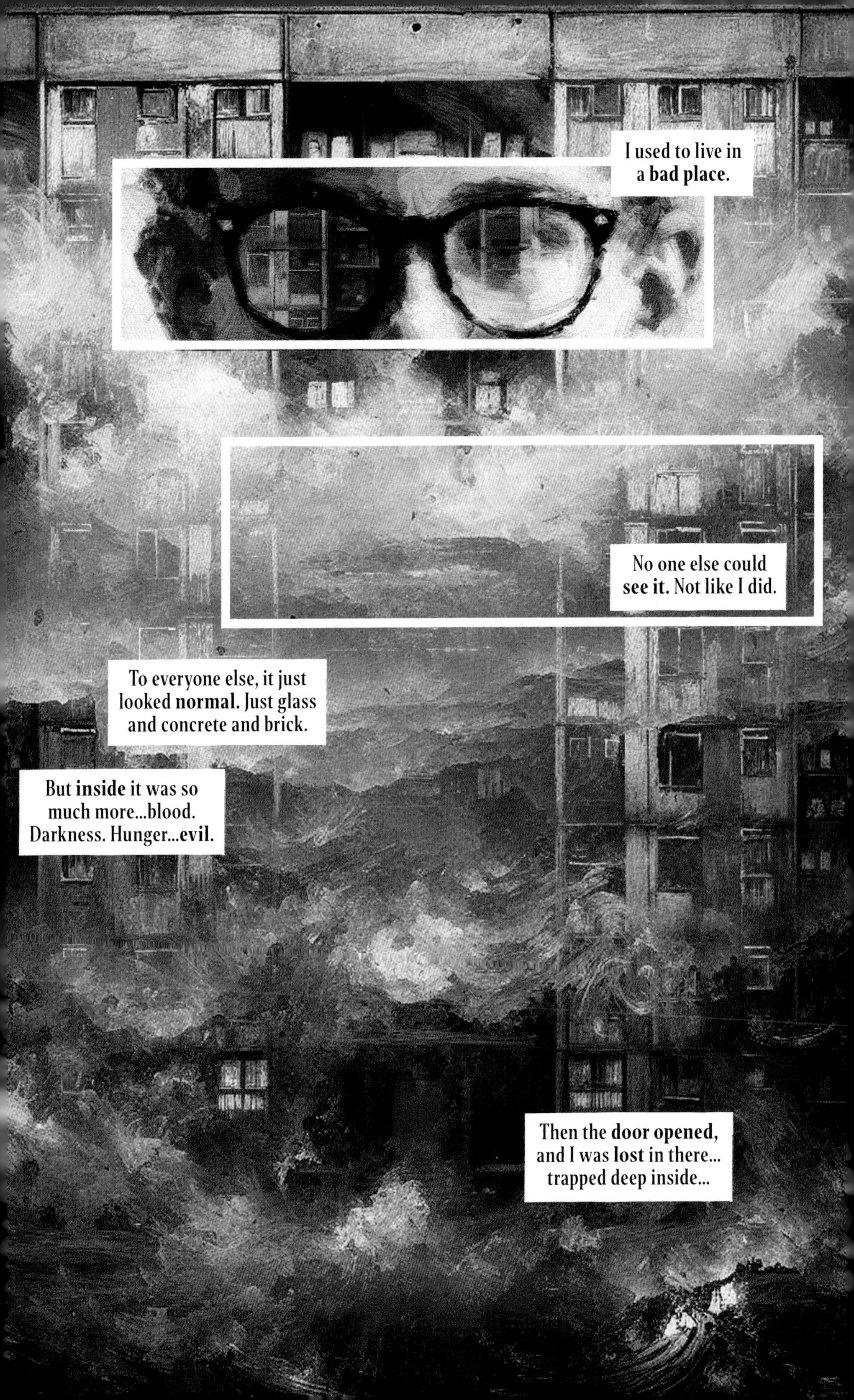
I used to live in a bad place.
No one else could see it. Not like I did.
To everyone else, it just looked normal. Just glass and concrete and brick.
But inside it was so much more...blood. Darkness. Hunger...evil.
Then the door opened, and I was lost in there... trapped deep inside...

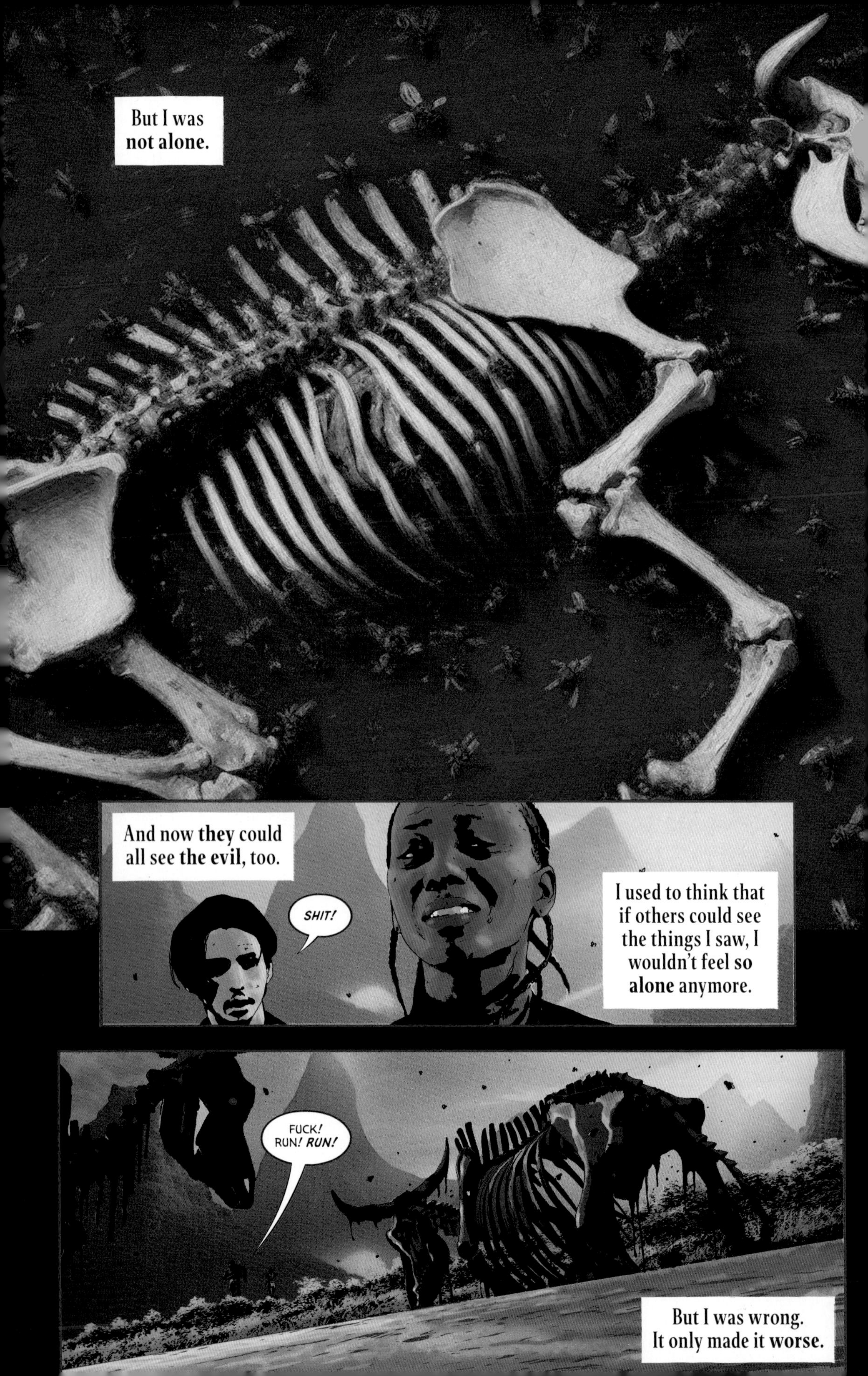
But I was not alone.
And now they could all see the evil, too.
SHIT!
I used to think that if others could see the things I saw, I wouldn't feel so alone anymore.
FUCK! RUN! RUN!
But I was wrong. It only made it worse.

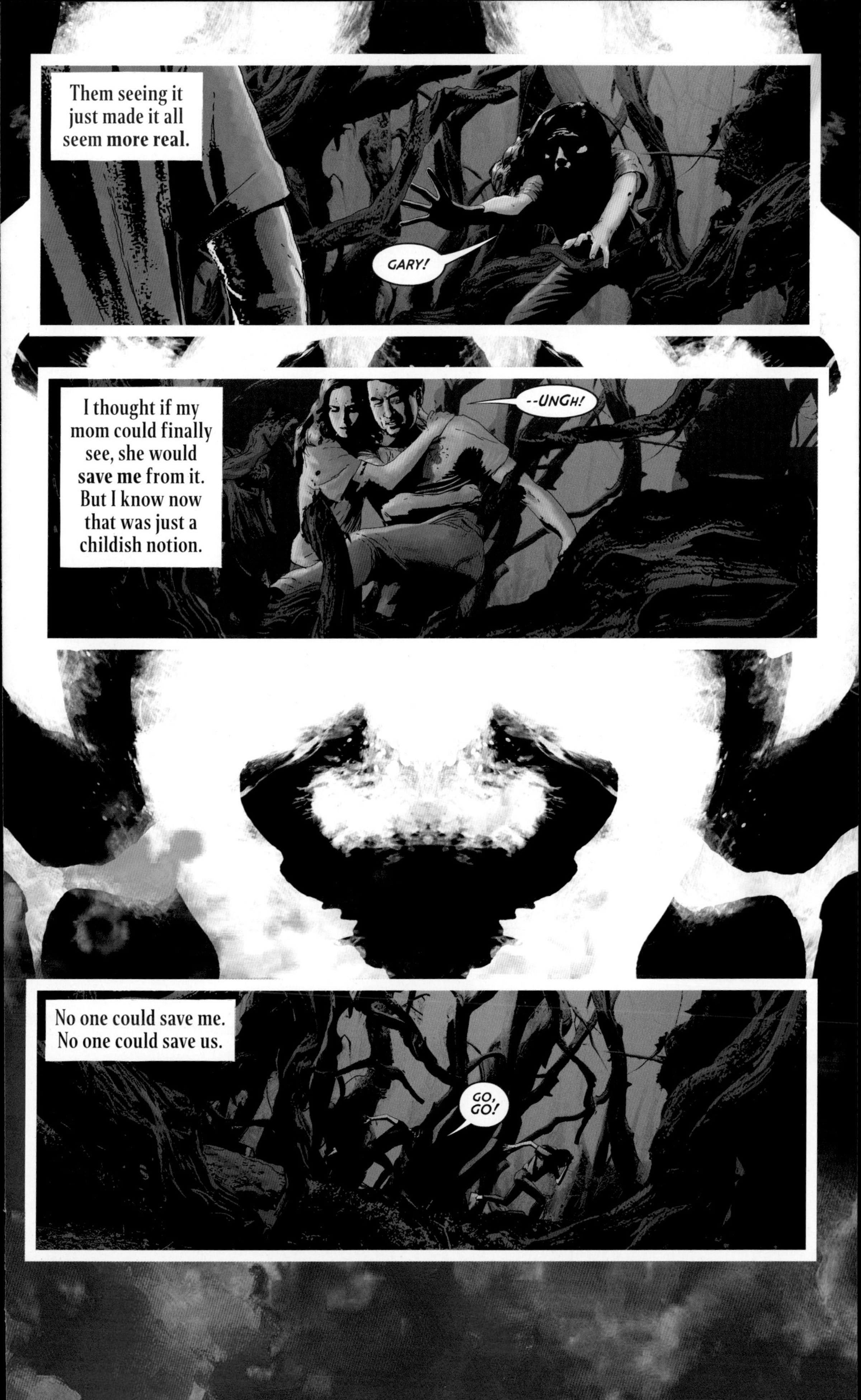
Them seeing it just made it all seem **more real.**
GARY!
I thought if my mom could finally see, she would **save me** from it. But I know now that was just a childish notion.
--UNGH!
No one could save me. No one could save us.
GO, GO!

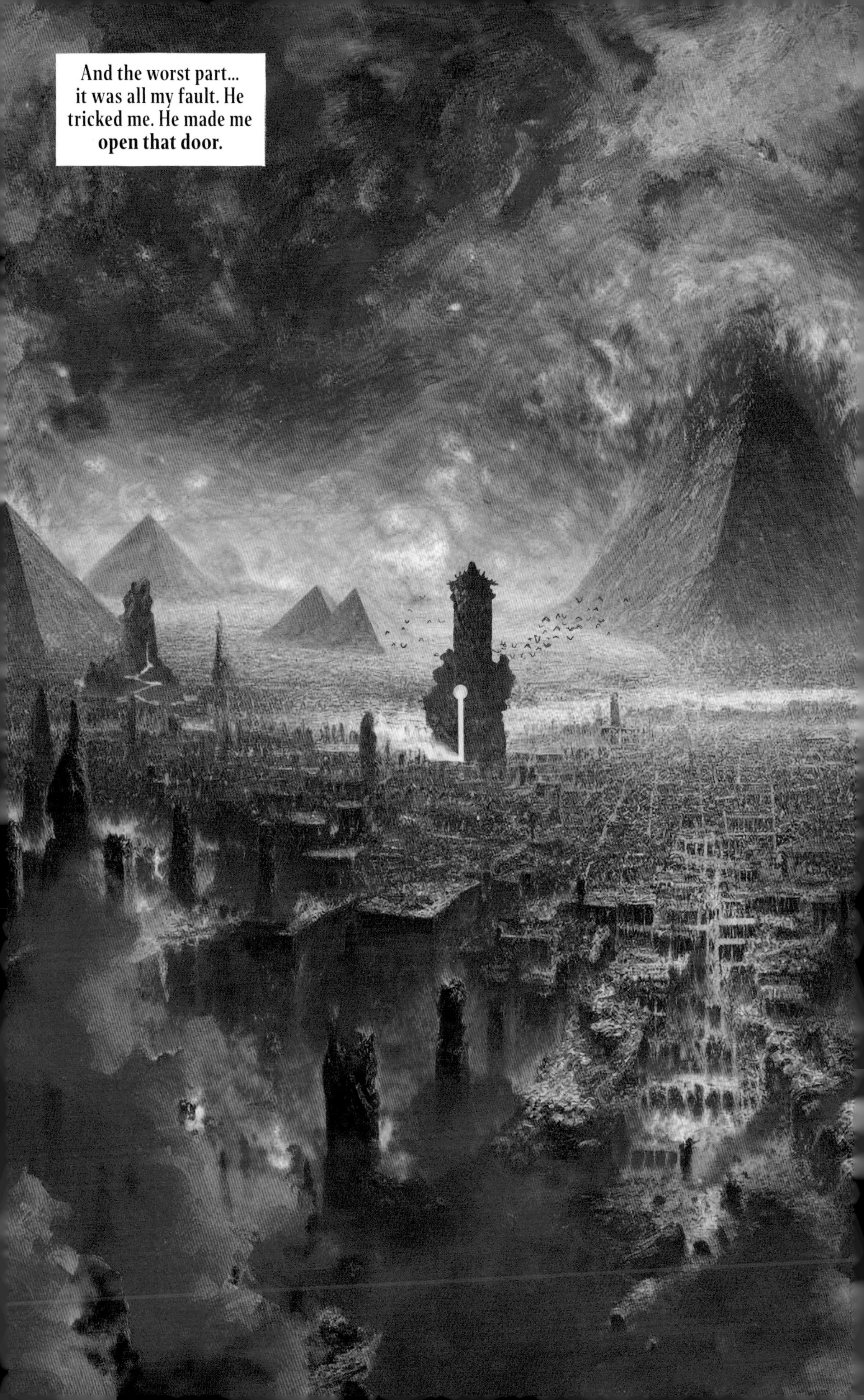
And the worst part... it was all my fault. He tricked me. He made me open that door.

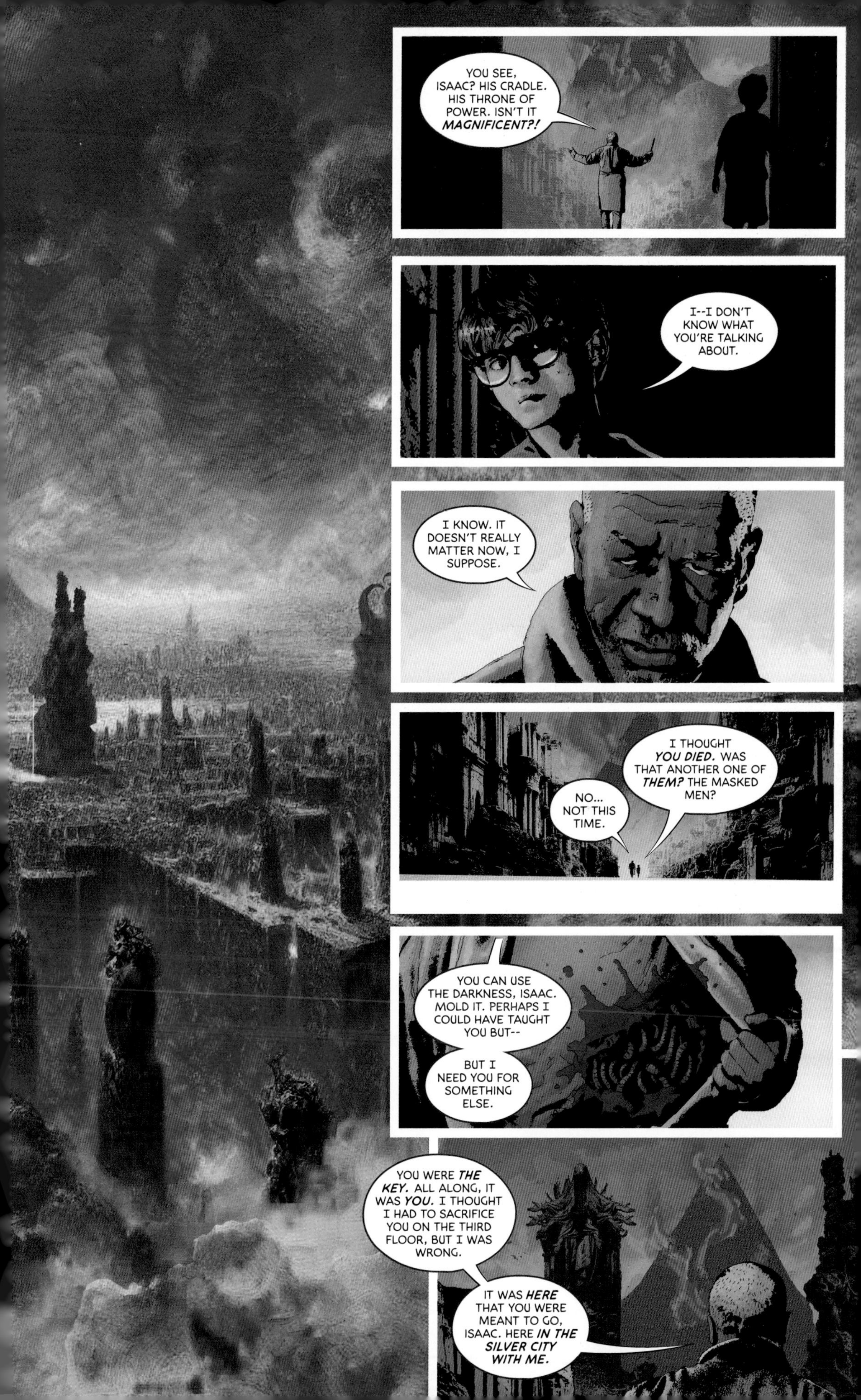
YOU SEE, ISAAC? HIS CRADLE. HIS THRONE OF POWER. ISN'T IT *MAGNIFICENT?!*
I--I DON'T KNOW WHAT YOU'RE TALKING ABOUT.
I KNOW. IT DOESN'T REALLY MATTER NOW, I SUPPOSE.
I THOUGHT *YOU DIED.* WAS THAT ANOTHER ONE OF *THEM?* THE MASKED MEN?
NO... NOT THIS TIME.
YOU CAN USE THE DARKNESS, ISAAC. MOLD IT. PERHAPS I COULD HAVE TAUGHT YOU BUT--
BUT I NEED YOU FOR SOMETHING ELSE.
YOU WERE *THE KEY.* ALL ALONG, IT WAS *YOU.* I THOUGHT I HAD TO SACRIFICE YOU ON THE THIRD FLOOR, BUT I WAS WRONG.
IT WAS *HERE* THAT YOU WERE MEANT TO GO, ISAAC. HERE *IN THE SILVER CITY WITH ME.*

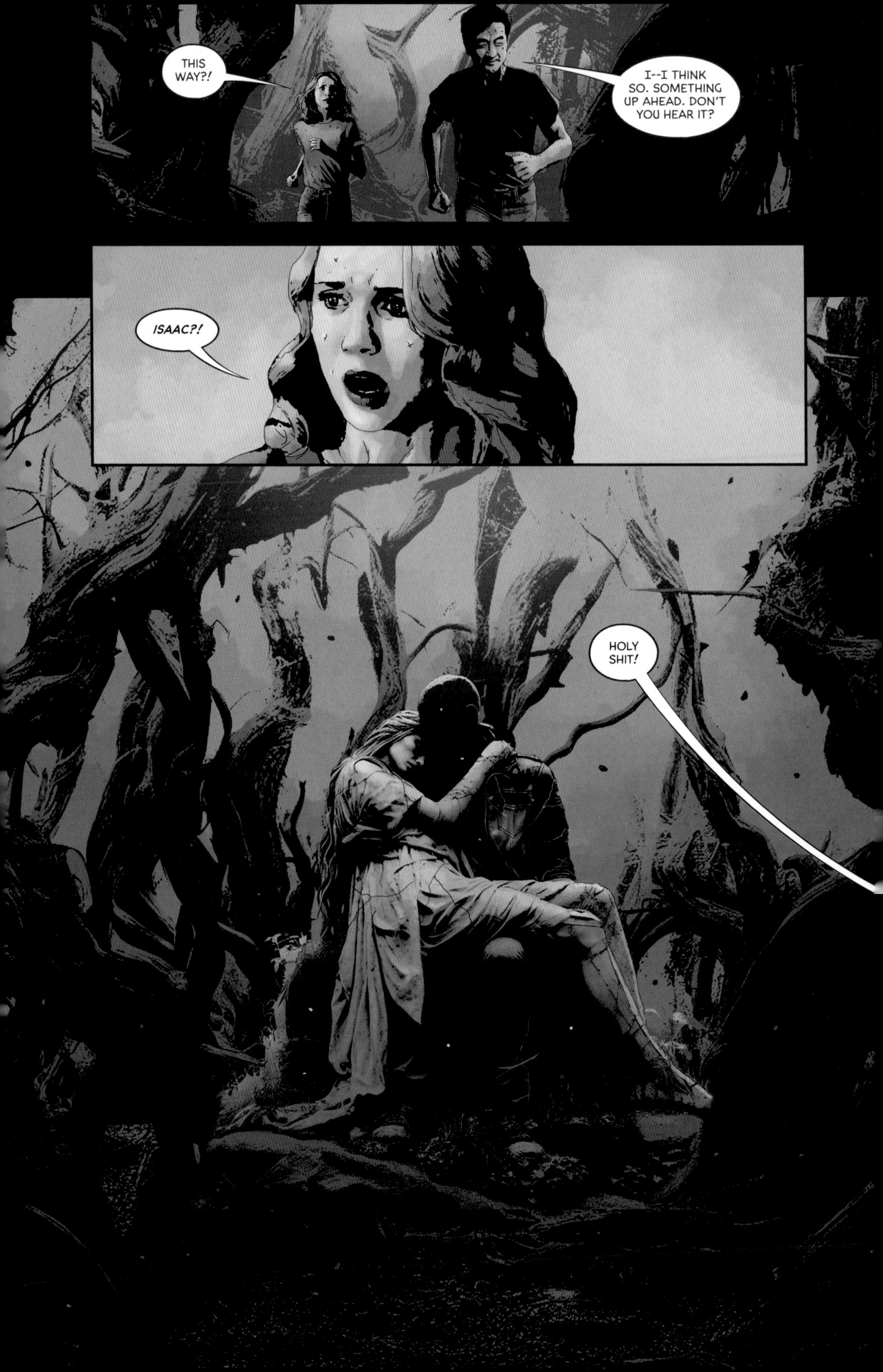
THIS WAY?!
I--I THINK SO. SOMETHING UP AHEAD. DON'T YOU HEAR IT?
ISAAC?!
HOLY SHIT!

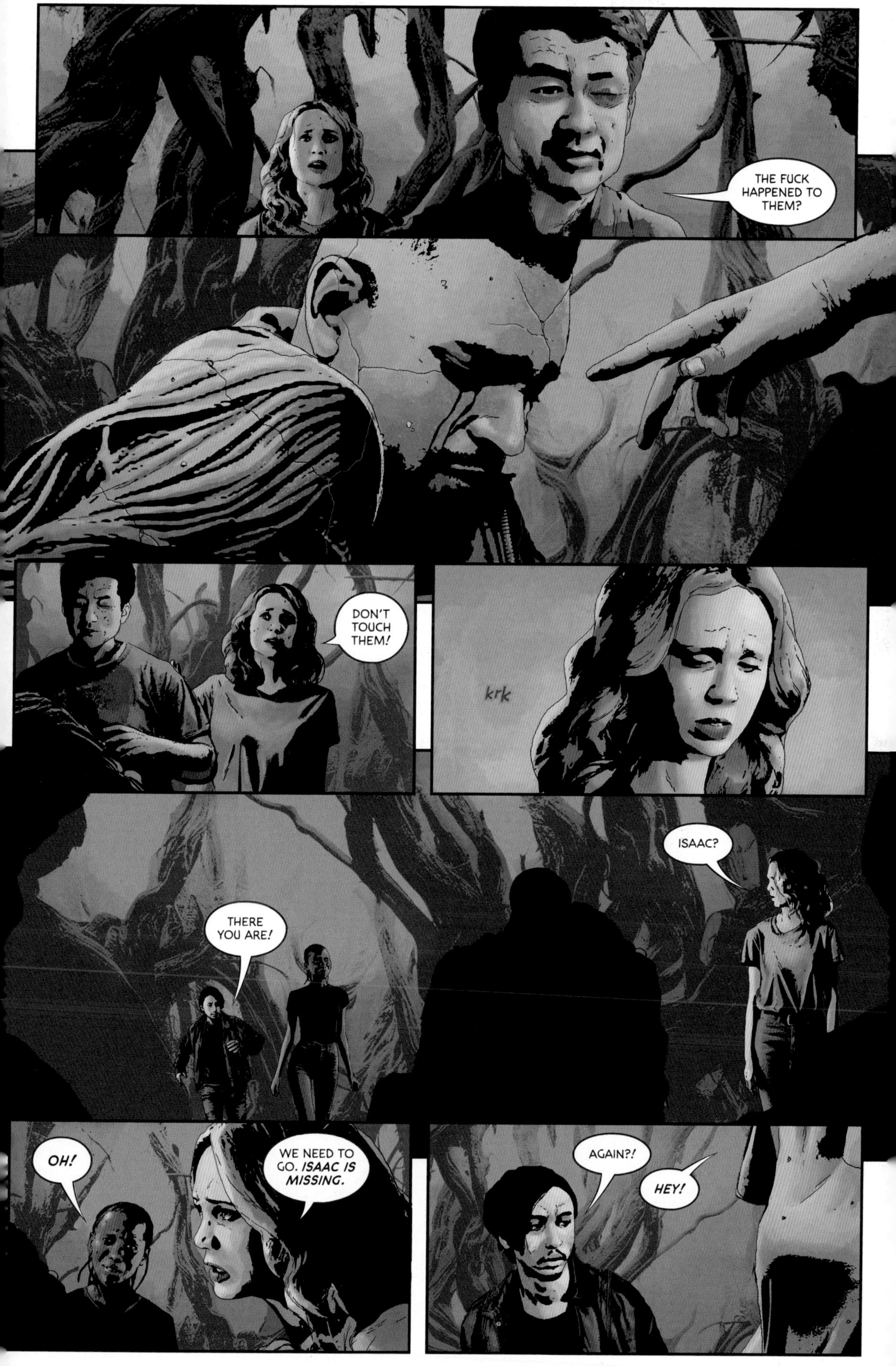
THE FUCK HAPPENED TO THEM?
DON'T TOUCH THEM!
krk
ISAAC?
THERE YOU ARE!
OH!
WE NEED TO GO. ISAAC IS MISSING.
AGAIN?!
HEY!

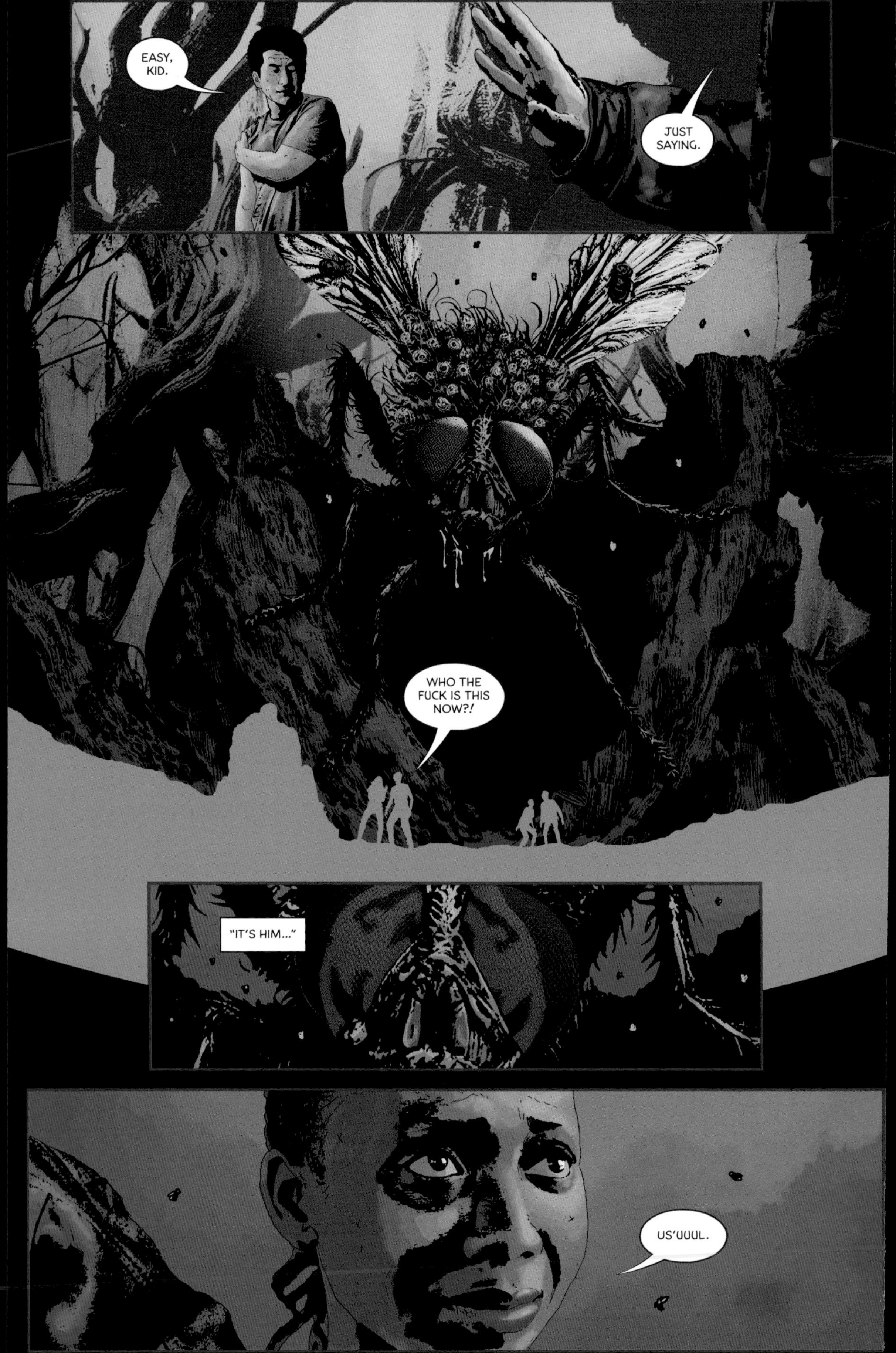
EASY, KID.
JUST SAYING.
WHO THE FUCK IS THIS NOW?!
"IT'S HIM..."
US'UUUL.

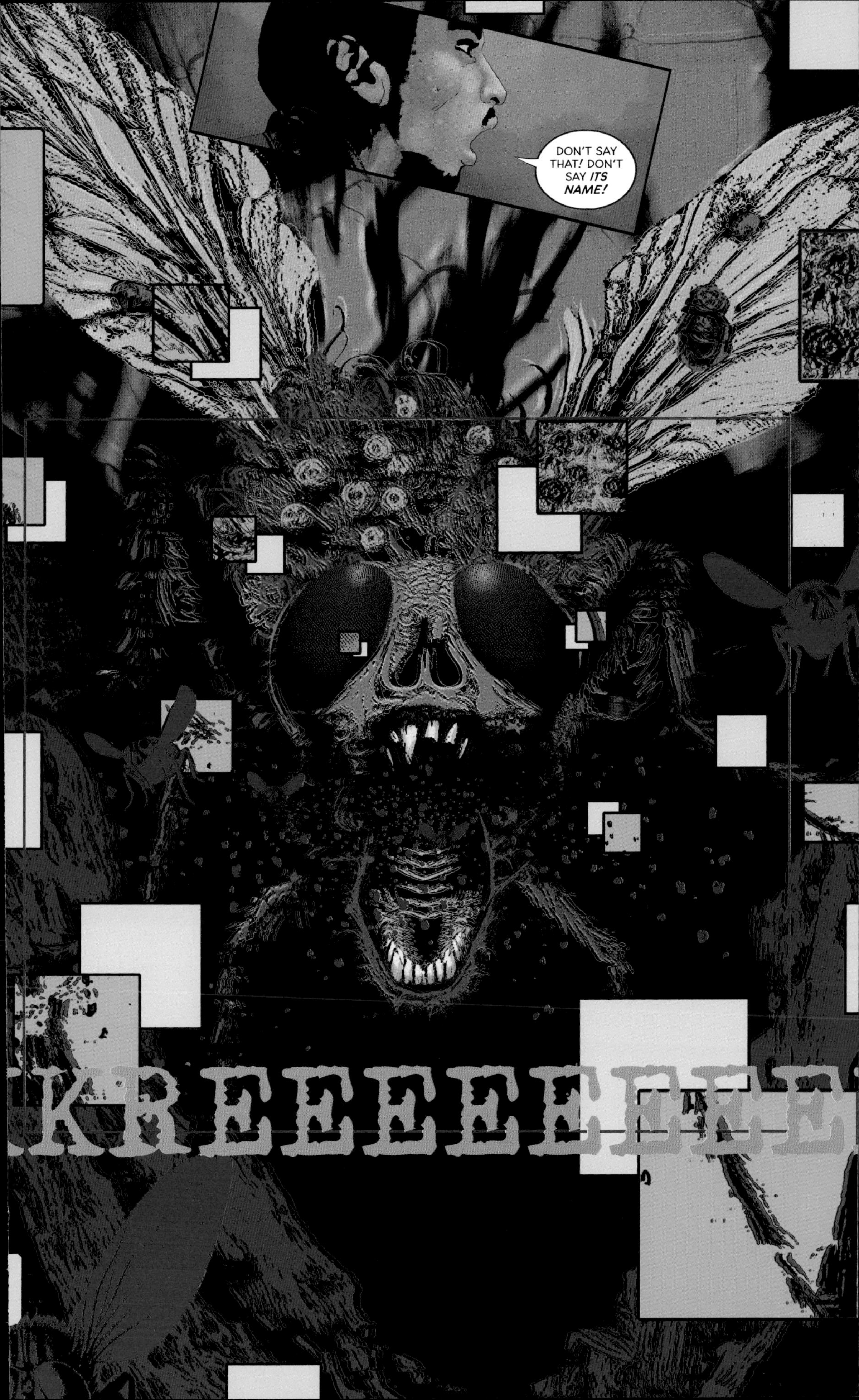
DON'T SAY THAT! DON'T SAY *ITS NAME!*
KREEEEEEE

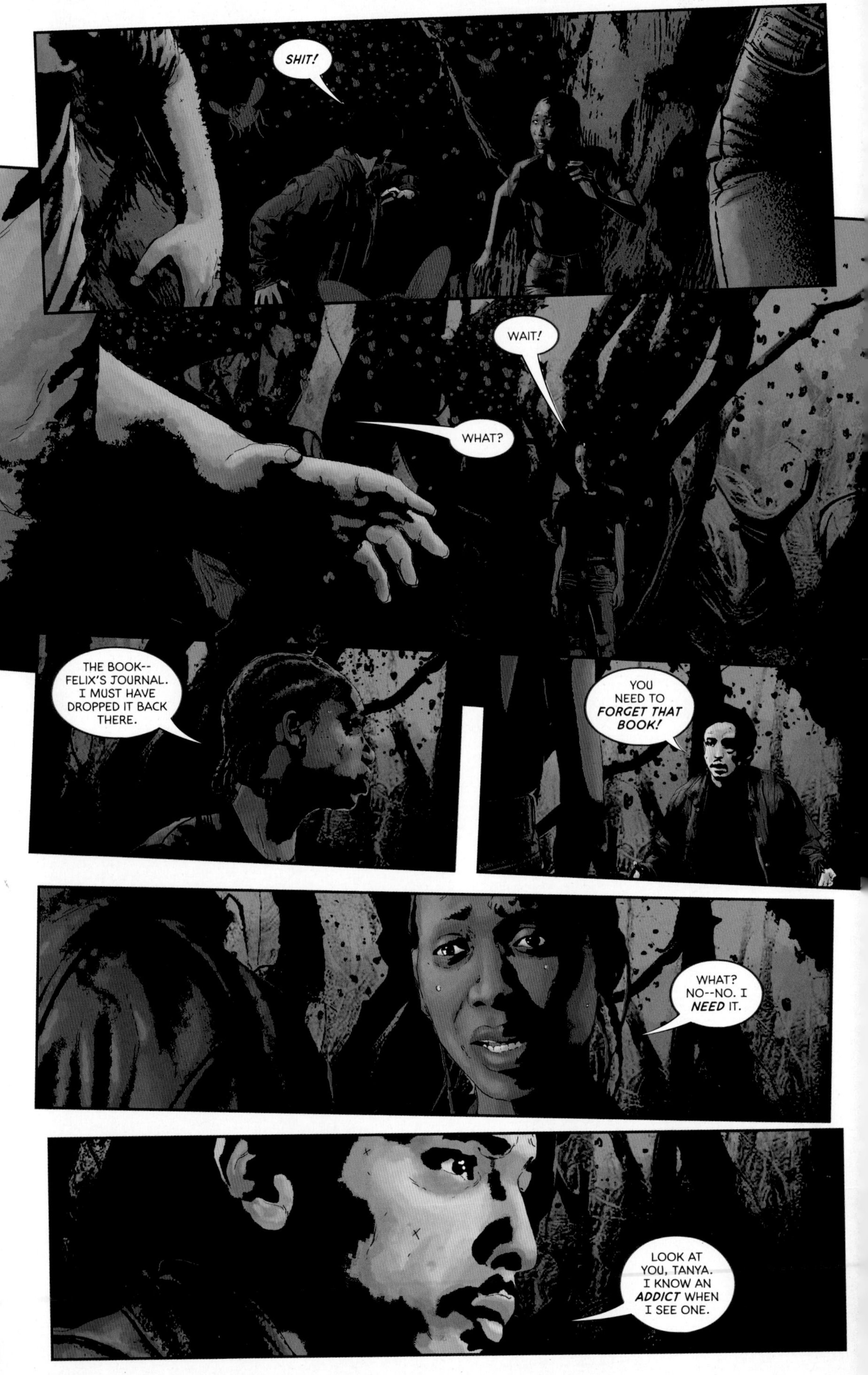
SHIT!
WAIT!
WHAT?
THE BOOK--FELIX'S JOURNAL. I MUST HAVE DROPPED IT BACK THERE.
YOU NEED TO FORGET THAT BOOK!
WHAT? NO--NO. I NEED IT.
LOOK AT YOU, TANYA. I KNOW AN ADDICT WHEN I SEE ONE.

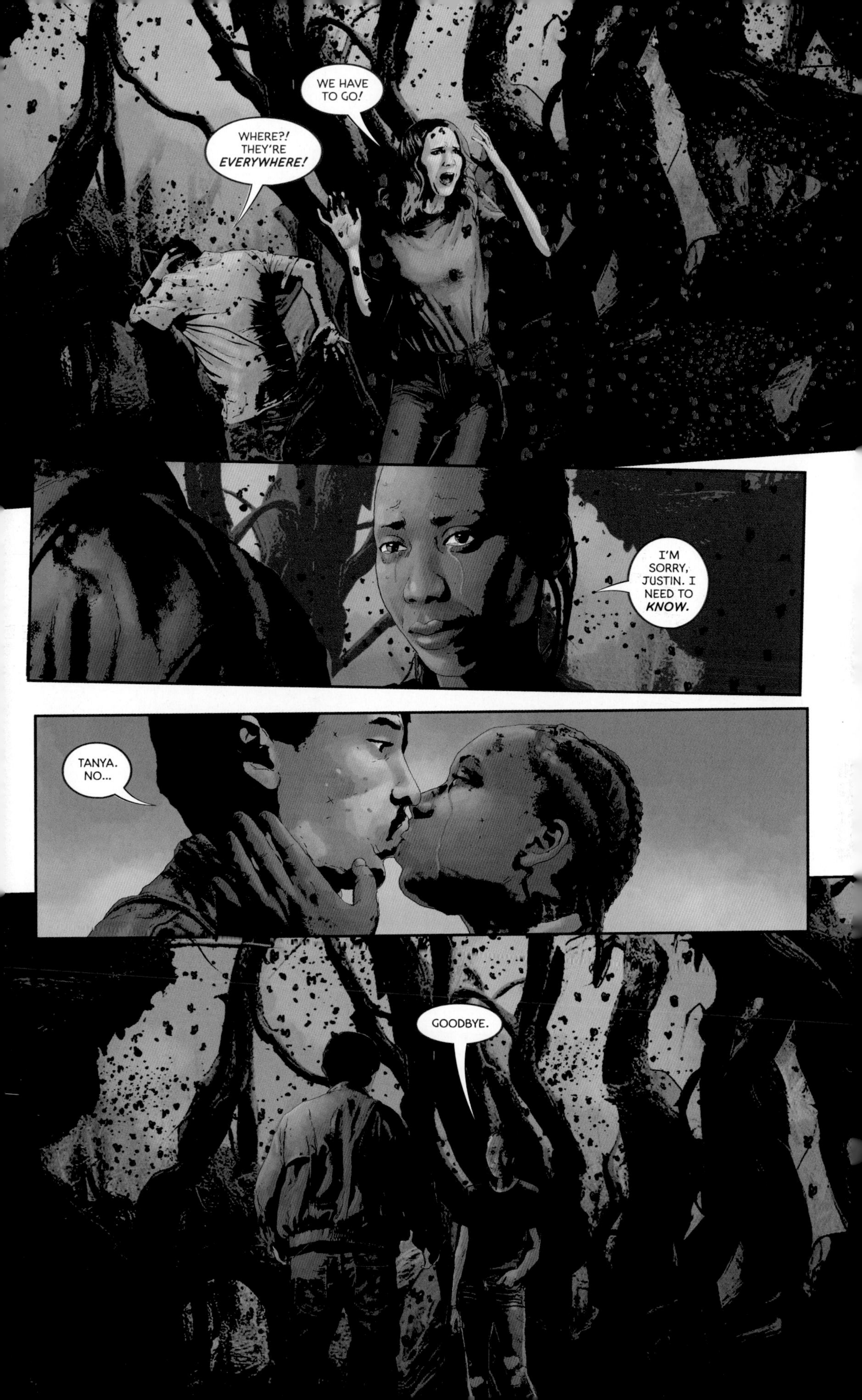
WE HAVE TO GO!
WHERE?! THEY'RE EVERYWHERE!
I'M SORRY, JUSTIN. I NEED TO KNOW.
TANYA. NO...
GOODBYE.

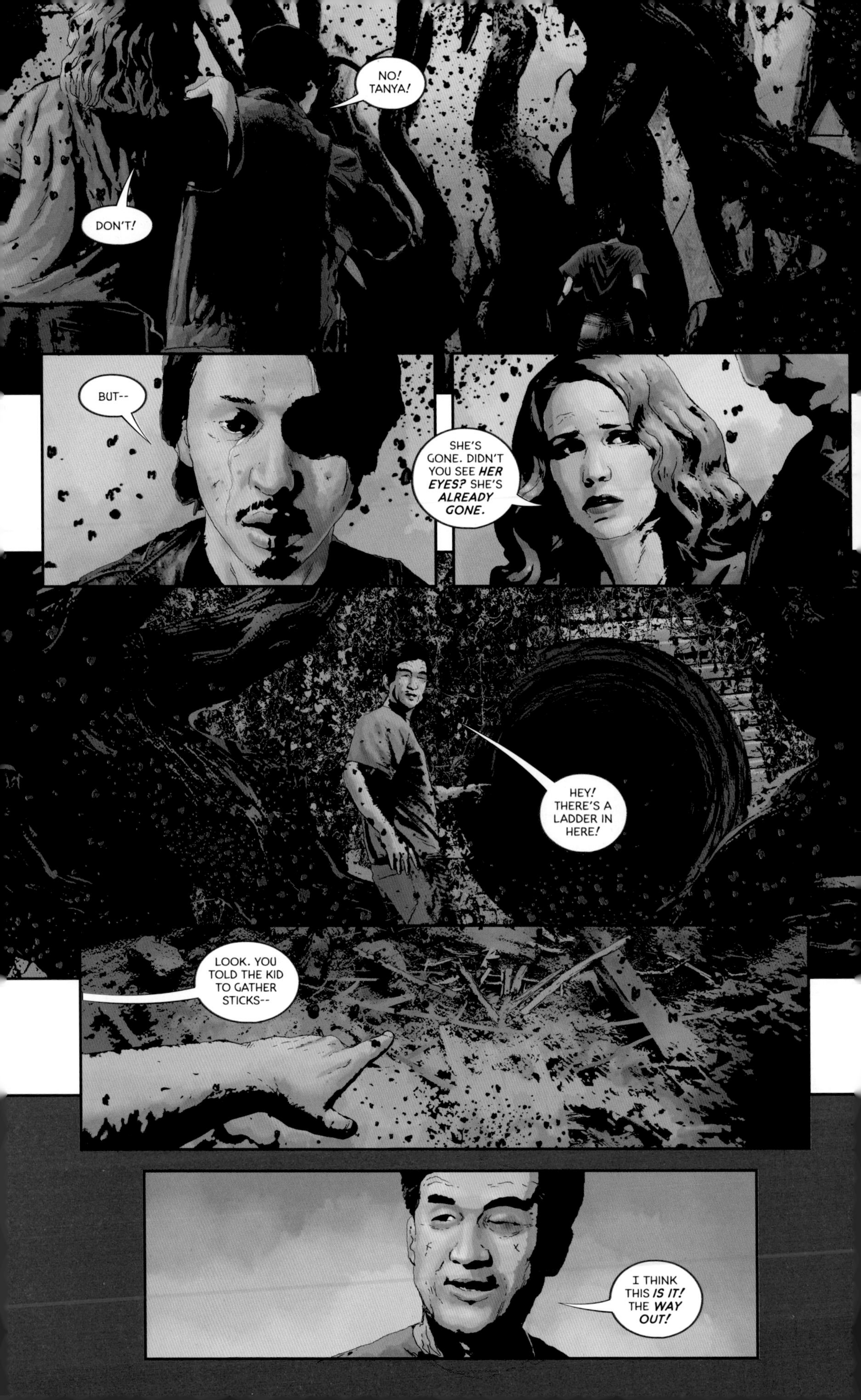
NO! TANYA!
DON'T!
BUT--
SHE'S GONE. DIDN'T YOU SEE *HER EYES?* SHE'S *ALREADY GONE.*
HEY! THERE'S A LADDER IN HERE!
LOOK. YOU TOLD THE KID TO GATHER STICKS--
I THINK THIS *IS IT!* THE *WAY OUT!*

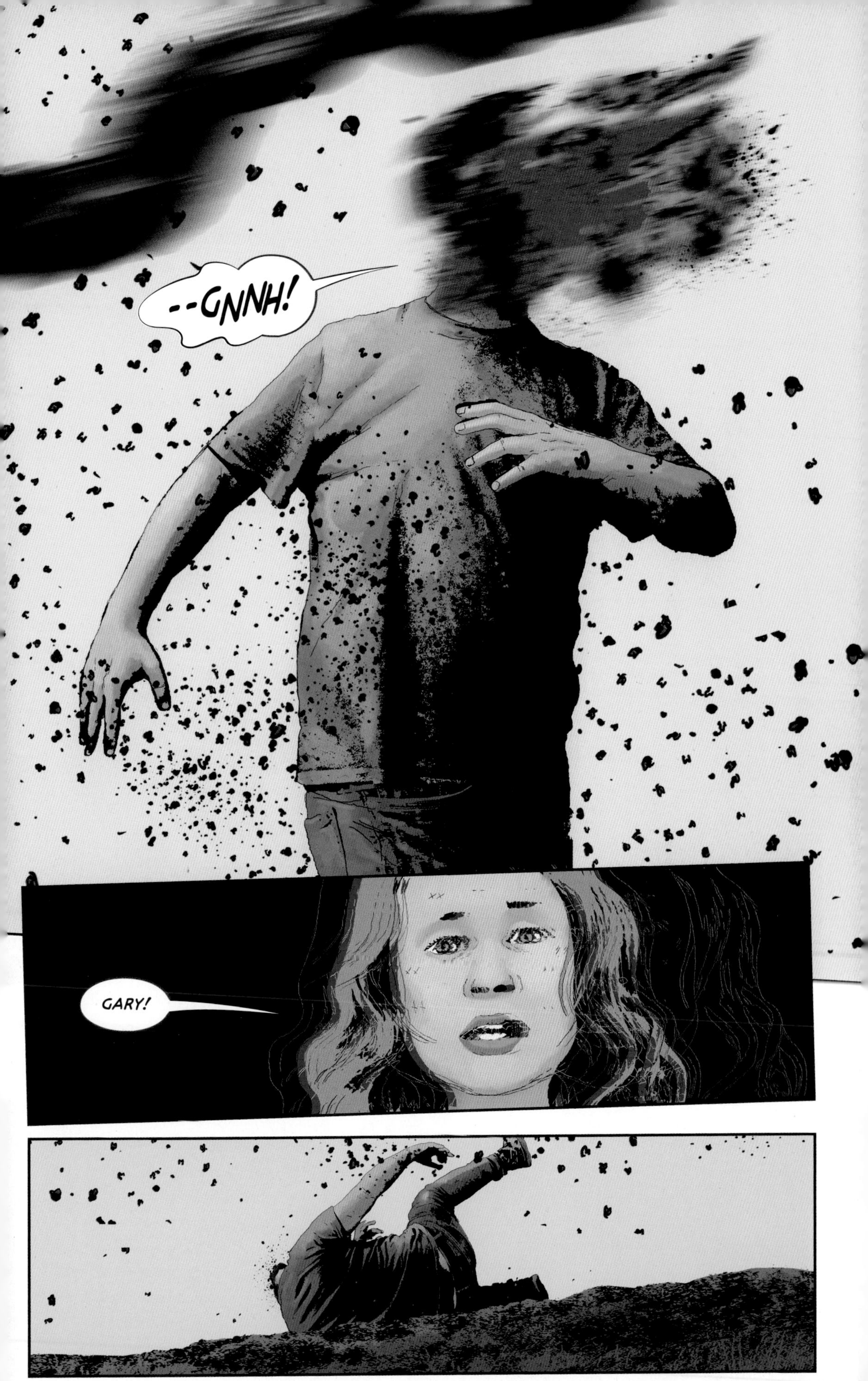
--GNNH!
GARY!

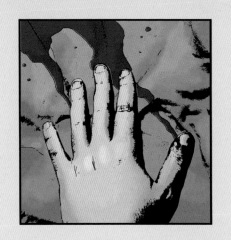

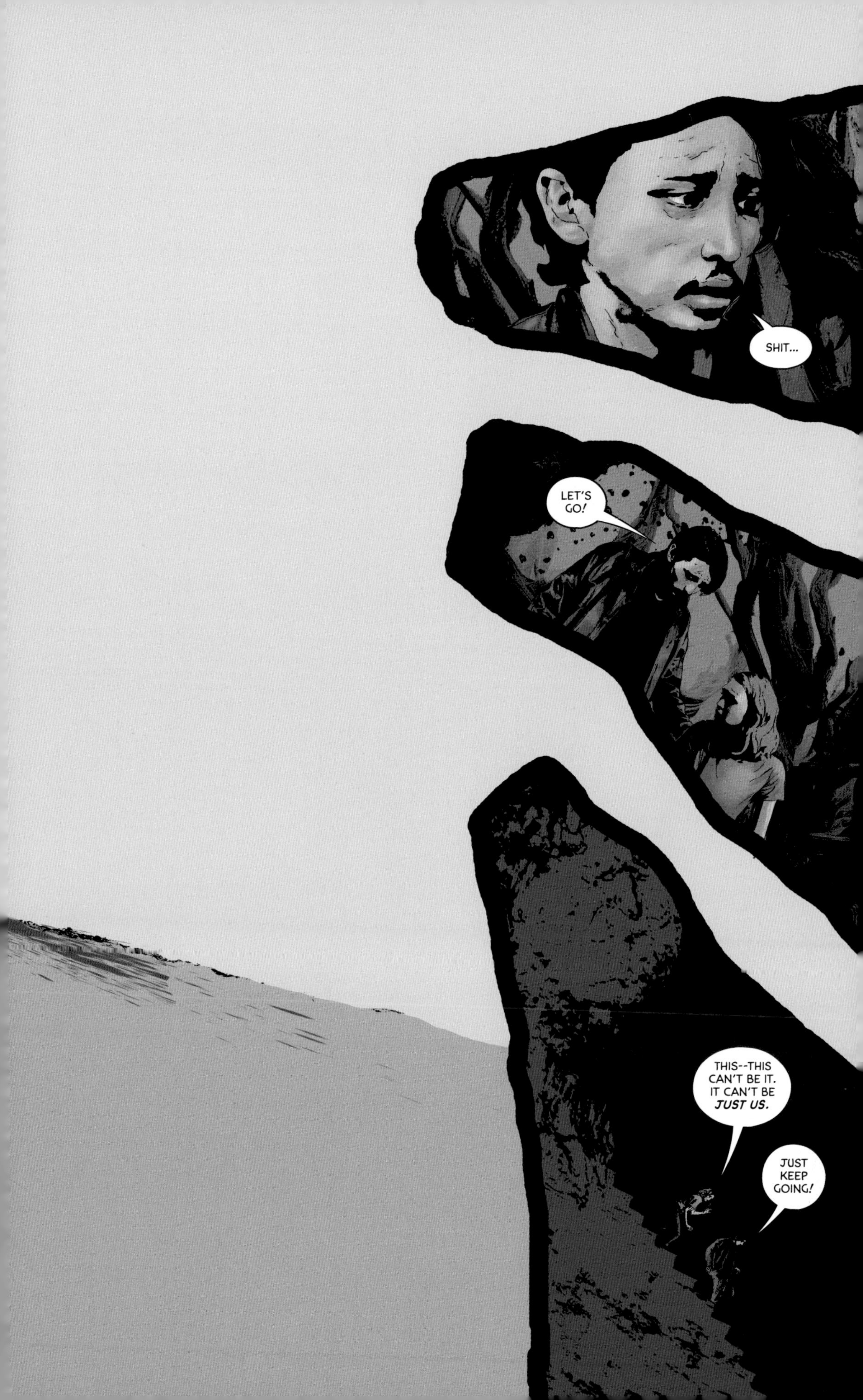
SHIT...
LET'S GO!
THIS--THIS CAN'T BE IT. IT CAN'T BE *JUST US.*
JUST KEEP GOING!

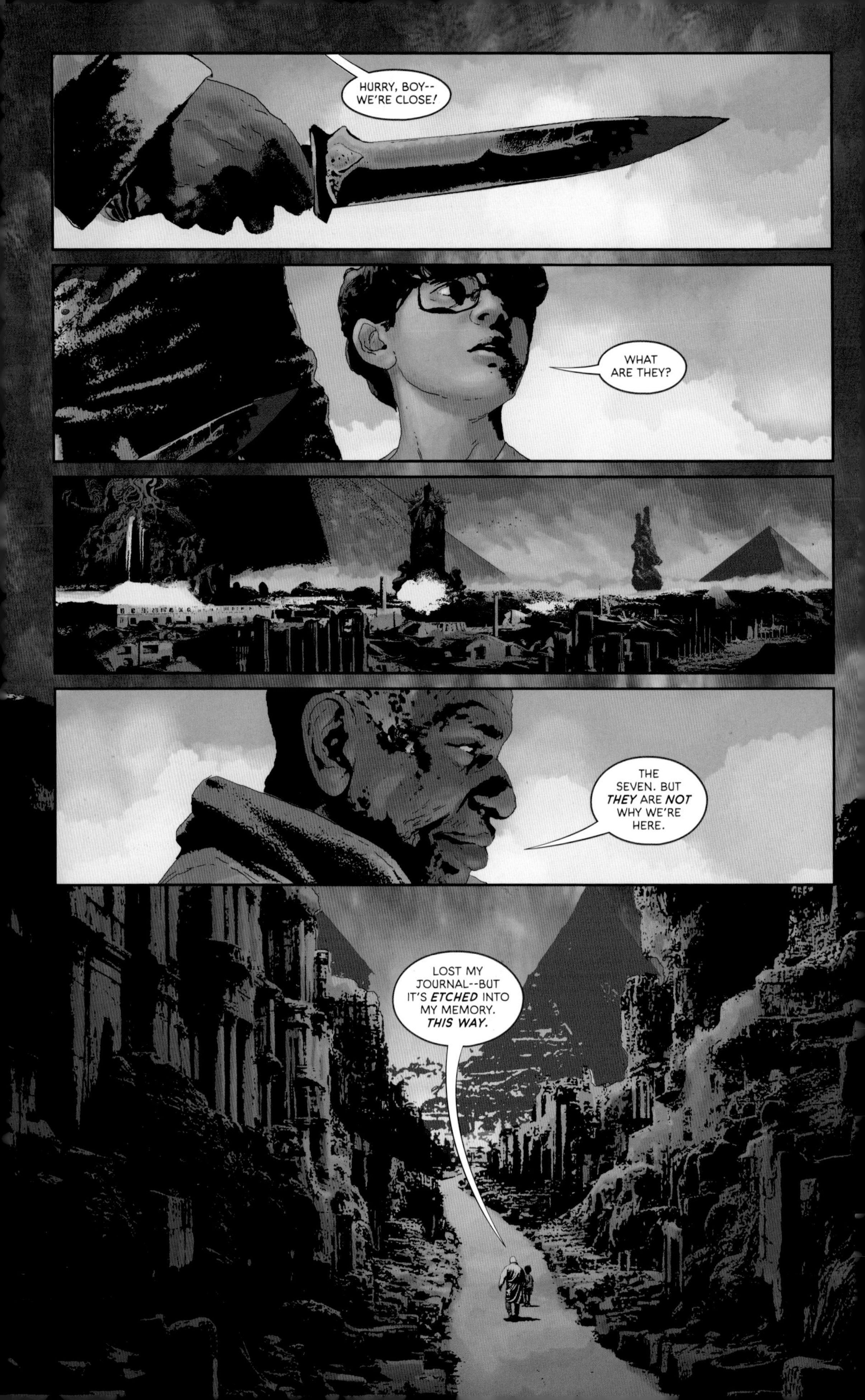
HURRY, BOY--
WE'RE CLOSE!
WHAT ARE THEY?
THE SEVEN. BUT *THEY* ARE *NOT* WHY WE'RE HERE.
LOST MY JOURNAL--BUT IT'S *ETCHED* INTO MY MEMORY. *THIS WAY.*

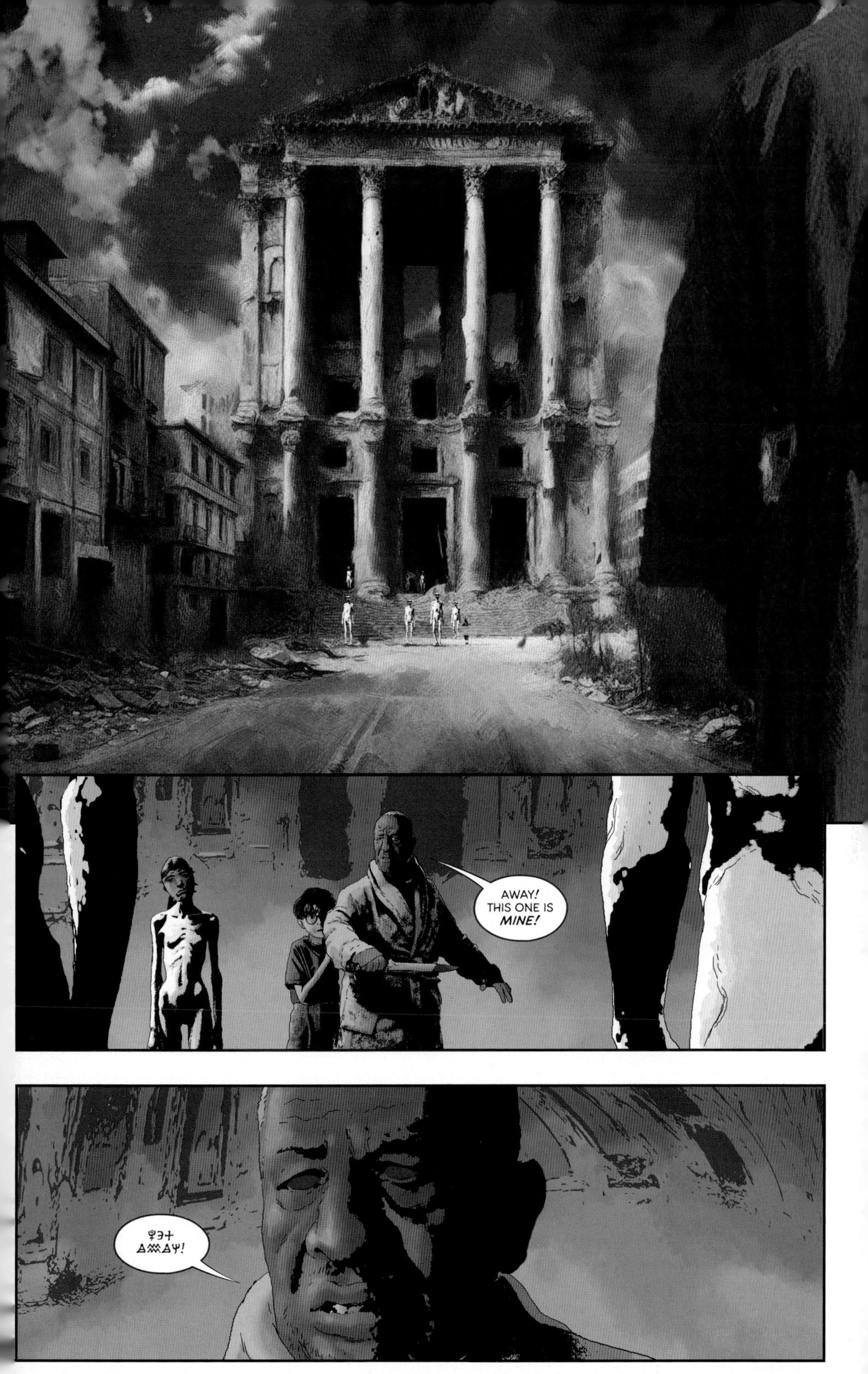
AWAY! THIS ONE IS MINE!

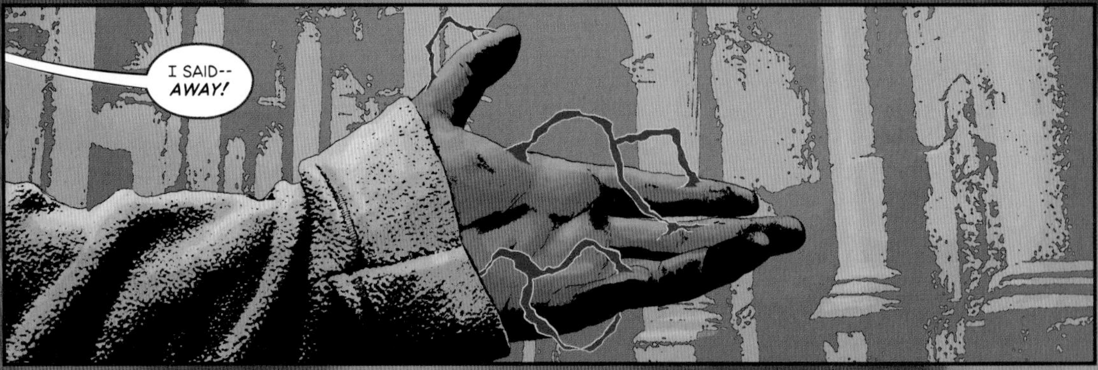
I SAID--
AWAY!

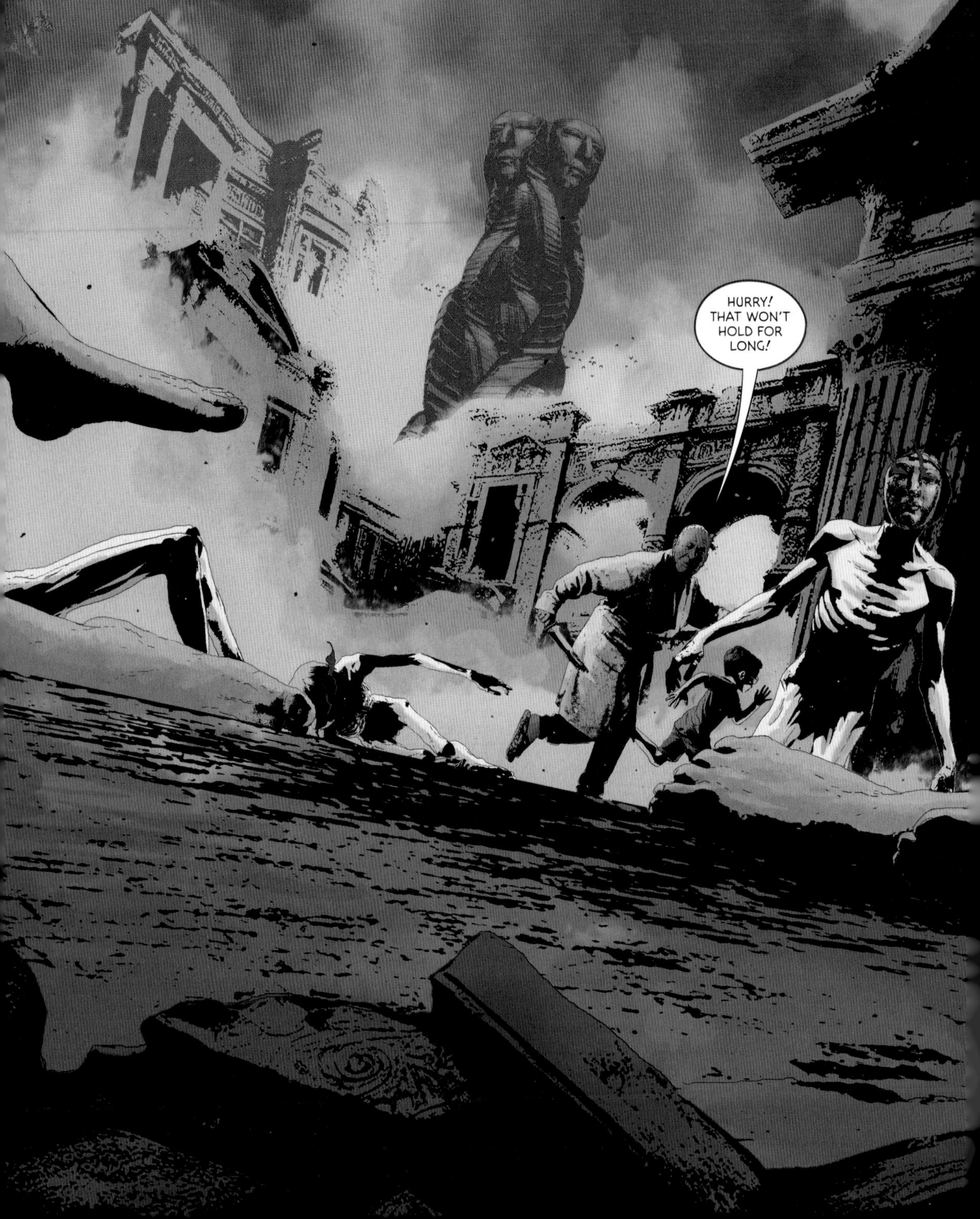
HURRY! THAT WON'T HOLD FOR LONG!

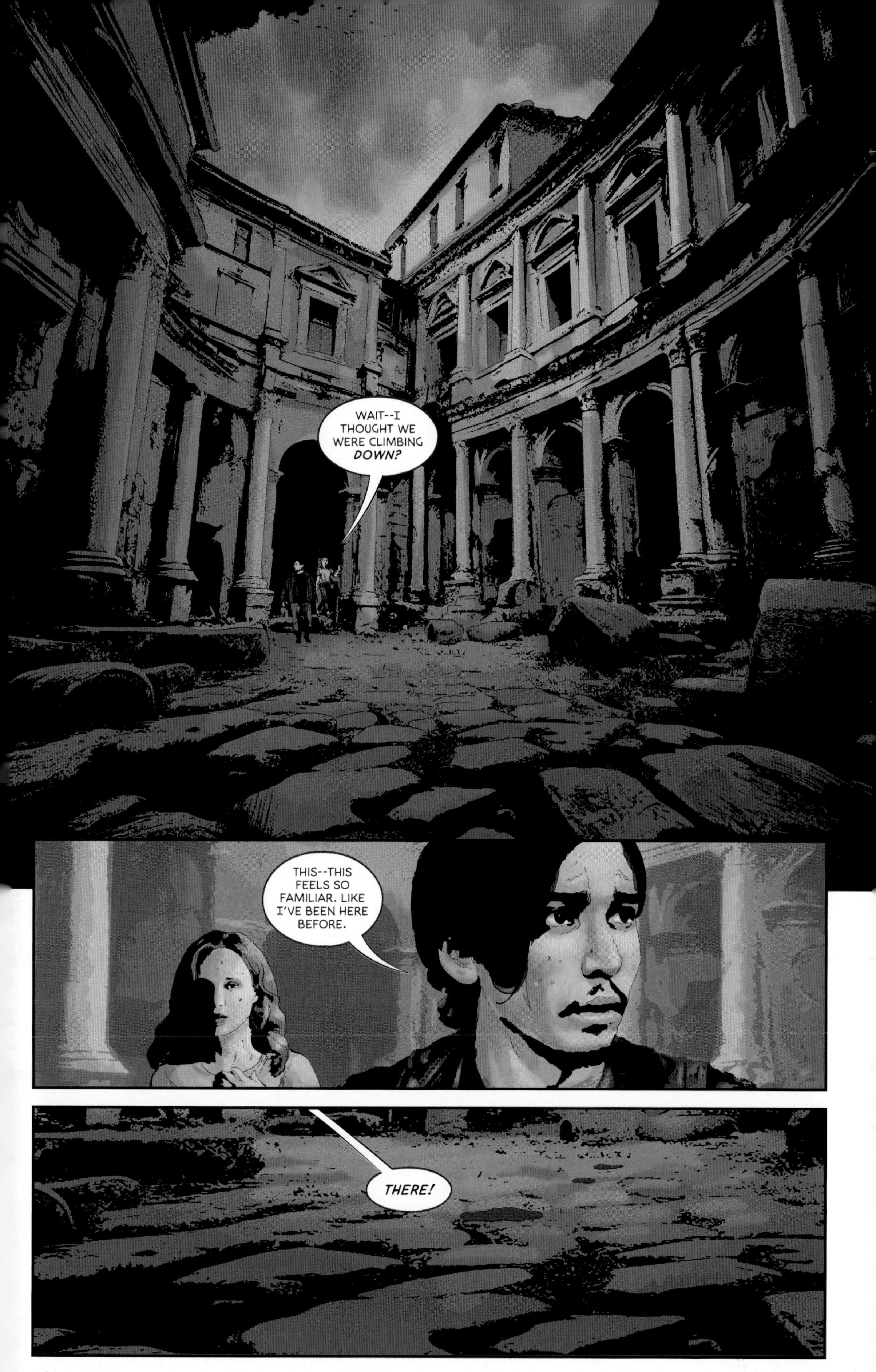
WAIT--I THOUGHT WE WERE CLIMBING *DOWN?*
THIS--THIS FEELS SO FAMILIAR. LIKE I'VE BEEN HERE BEFORE.
THERE!

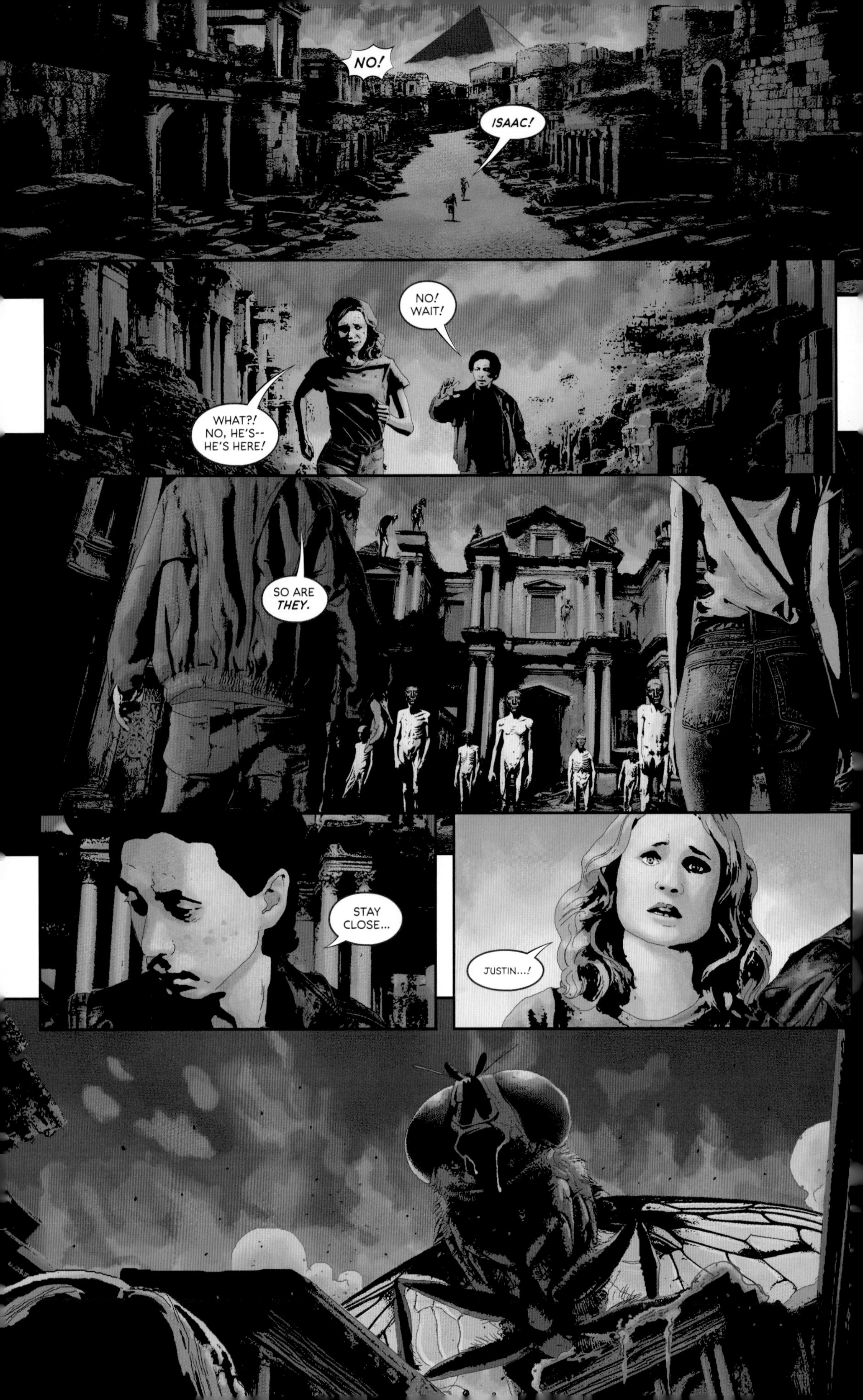
NO!
ISAAC!
WHAT?! NO, HE'S-- HE'S HERE!
NO! WAIT!
SO ARE THEY.
STAY CLOSE...
JUSTIN...!

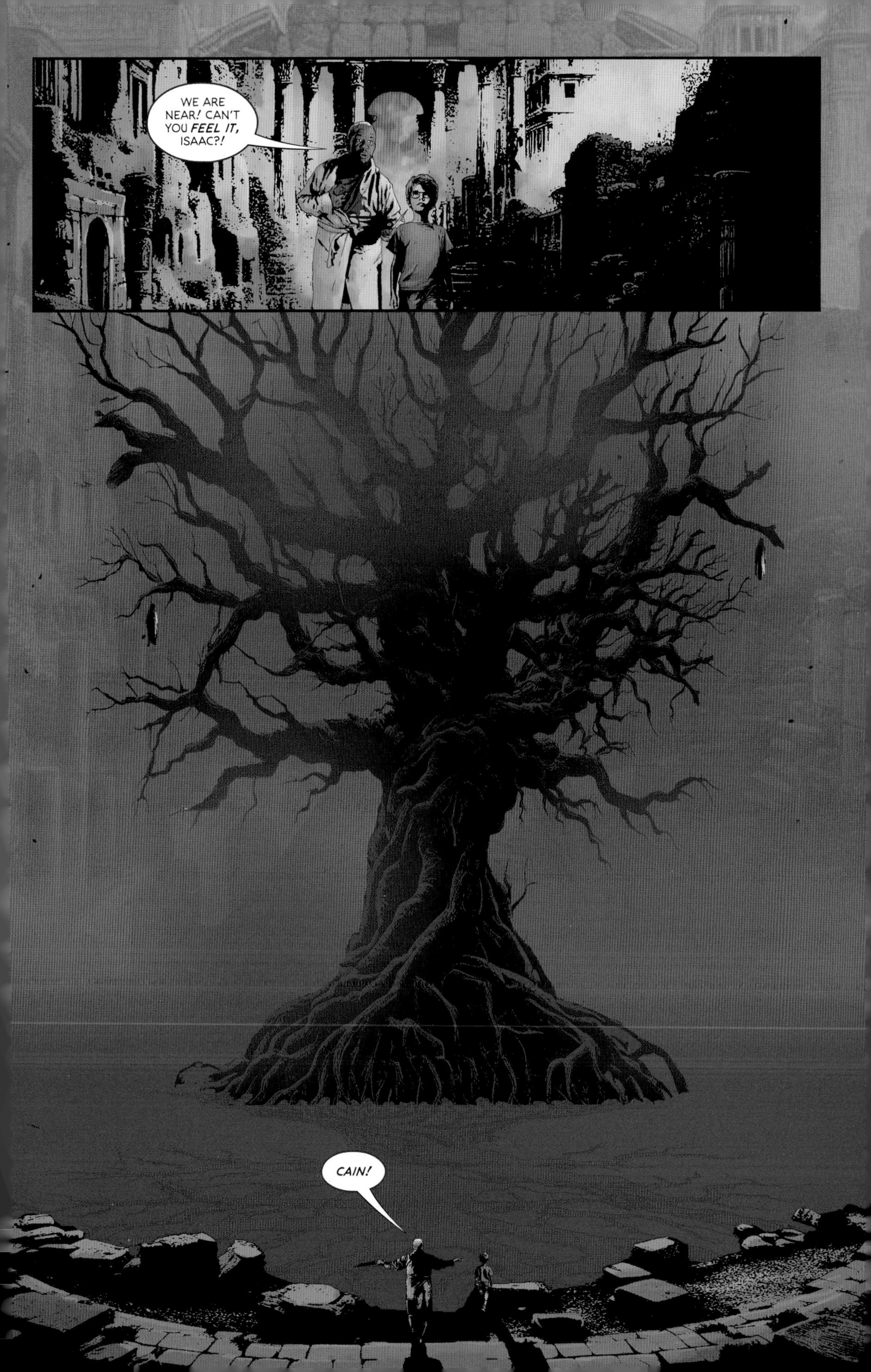
WE ARE NEAR! CAN'T YOU FEEL IT, ISAAC?!
CAIN!

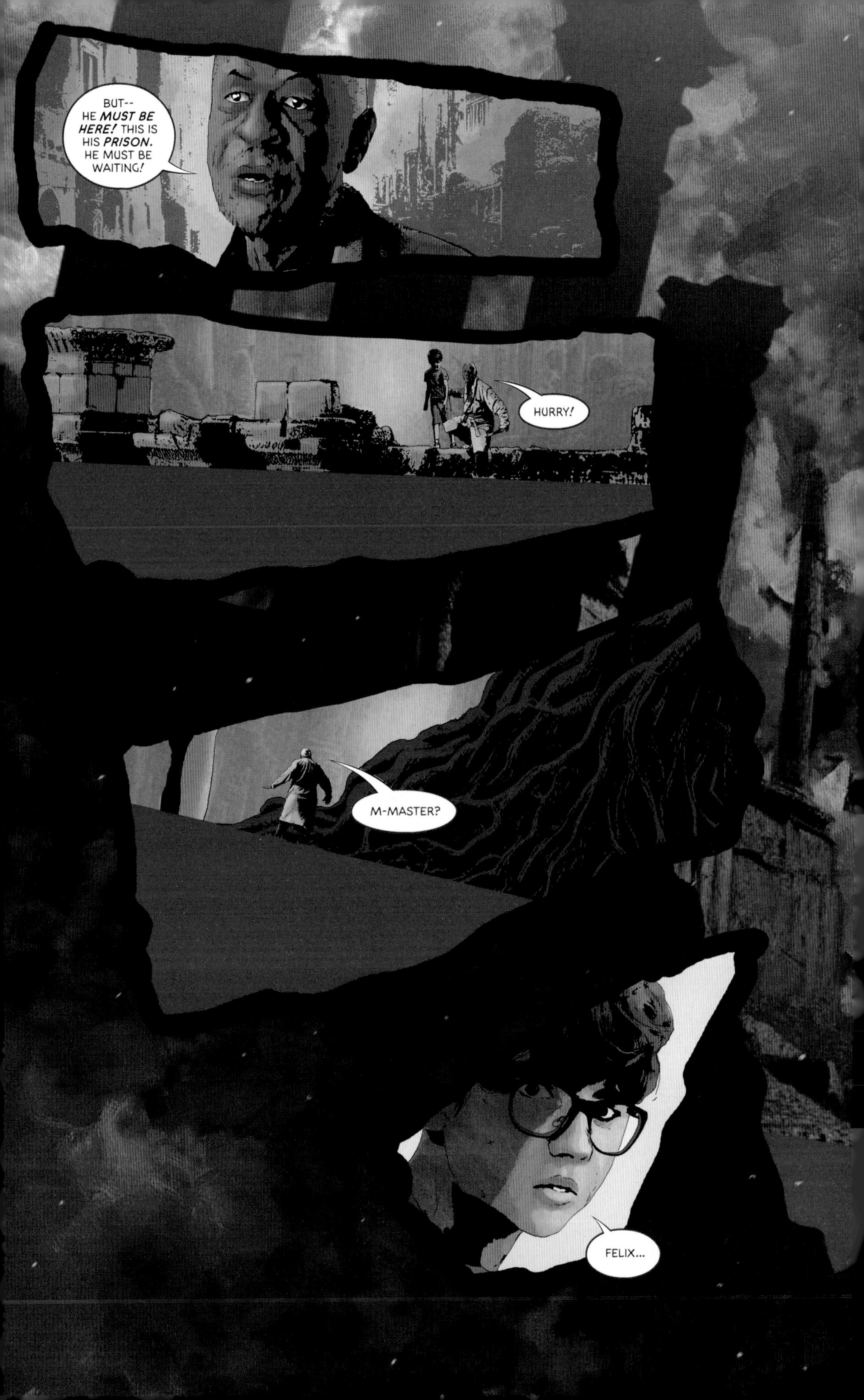
BUT-- HE MUST BE HERE! THIS IS HIS PRISON. HE MUST BE WAITING!
HURRY!
M-MASTER?
FELIX...

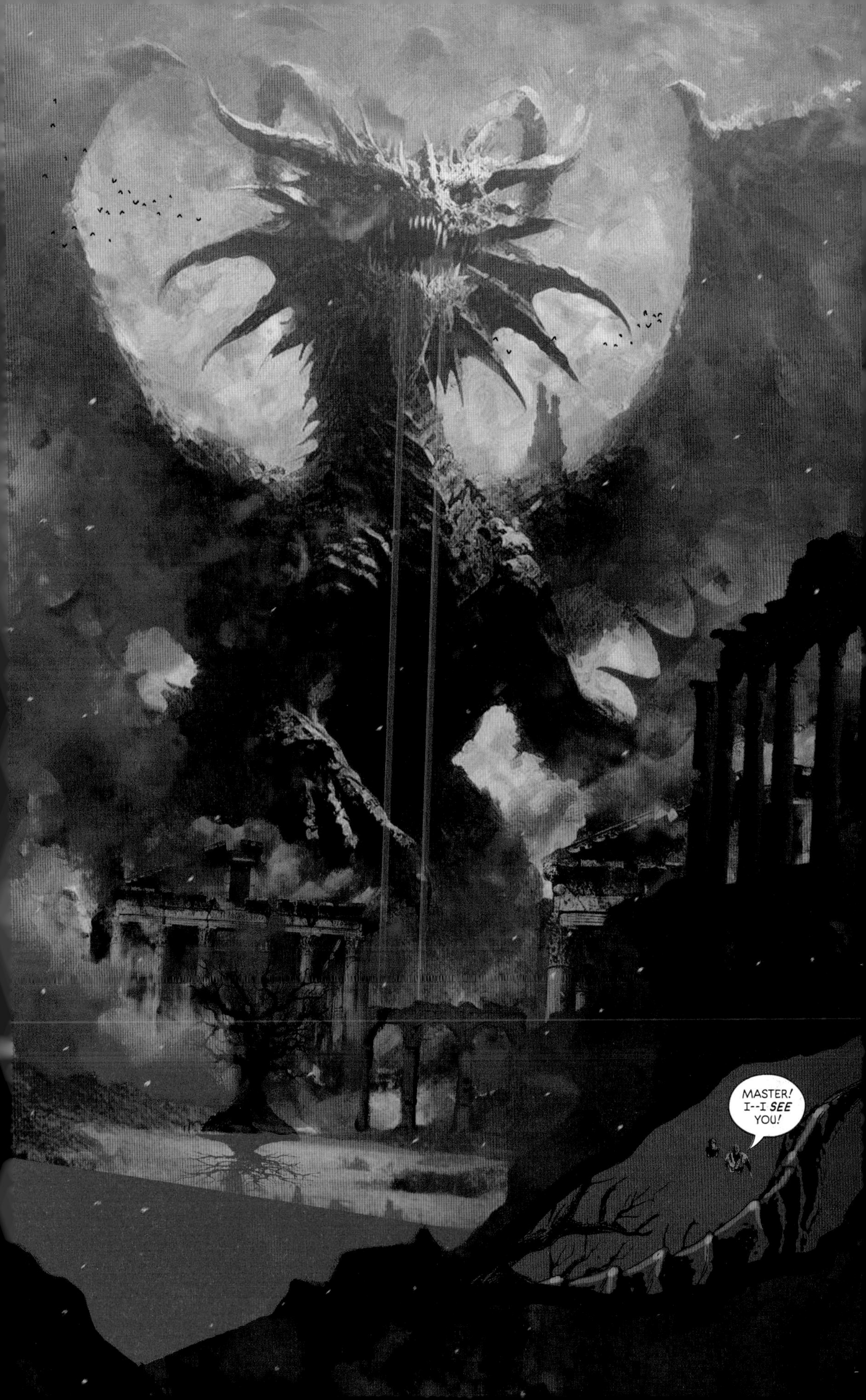
MASTER! I--I SEE YOU!

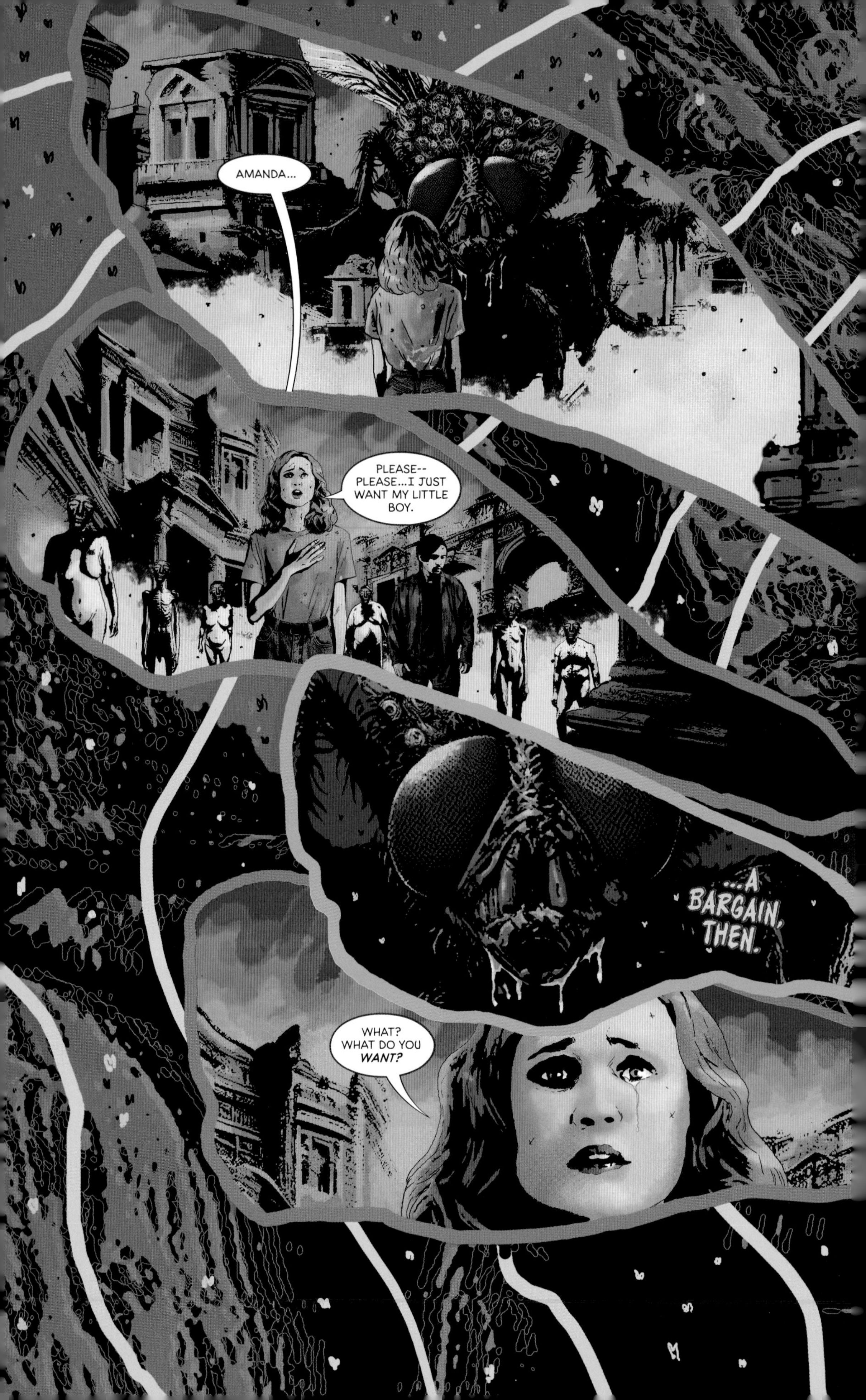

AMANDA...
PLEASE-- PLEASE...I JUST WANT MY LITTLE BOY.
...A BARGAIN, THEN.
WHAT? WHAT DO YOU WANT?

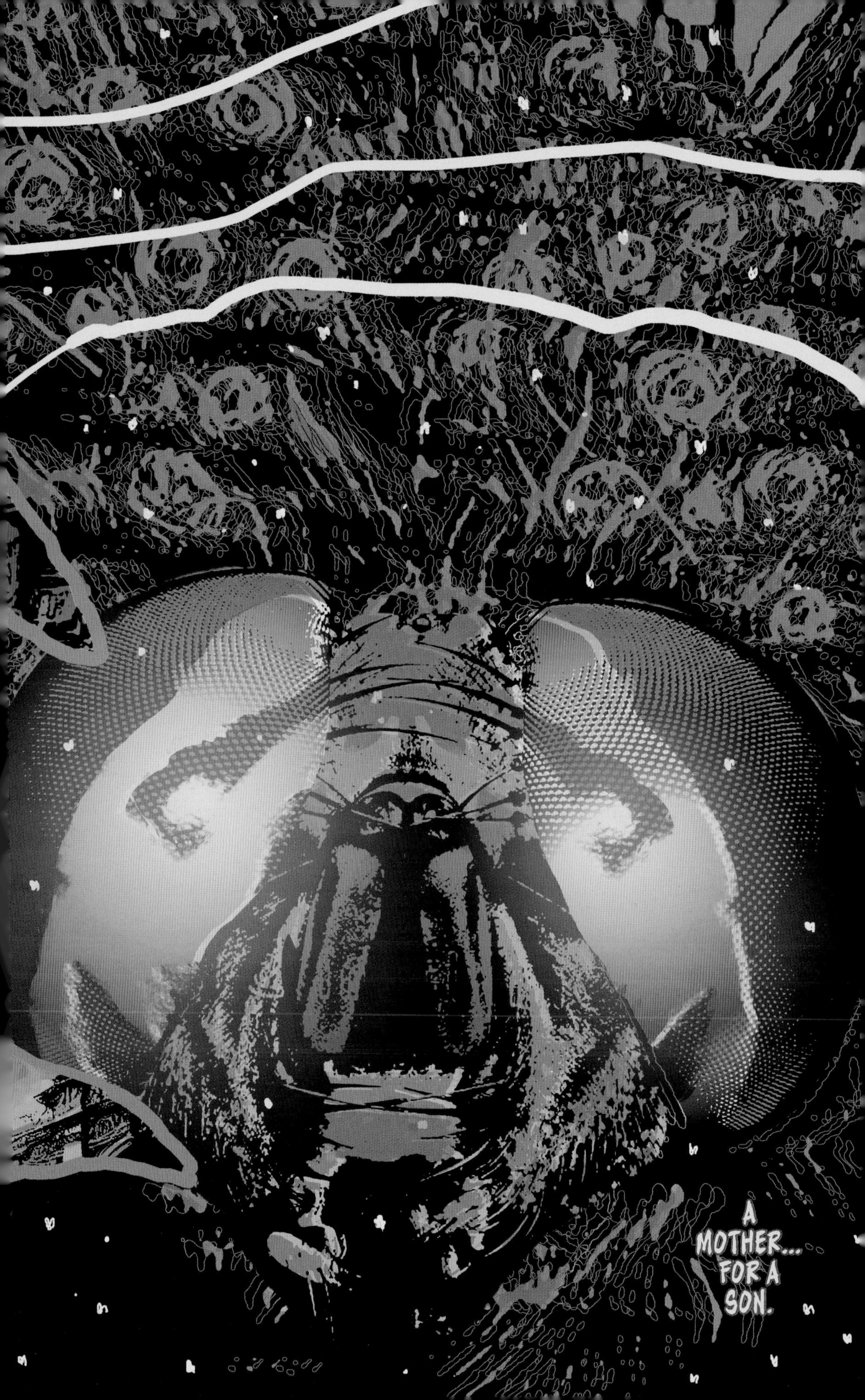
A MOTHER... FOR A SON.

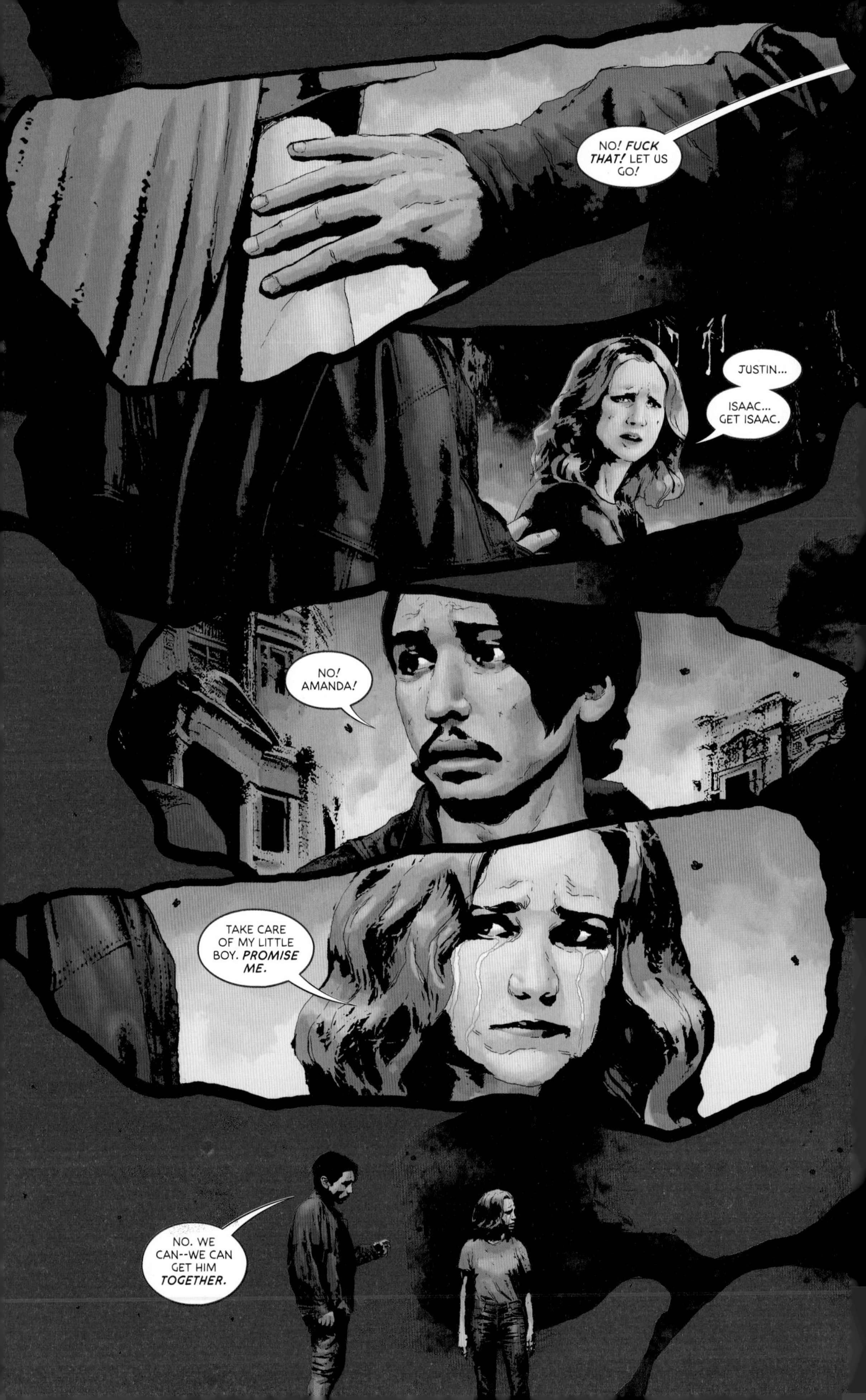
NO! FUCK THAT! LET US GO!
JUSTIN...
ISAAC... GET ISAAC.
NO! AMANDA!
TAKE CARE OF MY LITTLE BOY. PROMISE ME.
NO. WE CAN--WE CAN GET HIM TOGETHER.

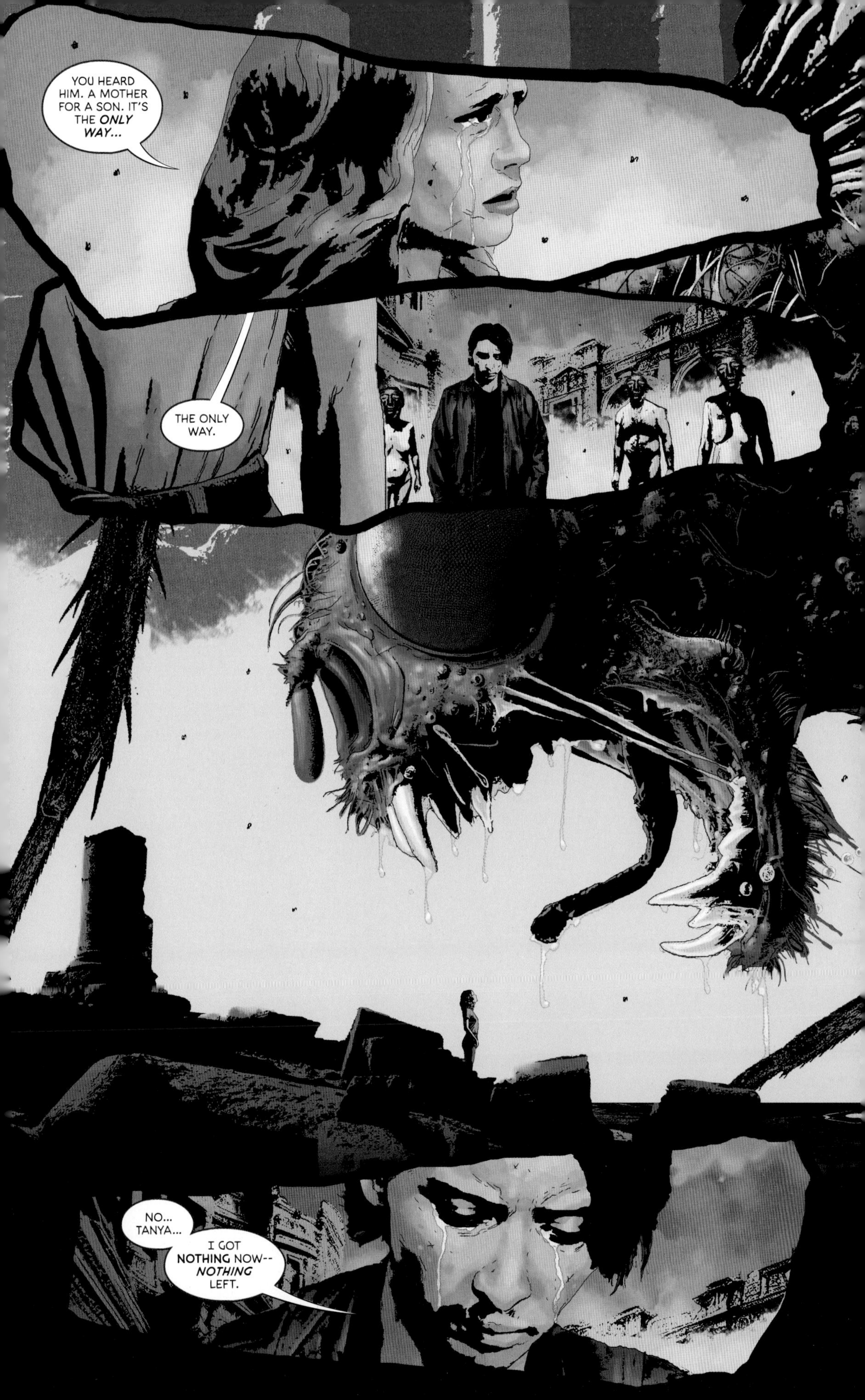
YOU HEARD HIM. A MOTHER FOR A SON. IT'S THE *ONLY WAY...*
THE ONLY WAY.
NO... TANYA...
I GOT **NOTHING** NOW-- ***NOTHING*** LEFT.

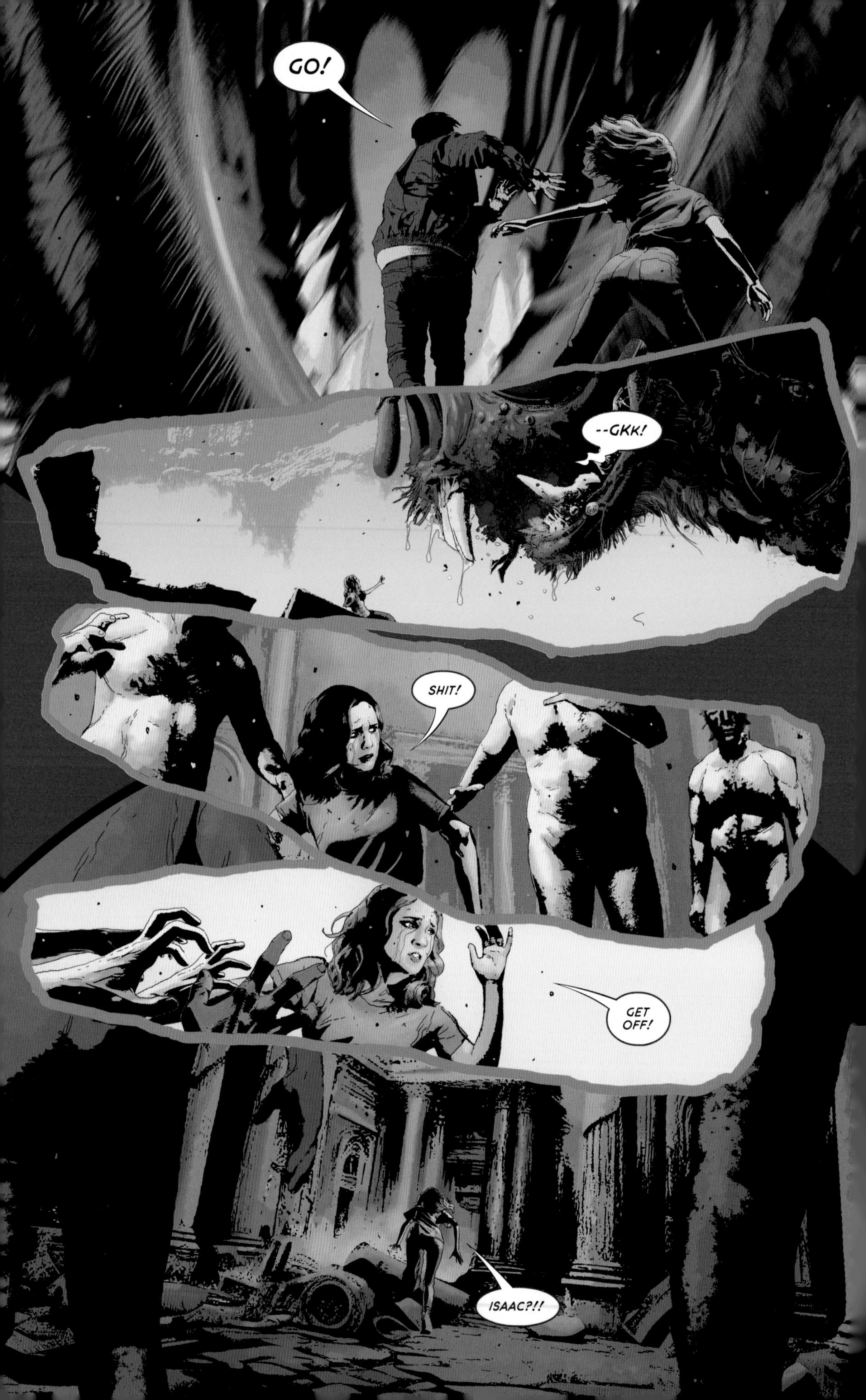
GO!
--GKK!
SHIT!
GET OFF!
ISAAC?!!

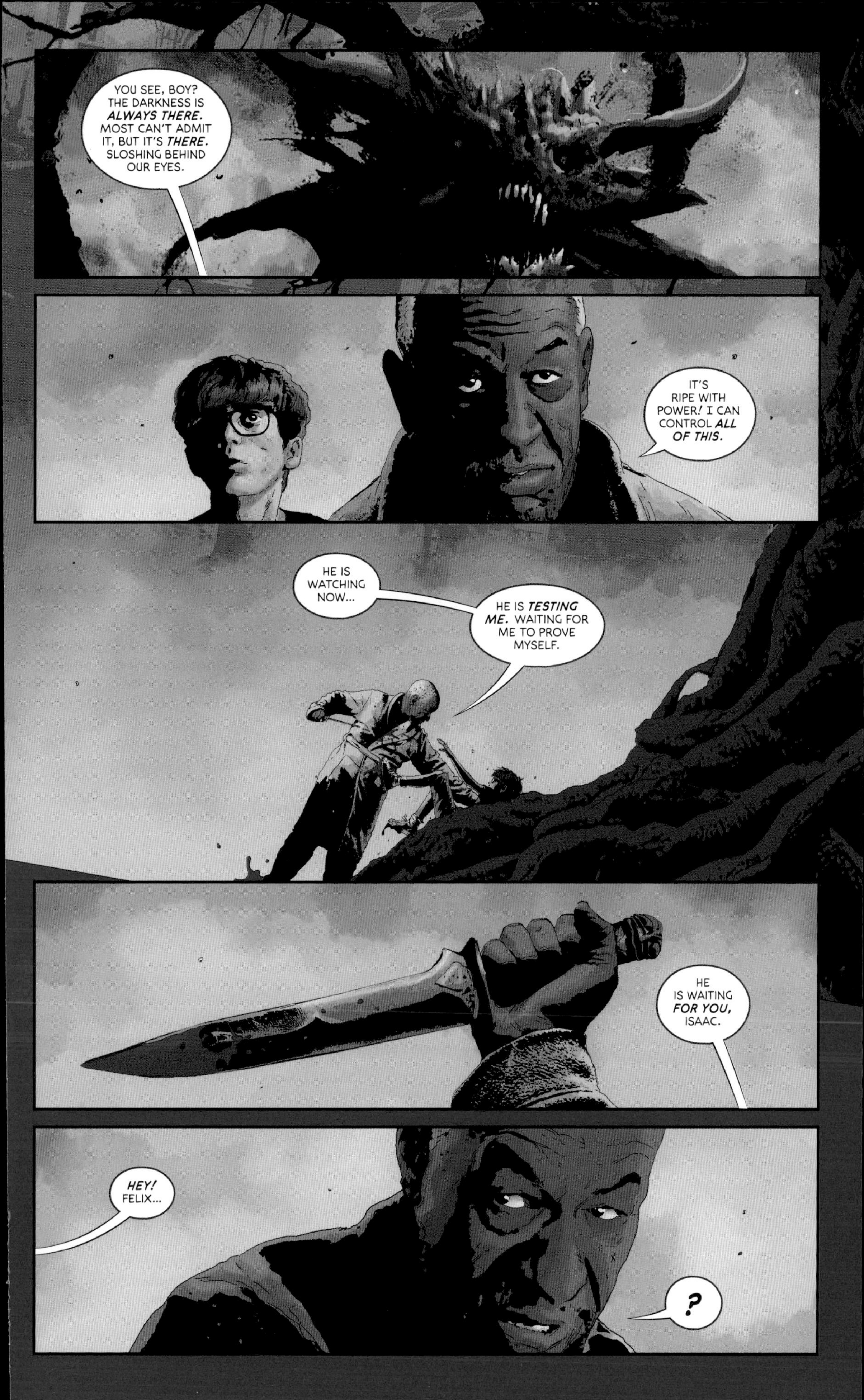

YOU SEE, BOY? THE DARKNESS IS ALWAYS THERE. MOST CAN'T ADMIT IT, BUT IT'S THERE. SLOSHING BEHIND OUR EYES.
IT'S RIPE WITH POWER! I CAN CONTROL ALL OF THIS.
HE IS WATCHING NOW...
HE IS TESTING ME. WAITING FOR ME TO PROVE MYSELF.
HE IS WAITING FOR YOU, ISAAC.
HEY! FELIX...
?

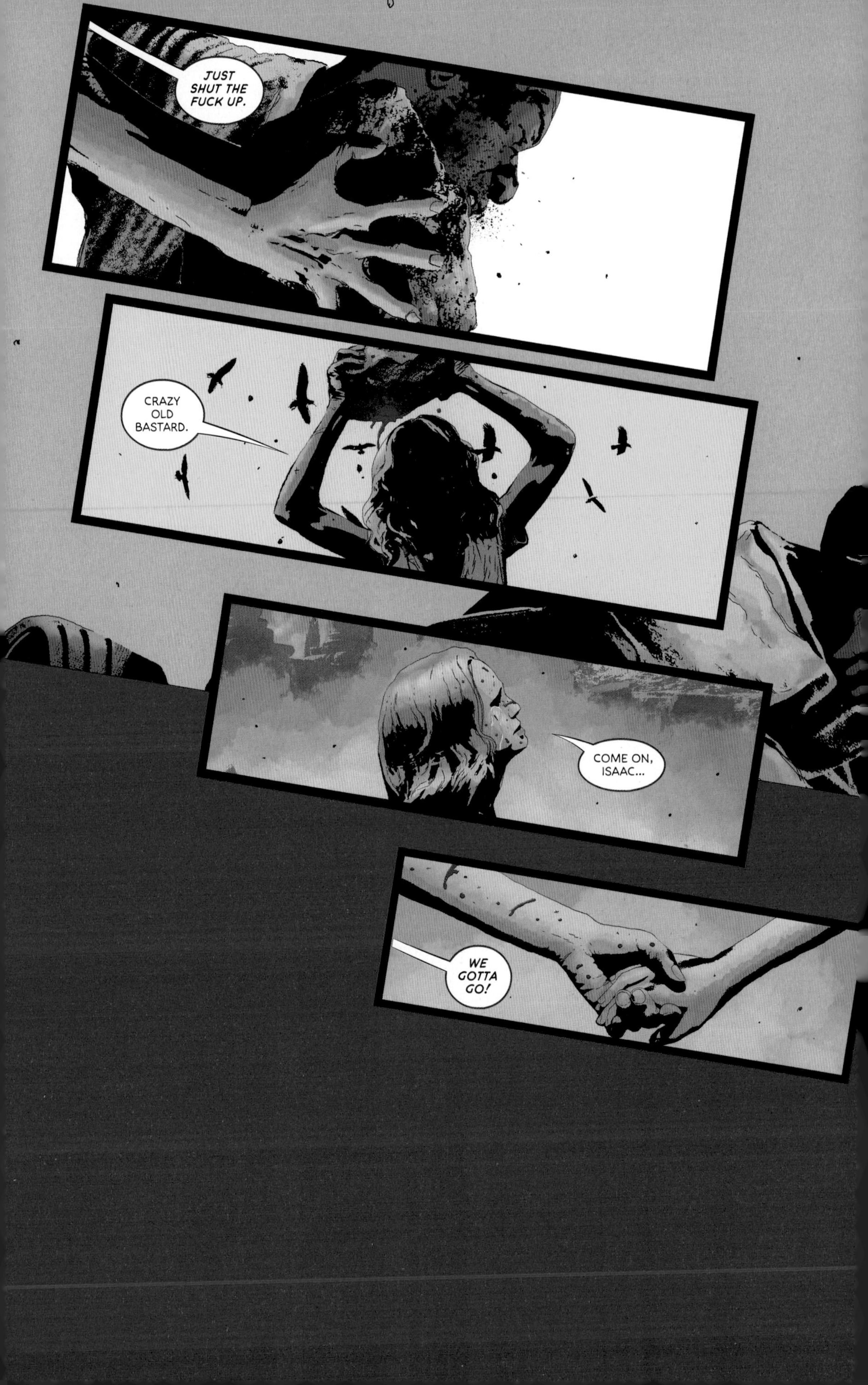
JUST SHUT THE FUCK UP.
CRAZY OLD BASTARD.
COME ON, ISAAC...
WE GOTTA GO!

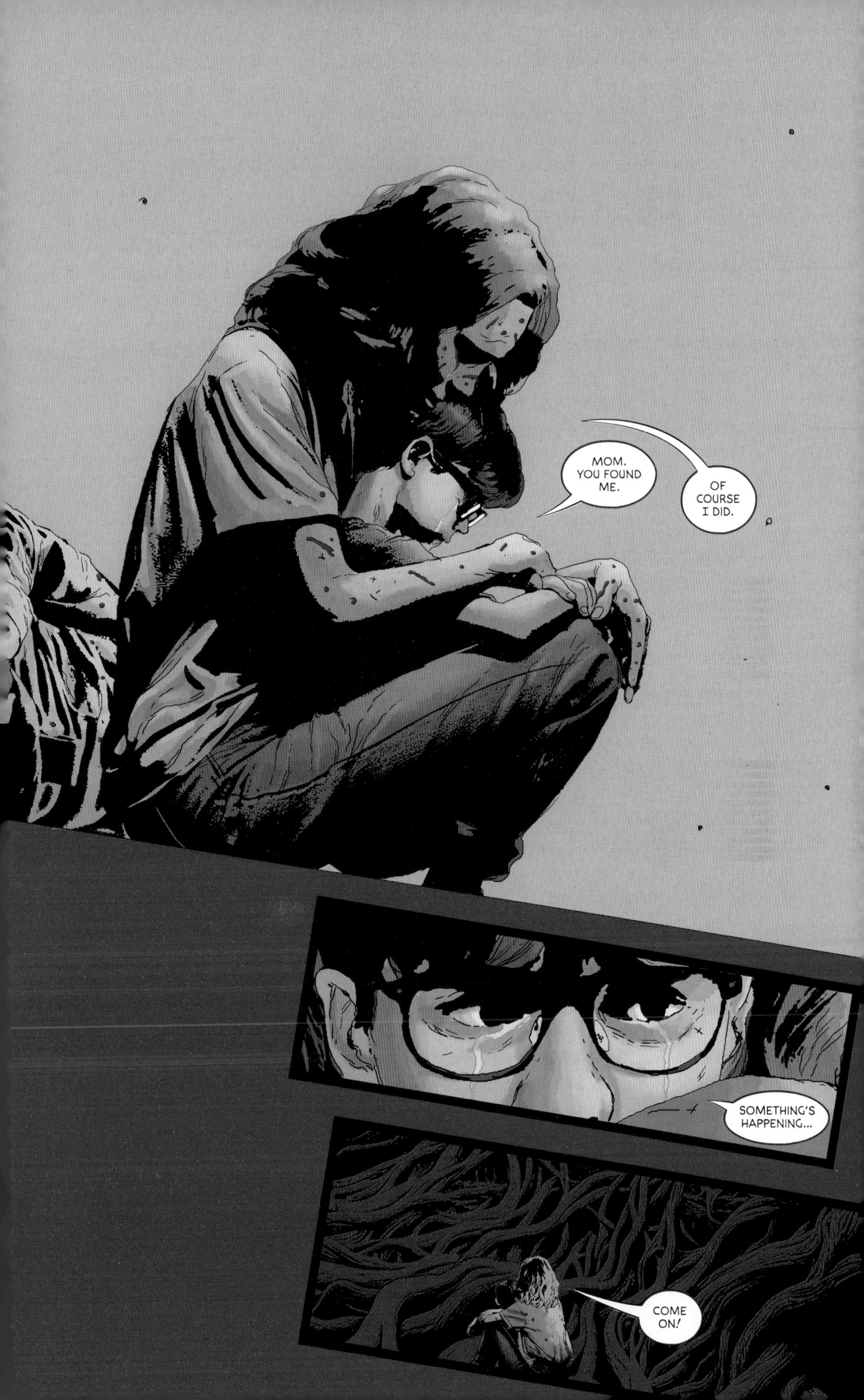
MOM. YOU FOUND ME.
OF COURSE I DID.
SOMETHING'S HAPPENING...
COME ON!

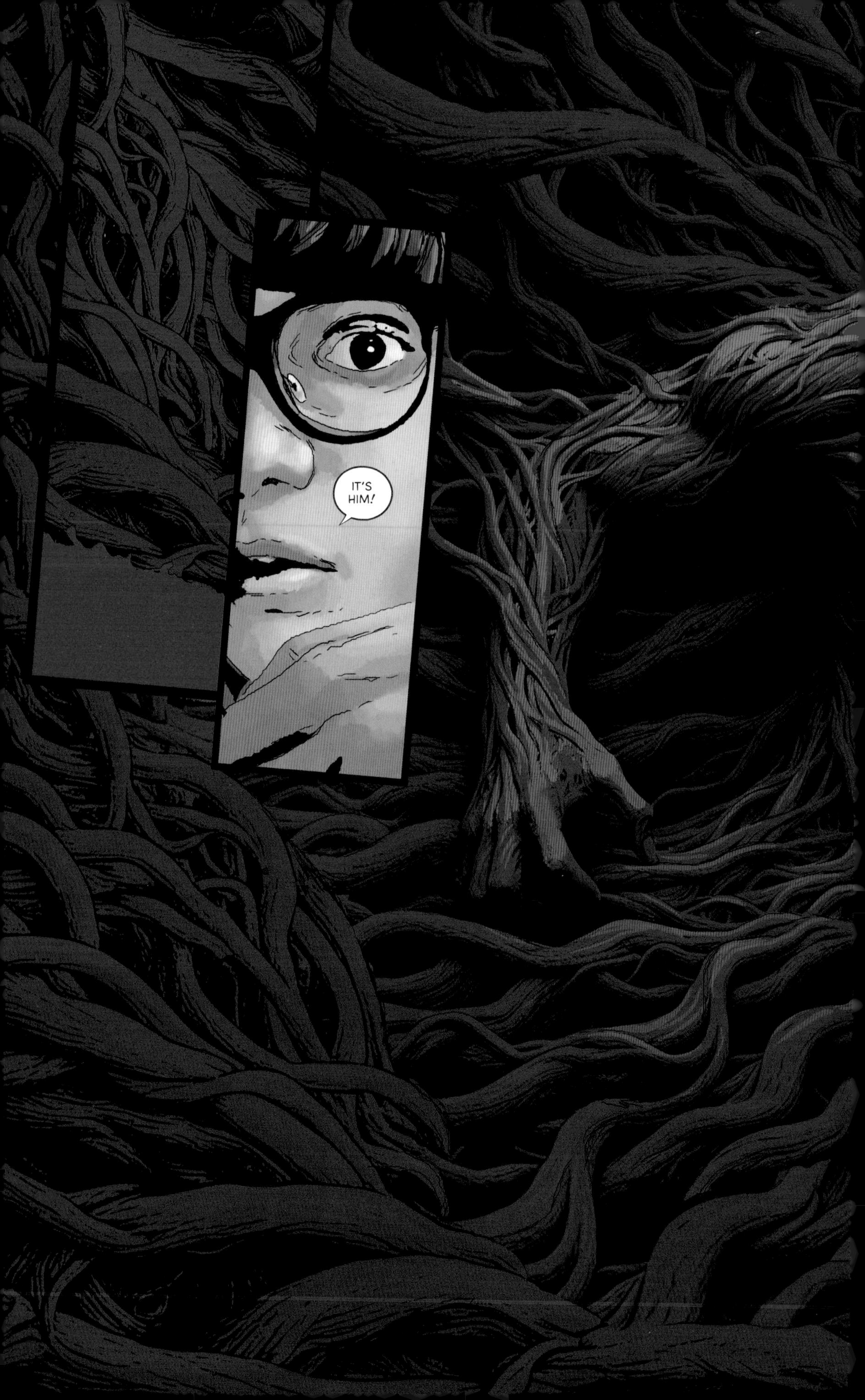
IT'S HIM!

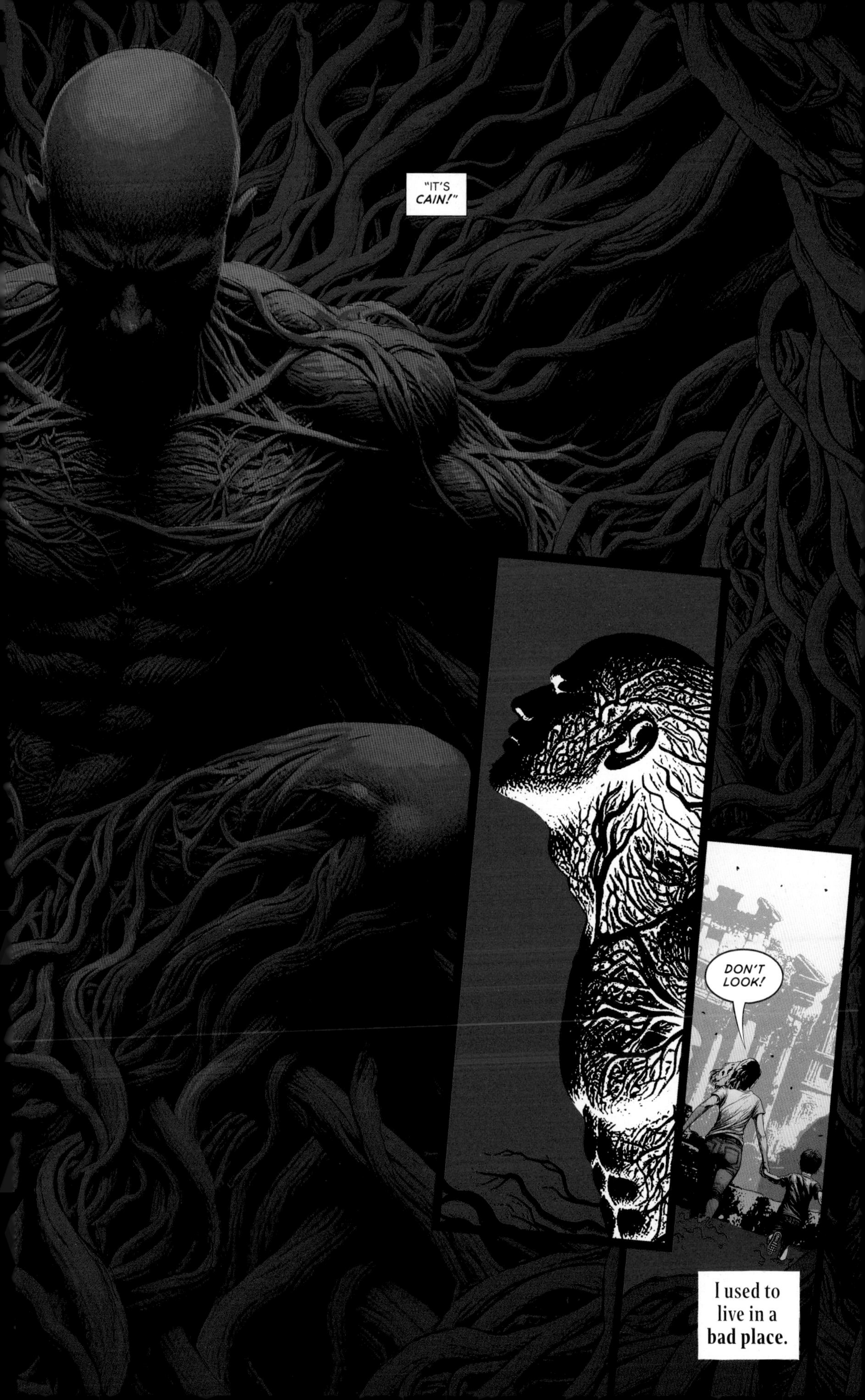
"IT'S
CAIN!"
DON'T
LOOK!
I used to
live in a
bad place.

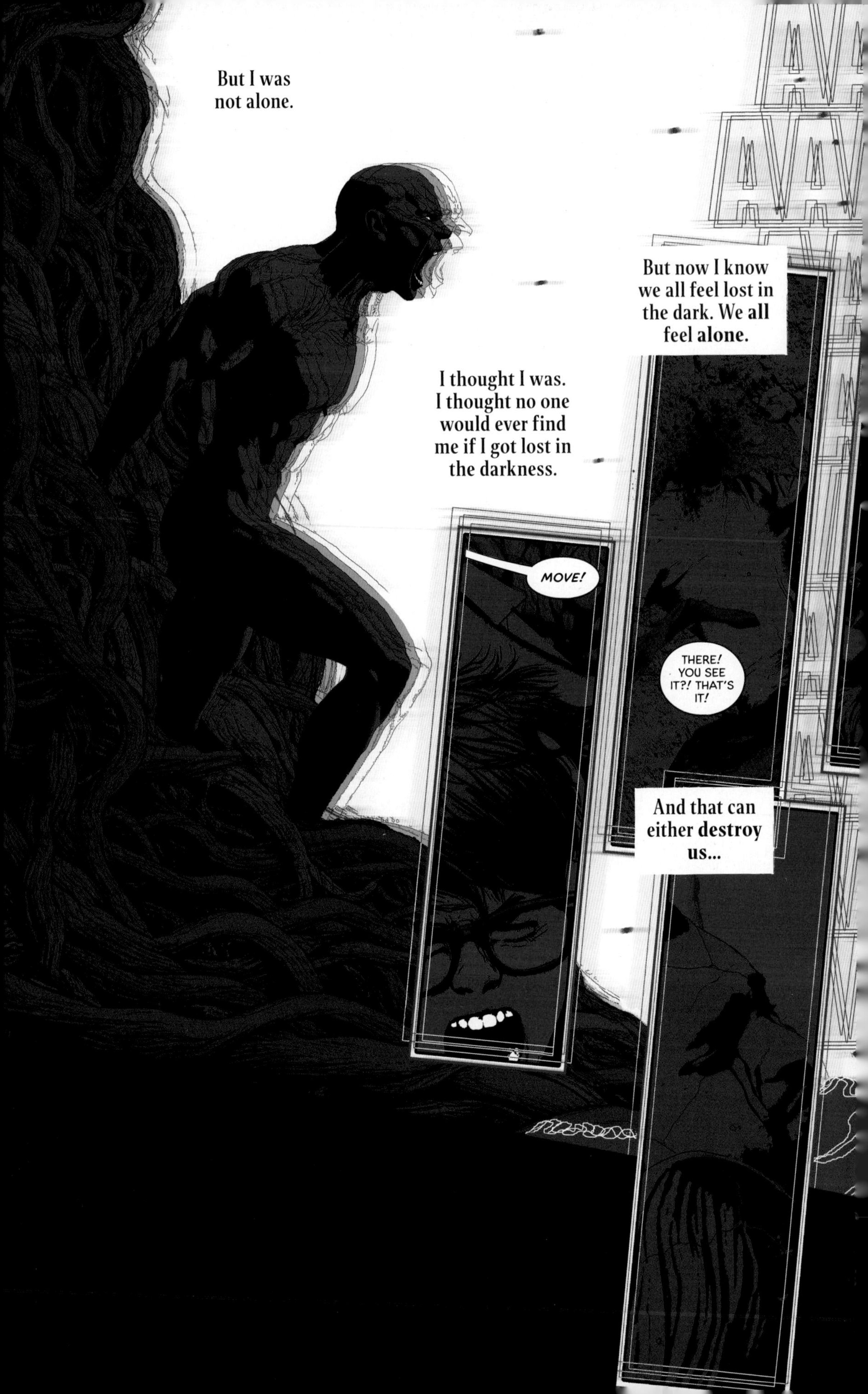
But I was not alone.
I thought I was. I thought no one would ever find me if I got lost in the darkness.
But now I know we all feel lost in the dark. We all feel alone.
MOVE!
THERE! YOU SEE IT?! THAT'S IT!
And that can either destroy us...

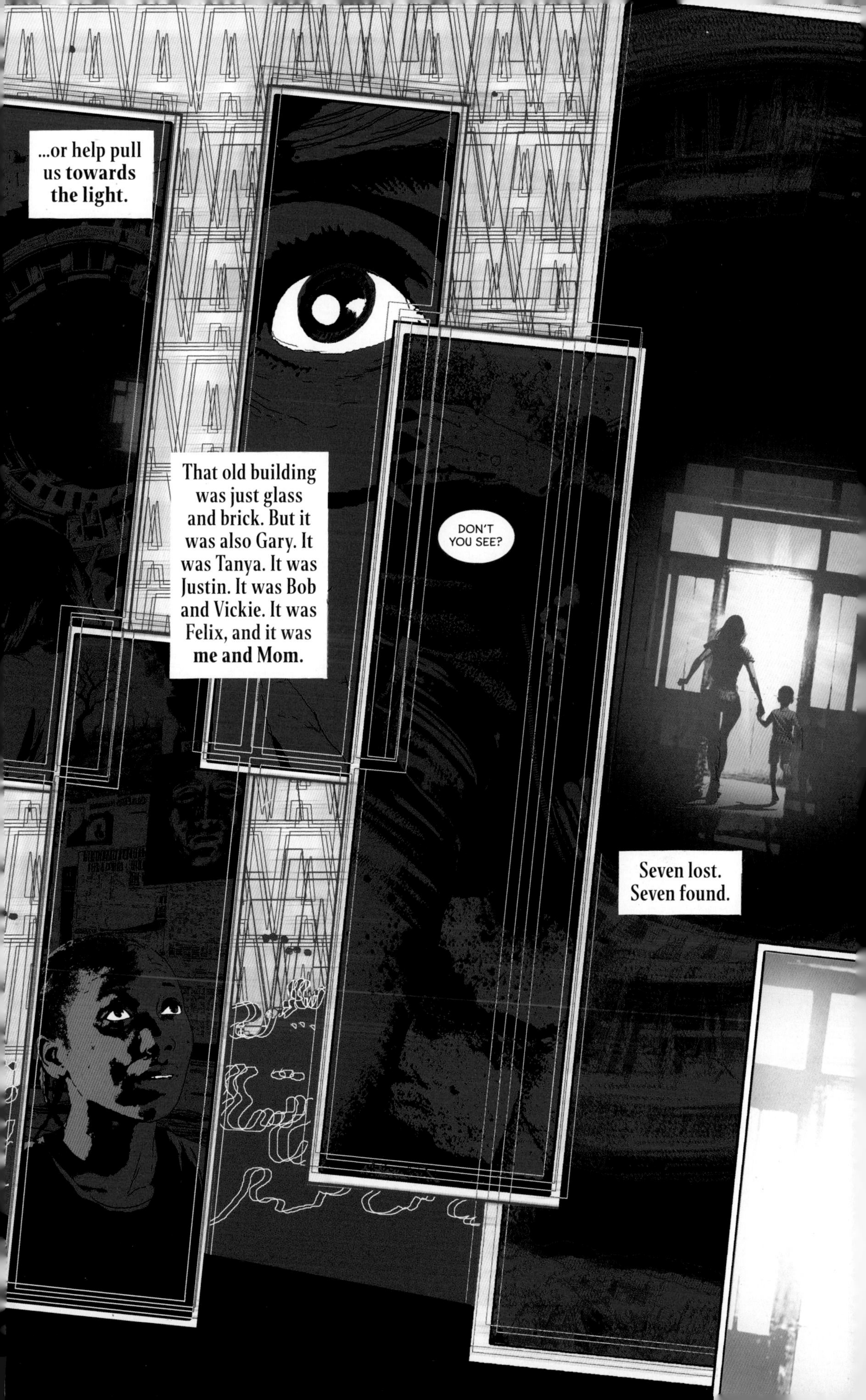
...or help pull us towards the light.
That old building was just glass and brick. But it was also Gary. It was Tanya. It was Justin. It was Bob and Vickie. It was Felix, and it was me and Mom.
DON'T YOU SEE?
Seven lost. Seven found.

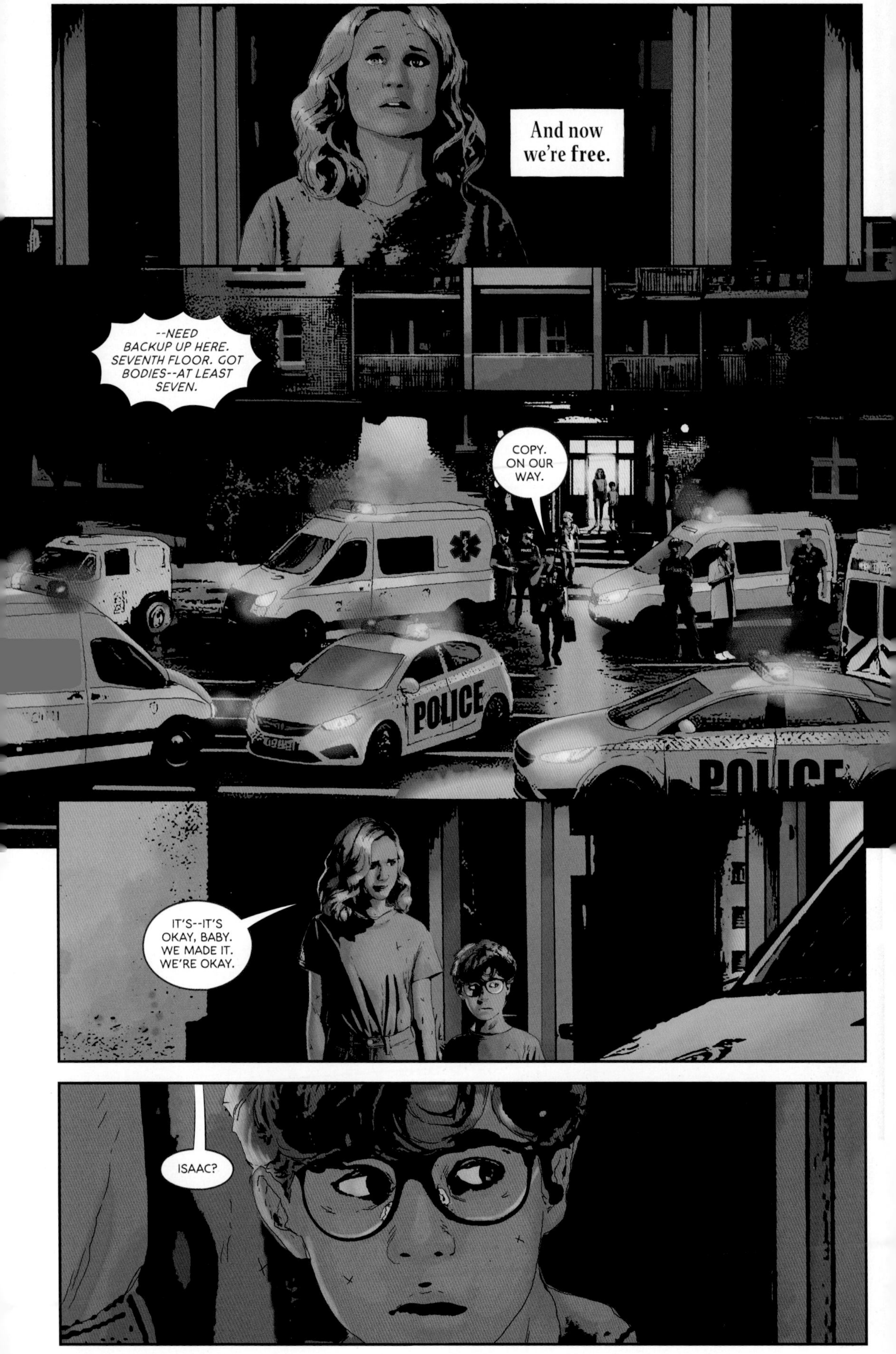
And now we're free.
--NEED BACKUP UP HERE. SEVENTH FLOOR. GOT BODIES--AT LEAST SEVEN.
COPY. ON OUR WAY.
POLICE
IT'S--IT'S OKAY, BABY. WE MADE IT. WE'RE OKAY.
ISAAC?

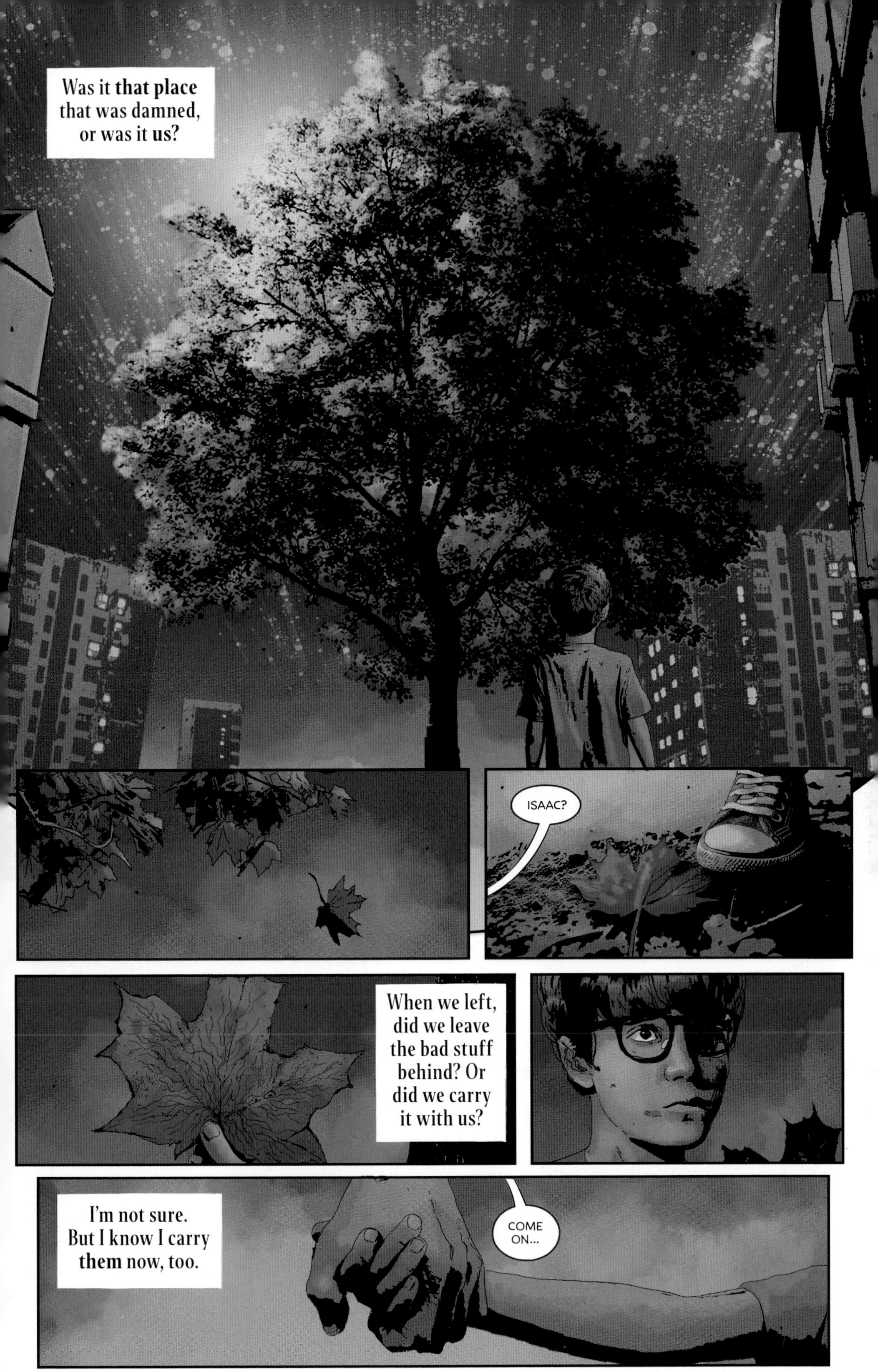

Was it **that place** that was damned, or was it **us**?
ISAAC?
When we left, did we leave the bad stuff behind? Or did we carry it with us?
I'm not sure. But I know I carry **them** now, too.
COME ON...

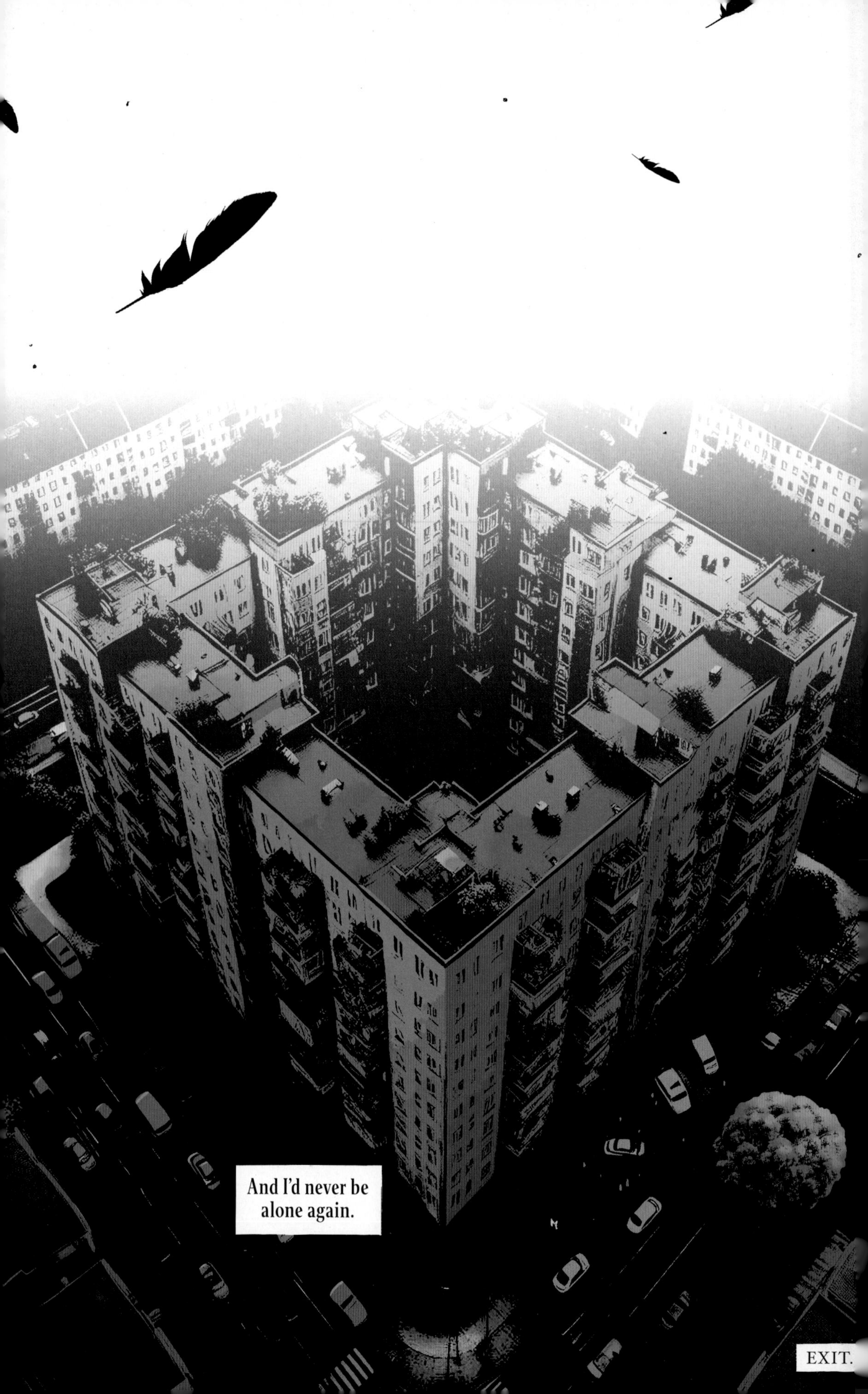
And I'd never be alone again.
EXIT.

Variant Cover Gallery

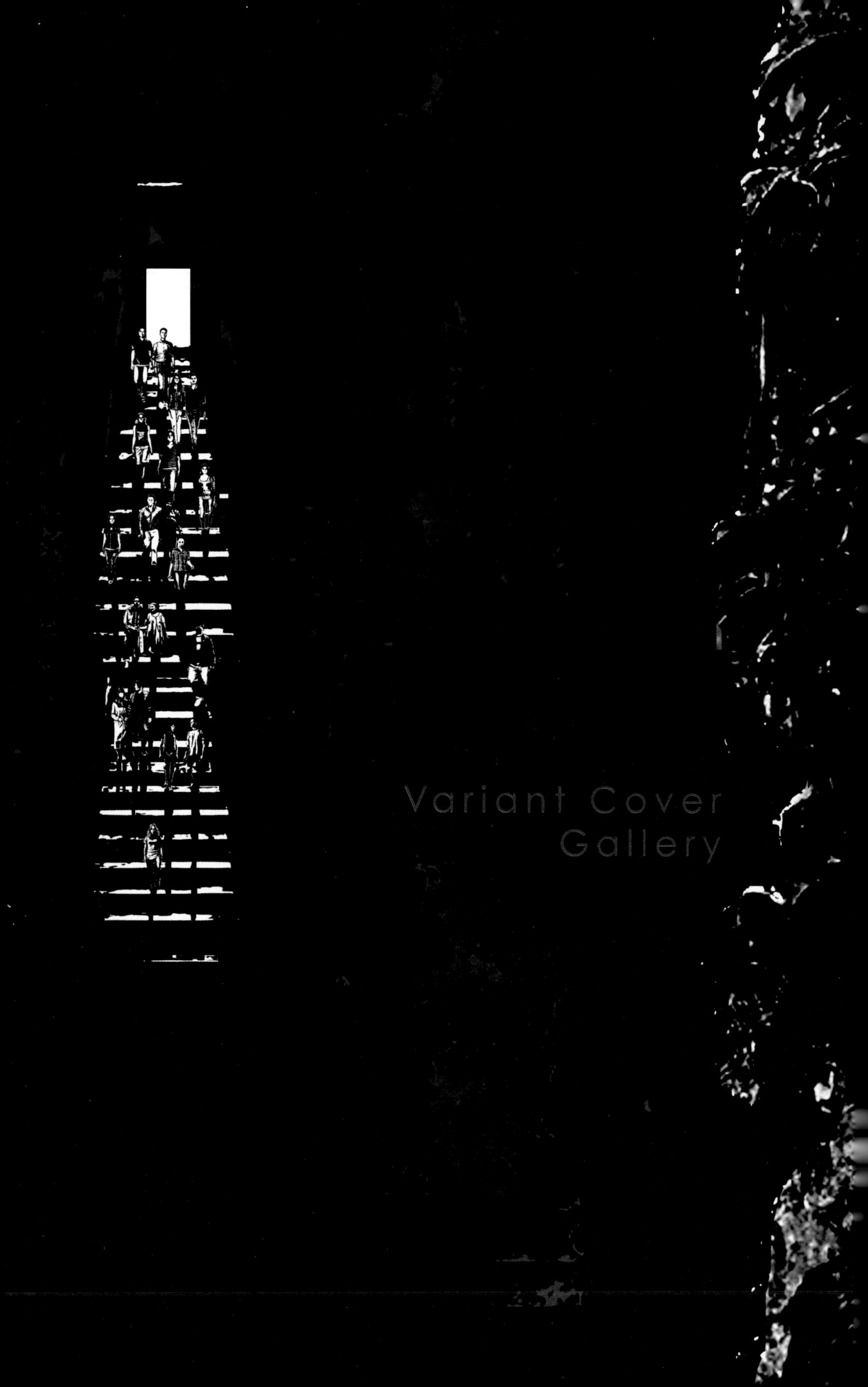

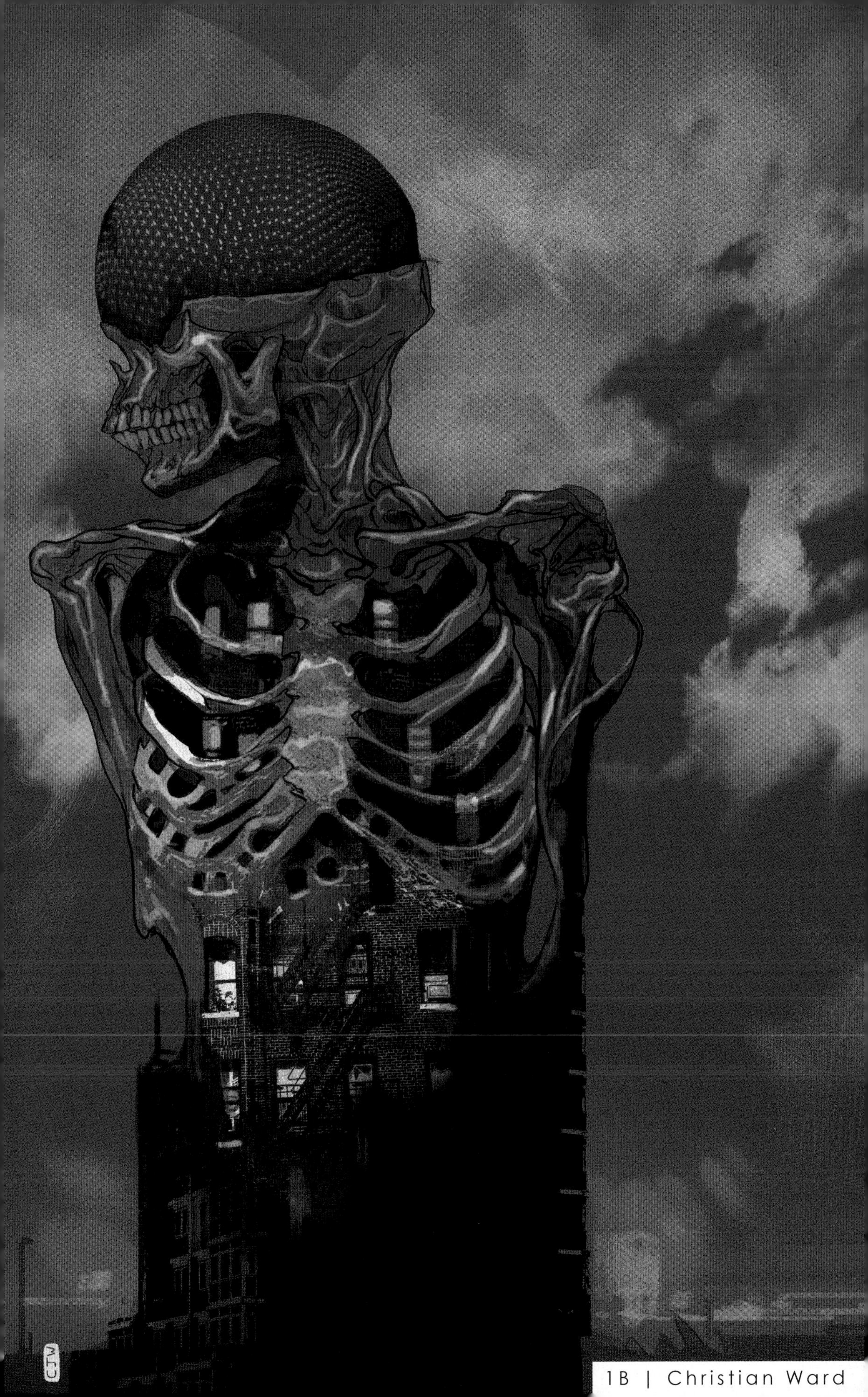

1B | Christian Ward

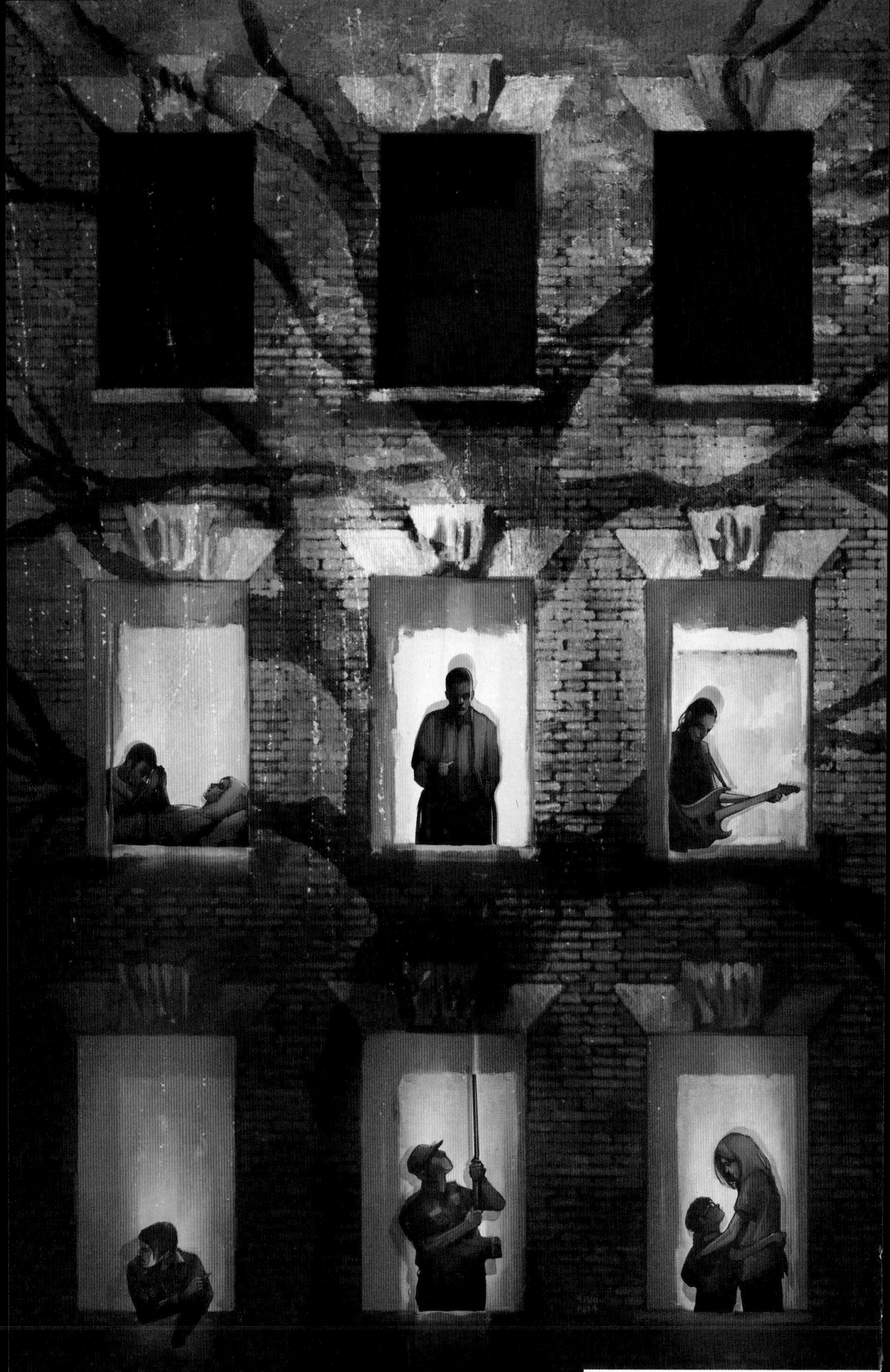

1C | Martin Simmonds

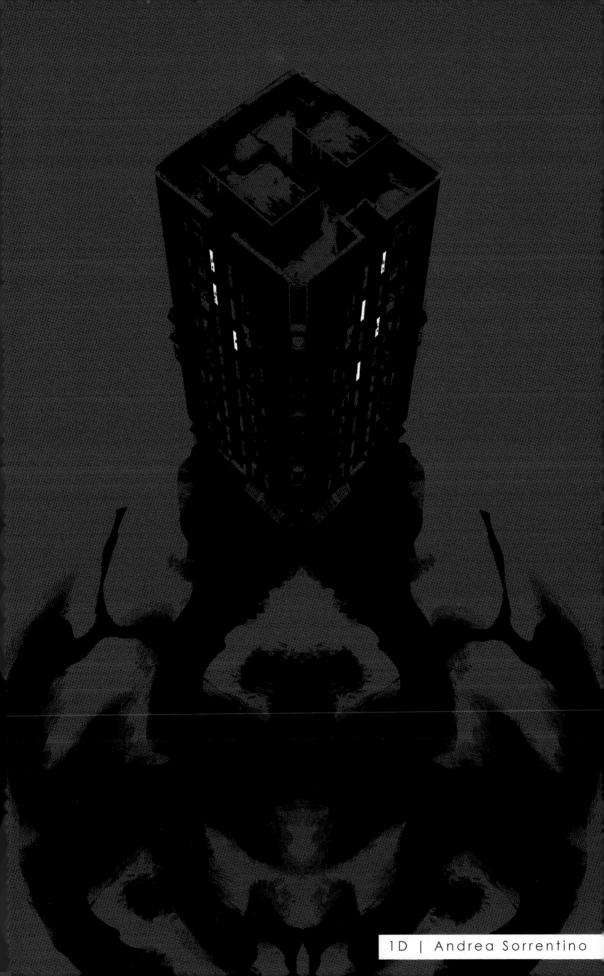

1D | Andrea Sorrentino

1F | Tradd Moore

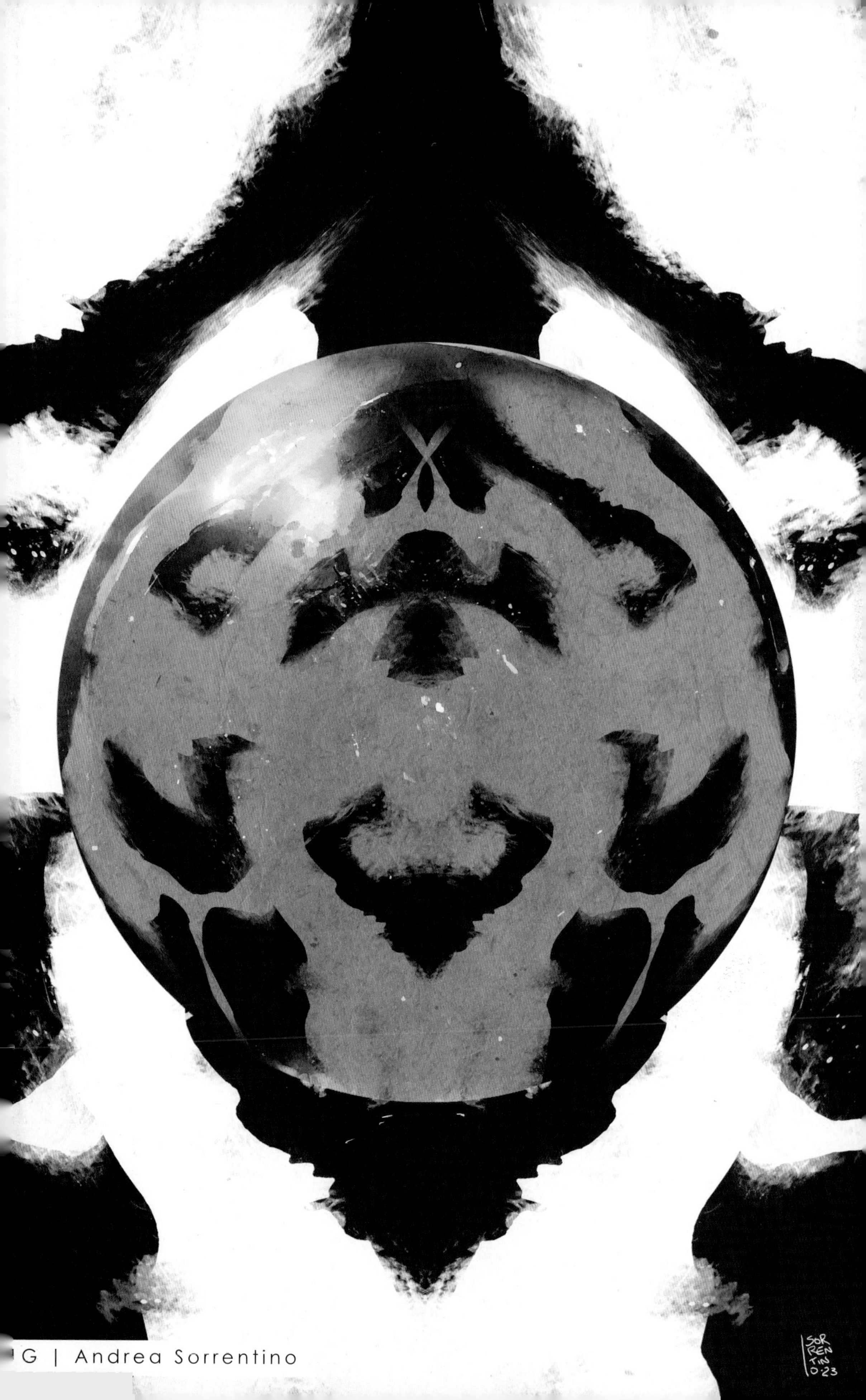
SOR
REN
TIN
O·23

G | Andrea Sorrentino

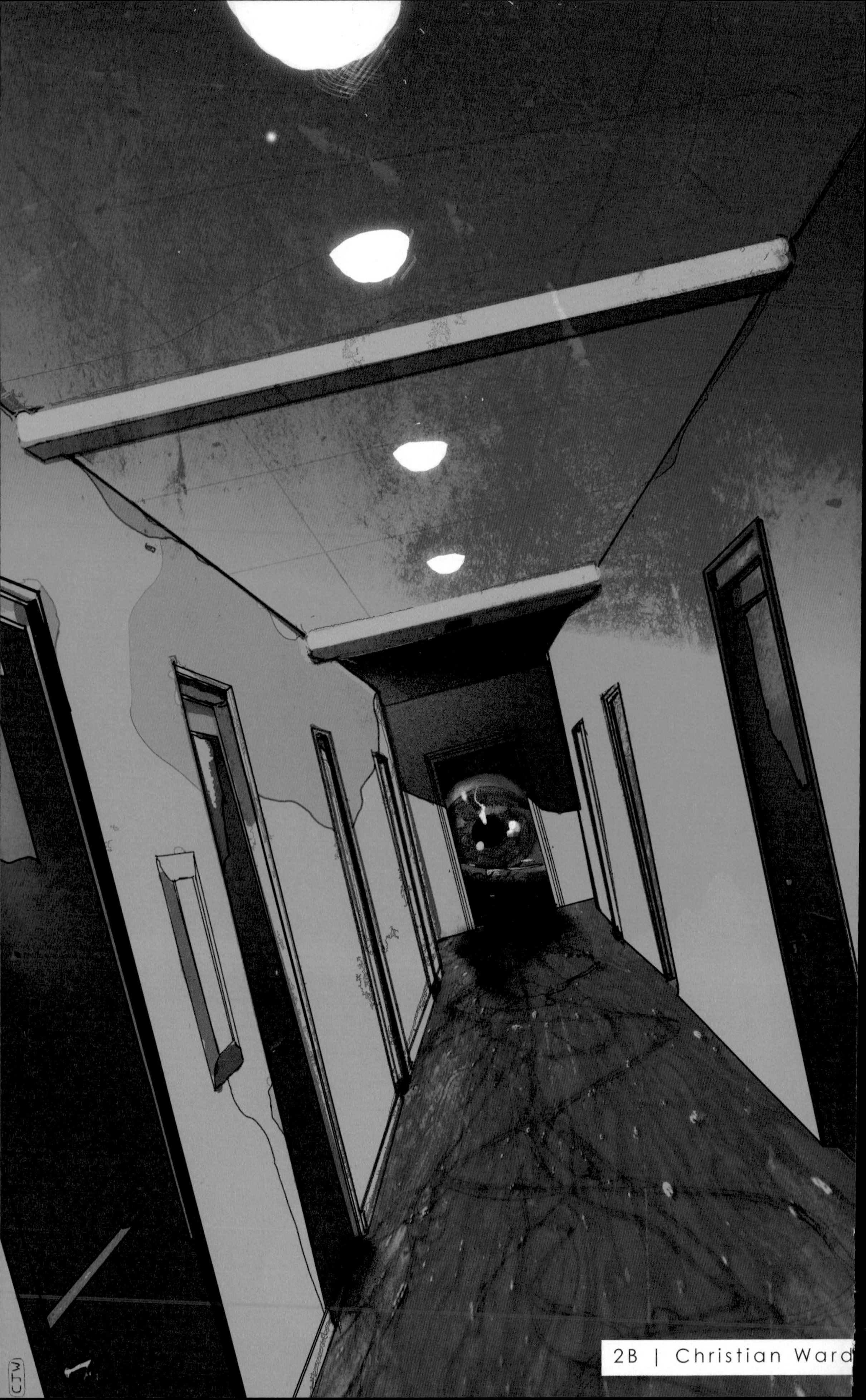

2B | Christian Ward

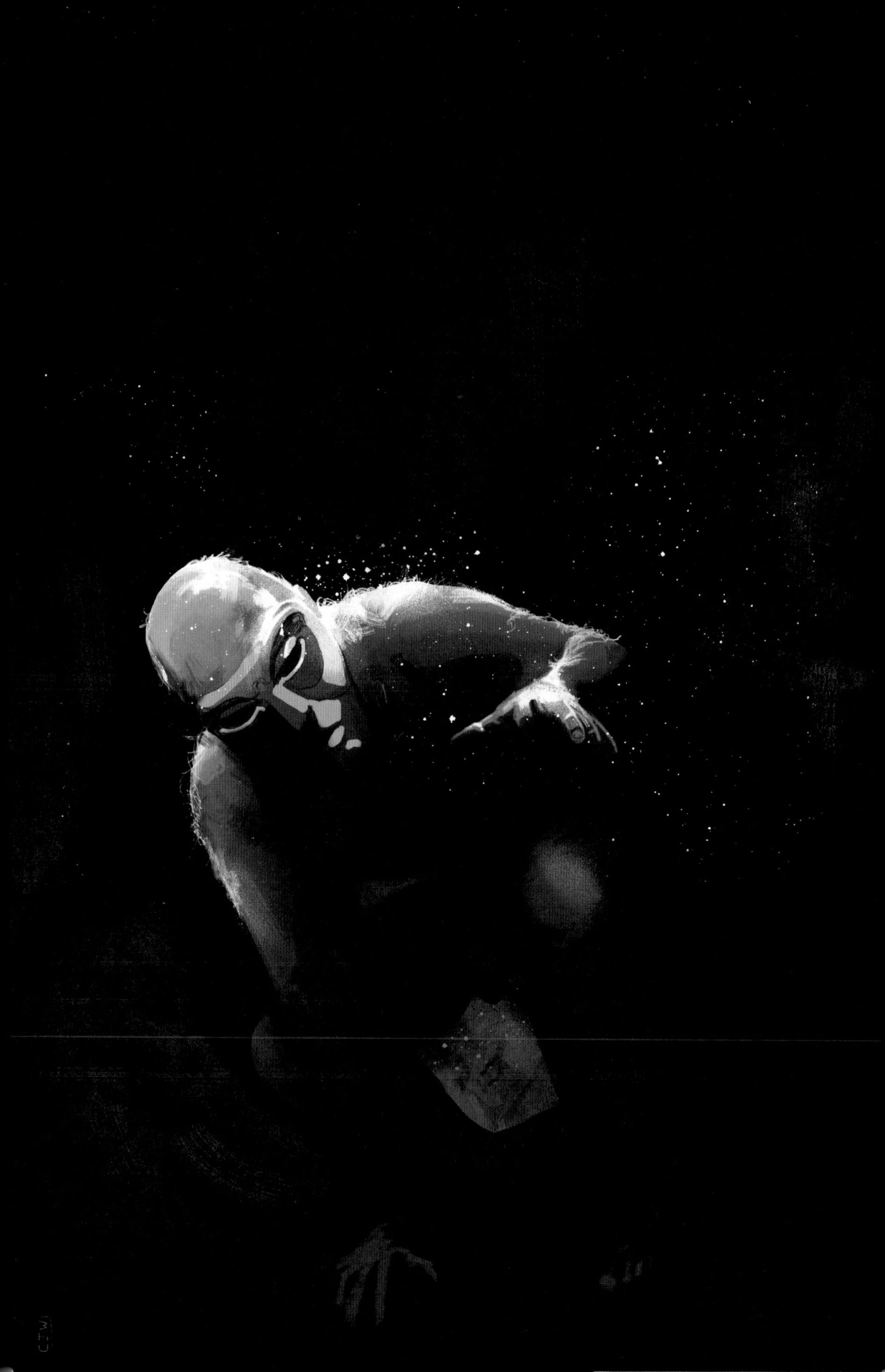

3B | Christian Ward

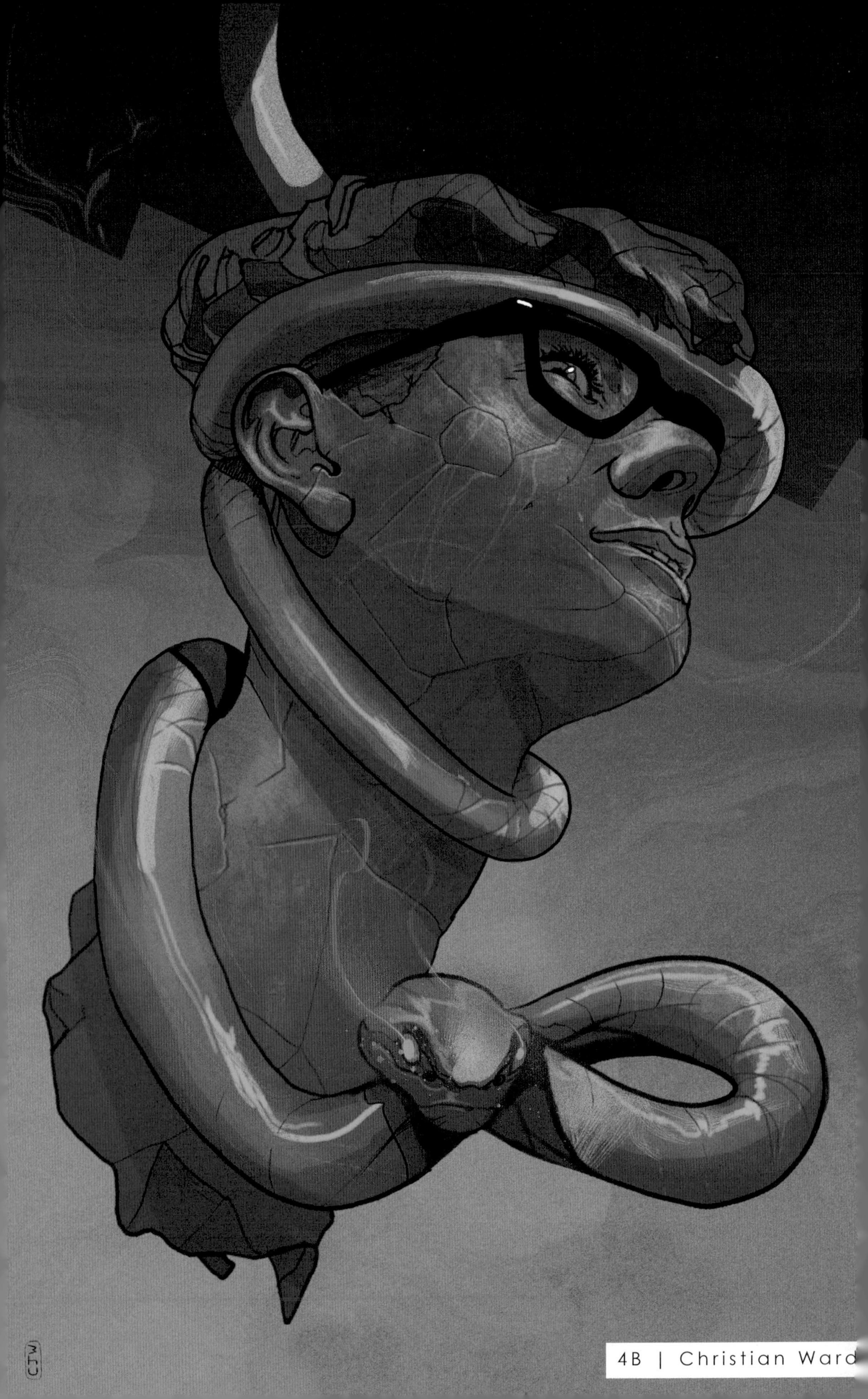
CTW

4B | Christian Ward

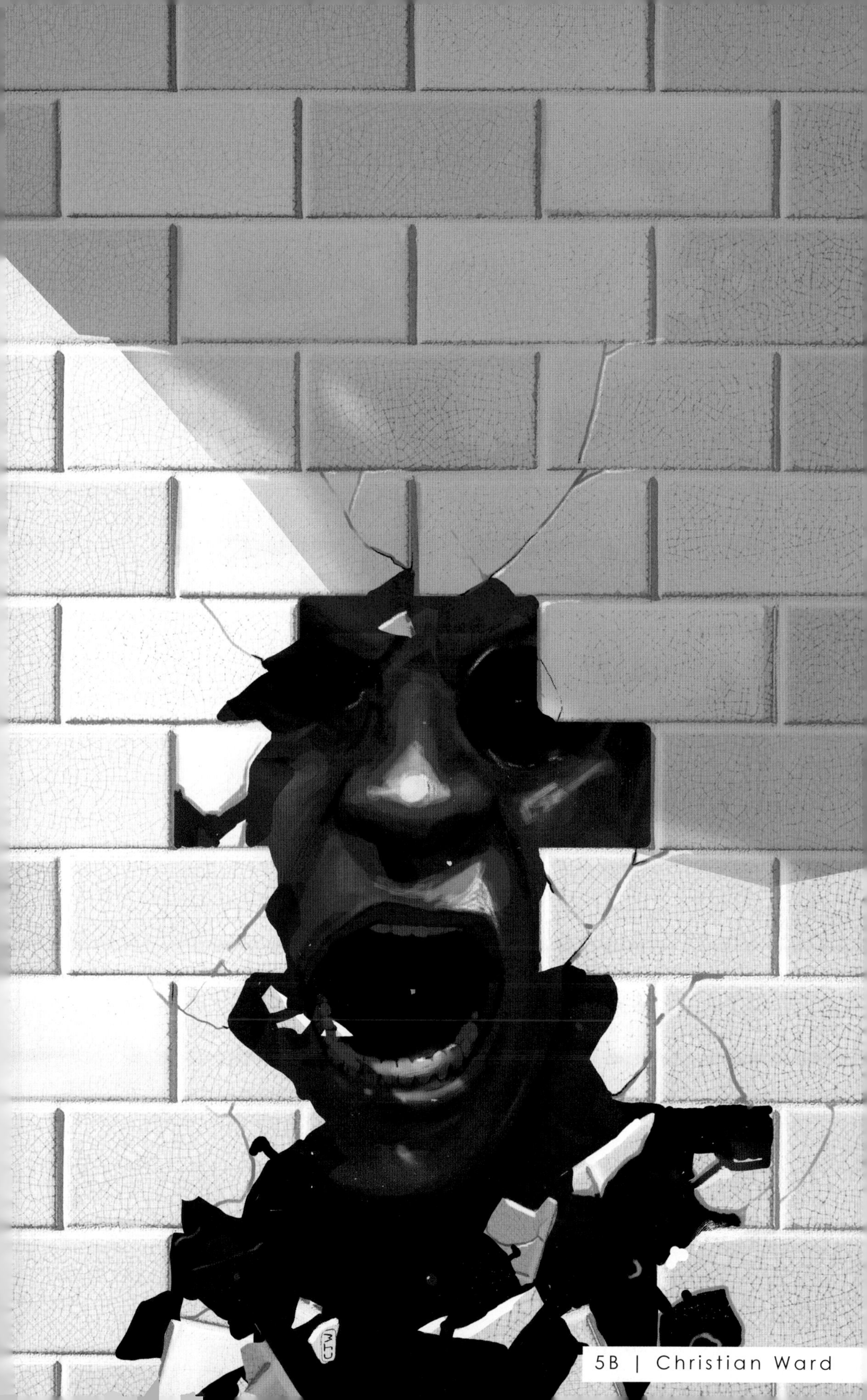

5B | Christian Ward

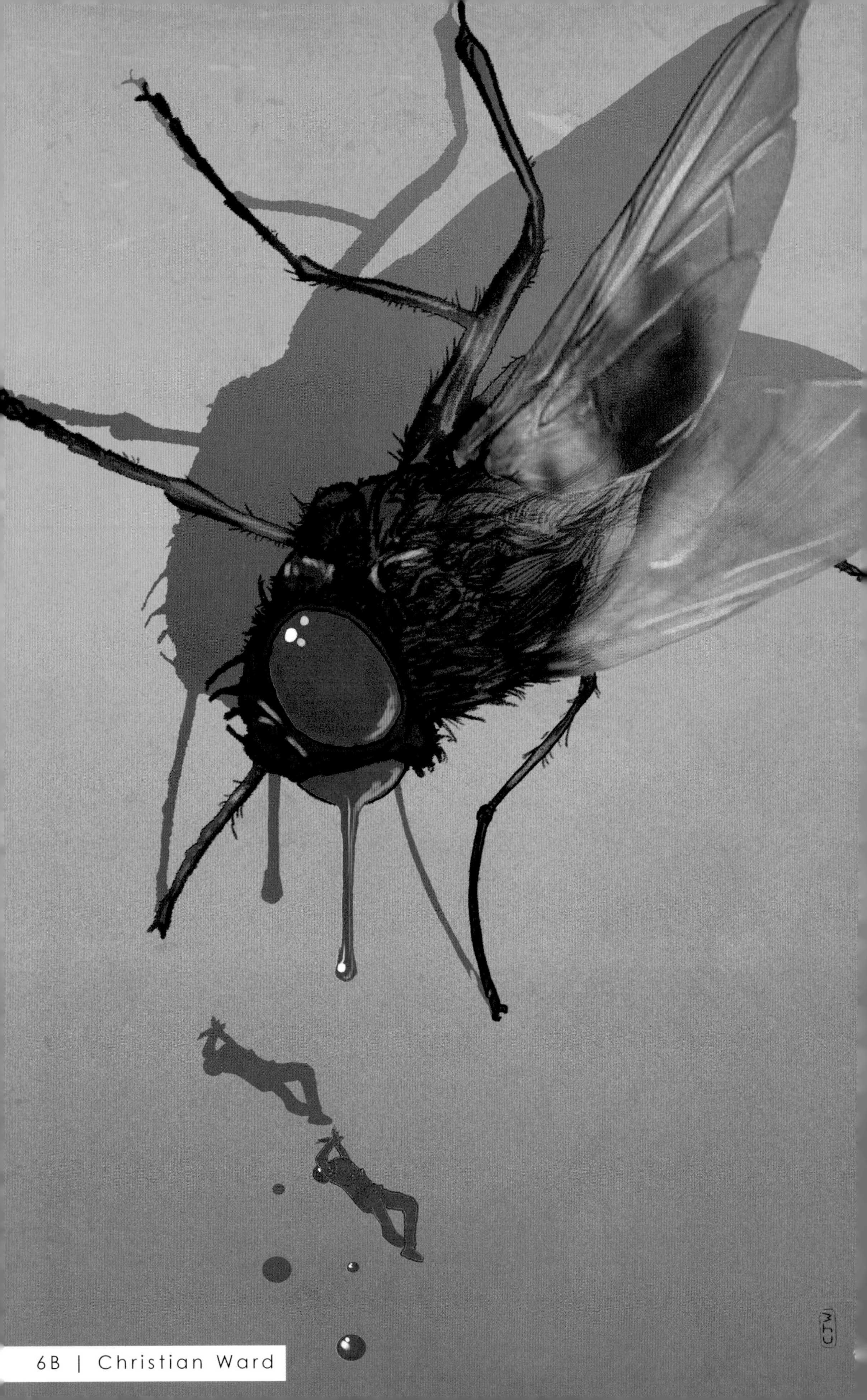
CJW

6B | Christian Ward

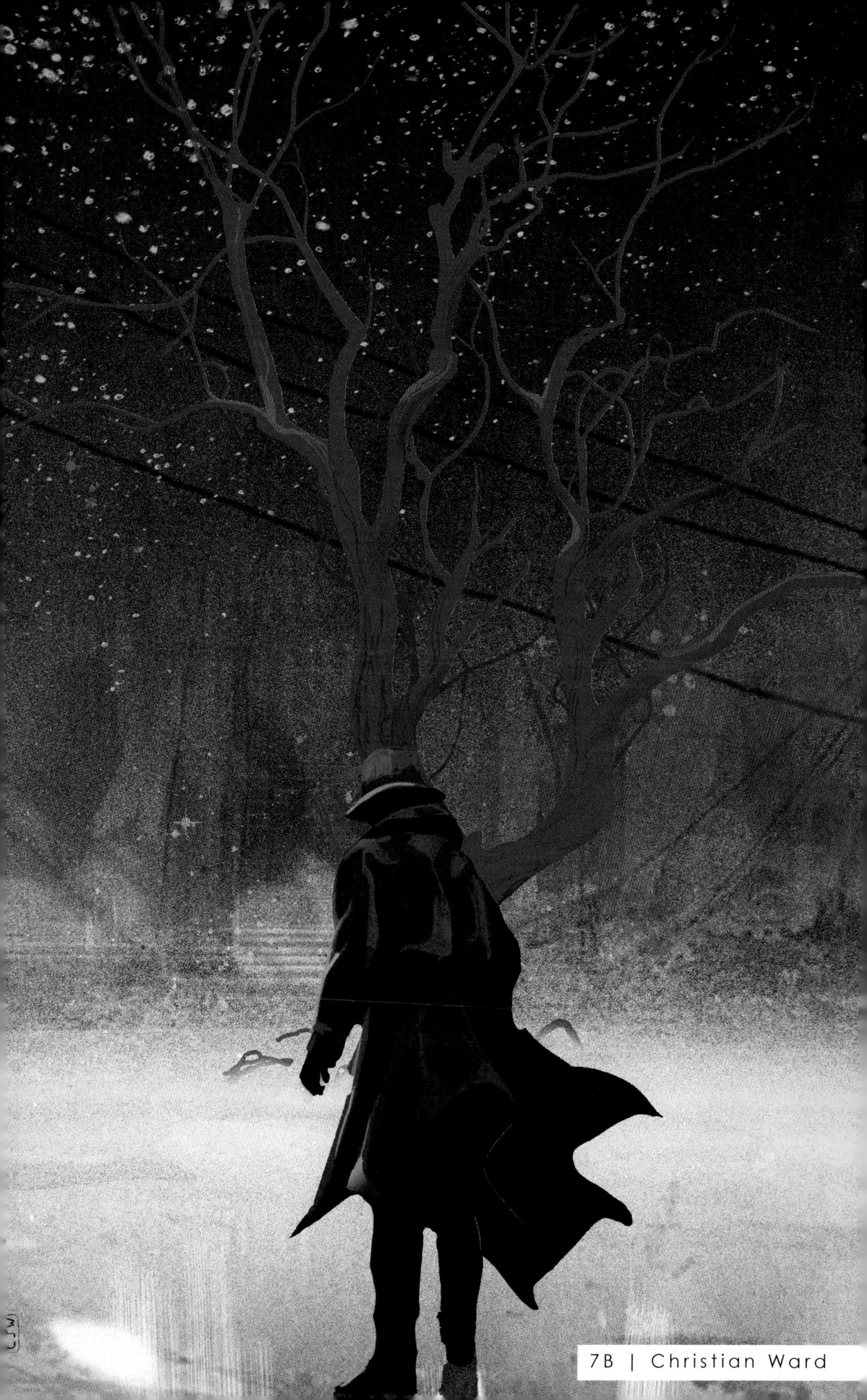

7B | Christian Ward

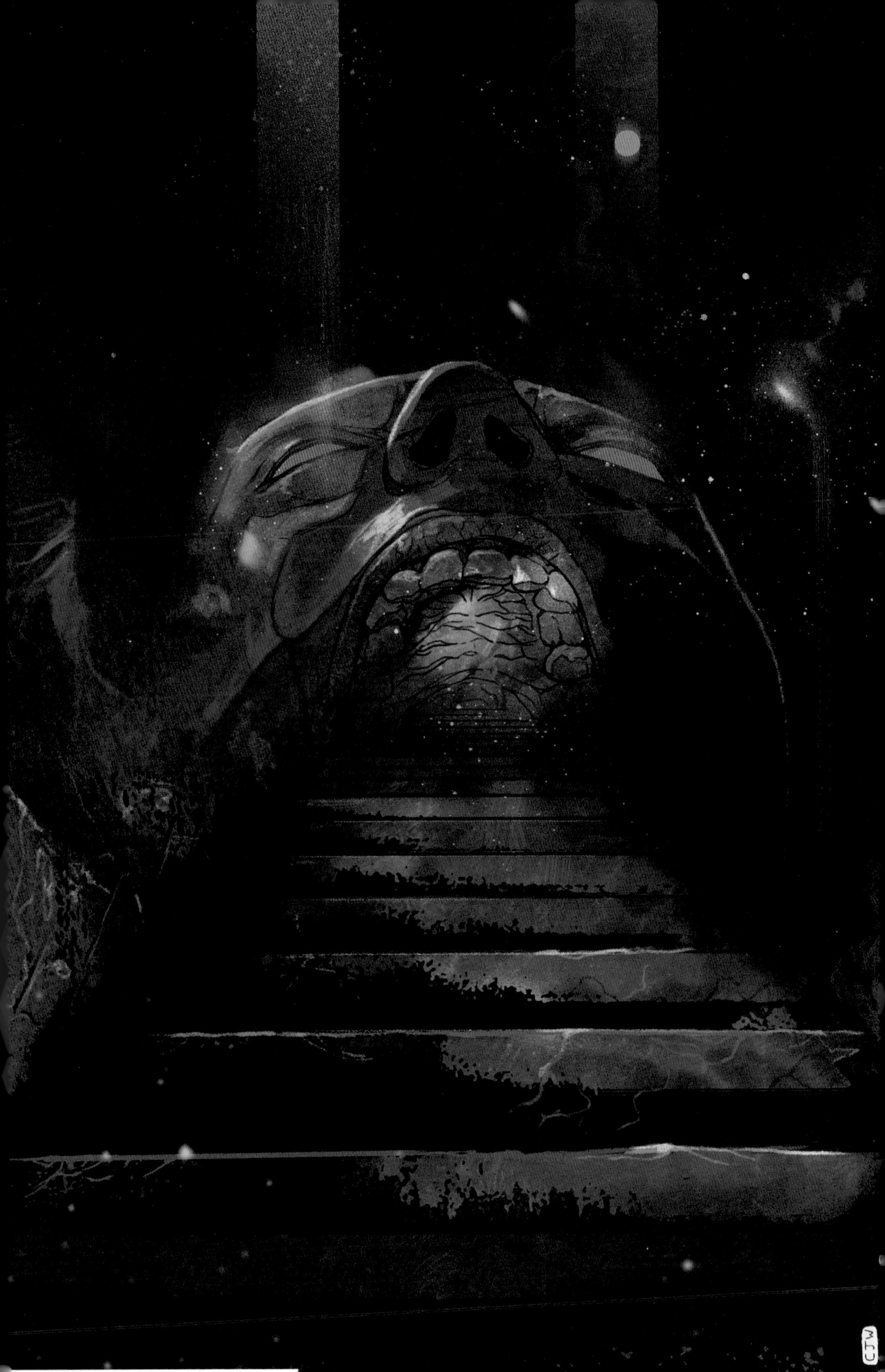

8B | Christian Ward

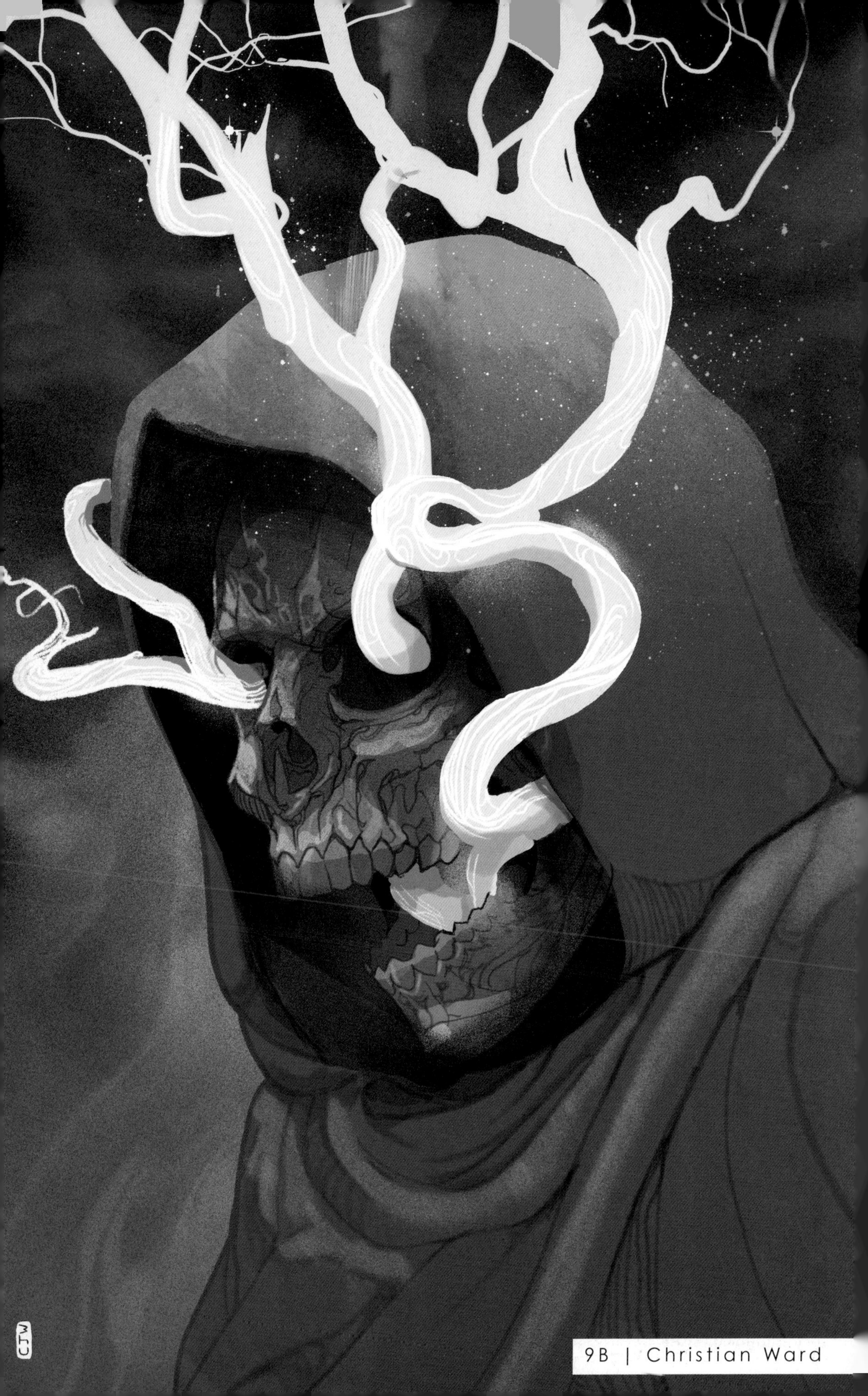
CJW

9B | Christian Ward

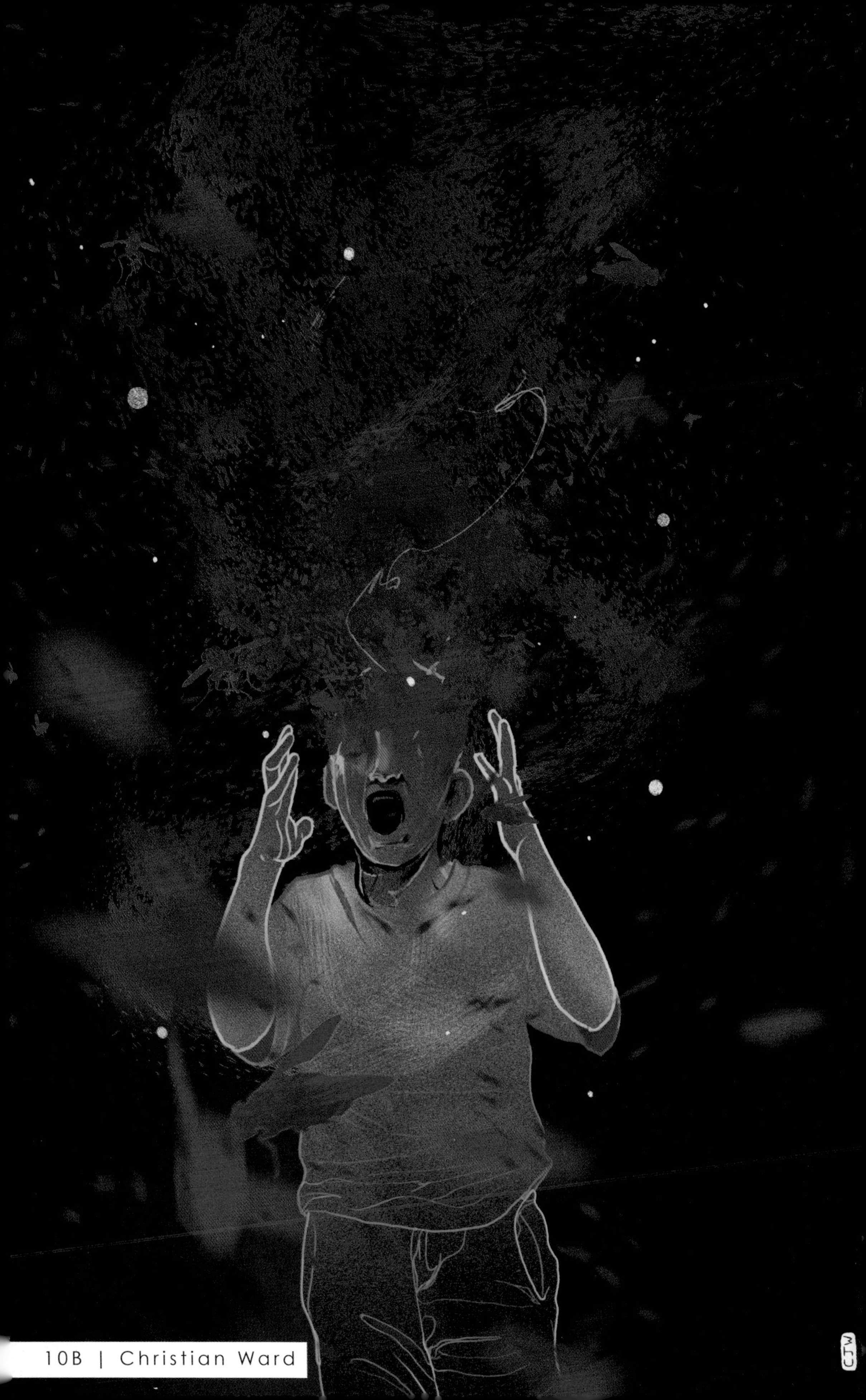
CJW

10B | Christian Ward

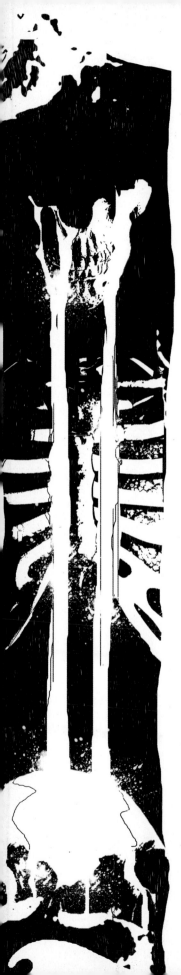

JEFF LEMIRE

is the creator of the acclaimed graphic novels *Sweet Tooth* (at Netflix from Robert Downey Jr.), the *Essex County Trilogy*, *The Underwater Welder*, *Trillium* and *Roughneck*, as well as *Descender* and *Ascender* with Dustin Nguyen and *Black Hammer* with Dean Ormston. Jeff has also written *Green Arrow*, *Justice League* and *Animal Man* for DC Comics and *Hawkeye* for Marvel Comics. He's also part of the creative team on *Cosmic Detective*, which he recently Kickstarted with Matt Kindt and David Rubín.

In 2008 and in 2013 Jeff won the Shuster Award for Best Canadian Cartoonist. He has also received the Doug Wright Award for Best Emerging Talent and the American Library Association's prestigious Alex Award, recognizing books for adults with specific teen appeal. He has also been nominated for 8 Eisner awards, 7 Harvey Awards and 8 Shuster Awards. In 2010 *Essex County* was named as one of the five Essential Canadian Novels of the Decade. He currently lives and works in Toronto with his wife and son.

ANDREA SORRENTINO

is the artist and co-creator of the critically praised and Eisner Award-winning *Gideon Falls* as well as the artist of other DC and Marvel hits like *Joker: Killer Smile*, *Batman: The Imposter* and *Wolverine: Old Man Logan*. He's renowned in the comic world for his tense, moody and suspenseful art and creative layouts that go beyond beat-to-beat storytelling and into evocations of deep, suggestive mental states.

Sorrentino lives and works just outside of Naples, Italy, precariously close to an active volcano.

DAVID STEWART

has worked as a colorist for over 20 years. He's worked on titles like *Hellboy*, *Shaolin Cowboy*, *Black Hammer* and *Ultramega*. He resides in Portland, Oregon with his wife and three black cats.

STEVE WANDS

is best known as a Harvey Award-nominated and Lammy Award-winning comic book Letterer with DC Comics, Image, TKO Studios, Dark Horse and others. When not working, he spends time with his family in New Jersey.

GREG LOCKARD

is a comic book writer and editor. As a freelance editor, his clients have included ComiXology Originals, Image Comics, Einhorn's Epic Productions and others. As a member of the Vertigo editorial staff, he worked on a number of critically acclaimed titles including *Dial H*, *The Unwritten*, *Sweet Tooth* and many others. *Liebestrasse*, published by ComiXology Originals, is his debut graphic novel as a writer and co-creator.